CLASSICAL COUNTY HISTORIES

GENERAL EDITOR: PROFESSOR JACK SIMMONS

ANTIQUITIES

HISTORICAL and MONUMENTAL

OF THE COUNTY OF

CORNWALL

ANTIQUITIES

HISTORICAL AND MONUMENTAL

OF THE

COUNTY OF

CORNWALL

W. BORLASE

With a new introduction by P. A. S. Pool and Charles Thomas

This edition originally printed by W. Bowyer and J. Nichols, London, 1769
Republished 1973 by EP Publishing Limited
in collaboration with Cornwall County Library

PUBLISHER'S NOTES

This is a reprint of the second edition of 1769
The first edition was published in 1754

The text and plates have been reproduced
from Cornwall County Library Copy Numbers
386616, 221993 and 645463. Full details are
deposited in Cornwall County Library

Copyright © in reprint 1973 EP Publishing Limited,
East Ardsley, Wakefield,
Yorkshire, England

Copyright © in introductions 1973
P. A. S. Pool and Charles Thomas

ISBN 0 85409 852 6

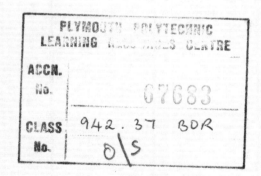
Reprinted in Great Britain by Scolar Press Ltd.
Menston, Yorkshire, U.K.

INTRODUCTION

THE MAN AND HIS WORK

William Borlase was born at Pendeen House, in the parish of St. Just about five miles from the Land's End in Cornwall, on 2 February 1695/6, second son of the local squire, John Borlase.[1] His paternal ancestry was that of a distinguished Cornish family claiming Norman descent, a junior branch having become established at Pendeen in 1637, when William's great-grandfather bought the house and laid the foundation of the extensive Borlase estate in West Cornwall. He died in 1664, his house having been damaged by Parliamentary forces as a reprisal after helping to raise a troop of horse for the King. His son, another John, rebuilt the house and died in 1693, and his son, the third successive John, lived from 1666 to 1755 and was the father of William Borlase.[2]

"John of Pendeen", as he was widely known, was for much of his very long life one of the leading personages of West Cornwall. He had extensive mining interests and made substantial purchases of land to add to the estate inherited from his father. He served as M.P. for St. Ives in 1705 and 1708 and was a J.P. for many years. He was of a somewhat uninhibited disposition and in his later years caused much anxiety to his sons. He married in 1690 Lydia Harris of Hayne in Devon. and of their 13 children the eldest and second surviving sons were Walter (1694–1776) and William (1696–1772), the latter of whom was the author of this book. Walter Borlase eventually became Vicar of Madron near Penzance and Kenwyn near Truro, Vice-Warden of the Stannaries, and a magistrate; as his father's heir and eventual head of the family, and by virtue of his public offices, he was in their time much more widely known than his brother William.

Nothing is known of William Borlase's childhood at Pendeen, but one may assume that the immediate proximity of Pendeen vau, an Iron Age "fogou" or souterrain, first roused his interest and curiosity in the works of early man. He was "put early to school in Penzance, where his master used to say he could learn but did not; he was then, more to his improvement, in the year 1709, removed to the care of the Rev. Mr. Bedford, then a learned schoolmaster at Plymouth". In March 1713 he matriculated at Exeter College, Oxford, which both his father and Walter had attended, and attained the degree of B.A. in October 1716 and M.A. in June 1719, "as soon as of the usual standing".

In 1718 there came to Oxford Sir John St. Aubyn, four years Borlase's junior but already since 1714 head of his family and owner of St. Michael's Mount, and clearly destined to become one of the leading figures in the life

---

1. This Introduction is a shortened version of a paper entitled *William Borlase, the Scholar and the Man*, published in *Journal of the Royal Institution of Cornwall* for 1966. Thanks are due to the Institution for permitting its reproduction in this form.

    The main source is the William Borlase Correspondence at the Penzance Library, Morrab Gardens. Individual references are given for all important extracts, the incoming original letters being cited as OL and the outgoing draft letter-books as LB. Most of the quotations without individual references are from an autobiographica letter written in 1772 (see note 29).

2. W.C. Borlase, *Borlase of Borlase* (1888), based partly on an unpublished MS. by Dr. William Borlase.

of West Cornwall. Despite the disparity in prospects, a firm and lasting friendship grew up between the two men, and for the rest of his life Borlase was closely associated with the St. Aubyn family.

Although he never went abroad, Borlase made several tours in England before his final return to Cornwall in 1722. He is known to have visited Salisbury and Wilton in 1718 and Warwick in 1719, and his travels may have been much more extensive, as the records of these years are very scanty. Being intended for the Church, he was ordained deacon in September 1719 and priest in July 1720; there is no record of his having served a curacy, but it seems probable that he acted as chaplain to the Marquess of Annandale, who died at Bath in February 1721. In 1722 he spent some time in London with St. Aubyn, his guide to the social life of the capital being Mrs. Martha Delahay, St. Aubyn's aunt.

In 1722 he became Rector of Ludgvan, a pleasant rural parish overlooking the shores of Mount's Bay about three miles from Penzance, where he was to live for fifty years, having secured "a sufficiency that set him above want (though below envy) all the rest of his life". On 28 July 1724 he married Anne, eldest surviving daughter and co-heiress of the Rev. William Smith, a native of Durham, late Rector of Camborne and Illogan.

Glimpses of Borlase's happy life at Ludgvan in the years immediately after his marriage appear in a letter to an uncle who was contemplating returning to England from the East Indies:

"I have had the pleasure of seeing some of the most considerable places in England, and I think there is hardly any place where I could so willingly wish that my lot had fallen as where it has. There is no part of England that abounds so much in the necessaries and at the same time has so many of the elegancies of life as that of Mount's Bay. The gentry, most of whom are our near relations, are of a free frolicking disposition. In the Summer time we meet (some ten or a dozen) at a Bowling Green, there we have built a little pleasure house and there we dine, after dinner at bowls, and by so frequently meeting together we are as it were like so many brothers of one family, so united, and so glad to see one the other. For my particular part since I have had the good fortune of a settlement it has required all my care and attention to gett my habitation, which was a most ruinous one when I came to it, in some tolerable order. I have now I thank God made it somewhat comfortable and easy and to my great satisfaction not only made the house tenantable, but from a wilderness or rather brake of briars and thorns have shap't out a little garden, where I may have plenty one time or other, and where I have at present some pretty airy walks, thriving plantations, and clear running water; neither is my water barren cold or uninhabited, but there are little fish in store which leap and play together in a little pond I have, and supply me with a little dish of excellent shots upon any emergent occasion. In my garden I spend most of my time without doors, having not the good fortune to delight much in hunting or in shooting, diversions which I am however far from finding fault with in others and for which our country is abundantly well provided."[3]

In 1730, being much troubled with rheumatic pains, Borlase went to Bath to

3. WB to George Borlase, 18 December 1727,
LB I 20.

seek treatment from his friend Dr. William Oliver (1695–1764), a native of Ludgvan who became a fashionable physician and invented the famous "Bath Oliver" biscuits. After this, "and by cold bathing in the sea, after his return, he, through the goodness of Providence, acquired such a firmness of constitution as served to carry him to the extreme of old age."

In May 1732 Borlase obtained a second living, the vicarage of his native parish of St. Just, which he held for forty years until his death, but he continued to reside at Ludgvan and curates served his other parish.

From his coming to Ludgvan at the age of twenty-six until he was over fifty Borlase spent such time as he could spare from his parishes, his garden and his family in the collection of material concerning the antiquities and natural history of Cornwall, but as yet with little or no thought of publication. In these early researches Borlase received much encouragement from St. Aubyn and Oliver and more active co-operation from his friend and neighbour Edward Collins, Vicar of St. Erth and "generally the companion of all antiquarian enquiries".

In undertaking the study of Cornish antiquities, especially those of prehistoric date, Borlase was working on almost untouched ground. Cornwall abounded in early remains of almost every type and period, but virtually nothing had been published except unsystematic references to individual sites in the works of Carew, Norden and Camden. Such recording of field monuments as had been undertaken by antiquaries like Lhuyd, Anstis and Tonkin remained in manuscript. The peninsula of West Penwith, where Borlase lived, is so immensely rich in antiquities that the task of recording and classifying them, which he began, has only recently been completed after more than two centuries of work by many devoted antiquaries. As early as 1728 Borlase was corresponding on antiquarian topics with Thomas Tonkin, the leading Cornish antiquary of the previous generation, but it was not until ten years later that he began the systematic recording of field monuments, coupled with speculation as to the rites of the Druids to whom he attributed the rock basins of artificial appearance which he had found on many granite outcrops. A later letter explains his early studies:

"It being my fortune to live at a great distance from places of publick resort, and my profession confining me to a small round, I found myselfe obliged to amuse myselfe with such remarkables as were within my reach, or utterly to abandon that share of curiosity which I had imbibed during the time of my education, and was grown too strong for me when I settled to be easily gott rid of. My turn was to antiquity, and I found in a short time that though we had few remains about us of any striking beauty or magnificence, yet that we had a great variety of monuments here which were of the most remote antiquity. Upon examining frequently those monuments and authors concerning them, I thought something might be added to the accounts I met with from a faithfull measurement and observation of the structure, shape, situation and some other peculiarities of these monuments, although at the distance I have allways lived from libraries my conceptions must needs be rude and new to those who have every book at their command."[4]

This lack of library facilities was a problem which Borlase had encountered some years before when first embarking on the serious study of an-

4. WB to William Stukeley, 10 November 1749,
   LB II 51.

tiquities and natural history, and in 1739 he had sent to the Archdeacon of Cornwall a long memorandum on the need for a County Library. Despite some influential support his efforts met with no success and Cornish scholars had to wait until 1792 for the foundation of the Cornwall Library at Truro, followed by the Penzance Library and the Royal Institution of Cornwall in 1818.

The earliest reference to research in natural history is a letter to Oliver in 1734, describing certain chemical tests Borlase had carried out on the water from a medicinal well in Ludgvan. It is however clear that his main interest was in mineralogy, a study for which the rich mines of both his parishes (especially the copper-mines on Lord Godolphin's land at Ludgvan) gave ample scope. In 1735 he received a request for a set of mineral specimens from Dr. John Andrew, a young Cornish physician whom Borlase had at one time hoped to induce to enter holy orders, but who was then studying at Leyden after a period at Bath with Oliver. At Leyden, Andrew was in contact with several eminent scholars, including Prof. Boerhave and Dr. J. F. Gronovius, both of whom were keenly interested in Borlase's Cornish minerals, and the latter of whom corresponded with him for some years. Borlase sent several boxes of minerals to Leyden, receiving in return botanical roots and seeds for his garden at Ludgvan. In 1737 Gronovius submitted some of Borlase's specimens to Linnaeus, who said "that he never saw at once such a fine collection".[5]

Borlase's letters show clearly that it was encouragement from Andrew and the spur of contact with leading Continental scholars that led him to the serious study of mineralogy, and this interest in turn brought him into contact with one of the greatest literary figures of the age. In December 1739 Oliver wrote to Borlase stating that Alexander Pope was collecting specimens for a mineral grotto in his garden at Twickenham, and urging him to "let our county have the honour to contribute all it can to the beauty of this grotto where the greatest genius of this age will often contemplate and admire the riches of our native soil". Before the end of the month Borlase had despatched to Pope the first of four consignments of minerals, together with suggestions as to their arrangement and display. The poet rendered effusive thanks, writing on 9 March 1740, "Your bounty like that of nature confounds all choice"; on 8 June he reported progress with the grotto, "in some part of which I must fix your name, if I can contrive it agreeably to your modesty and merit, in a shade but shining". This was done, for in December 1741 Oliver reported to Borlase "your name wrote in letters of gold in the grotto, an honour the greatest man might be ambitious of". Pope also sent Borlase an edition of his works.[6]

Six years later we find Borlase on his fifty-first birthday apparently preparing for a peaceful old age, yet in reality within a few months of the stimulus which was to introduce the decade of achievement in which he would perform his life's work:

> "As for my part, I am preparing for old age, that is, laying in a fund of amusements, such as may inable me to spend my time within doors to my satisfaction, since rambling abroad and good fellowship are become tiresome, and the severity of the seasons become more sensible. I read a little, I write a little, I paint a little, I collect a little, I think a little unless

5. S. Savage, "Linnaeus and Cornwall", *Svenska Linne Sallskapets Arsskrift* (Proceedings of the Linnaean Society of Sweden), xxxix–xl (1956–7), 7.

6. OL I 115, 135, 151; LB I 59, 68. See also Maynard Mack, *The Garden and the City* (University of Toronto Press, 1969), Chap. 2.

it be upon my friends and them I hope I shall never forgett, in short betwixt a little of one and a little of the other I find the days short enough in the midst of summer, and endeavour to lengthen them in the winter by rising early that I may fill every portion of time somehow or other, although the marks and traces I shall leave may be none of the most important, nor at all interesting to the rest of mankind."[7]

In May 1748 Borlase went to Exeter to attend the ordination of his eldest son, and there met two learned clergymen whose influence and encouragement were to extend his correspondence to wider circles of scholarship and induce him to undertake the publication of the results of his years of research. Charles Lyttelton (1714–68) became Dean of Exeter in 1748 and remained there until 1762 when he became Bishop of Carlisle, becoming also President of the Society of Antiquaries in 1765. Jeremiah Milles (1714–84) became Precentor of Exeter in 1747, and succeeded Lyttelton both as Dean in 1762 and as President of the Antiquaries in 1768. Junior to Borlase in years but by far his senior both in the Church and the learned world, they recognised in him a kindred spirit and affinity of studies worthy of the fullest encouragement, and he found in them lasting friends and correspondents whose influence on his later career was of exceptional importance.

Also in 1748 Borlase started a regular correspondence with Emanuel Mendes da Costa (1717–91), a London mineralogist of Portuguese descent who was recommended to him by the Bishop of Exeter. In July 1749 da Costa visited Borlase at Ludgvan, and on his return to London proposed him for Fellowship of the Royal Society, an honour to which he was elected in May 1750 after having submitted to the Society a treatise on *Spar and Sparry Productions, called Cornish Diamonds*. This was the first of thirteen papers contributed by Borlase to the *Philosophical Transactions* and also, at the age of fifty-four, his first published work.

Da Costa brought to Ludgvan a request from William Stukeley for details of certain Cornish antiquities. Stukeley was at that time well established, through his books on Stonehenge (1740) and Avebury (1743), as the leading antiquary of the country; Borlase was probably rather flattered at receiving a request for assistance from one so eminent, and sent Stukeley drawings of several Cornish sites. This brought a cordial letter from Stukeley, full of fanciful remarks about Druids and requesting further information. Borlase sent a full reply, but the correspondence between the two archdruids of eighteenth-century antiquarianism then came to an unexpected and unexplained end, despite the efforts of da Costa to induce them to resume it. Perhaps it would have been unreasonable to expect them to reconcile their doctrines and rites.[8]

By the end of 1750 Borlase had finally decided to publish his work, and circulated a prospectus inviting subscriptions, "a tedious way of proceeding indeed, and what gave him more pain, burthensome to his friends, but a method which did him much credit, by the number and rank of the subscribers". Later he circulated to the clergy and gentry of the county a very detailed questionnaire requesting information on the history, topography, natural history and antiquities of their parishes; as might have been expected, few replies were received, but some of these contained information of great value.

7. WB to John Andrew, 2 February 1747, LB II 12.   8. P.A.S. Pool, "The Borlase–Stukeley Correspondence", *Cornish Archaeology*, v (1966), 11.

Introduction

By the summer of 1753 the MS. of the *Antiquities* was ready for the printer and Borlase, who had first considered printing in London, finally determined on Oxford because of "the greater retirement and more easy access to books" and took the MS. there in July. The printing was carried out by W. Jackson, "a private press at which I found all the honesty, patience and expedition which my heart could wish", and the illustrations engraved under the author's supervision by James Green. The book was published in February 1754, upon which Borlase at once returned to Cornwall.

It is upon the *Antiquities of Cornwall* that William Borlase must be and has most often been judged as a scholar. The most fundamental fact in evaluating this book is that it was a pioneer work, the first chronological account of the antiquities of the county, the first book to describe and illustrate any significant number of them. Although Borlase's successors, especially in his own district, supplemented his work with much valuable research, nearly two centuries were to elapse before the publication of a book of similar scope, Hencken's *Archaeology of Cornwall and Scilly*, in 1932.

The most frequent criticism of the book is that Borlase's conclusions, especially those concerning Druids, were unduly speculative, inadequately supported by evidence, and in certain cases (e.g. the alleged artificial origin of rock basins) demonstrably incorrect. Although much of this criticism may be factually true, it ignores completely the fact that Borlase's field-work, as recorded both in his book and his unpublished MSS., was accurate and comprehensive, often giving us the only available details of sites since damaged or destroyed. It is unreasonable to blame Borlase for his attribution to the Druids of many sites now established to be of earlier date (such as stone circles) or natural origin (such as rock basins). These theories were, on the information available to him, attractive and tenable; the antiquaries of the eighteenth century knew nothing of the sequence of Stone, Bronze and Iron Ages, or of successive prehistoric migrations from Europe, but regarded the prehistoric inhabitants of Britain as a single indigenous race of "Ancient Britons", whose caste of priests, the Druids, was described by Caesar, Tacitus and other reliable classical authors. It is therefore hardly surprising that Borlase, having correctly deduced the stone circles and similar monuments to be prehistoric in date and religious or ceremonial in purpose, followed Stukeley and others in attributing them to the Druids; the available evidence supported this theory and Borlase had ample justification in putting it forward. So far as concerns the rock basins, which Borlase was the first antiquary to attribute to the Druids, while one must accept the statements of geologists that these are natural, the impression received from examination of them so overwhelmingly favours artificial origin that Borlase's discovery, recording and explanation of these sites can only be regarded as a scholarly achievement of the first magnitude, and the later disproving of his theories as an unfortunate and ironic sequel but not really relevant to an estimate of his work.

Borlase's own candid and logical attitude to the problem of antiquarian conjecture may be found in the preface to this book (p. ix). It is, however, true that many of his druidical theories are, by modern standards, unduly speculative and insufficiently supported by evidence. But he must be judged by the standards of his own time, and his conclusions make sober reading when compared with the wildly extravagant fancies of William Stukeley; Borlase's theories were much more closely linked with his fieldwork than were those of Stukeley, and he never

(x)

succumbed to Stukeley's besetting sin of seeing on the ground only the evidence which supported his own theories. Publication of Borlase's book made direct comparison with Stukeley inevitable, and Borlase received the warm support of Milles:

"Dr. Stukeley shakes his sententious head at you for thinking that the Druids were ever guilty of idolatry. He will not allow them to have deviated one step from the old Patriarchal Religion, and is clear that they had a knowledge of the Messiah – you will not think your character hurt by such a disagreement.

"You need not be in any pain on account of your differing from Dr. Stukeley about any point of Druid history. What you assert is founded on authority, but he makes a system out of his own head, and never cares whether he has any authority to support it. There is no imagination so wild that he will not lay down with all solemnity of truth, and treat it as if it were demonstrably certain."[9]

In 1755 Borlase was responsible for a suggestion that bore much fruit and showed him to be years ahead of his time as a geographer. For some years he had been in correspondence with Henry Baker (1698–1774), who in 1754 was one of the leading founder-members of "the Society for the Encouragement of Arts, Manufactures and Commerce" (now the Royal Society of Arts). In response to a request from Baker for suggestions as to projects deserving the Society's support, Borlase wrote lamenting the state of British Geography, "very low, and at present wholly destitute of any public encouragement", and suggesting that the Society should offer premiums for accurate surveys, in the hope that the Government would eventually sponsor surveys of the whole country. The Society adopted this suggestion after some delay, and the first premium was awarded to Benjamin Donn in 1765 for his map of Devon, but it was not until the formation of the Ordnance Survey in 1784 that Borlase's vision of a nationally-sponsored survey was fulfilled.[10]

Another branch of knowledge in which Borlase was well abreast of most scholars of his time was meteorology; for twenty years from 1752 until his death he kept a daily record of pressure, temperature, wind and rainfall at Ludgvan, an aspect of his work recently studied by Professor J. Oliver, who commends the care with which the entries were made, the meticulous observations on which they were based, and Borlase's spirit of scientific enquiry into meteorology, going beyond the mere collection of weather statistics.[11]

In 1756 Borlase published his second book, *Observations on the Ancient and Present State of the Islands of Scilly.* The fieldwork on which this book was based had all been carried out in 1752, when Borlase had spent two weeks at Scilly in the company of his friend and curate, Henry Usticke. The journal of this visit is preserved at the Penzance Library, and shows Borlase at the height of his powers carrying out intensive fieldwork over entirely fresh ground in a very limited time. His book on Scilly, based almost wholly on the records of this brief visit, was not the first, for Robert Heath's *Account of Scilly* had been published in 1750, but it remains to this day unequalled as a clear and accurate

9. Jeremiah Milles to WB, 23 March and 25 April 1754, OL III 57a and 57b.
10. W.L.D. Ravenhill, "Benjamin Donn", *Trans. Devonshire Assn.* 1965, 183; also his introduction to the bicentenary edition of Donn's map (Devon & Cornwall Record Society and University of Exeter, 1965), 3.
11. J. Oliver, "William Borlase's Contribution to 18th Century Meteorology and Climatology", *Annals of Science,* xxv (1960), 275.

account of the antiquities, scenery, history, social conditions, and maritime and strategic importance of the Islands, and was praised by no less a critic than Dr. Samuel Johnson as "one of the most pleasing and elegant pieces of local enquiry that our country has produced".[12]

In October 1757 Borlase went again to Oxford to supervise the printing of his *Natural History of Cornwall*, using the services of the same printers and engraver as with the *Antiquities*, and returned to Cornwall on completion of this task in the following April. Like the *Antiquities*, the *Natural History* was a pioneer study of very great importance. Dr. F. A. Turk has warmly commended Borlase's lack of concern with Tonkin's "apparitions, natural prodigies, monsters and superstitions", and the scrupulous accuracy and reliability of his observations and records.[13] Borlase's own attitude to this study is best shown in an extract from his introduction to the book:

> "To banish all hypothesis, whilst so many points of Natural History remain disputable and undecided, would be to obstruct one (and no inconsiderable one) of the avenues to knowledge. All cautious hypotheses must be pardoned for aiming at truth, although they miss the mark. But an hypothesis may be too bold, and when authors pretend to account for everything, they are not aware how indecently they intrude into the councils and peculiar province of their Maker. There are many secrets in nature, which man had better let alone, and wisely own his ignorance. God has given us a sagacity to discern, and faculties to use his works; but in a gross only, and collective state; he has given us no talents to track the first principles through their several migrations and meanders, to transmute, destroy and recompose the works of Nature; he did not design that we should presumptuously revise, mimick or make, but use, revere and celebrate his works. Natural History has its bounds, which if it exceeds, it gets wilfully into the dark, and consumes our time in endless and futile disquisitions; Natural History has its bounds, most apparent to those who know most of it; among the rest of its uses therefore (upon proper intimacy) it will certainly teach us a due estimate of our own weak abilities, short-sighted fancies, and at the same time the unlimited unfathomable depth and height of the works of God."

The great scope of the book is indicated by its full title:

> "The Natural History of Cornwall. The Air, Climate, Waters, Rivers, Lakes, Sea and Tides; of the Stones, Semimetals, Metals, Tin and the Manner of Mining; the Constitution of the Stannaries; Iron, Copper, Silver, Lead and Gold, found in Cornwall; Vegetables, Rare Birds, Fishes, Shells, Reptiles, and Quadrupeds; of the Inhabitants, their Manners, Customs, Plays or Interludes, Exercises, and Festivals; the Cornish Language, Trade, Tenures and Arts."

In fact more than half the book is concerned with geology and mineralogy, showing the direction from which the author had approached the study. Many of the illustrations are of Cornish houses, engraved to scale at the expense of their owners. Borlase's justification of these illustrations in a work on natural history ("it might be some satisfaction to posterity to see the patrimonial habitations

12. *Literary Magazine*, May 1756, 91.
13. F. A. Turk, "Natural History Studies in Cornwall, 1700–1900", *Journal of the Royal Institution of* Cornwall (1959), 237–242; see also his Introduction to the facsimile reprint of Borlase's *Natural History* (1970).

of their ancestors") seems a little illogical, but has proved fully justified.

Borlase's next concern was a munificent gift to his University, best described in his own words:

> "As soon as he returned, his first care was to send all the fossils and remains of antiquity, which he had described in his works, for the satisfaction of the curious, as well as his testimony of gratitude to his Alma Mater, to the care of the learned Mr. Huddesford, fellow of Trinity College and curator of the Ashmolean Museum, to be there reposited; for which he received the thanks of the University in a letter from the Rev. Dr. Thomas Randolph, then head of Corpus Christi College and Vice-Chancellor, dated 10 November 1758; and the fossils etc. were placed in a glass desk or cabinet for the more commodious examination. He continued to send everything curious in his department, as it came to hand, to the same repository."[14]

It was not for some years that his services to scholarship and to Oxford were recognised with an honour as unexpected as it was appropriate; in March 1766 he received the Honorary Degree of Doctor of Laws, thus at the age of seventy becoming known as "Dr. Borlase," by which style he is always remembered; as he put it, "an old man must die a young doctor".

Compared with his brother Walter, William Borlase played but a small part in public life. He was a welcome guest at Clowance, Tehidy and the other great houses of West Cornwall, and as a friend of Sir John St. Aubyn, who was M.P. for Cornwall from 1722 until his death in 1744, he took some part in elections and other political activity in the county. In 1744 there was a county by-election following the death of Sir William Carew. The candidature of his son, Sir Coventry Carew, was supported both by St. Aubyn, the other county member, and by Sir William Morice, to whose influence Borlase owed his living of St. Just, and Borlase was very embarrassed to receive a letter from the Duke of Bolton, patron of his Ludgvan living, requiring him in peremptory terms to support another candidate:

> "Sir William Carew, your late representative for the County of Cornwall, being dead, and all the gentlemen in the Whig interest having unanimously agreed to set up Mr. Carteret (Lord Carteret's son) to be chosen in his room, I therefore desire, and in gratitude shall expect, you to give your vote and interest for him at the next election, by which you'l oblige, your most assured friend, Bolton."[15]

This letter is a vivid example of how pressure could then be brought upon voters, and Borlase's dignified and tactful reply shows equally how an upright man could withstand it:

> "I have received the honour of yours and think myself very unfortunate that when your Grace was disposed to mention Lord Carteret's son to me to succeed Sir William Carew, I had no friend near to acquaint you with the obligations I lay under to the principal gentlemen who were likely to oppose him. . . . I am persuaded that if your Grace had been acquainted with these attachments you would have been so good to me as to leave me at liberty (as the other gentlemen must do) to serve my country in the best manner I am able at the approaching election; and

---

14. Borlase's autobiographical letter (see note 29).   15. Duke of Bolton to WB, 12 March 1744, OL I 238.

if I find myselfe obliged to depart from your Grace's recommendation (which I shall do with great reluctance) you will impute it not to a sense of any obligations superiour to those I have to you, but to the sincere, though perhaps mistaken, conviction of what I owe to my country."[16]

In the event, Carew was elected and served as Member until his death in 1748, Carteret receiving so little support that he described his journey to Cornwall as the most disagreeable one he had ever taken.

Borlase's interest in politics did not long survive the death of St. Aubyn in August 1744 and his decision to publish, but neither politics nor literature was allowed to interfere with his parochial work, and he remained a dutiful and conscientious clergyman until the end of his life. Although the incumbent of two parishes he was not a "pluralist" in the sense so often criticised; he worked Ludgvan without the aid of a curate for fifty years until the last few months of his life, and kept a most careful watch over the spiritual and material needs of his parishioners both there and at St. Just.

One of the most remarkable of all Borlase's letters is that to Mr. Bettesworth of St. Ives:

"I hope the rumours of your pretending to conjuration are not true, and I have so much charity as to believe that you have not been medling in the dangerous mysteries of a lower world, but rather, like a good Christian, defy and refuse all intercourse with the devil. Yet since there are such rumours, and you are said to take upon you to discover lost and stolen goods, I hope you will think that to retrieve and vindicate your character it will be necessary for you to use abundant caution that you give no encouragement to silly women to come to you on such foolish and wicked errants; and particularly I am obliged to desire that no such encouragements may be given to those persons who are the flock, and must be the care of your most humble servant, William Borlase."[17]

Borlase insisted on strict qualifications in his curates; in July 1766 he declared, "I take no curate who has in any wise leaned to or encouraged the Methodists or their teachers", and in 1761 he sought an assurance from the Bishop that a proposed curate "was not infected with Methodism", while at another time he expressed concern lest a candidate's Scottish accent might prove disagreeable to the congregation.[18] It is clear from these remarks that he had no sympathy whatever with Methodism, and that he deeply resented the activities of Wesley and his preachers, who were especially active in St. Just. An earlier letter is even more outspoken:

"The person who comes to it [St. Just] should have a due sense of the irregularity and ill tendency of Mr. Wesley's principles and practice, because this parish being populous, and few people of figure or knowledge is one of this quack's constant stages."[19]

Wesley's journals for 1745 refer to him and his followers being harassed by a magistrate called "Dr. Borlase", and it has often been assumed that this was William. In fact the evidence is conclusive that Wesley's references to "Dr. Borlase" are to Walter, who was at that time both a magistrate and a doctor, whereas William was never a magistrate and did not receive his doctorate until

16. WB to Duke of Bolton, n.d., LB I 73.
17. WB to J. Bettesworth, 4 March 1728, LB I 23.
18. LB III 212, 10, 205.
19. WB to Bishop of Exeter, n.d. April 1756, LB II 149.

over twenty years later. Some of Walter's actions were undoubtedly arbitrary and high-handed, but it must be remembered that at the time the country was full of rumours of Jacobite plots and invasions, the Pretender was said to be hiding near Penzance, and to a diligent and alarmed magistrate the possibility of the travelling preachers being Jacobite spies seemed as likely as it now seems absurd.[20] It is pleasant to record that John Wesley was an admirer of William Borlase's scholarship; in 1757, having looked over the *Antiquities*, he concluded that "he is a fine writer, and quite master of his subject".[21]

Of all the Borlase family least is recorded of William Borlase's wife Anne; no letter between them survives, and we have only William's reference to his studies being helped by "his happy connection with one who took more than her part of domestick cares", and a few compliments in letters from friends, such as that of Milles who described her as "the happy mixture of the Philosopher and matron". Until her death in 1769 she seems to have been an ideal scholar's wife.

Of their six sons, born between 1726 and 1732, two died as infants, two as young men, and two only survived their parents. Three entered the Church: William who died in 1756 aged thirty shortly after becoming Vicar of Zennor; John, who became Rector of St. Mewan and died in 1780; and George, who became a Fellow of All Souls and Vicar of South Petherwin and died in 1775. All three by their financial improvidence caused much anxiety to their parents, whose favourite son Christopher had joined the navy and died of a fever off the Guinea coast in 1750 at the age of twenty.

As well as his own family, Borlase's household normally included, from 1738 to 1751 at least, one resident pupil. These included Thomas Hawkins, the heir to Trewithen; Sir John St. Aubyn, son and heir to Borlase's patron; Sir Richard Vyvyan of Trelowarren; and John Prideaux Basset of Tehidy. Nothing shows more conclusively the esteem in which Borlase was held by his fellow-gentry than that the heirs to four of the greatest estates in West Cornwall were thus entrusted to his care.

For many years Borlase kept a Cornish chough as a pet, as shown by the following letter:

> "Our chough is now I think in its fourteenth year. It has sometimes been sick, Mrs. Borlase is the doctor, and when its appetite appeared to be disordered she has grated rhubarb made up with a little meal into a paste with success; if his spirits are low we infuse saffron into his water; and as he has free egress and ingress, he appears generally at dinner, knocking at the door if it be shut with his bill till 'tis opened; his place is to perch behind my chair, his favourite dish is the yolk of a boiled egg, which he will take off my plate without leave; if there is any white meat, particularly chicken or veal, he expects his share minced for him, and he flies upon the table and back to his perch without ceremony and manners. It is a bird that loves such familiarity and I apprehend cannot live in solitude where he has not liberties of ranging and varying the scene."[22]

From time to time these pets were despatched by Borlase to his friends in London; thus in 1757 at the request of Oliver he sent two young choughs to

20. J. Pearce, *The Wesleys in Cornwall* (1964), 14–17.
21. *Journal of John Wesley*, 16 September 1757;

Pearce, *op. cit.*, 128.
22. WB to Jeremiah Milles, 31 January 1763, LB III 91.

London for Mr. Legg the Chancellor of the Exchequer, but neither lived long despite their "sprightly wit and active parts".[23]

Borlase's last years were spent, not in the retirement which he had so richly earned, but in industrious activity scarcely less than during the strenuous decade of publication which preceded them. His life's work had been accomplished; he was contented with his lot, and had no wish for the ecclesiastical preferment which he could probably have obtained after his friends and pupils became deans, bishops, baronets and patrons of rich livings.

Inevitably Borlase's political and social views tended to become reactionary as old age advanced; thus in 1766 he complained bitterly to St. Aubyn:

"If you are not able to keep the mad Americans from disputing Acts of Parliament, it will not be worth your notice or that of anyone else to think of a seat in St. Stephen's Chapel."[24]

In the same year he wrote to Bishop Lyttelton complaining of the extravagance of the poor:

"We hear every day of murmurs of the common people, of want of employ, of short wages, of dear provisions; there may be some reason for this, our taxes are heavy upon the necessaries of life, but the chief cause is the extravagance of the vulgar in the unnecessaries of life. In one tin work near me, where most of the tinners of my parish have been employed for years, there were lately computed to have been at one time threescore snuffboxes. There may be in my parish about fifty girls above fifteen years old, and I dare say forty-nine of them have scarlet cloaks. There is scarce a family in the parish, I mean of common labourers, but have tea once if not twice a day, and in the parish almshouse there are several families and parts of families, but not one without their tea-kettle, and brandy when they can purchase it – in short all labourers live above their condition, and can it then be wondered at that wages price and hire should fall short of their wants."[25]

He also found himself unable to appreciate modern developments in literature, especially in fiction, as shown by the following:

"I have unfortunately such a veneration for the ancients that I don't sufficiently perhaps esteem the moderns upon which others lay out not only their money (that's nothing but to booksellers) but their time which should be very precious and their affections which should be more so. . . . Who reads Homer or Horace now, when he can take up Tom Jones? Who will read Xenophon's Cyrus, or run with delight to a Pastoral in Theocritus or Virgil, or to a tragedy in Sophocles, when he may saunter away his easy hours, and repose his brain with a David Simple, a Parson Andrews, a Pamela, and the chit-chat history of a chambermaid? Indeed these novelists and life scribblers have turned all sound literature out of doors, they teach people to read nothing but trifles, and increase the degeneracy of taste without rectifying the morals. To promote virtue and reading is the pretence, but to please foolish purchasers is the true motive, little heeding whether, whilst they are exhibiting the trials of constancy and chastity, they may not excite improper desires, and sapp

23. OL I 117a, 118a.
24. WB to Sir John St. Aubyn (the younger), 22 January 1766, LB III 192.

25. WB to Bishop Charles Lyttelton, 3 February 1766, LB III 193.

the foundations of modesty without whose support chastity will soon surrender."[26]

As death decreased the circle of his friends and infirmity reduced his own mobility, Borlase spent much time indexing his correspondence and sewing it into books, but his main recreation was painting, which he had first taken up on being provoked by the incompetence of a very bad portrait painter whom he encountered in 1747 and at once determined to excel. He swiftly obtained a high degree of competence in oils, and some of the family portraits which survive are attributed to him, but much of his work consisted of landscapes.

Borlase's most important literary production in his latter years was the revised and enlarged second edition of the *Antiquities*, published in 1769 and reproduced in the present volume. On this occasion he sold the edition to a London bookseller for a single payment of 100 guineas, and the proofs were sent to Ludgvan for correction, thus sparing him the burden of collecting subscribers and travelling a long distance to supervise the printer. He also prepared extensive additions and amendments to the *Natural History*, with a view to an eventual second edition, but this was never accomplished, and the additions remained unpublished for nearly a century.[27]

On 21 April 1769 Anne Borlase died at the age of sixty-six after some years of poor health; shortly before this, the household had been joined by William, elder son of John of St. Mewan, who remained as the companion of his grandfather's old age for the three years that remained to him. Thus in his bereavement Borlase found solace in "the instruction of a dutiful and apprehensive youth", and in 1771 at the age of seventy-five he was still rising at 6 a.m. to supervise the studies of his grandson, who would in return drive him about the parish, read the newspapers to him, and look after his painting materials.[28]

In January 1771 Borlase suffered a severe illness, which made it necessary for him to obtain a curate for Ludgvan, and also caused the cancellation of his last literary project. Years before he had prepared a short treatise on the Creation and the Deluge, originally designed as an introduction to the *Natural History* but not used for that purpose. This he now prepared for publication in revised form as *Private Thoughts of the Creation and the Deluge, by a Country Clergyman*. Unhappily illness made him unequal to the burden of proof-correction, and he was obliged to recall the manuscript from the printer. The work is a unique combination of the author's religious and scientific knowledge, a cogently-argued attempt to reconcile his implicit faith in the authority of Moses as an historian with the enquiring nature resulting from decades of scientific observation.

In May 1772, at the request of his friend William Huddesford of the Ashmolean, Borlase sent him a long and agreeably modest autobiographical letter, containing much information which would otherwise have been lost, and concluding "very little more can be hoped for by himself, or expected by others".[29] As the summer drew on his grip on life slowly lessened, and on 11 August he made his will. The end was now at hand; on 28 August he wrote his last letter, to Huddesford ("I grow more indifferent to the world and less able to bear

26. WB to Dr. William Oliver, 14 November 1760, LB II 178.
27. *Journal of the Royal Institution of Cornwall* Nos. 2–5 (1864–66) Supplements (reprinted as an Appendix to the 1970 Edition of the *Natural*

History—see note 13).
28. LB III 340, 345, 353.
29. LB III 358, printed in *Gentleman's Magazine*, lxxiii (1803), 1114.

company every day"), on the 29th he made the last entry in his cash book, on the 30th the last in the daily meteorological record, and on the 31st he died, at the age of 76 years.

As well as his books, Borlase left many unpublished MSS. of great importance, most of which are happily preserved. Undoubtedly the most noteworthy are his *Correspondence* for the period 1722–72 preserved at the Penzance Library, Morrab Gardens. These include drafts of outgoing letters and original incoming letters from many noted scholars, the whole constituting a full and detailed record of the life of an eighteenth-century scholar, gentleman and parson.[30] Other important MSS. are the *Parochial Memoranda* (British Museum), the *Cornish Language* collection (Cornwall County Record Office), the *Excursions*, the *Cash Book* and the *Meteorological Records* (Truro Museum), and the *Armorial and Genealogical* collection, the *Journal of a Tour to Scilly*, the *Description of Ludgvan*, and the *Creation and Deluge* (Penzance Library).

Borlase was a great scholar and also a great man. His books were pioneer works which after two centuries are still of high value to antiquaries and naturalists, and his reputation as a scrupulous observer and recorder remains untarnished by his lapses into the exotic realms of druidical speculation. He was, beyond question, the greatest Cornish scholar of the eighteenth century, linked by correspondence and occasional visits with other scholars but working for the most part in isolation, and his achievement is the more remarkable when one appreciates how far he lived from libraries, universities and other centres of learning and culture, and how these disadvantages postponed for many years his decision to publish. The chief characteristics of his long life were industry and contentment; he never spared himself in the service of his religion, his country, his family and his studies, and, in the words of the graceful tribute of Alexander Pope, he lived and worked "in a shade, but shining".

In conclusion there follows part of an obituary of William Borlase, found among the family records and possibly written by his brother Walter:

"He made the best use of his retired and delightful situation at Ludgvan, as a Pastor, a Gentleman, and a man of learning. He discharged the duties of his profession with a most rigid punctuality and exemplary dignity. He was remarkably attentive to the affairs of his parish and the regularity of his parishioners, was affable and easy of access and ready on all occasions to assist them with his advice both in their spiritual and temporal concerns. Though he was not admired as a preacher, yet several specimens he has left in manuscript prove that his studies were not confined to Antiquities or Natural History. He was esteemed and respected by the principal gentry of his county, and lived on the most friendly and social terms with those of his neighbourhood. He was lamented in the several relations of a kind father, an affectionate brother, an instructive pastor, a sincere friend, a man of erudition and a good citizen."

P. A. S. POOL

M.A., F.S.A.

30. Borlase corresponded with the following persons mentioned in *D.N.B.*: Joseph Ames, Henry Baker, Thomas Bentley, Charles Duke of Bolton, Gustavus Brander, Peter Collinson, Emanuel Mendes da Costa, David Durell, John Ellis, Richard Lord Edgecumbe, Richard Gough, Francis Earl of Godolphin, Thomas Hornsby, William Hudson, William Huddesford, John Hutchins, Smart Lethieullier, George Lavington, Isaac Lawson, Daniel Lysons, Charles Lyttelton, Matthew Maty, Jeremiah Milles, William Oliver, Thomas Pennant, Richard Pococke, Alexander Pope, Sir John St. Aubyn, William Stukeley, Thomas Tonkin, John Wall, Browne Willis, Francis Wise.

BORLASE AS ARCHAEOLOGIST AND
FIELD WORKER

It would be fair to describe William Borlase, not as an archaeologist, but as an antiquary, using the latter word without any of its more recent pejorative undertones. In the setting of his age, he must not only rank as a great antiquary; he was among the first to practise systematic fieldwork, in the sense of the planned first-hand recording of visible antiquities, area by area. With the explosion of knowledge, the extension of leisure to most of our population, and the progressive separation of specific disciplines from their older matrix of Natural Philosophy, we have become accustomed to the parcelling-out of fresh knowledge into tight little boxes. Biologists record our fauna and flora, not just through specific and generic labels, but against a background of fixed vice-counties or ten-kilometre squares. The contemporary distribution of a given species can, in a moment, be typed out in map form *via* a computer. Archaeologists, even if their sequential time-scale is just as liable to revision as Borlase's, match new discoveries against a vast corpus of comparanda and plot them with eight-figure references to our unsurpassable National Grid. Geologists have at their command a battery of scientific aids that render the immediate, macroscopic, inspection by eye and hand no more than a preliminary, perhaps inessential, step towards identification. We are, mercifully, still far from the point where there is nothing left for us to discover about the matter of Britain, but the once boundless arena open to the pioneer fieldworker has shrunk to negligible dimensions.

Borlase operated in a field – his own field, to which his position in society and his autochthonous descent gave him special claims and advantages – where, for all practical purposes, his boundaries were those that Divine Providence had set to the workings of the human mind. We need not concern ourselves so much with the prevalent mental outlook of his day, or with the lack of clear distinctions between evidence, inference, and speculation that makes much of his archaeological writing unfamiliar to a modern specialist; more apposite is the question of his whole approach to the external world. Given, of course, the limits imposed by dogma, and the facts of his being a priest of the established Church and his possessing a taste for metaphysics, his outlook was unitary, broad, and humane. If he chose to impose his own systematics on his researches, dividing what we should now regard as pure archaeology from pure genealogy and natural history, he did not hesitate to link these, and other, topics by way of cross-reference, and his unpublished field notebooks reveal him as basically the collector of *all* phenomena. Such an approach makes for delightful reading, and imparts strongly the true flavour of another age; but, as anyone who has ever tried it will confirm, it makes it desperately difficult, for example, to construct an index to any of Borlase's published work.

I stress these aspects of the man and his work because no *aperçu* of Borlase as an archaeologist will amount to very much if we appraise him through the canons of the late twentieth century. Nor can one entirely construct such an appraisal just from his major published work – his *Antiquities* (1754 and 1769), his *Scilly Isles* (1756), and to some extent his *Natural History* (1758). These books, produced – apart from the revision of the *Antiquities* – in a single decade, the peak of his working life, constitute an extraordinary personal monument by and to a country parson. But, curiously enough, a contemporary archaeologist, and especially a contemporary engaged mainly upon field-survey or rescue excavation, finds much greater kinship with Borlase in the notebooks. Fortunately we have the majority of these, either at the Penzance Library or at the Royal Institution of Cornwall, and increasing attention is being paid to them. There are also a few set pieces, like the remarkable description of St. Michael's Mount, where we possess, if not the holograph, a near-contemporary copy by one of the St. Aubyn family.

Borlase catalogued his antiquarian observations, as far as possible, on the basis of the ecclesiastical parishes. This is still a favoured method in fieldwork, not as a mark of devotion to the Church of England, but because it also formed the basis of the Tithe Apportionment Survey centred around 1840, and the tithe maps are still the starting-points for large-scale field research. He was also in the habit of what we may call "linear observation"; i.e., when journeying around the county, normally on horseback if for any distance, he carried a pocket notebook, and clearly allowed himself time to stop, to look, to sketch, to chat, and if occasion warranted to stray from the road. Later, at leisure, pencilled drawings could be inked in, or redrawn in ink. An exactly similar method of linear observation was employed widely by Lt.-General Pitt-Rivers in the later nineteenth century, and of course is still practised. For the parishes, it is clear that Borlase contemplated – as did Charles Henderson, fifty years ago – a massive parochial survey of all Cornwall. This was to have been part archaeological and part historical – his friends and correspondents at Exeter and elsewhere were asked for relevant transcripts from episcopal registers and deeds – and would, we can scarcely doubt, have had a strong linguistic element, reflecting the author's deep interest in every form of place-name as well as in the Cornish language. Given the primitive internal communications of Cornwall in the 1750s, and the extraordinary difficulties that Borlase would have encountered in visiting, say, the extreme northern or south-eastern parishes, far beyond his own wide network of relatives and kinsfolk, we can do little but applaud his courage and vision.

Borlase did actually make some preliminary moves. Taking as his model, obviously, the existing system of terriers, returns, and queries initiated by successive bishops at Exeter – there had been a terrier demand, following a visitation, in 1727 – he sent a circular to all incumbents, and selected gentry, throughout the county about 1753. It is sad to record that the result was even more disappointing than the outcome of similar endeavours in more recent times; as far as we can ascertain, only seven or eight replies were received. What was to have been the collated version survives as Borlase's *Parochial Memoranda*.[1] A typical entry would contain, first, concisely summarised findings from his own fieldwork; second, historical notes, augmented from Exeter documents or notes supplied to him by such friends as Dean Lyttelton or Jeremiah Milles; and, third, Borlase's views – largely speculative by present onomastic standards – on a variety of place-names within that parish.

Again, thrown back here on his own resources – and we must remember that he began to publish and to record seriously after he had passed his half-century, fortunately drawing upon mature field survey – it is probably the archaeological

1. Now British Museum MS. Egerton 2657.

Introduction

element that counts for most. Here is a telling instance. Folio 16 of the Egerton MS. deals with "Cambron *als* Cambourne" (Camborne). Section 1 of the entry describes a visit to a holy well and chapel called *Fenton Er* (= Fenton Ia, "(holy) spring of (Saint) Ia"). It does so with such accuracy that, although the site was entirely lost from the later eighteenth century, I was able in 1962 to re-discover it, using nothing more than Borlase's notes as my guide, and subsequently to recover a long and most important sequence of construction by excavation.[2] Again, Borlase notes the presence of a decorated granite cross by this chapel; this cross, which must weigh nearly a ton, was moved over two miles between *circa* 1750 and 1896, when it was found built into a well-head. It now stands in Camborne churchyard, and can be positively identified as St. Ia's Cross because it was fully and accurately sketched, and its context noted, by Borlase. Another of his MSS., a small field notebook,[3] apart from being a prime example of what I have called "linear observation", allows one to make with absolute confidence several similar identifications where monuments have since been moved, or altered, or destroyed.

When we turn to the *Antiquities*, we are perhaps seeing the man at one remove. This is not a record of fieldwork. It uses fieldwork and field observation, but primarily for illustration. The author, prompted by his friends to embody his findings in print, offers us a sequential narrative designed to illuminate the history of man in Cornwall, from the permissible beginnings to his own time, in the light of a literary backdrop drawn from his own wide (though by no means exhaustive) readings in classical and Biblical antiquity. His attitude is admirably set out, not so much in his Preface, as in the letter (November 1749) to William Stukeley quoted above.[4]

The important words in that letter begin with "faithful measurement and observation". The *Antiquities* is the product of its times; of course we know that rock-basins on granite tors were neither carved by Druids nor, in all probability, ever laved with the blood of their victims, and cliff-castles have long been divorced from Danes, even if their precise strategic functions remain matters of debate. Borlase's own views on the tin-trade of the ancients, along with Belerium, Ictis and the Cassiterides, were to be bettered a century later by another Cornishman, George Smith (in *The Cassiterides*, 1863). All this detracts hardly at all from Borlase the observer, Borlase the antiquary in the field, starting-point of a tradition of informed fieldwork which in his native Cornwall stretches, continuously, to today. He would have been delighted to know that the current "Parochial Check-List Survey" of Cornwall, about a third of which has been completed and about a quarter already published, is regarded nationally as a model.

One may perhaps end by emphasising again this note of continuity. Borlase set great store by Carn Brea, the several granite tors of which still exhibit his curious rock-basins, and he gives us considerable information on its antiquities and chance finds. As I write (December 1972) the Cornwall Archaeological Society is preparing its fourth season of investigation on this hill-top, confirming its nature as an extensive, and extremely early, Neolithic settlement; not a hill-fort, not a conventional causewayed camp of the period, but apparently a

2. cf. my *Christian Antiquities of Camborne* (Warne, St. Austell, 1967), ch.v, "The Excavation of St. Ia's Chapel".

3. Royal Institution of Cornwall, Borlase MS. no.41, *Excursions 1751–1758*.

4. See p. (vii).

complex and hitherto unknown form of (and here one must use the German term) *Hohensiedlung* involving agricultural plots, houses in small ramparted enclosures, a vast flint-working industry, and a range of pottery which will greatly extend the British repertoire. The eventual elucidation of the long sequence of disjointed occupations – they include the Iron Age and some form of medieval activity – will take into account those finds (of Bronze Age implements, of certain early British coins) reported, and reported with exactitude, by William Borlase. In similar vein, if it ever proves possible to undertake the badly needed re-examination, which would involve wholesale clearance and near-total excavation, of Chun Castle, the great circular granite fortress in the Land's End peninsula, Borlase's careful plan forms the starting-point. It did so for Edward Thurlow Leeds, who conducted partial excavations there in the 1920s, and it would have to do so on any future occasion. I choose but two examples, both of which concern major field monuments within the county. The same is true of the Isles of Scilly, where William Borlase's 1756 monograph more closely resembles a piece of straight archaeological rapportage. The editing, and publication, of his field notebooks, and of such major items as the St. Michael's Mount description, is now under active consideration. Fieldwork, in the last few years considerably rehabilitated in British archaeology as a pursuit at least equal in importance to excavation, owes a great deal to Borlase's patient and careful example; archaeology in the far south-west owes even more. We remember this antiquarian giant with both affection and gratitude.

CHARLES THOMAS
M.A., F.S.A.

ANTIQUITIES,

HISTORICAL and MONUMENTAL,

OF THE

COUNTY of CORNWALL.

CONSISTING OF

SEVERAL ESSAYS

ON

The FIRST INHABITANTS, DRUID-SUPERSTITION, CUSTOMS,
And REMAINS of the moſt Remote ANTIQUITY

In BRITAIN, and the BRITISH ISLES,

Exemplified and proved by MONUMENTS now extant in CORNWALL
and the SCILLY ISLANDS,

With a VOCABULARY of the CORNU-BRITISH LANGUAGE.

By WILLIAM BORLASE, LL.D. F.R.S. Rector of LUDGVAN,
CORNWALL.

" Miratur, facileſque oculos fert omnia circùm
" Æneas, capiturque locis, et ſingula lætus
" Exquiritque auditque virûm Monumenta priorum."   VIRG.

The SECOND EDITION, reviſed, with ſeveral Additions, by the Author; to which is added a Map
of CORNWALL, and Two new Plates.

LONDON,

Printed by *W. Bowyer* and *J. Nichols*:

For S. BAKER and G. LEIGH, in York Street; T. PAYNE, at the Mews Gate, St. Martin's;
and BENJAMIN WHITE, at Horace's Head, in Fleet Street.

MDCCLXIX.

T O

SIR JOHN ST. AUBYN, BARᵀ.

MEMBER OF PARLIAMENT

F O R

THE COUNTY OF CORNWALL.

SIR,

WHILST I was collecting the following Monuments, at my leisure hours several years since, I seldom added any thing to the number without communicating it to Your late excellent Father; who, curious as he was in most parts of knowledge, and particularly fond of this his native County, received double pleasure from every thing remarkable in Art, Nature, and Antiquity, which it was found to contain.

I was then in hopes of writing somewhat concerning this County, which might in time make its appearance under the unexceptionable Patronage of one, who had represented it in Parliament for many years with such an universal Reputation, as could proceed only from the most distinguished Abilities,

and

and the moſt eminent Integrity in the uſe and application of them.

But his death put an end to thoſe hopes; and
whilſt, for want of ſuch a Patron (after I had thrown
theſe Papers into the following order), I was heſi-
tating whether I ſhould publiſh them or not; You
were pleaſed, Sir, to fix me in the deſign, by encouraging the Publication in the moſt friendly and
generous manner.

In dedicating therefore this Work to You, at its
firſt appearance, I did but comply with the rules of
Gratitude; and as the Favours I have received from
You ſince, in a courſe of fifteen years Friendſhip,
would make it ſtill more unpardonable to place any
other name, where Yours ſo juſtly ſtood before, I
readily embrace this opportunity of renewing my ac-
knowledgements to You, and ſubſcribing myſelf,

S I R,

Your moſt obliged, and

Obedient Humble Servant,

William Borlaſe.

[v]

TO

THE READER.

THERE is no study more instructive and entertaining than that of Ancient and Modern History; and, though the latter may be more interesting, easy, and pleasant, yet the former is also a most necessary part of Knowledge, as it enlarges our prospects, furnishes us with a great variety of examples both of Virtue and Vice, produces frequent instances of Science and Errour, discovers the manner in which great actions have been conducted, and great attempts have miscarried.

Now, the study of Antiquity is the study of Ancient History; and the proper business of an Antiquary is, to collect what is dispersed, more fully to unfold what is already discovered, to examine controverted points, to settle what is doubtful, and, by the authority of Monuments and Histories, to throw light upon the Manners, Arts, Languages, Policy, and Religion, of past Ages.

ANTIQUITIES may be either considered as Foreign or Domestic; such, I mean, as relate to other people and countries, or are peculiar to our own.

IT is the usual observation of Foreigners, that the English Travellers are too little acquainted with their own Country; and so far this may be true, that Englishmen (otherwise well qualified to appear in the world) go abroad in quest of the rarities of other countries, before they know sufficiently what their own contains; it must be likewise acknowledged that, when these foreign tours have been compleated, and Gentlemen return captivated with the Medals, Statues, Pictures, and Architecture, of Greece and Italy, they have seldom any relish for the ruder products of Ancient Britain. Thus what is foreign gets the start of what is at home, and maintains its prepossession. My situation in life (whatever my inclinations might be) confined me to a different track; I saw myself placed in the midst of Monuments, the Works of the Ancient Britans, where there were few Grecian or Roman Remains to be

b   met

met with; my curiofity, therefore, could only be gratified by what was in its reach, and was confined to the ftudy of our own Antiquities; and thefe papers are the fruits of that ftudy.

WHETHER thefe fruits (if I may carry on the allufion) may fuit the tafte of all, I much queftion; but, however fond we may be of the fuperiour flavour and beauty of what comes from abroad, it would be very unwife in us to exclude every thing from our entertainments which *our own Country* produces.

Book I.

To fix me in the choice of this fubject, not only my fituation in life, but the manner in which it has been treated of by others, has greatly contributed. For, firft, as to Cornwall, I found its Hiftory and Monuments but faintly touched in the *Survey* of Mr. *Carew*, a gentleman of great learning and ingenuity, and extremely capable of defcribing his Country, if the infancy of thefe ftudies, at that time [a], had afforded him fufficient light, and proper materials.

THE better part of *Norden's Survey*, which comes next, is a meer tranfcript of Mr. *Carew*; and from the other parts of this Work very little of moment is to be learnt.

THESE Authours have written profeffedly of *Cornwall*; and where this County is treated of collectively with many others, making only a *part* of the *whole*, as in the general writers of England, *Leland*, *Camden*, *Speed*, &c. fuch Memoirs of it muft be ftill more incompleat.

Book II. and III.

As to the Hiftory of the *Druids*, I found that branch in a worfe condition; moft Authours having contented themfelves with enlarging upon feveral paffages in *Julius Cefar's* account of this ancient Priefthood, and what *Pliny* has left us on the fame fubject, fo regularly, that their attempts in the Druid Hiftory may juftly be looked upon as no other than Paraphrafes upon what had been faid before, without eftablifhing any difputed fact, or difcovering any thing new, by having recourfe to the Monuments which the Druids left behind them [b].

THAT valuable collection of Antiquities by *Montfaucon*, for which the Learned are fo much obliged to him, contains but few

[a] About the year 1600.
[b] See Elias Schedius de Diis Germanis. — Smith's Syntagma de Druidis. — A Collection of French and German Writers, in Frickius de Druidis. — Sheringham. — Sammes, &c.

ancient

ancient Druid Monuments, and thofe the meaneft Defigns, and worft Engravings, of that voluminous Work.

THE Authour of the *Religion of the ancient Gauls* c labours under the fame deficiency, and is rather too redundant in his own Diſſertations, whilſt the too timorous Authour mentioned before him will fcarce hazard a fingle conjecture ; an excefs of caution, which, in one of fuch modefty and knowledge, is much to be lamented.

MR. *Toland* d has written on this fubject ; but I doubt whether ever he copied or meafured one Monument ; and the authorities upon which he afferts many extraordinary particulars have never yet been produced.

THE Reverend Mr. *Rowland* e took a better method to advance this kind of Learning ; he examined a great variety of Druid Monuments in Anglefea, has defcribed them as particularly as he could (though his Drawings are extremely ſhort of the reſt of his performance), and gives the world many pertinent obfervations upon them. He underſtood the Britiſh and learned Languages, and has made a proper application of both, in order to give light to his fubject.

MR. *Martin*, in his Defcription of the Weftern Ifles, fpeaks of many remains of the Druid Superftition in thofe Ifflands ; but, as I remember, there is but one Drawing engraved f, and that a very faulty one, by no means correfponding with the verbal defcription. In ſhort, fo little ufe has been made of the Druid Monuments (undoubtedly the beſt fupports of their Hiftory), that the more I read of thofe Authours, the more fully I was convinced of the neceſſity of copying the original Monuments, which lay round me, and offering fomething to the Publick, which their undeniable properties fuggefted, and, I hope, will ſtill maintain.

I MUST not forget to acknowledge, that this branch of Antiquity (as well as moſt others) is greatly obliged to the labours of the learned and ingenious Dr. *Stukeley*, particularly in his *Stonehenge* and *Abury*; and that *Keyfler*, in his Antiquities, fupports his judicious Remarks with very entertaining inftances from the Cuftoms and Hiftory of the Northern as well as other Nations.

c In Two Volumes, Quarto, by Monf. Martin.
d Hiftory of the Druids, Octavo.
e Mona Illuftrata, Quarto.
f The Temple at Claffernifs.

THE

Book IV.   THE fourth book is intended to confirm a point of Hiftory hitherto difputed, by fhewing, that the *Romans* were not only in *Cornwall*, but conquered it early; and, by their Coins, Sepulchres, and other Remains, appear to have fubdued every part of it.

NEXT follow fome Obfervations on the Military and Religious affairs of *Cornwall*, preceding the Norman Conqueft, with fome gleanings of Hiftory relating to the Civil Government of this County, its Princes, and Wars, in as much order as my Reading would afford.

THE remaining fheets I have dedicated to the Recovery and Prefervation of the *Cornifh Language*, of which more will be premifed to that part of the Work g.

THIS is the *fhell*; what it contains, muft here befpeak the candour of the learned Reader.

GREAT perfection cannot be expected, where the Subject is fo obfcure, the Age fo remote, and the Materials fo difperfed, few, and rude; where we muft range into fuch diftant Countries for Hiftory and Examples, and into fo many Languages for Quotations.

SOME of the miftakes and errours, I muft take wholly upon myfelf. The literal errours of the Prefs, the Printer and I muft take betwixt us.

SOME Mifquotations of Page and Book, as my fituation did not always afford me Originals, nor indeed often the moft correct Editions, may juftly be charged upon the Authours upon whofe credit I was obliged to depend.

I ALLOW that I have frequently ventured to differ in opinion from fome of the firft rank of Literature, becaufe I think every Authour, in juftice to the Publick, is obliged to give his own fentiments, rather than implicitly follow thofe of other people; but, whenever I differ, I hope it is with decency, I am fure it is not without fome reluctance.

I HAVE neither neglected the learned nor unlearned; but have gathered what plain truths I found in each, and endeavoured to

g See, in p. 413, the Preface to the Cornifh Vocabulary.

illuftrate

illuftrate my Subject with both; but never copied either, that I can recollect, without taking care that every Reader fhould know it.

I have been always ready to fubmit my papers to revifal and correction; and many Gentlemen, allowed to be well verfed in ftudies of this kind, can teftify, that I have oftener entreated their affiftance in this refpect, than I have been able to obtain it.

In treating of the Superftition and *Rock-Monuments* of the *Druids*, I may feem too conjectural to thofe who will make no allowances for the deficiencies of Hiftory, nor be fatisfied with any thing but evident Truths; but, where there is no Certainty to be obtained, Probabilities muft fuffice; and Conjectures are no faults, but when they are either advanced as real Truths, or too copioufly purfued, or peremptorily infifted upon as decifive.— In Subjects of fuch diftant Ages, where Hiftory will fo often withdraw her taper, Conjecture may fometimes ftrike a new light, and the truths of Antiquity be more effectually purfued than where people will not venture to guefs at all. One Conjecture may move the veil, another partly remove it, and a third, happier ftill, borrowing light and ftrength from what went before, may wholly difclofe what we want to know.

It is a very defirable character which Dr. *Plot* [h] gives of the writings of the famous Dr. *Willis*, that " in them there is " nothing trivial, moft new, and all moft ingenious." I am afraid, that in the following Treatife more things will appear trivial than new, and more new than ingenious, efpecially to thofe who will not admit the neceffity of minute and circumftantial Defcriptions and Meafurements.

But notwithftanding this—fome *Monuments* fcarce fo fully explained in others, fome new, that is, firft difcovered, others illuftrated by citations from the moft learned Ancients, not hitherto fo applied, and fome difficulties in Hiftory cleared up, will, I hope, be found in the following Work; and I flatter myfelf, upon the whole, that future Writers upon the *Britifh* Antiquities may find their tafk fomewhat the eafier for thefe *Obfervations*.

[h] Oxfordfhire, p. 309.

c   CONTENTS.

CONTENTS.

BOOK I.

CHAP. I. pag. 2. GEneral Obſervations on the Hiſtory of Britain; the Name of Britain, various Opinions of Camden, Bochart, &c. *Brit*, likely from the Hebrew; and *tania*, an uſual, additional Termination, pag. 5.

II. p. 6. Of the ancient Inhabitants; their Relation to the Eaſtern Nations, p. 6. The general Diſpoſitions of Mankind in the firſt Ages after the Flood, wandering and unſettled, p. 8. therefore Mankind ſpread quickly, peopled the Weſt and North of Europe ſoon, and the Iſlands adjacent, and then perhaps America, p. 9.

III. p. 10. Firſt Inhabitants from Gaul, p. 10. Tacitus's Opinion of the Origin of the ſeveral Inhabitants, from Spain and Germany, as well as Gaul, examined, p. 11. England not joined to the Continent ſince the Flood, p. 13. Cornwall not planted with Inhabitants from Phenicia, ibid.

IV. p. 14. Of the Gauls, p. 14. ſame as Celts and Cimbrians, ibid. Britain peopled before any Irruptions or Remigrations of the Celts, p. 17.

V. p. 18. What the antient Inhabitants of Britain thought of their own Original, p. 18. That they were ſprung from Dis, the Earth, or God of the Earth, ibid. The Germans and Romans had the ſame Notions, p. 19, 20.

VI. p. 21. Reſemblance which the ancient Cimbri or Celts bore to the Eaſtern Nations; how far the Monuments of Aſia and the Eaſtern Parts of Europe may contribute to illuſtrate the Antiquities of the Weſtern Nations, p. 21. that Reſemblance from Mankind's continuing ſome Centuries in one Nation and Society after the Flood, p. 23. whence Likeneſs in Tongue, Cuſtoms, and Religion, p. 24, 25.

VII. p. 25. Of the Story of Brute; if any Truth in it; very little and inconſiderable muſt have been his Power, p. 26. Of the Arrival of the Phenicians, p. 27. came into Cornwall early; but whence uncertain, p. 27 and 28. their Trade, p. 29. to the Caſſiterides, among which they reckoned the Weſtern Parts of Cornwall, p. 30. Few Monuments left behind them, and why, p. 31, 32.

VIII. p. 32. Of the Grecians, their Navigation, p. 33. what Time they might have come to the Caſſiterides for Tin, ibid. Cornwall and the Scilly Iſles the Places of their Traffic, p. 34. they left few Monuments, and why, p. 35.

IX. p. 35. Of the Romans; that they poſſeſſed themſelves of Cornwall, p. 35, 36, and 37.

X. p. 38. Of the Saxons. their coming into Britain owing to the Invitation of Vortigern, Earl of Cornwall, choſen King of Britain, p. 38. Britans fly before the Saxons into Wales, Cornwall, and Armorica, which laſt received it's Britiſh Inhabitants from Cornwall, p. 39. Wars of the Corniſh with the Saxons, p. 41. till finally conquered by Athelſtan, p. 48.

XI. p. 44. Of the Danes, p. 44. Invited to land by the Corniſh, p. 41. Intrenched and fortified their Landing-places, though in Alliance with the Corniſh, p. 45. had many Caſtles in the Weſt of Cornwall, ibid. wintered there, p. 47. turn Enemies to the Corniſh after Athelſtan's Conqueſt, and deſtroy Cornwall, p. 48.

XII. p. 49. Of the Normans. A ſhort View of the unſettled Situation of the Britiſh Crown, immediately preceding the Conqueſt; the Normans coming in eaſily, and by one Victory give a new Turn to the Monuments of Britain. A new Way of building Churches, Monaſteries, and Palaces, introduced. Croſſes richer, Sepulchres inſcribed, Dates affixed, French Tongue encouraged and enjoined, p. 49, &c.

XIII. p. 51. Moſt Monuments in Cornwall, and elſewhere in Britain, owe their Riſe to the antient Britiſh Religion, which was Druid, p. 51, 52.

B O O K   II.

CHAP. I.   WHENCE the Britifh Religion had its Rife, p. 53. from the antient Idolatry of the Eaft,
pag. 53.   ibid. What that ancient Idolatry was; its firft Rife, p. 54. its Motives and Principles, p. 55. Gods, and the Order in which they became fo, p. 56. Image-Worfhip fubfequent
to Ghoft-worfhip, p. 57. but foon became more univerfal, p. 58. Magic next, ibid. then
Fire-Worfhip, p. 59. Elements deified, ibid. Stones, and Beafts, Birds, and Reptiles, p. 60.
Worfhip of thofe numerous Gods how introduced, p. 61. how degenerate and polluted, ibid.
why the fame or like Idolatry in all Nations, p. 62. Human Victims not the Cuftom of the Druids
only, but of all Nations, p. 64. therefore Druidifm, or the Britifh Religion, is but a Branch of
the firft general Idolatry, p. 66.

II. p. 66.   Name and Claffes of the Druid Priefthood; Meaning and Derivation of the Word Druid, p. 66,
67, 68. Claffes three, Druids, Bards, and Eubates, p. 68.

III. p. 69.   Countries inhabited by the Druids. No Druids anciently in Germany, 69. but the German Religion effentially the fame with that of the Gauls and Britans, 71. as being originally Celtic, but
much improved by the Druids, p. 72. Druids, a Priefthood peculiar to the Gauls and Britans, and
common to every Part of Britain, ibid.

IV. p. 73.   Antiquity of the Druids; much more antient than Pythagoras, p. 74. but fubfequent to the
Divifion of the ancient Celts into Germans, Teutones, Spaniards, &c. p. 75.

V. p. 76.   Original of the Druids; not from the Jews, p. 76. nor Greeks, ibid. nor any foreign Nation,
but inftituted either in Britain or Gaul, p. 78.

VI. p. 78.   Druidifm had its firft Rife in Britain, and not in Gaul, p. 78.

VII. p. 80.   Dignity and Power of the Druids; they were the firft Order of the Britifh Nobility, p. 80.
educated Youth, decided all Contefts, excluded from Sacrifices, explained Omens, fared fumptuoufly; were exempted from the Burthens of War, but of great Influence both in War and Peace,
p. 80, 81. the Government of their Order; their general Affembly the laft Refort of Judgment, p. 82.

VIII. p. 83.   Druid Difcipline, Quality and Admiffion of their Difciples; Privacy, Time, Manner, and
Place of Inftruction, p. 83. taught by Verfes, *memoriter*, not by Writing, p. 84. Pythagoras and
Socrates did the fame, ibid. all their Religion and Morality in Hymns, and in what Metre,
p. 85; exceedingly ftrict in their Difcipline, and fevere in punifhing the Breaches of it; Lovers of
Silence, p. 86.

IX. p. 86.   Of the Druideffes, none proved by Keyfler to have been among the Germans, p. 86, 87, 88, 89.

X. p. 89.   Druid Learning; their Letters, p. 90. whether, and how far, they underftood the Greek Tongue,
p. 90, 91. Irifh Druid Letters, p. 91. Lovers of Verfe and Rhetoric, p. 92.

XI. p. 92.   Their Phyfical Knowlege; underftood the Nature of Eclipfes, Geography, Ethics; thought the
World had a Beginning, and was to have an End, by Fire; computed Times by Nights, as the
other Antients did, not by Days, and their Reafons for it, p. 92, 93. the Beginning of their
Year, July; Moon, fix Days old; a Generation with them, thirty Years, p. 92.

XII. p. 92.   Their Botany, Fondnefs of the Vervaine, p. 93. folemn gathering of the Mifletoe, p. 94.
gathering the Selago, p. 95. and Samolus, p. 96. Their Anatomy, ibid.

XIII. p. 96.   Moral and Religious Doctrines, Juftice, Confidence in a future Life.

XIV. p. 97.   The Immortality and Tranfmigration of the Soul, how far adopted by the Druids; Immortality
undoubtedly held by all, and a diftinct Principle from the other, p. 101. the Tranfmigration held
by fome, and that in two Senfes, ibid.

XV. p. 103.   Druid Doctrines not only taught by Verfes, *memoriter*, but by Allegory and Mythology, p. 103.
as appears by Lucian's Hercules Ogmius, ibid. Portal of Montmorillon, [Plate V. p. 53.]
explained, p. 104, 105. Cernunnos, [Plate VI. p. 107.] explained, p. 106.

XVI. p. 107.   Druid Deities, Idols, and Symbols, Mercury, Apollo, &c. p. 107. Symbols, the Cube and
Oak, ibid. that they worfhiped the Serpent, and the Bull, not unlikely, p. 110. certainly
Stones, Rocks, Fountains, and Fairies, ibid.

XVII. p. 110. Druid Places of Worſhip, Groves, p. 110. why, ibid. that they had Temples, p. 111, 112, 113. Keyſler's and Mr. Martin's Objections examined, ibid. Dr. Stukeley's three Claſſes of the Druid Temples, p. 114, 115. Temples, not accurately placed, p. 115. on the Tops of Hills, p. 116. Sacred Woods incloſed, ibid. Karn-brê Hill deſcribed, [Map, Plate VII. A Z, p. 117] referred to, and explained, p. 117, 118, 119, 120. Druids had no incloſed Temples, and why, p. 120. Contents of their Groves, Rude Stone-Idols, ibid. Altars for Burnt-offerings, Libations, and ſmall devoted Gifts, p. 121. Ordinary Places of Idolatry; Rocks, Fountains, Trees, and Croſs-Roads, p. 121, 122. many Places of Devotion, as Circles and Altars, near one another, and why, p. 122, 123.

XVIII. p. 123. The Druid Worſhip; Time of Worſhip; Women admitted, and why, p. 123. Vulgar to keep their Diſtance, 124. in what Order their Rites proceeded, ibid. Druid Habit, ibid. of Men and Women, p. 125. the Magic Rod, ibid. Several Kinds of Victims, Animal and Human; Reaſons which tended to confirm them in this dreadful Cuſtom, p. 125, 126. Cloſe of their Sacrifices, generally Intemperance, p. 127.

XIX. p. 127. Superſtitious Turnings of the Body during the Time of Worſhip, of the Druids, Greeks, and Romans, p. 127, 128, 129. Remains of this Cuſtom in the Scottiſh Iſles, p. 129, 130. of two Kinds, ibid. the Cuſtom of the three Turns very ancient, p. 131. (from Virgil and Ovid, p. 132.) Why the Druids turned Sun-ways, and why retrograde, conjectured, ibid. and ſupported from Tacitus, Keyſler, &c. p. 133. To what theſe unedifying Cuſtoms were owing; likely to the perverting or miſunderſtanding certain Portions of Scripture, p. 134.

XX. p. 134. The Holy Fires of the Druids; the Occaſional Feſtival Fires, made in ſeveral Parts of England, Remains of this Druid Rite, p. 135. when kindled, and how attended, in Cornwall, p. 135, 136. Karn Gollewa, and Karn Leſkys, Scenes of Fire-worſhip, p. 136. the latter deſcribed, and Plate IV. Fig. I. explained, ibid. Sharpy-tor, p. 137. Fire-worſhip common among the Canaanites, ibid.

XXI. p. 138. Divination, Charms, Incantations, and Predictions, p. 138. Divining, from the Entrails of the Victim, ibid. by Augury, by the Number of Criminal Cauſes, ibid. by Lots, p. 139. by white Horſes, p. 140. from the Waves, Eddies of Sea, River, and Well-water, ibid. from the Convulſions of the dying Victim, ibid. by the Running of a Hare, p. 141. by ſingle Duel, ibid. Charms of the Anguinum, ibid. Remains of this Rite in Cornwall, p. 142. Incantations of Stones, p. 143. Logan Sones, ibid. Holed Stones, ibid. Divinations from the Brain, and other Parts of Animals, p. 143. and Note P.

XXII. p. 144. Reſemblance betwixt the Druid and Perſian Superſtition, in Temples, Prieſts, Worſhip, and Doctrines; whence this Reſemblance, p. 149. Dion. Halicarn. examined, ibid. The Source gueſſed at, by diſtinguiſhing the ſeveral Parts of Gentiliſm in which they agree, p. 150, &c.

XXIII. p. 152. The Druids Declenſion and Extirpation; Altar of Tiberius repreſenting the ſame [Plate VIII. p. 157.] explained, p. 153. laſt Place we read of them, Ireland, where they were ſilenced by St. Patrick, p. 155. The many Monuments they muſt have left behind them, 155, 156, 157.

B O O K III.

CHAP. I. OF Rude Stone-Monuments in general, p. 158, 159.
pag. 158.

II. p. 160. Single Stones-erect, or rude Pillars, Religious Monuments, p. 160. Idolatrous, p. 161. Example of Do. in Cornwall, at Men-perhen, Sharpy-tor, and Wringcheeſe, p. 162. Memorials of Civil Contracts, p. 163. Marks of Places of Worſhip, p. 164. Of Places of Election and Council, ibid. Sepulchral, p. 165. Military Memorials, p. 166. Boundaries, 167. Scope-liſmus, p. 168.

III. p. 168. Rock-Idols common among the Orientals, p. 169. One remarkable Speaking-Stone in Wales, p. 170. Another in Norway, with the ſuppoſed Prophecy, p. 171. Why Rocks firſt became Emblems of Divine Powers, p. 172. Rock-Idols in Cornwall, many probably dedicated to Saturn, Mercury, or Mars, 173. Mên-Stone in Conſtantine, [Plate XI. Fig. I.] explained; another in Scilly; what they ſignified, conjectured, p. 173. Wring-Cheeſe, [Plate XII.] deſcribed; what intended to ſignify, ibid. Toll-Mên, two in Scilly, p. 174. [Plate XII. Fig. II. and III.] deſcribed. That in Conſtantine meaſured and explained, p. 174. Whether fixed by Art or Nature, conſidered, p. 175. Whereto the Paſſage underneath it might ſerve, ibid. Mên-an-tol of Maddern, [Plate XIV. Fig. I. and II.] planned, elevated, and deſcribed, p. 177. Served ſeveral ſuperſtitious Purpoſes; for Libation, ibid. Initiation, Dedicating, Sanctification, and Reſtoration of Health, ibid. Likely alſo Oracular, p. 178. The holed Stone at Roſmodreuy Circle, [Plate XIV. Fig. III.] explained, ibid.

The

IV. p. 179.　The Logan, or Rocking Stones; some among the Ancients; two Sorts, natural and artificial, p. 180. Treryn and Bosworlas, natural, ibid. Karn Lehau, artificial, ibid. St. Agnes Logan Stone in Scilly, [Plate XI. Fig. IV.] Men-an-bar in Sithney, [Plate XI. Fig. V.] described, p. 181. Mistakes concerning the last noted, p. 182. Druid Monuments, and their Use, ibid.

V. p. 183.　The supposed Virtue of Stones and Gemms; the Opinion borrowed from the Urim and Thummim of the Jews, p. 183. Adopted by Zoroaster, Zachalias, ibid. The Persians, the Druids, and the Germans, p. 184. Remains of it; the great Esteem of the Hematites, and the Fatal Stone, with its Oracle, p. 185.

VI. p. 185.　Monuments of Two, Three, and several Stones; Trewren, a Two-Stone Monument Sepulchral, [Plate X. Fig. IV, and V.] described, p. 187. Some Goals, ibid. Three-Stone Monuments, Sepulchral, or Idolatrous; some Memorials and Religious, ibid. Design of Wormius's Monument at the End of Chap. VII. guessed at, p. 180. Number and Shape of the Stones, why different, p. 189. Strait-line Monuments, their Intent, ibid. Nine Maids, [Plate XVII. Fig. I.] ibid. Stones erected as Portals; their Design, 190. Karn-Boscawen Monument, [Plate XIV. Fig. IV.] described, ibid. Its probable Use, ibid.

VII. p. 191.　Of Circular Monuments, Sect. I. Number and Distance of Stones, p. 191, 192. How named in Cornwall, Sect. II. p. 193, 194. Their Intent and Use, Sect. III. p. 194. Some Religious, as the Altars at Mount Sinai and Gilgal, p. 195. Why round, and the Limits marked with Stones erect, p. 196. Those of Grandeur and Magnificence Religious, p. 197. Stone-henge, a Druid Temple, and prior to the Romans and Saxons, ibid. Why of different Sizes, ibid. Particular Sorts of Religious Circular Monuments, Boskednan Circle, [Plate XV. Fig. II.] p. 198. Kerris Roundago, [Plate XII. Fig. II.] described, ibid. Salakee Temple in Scilly, [Plate XI. Fig. II.] described. The Hurlers, [Plate XII. Fig. VI.] p. 199. Botallek Circles, [Plate XVI.] explained, ibid. Circles with Altars, p. 200 Trescaw in Scilly, [Plate XII. Fig. IV.] explained, ibid. Karn Menelez, [Plate XII. Fig. V.] ibid. Classernis Temple, [Plate XVII. Fig. V.] p. 201. Wormius's and Speed's Mistakes, in calling them Trophies, p. 202. Places of Council and Judgment, Sect. IV. ibid. Altars in the Fora, p. 203. Stones to stand by (Boscawen un, Plate XV. Fig. III.) p. 204. to stand upon, p. 205. to sit upon, as Tredinek Circle, [Plate XV. Fig. I.] ibid. Bodinar Crellas, [Plate XVII. Fig. IV.] explained, p. 206. Senor Cirque, [Plate XV. Fig. IV.] its Intent probably, ibid. Some Theatres and Amphitheatres, and why, p. 207. St. Just Amphitheatre, [Plate XVIII. Fig. I. II.] explained; its Use, to hear Plays, and for British Exercises, p. 207. and for Duels, p. 208. Some Sepulchral, by Ashes, Urns, &c. found in them, p. 209. Little Circles at Bartiné, at Botallek, at Altarnun; likely, originally Sepulchral, p. 210.

VIII. p. 211.　Of Barrows, a Monument found in most Countries, p. 211. Name, p. 212. Construction, p. 213. From the adjacent Grounds; several Sorts, p. 216. Place, p. 217. Size, ibid. Scilly Barrows, [Plate XX. Fig. I. and II.] described, p. 219. To what Nations they are to be ascribed, p. 220. Secondary Uses of Barrows, p. 221.

IX. p. 223.　Of the Cromleh; its Place, p. 223. Construction and Name, 224. Found in many Nations, ibid. Kits Cotty House, [Plate XXII.] ibid. Not Altars originally, p. 225. Proved from Chûn Quoit, [Plate XXIV. Fig. X.] of Crum Cruach, p. 226, 227. A Sepulchral Monument, p. 229. Molfra Cromleh, [Plate XXIV. Fig. IX.] described, p. 230. Lanyon Cromleh, [Plate XXI. Fig. I.] p. 231. Senor Cromleh, [Plate XXI. Fig III. and IV.] p. 232. Chûn Cromleh, [Plate XXIV. Fig. X.] ibid. Human Bones found in one in Ireland, p. 233.

X. p. 233.　Of Urn-Burial; Urns how and where placed, p. 234. Chikarn Urns, ibid. Gwythian Urn, p. 236. And what to be thence inferred, ibid. Bones how disposed, p. 237. Mên Urn, ibid. Various Contents of Urns, p. 238. Some Bones more burnt than others, and why, p. 239. Accounted very unhappy not to have the Dead much burnt, from Homer, p. 240.

XI. p. 240.　Of the Rock-Basons, found in several Parts, p. 240. Two Sorts, some with Lips, others with none; where placed, p. 241. Their Shape and Size, p. 242. For what Use not fit, p. 243. The Antiquity and Frequency of Water-Purifications, p. 245. Varieties of Holy-Water, p. 248. Spring and Sea Water, ibid. Dew, p. 249. Rain and Snow Water, p. 249, 250. That the Druids had the Rites of external Purifications, p. 252. Of the General Use of the Rock-Basons, p. 254. The Use of those which have Lips, p. 255. Use of those which have no Lips, p. 256. Some shaped as if to receive the Human Body, ibid.

XII. p. 258.　Of the Gold Coins found at Karn-brê, p. 258. Their Description, p. 259. Not Phenician, p. 263. nor Greek, nor Roman, p. 265. A Passage in Cesar examined, ibid. Camden's and Speed's Coins examined, p. 267. Which are British, p. 269. Of the Resemblance which the Karn-brê Coins bear to the Gaulish, and the Reason of it, p. 271. Of the Age of these Gold Coins, p. 273. Of the several Charges or Symbols of these Gold Coins, p. 275, &c. and why

why all of or belonging to the Chariot, p. 279. Of the Head, Diadem, Clasp, curled Hair, Habit, Trees, Spices, Balls, Pearls, and Laminæ, p. 280, 281.

XIII. p. 281. Of the Brass Celts found at Karn-brê, p. 281. How far to be assigned to to the Romans, 282. Where found, and with what, p. 283. Various Opinions of their Use, p. 284. [Plate XXIV. Fig. I. and II. &c.] described, p. 286. Their Size, Socket, Edge, Ring or Eye, and their Uses, p. 286, 287. A Stone Celt, p. 287. Why commonly made of Brass, p. 289.

XIV. p. 292. Of the Caves of the ancient Cornish-Britans, p. 292. Bolleit and Bodinar Caves, ibid. Pendeen Vau, or Vou, [Plate XXV. Fig. I.] described, p. 293. Their Use for Retreat in Time of War, p. 294, &c.

BOOK IV.

CHAP. I. pag. 298. OF Roman Coins found near Mines in Cornwall, p. 298. Roman Coins found near Harbours, p. 300. Mopas Coins, p. 302. Trewardreth Coins, ibid. Of scattered Coins, p. 303.

II. p. 306. Of Roman Sepulchres and other Remains, p. 306. Sancred Urn, p. 307. Kerris Urn, ibid. Golvadnek Barrow, ibid. Roman Remains found at Karn-brê, p. 309. Roman Pateræ, ibid. Some Fragments, p. 311.

III. p. 311. Roman Camps and Fortifications in Cornwall, p. 311. Little Dinas, p. 312. Binnoway and Wallsburrow, ibid. Lancefton, p. 315. Wolvedon, ibid. St Agnes Klêdh, ibid. Shape of Roman Fortifications, p. 315. Boffens Fort, p. 316. Latin Inscription in Greek Letters found on a Tin Patera, p. 317.

IV. p. 321. Of the Roman Geography of Cornwall, and the ancient and present Limits, p. 321. Of the Voliba, Uxela, Tamare, and Isca of Ptolemy, p. 322. That Exeter is the Isca Dunmoniorum of the Itinerary, p. 323. Ancient and present Name of the County, whence, p. 324. How far Cornwall extended, p. 325. Of Stratton, whether a Roman Town, p. 326.

V. p. 327. Roman Ways, their Uncertainty, p. 327. Structure, p. 328. Roman Ways, West of Exeter, p. 330. Antoninus's Itin. Peutinger's Table, Ptolemy, and the Anonymous Ravennas, examined, p. 330, 331. Richard of Westminster, p. 332. Part of a Roman Road, likely, betwixt Lostwythyel and Liskerd, p. 333. and betwixt Bodman and Lostwythyel, p. 334. A Northern Roman Road, through Stratton, p. 336.

VI. p. 330. When Cornwall was in all Probability first conquered by the Romans, p. 338. Antique Intaglio of a Griffin, p. 342.

VII. p. 343. Ancient Castles in Cornwall: Cliff Castles, as Treryn Castle, &c. p. 344. their Use, p. 345. Hill Castles, as Bartiné, Caerbrân, Castle-andinas, and Castle Chûn, p. 346, 347. by whom built, and for what End, p. 348.

VIII. p. 350. Of Walled Castles, for Defence and Residence, p. 350. Castle Karn-brê, ibid. Tindagel, p. 352.

IX. p. 354. Castles which have Keeps, as Trematon, p. 354. Reftormel, p. 356. Bofcastle, and Lancefton Castle, p. 358. The Name, p. 362. Antiquity and Use of such Castles, p. 363.

X. p. 366. State of Christianity in Cornwall, before the Norman Conquest, p. 366. Saints who preached or suffered in Cornwall, p. 369. Of the Monasteries of the fifth Century, p. 372. British Churches in Cornwall, under the Saxons, p. 374. A Bishoprick erected in Cornwall, p. 377.

XI. p. 380. Of Religious Houses founded in Cornwall before the Norman Conquest: Of Padstow Church and Monastery, p. 380. Of Bodman Priory and Cathedral, ibid. St. German's Priory, p. 381. Of the Deanry of St. Berian, p. 384. Bonury, p. 385. Of St. Stephen's near Lancefton, ibid. Priory of St. Michael's Mount, ibid. Carantoc Deanry, p. 387. St. Neot's, ibid. St. Piran, p. 388. St. Kiaran, alias St. Keveryn, ibid. Priory at Scilly, p. 389. St. Probus, ibid. Constantine, p. 390.

Inscribed

XII. p. 391.   Infcribed Monuments before the Norman Conqueft, p. 391. Ifnioc, ibid. Cirufius, 392. Rialobran, p. 393. Quenetau, p. 394. Cnegumi, p. 395. Catin, ibid. Doniert, 396. Alroron, p. 399. Ruani, 401. Leuiut, ibid.

XIII. p. 402.   The Civil Government of Cornwall, from the Time of Brute, p. 402. A Catalogue of the Kings of Britain, with the Princes and Affairs of Cornwall, according to the Order of Time, to the Norman Conqueft, p. 404.

XIV. p 413.   Cornifh Vocabulary, p. 415.

HISTORICAL

Plate III. pa. I.

Delin. W.B.   *J.^a Green Sculp. Oxon*

HISTORICAL OBSERVATIONS

RELATING TO

BRITAIN.

BOOK I.

General Observations on the Hiftory of Britain.

IN order to illuftrate the ancient monuments which are to be found in Cornwall, it will be neceffary to take a fhort view of the moft important circumftances in the hiftory of this ifland of Britain. The original of a people muft be confidered and carefully traced, becaufe whatever monuments are difcovered to have been among the anceftors (I mean the firft planters of countries) will in all probability be found among the pofterity. To difcover the original of a nation, the name, the national language, the neighbouring people, the refemblance of its manners, laws, monuments and religion to thofe of the moft early ages (though in diftant countries) may all contribute ; but, above all, authentic records (if they can be found) will moft effectually fatisfy our enquiries.

Befides the original people from whence any nation is derived, we have a farther enquiry to make, which is, into what changes and alterations the people fo derived, have either by war and conqueft been forced, or by mutual converfe, trade, and alliance have infenfibly and gradually paffed ; becaufe every fuch alteration will difpofe a people to erect different kinds of monuments, according to

the

the different cuftoms which they have contracted by inclination and commerce, or which have been impofed upon them by their con-querors.

Thefe things being neceffary to give fome light into the fubject of the following papers, it will be worth our while to confider what may really be difcovered, what may fairly be implied, what proba-bly be fuppofed; but to enter particularly into the Britifh hiftory, or endeavour at a regular feries of perfons, times and facts, would be as vain in a writer, as it would be unpardonable with regard to the reader. The ifland of Britain is mentioned very feldom, and in a few words by the Greek authors now extant[a], fo that authentic records, relating to our ifland, we have none beyond the times of Julius Cefar; fome few remarks of Tacitus we have next; fome hafty, and general obfervations in the Roman writers of the fubfe-quent ages, but none after Tacitus exprefsly, except Gildas, till Bede; and afterwards too many fictions of name, time, and fact (it is to be feared) in the monkifh times, publifhed to the world for hiftory; fo that there is fcarce any hiftory more disfigured by fable, and more uncertain as to facts, and time, than the Britifh hiftory, and every one muft now defpair of entering into the particulars of it with any fanguine hopes of certainty. However, Cornwall being one of the two places to which the natives of this ifland who furvived the Roman and other conquefts chiefly retired, in order to preferve the little remains of Britifh blood, and liberty, and having retained the language of the ancient Britans down to the prefent times, we may fafely conclude, that the hiftory of Cornwall is naturally in-cluded in, and muft principally be drawn from, that of Britain in general, however imperfect.

C H A P. I.

Of the Name of Britain.

THE original of names is neither the moft entertaining, nor the moft inftructive part of knowledge; but as in the feveral opinions of learned men on this head, fome traces of the ancient hi-ftory of our ifland, may now and then be difcovered, it may not be amifs to fay fomewhat on that head, though, by reafon of the great uncertainty of fuch matters, very little may fuffice.---In the derivation of names no great agreement among the learned is to be expected. I here induftrioufly omit feveral derivations collected with great care by Camden, and his editor, Mr. Speed, and others, where the curious reader may take his Choice of thofe words which

[a] Ariftotle, Polybius, Athenæus, &c.

will

will give him moft fatisfaction; and fhall only make a few obfervations on the fuppofitions of Camden and Bochart. Firft then, if brit
or brith fignifies painted, as Mr. Camden (page xxxv, &c.) affirms,
it is not unlikely that our ifland was called by the later Greeks (for
Albion was its firft name as Pliny fays) Britania, becaufe the inhabitants painted their bodies, this being a cuftom fo fingular, as might
well ferve to diftinguifh them from other nations, which is the fole
end of fuch names: add to this, that thofe who retired before the
Romans, and were pent up in the northern parts of Scotland, were
called by the Romans Picts, to denote, as well their cuftom of
painting their bodies, as to diftinguifh them from the other branches
of the Britans, who were more fupple, and willing to leave their
own national cuftoms, and conform to thofe of the Romans. This,
therefore, is a very natural fuppofition of Mr. Camden, if the cuftom
of painting were general among the Britans, as well as peculiar to
their nation, and the word brit, or brith fignified painted. But it
is by no means agreed, that either of thefe words fignifies painted,
in the Britifh tongue [b]: and farther, what the ancient native Britans
called themfelves, and their country, we no where find; but if
they had the cuftom of painting themfelves from the Celts, or Gauls,
or from the Scythians, as Bede and Dr. Stillingfleet imagine, it can
fcarce be conceived why they fhould call themfelves painted, or their
country that of painted men, when their next neighbours the Gauls,
the Geloni, Agathyrfi, and Scythæ, had the fame fafhion, and that
famenefs would prevent all diftinction: and, indeed, though fome
rich and fanciful perfons among them might paint themfelves, yet
it can fcarce be fuppofed that this was a national, univerfal cuftom [c].
It is more eafily to be imagined, therefore, that brit or brith fignifies
fomewhat of the natural fituation of the ifland, than any thing fo
variable as the cuftom of the inhabitants. It is further to be obferved, that the Greeks and Romans in forming the names of places
built upon the foundation, which they found ready laid to their
hands, either by fome adjunct making the ancient word more expreffive, or contenting themfelves to improve the found only by a
more mufical termination; fo that brit is very likely to be found (if
not in the Britifh) in fome other language, akin or parental to it, as
we will endeavour to fhew by and by.

Bochart has recourfe to the Greek name of this ifland, Βρεζανικη,
in order to derive it, with the greater probability, from Baratanac,
in the Phenician tongue fignifying a land of tin: but it may with
reafon be objected to this great man's fuppofition, that the termina-

---

[b] No Britifh word begins with a B as a radical letter: Humph. Lhwyd, Breviar. Sammes, 46.
Yet it muft be owned that Dr. Davis in his Dictionary, and from him Mr. Ed. Lhwyd fays,

Archæol. p. 20. col. 3. W. Brith, painted;
brith, fpeckled. pag. 33. col. 3. Ib. and brithilh,
Angl. "Spot fifh, fcil. a trout." pag. 34. ib.
[c] Sammes, pag. 70 to 74.

tion

tion of Βρεϊανικη is very common among the Greek derivatives [d], and
the κ, here, implies not the fame confonant neceffary in the theme,
or root from whence the word is taken, and to the root it is that
we muft refort for the truth of a derivation ;—befides this, it is not
very clear in Hiftory that the whole ifland of Britain was ever famous in all its feveral parts, or, indeed, in many of them, for the
production of tin ; and it can fcarce be fuppofed that what, fuch
a fmall corner of it as Cornwall, and the Scilly Ifles, was remarkable for, fhould have credit enough to give name to an ifland
fo many times larger than themfelves. Where a whole, or the
greateft part of a country, was anciently very remarkable forplenty
of fome peculiar commodities, as corn, wine, honey, and the like,
there, that a name fpecifying that commodity, fhould fix upon it,
is not improbable ; it is therefore not unlikely that the little Scilly
Iflands fhould receive the name of Caffiterides from their tin ; but
that the vaft ifland of Britain fhould receive its name from a metal
found only in the moft remote, and fcattered extremities, does not
feem to be probable.

These are the moft confiderable derivations of the word Britain ;
and although it is more eafy to fhew the difficulties, and infufficiency
of other etymologies, than to eftablifh one unexceptionable in their
room : yet, as we are now engaged with names, it may not be amifs
to refer it to the learned as a thing to be confidered, whether the
former part of the word Britain may not be found in the Hebrew
language, which, as we are well affured, is the ground of the Phenician, and ancient Celtic. In the Britifh tongue there are many,
(See Rowl. Mon. Ill. p. 278.) fome fay 300 Hebrew Roots to be
found, which will make it not unlikely, to find the root of Brit
in that facred language. There ברא in Pihal, fignifies to cut off,
or divide, and with the ת added, (an ufual termination of nouns
derived from verbs, as ברית fœdus, &c.) will fignify a divifion, or
feparation ; and doubtlefs this is the firft idea that ftrikes us, when
we compare the fituation of Britain with that of its neighbouring
countries on the continent, from which it is fo entirely divided :

Et penitus toto, divifos orbe Britannos.

The latter part of this word is—tania ; a termination, not unufual among the Greeks, fignifying probably, no more than a region, or extent of land, as Camden rightly obferves. Thus Mauri-
tania is the land of the Moors ; Aquitania the land of waters ; Lufitania from lufus, (fays Pliny, lib. iii.) ; Baftitania, and Turditania,
two provinces of Spain, from the Turdi and Bafti. (Speed, pag. 9.

[d] As Ατ]ικ☉, Αθλη]ικ☉, Αιολικ☉, &c.

Rowland

Rowland Mon. illuft.) Now, if it fhall not fatisfy the reader to derive this tania from the Greek verb τεινω, we are inform'd by Pezron that ftan or tan fignifies, in Celtic, a region; and fome others alfo think, that tyn, or tain, or tania, does alfo fignify the fame thing, from Tany fpreading; if fo, I would only obferve that as the Celtic is fuppos'd to have contributed largely towards forming the Greek, Latin, and moft European tongues, the Greeks might have form'd their τεινω as well as their τανια from tany or tan in the Celtic, and apply'd it to countries, to which the figure of thofe countries made it juftly applicable. 'Tis therefore fubmitted, whether Bre-tania (as the Greeks write it) may not fignify a country divided from the continent, and extended in length, both which appellations may certainly with as much propriety be apply'd to Britain, as to any country in the world; for as the Sea feparates it from Gaul, and the continent, fo 'tis to be obferv'd that the land does not lye round, fquare, or in any compact figure, but very much extended, and ftretch'd out in length, as every map will inform us. But whatever the name of Britain may be deriv'd from, the long continuance of it, even from its firft appearance in hiftory, down to the prefent time, whereas all, or moft other countries have loft their original appellation, is thought by fome to be for the honour of the nation, and therefore much admir'd and envy'd by foreigners g.

Thus much for the variety of opinions concerning the name of Britain, from which, if we learn nothing elfe, we may certainly learn this ufeful leffon, that as the original of names appears to be very obfcure and uncertain, and the moft lucky conjecture is not likely to make us much wifer or better, it is by no means worth the while too tenacioufly to perfift in one's own fenfe, or to labour induftrioufly to obtrude it upon others.

CHAP. II.

Of the ancient Inhabitants of Britain.

WE are not likely to find greater certainty and fatisfaction in our enquiries about the firft inhabitants, than about the name of this country; but, indeed, Britain is not fingular in this point, nor our hiftory more defective than that of our neighbours; the firft planting of countries lying at too vaft a diftance in the fpace of time to admit of a diftinct view. In this profpect, as in others upon land

Scawen's MS. &c. penes C. Lyttelton, LL. D. Epifcopum Carliolen.

or water, what we fee with our utmost ken, we know not whether they be the real hills or mountains of the land we are bound to, or whether they may prove any thing more than fome deceitful clouds that may difappoint our expectations.   I fhall not therefore detain the reader long in thefe obfcure paths, but only endeavour to trace the inhabitants of this ifland fo far back, as to fhew their relation and refemblance to thofe eaftern nations of whom we have fome profane as well as facred hiftory remaining; like cuftoms, and like monuments appearing upon the records of fome countries, and exifting in reality in others (though at a great diftance) affording us the fureft light, and the moft reafonable deductions towards il-luftrating the antiquities of all countries which bear fuch an affinity.

It is in vain to enquire at what time this ifland of Britain firft re-ceiv'd it's inhabitants; but in all probability it was not a long time uninhabited, after its neighbouring nations, Gaul, Germany, and Spain were once peopled; and, confidering the temperate climates of thefe nations, the fertility of their foils, and the quick increafe of mankind, but more efpecially the will of God, which plainly appears to have been, that, what he had ordain'd for the ufe of man fhould be us'd and enjoy'd [h], this cannot be fuppos'd to be very

The weftern parts of Europe inhabit-ed foon after the difperfi-on. long after the difperfion of mankind at Babel.   The difperfion hap-pen'd, according to the Hebrew chronology, about the 101ft year after the univerfal deluge [i]; but this being much too early for a fufficient number of perfons, even to have form'd one large king-dom, much lefs fo unwieldy and tumultuous a number, as required a miraculous difperfion from heaven, and was fufficient to form many colonies and kingdoms in the different climates of the world, the Samaritan computation is reckoned more worthy to take place, and this fets the birth of Peleg (at whofe birth this difperfion hap-pened) about the four hundredth year after the flood: this will af-ford time for mankind to increafe, and, forgetting the fmart of God's judgements, to form ambitious defigns againft the decrees of hea-ven; time to combine together, and think their numbers would protect them from any future defolations [k]; in fhort, about 400 years after the flood, mankind may well be fuppos'd proud of their numbers, and God thought fuch numbers fit to be divided (as be-ing fufficient to plant the moft confiderable parts of the world), and that the world itfelf, as well as the Inhabitants thereof, might be equally benefited by fuch a feparation.   After this difperfion at

[h] "And God bleffed them, and God faid "unto them, Be fruitful and multiply, and *re-*"*plenifh* the Earth", fill it, fays the Hebrew. Gen. i. 28. So again immediately after the De-luge "God bleffed Noah and his Sons; and faid "unto them, Be fruitful, and multiply, and "replenifh the earth." Gen. ix. 1.
[i] Bochart is of the fame opinion. Geog. Sac. Lib. II. Ch. xiv.
[k] See Univerfal Hift. Lib. I. Ch. ii.

Babel,

Babel, it could not be many years before such a country as Europe was possess'd in all, at least its most temperate parts[1]. Some people, indeed, are for allowing several ages for this. They say that before mankind spread into different climates, and would forego their habitual settlements, friends, and relations, they must be much press'd by numbers; consequently, time must be allowed for their increase, (without supposing the interposition of an unnecessary miracle, which is absurd) nay for such an increase, as must have made it uneasy for them to stay together, which, after the first plantation of the earth by the posterity of Noah, and indeed after the dispersion too, must have been some hundreds of years at a moderate computation. But in this opinion, the dispositions of mankind in those early ages, and the determin'd will of God to have all (at least the most considerable) parts of this world possess'd, cultivated, and, like houses made wholsome by habitation, do not seem to have weight enough allow'd them. For, first, in those early ages, after the flood, a vast and quick increase of numbers may be justly allow'd to mankind; owing, as may be suppos'd, to their longevity, and their bodies continuing strong and nervous, some ages longer than they do at present: besides, soon after the dispersion, we can't but imagine that it became the general disposition of mankind to migrate from one country to another; curiosity either inspiring them with a desire of exploring different regions, hoping still to find what was better, that they might at last chuse which was best of all, and settle there, and in continual apprehension as they were in those unsettled times, least other names, and nations should prevent, and take the title of first possession from them: at the same time, as they journey'd, 'tis natural to suppose, that one portion of land might suit one, or more families, one country another tribe, and a third might have something particularly agreeable to another set of men. Mankind (at least as various then as now) as they pass'd from one country to another, left none without some inhabitants, there being hardly any situation or climate which would not engage some particular tempers to settle in it; not to mention, that the aged and weary, with those whom they could influence, would willingly put an end to their journeyings, wherever their fatigues were imagin'd to be, or really were, insupportable. All this while, for the same reason that God

---

[1] Japhet (under the name Iapetus, famous in Europe, according to many learned men (Bossuet's Universal Hist. p. 10.), having himself peopled the greatest part of the west.—Bochart is also of opinion, that of the seven sons of Japhet, two, viz. Thiras and Javan, came into Europe. Thiras took possession of Thracia and Mysia, and the north of Europe. Javan the southern parts, Greece, Italy, Gaul, and Spain. Geogr. Sacr. Lib. III. Cap. i. — " Mankind journey'd, (says Theoph. Antioch. quoted in Camden last edit. page 12.) " till they came even to Britain. Ex omnium " Historicorum fide certum est Gomerum, seu " Aschenazen, cum aliis Noemi nepotibus Gal- " liam primos inhabitasse."

Bulæus in Friek, p. 154.

3

dispers'd

difpers'd them firft from Babel, God's pre-difpofing power attended them; made them curious after foreign countries, and willing and earneft to make new fettlements, even before the firft fettlements of the immediate defcendants of Noah can be fuppos'd to be regularly eftablifh'd, or form'd into well-govern'd focieties: it was indeed in fome meafure neceffary for the prefervation both of man and beaft, that this wandering temper of mind fhould prevail, and this is the reafon that we find the patriarchs Abraham and Jacob fo unfettled, changing their countries fo eafily, whenever the want of provender or victuals pinch'd themfelves or cattle. This is the reafon that Efau or Edom went from his father's habitation, and fettied far to the fouth, and the Scythians, of the fame ftock with thofe who peopled the weft of Europe, liv'd in their waggons, in a ftate of continual motion, down to the times of Auguftus [m]; and this cuftom of the Scythians I muft obferve could be no new thing, no improvement of what was before, but very likely the manner in which the firft difpers'd from Babel convey'd their wives, children, and aged, and continued ever after fo to do. Thus then, the in-creafe of numbers, man's natural curiofity, the inability of the earth to maintain any great numbers in one fpot, 'till the invention of tillage, and above all, the gracious defign of the deity to have all his earth inhabited, co-operating to one and the fame end, it became the fafhion of the age, after the difperfion, to migrate; and we may reafonably conclude, that they no fooner had refted themfelves a little, after their long travels, but thinking every thing better which was to come, and at a diftance, than what they then enjoy'd, a great part of their numbers ftill mov'd on, not only through plains, and over mountains, but we have reafon to believe, that in thefe early times they boldly attempted the rivers and lakes, making ufe of floats, and fuch fhips, as they had either by tradition learn'd Noah's ark to have been, or fuch, as their moft ingenious mecha-nicks could then contrive: here alfo, we may imagine that there was no mountain fo high, nor any lake fo wide, nor any river fo rapid, but that the bolder and more intrepid fort would pique themfeves upon getting over the difficulties they met with. This fet the ingenious to invent proper machines, and veffels, to put fuch adventurous defigns in execution; and that this muft foon have happen'd, after the difperfion, nay at the very difperfion itfelf, will appear to every one, who will give himfelf the trouble to furvey the country of Mefopotamia; from whence, without boats or fome contrivance of the fame kind, no people could con-vey themfelves into any country beyond the great and navigable rivers of Tygris and Euphrates. Sailing, 'tis true, was the invention

[m] Hor. Car. Lib. III. Ode 24. See Herodotus.

of

of after ages, and is afcrib'd to Dedalus, the generation before the Trojan war; but boats, or fmall fhips, with oars, were much more ancient, and things which Noah and his fons, having experienc'd the fecurity of the ark (built by God's own appointment and direction), could by no means be ignorant of, nor their defcendants be carelefs enough to want the fervice of, in their peregrinations [m]: but to return, — fo reftlefs and inquifitive after new countries muft the firft ages after the difperfion have been, that they no fooner faw an ifland but we muft imagine fome of them were fir'd with a defire of furveying and poffeffing it. As foon, therefore, as the pofterity of Japhet had fpread themfelves over the weftern parts of Europe, and had poffefs'd the fea fhores of Gaul, they faw no doubt the oppofite coafts of Britain, and were foon inclin'd to adventure over, and fee what fort of country it was, and how well it deferv'd to be inhabited : this appears to have been the prevailing paffion of the age. To have waited 'till their firft fettlements were compleated, to fear the injuries of different climates, to be captivated with the eafe and plenty which they might almoft every where in the fouth of Europe have enjoy'd, to be terrify'd by the Alps, Apennine, or Pyrenean hills, by the width of rivers, and arms of the fea; to fit down contented 'till their prodigious increafe of numbers fhould make them divide again, and brought them under a neceffity of moving on farther; all thefe feem to be difpofitions fuiting well enough an age of luxury and eafe, but foreign and unnatural to the firft ages after the flood, and entirely oppofite to the principal intention of God at the difperfion, which was, to have the feveral parts of his terreftrial globe poffefs'd, cultivated, and improv'd.

Britain ftocked with inhabitants probably foon after Gaul.

And here, perhaps (fince the peopling America is a circumftance in hiftory fo difficult to account for), it may well deferve the thoughts of the learned, whether, whilft this travelling humour prevailed, the great continent of America might not have received its firft inhabitants from fome hardy adventurers, who, coafting from the northern parts of Afia and Europe, into the American continent, and foon after divided by the polar fnows from the reft of mankind, at a time when letters were fcarce known, no records kept, and no religion fettled, kept journeying ftill towards the fouth, in a fhort time loft all traces of the parents they fprung from; and were indeed loft to them 'till the great difcoveries of Columbus. But however that be, 'tis reafonable to imagine, that the iflands near the continent, and to be feen from thence, were foon peopled after the continent was inhabited, and that Britain, among the reft had her inhabitants as foon as, or but very little after, Gaul.

[m] A fhip was the fymbol of Saturn, who was Noah. Bochartus, Stillingfl. Orig. Sacr. 592.

Janus was alfo Noah; and Plutarch in his Roman Queftions, fays, that the ancient coins had on one fide the image of Janus with his two faces; on the other, the hinder part of the fhip. Ib. ut fupra. Stillingfl.

D

CHAP.

C H A P. III.

First Inhabitants from Gaul, and Gaul only.

AS we received our first inhabitants much about the same time with Gaul, because from thence our shores are to be discover'd, so it is also most likely, that we had our first inhabitants from Gaul, and for the same reason [n] : for as soon as the cliffs of Kent were observ'd from the opposite shores, the same restlessness (for it can't be call'd necessity) which may be said rather to have scatter'd inhabitants over the face of the earth, than to have planted it regularly, and replenish'd it, brought them over into Britain. These were likely the first inhabitants which this island receiv'd after the flood ; for should we allow with Tacitus, that the northern inhabitants came from Germany, the eastern only from Gaul, and those of the south from Spain (an opinion not easily maintain'd), yet the Gauls must have come in first ; it being more probable that those parts which lye within sight of the continent should first prompt the adventurous to cross the straits, than that the other parts should be planted first by persons, who had nothing before their eyes to make them attempt so dangerous a passage.

Thus much then is most agreeable to truth, that our first inhabitants came from Gaul [o] ; it being but a short passage betwixt the shores, and Britain plainly thence to be discerned by the naked eye, and what Tacitus [p] gives, as reasons that the inhabitants should come from three different places, because of the resemblance the inhabitants of the north bore to the Germans, those of the east to Gaul, and of South Wales to Spain, will prove no more, than that these parts of our island, being oppos'd to the different countries of Germany, Gaul, and Spain (tho' indeed the Silures can scarce be said to be oppos'd to Spain but in one certain sense, which will be taken notice of presently), had by their mutual correspondence, trade, alliances, or conquests, contracted a resemblance of manners, or, as he himself supposes [q], from a like climate, had a likeness of complexion, stature, and constitution. Others have thought, that the Phenicians, others that the Grecians planted some part of the sea coasts, leaving colonies behind them, but the great uniformity (even in the most important

[n] Britannos Gallicæ esse originis conjectat Jornandes. Hist. Goth. Cap. ix. says Bochart, page 165.
  [o] Bochart, page 1187. Camd. Pr. p. xv.
[p] Vita Agricol. Cap. iv.
[q] Seu procurrentibus in diversa terris positio cæli corporis habitum dedit.

articles)

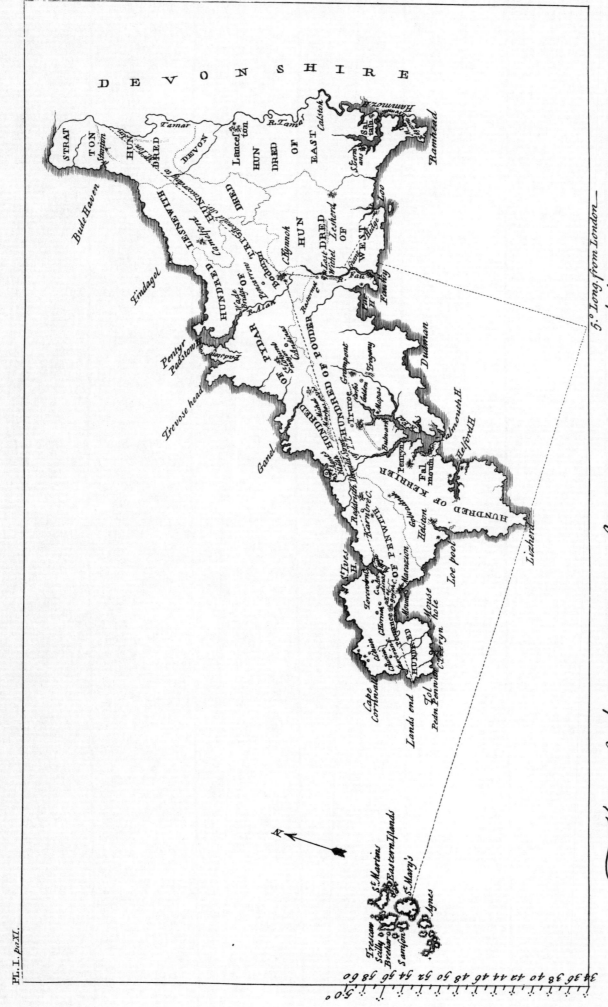

Map of the COUNTY of CORNWALL and the SCILLY ISLANDS

⊙ Ancient Casts U ✱ Where Roman Coins have been found ⸝⸝⸝⸝⸝⸝ Where Roman Ways are suppos'd ‖ C.Castle ‖ R.River. ‖ H.Harbour.

articles) to be obſerv'd among the ancient Britans, proves them of one original ; therefore that the inland inhabitants were Αυτοχθονες, and Aborigines, and the maritime parts peopled from different countries, is a groundleſs ſuppoſition ; for indeed there are no footſteps of any more than one language, one prieſthood, one ſort of monuments every where among them ; and wherever the ancient Britans were neceſſitated to retire, as into the north of Scotland, Wales, Cornwall, Cumberland, and Bretagne in Normandy, there the remains of one and the ſame language common to all are ſtill to be found; there the ſame monuments, civil, military, and religious, remain; and therefore the ſame cuſtoms, and religion, are to be inferr'd, and all contribute to ſhew that they had one original.

As we came from Gaul, ſo we had the ſame language which the ancient Gauls us'd [r]. Thus the leaders of the Gauls who ſack'd Rome, had names which were of Britiſh derivation ; and this made Mr. H. Lluyd imagine them to be Britiſh kings [s], whereas at that time, Gaul and Britain, and partly Germany too (for they were the Galli Senones, a people of North Germany, as Tacitus aſſures us, who ſack'd Rome [t]) had the ſame language, as ſprung from one common ſtock, and this language continued equally the tongue of both nations 'till Ceſar's time. Tacitus [u], ſpeaking of our reſemblance to the Germans and Spaniards produces (as is carefully to be obſerv'd) only ſome conſtitutional likeneſſes, as that the northern Britans have large limbs, long yellow hair, like the Germans; the ſouthern people of Wales (viz. the Silures) were ſwarthy, with curl'd hair like the Spaniards ; and even theſe were but imaginary reſemblances, and on which Tacitus lays very little ſtreſs : but when he treats of the coming in of the Gauls, there he inſiſts on the probability of the fact, intimating, that there was not much to be ſaid for the other opinions [w] ; in which it is to be obſerved, that we have no German or Spaniſh language ſo much as intimated to have remain'd in thoſe parts of Britain, which, if the people had been intruders from Germany and Spain into Britain, they muſt, in ſome meaſure, have preſerv'd, all nations being willing to retain their native language ; but when he comes to the parts oppoſite to Gaul, there he mentions an agreement in language, cuſtoms, and every thing elſe almoſt, betwixt the two nations. And when the Saxons had driven the ancient Britans into Wales and Cornwall, they were call'd Galli ; Wales, Gallia ; Cornwall, Cornugallia ; all expreſſing the ancient Britans to have been one and the ſame people, as to origin, with the Gauls upon the continent. Some

[r] Boch. Vol. I. page 1200.
[s] Humph. Lluyd, Brev.
[t] See Elias Sched. page 7.

[u] Vit. Agric. ut ſupra.
[w] " In univerſum tamen æſtimanti Gallos " vicinum ſolum occupaſſe credibile eſt."

may

may think that it derogates from the dignity of our country to allow of a Gaulish original, but, be the consequences what they will, whenever we are in search after TRUTH, although we discover her in ruins and rubbish, we must acknowledge, and revere her.

The Gauls in Cesar's time knew little of Britain;   If it should seem surprizing, that in Cesar's time the Gauls knew so little of Britain, that he could get from them no precise informations, what sort of men, places, ports, or harbours, this island contain'd; it may be answer'd, that the Gauls (as Cesar himself assures us) were perpetually engag'd either in publick national wars, or in intestine and private quarrels; that people of such a cast have neither leisure, nor curiosity to inspect their neighbours affairs, especially those which have no intimate connexion with their own; that they know little of countries but those thro' which their incursions are generally made; that the Britans being happily divided from such people by the sea, their aid was not usually sought; never perhaps, unless against so formidable an enemy as the Romans, at which time, the Britans afforded the Gauls all the assistance they could, as, doubtless, foreseeing that if the Gauls were once conquer'd, they themselves could not long be free: it may be answer'd also, that such inhabitants as pass'd from Gaul to Britain, at the first plantation, came many centuries before, and had worn out that relation of blood and friendship, which, in the beginning, must have subsisted betwixt persons of the same nation.

That the Gauls used to trade hither, Cesar informs us [x], and conven'd all the merchants, hoping for some satisfaction in his enquiries about Britain, but in vain; they knew, or at least pretended to know, nothing more than the maritime coast opposite to Gaul, their business being to exchange merchandizes, and return, not to make any curious remarks on the extent of the island, the diversity of inhabitants, their discipline of war, and the commodiousness of their harbours. If none, therefore, but these traders were accustomed to come into Britain, 'tis no wonder that in process of time the Gauls became so much estranged to this island, altho' first peopled by them: Britain affording room enough to its inhabitants to spread and employ themselves, and producing every thing necessary for their use, was a little world to itself; and the Gauls having more intercourse with those neighbours who were less divided from them, neglected a correspondence, which could not be carried on without the danger of the sea. The Britans, situated as they were, could not be often their enemies, and their aid, and assistance in time of need, must have been precarious, therefore they were not much to be depended upon as friends: so that with regard to the Gauls, the situation of the Britans did not permit them often either to be friends or enemies;

[x] Lib. IV. de Bell. Gall.

4   and

and it is therefore the lefs to be wondered at, that two nations, fo divided, fhould become fo little known to each other as they were in Cefar's time.

However, it may be reafonably fufpected, that the Gauls were not very ready to give Cefar all the informations in their power; for fome intercourfe was always maintain'd, and Britain affifted the Gauls againft the Romans, which was Cefar's chief pretence for invading the ifland, tho' ambition was his true and real motive. The Gauls had their priefthood of the Druids from Britain, as Cefar tells us; and whenever any difficulty arofe relating to the Druid fect or difcipline, they fent fome perfons into Britain to be more exactly inform'd of the truth [y]. This maintain'd a fort of religious correfpondence betwixt the two nations, which, together with their trade, confeffedly carried on by the Gauls, will fhew, that betwixt Gaul and Britain there was a more open communication, than betwixt Britain and any other nation.

and inform'd him probably of lefs than they knew.

To bring thefe firft inhabitants out of Gaul into Britain with greater eafe, fome will have this ifland join'd to the continent by an ifthmus or neck of land which reach'd from Dover to Calais; but as this has no foundation in hiftory, nor any neceffity to juftify it, or reconcile us to the fuppofition that ever any fuch union fubfifted fince the deluge, I fhall not take up the reader's time with refuting, what the learned Verftegan is fo fond of, and might as juftly demand our notice as moft authors, if he had been as good a naturalift as antiquarian. The refemblance and uniformity in the ftrata of the cliffs in Britain, and the oppofite ones of Gaul, is allow'd, but will not prove or infer any union fince the deluge, which it ought to do, if it be admitted as an argument in favour of transferring more eafily the inhabitants of Gaul into Britain. Indeed, there is no more occafion to fuppofe Britain join'd to the continent, than to fuppofe the Grecian iflands neceffarily join'd to the continents of Ionia and European Greece, in order for them to receive their firft inhabitants with the greater facility.

That the weftern parts of this ifland (viz. Devon and Cornwall) were firft difcover'd by the Phenicians [z], and by them inhabited, has no other foundation than that the names of places in thefe parts may be deriv'd from Phenician words, which is too deceitful a ground to build on, efpecially confidering they may all be found in the Britifh tongue, which, as fpoke in the feveral extremities of the ifland (where the Phenicians never traded), has great affinity with the Hebrew; and therefore we muft take care how we attribute to the Phenician traders, names which may be found in our own Britifh, a language deriv'd in a great meafure from

[y] Cæfar, Lib. VI.   [z] Samm. page 59.

E   the

the Hebrew, to which primarily the Phenicians alfo owed their whole language [a].

CHAP. IV.

Of the Gauls.

IT being moſt probable that Britain had her firſt inhabitants from Gaul, we will next enquire into the original of the Gauls, and endeavour to trace them as far as we can ; becauſe the more we can diſcover of them, the more we ſhall know of ourſelves, there being but one fountain to both theſe ſtreams.

The ſame people which the Romans call'd Gauls, were in their own tongue call'd Celts, even in Ceſar's time [b] : and the name of Celts was anciently of great extent, comprehending all thoſe nations who were ſometimes diſtinguiſh'd by the name of Scythians, Celto-Scythians, Getæ, Galatians, Gallogrecians, Celtiberians, Teutones, Germans, and Gauls [c] : but this great portion of mankind was ſtill more anciently, and when more united, call'd Cimbri ; and this laſt name reaches up to the DISPERSION, being deriv'd, as moſt authors agree, from Gomer, the leader of thoſe who came from Babylon, into the weſtern parts now call'd Europe : ſo that the Celts are deſcended from the Cimbri ; and tho', ſoon after, the name of Celts prevail'd, and was adopted by the greateſt part of this people and their deſcendants, yet ſome part of theſe weſtern nations retain'd the name of Cimbri, and were a moſt powerful nation as late down as the time of C. Marius ; and traces of this firſt name are ſtill found in the appellations of ſome countries and people ; and thoſe who choſe the name of Celts were ſometimes called Cimbrians, and the Cimbrians Celts, as being but one people originally, diſtinguiſh'd afterwards by two names. This is ſufficiently prov'd [d], for in the Cimbrian war (as it is call'd by moſt hiſtorians) Cicero ſays, that Marius vanquiſh'd the Gauls, inſtead of calling them Cimbrians. The ruffian hir'd to kill Marius, Lucan calls a Cimbrian ; Livy and Plutarch call him a Gaul. Thoſe who plunder'd Delphi, under Brennus, are generally call'd Gauls, but Appian in his Illyricks calls them Cimbri. Now the Gauls and the Celts are two words from the ſame theme. Let this ſuffice as to the name. As to the countries, they were ſpread from the ſea ſhores of Britain, and Gaul, as far eaſt as the

[a] See Mon. Illuſt. Bochart, Vol. I. p. 329.
[b] Ceſ. de Bell. Gall. Lib. I.
[c] Plin. Lib. IV. Cap. XII. Eli Sched. (ex Diod. Sic. Lib. V.) page 6. Luc. Flor. Lib. I. Oroſius, Lib. V. Salluſt. Jugurth. Eli Sched. pag. 8 and 10. Shering. 54.
[d] See Camd. Brit. page 7. and Speed's Chr. page 12.

Palus

Palus Meotis, at the extremity of the Euxine sea; where, from one branch of them, the Cimmerian Bosphorus takes its name: under the name of Cimmerii, they inhabited the northern coasts, even to the sea which lyes off Archangel in Russia: Celtiberia, a great part of Spain, was so call'd from a branch of the Celts, which settled on the river Iberus: Gallia Narbonensis was another southern settlement of the same people [e]: there were also the Celtæ Cisalpini, and Transalpini; so that if we except the southern parts of Italy, Greece, and the isles of the Ægean sea (which had perhaps their inhabitants from the Syrian continent), all Europe may justly be said to have been peopled by the ancient Cimbri, or (as they were soon after call'd) Celtæ.—The Gauls, then, were the same as the Celts, and the Celts the same people originally as the Cimbri.

The beginning of this considerable nation is not to be determin'd with any exactness as to time, or their common parent; but Josephus [f], from the traditions of the Hebrews, says that Japhet, son of Noah, had seven sons, who planted themselves partly in Asia, from the mountains Taurus and Amanus, to the river Tanais, and partly in Europe as far as Cadiz, at the Straits Mouth. By this ancient testimony it will be probable, that the first inhabitants of Europe were one of these portions of mankind, which were dispers'd from Babel, and coasting round the Euxine sea, directed their general course towards the north, as other portions did to the other parts of the world. Having got round the extreme parts of the Euxine sea, which first oppos'd itself to their northern passage, part stay'd in Scythia, whilst others steering westerly (and in every country some chusing, as we may imagine, to leave the main body, and stay behind) great numbers continued their course, till they came to the western coasts of Gaul: thus, this vast country of Europe was at first thinly besprinkled with people, God Almighty dividing them into small parties [g], in order to erect little kingdoms, and states more proportioned to the arts and knowledge of governours, and more convenient to promote industry and obedience in the general mass of mankind, than when less divided, or throng'd together in one vast unwieldy empire: accordingly, these several divisions soon finding themselves much scattered from their late fellow travellers, form'd so many little societies, and distinct governments, which kept no records or publick registers relating to their original, being wholly taken up with tilling lands, and feeding cattle, wildly intent upon present qualifications, and regardless of what was past. Such a situation admitted not the least attention to letters, and the

e Eli. Sched. page 16. de diis German.   f See Sheringh. page 403.   g Gen. xi. 8, 9.

liberal

liberal arts (which neither fhoot nor flourifh but under the fhelter of peace and government); thefe things, I fay, inevitably produc'd an utter oblivion of their being deriv'd from one common ftock. At the fame time the different climates in which they fettled foon begot different conftitutions of body, and different temperatures of mind; hence the difference of their cuftoms and manners: different manners made different prohibitions and different penalties neceffary; hence different laws. From the little intercourfe maintain'd betwixt the feveral branches that firft peopled Europe, their language, at firft one and the fame (I mean the Celtick), became differently pronounc'd, differently modell'd by their leading and moft ftudious men; fome words were forgot, and in thofe firft ages (having no books, without which a language cannot continue long the fame) new words muft be fram'd, as often as neceffity oblig'd, and every ftate muft have a particular name, to diftinguifh it from others: hence they became fo many different nations, and each nation, jealous of it's own honour, contended with its neighbours for dominion, antiquity, and country. Frequent enmities effac'd all remembrance of blood, and made them too often induftrioufly alter their language, cuftoms, and religion, left they might feem too like, and therefore to have borrow'd from their neighbours: thus the Celtæ or Cimbri (as well as the reft of mankind) became fo many diftinct nations, their laws, manners, names, language, and religion all different, though the people were fprung from one ftock, and but fo many different branches from the fame root.

By what degrees thefe changes happen'd to that part of Noah's pofterity which peopled Europe, or in what length of time they had overfpread the country, is hard to determine; but though they can't be fuppofed to have extended themfelves through fo large a tract of land fuddenly, and in a few years; yet, it being God's manifeft defign (as is before obferv'd) that each part of the earth fhould have it's fhare of inhabitants without any longer delay [h], it can hardly be imagin'd, that they were more than a century, or two at moft, making their way from Babel to the uttermoft coaft of Gaul: this feems the more probable, becaufe of the many Hebrew roots found in the old Celtick (the mother tongue whence all the languages of Germany and Gaul are deriv'd [i]): now, it is not likely, that thefe Hebrew roots would have been retain'd in

---

[h] As to this, Mofes is fo exprefs that he repeats God's fcattering them from Babel, upon the face of all the earth, in two immediately fucceeding verfes. Gen. xi. 8, 9. " So the Lord " fcattered them abroad from thence upon the " face of all the earth: and they left off to build " the city. Therefore is the name of it call'd " Babel, becaufe the Lord did there confound " the language of all the earth: and from thence " did the Lord fcatter them abroad upon the " face of all the earth."

[i] Bochart, Sac. Geog. Lib. I. Cap. xliii.

fuch

such abundance, if they had been many centuries upon their journey, languages altering, we know, in proportion to their age, especially where no books of genius appear to fix the language, and to which recourse may be had, as to a just standard of purity, and elegance.

That this people (the Celts or Gauls) increas'd prodigiously is the opinion of all history [k], their northern climates more conducing thereto, perhaps, than hotter countries; and to this quick increase were principally owing the several irruptions which they made into the east and south. But here I would beg leave to observe, that 'tis not likely that this, or any other populous nation would make invasions upon inhabited countries, as long as they had before their eyes any countries or islands unpeopled, in which they might bestow their superfluous numbers, and make so much more commodious and secure settlements; long before these eastern eruptions, therefore, they had probably spread their offspring into the isles of Britain, and Ireland, and when they had at last no farther country at hand, into which they could transplant their numbers, they recoil'd, as having no farther west to go, and began their eruptions; some threw themselves into the eastern countries, and sat down at the Cimmerian Bosphorus; another part pierc'd as far as Galatia; some, at one time plunder'd Greece, and were call'd Gallo-Grecians; some made a settlement in Spain, and gave rise to the people thence call'd Celtiberians: and at another time a branch of the same people took and plunder'd Rome, and settled in the north of Italy. The same people, in later times, and for the same reasons, under the name of Hunns, Goths, and Vandals, overwhelm'd the tottering empire of Rome, which doubtless they would never have attempted at such hazard, had they any country or island before them, in which they could distribute, with safety, some of their multitudes. We may therefore, by parity of reason, conclude, that the Cimbri or Celts, as they were afterwards call'd, peopled Britain, and afterwards Ireland, before ever they made any irruption, either into Asia, or the southern parts of Europe: and this conclusion, if true, will serve to shew us that before the Cimmerian Bosphorus had its Cimmerii, Spain its Celtæ, and Galatia its Gauls, Britain was inhabited. The reasons on which this conclusion stands are obvious, no people being willing to face all the dangers and hardships of war to procure themselves habitations, whilst at the same time there lyes an uninhabited, plentiful, and well situated country near at hand, which they may take possession of without opposition.

[k] Posidonius, Eli. Sched. page 10.

F

Such

Such is the train and feries of this people which we have from hiftory; from the Cimbri came the Celts, from the Celts the Gauls. The Celts are confeffedly very ancient; and yet, as Appian Alexandrinus fays [l], they were defcended from the Cimbri; which was therefore the moft ancient name of the firft planters of Europe, and deriv'd probably from the name of their chief leader Gomer, eldeft fon of Japhet, to whofe lot Europe fell, as moft authors agree. From the Celts came the Gauls, and from the many refemblances betwixt the Gauls and Britans, the Saxons and others call'd the Britans Gauls. The Britans however have ftill higher eftimation of their own antiquity, and know no other name for their people but Cumbri [m]; by this appellation afferting their defcent from the Cimbri, and not acknowledging an original even fo modern as a Gaulifh, or even Celtic.

CHAP. V.

What the ancient Inhabitants of Britain knew, or thought of their own Original.

IN Cefar's days the Gauls had quite loft fight of their original, all of them giving out [n], that they were fprung from Dis; that is, from the Earth [o], according to their meaning, but Cefar feems to mean Pluto, or the God of darknefs [p]. The inland inhabitants alfo of Britain, call'd themfelves e Terrâ nati, although the maritime parts, with greater judgment, acknowledged themfelves fprung from the Gauls. Now both thofe who afferted that they were defcended from Dis, and thofe who called themfelves e Terrâ nati, meant the fame thing, acknowledging equally that they could not tell how, or when they came thither: " Αυτοχθονας appellat " (viz. Cefar, fays Leland of the Britans) tanquam in terrâ ipfâ " genitos, quòd antiquioris originis effent quàm ut generis fui pri- " mordia cognofcerent [q]." " Acheloüs Terræ fuiffe filius dicitur, " ut folet de his dici, quorum per antiquitatem latent parentes:" fays Servius ad Virgil. Georg. I. ver. 9.

Some indeed will have Dis to be the fame as Tuifco, or Tuifto: if fo, Tuifco being the generally allowed father of all the German nations [r], the Druids, who inform'd the Gauls [s], that they were fprung

---

[l] Speed, page 13.　　[m] Ibid. page 12.

[n] Cef. Bell. Gall. Lib. VI.

[o] See Tully, de Nat. Deor. Lib. II. Pantheon, page 251. Cef. Eli. Sched.

[p] Unlefs Dis-pater be the fame among the Gauls, as Dies-piter (viz. Jupiter) among the Greeks (as Ecchart imagines) which is not fo likely.

[q] Shering. page 396.

[r] Suppos'd to have liv'd before Abraham. See Cluver page 6. and Sheringham, ibid. ut fupra. Cluverii conjectura. Teuth idem eft qui Græcis Θεος; Τους, Dorice Δυς: Latinis Deus feu Dius & Dis.

[s] Cef. Lib. VI.

from

from Dis, preferv'd it, doubtlefs, among their traditions, that the Germans, Gauls, and Britans, were all defcended from that nation, which under the conduct of Tuifco peopled all the weftern parts of Europe; and this will be ftill a more exprefs teftimony to all our former reafonings about the Gauls and Britans being but different colonies of one people. Some writers, however, treat the whole ftory of Tuifco as fable, and the forgery of Annius of Viterbo, and Aventinus, who, by inventing names and facts, and applying them to traditions, which had perhaps truth at the bottom, have (as fome of our Britifh Hiftorians are faid to have done) brought the tradition itfelf into fufpicion and contempt: but Tacitus is a very good evidence, that it was in his time the opinion cf the whole German nation, that they were fprung from Tuifco, or Tuifto[t]. "Celebrant Carminibus antiquis (quod unum apud illos "memoria et annalium genus eft) Tuiftonem Deum, Terrâ edi- "tum, et filium Mannum originem gentis, conditorefque." If any one can doubt whether Tuifco, and Tuifto, are the fame, he feems to me more fcrupulous about a fingle letter, than in mat- ters of fuch antiquity, and among nations fo little exact in writing, there is occafion to be. Thus far, then, it may be excufable to lay fome ftrefs upon Tuifco, namely as a general tradition among the Germans, that from him they had their original, and that he was either Dis, or his fon, being faid by Tacitus to be Terrâ editus[u]. But whether Tuifco be the fame as Dis, or not, or Thoth, the Egyptian Mercury (as Bochart, page 463. imagines); which Mercury, I muft obferve, was a great traveller, and the God of travellers, and reckon'd fo perhaps, as being one of the leaders of the migration from Babel; it comes to the fame point, that the Germans, Gauls, and Britans had equally loft all notice whence their firft inhabitants came; the Gauls and Britans faying that they were from Dis, or e Terrâ nati, the Germans that they were from Tuifco, and he, e Terrâ editus. What thefe weftern nations meant by Terrâ nati, was probably the fame opinion which many of the ancients held, that the firft inhabitants of countries were not defcended from parents in the ufual manner, but coeval with the world, and fprung out of the ground like trees and flowers; a cor- ruption, this, of that great truth, that the body of man was form'd in the beginning of the world by his Creator, and the materials taken from the earth[w].

The Grecians had the fame falfe philofophy among them, and their poets adorn'd it with fable, and that fruitful invention fo na- tural to their country. Their Titans were fons of the earth, Jafon

[t] De Mor. German.
[u] If any one defires to enter further into this fubject of Dis and Tuifto, Teut, Teutates, &c.
he will find it treated of at large, Pellout, Vol. II. Chap. VI.
[w] Gen. II. 7.

sow'd the teeth of the Dragon in Colchis, as Cadmus had done before in Thebes, thence sprung a race of armed men; fables all, and built upon one and the same tradition, with that which gave rise to this opinion of the Gauls and Britans, and shew that mankind in different and distant countries did believe that their forefathers, for whose original they could not account, were Terrigenæ, or born of that earth, which in truth affords only nourishment to compose the meaner and more ignoble part of us at present; as it did at first, materials for the forming hand of God.

It must be observ'd also that Terra [x] was among the Germans one of their Majores Dii, or superiour deities, which they respected and ador'd as the giver of all things; and when they enter'd the sacred groves to worship, if by chance they fell down on the ground (as might be no unusual thing for those, who could not approach the consecrated shades, without some sort of chain or shackle, to shew their subjection to the deity of the place) it was not lawful for them to arise, or to be lift up from the ground during the continuance of the holy rites: " Per humum evolvuntur [y], eoque omnis " superstitio respicit, tanquam inde initium gentis, ibi regnator om- " nium Deus, cætera subjecta atque parentia." Thus the Germans (and the Gauls very likely were infected with the same superstition) look'd upon Terra as their God, and their meaning by Terrâ nati might (when they regarded the first cause) probably be, that those first founders of their nations were the natural offspring of the Gods; an opinion too common, among the heathens, to need any proof, and another corruption of that great truth, that mankind, in its first origin, was the handy-work of God.

The Britans, then, had the same false opinions concerning their origin which the Gauls had, the Gauls said they were deriv'd from Dis, the Earth, or God of the earth; the most ancient inhabitants of the midland parts of Britain thought their original was from the Earth. The Germans thought themselves sprung from Tuisco, and he from the Earth. The Greeks call'd their first ancestors, for the same reason, Αυτοχθονες; the Romans theirs, Aborigines; all plain intimations that they knew not whence they were. And thus much for the meaning of what (as Cesar says) the Britans thought of their first origin, which may be better trac'd perhaps, by considering in the next chapter the several points in which they, or their ancestors resemble, and agree with the eastern nations, than by taking their own opinion for their original.

[x] Cesar.   [y] Tacitus de morib. German.

CHAP.

C H A P. VI.

Of the resemblance which the ancient Cimbri, or Celts, bore to the Eastern Nations; and how far the Monuments of Asia and the Eastern parts of Europe may contribute to illustrate the Antiquities of the Western Nations.

IF it does sufficiently appear that the resemblance betwixt the Celts and Eastern nations, in language, manners, monuments, and opinions, is no forc'd, distant, and imaginary, but such a real and close resemblance as usually proceeds either from descent, or intimacy, and converse, then it will be manifestly within the rules of reason to conclude, either that both these people had been, in former ages, parts of one community; or all along maintain'd such an open commerce with each other as is necessary to produce a strict uniformity in those general, national points: but, as no such open commerce appears to have been between the Celts and the Eastern countries, notorious enough to influence such multitudes of people to a resemblance of language, manners, monuments, and opinions, that resemblance cannot be accounted for, but by concluding them to have been once one and the same people: and when this people separated into many nations, and became dispers'd into many countries, each portion carried that religion, those customs, opinions, and language with them, which they had, when, being united in a much larger mass, they dwelt in one country.

As the settlement of this point will be of no little consequence, let us first take a short view of mankind united in one common society, and then consider what general resemblances they are likely to have retain'd, after their disunion and separation from each other.

Mankind continued together for some centuries after the deluge, and compos'd only one nation, seated in that country which was watered by the rivers Euphrates and Tigris, sometimes call'd in general Syria, but more particularly distinguish'd by the several names of Armenia, Assyria, and Chaldæa [z]. Being the Children of one family (that is of Noah and his sons) notwithstanding the early difference which appear'd betwixt Cham and his other two brothers, their language was the same [a], and doubtless their religion, their customs and manners could not be very different, as long as they continued together: and together they continued, till vainly presuming to build a city, and a tower whose top was to reach up even to heaven, and defeat the decrees of the Almighty, God thought proper to con-

[z] See P. Mela and De L'isle's maps. [a] Gen. xi. 1.

G

found

found all such airy schemes, and by miraculously introducing different languages (or at least different dialects of the former universal language) made it necessary for those who spoke one and the same tongue, to consort together, and separate from those, the speech of whom they could no longer understand. Thus was mankind reduc'd to a necessity of forming as many different parties, or little nations, as they found languages among them; and being united thereby, as by so many links or chains, found themselves under an equal necessity of moving off into different countries, to prevent confusion, enmity and bloodshed. This introduction of different languages (I would here observe) was of itself sufficient to answer the end proposed, which was to distribute mankind more equally over the face of the earth; and therefore other changes in a sudden miraculous manner have no room to be suppos'd, as we shall see by and by.

Again, tho', at the dispersion, their language was altered so as that one party or family could not understand the speech of any other, yet it is by no means necessary, to produce the effect designed, that all the different manners of speaking should be radically new, and in their grounds essentially different from that sacred language which mankind first received from God himself, and in which they convers'd so often with the deity. Some learned men, I know, have thought that they were entirely all new languages which at the dispersion were impos'd, and the old one destroy'd; but on the other hand, many have with great justice observ'd, that the Hebrew language was the mother of all languages [b]; and those who contend for the Syriac [c], seem to contend against reason, the Syriac, Armenian, and Arabian tongues appearing to be but so many different dialects of the Hebrew; and it is evident by the many Hebrew roots, which shew themselves in the northern languages, as well as those of the east, that however our languages may be now innovated, mix'd, and alter'd, yet they have the Hebrew language at the bottom, as the general ground-work of all [d].

Further, it is now generally allow'd, that the ancient Celtic [e], Getic or Gothic language, is that which, variously modify'd, gives rise to the Dutch, Swedish, French, and British tongues, and in the last of these, 300 roots of the Hebrew tongue have been insisted upon by some persons [f], and doubtless by the diligence of others, more may

---

[b] Nosse possimus linguam Hebraicam omnium linguarum esse matricem. Hieron. Cap. iii. Sophoniæ. See Eli. Sched. p. 174 and 175.

[c] As Theodoret, &c. Vide Selden de Diis Syris, Prol. Cap. xi. Eli. Sched. page 167, &c.

[d] " Nec modo Indicam, Persicam, Babylonicam, Armenicam, Syram, Arabicam, Hebrææ junctissimas linguas, sed et Gothicam linguam, ac hujus rei multa extare apud Procopium, Agathiam, et Jornandem documenta." Francisc. Junius, Præfat. Grammat.

[e] Pezron. Rowl. 317.

[f] Rowl. Mona. page 278.

still

still be difcover'd; which great conformity in languages, nothing could have occafion'd in fuch diftant countries, from India even to Britain, but their being deriv'd primarily from one nation and one country.

At the difperfion from Babel, mankind was fplit into many diftinct nations, by the different languages impos'd, but it can't be fuppos'd that every thing elfe became different in the fame fudden and miraculous manner: fo thorough a change would have multiply'd the miracle without reafon; and indeed there are no grounds from facred writ to fuppofe it; therefore, as to their cuftoms, the effentials of their religion, and their manners, mankind continued the fame as before the confufion of tongues; and wherever they were difpers'd, there they carry'd, and for a long while retain'd, the manners and cuftoms which were common to them all, when they made but one nation in the plains of Shinar.

In moft particulars, then, mankind continued the fame, or very like, till new climates, different governours, the accidents of war, and the cultivation or neglect of arts introduced alterations, and more or lefs effac'd that univerfal refemblance.

If we meet, therefore, with many cuftoms, religious, military, and civil, generally practis'd by the inhabitants of Syria and the eaftern world, and equally follow'd by the weftern inhabitants of Gaul, Germany, and Spain; if we find monuments of the fame kind in Africa and Sweden, or ftill more diftant regions, we are not to be furpriz'd; but to confider that mankind travel'd from Babel equally inftructed in all the notions and cuftoms common to them there, and that 'tis no wonder if fome of the deepeft-rooted principles, and the moft prevailing cuftoms reach'd even as far as mankind extended themfelves; that is, to the utmoft extremities of the earth.

This feems to be the reafon that fome great points of religion and practice have univerfally obtain'd throughout the whole race of mankind; fuch as the immortality of the foul; propitiating the Deity by facrifices; confecrating particular places to worfhip, performing obfequies, and erecting monuments to the dead; they were ufages and opinions common to mankind united, were with them difpers'd, and took root wherever they fettled.

Thus then the great refemblance obferv'd above, in the grounds and roots of languages, in diftant countries (which do not appear by hiftory to have had any communication or correfpondence) the refemblance of cuftoms, opinions, and monuments too (as will appear hereafter by their comparifon) nay the names of their principal Gods and Heroes being found the fame, almoft in all countries g, all

---

g With the Greeks, Jaw [and Διος]; with the Mauritanians, Juba; with the Latins, Jovis [and Deus]; all manifeftly from the moft holy Tetra-grammaton יְהֹוָה Jehovah of the Hebrews. Eli. Sched. 892.

thefe

thefe criterions are fo many evidences not only of mankind's being once united in one community, but after their difperfion,
of preferving thro' all their journeyings, even to their moſt diſtant
fettlements, a general refemblance in manners, opinions, language
and religion.

Hence fome very ufeful obfervations may be drawn.

Firſt, That, in proportion to the ſtrength of this refemblance,
and the clearnefs of thofe evidences, mankind may be fuppos'd to
have arriv'd fooner, or later, to their prefent fettlements.

For, wherever traces of thofe Eaſtern and univerfal cuſtoms
are well preferv'd, and the prefent remains (be they what they will)
bear a near refemblance to what we read of the ancient inhabitants of Syria, there we may fafely judge, that the inhabitants were
not a long while upon their migration, but advanced with expedition,
and fettled, whilſt the common cuſtoms of mankind were as yet
lively, and in full ſtrength among them — but where the veſtiges
of the old Syrian manners and language are fcarce at all to be per-
ceiv'd, there we may imagine they came flowly (not till after many
ages, feveral ſtops, and difficulties) to their prefent countries, and
were not fettled till they had loſt the cuſtoms, and worn out thofe
impreffions, which they muſt have brought with them from the
general mafs of mankind.

2dly, That thofe monuments are moſt ancient, which bear the
greateſt refemblance to the monuments of the Eaſt, as being neareſt
of kin to that fimplicity, with which monuments were erected in
the firſt ages of mankind, as authentick hiſtory, and the remains
themfelves of fuch monuments do teſtify. Another obfervation
muſt here occur, which is,

3dly, That mankind, having been once united, and living together as one fociety, their cuſtoms, manners, laws, language, and religion the fame, it may not be an improper manner of explaining monuments and antiquities in the Weſt (in countries efpecially where we
have little or no other hiſtory to guide us) by having recourfe to the
facred, and other hiſtories of the Eaſtern nations; where, if we find
the figure, materials, fituation, or dimenfion of monuments, very
much of the fame kind with thofe which it is our intention to explain,
we need not doubt but they proceeded from one defign, and that they
are (tho' in the moſt diſtant countries) the remains of one and the fame
cuſtom, anciently common to mankind in their more united ſtate.

4thly, That the refemblance which the ancient Cimbrians, Celts,
and Gauls, preferv'd to the Eaſtern nations, is very evident, as well
from the Celtic language, being fo much indebted to the Hebrew
(as is mention'd above), as from what we are elfewhere affur'd of by

4   the

the curious. " Narrat Lazius (fays Sheringham, page 112.) Cimme-
" riis et Phrygibus unam eandemque fuiſſe linguam ;" which ſame-
neſs of language, in people divided by ſo many different nations
and countries from each other, could proceed from no cauſe ſo
obvious and probable, as that they had been once united. In religion,
the reſemblance of the Gauls to the Eaſtern nations is altogether
as great; for tho' the Sect of the Druids had rais'd ſuch a ſuper-
ſtructure as diſtinguiſh'd their Prieſthood, Diſcipline, and Worſhip,
from all others, yet the foundation was old, and before deſcrib'd.
The immortality of the ſoul, and a future world, was one of the
principal doctrines of the Druids [h], as we ſhall ſee at large hereafter.
As to ſacrifices, they not only endeavour'd to propitiate the deity by
them, but like the people of Canaan and Moab, dyed their altars
with human gore. Groves they choſe to worſhip in, as the Canaanites did; and this the Druids (ſtricteſt perhaps of all ſects),
carry'd alſo into exceſs, performing their ſacred rites not as others
did in encloſed and cover'd temples, but only under the conſecrated oak. Obſequies they had in ſuch regard, that whatever was
moſt precious, and moſt eſteem'd by them, during life, ſuch as
horſe, armour, domeſtic utenſils, nay their moſt beloved ſlaves, were
forc'd to attend their dead maſter into the funeral pile [i] : but I only
touch theſe things now, this reſemblance between the Eaſtern and
Weſtern Religions, will ſtill ſhew itſelf more ſtrongly, when we
come to the religion of the Britans.

CHAP. VII.

Of the Story of Brute, and the Phenician Trade to this Iſland.

IT is the more difficult to diſtinguiſh intruders from the original
inhabitants, and to determine what invaders in ancient times
have paſs'd from their own, into another country, becauſe the higher
up in time our enquiries reach, the more we find mankind alike, as
being but ſo many ſeveral portions, juſt divided from the ſame maſs,
nor as yet diſtinguiſh'd from each other by the different impreſſions
which after-times introduced; their rites, manners, languages, little differing in the primitive ages; and nations born in different, and
diſtant countries, uniting ſoon, and becoming one people, without
making any conſiderable alterations; people ſettling then, like con-
genial liquors, without any violent ſtruggles; on the other hand,
as our enquiries deſcend thro' the more modern periods of time,

[h] Ceſ. de Druid.　　[i] Ibid. Lib. VI.

H　　　　　　nations

nations mix with more difficulty, and produce more fenfible alterations on one another, by conqueft, alliance, and commerce.

However, the hoftile invafion of fome ftrangers, and the frequent
arrival of others, on account of commerce, muft have introduced
alterations among the original inhabitants, in proportion to the age
they liv'd in, and monuments agreeable to the cuftoms of that
country from whence the ftrangers came.

Of the Tro-
jans. If Brute fhould be allowed to have landed, and made a fettlement
in this Ifland, as fome learned men have thought [k], yet with the fmall
number of followers which fuch a fugitive could perfuade to follow
his fortunes, he can fcarce be imagin'd to have feiz'd by violence, or
retain'd by conqueft, any confiderable part of fo large an ifland; he
may with more likelyhood be fuppos'd to have fettled here by the
friendly entertainment, and confent of the firft inhabitants, in the
fame manner as the Phenician and Grecian colonies did tranfplant
themfelves into Thrace, Libya, Sicily, and Spain. The ifland being
in thofe early days thinly peopled, a colony of men more civiliz'd, and
fkill'd in the arts of peace and war, than thofe of the Weftern world,
was not unlikely to take footing in the moft convenient place they
found, and upon very good terms alfo, with the original inhabitants.
This is the firft entrance of ftrangers into Britain, which either
hiftory or tradition affords us; and fuppofing this ftory true (as
being thus far attended with no improbability) it muft be granted
that the curiofity, and reciprocal wants of the ftrangers and inhabitants, would beget fuch an intercourfe as mutually to affect the
language, manners, and cuftoms of both. It could not be wonder'd at, therefore, if fome Britifh cuftoms were like thofe recorded
of the ancient Trojans.

Of the Phe-
nicians, and
the time they That the Phenicians came here very early, is much better founded:
the Tyrians, born for commerce, and like their Venus fprung out of
came to the the fea, were indefatigable in their expeditions: let us trace them back
Weft of Eu- as far as we can, in order to throw fome light upon their naviga-
rope. tions into this weftern part of the world. The Phenician Hercules
is fuppos'd [l] to have vanquifh'd Antæus, king of the Weftern parts
of Africa, more than 300 years before the expedition of the Argo-
nauts, which we know was a whole generation before the Trojan
war, by which Bochart fufpects that the Phenicians muft have been
very converfant in the weft of Africa before Jofhua's time: and
that they came as far weft as Tingis (now Tangier) at the Straits
leading into the Mediterranean fea, about the time of Jofhua,
appears likely at leaft [m], if there were really two pillars with this

---

[k] Edward the Firft's letter to the Pope, Leland, Sir John Price, Sheringham, &c.

[l] Bochart, Vol. I. p. 326.
[m] See Bochart, p. 325. Geogr. p. 166.

Phenician

Phenician Infcription, " We are thofe who fled from the face of
" Jofhua, the fon of Nave." Eufebius, it muft be own'd, writes
to the fame purpofe [n]; that fome Canaanites fled from the children
of Ifrael, and inhabited Tripoli in Africa. However that be, moft
likely it is, by the temple erected at Tarteffus, on the European
fide of thofe Straits, to the Tyrian Hercules, and by the general
tradition in all countries of his pillars being fet up near the fame
place, that the Phenicians came fo far Weft, in the moft early
ages of the world. Of this alfo the names of places thereabouts, all
of Phenician derivation, may be farther proofs, to fuch as delight
in arguments of that kind. Having penetrated thus far fo early,
we are well affured by the many colonies they planted foon after
each other, at New and Old Carthage (which was built fifty years
before the taking of Troy, as Appian fays) at Tangier, at Malacha,
Gades, and other places [o], that it was not the cuftom of this nation
to ftand ftill; they were always for making new fettlements, new
plantations [p], but the certain date of their difcovering the Britifh
Ifles is not to be found: however, having brought them to the
wefternmoft parts of the Mediterranean fea, let us now proceed to
trace the Phenicians into the Atlantic.

Strabo fays [q], that the Phenicians ventur'd outfide the Straits
Mouth foon after the Trojan war; but when they firft began to
trade here in the Britifh iflands is uncertain, fome think not till
the year before Chrift 450 [r], but very likely fooner.

When they may be fuppos'd to have firft difcover'd Britain.

About 600 years before Chrift, Pharaoh Nechao, king of
Egypt (the fame who flew Jofiah king of Judah) order'd fome
Phenicians to fet out from the Red Sea, to go round Africa, to pafs
by the Straits of Hercules, to penetrate into the Northern Seas, and
to bring him an exact account of their voyage: about this time
therefore, if not before, 'tis not unlikely that the Phenicians finding, by this voyage of their countrymen, the Weftern or great Atlantick Ocean not fo turbulent and unnavigable as their forefathers
had taught them to believe, were either then, or foon after, tempted
to undertake a northern voyage, and coafting along the banks of
Spain, and France, might firft difcover the Britifh Ifles, and, upon
difcovery begin to trade, which was the principal end of all their
voyages. There is another remarkable voyage of the Phenicians
mentioned in ancient hiftory, but continued down to us with great
uncertainties of circumftance, and time: Himilco was fent forth
from Carthage to make a voyage to the North, at the fame time

[n] Græc. Chron. p. 11.
[o] Bochart, p. 326.
[p] Hoc pene unicum gentis ftudium ab ipfa fta-
tim origine innatum fuerat ut quoquo verfum in
omnes partes terrarum orbis vela facerent, et co-
lonias deducerent. Ibid. præfat. 327.
[q] Bochart, p. 638.
[r] Carte, p. 46.

that

that Hanno, a Carthaginian General, was difpatch'd, the contrary way, to explore the Southern coafts; but at what time thefe two leaders liv'd, whether a little before the fecond Punic war (as indeed the names feem to intimate) or much more anciently in the time of Darius Nothus, is very undetermin'd, as Camden thinks, as alfo whether the Periplus of the latter, written in Punick, fhall be of any authority, tho' by Feftus Avienus affirm'd to have been perus'd by him. However, if the Phenicians had been near the Straits Mouth, above 800 years before the reign of Pharaoh Nechao (viz. in the time of Jofhua *), it is not likely that fuch enterprizing failors fhould make that their Ne plus ultra, for fo many ages: they had a colony at Gades, without thefe Straits, in their delicious Bætica lying on the Atlantick Ocean, as anciently almoft, if not altogether, as the before-mentioned age of the Tyrian Hercules's arrival at Tingis; therefore they may be fairly fuppos'd to have difcover'd Britain, more than 600 years before Chrift: and, if we place their difcovery no higher up than this, the Phenicians muft be allowed to have traded with us folely, and without the leaft participation of other nations, for more than 300 years, as will appear when we come to confider the time when the Grecians fucceeded them in this traffick.

What parts of Britain firft difcover'd by the Phenicians, and traded to, and for what.   If the Phenicians, in their northern voyages, coafted along the fhores of Spain and Gaul (as was doubtlefs the moft ancient way of navigating), then the fhores of Britain oppofite to Gaul muft have been firft known to them; but at whatever part of our ifland they firft arriv'd, the Weftern parts had certainly the greateft fhare of their commerce, if not the whole. The Phenician bufinefs into thefe parts was not conqueft and glory, but trade; and from Gades they traded to Britain, bringing Salt, Crockery, and Brazen ware [s]; what they came for was Tin, Lead, and Skins, but efpecially the former, which was foon found to be fo ufeful a Metal, that it grew famous over all the then known world, and encouraged the Phenicians to continue, and engrofs the trade to this Ifland.

Tho' lead was a metal found anciently in fome parts of Gaul and Spain, yet it was with great difficulty come at. " Laboriofius in " Hifpania erutum totafque per Gallias (fays Pliny, Lib. XXXV. " Cap. xvii.) fed in Britanniâ fummo terræ corio, adeò largè, ut lex " ultro dicatur, ne plus certo modo fiat." The parts of Britain anciently famous for Lead were the country of the Coritani, men of Lincolnfhire, Derbyfhire, and that neighbourhood; the Ordovices, North-Welfh; and the Brigantes, or Northumbrians [t].

[s] Strabo, Lib. III.   [t] Bochart, p. 649.   * Pag. preced.

But

But the principal inducement for the Phenicians to frequent our coasts was Tin, a Metal far tranfcending both the beauty and the ufe of Lead: this Metal was anciently alfo found in Lufitania[u], and Gallecia, but in too fmall quantities to fatisfy the expectations of fo many cities, and countries, as were defirous to have it. The Phenicians therefore, having difcover'd abundance of Tin in fome fmall Britifh iflands, among which they probably reckon'd the Weft of Cornwall, as we fhall fee in the fequel of this work, carry'd on fo confiderable a trade here, that from thefe little iflands only, they were enabled to fupply the greateft part of the world with this ufeful Metal: all the cities and nations of the Mediterranean had their Tin chiefly from the Phenicians, and they from the iflands of Britain; I fay chiefly, for tho' Spain yielded fome little fhare of this commodity, yet it muft have been a very fmall quantity, or the Phenicians from Gades would doubtlefs have fupply'd themfelves at home, and never have crofs'd the Atlantick Ocean at fuch hazard and expence, in the infancy of navigation. This Metal was not only fent up the Mediterranean, but exported even as far as India itfelf, for India has naturally none of it, but purchas'd it by her Diamonds, and precious ftones[w]. Such an extenfive trade required proportionable fupplies; and as we read of no Tin-mines worth notice, Eaft of the Dunmonii[x], all the Phenician trade for this Metal muft have been confined to that country now call'd by the two names of Devonfhire and Cornwall, and the fmall iflands adjacent to Cornwall, now Scilly (or Sylleh) Iflands. Among thefe, the iflands were moft productive, and therefore moft famous in hiftory; and from the Tin they yielded, call'd Caffiterides. They were either nam'd fo by the Grecians[y], from the Greek word Κασσίτερον (Tin), or (it being confefs'd that both the Chaldeans and Arabians, call Tin by a name of like found[z]) fo nam'd by the Phenicians themfelves, which I muft obferve is fo much the more probable, becaufe we find thefe iflands call'd Caffiterides long before the Grecians either traded thither, or knew where the iflands lay; for Herodotus, who liv'd about 440 years before our Saviour, fays, that he knew nothing of the iflands Caffiterides, from whence their Tin came[a]. Now, with great deference to Bochart's judgment, let it be obferv'd, that 'tis highly improbable the Greeks fhould give name to iflands they knew not where to find, and confequently had no communication withal, but thro' means of the Phenicians. Solinus calls them Infulæ Silurum, or Infula Silura, of which the prefent name Scilly may feem to retain enough to juftify him: but 'tis

[u] Portugal. Pliny, Lib. XXXV. Cap. XVI.
[w] Pliny, Lib. XXXV. Cap. XVII.
[x] Cornifh men, Cornwall comprehending Devon and Cornwall.
[y] Bochart, p. 650.

[z] קסטורא קיסטירא
[a] 'Ουτε νησας οιδα Κασσιτεριδας εουσας εκ των ὁ κασσιτερος ἡμιν φοιτα. In Herod.

I   much

much to be fufpected, whether the ancient Geographers knew the real fituation of the Silures, and whether the Scilly Iflands were not miftaken for iflands adjacent, and belonging to the true country of the Silures, or South Wales. However, if there be any truth in what Tacitus relates, viz. that the Silures were oppofite to Spain, it can only be true of the Silures of the Scilly Iflands; and if fome of their inhabitants were like the Spaniards, it is n t near fo furprizing as that the inhabitants of South Wales fhould be fo. The Pheni-cian colony at Gades might probably fend over fome of their in-habitants to iflands which afforded them fo great a profit, in order the better to fuperintend, and engrofs fo profitable a commerce: their defcendants might retain, even to the time of Tacitus, the fwarthy complexion, and curl'd hair of the people they were fprung from; here we find a refemblance which has hiftory to fupport it, and no folecifm in Geography to weaken or reject it.

From thefe iflands the Phenicians had their treafures of Tin [b], and were exceeding jealous of their trade, and therefore fo private, and induftrious to conceal it from others, that a Phenician veffel thinking itfelf purfued by a Roman [c], chofe to run upon a fhoal, and fuffer fhipwreck, rather than difcover the leaft track, or path, by which another nation might come in for their fhare of fo bene-ficial a commerce.

In the next place, I would here obferve, that we are not only to reckon the Scilly Iflands, but the adjacent Weftern parts of Cornwall among the Caffiterides; for the ancient workings for Tin, in the Scilly Iflands, are neither deep, nor many, nor large [d]; and therefore it cannot be conceiv'd that the Tin for fo many ages, could have been raifed there, in quantity fufficient to fupply the demand: it may be conjectur'd therefore, and the conjecture fup-ported by many arguments, that the Continent [e] being in view from thefe iflands, and appearing to them not very extended, but narrow, and like an ifland (as indeed the juttings out of Cornwall, thither-ward, plainly do, to every eye), the active Phenicians foon reforted thither, and finding the fea on either hand of them, and taking it for granted that this land was every where encompafs'd by the the fea, counted it no more than one of the clufter of iflands, and rang'd it among the Caffiterides, finding it rich in the fame trea-fures; and therefore deferving the fame name. Ortelius, there-fore, not without reafon, makes the Caffiterides, to include not only the Scilly Ifles, but alfo Devonfhire and Cornwall.

Few Phe-nician re-mains.   The Phenicians having made thefe iflands their principal feat of traffick, for fo many ages, if any veftiges of the Phenician religion,

[b] Strabo, Lib. III. de Caffiter.
[c] Strabo, ibid.
[d] See the ancient and prefent ftate of the Scilly Iflands, p. 73, &c.
[e] So the people of Scilly call the Weftern part of England.

4

cuftoms,

cuftoms, buildings, or language be any where to be difcover'd in the
Britifh Iflands, they muft needs, one would think, be found in thofe
ifles, or in the adjoining continent neareft to them, where doubtlefs
the fame trade alfo reach'd; but there is one reafon which will hinder us from expecting to find any great matters of this kind at Scilly,
tho' fome things of this fort there are; and that is, that fmall
iflands are liable to many alterations, which a greater fcope of ground
is exempted from. In fhort, improvements of tillage, and planting,
and fortifying, and incroachments of the fea, and fand, muft have
chang'd the face of things extremely in fuch narrow fpots, fince the
Phenician times; but thefe ifles, as well as the adjoining continent,
have preferv'd fome monuments which may not improbably be attributed to the Phenicians, as will be feen in the fequel of this
work. A continual commerce, for fome hundreds of years, muft
have occafioned fome of the Phenician nation to fettle here, and
this fettlemennt muft have produc'd fome mixture of the two languages, as thofe that fettled muft alfo probably have erected fome
of their own national Deities, the human mind being not able to
reft in any climate, without fome religion: accordingly, many words
in the prefent Britifh, are evidently of Tyrian derivation, and many
rude Obelifks, are ftill notwithftanding the pillaging of modern builders, to be feen in Cornwall, and fome in the iflands, which in all
probability were the Symbols of the Phenician Deities, as will appear
when we come to treat of Erected ftones, and fuch as they ufually
worfhip'd; it being the notorious infatuation of the Canaanitifh
nations, to pay divine honours to fuch rude ftones. Again, if fome
places, where the Phenicians were moft converfant, retain names of
Phenician original, we are to attribute this either to the Hebrew,
that general fource of all languages, or to the commerce of the
Phenicians with the firft and native inhabitants, and are by no
means (with fome authors) to fuppofe the Phenicians the firft
planters of our ifle; their bufinefs being to improve upon the
natural products already known by the natives, import trifles, as
we know they did into Britain, and carry back the moft precarious
commodities to their own markets, not to plant defolate iflands with
fuch ufeful merchants and failors as their citizens confifted of.

Laftly, as the records of Phenician hiftory are very few, and fcarce
any thing more than a few fragments preferv'd in the Greek and Roman writers [f], and as the ages in which they flourifh'd here, are
very remote, it is not to be expected that a great many monuments
of their erecting fhould be now extant. If they built any cities,
the common cuftom of Tyrians, as the fhores of Spain and Africa
teftify, or fettled Colonies, or erected Temples, as is not unlikely, yet

[f] Bochart, p. 327.

the

the defolations of age and war as well as fea (near which they always built), may well be fuppos'd to have obliterated every thing of this kind, unlefs the names of thofe things, fometimes lefs fubject to ruin than the things themfelves, may chance to have efcap'd:

Tantum ævi longinqua valet mutare vetuftas.

But fome few monuments, as I faid before, there are, which from their great fimplicity may be well judged, as ancient as the Phenician times, and from the Phenicians being us'd to have fuch in their own country (as will appear from ancient authors) may be very rationally fuppos'd of Phenician original.

C H A P. VIII.

Of the Grecians.

THE Phenicians were not more happy in their voyages, than they were induftrious to conceal the fuccefs of them from the reft of the world; hence it was that the Greeks appear to be fo much in the dark as to Navigation, and Geography, for many years after the Phenician trade was at its height: that Herodotus treats as a fable what the Phenicians faid, that in encompaffing the South of Africa, they had the fun on their right hand; which was however moft certainly true: that Strabo denies it abfolutely, and Polybius doubts whether or no the South of Africa be encompaffed with Sea. Nor were they better acquainted with the Northern Ocean; for Herodotus acknowledges, that the Greeks knew nothing of the extreme parts of Europe, nor of the places whence the Amber and Tin was brought; that is, the Northern coafts of Germany on the Baltic, and the Britifh Ifles: and Ariftotle, who liv'd when Greece made the greateft figure in every other part of Literature, and was himfelf a moft diligent enquirer into every thing curious and ufeful, knew fo little of what fea or country might be beyond the Pillars of Hercules, that he thought the places in that neighbourhood were contiguous to the Eaftern parts of India g; fo ignorant was he of the real circuit and extent of the earth. However, the Grecian trade to this ifland for fome time before Julius Cefar is undoubtedly to be prov'd, though at what time it began is very uncertain.

About 900 years after the Phenician Hercules, 600 after the Trojan war, and 550 before Chrift, the people of Samos fending a colony into Egypt, they were driven by the winds down the Mediterranean, and quite through the Straits of Gibraltar, which was the

g Bochart, p. 326, and 648.

firft

firſt paſſage the Greeks made into the Weſtern Atlantick Ocean, but about theſe Straits they ſtuck and ſettled for ſome ages, without making further progreſs, as may be fairly induc'd from Herodotus and Ariſtotle abovementioned. About the time of Alexander the Great, Pytheas, a famous Aſtronomer of Marſeilles, undertook a Nor-thern voyage, and ſail'd ſo far North, that he ſaw the Sun diſappear, only for a moment of time, and immediately to riſe again, which muſt be as far as 68 degrees North Latitude, where, in the ſummer, there is no night, when the Sun is near, or in the tropic of Cancer, the Sun then performing his whole courſe above the Horizon. This probably was the firſt time that the Greeks ventur'd into the Northern ſeas ; but afterwards, incited by the ſucceſs, or conducted by the curious obſervations, of ſo great a man as Pytheas, the Greeks were bold enough to attempt frequent voyages of this kind ; and, being naturally ingenious, were ſoon ſkilful enough to perform them with as much facility and exactneſs, as might be ex-pected from the infancy of their aſtronomical ſtudies. It is very ſtrange therefore, if true, that the Greeks, who made a voyage thro' the Straits as anciently as Alexander's time, ſhould not ſail to Britain before the time of Ptolemy Lathyrus, king of Egypt, who liv'd about 117 years before our Saviour : yet, ſo ſays Bochart [h], and, if he is right [i], it will ſhew how ſecret the Phenician navigators kept this trade. Mr. Camden places the coming of the Greeks ſome-what higher than Bochart, and thinks that they arriv'd here about 160 years before Ceſar. Sammes [k] thinks Mr. Camden miſtaken, and that they came here as early as Pythagoras, who flouriſh'd about 600 years before our Saviour ; but brings no authority, and indeed this is by much too early for their timorous navigation. It may however be here obſerv'd, that the Greeks muſt have been well acquainted with Britain, at leaſt as anciently as Mr. Camden mentions. Pliny ſays, that Britain was famous in Greek Monuments long before the times of the Romans ; and Polybius, who flouriſh'd about 200 years before our Saviour, a Greek by nation, though a conſtant companion of Scipio Africanus, promis'd to write of the Britiſh Iſles, and της κασσιlηρυ καlασκευης (the methods of preparing Tin) and made good his promiſe, as Strabo ſays ; a taſk which ſo cautious a writer as Polybius would never have undertaken, had there not been ſufficient materials, at that time to be procur'd, for the ground-work of ſuch a hiſtory.

How long ſoever the Greeks traded hither, it does not appear Few Greci-that they left many monuments behind them, if any at all, unleſs an Remains. the number of Greek words interſpers'd in the Britiſh language may

---

[h] See Diod. Sic. Lib. V.   [i] P. 650.   [k] P. 101.

be

be adjudg'd to be such, and to have proceeded from this commerce[1]. Let us enquire into the original of this mixture (suppos'd to be the most evident remains of the Greeks in these islands) and see whether there may not be other causes, as well as commerce, to which this insertion of Greek words into the British language may be imputed: their trade for Tin cannot be allowed to have extended beyond the confines of Devonshire, no Tin having been discover'd, or work'd, that we know of in any other part of our island; at least not in such quantities as to draw the attention of the Greeks; and how little an intercourse with so small a district, could affect the whole British language is very apparent.

Certain it is, the Greeks were not a little proud of their language, and thought it a glory to their country to disperse, and introduce it wherever they came; and indeed, the copiousness, elegance, and sonorous cadence of their tongue, at once facilitated their endeavours, and made other nations so fond of it, that the publick records, and inscriptions in many places were Greek, altho' their national tongue serv'd their other inferior purposes, of conversation, and business. The Gauls us'd the Greek letters in Cesar's time, who found their rolls of soldiers, with the number of their women and children written in Greek characters; and for a few centuries before Christ, as the conquests of Alexander and his captains had spread this excellent language thro' Egypt and all the East, so the colonies of the Peloponnesians (with those of the other Greeks) and their Academies, to which the polite world resorted, had made it equally acceptable in the West, so that, for two or three centuries before our Saviour, it was the universal fashion of the world to write in Greek. We may therefore safely say, that the British had not all their Greek words from the trading Greeks; the truth indeed seems to be, that the use we made of Greek in these islands, was owing to several distinct causes; partly to commerce, and in some measure to the Druid intercourse with the Gauls, whose records were in that character. Besides this, the Greeks might have borrow'd some words from the Gallo-Grecians, a Celtic nation, which may well account for many like words in the Greek and British, to say nothing here of the great resemblance of many Greek words to the Phenician, from which last nation we know the Grecians had their very letters.

As for other remainders of the Greeks, we find few or none; for as Tin was what they sought and dealt in, Cornwall and the Scilly isles were doubtless the places of traffick; but here we find no foot-steps of any Grecian Monuments, neither Inscriptions, Coins, nor any other remains, which can shew that the Greeks ever made any settlement here. And, indeed, when trade is the only business, where there are

[1] See Sheringham's List, p. 101, &c. Sammes, p. 86, 87. Rowland's Mona.

no

no colonies planted, no encampments, no battles fought, no temples built, or settled worship introduc'd (all which things are quite foreign to the education and intentions of the man of trade) it is unnatural to expect that people, let them be Phenicians, Greeks, or Romans, should employ themselves in erecting many monuments.

CHAP. IX.

Of the Romans.

THE Romans came into this island with intentions very different from those of the Greeks, and Phenicians, and, under the conduct of Julius Cefar (ever fond of new conquests), invaded it about the year before Christ 55 [m]; and after some struggles, reduc'd the greatest part of it, in the time of Claudius, into the form of a province. But since it has been all along doubted, whether the Romans extended themselves so far West as into that county whose monuments are to be the principal subject of our present inquiry, it cannot be foreign to our purpose to examine this point of history, and to shew first, the improbability of the Romans leaving Cornwall unsubdued; and next, the several proofs which may be produc'd to shew that Cornwall was indeed well known to, and posses'd by them. I am sensible that the learned [n] are of opinion, that the Romans never came West of the river Tamar, at present the Eastern limit of this county: but with great submission, we must attribute this opinion to the distant situation of this country from the feats of learning, and the frequent difficulty of procuring proper informations concerning it. At what time the Romans first possessed themselves of Cornwall, must indeed be difficult to fix, since their being here at all, has been so long doubted of; but as all historians agree, that the southern part of Britain was conquer'd by Claudius Cefar, 'tis not unlikely that Cornwall, the southernmost part of all this island, may be included in this computation.

When Agricola's fleet made their tour round Britain in the reign of Domitian, they could not pass by unobserved, some of the noblest harbours in the world, such as Falmouth, Hammoze, and such secure stations, as Fowey, Helford, and some others of that kind; nor would a General so curious, so diligent to improve incidents, and turn every discovery to the benefit of his country, and the glory of his government, neglect to dispatch proper guards to seize upon, and make use of, such havens as these. It further appears that Agricola's fleet sail'd thro' the British and St. George's Chanels, attending Agricola's march [o]. Now if the march of his troops, and

[m] Fifty-nine, says the Chron. Table Scr. post Bedam. Sixty says Bede: so also the Saxon Chron.
[n] Camd. XXXIX.
[o] Horsley's Brit. Rom. p. 43.

the navigation of his fleet was well concerted, and had proper connexion, then his army muſt have been on all the coaſts of Cornwall,
as we ſhall find when we come to examine the Roman conqueſt of
Cornwall more particularly P.

Again, if we may conclude any thing from the words of Tacitus q, " Fert Britannia aurum, & argentum, & alia metalla pre-
" tium victoriæ," we muſt think that the Romans made ſure of
the moſt conſiderable mines, as well as harbours, in Agricola's
time, if not before.

Again, Galgacus, in his celebrated ſpeech r, has theſe words,
" Neque ſunt nobis arva, aut Metalla, aut Portus, quibus exercen-
" dis reſervemur :" intimating that the Paſture, the Metals, and the
Ports, in other parts of the iſland, had prov'd but ſo many temptations to the avaricious Romans ; but that there was no ſuch thing
in the country where they were, they had only a General, and an
army, but that they were free as yet ; whereas thoſe who were rich
and abounded in mines, were already brought into ſlavery : " Hic
" dux & exercitus, ibi tributa & metalla, & cæteræ ſervientium
" pœnæ." Now what Metal was this iſland (tho' not perhaps with-
ſome ſome Gold and Silver, as at preſent, in ſome few places) famous
enough for, to engage the arms of the Romans, but Tin ? And
what place ſo celebrated for Tin as Cornwall and its little iſles, the
Caſſiterides ?

In the Origines Britannicæ, Dr. Stillingfleet thinks that Veſpaſian
conquer'd both the Belgæ and Danmonii (from Suetonius in Veſpaſ.)
which Dr. Muſgrave s endeavours to refute, and reckons for nothing
the teſtimony of Geoffry of Monmouth t, and Ponticus Virunnius u ;
but the learned Dr. Muſgrave had forgot that he had ſaid (Vol. I.
p. 211.) " Romani in omnem fere angulum hujuſce inſulæ ſe in-
" ſinuarunt," and here lays his ſtreſs upon the want of Roman Antiquities diſcovered in the time of Mr. Carew, and Mr. Camden, in
whoſe time the reſearches after Antiquities were in their infancy,
and there was, I think, but one Coin of the Roman Emperours found
in all Cornwall ; it is certain, therefore, that Dr. Muſgrave deter-
mines a point, without giving fair play to what might afterwards
be diſcovered.

It muſt be allow'd that no Baſs-reliefs, or Altars of Roman
ſtructure, have yet been diſcover'd in Cornwall, which may with
ſome be an argument that the Romans never came ſo far Weſt ;
but this argument will prove too much ; for by the ſame rule
of judging, the Romans never were at Exeter w, and many

p Book IV.
q Tacit. Vit. Agric.
r Ibid.
s Vol. III. p. 123.
t Lib. IV. Cap. XVI.

u Brit. Hiſt. Lib. IV.
w Leland, in his Itinerary, mentions a Roman Inſcription on a ſtone fix'd in the city
wall, behind Bedford-Houſe in Exeter, but 'tis
now gone.

other

other places[x], where none of the above indications are to be met with, and yet, from Antoninus's Itinerary, and other evidences not to be gainfay'd, we know the Romans had their Caftra Stativa at Exeter: but the multitude of Roman Coins found lately in the feveral parts of Cornwall, and the date of them correfponding with hiftory, and pointing out the very occafion which drew the Romans here at that time, one Roman infcription on a Patera[y], fome Sepulchres alfo, with all the ufual indications, as Pavements, Urns, Caves, and Utenfils found in them, fome Forts, and Encampments, fome Ways, which carry a great probability of their being Roman, will hereafter appear in their proper place[z], and be fuch plain evidence of the Romans being in Cornwall as cannot be contradicted.

It is a very groundlefs fufpicion, to imagine that the eftablifhing this truth can do any difhonour to our country; for when the laft ftruggles for liberty were at an end, and the conqueft fix'd, the Romans were generally gentle and gracious mafters; the worft of them would take care that no people or nation fhould invade their provinces with impunity, and that their fubjects fhould be fuch to none but to themfelves; and the better fort of Governours employed themfelves to introduce arts, to familiarize their own cuftoms to the natives, and gradually to extirpate ignorance and barbarity; fo that, in fhort, 'tis not very difficult to afcertain, whether the Britans, by lofing their liberties to fuch mafters, were not in reality gainers: but, if they had loft their liberties and laws, without any recompence, as they afterwards did to the Saxons, Danes, and Normans, Truth and Fact muft be acknowledg'd, and teftimonies from Antiquity muft have their proper weight allowed them. The Romans continued here fo long, and their government was fo well lik'd, that after[a] 464 years (from the entrance of Julius Cefar, 54 years before Chrift, to the year 410) the Britans, though formally difcharg'd from all allegiance to the Roman Empire, were extremely loth to part with fuch mafters; and the Romans, out of compaffion to the miferies they fuffered from their neighbouring enemies, fent them, at feveral times, fome troops to affift them, but, in about twenty years after, took their laft leave, and return'd no more.

---

[x] Worcefter was undoubtedly a Roman town; and yet there are no veftiges of any kind remaining of that people, except a few Coins dug up of the latter empire.

[y] Found at Boffens, in the parifh of St. Erth about three miles North Eaft of St. Michael's Mount, of which fee, Lib. IV. Cap. III.

[z] Lib. IV. Cap. I.—VI.

[a] Mr. Camden, p. cviii. fays 476.

L

CHAP. X.

Of the Saxons.

THE Romans had no sooner retir'd from Britain, than the Scots and Picts, in hopes of bettering their condition, made frequent inroads from Scotland. The Britans had now, for some ages, been accustomed to recruit the Roman armies abroad, with the choicest of their youths; and being seldom inur'd to bear arms at home, where they had no encouragement to study the profession of a soldier (their masters, the Romans, for political reasons, secluding them as much as possible from the art of war) they found it a very difficult matter, after a disuse of so many ages, to bring themselves to any tolerable relish for the duties of the field; so much more does war depend upon use, and experience, than upon natural genius. At the same time, their troublesome neighbours in the North had preserv'd their warlike disposition in its proper force, by their continual struggles with the Romans, as well as their frequent invasions of Britain, for the sake of plunder. The Britans, seeing themselves under these disadvantages, and despairing of ever being a match for their enemies, whose barbarity they were every day experiencing without any hopes of ever satisfying their thirst of spoil, determin'd to call in foreign aid; and the Saxons having been for some ages remarkable at sea, had also by this time got the name of the most valiant nation on the continent. The Saxons, therefore, then seated on the German shores opposite to the North-eastern parts of the island [b], being a populous nation, soldiers of fortune, and us'd to sea-expeditions, seem'd most likely to afford that speedy and effectual assistance, which the Britans so much wanted.

After the Romans were withdrawn, the Britans had chosen Vortigern Earl of Cornwall for their king, who, betwixt the years 430 and 452 (Chronologists differing in the precise year [c]) thought it necessary to call in the Saxons to aid him against his enemies the Scots and Picts. The Saxons willingly embrac'd the opportunity, and having done great service to Vortigern, expected to be rewarded in proportion to their own estimate of that service; but, as conquering soldiers are not soon satisfied, their pretensions were easily rais'd high enough to disgust the Britans, who had employed them. As soon, therefore, as the Saxons had humbled the Picts and Scots, it was no difficult matter for a people bred to war, as they were (and consequently not long pleas'd with peace) and, besides, enamour'd with the spacious, and plentiful country of Britain, to find

[b] They then dwelt in Slefwick, Jutland, and to the North of the present city of Hamburgh, viz. the Cimbrick Cherfonese, now mostly included in the Dutchy of Holstein. Ush. Prim. Cap. XII. p. 392.

[c] Usher's Prim. Cap. XII.

sufficient

sufficient pretences to quarrel with the unactive Britans, under so indiscreet a Prince as Vortigern; accordingly, they made no scruple to employ their arms to conquer those, whom they were but just before call'd in, to defend: to this war the Saxons had this further encouragement, that from the native country on the continent, then full of people, as many as were either willing to assist their countrymen, who first came hither, or desirous to improve their own circumstances, could find an easy passage into Britain, by means of their shipping, which their continual piracies had made it necessary, as the plunder had made it sweet, for them to maintain in full force.

By such fresh supplies the Saxons found it no hard matter to keep their footing, and about the year 460, treacherously murder'd, as it is said, 300 of the principal British Nobility, on the plains near Salisbury; the Britans therefore (who had hitherto liv'd promiscuously and quietly, with the Romans) found it necessary to retire before the Saxons. Some fled into Scotland, others into Holland, and some into Armorica in Gaul, afterwards from them call'd Britain, now Bretagne: on which part of our history I must beg leave to make a remark or two before I proceed, because the date of the fact requires it in this place.

Here then, that is, at or near this flight of the Britans from the Saxons, we are to place (as I think) the first considerable settlement of Britans in Armorica, they being never mention'd in history as inhabitants in any part of Gaul before this time[d]. Some, indeed, are of a different opinion[e], and think that Pliny mentions (though obscurely) the Britans in Gaul. Constantine the great, it must be allowed, and after him Maximus carry'd out of this island many parties of soldiers, and when they had serv'd them faithfully, and were discharg'd, those Emperours might, as some think[f], settle them in Armorica; but it is by no means likely, that the remnants of these recruits could be in number sufficient, to people, or subdue, or give name to all the country of Armorica[g]; it is much more probable, and indeed agreeable to history, that when the Saxons had conquer'd the greatest part of the island, the Britans thronging into the sea coasts of Hampshire and the Western counties, particularly Cornwall (whereto they retired, as loth to leave their native ground, as long as they could keep it), went over in such numbers, as soon made them the most consi-

[d] Usher. Antiq. Cap. XII. Camden 12mo, p. 38.
[e] La Ramee, and others.
[f] Hist. de Bretagne, par D'Argentre, p. 2.
[g] It must be allow'd that the learned and judicious Lhuyd, in his comparative Etymology, p. 32. col. 3. thinks that the Britans, who left this island, and possess'd themselves of Armorica, pass'd thither before the Saxons came in: but as far as appears to me, he had not sufficiently consider'd that the Migrants pass'd into the province called now Bretagne, through and from Cornwall principally, a circumstance evident (among other proofs) from the near resemblance of the Cornish and Armorican dialects, the names of places frequently the same, the constant alliance and friendly intercourse of both countries (which cannot be accounted for, if the inhabitants of Armorica proceeded indifferently and equally from all parts of Britain) and that nothing could make the Britans leave their native and so plentiful a country, in such numbers as were necessary to obliterate the ancient name of their country, and give it that of strangers, but war and compulsion.—Let the Reader judge.

derable

derable part of the inhabitants in that diſtrict, and from this time or ſoon after that part of Gaul oppoſite to Cornwall, and before call'd Armorica, began to be call'd Bretagne ; and has ſtill that name ; and the ſame language common to both people, and the friendly, and frequent intercourſes of trade, and alliance, even to the laſt generation with the Corniſh, ſhew the Armoricans, and Corniſh Britans to have been formerly one people. "Cornwall (ſays Mr. Scawen, MS. p. 40.) "hath received princes from thence (viz. Armorica), as they from us; "mutual aſſiſtances given and taken in former times, mutual inter- "changes of private families, now extinguiſh'd." "The Armoric "Britans (ſays M. Lhuyd, Pref. to Etymologicon, p. 267.) do not "pretend to be Gauls, but call the neighbouring provinces ſuch, and "their language Galek ; whereas they term their own Brezonek "[that is Britiſh], as indeed it is, being yet almoſt as intelligible to "our Corniſh, as the illiterate countrymen of the Weſt of England, "to thoſe of the North." The Britans of Armorica, therefore, fled before the Saxons into Cornwall, and thence into Armorica, in ſuch numbers as were ſufficient to poſſeſs, and give name to that country, and the ſtory (ſo much inſiſted upon by the Britiſh Hiſto-rians [h]) of Maximus's coming into Britain, and then carrying over Conon Meradoc and Britiſh ſoldiers enough to people and ſubdue Armorica, is a meer fable, improbable in all its circumſtances, and unſupported by any hiſtory of credit [i]. But to return,

The greateſt part of the diſconſolate ancient inhabitants retir'd into Wales, and Cornwall; and from this time they are to be under-ſtood, as inhabiting and ruling only there, and having only one King, ſometimes choſen out of Wales, and ſometimes out of Cornwall; and to this King, common to both countries, whatever little parties of Britans were diſpers'd elſewhere [k], acknowledg'd, and paid a kind of allegiance, though not properly inhabitants either of Wales or Cornwall. To enter into a detail of all the Battles fought with the Saxons, and affecting the intereſt of the Corniſh Britans, would be foreign to our preſent deſign ; but a ſummary account of this matter may ſerve to collect and recover ſome parts of our hiſtory.

After Vortigern had ended his unfortunate reign, his ſon Vortimer and ſome other valiant men [l] did their utmoſt to recover their coun-try, and protect their religion, ſtruggling perpetually, tho' in vain, againſt the Saxon incroachments; but after this deſtructive war had continued near two hundred and forty years, Cadwallader of Wales, laſt ſole Monarch of the Britans, died about 689, and the Britans

[h] Pontic. Virum. p. 37 to 39. &c.
[i] " In all the proceedings of Maximus, I ſee "no ground for ſettling colonies of Britans in "Armorica." Stillingf. Ant. Brit. p. 184.
[k] " Cumberland was then poſſeſs'd by Bri-

"tans, and had Princes of its own till near the "Norman Conqueſt."
[l] Aurelius Ambrof. Uter. Pendragon, and Arthur firſt King of Cornwall, then of all the Britans, &c.

never afterwards attempting to set up one national king, shews how low their affairs were reduc'd by the Saxon wars. From this time Wales became divided into two[m], and soon afterwards into more principalities (each of their petty Governours however having the name of King), and Cornwall, having no longer any King in common with the Welsh-Britans, became a distinct principality, generally under one prince, and sometimes under more. Here ceas'd, in a great measure, that connexion which had subsisted for so many years betwixt the Welsh and Cornish; and acting, after this, under different rulers, they were no longer able to act with that force against the Saxons which they had formerly done, when more united. About this time, however, aid came to the Cornish from another quarter. The Armorican Britans came over into Cornwall under Ivor their King, and his kinsman Ynor; and though Leland [n] denies any such remigration of the Armoricans, it is not at all improbable that this people, at the solicitation of the Cornish, should attempt to rescue from the Saxon tyranny a country to which the greatest part of the Armoricans ow'd their original about 250 years before. With this assistance the Cornish recovered their country, and the East of Devonshire from the enemy. But their success was of short continuance, for they found a severe scourge in Ina King of the West Saxons, who defeated them entirely in 710, and got much renown by his wars with the Cornish [o]. In the year 720, Adelred, King of West Sex, invaded the Cornish, but was repulsed by Roderic Molwynoc, " King (or General) of the Britans " in the West part of England," and Prince of North-Wales, who was afterwards, however, " driven by the Saxons to forsake the " West-country," and retire into his own inheritance in North-Wales [p]. Cuthred King of West Sex obtained a considerable victory over the Cornish in the year 743. The same Cuthred is said to have conquer'd part of Cornwall, and united it to his kingdom of West Saxony, in the year 753; and from this time the Saxons look'd upon some of the Eastern parts of Cornwall (which were beyond the river Ex [q]) as their own, and upon every invasion of the Danes and Cornish, dispatch'd forces into Devonshire to oppose them. About the year 766, Kinewulf King of West Sex had some troublesome dealings with the Cornish; for in this year he gave several parcels of land to the church of Wells, by a charter which runs thus, " [r] I Kinewulph, King of the West-Saxons, for the love of God, and " (which shall not be here particularly mentioned) some vexations of " our Cornish Enemies, do, by the consent of my Bishops and noble- " men, make over by gift, a certain parcel of ground to the Apostle " and servant of God, St. Andrew, &c."

[m] North and South Wales.
[n] Sheringham, p. 393.
[o] Rapin, vol. I. octav. p. 209.
[p] Carad. Llang. Edit. Powel, p. 25.
[q] The part East of Exeter.
[r] Camden, p. 84.

M

Not

Not long after, the Cornifh, the better to oppofe the Saxons encouraged the Danifh pirates to land, and bring over every now and then frefh forces from their country, into Britain; a fufficient inftance how little the fatal mifcarriages of former times do influence a precipitate, and ill-govern'd people. The Cornifh fmarted fo much under the Saxons, that one would think they could not have forgot how dangerous an impatience it was in their anceftors to feek that redrefs in war from foreign foldiers, which might have proceeded, though more flowly, yet with more fecurity, from exerting their own innate virtue and fortitude. The Danes firft arrived at the fhores of Weft Saxony (under which name the Saxons began now to comprehend all the ancient kingdom of Dumnonia) in three fhips, when Beorthricus (or Brithric) was king, in the year 787, and had not long been us'd to the coafts, before the Cornifh made a league with them [s]; for in the year 806, a fleet arriv'd in Weft Wales (fo the Britifh Writers frequently call Cornwall) which encourag'd the Cornifh to an infurrection againft Egbert, firft king of England, as uniter of the Saxon Heptarchy. This formidable union drew all the power and fkill of Egbert that way; and thefe, at laft, after the war had continued fome years, proving too ftrong for the Cornifh valour [t], Egbert over-run all Cornwall about the year 813[u]. After this, either the reftlefs nature of Egbert, or the fituation of his affairs calling him elfewhere for fome time, the war feems to have been rather interrupted than ended. In the 24th year of Egbert there was a confiderable battle fought betwixt the Britans and Weft Saxons of Devonfhire, in which many thoufands fell on each fide, and the victory remain'd uncertain: this battle was fought at Gavulford [w] (or Camelford [x]) in Cornwall. Notwithftanding all this, the Saxons having gotten footing in Devonfhire, the Cornifh Britans, affifted by the Danes, who at this time came at the particular inftance of the Cornifh [y], march'd Eaftward in the year 835 to difpoffefs them, and at firft overcame the Saxons, but foon after at Hengftone-Hill, a few miles to the weftward of Tamar, were totally overthrown; and to reftrain them for the future, Egbert enacted this fevere law, that no Britan fhould pafs the limits of his country, and fet foot on the Englifh ground upon pain of death; about fixteen years after this, the old inveteracy of the Cornifh Britans againft the Saxons continuing, they feem to be again involv'd, for we read that Cheorl, call'd by Huntingdon [z] the Conful, by Hoveden [a] the Earl of Devonfhire, fought againft the Danes, and obtain'd a fignal victory. There was a national enmity betwixt the Britans and the Saxons; to cherifh

---

[s] Sax. Chron. p. 64. about the year 806, fays Mr. Camden, Eng. 206.

[t] Fortiffimos fortiter effugavit, fays Hoveden, p. 237 of Egbert and the Cornifh.

[u] Sax. Chron. p. 69. A. D. 809, fays Rapin, p. 214.

[w] Sax. Chron. at the year 824 or 5.

[x] Camd. 12mo. p. 82. " Camelford alicubi " Gaffelford."

[y] Rapin, vol. I. octavo, p. 299. Philofoph. Tranf. Numb. 458. Hen. Hunting. p. 198.

[z] P. 200.   [a] P. 258.

which

which it was the interest of the Danes, as much as it was the natural inclination of the Britans: these two nations therefore, united by inclination and interest, omitted no opportunity of attacking the Saxon territories whenever they either found them unguarded or distress'd, and themselves in a hopeful condition to invade and conquer.

In the turbulent former part of king Alfred's reign, when the Danes were so busy, and triumphant over the English, it cannot be suppos'd that the Cornish and Welsh Britans were idle spectators. We find the Danes after a truce, wintering at Exeter, in the 4th of King Alfred, A. D. 876. and without doubt by the encouragement of the Cornish party there. Hither their ships also immediately tended with fresh supplies, though frustrated of their design by a tempest, in which 120 ships were wreck'd; nor did their land-army marching towards Exeter [b], fare much better, being encounter'd by Alfred, and oblig'd to give hostages to depar with all speed. This seems to have given the Saxons the chief power in Exeter, for in the 21st of Alfred, the Danes laid siege to Exeter, but fled at the approach of Alfred, who was by this time become a powerful king.

The Welsh as well as the Cornish had been from time to time assisted, and encouraged by the Danes in their common cause, against the Saxons, and therefore were never left quiet by the Saxons as soon as they had vanquish'd, or by league, or otherwise got rid of the Danes [c]. The Britans of Cumberland had also put themselves under the protection of the Danes, and submitted not to the Saxons till the time of Edward the elder, son to Alfred the Great [d]. At length, a formidable confederacy was form'd against King Athelstan, in the year 938 [e], in favour of Anlaff, in which the Irish, Scots, Welsh, Danes, and Cornish united, but in vain: Athelstan first overthrew the forces of the north, where the allied nations lost Constantine King of Scotland, six Irish or Welsh Kings, and twelve Earls, and General Officers: he then marched against the Cornish Britans, who had assisted the confederates, took Exeter (which before they had inhabited upon equal terms with the Saxons [f]) from them entirely. About this time also he bounded the Welsh by the river Wye, taking all, betwixt that and the Severn, from them; for the same reasons, and to punish those alike, who seem'd alike guilty, he excluded the Cornish for ever from any right to Exeter, which had been their capital for so many centuries; he took also all that goodly country betixt the rivers Ex and Tamar from them, and made the Tamar their future boundary, which has ever since been so accounted. This was so considerable an alteration in the circumstances of Cornwall, that

b N. B. The first detachment of the Danes, after a truce with Alfred, came from the East, and lodg'd itself at Exeter; aud 'tis likely their troops from Wales and Cornwall march'd to join what had been admitted into Exeter.
c Rapin, vol. I. p. 361.   d Ibid. p. 362.

e Some say 940, some 933.
f Malmesbury, p. 28. Speed, Chron. p. 341. "At this time also Adelstan did remove the "Brytaines that dwelt in Excester and there- "aboutes to Cornewale. Carad. Langar." Edit. Powel, p. 51.

nothing

nothing lefs than an entire conqueft could have produc'd it; from this time therefore we are to confider Cornwall under the Saxon yoke[g]. Athelftan, having made a thorough conqueft of Cornwall, took fhipping for the ifles of Scilly, that he might not leave any fpot unfubdued that belong'd to it. This happen'd, after the Cornifh Britans had maintain'd a perpetual ftruggle againft the Saxons, for the full fpace of 500 years, from their firft coming into Britain. An enmity this, of that inveteracy and continuance, as is fcarce to be equall'd in hiftory; it reach'd down to the year 938, and the Saxon Monarchy foon after giving way to the Danifh, it cannot be expected that many Saxon Monuments fhould be erected in a country fo averfe from the beginning to the Saxon Government, and fo little a while under its dominion: and indeed we have no Saxon monuments among us, that have come to my knowledge (excepting a few fragments of buildings which favour of the Saxon ftyle of architecture) unlefs the foundation of colleges and monafteries, and donations to churches, may be call'd fuch.

CHAP. XI.

Of the Danes.

The manner of the Danifh invafions, and the military works it occafioned.

THOUGH the Danes landed in Weft Sex in the year 787[h], yet they winter'd not here in Britain (which is however to be underftood of the Eaftern Coafts, near the heart of the ifland, and not of the Weft as we fhall fee in the fequel) 'till the year 854, as is particularly taken notice of by the hiftorians[i]. It feems, it was their cuftom to return every year to their own country, either to carry off their fpoil, to vifit their wives and children, to recruit their forces, or to repair their fhips, which could not be fo well done, or fo fecurely attended to, in a foreign and enemy's country. This frequent failing to and fro brought them acquainted with all the fecure landing places on the coaft, where, if the winds would not permit them to land in one place, they foon knew where, in fome other adjacent creek, they might fhelter their fhips, and difbark their men with more fafety and conveniency; if they could not fecurely put on fhore a great number in one place, 'tis natural to imagine that they would divide into parties, and land as near one to the other as poffible: this, the many landing places fo very little diftant from each other round the extremity of Cornwall (call'd the Land's End) do abundantly teftify: as the Danes were fo frequently obliged to land, and embark again, another thing occurs to every one who will

In Cornwall.

[g] " Cornwalli, in hoc tantum reprehenfibiles, " licèt vires omnes ad patriæ falutem tuendam " animosè contulerant, in Saxonum poteftatem " conceflerunt, utpote qui numero non va- " luerunt, nec Regio fatis a naturâ munita eos " tutare poterat." Camden.
[h] Sax. Chron. p. 64.
[i] Hen. Hunt. p. 200. Heveden, p. 237.

confider

confider their works (for works are records and oftentimes the only remaining proofs and grounds of hiftory), and 'tis this, that not caring eafily to quit any land where they had once got footing, and yet knowing well enough to provide for a fecure retreat to their fhips on all events, they not only intrench'd themfelves on the hills, but foon learn'd (fo inftructive is neceffity) to intrench and fortify their landing places, many evidences of which are ftill vifible, and fome of their works entire, on the weftern fhores of Cornwall; and where the cliffs are of clay or loofe moldering ftone, the fea, as appears by the remaining veftiges, has wafh'd away a great part of feveral of them. If any one wonders what occafion the Danes had to fortify thus, while they were allies to the Cornifh, let him recollect, that being much addicted to plunder and cruelty, even where they were invited as allies, fomething of this kind was neceffary to protect themfelves from that juft retribution which the injur'd natives might otherwife have oblig'd them to. It was alfo neceffary for them to fortify, in order to awe the natives, and make it difficult for them to renounce their alliance. Thefe military works are by the prefent inhabitants all call'd caftles, are numerous in the Weft of Cornwall, and as they are more modern than the Phenicians, Greeks, and Romans, and could ferve no purpofe of the native Britans, muft have been erected by the Danes; for it does not appear, that the Saxons did make any confiderable debarkation of troops in Cornwall, they plunder'd and ravag'd the fhores, and fea-port towns, about the times of the Conftantine family, but retreated to their fhips foon: whereas the Danes came in numbers, and join'd the natives, and being better inftructed in the arts of Invafion erected caftles (even during their alliance with the Cornifh), it being the cuftom of the Danes to encamp and fortify the hills wherever they came, though without any intention to ftay there any long while [k].

The Danes, by their frequent embarkations, had not only obtain'd a thorough knowledge of the coafts of our ifland, but here in Cornwall they had this further advantage, that by their landing in the Weft, and marching fo often Eaftward to fight the Saxons, they were become perfectly acquainted with all the paffages and ftrong holds of fo narrow a country as Cornwall; and thefe two advantages (which the unfortunate fiding of the natives with the Danes, for fo many years, could not but give them) were too confiderable and evident, to be neglected by a nation fo addicted to pillage abroad, and fo meanly accommodated at home; and it is too plain, from their caftles and entrenchments on every hill almoft in the hundred of Penwith [Cornwall], as well as by their

[k] Sax. Chron. Ann. 878. p. 84.

N

landing

landing places abovementioned, that they were guefts not eafily to be got rid of; and although the Cornifh were not at all times inclin'd, or able to face the Saxons, and had not therefore at all times occafion for the Danifh powers to help them; it is however probable, that the Danes chofe not to quit the country entirely, but foon learn'd to leave confiderable parties of their countrymen in their encampments here, under pretence of being a guard to the inhabitants, but really in order to fecure a fafe return to thofe who re-embarked for Denmark, whenever they fhould chufe to come again into Britain. As cruel as the Danes were in thofe days, it does not appear from hiftory, that they dealt as feverely at firft with the Cornifh, as they did with the Eaftern parts of the ifland; for, as foon as ever they landed in Norfolk, Suffolk, or farther to the North on that coaft, we hear of their deftroying every thing facred and civil, with an unparallel'd barbarity; but when they landed in Cornwall, they feem'd to have always march'd into Devonfhire to fight the Saxons, and however faithlefs they were in other treaties, it does not appear that they ever broke with the Cornifh, 'till after the total conqueft of it by Athelftan, which was more than one hundred years after their firft alliance againft Egbert. Indeed, in the year [l] 876, the Danes are faid to have attempted Exeter and taken it, but this will not infer, that they were then at enmity with the Cornifh; for that city was at that time divided betwixt the Saxons and the Cornifh [m] (much, without doubt, to the diffatisfaction of the latter), and the Danes retir'd to Exeter, as to a place of fafety and alliance, and entered the caftle there without any refiftance [n]; and, that they then took only that part of it which belong'd to the Saxons, is evident; becaufe Alfred King of Weft Sex, immediately purfued them thither, compounded the difference for that time, and took Hoftages of them. In the year 878 [o], the brother of Inwærus, and Healfdenus a Danifh commander of 23 fhips, was flain in Devonfhire, with 840 men: again, in the year 894, we find that the Danes attack'd a certain fortification in the North of Devonfhire with 40 fhips, and with 100 other fhips laid fiege to Exeter; which fhews only that Exeter was at that time principally under the jurifdiction of the Saxons, and for their fakes King Alfred immediately march'd thither, and made the Danes raife the fiege [p]; and, indeed, the Danes being fo often recorded to be in Devonfhire, looks as if they had made this their frontier, in order to cover their friends in Cornwall, and preferve it as a fecure retreat, in cafe they fhould be defeated, as oftentimes they were, though to little purpofe, as long as they continued mafters of the fea.

[l] Sax. Chron.
[m] Malmfbury.
[n] Sax. Chron. ad ann. 877.
[o] Sax. Chron.
[p] Ibid.

Though

Though it was the general custom of the Danes [q] who infested the shores of the West Sex, to return every winter to Denmark for more than 60 years after their first landing, yet we may imagine that those who landed in Cornwall at the desire of the Britans, in order to assist them against the Saxons, might not have such cogent reasons, annually to desert this island, as the others had; we may reasonably suppose, that the inhabitants would not refuse to supply with provisions, and the other necessaries of life, in winter, those who were always ready to fight their battles in summer: nay, it is not unlikely that the Britans thought themselves more secure from any attempt of the Saxons, when they had a body of Danes among them, than when they were left to themselves; besides, the Danes could recruit their forces among their allies, at least refresh them with ease from their fatigues, or employ them usually in erecting proper fences on the hills against winter, and the enemy; they might here too repair their shatter'd ships with some security, the Cornish havnig many good harbours on the coast: for these reasons, therefore, well as what is mentioned before, viz. the Danes being an acquaintance not easily to be shook off, we cannot scruple to attribute a longer and more familiar converse to the Danes and Cornish, than to the Danes and any other part of Britain; so early an alliance here soon after they first landed, gives strong reasons to support this conjecture, as the multitude of circular fortifications, some of which are wall'd round with very good masonry [r], and look more like a settled habitation, than a hasty Vallum thrown up for a temporary encampment. Nor were these fortify'd hills without their use, though in an allied country; for, in these several strong holds, considerable parties of Danes might well chuse to winter, rather than in towns, as places where military discipline might be better maintain'd, as well as fewer injuries done to the natives. By means of these castles the Danes had indeed the command over the Britans in Cornwall, yet still look'd upon them as allies, as long as they continued in a condition o assi stthem gainst the Saxons; but after Cornwall became entirely under the Saxon yoke, however obsequious the inhabitants might be disposed to act, the Danes look'd upon all the tyes of amity as dissolved, the Britans as servants to other masters, and Cornwall as a province of West Sex; and accordingly from this time landed here, as elsewhere, to plunder and destroy. In the year 981, they committed great ravages, burnt Bodman, then a Bishop's See. In the 19th year of Ethelred, A. D. 997, the Danish fleet sailed round Cornwall, and came into the mouth of the Severn,

[q] H. Huntingdon, p. 200; and Hoveden, p. 231.   [r] Chûn Castle, and Castelandinas, &c.

4   robbing,

robbing, as they went along, Cornwall, Devonshire, and South Wales[s], all three formerly their allies upon all occasions. And from the time of the Saxon conquest, the fortified hills serv'd them, not only to retain their soldiers in duty and order, and to awe the natives, but as places of refuge to secure themselves against their enemies, and preserve their booty, and pillage; and now 'tis likely that their landing places were more effectually secur'd.

For more than a hundred years the Danes continued their usual abode in Cornwall as friends; and after Athelstan's time, till the Saxon and Danish Monarchy became blended in one, as enemies; from this continual intercourse, and the fix'd residence of their garrisons, 'tis no wonder that there should be erected here many and various kinds of Monuments by the Danish nation. And, indeed, as history teaches us, that the Danes were more conversant and longer resident in Cornwall than elsewhere; so the variety of Danish Monuments, still extant here, abundantly confirms the truth of that history. Here likely they buried their valiant leaders, sometimes under Barrows, now and then in Kist-vaens, or stone-chests, some under erected stones, several of which are to be placed to their account, and many of each sort still remain, as will be particularly exhibited among the Sepulchral Monuments. Here they held their assemblies for chusing and inaugurating their chief commanders; and, doubtless, either made or used the circles of erected stones for that purpose; and hence it is that we have some distinguish'd by an Obelisk in the middle, or the Kongstolen[t], as in Denmark.

Here they fortified, with a Ditch and Vallum, their several landing places, and as they advanc'd, they fortify'd the hills with such propriety and judgment, that no less than eight castles as they are call'd (though they are rather strong entrenchments), are to be seen within five miles round the town of Penzance, all of a circular form, and so plac'd on the hills, that they are in sight of each other, about two miles asunder, so as to be able to communicate proper signals; the most distant not more than eight miles from each other; some enclos'd with a very thick wall or walls of masonry, wide ditches, and such other works round them as plainly bespeak leisure, security, and the peaceable permission of the natives; all these things sufficiently shew how powerful they were, in these Western parts of Britain, and at the same time how willing and desirous they were to continue their power, and perpetuate their possession. Plunder and power were the sole, and darling objects of the Danes; and by degrees they came to use the Cornish as bad as the rest of the kingdom; and to establish the one, that they might glut themselves with the other, they practis'd every kind of severity (which the hottest rage of war

[s] Speed, p. 359.　　　[t] Wormius, Mon. Dan.

only

only can excuse) unprovok'd, and, upon common occasions, fire, sword, and desolation, attending them wherever they march'd; so that Cornwall is suppos'd to have been at last utterly ruin'd by them, and to have continued as a forest uncultivated, and thinly peopled, for several ages. After the Danes arrived at the sovereignty, being then become Christians as well as kings, they look'd on the natives as their subjects, and consequently must think, that to harm and plunder them, would be proportionably to injure, and gradually to destroy themselves; thenceforward their depredations ceas'd, their Monuments took another turn, became Christian, and inscrib'd; and the Danish Line expiring soon after, as well as the Saxon, yielded an easier admittance to the Normans, of whom now, though too modern to say much of, we must take some notice, forasmuch as they also introduc'd some Monuments.

C H A P. XII.
Of the Normans.

THE last great alteration which our country underwent, was occasioned by the coming in of the Normans, which being owing to the failure of the Danish, as well as the interruption, and weakness of the Saxon line, it may be necessary to give a short view of the several successions immediately preceding the Conquest. After the weak reign of Ethelred, in which the Danes carried all before them, his son Edmund, surnam'd Ironside (from supporting his feeble and dishearten'd party with so much patience and fortitude) succeeded, and dying in the year 1017, after a strenuous but short reign, of less than twelve months, left the English party so forlorn, that Canute, son of Swane King of Denmark (at that time chief of the Danish forces in England, and already admitted into a partnership of the kingdom) was immediately acknowledged sole monarch of England, although Edmund had left two sons, and a brother, who afterwards was rais'd to the throne. Canute held the crown till 1036, and was succeeded by Harold (from his swiftness in running, surnam'd Harefoot) as some think [u], son of Canute by a former marriage, which others doubt of [w]. He reign'd about four years and four months, and left the crown to Hardacnute, son of Canute, by Ælgiva, or Emma, widow of King Ethelred, who after reigning near two years died, and with him expired the Danish Royal Line, and the crown return'd to the Saxon. Edward the Confessor, so nam'd for his piety, son of King Ethelred, by Emma, and half brother to Hardacnute, being chosen King, in the year 1041, and dying without issue in 1066, devised the crown [x], as 'tis

[u] Hen. Hunt. p. 209.
[w] Sax. Chron.
[x] Et juxta quod ipse ante mortem statuerat in regnum ei successit Haroldus. Hoveden, p. 258. See Sax. Chron.

O

said,

said, to Harold, eldeſt ſond of Godwin Earl of Kent [y]; but whether Harold received the crown by grant from King Edward, or ſeiz'd it, preſuming the greatneſs of his reputation in arms might reconcile people, in a little while, to the weakeſt title, if he could plead poſſeſſion, he held the crown only forty weeks and one day, being ſlain in battle againſt William Duke of Normandy [z], who with this ſingle victory got the crown; with ſuch eaſy tranſitions, in thoſe times, did the imperial crown of England paſs, not only from one hand to another, but from one family and nation to another; inſomuch that within 50 years the crown was poſſeſs'd by a Saxon, a Dane, a Saxon, and (as Harold had no pretence to the Saxon or Daniſh Blood-Royal) by the private family of Godwin, and laſtly by the Norman line: ſo that the crown, in one generation, was poſſeſs'd by five families, each diſtinct from it's preceding one, and each king (if you except Harold) of a different nation from his predeceſſor.

William the firſt, of the Norman race, being acknowledg'd King, made it the principal buſineſs of his reign to ſettle in Britain (as the moſt likely way to ſecure the crown to his own family) his countrymen who had attended, and further'd his expedition, and to introduce his country's cuſtoms, laws, and language: and as the Normans were at this time Chriſtians, and much more civiliz'd than either the Saxons or Danes at the time of their invaſion, it can't be thought that our country ſuffer'd ſo much from them, as from the others, or that the alterations introduc'd were of ſo wild, barbarous, and deſtructive a nature as what the former dreadful convulſions had been attended withal. As the ſciences were in this age more cultivated among the Normans, than here in England, they improv'd our manner in works of art and taſte [a], they introduc'd a nobler and more elegant kind of building and deſigning [b], than we had been us'd to

[y] Godwin Earl of Kent, of great power in his time, married to his firſt wife the ſiſter of King Canute, but had only one ſon by her, who was drown'd in the Thames: by his ſecond wife he had Harold (who ſucceeded Edward the Confeſſor), and many other ſons.

[z] To whom, William of Malmſbury ſays (p. 53.), that Edward the Confeſſor, after the ſudden death of Edward, ſon of Edmund Ironſide (whom he deſign'd his ſucceſſor, and for that reaſon had ſent for him from abroad) granted the ſucceſſion to the crown of England; and queſtions whether Harold had any grant at all from Edward, though the Engliſh gave out as much. Ibid.

[a] " Videas ubique in villis eccleſias, in vicis " & urbibus Monaſteria novo ædificandi genere " conſurgere.—Normanni veſtibus ad invidiam " culti.—Domi ingentia ædificia."—William of Malmſbury, p. 58.

[b] " Hiis diebus Anglici parvis, baſis & abjectis " domibus utebantur cum victualium habun-" dantia. Veſtibus etiam ſolebant uti protenſis " ad medium genu brachiis oneratis armillis " aureis. E contrario Franci & Normanni

" amplis & ſuperbis ædificiis modicas agebant " expenſas, ſed in cibariis delicati." J. Rous, Antiq. Warwick. p. 106.

" Biſhop Stillingfleet, in his diſcourſe of " the true Antiquity of London [Fol. Edit. " Vol. III. pag. 934.] declares his opinion, " That the new way of Building intro-" duced by the Normans related only to the " Roofs of Churches, and not to the Walls; " that is, the Saxons did not underſtand the " way of turning ſuch great arches with ſtone, " as were in the new Church of St. Paul's, " built by Mauritius; but they knew how to " build Churches with ſtone, and with arches, " &c. There is not the leaſt doubt of the " ſame Style of Architecture continuing after " the Norman Conqueſt as prevailed in the " Saxon age, only the latter was upon a more " enlarged Plan. The middle of Henry the " Firſt's reign, I fear, is too early for the in-" troduction of the Gothick Architecture, in " contra-diſtinction to the Saxon or Normanno-" Saxon, which was a very debaſed and cor-" rupted Roman Architecture. — The White-" tower, in the Tower of London, was cer-

be-

before; from this time therefore, our Monuments have no more the rudeness and disproportion of the natural stone; they no longer remain uninscrib'd, silent as well as monstrous; they want dates indeed, but are generally inscrib'd; surnames are added, but what shall particularly distinguish all inscrib'd Monuments erected by the Normans, is the old French, which, in all the law courts, and elsewhere, on all occasions, this king labour'd most assiduously to introduce, in place of the Saxon or English language. Those inscrib'd in French are likely to be near the Conquest, if the characters will suit that age, for notwithstanding all the struggles of the Norman line, the Saxon tongue gain'd ground again, and in a little time nothing but the law remain'd in French; a certain sign how difficult it is to make thorough alterations in language, and that chains are easier impos'd on the hands, than on the tongues; the other works of the Normans, such as Monasteries, Palaces, Courts of Justice, Churches, Crosses, and the like, are too little different from the works of the late, or present age, to require any particular notice here.

CHAP. XIII.

Of the British Religion.

AS many sorts of Monuments which we have now existing, are owing to the different nations which have successively settled in Britain (Phenicians, Greeks, Romans, Saxons, Danes, and Normans), so, many of them must have arisen from the Religion which obtain'd among the ancient people of this island.

From the sway that religion has, and always has had, in the actions of mankind, it will not be wonder'd, if ancient Monuments, in a great measure, owe their rise to, and are diversify'd, by the several rites, ceremonies, and particular institutions of the national worship, whatsoever that is. For all religions (though founded on one universal principle) have something peculiar to themselves (as every thing must have which is liable to be warp'd and tinctur'd by the humours of powerful and presumptive men); and whatever is subservient to the offices of religion, whether Temple,

" tainly of the first Norman age, and that agrees " with the Saxon mode; so does all that part of " Lincoln Cathedral, which was erected by " Remigius, and several others which might be " instanced. In King Stephen's time I find " some intermixture of Gothick with the Nor- " manno-Saxon, and earlier I can't trace it." Right Reverend Dr. Lyttelton, Bishop of Carlisle to the Author, October, 1765.

Some think, therefore, that the words before of Malmsbury are too general; and that the same kind of architecture which was in use before the Conquest continued, with some little variation only, till the middle of Henry the First's reign. And it is not unlikely, that some time was necessary to change the general custom in this point, as well as in all others. However, where the Normans did build, they followed their own country style, no doubt; but in what particulars it differed from the Saxon manner, is not now so easy to determine.

Altar,

Altar, Prieſt, ſacred Utenſil, or Rite, will have ſomething in it
diſtinct, and peculiar to that religion from whence it proceeded.
It will now be neceſſary, therefore, to enquire, what the moſt
ancient religion of this iſland was.

The ancient Britiſh Religion was of the Gentile kind, near
kin to the idolatry of the Eaſt, and every thing of a religious
nature was directed and managed by a Prieſthood of great antiquity
and fame amongſt the ancients; they were call'd Druids, of whom
a particular account follows in the next book.

END OF THE FIRST BOOK.

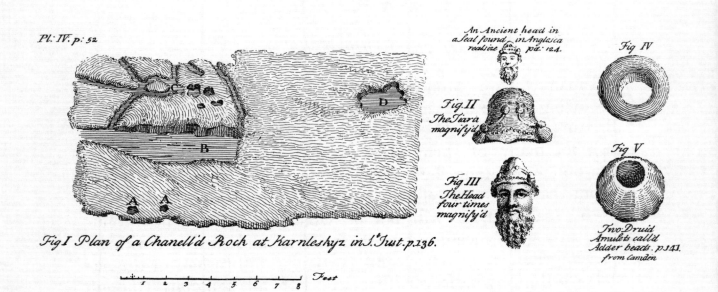

Pl: IV. p: 52

An Ancient head in
a Seal found in Anglesea
real size   pa. 124.

Fig II
The Tiara
magnify'd

Fig III
The Head
four times
magnify'd

Fig IV

Fig V

Two Druid
Amulets call'd
Adder beads. p.141.
from Camden

Fig I Plan of a Chanell'd Rock at Karnleskyz in St. Iust. p.136.

1 2 3 4 5 6 7 8 Feet

8   6   5   4   1   2   3   7

Bas Relieve on the Portal of the Temple of Montmorillon in France Montf.ⁿ Supplem.^e Tom.n.p221. Frick.p:49.explain'd p.104

OF THE
BRITISH RELIGION.
BOOK II.

CHAP. I.

Of Idolatry in general.

IF we take only a tranfient view of the Druid fuperftition, without at the fame time examining the hiftory of other countries,
and comparing Druidifm with the idolatrous rites of the Eaft,
we fhall be apt to think the Druids ftand alone in all the inftances
of barbarity, magick, and grove-worfhip, fo juftly laid to their
charge; the frequency of their human facrifices fhocks us, their
magick exceeds belief; their oak-worfhip looks fingular and abfurd; and their difcipline, cuftoms and tenets have the air of peculiarities to be found no where but in their fect.

In order, therefore, to make a proper eftimate, and form a right
judgment of this Idolatry of Britain, it will be neceffary to give a
fhort furvey of the rife of Idolatry in general; the falfe Deities that
were at different times fubftituted in the room of the true one; the
manner in which the Gentiles worfhip'd thefe falfe Deities, and the
remarkable refemblance that there was betwixt all the feveral forts of
Idolatry. From thefe particulars it will evidently appear (which is
of great concern to the prefent fubject) that Druidifm acknowledg'd

P   the

the fame Deities, us'd the fame worfhip, and therefore muft have had the fame original, as the cuftoms, tenets, rites, and fuperftition of other gentile nations.

SECT. I.
First rife
of Idolatry.

The Eaftern authors affirm that Idolatry was practis'd before the flood, and that the children of Seth were feduc'd to it by the Cainites; and indeed, it is very likely [a] that the fons of God were call'd fo, as having retain'd the true religion, in contradiftinction to thofe who had degenerated from it. Cain's infolent behaviour to his Maker [b] makes it alfo probable, that he was not like to keep himfelf or his pofterity long in the true religion. 'Tis alfo faid, that every imagination of the thoughts of man's heart was continually evil [c]; that all flefh had corrupted his way upon the earth [d]; and of all abominations, there is none fo productive of exceffive wickednefs as Idolatry, which promotes, and even confecrates the greateft vices, fuch as lewdnefs, murder, and debauchery; and it is not eafy to conceive how mankind could be fo totally immers'd in wickednefs, as they were before the flood, and retain at the fame time the True Religion.

But however that be, whether Idolatry began before the flood, or not, we have undoubted reafon to think, that people began foon after the flood to depart from the fear, and true worfhip of God; for fcarce was Noah laid in his Grave [e], but the children of men [f] (that is, thofe of the falfe religion), inftigated by fome motives which were difpleafing to God, enter'd into a combination to build a city, and tower, whofe top was to reach up to heaven. What their principal intention was does not plainly appear; whether for a refuge in cafe of a fecond deluge [g]; or to make for themfelves a memorial [h], or to erect a monument to the honour of the Sun, as the chief caufe of drying up the deluge (which fome learned men [i] have fuppos'd, becaufe the pyramidal form of this tower refembled fire); or laftly, whether they defigned this tower as a temple for fome Idol: whatever were the motives, the fact was contrary to the will of God [k], and their defign fuch, as tended to revive and promote that general corruption of faith and manners, which had been fo lately and juftly punifh'd by the univerfal deluge.

[a] Gen. vi. 2.
[b] Ibid. iv. 5, 9.
[c] Ibid. vi. 5.
[d] Ibid. v. 11, 12.
[e] Some think that the foundation of Babel was laid not more than ten years after Noah's death; moft people agree, not more than twenty-eight.
[f] Ham and his pofterity, viz. Canaan, who by the curfe of his grandfather Noah appears to have been undutiful, and very wicked. Gen. ix. 25, 26.
[g] Jofeph. Antiq. Lib. I. Cap. V. Univerf. Hift. p. 143.
[h] As the vulgar tranflation, Gen. xi. 4. feems to intimate.
[i] Tenifon of Idolatry.
[k] " This they begin to do, and now nothing " will be reftrain'd from them, which they have " imagin'd to do." Gen. xi. 6.

The

The Babylonians defcended from Cufh, the eldeft fon of Ham, claim the firft and higheft antiquity; and it muft be allowed, that from them all the Eaft and the North received their firft Idolatries. Egypt will allow no fuperiour in antiquity, as to religious rites and government; and if Ham, the youngeft fon of Noah, was king of Egypt[1], none can go far beyond it. The Egyptians fpread their abominations after many ages into Greece, and Greece communicated the infection to the Weft. The Phenicians lay claim alfo to the precedence in this matter, and fay, that the firft temple was erected in Phenicia: they are defcended from Canaan the youngeft fon of Ham, and were not only remarkable for their dangerous corruptions at home, as early as the time of Jacob and Mofes, but by the improvements they firft made in navigation, were enabled to communicate the poifon of their fuperftition, as far as the extremities of the then difcover'd world.

The general and chief motives for revolting from the worfhip of the true God, were the tranfcendent purity of God, and the ftrictnefs of life and manners requir'd in his adorers; people, therefore, who delighted in violence and wandering lufts, were foon glad to drop fuch a fyftem of reftraint, as the true religion, and by general confent frame to themfelves a more free, various, and extenfive manner of worfhip, fuch as might permit their paffions to range and expatiate at pleafure: this could not be done, they found, whilft they continued to ferve the true God, as he had directed; the bufinefs, therefore, of the inventive and powerful, was to fet up a new fort of Deities, who were to be pleas'd upon eafier terms; at leaft, who would not refent the frequent tranfgreffions of man in fo fevere a manner as God feem'd to have done, in the fall of Adam, in the curfe of Cain, and in the univerfal deluge.

SECT. II.

Chief motives to Idolatry.

This being all that is neceffary to obferve concerning the rife and firft motives of Idolatry, or that falfe religion which afterwards took poffeffion of all the world, excepting only the little nation of the Hebrews, let us now confider what that falfe religion was, and wherein its oppofition to the true confifted.

We muft not imagine that the falfe religion differ'd (as foon as it began) in every point from the true, nor that all the truths of the firft, and pure religion, were at once entirely rejected; but rather, that, admitting the great and fundamental truths, the children of men rais'd fuperftitious fancies of their own thereupon; invented and infifted upon fables, admitted great impurities in manners and worfhip, and in the end become wholly immers'd in every kind

SECT. III.

Principles it proceeded upon.

[1] Prid. Part I. Book VII.

of

of corruption, every extravagance of sin, and every absurdity of errour.   Thus, for instance, ——— They deny'd not the Being of a God, but made to themselves many Gods.

That there was a mediator necessary, was a tradition from the very first ages; and this tradition arose (likely) from the promise of God (Gen. iii. 15.), and was confirmed by man's general consciousness of his own infirmities and sin, and his want therefore of some person to interpose, and reconcile so frail a creature to a God of infinite purity [m].   This tradition, the first Idolaters did not deny, but chose mediators of their own fancy, the Sun, the Planets, and departed Ghosts: framing to themselves a multiplicity of tutelary, guardian Demi-gods.

Sacrifical rites were as old as the world; they abolished not sacrifices, but polluted them by debaucheries, and murder, and transferr'd them from their proper object, God the Creator, to the creature.

They acknowledged a Providence, and themselves in perpetual want of it, as to health, the necessaries and conveniences of life; they had therefore Gods for every purpose, of every shape, as well Colossuses [n] as of a portable size [o]; and in all places, that they might be at hand to help them upon any emergency.

That the soul was immortal, and that there was a future life, was a truth too evidently taught from the first beginning to be denied; but to make it subservient to the ends of false religion, they presently imagined, and made it part of their Divinity, that the ghosts of good, great, or ingenious men (whether good or wicked) being suppos'd in a state of happiness after death, were capable of assisting, protecting, and enriching men in this life, whence the worship of the Manes, Heroes, and Demi-gods.

They deny'd not the necessity of worship and supplication, but introduc'd all manner of impurity, violence, and imposture, and prostituted the sacred office of prayer, due only to God, upon Planets, Devils, Brutes, and senseless Images.   This was the first state of Idolatry, by which it appears how much easier it was to pervert truth, to obscure and mix it with the most egregious errour, than to abolish it.

SECT. IV. Their Gods, and the order in which they were deify'd.

The first capital errour in religion was departing from the unity of the Godhead, that is, worshiping more than one Deity; and the first thing that obtain'd to be put on an equal footing with it's Creator

[m] "The necessity of a Mediator between God "and Man, was a general notion which obtain'd "among all mankind from the beginning." Prid. "Connex. Part I. Lib. III. p. 177. 1st edit. 8vo.

[n] See Nebuchadnezzar's image in the plains of Dura.   Dan. iii. 1.
[o] Laban's Teraphim.   Gen. xxxi. 30.

was

was the Sun P, a body by its superiour splendour and heat, by its Celestial bodies. apparent, and orderly motion (circumstances of great glory to its Maker, but of none to its self) most apt to mislead weak minds from surprize and admiration into reverence and worship. To the Sun, the Moon, and other Planets were soon added, and all suppos'd to be actuated by souls, or intelligent spirits of a middle nature betwixt God and Man q; they were, therefore, concluded more proper to receive the addresses of weak and sinful man, whose petitions were too imperfect to reach the throne of the supreme God, without such a mediatorial introduction. To the making of these celestial bodies Deities, no doubt their beneficial influences upon fruits, plants, and animals, must be suppos'd to have contributed; it being the most obvious and easy errour, to worship what they saw, and felt the benefit of, as Cesar observes of the Gauls. " Deorum numero eos solos ducunt, quos cernunt, " & quorum opibus aperte juvantur, Solem & Vulcanum & Lu-" nam." Com. Lib. VI.

Some think that Image-worship succeeded next r, for that finding these new Deities as much absent from them as present (the Sun and Planets passing as much time below the horizon, as above) they invented Images to be always present with them, that so, upon any emergency, they might have a Deity at hand, to consult and implore: to these Images they gave names and qualities, which they still bear; whence it happens, that Jupiter, Mars, Mercury, &c. are Gods to be found among all nations. The Images of the Sun are reckoned most ancient, by those who think Image-worship prior to the worship of the Manes; and the Israelites being much addicted to worship them, they are generally forbid at the same time, and in the same place with the groves, as if they were a part of the Grove-worship. Isai. xvii. 8. and xxvii. 9 s.

But, as the images of the Sun and Planets *, as well as of the The persons and manes of heroes. other sorts, though distinguish'd by the proper Symbols, were generally at first of the human form, others think that worshiping out of flattery or affection the persons of absent as well as present Kings or victorious Generals, and the Ghosts of them after they were

---

P　　'Ου τον παντων Θεων.

Θεον προμον 'Αλιον. Soph. Oed. Tyran. Act l. Sc. 3.

The Chorus here swears by the Sun, as that God who stood forth in front of the Heathen Gods. Dacier says, " Le plus grand des dieux," but it is more agreeable to the original to call him the first, or foremost of the Gods.

" A very learned and ingenious man (Gisb. " Cuperi Harpocrates) has lately attempted to

" shew, that all the Gods of Antiquity center " in the Sun." Lett. of Mythol. p. 89.

q Prid. Connex. Lib. III. Part I. p. 177. 1st edit.

r Ibid. p. 187.

s They are call'd חמנים " Subdiales statuæ, " quasi solares vel soli expositæ." Buxt. Lex. Simulachra solaria: i. e. in honorem solis facta. Jun. Trem.

* Wisdom, xiv. 15, 16.

Q　　　　　　　　　　　　　　　dead,

dead, preceded, and gave rife [t] to Image-worſhip, and it ſhould ſeem reaſonable to ſuppoſe, that they muſt firſt have worſhiped Perſons, before they pay'd adoration to their Statues.   As ſoon as the Hero was dead, the ſame people, which had a veneration for him when alive, were ſoon perſuaded by their ardent leaders, to pay him divine honours after his death, eſpecially whilſt the remembrance of his perſon, and the glory of his actions were recent in every one's mind ; and (leaſt the peoples reſpect and affection, which were the grounds of their worſhip, might cool and languiſh in time) Images were invented to keep freſh and lively the idea of what was dead; they were intended to perpetuate the beauty, ſtrength, ſize, and ſpirit of the departed ; now it is not likely, I would ſay, that the prieſts or great men ſhould make uſe of this device of Image-worſhip, till they found it neceſſary, to continue, and ſtrengthen their ſuperſtition.   Thus from the Manes or Ghoſts, their wandering worſhip was ſoon laviſh'd upon Images ; and having Images to repreſent their human Gods, the faſhion ſoon ſucceeded of making Images alſo to repreſent their planetary Gods. Now all theſe Images were made in human ſhape, becauſe the imagination of man was not able to conceive a more excellent form, nor to give more exalted ideas of their abſent Deities, than by repreſenting them in the likeneſs of man.

Images firſt worſhiped as Memorials, afterwards as Deities of Intelligence and Power.

This I conjecture to be the moſt natural and likely method for Idolaters to have proceeded in the firſt ages [u], but I muſt here obſerve, that ſoon after the Images of their Gods were introduc'd, they were conſecrated with great pomp, various ceremonies, feſtivals, and ſolemn ſupplications, and every one of the numerous aſſembly was to pay his adorations before the new Deity.   Theſe adorations might, in the beginning, be directed primarily to the Perſon or Planet whoſe image was ſet up, and only a ſecondary worſhip paid to the Image itſelf; but the repreſentative ſoon became equal to the principal, and the copy took place of the original; for in a little while it became the general opinion, that by means of incantation, and magical charms, the power and influence of the Sun, Moon, or Demi-god, was brought to reſide in thoſe Images, after they had been ritually deify'd.

Image-worſhip ſoon ſpread itſelf over all the Eaſt, thence into Egypt, and from Egypt into Greece, and became the univerſal religion of the Gentile world, till the Magi of Perſia form'd a conſiderable oppoſition to it, teaching, that no Image ought to be

---

[t] The original of Idolatry came from the conſecration of ſome eminent perſons after death, according to Sanchoniathon. See Stillingfleet, Orig. Sacr. 4to edit, p. 32.

[u] Firſt they worſhiped Planets, then the Manes of Heroes, then Images both of Heroes and Planets.

ador'd

ador'd, but that both the good and bad Principle (or God, for they held both to be Gods, calling the firſt Oromazes, the ſecond Arimanius), were to be worſhiped only by fire. Thenceforward the worſhipers of Images were diſtinguiſh'd by the name of Sabians, and the worſhipers by fire ſtil'd Magians, and in India and ſome parts of Perſia ſome remains of each Sect ſtill continue.

Magick [w], Witchcraft, or the ſcience of correſponding with Evil-ſpirits, ſome think is as ancient as the antediluvian world; and indeed, amidſt the numerous corruptions of thoſe early ages it is not improbable, that the rapacious, gloomy, anxious, and vindictive, ſhould embrace this horrid commerce with Demons, an intercourſe which (whether imaginary or real) deluded them with the proſpect of ſuperiour knowledge, of poſſeſſing what they luſted after, of curſing their enemies, and executing all their envy, malice, and revenge, by incantations not to be reſiſted by human talents; this was a total deſertion from the ſervice of God, and liſting into that of the Devil, and proves that when mankind had thrown aſide the unity of the Godhead, they could not only condeſcend to worſhip the meaneſt productions of nature, but the moſt deteſtable and bandon'd of all beings. *(margin: Demons.)*

It muſt next be obſerv'd, that the Gentiles, from the remoteſt antiquity, worſhip'd Fire or Light; at firſt, perhaps, only in the Sun, as the fountain of light and heat; afterwards they never worſhip'd without fire on the altar, as the medium to tranſpire their addreſſes unto the deity; ſoon after (for errour is infinite, and one miſtake in ſuch ſolemn caſes begets another) the Fire itſelf was worſhip'd. *(margin: Fire.)*

Hyde, indeed [x], denies that the Perſians worſhip'd fire, calling it not the Cultus Divinus, but the Cultus Civilis: but this nice diſtinction can ſignify no more with regard to the generality, than that in their religion there were different degrees of reſpect and adoration, more and ſtricter rites and ceremonies attending the worſhip of ſome Deities, than what were allowed to that of others. For as they allowed their holy fires to be the Schechinah or habitation of God, it was very difficult, if not impoſſible, to keep the mind of the vulgar, and leſs contemplative, from paying a kind of adoration to them; and therefore the Perſians were indeed worſhipers of Fire [y].

[w] Magick had ſeveral parts, as Aſtrology Witchcraft, Palmiſtry, Hydromancy, Augury, &c. The chief part of the Druid Magick conſiſted in foretelling, from the entrails of human victims.

[x] De Vet. Perſ. Rel.

[y] Prid. Connex. and Montfauc. Tom. II. p. 394.

Nimrod,

Nimrod, grandſon of Ham, is ſaid by St. Auguſtine to have been the firſt who compell'd his ſubjects to worſhip Fire in Chaldea.

Air, &c. The other elements, Air, Earth, and Water were alſo deify'd, it becoming a cuſtom very ſoon, to make Gods of every thing which appeared either capable of doing harm, or neceſſary and beneficial **Plants.** to human life : the ſame reaſon made them proceed to deify plants and herbs [z], led thereto by their experienced medicinal virtue, by the beauty of flowers, or (in hot countries) by the friendly ſhade of trees.

Erected Stones. They deſcended ſtill lower, and making rude and ſhapeleſs ſtones the repreſentations of their fancied Deities, ſoon learn'd to forget and think no more of the abſent repreſented Deity, and paid their adoration to the Symbol, the huge lifeleſs lump of Stone ; this kind of Idolatry was very ancient among the Egyptians and Phenicians [a]. It would be uſeleſs in this ſurvey of Gentiliſm, to purſue the Egyptians through all the variety of creatures, Beaſts, Birds, and Reptiles which they worſhip'd ; and it is now time to ſee in what manner they worſhip'd this confus'd multitude of Gods.

SECT. V. Having chang'd the object of their devotion, and adopted the **Worſhip.** Creature for their Deity, inſtead of the Creator, they preſerv'd however, ſome general Reſemblance to the true manner of Worſhip. They worſhip'd by Sacrifices, by Meat and Drink Offerings, by Proſtration, by Supplication, by Feſtivals, and in publick aſſemblies.

The great buſineſs of the Devil was not to obliterate what went before, but to turn, change, and pervert in the moſt ſecret, eaſy, and imperceptible manner, every rite, doctrine, and inſtitution, ſo as it might beſt promote Immorality, Deluſion, and Impiety. And indeed, this was no hard matter to do, when once mankind had departed from that one great truth, the unity of the Godhead. This principle would have kept them ſteady, excluded every fanciful impoſture, and permitted nothing in worſhip which was not agreeable to that God, who had ſo ſufficiently revealed his will from the beginning of the world, that no one could be at a loſs to know what was acceptable to him, and what was diſpleaſing ; but having accumulated to themſelves an infinite number of Gods, 'tis hardly credible to what an exceſs of errour and pollution in worſhip, they were ſoon expos'd. Every new Deity had his peculiar attributes, his prevailing paſſions aſſigned, and was to be worſhip'd after ſome new and diſtinct method, ſo that it ſoon became a myſtery and ſcience (and no doubt was continued as ſuch by the lucrative in all places)

---

[a] Some ſay before the flood. Sanchon. Euſeb. præp. Evan.   [z] See Erected Stones. Lib. III.

to underſtand by what rites each particular God was to be approached [b]. Every new rite multiply'd error, for every method of worſhip muſt be wrong, that is, either abſurd or wicked, which has an improper object; for there is no worſhiping a falſe God with true Religion; no ſerving Idols with pure devotion. Inſtead, therefore, of the true fear of God, a gloomy kind of awe, and religious dread, conſiſting of Grove and Night-worſhip, was introduced.

Inſtead of the Sabbath, which was intended to recall people from their wordly buſineſs to a ſerious recollection of, and thankſgiving for the Creation, Feſtivals to their Demi-gods were inſtituted.

Inſtead of the few Altars which were erected by the ſervants of the living God in a few places (ſuch as were ſanctify'd by the appearance of God, or his Angels), the Heathens erected Altars on every high hill, and under every green tree; and this multiplicity of Altars tended evidently and neceſſarily to vary the ſervice performed at them, each officiating prieſt ſtriving to make his Altar finer, and by the novelty of ſome rite and ceremony, to render it more engaging, and better frequented, than that of his neighbours.

Inſtead of the true purity of heart, a falſe ſuperficial purity was ſubſtituted, conſiſting of ablution, white garments, outward ſprinklings, and luſtrations.

Inſtead of ſacrifices (moſt acceptable to God by the holineſs of mind, and innocency of the hands that offer them) the ſacrifices of the heathens were ordain'd to conſiſt, not of ſheep, or oxen, as at firſt, but of thoſe things which were moſt precious to the heart of man, as human victims, and even their own children [c].

The worſhip of the Sun, performed when he was in the meridian height of his power, ſoon taught men in thoſe hot countries of the Eaſt to raiſe their Altars, and perform their devotions in Groves; and, after Sacrifice, Luxury and Debauch enſued.

The worſhip of the Moon was performed in the night; this introduced every kind of pollution, which the day in ſome meaſure would have ſhamed.

---

[b] The Egyptian prieſts were particularly ſecret, and almoſt impenetrably reſerv'd with regard to their rites.

[c] Sacrifices were to conſiſt, at firſt, and likely by God's appointment, of beaſts without ſpot or blemiſh, and offerings of the beſt of fruits; hence came the cuſtom among the Gentiles (whoſe rites were but the diſtorted copies of the great originals us'd by the people of God) to think that nothing was too precious for a ſacred offering, and that to ſacrifice what was deareſt to man would be moſt acceptable unto God: hence offering up the moſt beautiful captives, the firſt-begotten ſon, the moſt noble youths, and the deareſt friends.

R
When

When Demons began to be worſhiped, Divination, Oracles, Incantations, and all the groundleſs fancies of Augury [d], naturally followed.

When Fire became a Deity, the children of the Idolater were offered and burnt, that the Deity might have them, and be propitiated.

But nothing contributed more to produce and eſtabliſh thoſe abominations than the deifying men, and, to complete the aſſembly, women. For their Heroes (though fortunate leaders, or inventers of uſeful arts) being ſome of the race of the firſt Idolaters, muſt have been exceedingly corrupted in Morals and Religion, and were no ſooner made Gods after their deceaſe, than their vices were adopted, imitated, conſecrated: hence it naturally became the faſhion to juſtify, to practiſe, to form a rite of worſhip of thoſe very Immoralities which their new-made God was remember'd to have addicted himſelf unto. If he was cruel and bloody, he was to be ſacrificed unto by human victims; if he was luſtful or drunken, proſtitution was to attend his feſtival, and his propitiation was to be a ſcene of intemperance and debauch; if he had been avaritious, the innocent and weak were to be plundered to make a rich offering to his altar. In ſhort, if we conſider the great indulgencies which ſuch a religion as this of Gentiliſm granted to every paſſion; that there was no vice, but what could plead in its mitigation, that it had been the favourite of ſome of their Deities, it is no wonder that Idolatry began ſo ſoon, that it ſpread ſo univerſally, and ſo totally corrupted both the practice and the worſhip of its followers.

SECT. VI.

Why the ſame, or like Idolatry in all Nations.

It would be more ſurpriſing, that in ſuch a variety of Deities and Idols there ſhould be preſerv'd ſo near a reſemblance in the method of adoration [e], betwixt the moſt diſtant nations. This, I ſay, would indeed be very ſurpriſing, if we did not at the ſame time recollect, that all Idolatry began as early as the family of Ham; proceeded upon the ſame general motives of licentiouſneſs; that the Sun and Planets, open to every eye, were the firſt Gods, and eaſily continued the firſt deluſion, as attracting in every region the notice and adminiſtration of the ignorant and wicked; that one and the ſame principle, Polytheiſm, will produce a multitude of corruptions in all places; that Grove-worſhip, being the conſequence of worſhiping the Sun, produc'd every where debauch; worſhiping the Moon, proſtitution; worſhiping Demons, magick

[d] Augury was founded at firſt (as ſome ſuppoſe) on the tradition, of Noah's ſending forth, firſt the crow, and then the doves from the ark, with a very innocent intention to prove the decreaſe of the waters.

[e] Sacrifices, Fruit, and Meat-offerings, Grove-worſhip, unclean Myſteries.

and

and divination; deifying wicked men, immoral rites; that facrifices (having been the univerfal cuftom of every falfe and mimick religion, as well as the true) degenerated eafily into the barbarity of facrificing human victims, as being fuperiour in their nature to thofe of the brute kind; that, afterwards, their drink-offerings were the blood of their victims, and that every kind of cruelty muft become familiar to thofe, who could make Religion confift in murder, and look'd upon the moft unnatural butchering their own children, as the higheft proof of devotion to their Gods.

We may obferve in the next place, that all this fyftem of abfurdity, impurity, and inhumanity, was not only propagated every where upon the fame principles, but all conducted by one hand; I mean the authour of errour, the father of lyes, as he is called; when we confider all this, we fhall no more wonder to find the fame fuperftitions and abominable worfhip in the farthermoft parts of India, and in the wefternmoft parts of Europe: the fame in Babylon, Egypt, and Phenicia; the fame in Greece, Germany, and Britain: what the Brachmans were in India, the Druids were in Gaul; what the Magi did in Perfia, the fame, or even more, fays Pliny, did the Britifh Druids: in fhort Grove-worfhip, with all its train of horrors, divination, the myfterious rites of ma gic, human facrifices and proftitutions, are to be found, more or lefs, in the religion of all countries, and for the fame reafons; the authour was the fame, and alike the principles: the root was corrupted, and from thence the infection was fpread into all the moft diftant branches of mankind.

It has been long difputed, whence the Druid difcipline and fuperftition had its rife; but if we compare it with the ancient Gentile Religion, every Tenet and Rite which the Druids taught and and practifed, every Deity which they are faid to have worfhiped, we fhall find to have been common to them, and the moft ancient Idolaters of the Eaft. The moft diftinguifhing parts of their (the Druids) fuperftition, are the Grove-worfhip, and their human Victims; the firft of thefe was fo common among the Canaanites in the time of Jofhua, and attended with fo much impiety and lewdnefs, that it made their utter extirpation infifted upon by the only true God, infinitely merciful and benevolent. One reafon why the Druids were fo fond of Groves (of Oak efpecially) was becaufe of the Mifletoe which grew on the Oak Trees, to which they paid a fort of worfhip, but even in this they are not alone: the Perfian and Maffagetes thought the Mifletoe fomething divine, as well as the Druids: the Grecians had their vocal Oaks at Dodona, that gave forth oracles; and the Arcadians thought

The Druids like other Idolaters.

In Grove-worfhip.

4

thought that ſtirring the waters of a fountain with an Oak-bough, would produce rain. Evander was ſacrificing in his Groves, without the city, when Æneas came to him [f]. The ancient Tyrrhenians had the ſame cuſtom; the firſt temple in Egypt, that of Jupiter Hammon (or Ham the firſt king) was in a ſacred Grove.

Human victims.

As for the cruel cuſtom of ſacrificing human victims, 'tis true that it cannot be enough condemned and deteſted, and that the Druids continued this horrid practice longer than any nation or ſect we know, and perhaps practiſed it more frequently; but 'tis as true, that we hardly read of any conſiderable nation, but what has had the ſame cuſtom (at leaſt upon extraordinary occaſions) recorded of it [g]. The Egyptians had this abominable cuſtom [h], as alſo the Phenicians [i], whoſe King, Chronus [k] (or Saturn), ſacrificed his own ſon during a publick calamity [l]: and when Saturn became a God, is it any wonder that he ſhould be ſuppos'd to delight in ſuch ſacrifices? From the Phenicians the Iſraelites [m] learn'd to devote, and offer by fire, their own children to Moloch [n], another name for Saturn. From them the Carthaginians tranſplanted alſo with their colony the ſame bloody rites, and in the firſt ages of their commonwealth, uſed to ſacrifice to their God Saturn the ſons of their moſt eminent citizens; in after-times they ſecretly bought and bred up children for that purpoſe. In the year before Chriſt 308, thinking to reform more effectually what was amiſs by a publick ſacrifice, the Carthaginians offered two hundred ſons of the nobility, and no fewer than three hundred more offered up themſelves voluntarily. Diod. Sicul. Lib. XX. Cap. I.

The ſame author gives us a particular account of the manner in which this barbarous offering was made; the children were put into the hands of a brazen ſtatue of Saturn, and the hands being ſo contriv'd as to bend downwards to the earth, the unhappy victims dropt eaſily through, and fell into a furnace prepared for them below [o].

---

[f]. Æn. VIII. ver. 102. Ibid 597, & Æn. XI. ver. 739.

[g] Vide Smith's Syntagma de Druid. p. 77, &c.

[h] " Ægyptii vivos homines Typhoni ſuo " comburere ſolebant." Bulæus in Frik. 162.

[i] See Lev. xviii. 21. Deuter. xviii. 10, 11. 2 Kings. xxiii. 10.

[k] Chandler (and others) think him Ham. Anſwer to Moral Philoſ. p. 184.

[l] It was cuſtomary (ſays Phil. Bibl. from Sanchoniath.) among the Phenicians in great perils of the ſtate, to ſacrifice ſome one of their deareſt friends and relations to Saturn. See Pool, ad Deuter. xviii. 10.

[m] See the Scripture Hiſt. paſſim. 2 Kings xvii. 31. Pſ. 106. 37. Jer. vii. 31.

[n] " Non dubitandum quin ſit Saturnus." Pol. Ibid.

[o] Ibid. Lib. XX. Cap. I.

" Mos fuit in populis quos condidit advena Dido,
" Poſcere cæde Deos veniam, ac flagrantibus aris,
" Infandum dictu, parvos imponere natos !"

Sil. Ital. Lib. IV.

The

The Perfians had the fame horrid cuftom P; the Scythotauri offer'd ftrangers to Diana, the Laodiceans a virgin to Pallas q; the Thracians, and thofe who liv'd on the river Boryfthenes had the fame facrifices r. The Grecians alfo admitted the fame dreadful rites.

Iphigenia was to have been facrific'd to Diana by her father Agamemnon, to obtain a favourable wind s; the Arcadians facrific'd a boy to Jupiter Lycæus t; the Indians and the Cretans killed men overcharg'd with banqueting, and young boys, to Saturn on his feftivals: in Chios and Salamis they cut the throats of men; and then tore them to pieces as an offering to their Gods.

A temple dedicated to the fame Divinity there was in Arcadia, in which girls were whip'd to death, as boys were in Sparta, at the altars of Mercury and Orthia Diana; and Ariftomenes of Meffene is reported to have flain three hundred men at one facrifice to Jupiter Ithometes; the Lacedemonians alfo were mad enough to facrifice human victims to Mars. In the anniverfary feaft of Bacchus, the Greeks facrific'd living men. The Cimbrians did the fame; and if we may believe Spanifh writers, the American Indians of Peru were taught the fame leffons of inhumanity, and feldom facrific'd lefs than two hundred children upon the acceffion of a new Inga or Emperour. To mention no more, the Romans were as guilty in this particular as other nations. Tit. Liv. relates, that human victims were offered up after the defeat of Cannæ. And Dionyf. of Halicarnaffus (in his firft book of Roman Antiq.) informs us, that Jupiter and Apollo fent dreadful calamities into all the coafts of Italy for this reafon, namely, becaufe the tenth part of the natives was not offered up in facrifice. And this cuftom continued at Rome many ages, for the Romans were not forbid human facrifices 'till the Confulfhip of Cn. Corn. Lepidus, and Pub. Lic. Craffus in the 657th year of their city, 97 years before Our Saviour, whence Pliny (Lib. XXX. Cap. I.) infers that the Romans ufed human facrifices 'till that time u.

P Al. ab Al. vol. II. pag. 750.
q Pompon. Mel. lib. II. cap. i.
r Pliny, lib. VIII. ch. xxii.
s 'Ωδ' ην τα κεινης θυμαια, fays Sophocles, Electra Act II. pag. 77.
" On n'offroit pas alors d'autres victimes a " cette Deeffe." Dac. tranflat. None but virgins were at that time acceptable victims to Diana.
t See Pliny, lib. VIII. pag. 22.
u Some think the Gentiles borrow'd this dreadful rite from the hiftory of Abraham and Ifaac; but if this had not been a rite ufual among the Heathens before, Abraham would not have been commanded to it, nor probably obey'd, without fome more particular and cogent reafons given by God for fuch a fhocking facrifice; but there is not the leaft argument recorded in fcripture to enforce, what an injunction entirely new and fo unnatural might well require, to make it prevail over fo righteous a man. The cuftom therefore feems more ancient, and God feems to have commanded this action not only for the tryal and juftification of the patriarch, but that he might thereby have an opportunity of convincing him how much he abhorr'd fuch facrifices of the heathen, by interpofing in a miraculous manner, to prevent the innocent fon from dying an immature and violent death, and the obedient father from imbruing his hands in the blood of his only fon.

S   As

Magick,&c. As the Druids were by no means fingular in their facrifices, fo neither in their magick, their purifications, difcipline, and places of worfhip; of all which traces are to be difcovered in the ancient hiftory of the moft confiderable nations; and, therefore, whilft we have been following the fteps of Gentilifm, and Idolatry in general, and attending it from its firft beginning 'till it had fpread its poifon into all countries, I can't but think that we have been at the fame time laying before the reader the original, and nature of the Druid fuperftition. The feeds of Idolatry are the fame in kind, and nature; and though they thrive more luxuriantly in fome foils than in others, and contract fome mixtures and peculiarities from the Climate they grow in, enough to diftinguifh the Idolaters into different fects, yet the plants are of the fame tribe; and indeed, Druidifm has all the ftrongeft features to fhew in evidence of its birth, that it is but a branch of the firft general and moft ancient Idolatry: 'tis but a fect (though eminently diftinguifh'd by the learning and ftrictnefs of the priefts) that differs in fome ceremonials and ordinary particulars from the fects of other nations, who either fettled in the Eaft, where mankind firft inhabited, or pafs'd from thefe firft fettlements into the moft diftant countries, carrying the fame religious effentials throughout the whole Gentile world.

For all this the reafons have been given before, namely, becaufe thefe effentials were found to fuit beft with the licentious temper of mankind, and were fecretly promoted in every nation by one and the fame power of darknefs, Satan well knowing that his iniquitous fyftem would moft eafily conduce, in this life to the utter corruption, and in the next to the certain perdition, of its unhappy followers.

Of Druidifm we now come to treat more particularly, and circumftantially.

C H A P. II.

Of the Name and Claffes of the Druid Priefthood.

THE name Druid is by many fuppos'd to be deriv'd from the Greek word Δρυς, an oak; an opinion which has been adopted by fome learned men [x]: becaufe the veneration of this fect for Oak, the tree, leaves, and excrefcencies of the Mifletoe exceeds every thing of that kind which we read of other nations. But Strabo is of opinion, that in the names of foreign nations (all which the Greeks call'd barbarous) we are not to feek for Greek

---

[x] Pliny, lib. xvi. Sheringham, &c.

etymolo-

etymologies [y]: and, indeed, this derivation, though so obvious, is thought much too modern [z], the Druids having been famous from the most remote antiquity; long before Greece could boast of her wise men, or philosophers, who were really beholden to the Druids, and copied them in many particulars [a]: and therefore it is not likely that they should borrow their name from a nation which they so much surpass'd in antiquity.

As the Druids were Priests of Gaul and Britain, it is more probable that their name was taken from the Celtick language, upon which the language of the Gauls and Britans (originally the same) was grounded : in this language Derw signifies an Oak [b]; and Deru as the Armoricans write it [c], Derven and Derwen as the Cornish and Welsh, has the same signification still, and therefore some have suppos'd them to have call'd their priests Derwidden, in Latin Querquetulani [d]. Some derive Druid from the British Tru, and Wis, (viz. wise men [e]) to which subscribes Baxter, saying that the Druids were call'd in British Deruidhon, i. e. persapientes [f]. The Turkish devotees call'd Dervises are suppos'd to derive their name from the same fountain. " Sacerdotum genus apud Turcas ab antiquissimis tempo- " ribus conservatum Dervis, & nomine, & re Druides." Keysler, p. 152. In Scotland they were call'd Durcerglii [g]. In Spain, Turduli, or Turditani [h]: where we must observe, that what is Der or Dre with the Celts, is with the German Celto-Scythes, Deur, vel Door, so that with them the Druids were call'd Deurwitten [i]: the first syllable of all which partakes of the root from whence the other names of this priesthood are so evidently deriv'd [k].

There are other opinions about this name. The primitive word Drud (in the plural Drudion) is thought to have several significations. First, it signifies a Revenger; 2dly, Cruel; 3dly, Valiant, or Hardy; 4thly, Dear, or precious [l]. Some * derive it from the Celtic word Trewe, that is, Faith; or from Drut, a Friend; others from the Hebrew Derussim, Drussim, or Drissim, that is, people of contemplation [m]; and the learned Keysler (pag. 37.), says that Draoi, (Deuteron. xviii. 11. Bibl. Hibern.) in the plural number Draioithe, signifies a Magician or Inchanter, from which, Cesar and others, made the word Druides.

[y] " Placet Strabonis consilium, qui negat in " appellationibus gentium barbararum quærendas " esse etymologias Græcas." Hoffman in Druid. pag. 111. Frickius, pag. 27.

[z] Elias Sched. De diis Germanis, pag. 258.

[a] " Antiquissimi enim hi (viz. Druidæ) apud " Celtas, doctores, & ipsis Græciæ sapientibus " excellentiores, qui postea longo temporis decur- " su secuti sunt Druidarum sectam." Sched. ibid.

[b] Frickius, pag. 24.

[c] Sammes, pag. 104.

[d] Sheringham, pag. 105.

[e] J. Gorop. Becanus not. on Cæf. Comm. edit. Delph. lib. 6.

[f] Glossar. pag. 107.

[g] Hect. Boeth. lib. ii. Eli. Sched. 256.

[h] Sched. lib. ii. chap. ii.

[i] Baxter, ibid. 107.

[k] Druwydd, Drudau, Drudion, Drudon, and Derwyddon were equally names of the Druids. Rowland, pag. 247.

[l] Jones to Tate in Toland of the Druids, pag. 187, 188. * Bucherus in Frick.

[m] Hoffman, ibid. ac supra.

However,

However, it is moſt likely that the Druides were call'd ſo from their ſuperſtitious regard for the Oak-tree, and that they had not their name from the Greek word Δρυς, but from the Celtic Deru, in the firſt ſyllable of which the E muſt be pronounced very ſhort, if at all, like the Hebrew Shevah.

Druid, then, (whenceſoever deriv'd) was the general name of the Britiſh Prieſthood, and there were three degrees of Druids[n]. The ſuperiour claſs was call'd *The* Druids, by way of eminence[o]. They had under, and next to them, the Bards; who, though inferiour in rank, are ſaid to be prior in antiquity[p]. They were remarkable for an extraordinary talent of memory[q]; and therefore, in all probability, particularly employ'd to teach their young diſciples, who were chiefly to learn to Remember, as the principal qualification in ſocieties where no written rules were allowed. Theſe were alſo the poets of the Britans and Gauls[r].

The Eubates, or Vates, were of the third and loweſt claſs, their name, as ſome[s] think, deriv'd from Thada which amongſt the Iriſh commonly ſignifies Magick, and their Buſineſs was to foretell future events; and to be ready on all common occaſions to ſatisfy the enquiries of the anxious and credulous[t].

Theſe are the ancient diviſions of the Druid Prieſthood, and theſe, all the names which we meet with in ancient hiſtory; but when any family had been long prieſts to a particular Deity, as Apollo, Mercury, and the like, that family look'd upon itſelf as peculiarly conſecrated to the ſervice of that God, and the Druids took names to themſelves, and children, deriv'd from the name of the God they ſerv'd[u]. But that this was a modern cuſtom, introduc'd after that the Druids, mixing much with the Greeks and Romans, had departed from their ancient ſimplicity, is certain, and we are not now enquiring after the modern, but the ancient Druids.

---

[n] Τρια φυλα των τιμωμενων. Strabo, lib. iv. on which Leland (De Script. Britann. p. 6.) makes this remark, " Strabo videtur tria illuſtrium in " literis virorum genera recenſere." Frickius, p. 33. & Martin de la Relig. des Gaules, tom. I. pag. 173, &c.

[o] Ingeniis celſiores.

[p] Sammes.

[q] Rowland, p. 61.

[r] " Cum dulcis lyræ modulis cantitarunt, lau- " dationibus rebuſque poeticis ſtudent." Ammian. Marcell. The Welſh ſubdivided this claſs into three parts: " Firſt, the Privardd, Prince of learned " men, or firſt inventor: 2dly, the Poſvardd,

" imitator or teacher of what was invented by " the Privardd: 3dly, the Arwyddvardd, that " is, an Enſign Bard, or Herald at Arms." Jones in Toland, ibid. 192. But this, I believe, is a diviſion unknown to the ancient Druids.

[s] Keyſler, Antiq. Septentrion. p. 36.

[t] Some reckon the Eubates the ſecond rank; " The Bards were Singers, the Eubates Prieſts " and Phyſiologers, and the Druids to their Phy- " ſiology added Ethicks." Rowl. p. 65. But as their office was inferiour to that of the Bards, I have, with ſeveral others, plac'd them in an inferiour claſs.

[u] Rel. des Gaul. p. 388.

CHAP.

C H A P. III.

Of the Countries inhabited by the Druids, probably only Gaul and Britain.

THAT the Druids inhabited and in facred matters prefided over Britain, and the Britifh Ifles, as well as all Gaul, is not to be doubted. 'Tis alfo afferted by fome moderns, that there were Druids in Spain[w]; but this remains to be prov'd, and if there were really any, they pafs'd from Gaul to Spain, by means of the vicinity of fituation, and muft have been modern and inconfiderable, by their being taken fo little notice of in hiftory, and not near fo ancient, noble, powerful, and well difciplin'd, as in Gaul and Britain.

It is much debated, whether there were any Druids in Germany[x]; **No Druids in Germany.** Cefar is very exprefs that the Germans had no Druids, but in this he is thought to be miftaken[y], and to be flatly contradicted by Tacitus, who in his account of the Germans fhews a great deal of accuracy, and appears to have been rather better inform'd, as to his fubject, than Cefar[z]. Tacitus is certainly very faithful and particular, but he does not appear to contradict Cefar, nor Cefar to have faid any thing but what was truth: thefe two great authors may be reconcil'd, as it feems to me, with little trouble. Cefar's words are thefe, " Ger- " manos neque Druidas habere qui rebus divinis præfint, neque " facrificiis ftudere;" that is, the Germans have no Druids, no fuperiour, noble order of priefts, famous for difcipline and learning, invefted with an abfolute authority in all facred affairs: " neque " facrificiis ftudere," they did not mind their facrifices much; they were not curious and learned in explaining the circumftances that occurr'd during their facrifices; they were not folicitous about, nor well vers'd in, the art of predicting future events from the entrails of the victims, as the Druids, and other Gentile nations were: this is all Cefar fays; he does not deny that they had priefts, but he fays they had no Druids; he does not deny that they had facrifices, but he fays they were unfkilful and unlearned; they did not apply them-

---

w " Hifpani quippe a Celtis traxerunt originem " & unà religionem eorum hauferunt." El. Sched. lib. ii. ch. ii. " Celtiberi dicti a com- " miftione Celtarum & Iberorum." Ibid. ex Diod. Sic. lib. v.

x Leibnitius, Wachterus, Calvoerius, and other learned men among the Germans deny it. Chr. Aug. Fabrettus, Dithmarus, Eli. Schedius,

Frickius, p. 44. and Keyfler, p. 378. hold the affirmative, but are far from proving it.

y " Contra cæterorum fidem tradit." viz. Cæfar. Sched. 254.

z " Plura igitur ac certiora de religione Ger- " manorum Tacito nota quam Cæfari." Lipfius in not. ad Tacit. de M. G. cap. viii.

T   felves

felves to ſtudy their ſacrifices, nor endeavour to reap that information concerning futurity, which their ſacrifices might have afforded them ; and this is very true, the German nation continuing, even to the times of Tacitus, a plain, ſimple, uncultivated, and an un-learned nation, as appears all along in his account of them [a]; nor is what Ceſar ſays here, contradicted or refuted by what Tacitus ad-vances.   For Tacitus does not ſay that that the Germans had any Druids, any diſtinguiſh'd order of prieſts, form'd into ſocieties [b]; ſo ſtrict as to their rites, and their ordinary aſſemblies ; ſo exact in ob-ſerving every thing relating to the Oak ; ſo ſtudious, learned, and contemplative, concerning the works of nature ; ſo intent upon the education of children, all regularly ſubordinate to one Arch-Druid, and of ſuch authority in times of peace and war, that in Britain they were the firſt order of the ſtate.   Neither does Tacitus mention the other inferiour orders of Druids, viz. the Bards, and the Vates, that I can recollect: whereas Strabo, Diod. Siculus, Lucan, Ammian. Marcell. &c. all mention them as belonging to the ſect of the Druids. But the ſame Tacitus, deſcribing the Battle of Angleſea in Britain, ſtrait mentions the Druids, " Druidæ, inquit, circum," &c. and if the Germans had Druids he would not have omitted them.   Tacitus ſays indeed, that the Germans had prieſts, and ſo had all nations ; but this will no more prove that the Germans had Druids, than that the Egyptians, Greeks, or all the world had this order among them, becauſe they had alſo prieſts.   The maſter of a family might divine by lots among the Germans in all private domeſtick affairs [c], and the prieſts were only conſulted in publick exigencies, but no ſuch thing was permitted among the Druids ; and among the three ſeveral ways of divining mentioned by Tacitus, there is nothing mentioned of foretelling future events from any part of their ſacrifices ; which ſilence of Tacitus does really confirm what Ceſar obſerv'd, that they were not ſtudious nor intent upon explaining their ſacrifices.

Conradus Celtis (Deſcr. of Nuremberg) advances it as an indiſ-putable truth [d], that the Germans had no Druids, but from the time of Tiberius, when that ſect paſs'd over thither from Gaul, in order to celebrate their myſteries (forbidden by that Emperor), with the greater ſecurity.   To this opinion there is one objection, which is certainly of great weight ; it is this, that Germany's receiving ſo conſiderable a change in its civil and ſacred polity, as muſt have come in with Druidiſm, could never eſcape ſo correct and penetrat-ing an hiſtorian as Tacitus ; if ſuch an innovation had happen'd ſo

[a] Les hommes & les femmes (dit Taeite) ſont egalement ignorans, des ſecrets des lettres. Caſtlen. Coutumes. de Gaulois, p. 57. Ænée Sylve aſſure que du temps d'Adrian la civilité & les lettres vinrent en Germanie. Ibid.

[b] Sodalitiis aſtricti, conſortiiſque. Ammian. Marc. lib. xv.
[c] Tacit. de M. G.
[d] Rel. des Gaules, p. 212.

few

few years before him as the reign of Tiberius, Tacitus could not have pafs'd it over in filence; but he never mentions any Druid among the Germans, from which we are to conclude, that there were either no fuch perfons there, or too few to deferve the notice of his hiftory.

But the truth of it is, although the Germans had no Druids, although that order of priefts was not eftablifh'd among them, and confequently their religion wanted many fuperftitious ceremonies, and much of that erudition in idolatry, which the authority, learning, and invention of that priefthood had introduc'd in Britain and Gaul, yet the religion of the Germans was, in the fundamentals, one and the fame with that of the Gauls and Britans. Their principal Deity was Mercury, they facrific'd human victims [e], they had open temples [f], and no Idols of human fhape: they confecrated Groves [g], worfhip'd Oaks [h], were fond of the aufpicial rites [i], computed by nights, not by days [k].

The Religion of the Germans as to fundamentals the fame as that of the Gauls and Britans.

No one that obferves this great conformity in fuch effential points can doubt but that the religion of the Germans was at the bottom the fame [l] as that of Britain and Gaul, although all the tenets and cuftoms which were introduc'd by the Druids, and diftinguifh'd them from any other priefthood, had not taken footing in the ancient Germany. If we find therefore the fame kind of Monuments in Denmark, Sweden, Norway, and in Germany properly fo call'd [m], as we find in Britain, and Gaul, we may attribute them all to a religion effentially the fame, although it cannot be prov'd that the Druids were eftablifh'd, nor the priefthood equally dignified, and learned in all. The fame religion (that of the ancient Celts) is to be trac'd as far as the Northern parts of Lithuania [n], and the Ruffians retaining for many ages after Chriftianity the like idolatrous veneration for their groves, refus'd to admit the Chriftians into them, though focial enough in other particulars, thinking that their facred places, and their divinities would be violated by the prefence of thofe who were of fo different a religion [o]. In a word, there was no nation in the Northern and Weftern parts of Europe which had not (as the

---

[e] " Deorum maxime Mercurium colunt." Tacit. ibid. cap. ix. (in the fame words Cefar of the Britans and Gauls, lib.vi.) " cui certis die- " bus humanis quoque hoftiis litare fas habent."
[f] " Nec cohibere parietibus Deos, neque in " ullam humani oris fpeciem affimilare ex mag- " nitudine Cœleftium arbitrentur". Ibid.
[g] Lucos & nemora confecrant. Tacit. ibid.
[h] — — — — " Lucofque vetuftâ " Relligione truces & Robora numinis inftar " Barbarici"—— Claudian de Sylva Hercynia. Lipf. not. on Tacitus, ibid.
[i] " Aufpicia fortefque ut qui maxime obfer- " vant." Tacit. ibid.

* The Sclavonians (a people of Germany) worfhip'd Oaks, inclos'd them with a court, and fenc'd them in, to keep off all unhallow'd accefs. Not. on Tacit. Variorum, ch. ix.
[k] See Tacit. ibid.
[l] " Le mème fond de religion qui etoit en ufage dans les Gaules, l'etoit auffi dans toute la Germanie mème chez prefque tous les peuples feptentrionaux." Rel. de Gaul. vol. II. p. 94.
[m] Anciently much larger. See Cluver, and Wells, Compar. Geog, &c.
[n] Cromer, lib. xv. in Sched. p. 346.
[o] Helmoldus de Ruffis, in not. var. ad Tacit. de M. G. ch. ix.

ground-

ground-work of their religion) the fame kind of idolatry as the Druids profefs'd in Gaul, and Britain P; although the order, fect, and difcipline of the Regular Druids never extended itfelf beyond the bounds of Gaul and Britain, as the German authors contend.

Cefar, Strabo, Pliny, and Pomponius Mela mention them only in Gaul and Britain; and the Germans have no reafon to think that they are injur'd by Cefar, and depriv'd of their ancient and famous order of Priefts unjuftly, 'till they can produce pofitive proof in favour of themfelves from the ancients, which, as far as I can learn, will be no eafy matter.

It may be of fervice therefore here to make one general obfervation, viz.   That whatever religious ceremonies and tenets we find recorded to have been among the Germans and northern nations, they are parts of the old Celtick religion, common to all the Weft of Europe, and confequently to the Druids, and therefore the fuperftition of Germany and the Northern countries may give great light into that of the Druids, and may juftly be referr'd to, as they frequently are, in this work.   But this argument will not bear being inverted; the inverfe is not true, for what we find recorded of the Druids can by no means be afferted of the Germans, and Northern nations.

The Druids built much upon, and improv'd the Celtick plan, added fcience and contemplation, feparated themfelves into a diftinct and noble order, held annual councils about facred things, refin'd the plain homely rites of their forefathers, and carried the erudition of their myfteries to a height unknown to nations invariably retentive (as the Germans were) of their firft fimplicity; content to make war, and hunting, the principal aim of their lives; affording religion, arts, and fpeculation, but a fmall, if any portion of their time and thoughts.

In fhort, what is faid of the ancient Germans, &c. as to things divine, may be faid alfo, for the moft part, or reafonably inferr'd (as of Celtic original) to be true of the Druids; but all that is faid of the Druids can by no means be probably inferr'd of the Germans.   If the reader keeps this diftinction always in fight, it will prevent miftakes.

The little ifle of Anglefea is thought to be the chief refidence of the Britifh Druids q, and indeed Tacitus mentions them only here, becaufe here the battle which he was to defcribe was fought; but they were a Holy Order common to all the nation of the Britans,

---

P Their Cromleches, Cirques, and Erected ftones are to be feen in Norway, Sweden, Denmark.—See Wormius's Mon. Danica. Olaus Magnus, paffim: and in Rudbeckius's Tables XXXV. and XXXVI. are Squares, Circles, Triangles, and Ellipfes of Stones-Erect.

q Humph. Lluyd's letter to Abr. Ortelius, Tac. vol. I. p. 592. Rowl. Mona.

and diffused every where, as appears not only from History, but from Monuments extant in every corner of the island, and particularly in Cornwall.

CHAP. IV.

Of the Antiquity of the Druids.

IN all our general enquiries after the Druids, we must carefully distinguish between the Priesthood, and the Religion which that Priesthood professed. That the Religion was a branch of the first Eastern Idolatry, which obtained soon after the flood, is plain[r], and by its overspreading all the countries, which that ancient and populous Nation (the Celtæ) inhabited, appears to have been brought with them from the East, at their first migration[s], and when the Celtæ had parcelled themselves out into Germans[t] and Gauls, and were afterwards subdivided into Swedes, Danes, and Britans; the same Religion passed with these off-sets which the Celts planted, and this is the reason that the ancient Religion of these nations was really in essentials one and the same; but it will not thence follow that the Priesthood was also the same in all these countries, nor that Druidism is as ancient as their Idolatry. When we are therefore enquiring into the antiquity of Druidism, it is into the antiquity of that religious Sect, that order of Priests and Philosophers, and not into the antiquity of their Religion, which in the principal parts is certainly as old as the first Idolatry.

The want of this distinction has led the Germans into a mistake, arguing very inconclusively from the Religion's being the same with that of Gaul and Britain (as doubtless it was) that therefore the Germans had Druids, which (as has been before observed) does no more follow than that if all Europe were of the Christian Religion, therefore all Europe must have the Benedictine or Jesuit order in every nation, nor is it warranted by any ancient author that I have seen.

That there were Druids remarkable for their learning, and even antiquity, before the time of Pythagoras, who lived near 600 years before our Saviour, is extreamly probable[u]. A certain man called

---

[r] See cap. i. lib. ii.

[s] Schedius thinks the Druwyds derived from Tuifco, who was the leader of the Celts from the East, because the Religion came together with him, and that nation; confounding the Priesthood and Religion, as usual, p. 257.

[t] The Germans were called Κελλοι and Κελλικοι down to Plutarch's time.

[u] "Pherecydes Pythagoræ præceptor primus

"publicavit Druidarum argumenta pro animæ "immortalitate." Hoffman's Dict. in verb. p. 111. "Cæterum cuilibet vel modicè perspicaci pate- "bit Druidas philosophatos plus mille annis an- "tequam Eruditio Pythagoræ innotuisset in "Italia." Steph. Forcatulus de Gall. Imp. & Philof. p. 41. "Plus octingentis ante annis Phi- "losophati sunt quam Græcie lementa literarum "Cadmo fuerint assecuti." Jo. Picardi Celto-

U   Alexander

Alexander Polyhistor in Clemens Alexandrinus [w], says that Pythagoras heard both the Druids and the Brachmans [x]. Now, we can scarce imagine that so curious a traveler as Pythagoras could be induced to traverse almost all the then known globe, in order to converse with them, and examine the principles upon which they proceeded in the search of wisdom, by any thing less than because both the Brachmans and Druids made at that time a considerable figure in the discourses and writings of the learned. I would only observe upon this passage, that what is said here is very agreeable to the general character of that indefatigable Philosopher [y]. He first traveled into Egypt to converse with their Priests, thence into the East to hear the Brachmans, the Priests of India; and it is not at all improbable that his insatiable curiosity would not let him rest till he had seen also the other extremity of the world to converse with the Druids, gathering every where what he thought divine, good, and wise, and communicating the doctrines he treasured up, where he found the people docile and willing to be wiser.

" Abaris formerly traveled thence (viz. from an island opposite
" to Gaul, and most likely Britain) into Greece, and renewed the
" ancient league of friendship with the Delians [z]." Now this Abaris was a man famous in his time, of Northern extraction, Priest of Apollo, (therefore by some conjectured to have been a Druid [a]), and is reported to have been very intimate with Pythagoras, who made no scruple to communicate to him freely (what he concealed from others, in Fables and Enigma's) the real sentiments of his heart, and the deepest mysteries. But whether Abaris was a Druid or not, or what parts, if any, of the Druid system might be owing to his private communications with Pythagoras, there are some tenets of the Druids which will make it very probable, that Pythagoras did really converse with this Priesthood; and as he might have been indebted for some points of knowledge to them, so he communicated to them some of those doctrines which he had learned elsewhere. The Metempsychosis, or transmigration of the soul (as will hereafter more particularly appear, when we come to treat of the Druid learning) it is very likely the Druids owed to Pythagoras. For that

pædia lib. ii. in Frickio, 199. " Gallorum Phi-
" losophos etiam Philosophis Græcis priores
" existimant nonnulli Græci Scriptores, ut Ari-
" stoteles apud Diog.Laertium, qui non a Græcis
" ad Gallos Philosophiam deveniffe, sed a Gallia
" ad Græcos prodiiffe scriptum reliquit." Not.
Cæf. Comm. lib. vi. Edit. Delph. 8vo. p. 119.
Coutumes des Anciens Gaulois La Ramée par
Castlenau, 52. " Aristote avoit ecrit en son
" Magicien (selon que Laert le reconte) que la
" Philosophie a pris son Origine de Semnotheis
" des Gaulois anciens."

w Strom. lib. i. p. 357.
x Cæf. Comm. Edit. Delph. 8vo. p. 123.
Γαλαίων και Βραχμανων ακηκοινχι. Brahamæi seu Bra-
mæi Arabici dicuntur, quasi ab Abrahamo Patri-
archa nomen & originem suam derivarent.
Smith's Syntagma de Druid. Mor. p. 49.
y " Pythagoram peregre profectum omnibus
" mysteriis Græcis & Barbaricis fuisse initiatum."
Diog. Laert. ibid. in Cæf. Comm.
z Diod. Sic. Lib. ii. chap. iii.
a Toland of the Druids from Porph; r. p. 161.

Pythagoras

Pythagoras borrowed this tenet from the Druids is not near fo probable, though advanced by fome learned men [b], who are perhaps too fond of every occafion to exalt the Druids. The extream fondnefs of the Druids, for white colours in their garments, and victims, favours alfo of the doctrines of Pythagoras. Some other rites, as we proceed, will appear perhaps to have been borrowed of Pythagoras, but that their whole fyftem was of his framing, or indeed of Grecian original (i. e. derived from the Greeks [c]), is by no means likely, for if they had not been at that time a famous fect, Pythagoras had never gone into their country to converfe with them; and before the time of this philofoper, they could not have borrowed much from the Greeks, for the Greeks before Pythagoras were in no capacity of communicating much learning or religion, having very little of either at that time in their own nation.

The great refemblance betwixt the Druids, Perfians, Gymnofophifts, Brachmans, and Egyptians, is a ftrong argument in favour of their antiquity; for if it be true that the Druids had not their tenets in general (but only fome particular ones) from Pythagoras, the principles of thefe diftant nations muft have been difperfed with them from Babel, or how could there be fuch a conformity between Iflanders in the Weft, and the moft remote nations of the Eaft, who do not appear to have had the leaft communication afterwards?

The Germans fuppofe the Druids as old as the migration of the Celts from the Eaft, miftaking continually the inftitution of the Priefthood, for the Religion of thefe Priefts: however, certain it is, they were very ancient in Gaul and Britain. Ariftotle writes of them in his book of magick [d]. All the Gauls faid " that they " were fprung from Dis (fays Cef. lib. vi.) which they had by tra- " dition from the Druids;" now this referring to the ancient Druids in the time of Cefar implies their great antiquity, it being fufficient, they thought, to fay, that the Druids for a long feries of ages had ftill delivered it as their opinion, that Dis, or Pluto (as Cefar is thought to mean [e]), was their father.

To fix the Æra of their antiquity would be a vain attempt, and therefore I fhall only make this obfervation, that if the Druids were

[b] " AnDruidæ Dogma, viz. Metempfychofin a " Pythagora acceperint, an a Druidibus Pythago- " ras in dubio mihi eft." Not. in Cæf. Comm. ut fupr. p. 123. " Falfiffimè omnium perhiberi Drui- " das Philofophiam fuam debere Pythagoræ." Frick. p. 38. " Pythagoras hanc ipfam Doctrinam " (viz. Metempfychofin) a majoribus noftris " haufiffe videri poteft, fi Clem. Alex. Strom. " lib. vi. & Eufeb. Præp. Evang. lib. x. ch. ii. " fequamur." Keyfler, p. 116.

[e] As fome think, viz. Diod. Sicul. Ammian. Marc. Valerius Maxi. & e recentioribus Seldenus ille etiam, & alii.

[d] " Ariftoteles in libro de Magia de eifdem (viz. " Druids) fcribit." Lel. de Sacr. Brit. p. 4. Celfus oppofes to the Antiquity of the Chriftian Religion, the more famous Antiquity of the Galactophagi, Getes, and Druids. Τ℧ς μεν Ὁμηρ℧ Γα-λακλοφαʃ℧ς και τ℧ς Γαλαῖων Δρυϊδας και τ℧ς Γέʃας, σοφωῖαʃα λεγει εθνη ειναι και αρχαια. Celf. ap. Orig. lib. i. p. 14. which though no argument againft the antiquity of the Chriftian Religon, is a good argument that the antiquity of the Druids was allowed to be very great in the days of Celfus, as Frickius rightly judges, p. 37.

[e] Ch. v. p. 18. book i.

really

really Celtic Priests, they would have spread with the several divisions of that mighty nation, and their traces would consequently appear equally strong and lively in every country where the Celts settled, but as we have no warrant from history (at least as I think) to suppose this Priesthood settled anciently any where but in Gaul and Britain, they cannot be so ancient as they are supposed by the Germans [f]; they must rather be supposed to have had their beginning after the Celts divided into Germans, Gauls, Cimbrians, Teutones, &c. and their subdivisions, each fragment of that vast structure making a powerful and numerous nation; but the Druid Priesthood taking place only among the Gauls and Britans.

CHAP. V.

The Original of the Druid Doctrine, and Priesthood.

IN what country this Order had its first rise and institution, whence their Rites and Doctrines, we will now enquire.

Not from the Jews. Some think they derived their rites from the Jews [g], founding their conjectures upon the resemblance of the Jewish and Druid ceremonies; but the little commerce which the Jews had, and were obliged to have, with other nations; nay the contempt and hatred which they met with from the Gentiles for their singularity of worship, and the strictness of their reclusive law, must convince us that we are to look for the rise of Druidism elsewhere.

Not from the Greeks. Several learned men [h] have with more reason thought it derived from the Greeks, induced thereto not only from the name of the order, which they looked upon (too hastily) as of Greek derivation, but from the conformity of their opinions to those of the most celebrated Greek philosophers, and their worshiping the same Gods. In order to give what light we can to this affair, let us go on with the distinction before-mentioned [i], which will prevent much confusion, and allow that many of the Druid rites, opinions, and their Deities also, are the same with those of the Greeks; but indeed it must be here remembered that the same Deities, Mercury, Sol, Jupiter, &c. were among the first false Gods [k], and being dispersed as such into all nations with the first Idolaters, retained their usurped dignity all over Europe, most part of Asia, and the most known parts of Africa; so that no conclusive argument can be drawn from

---

[f] " Arbitror institutos fuisse (viz. Druidas) a " Tuscone." Sched. p. 257. " Antiquissimi " enim hi apud Celtas Doctores." ib.

[g] " Quæcunque vel ex Persis Magi, ex Baby- " loniis vel Assyriis Chaldæi, vel ex Indis Gym- " nosophistæ, & e Gallis Druidæ, & qui Samo- " thei dicuntur, invenerunt, ea ipsi a Judæis

" (nam primi omnium Philosophi fuerunt & " Ægyptus Judæos Prophetas habuit) accepere." Sched. lib. ii. ch. ii. a Johanne Metello.

[h] Sheringham, p.104, 107. Sammes, &c.
[i] See Ch. iii. and Ch. iv. p. 73.
[k] See Ch. i. lib. ii.

thence.

thence. Again, if the Druids are to be plac'd higher in antiquity, and were eſtabliſh'd here, long before the Greeks made any figure in the learned world (as is very probable), and before they ſent forth colonies, or were civiliz'd enough to cultivate their own Religion; it is not at all probable that the Druids ſhould have owed much of their regulations, doctrines, or eſtabliſhment to the Greeks: it may be true that they borrow'd ſome tenets from Pythagoras, as Pythagoras himſelf did before from the Egyptians and Eaſtern ſages. It is alſo likely that they improv'd and extended their ſyſtem, and adopted ſome foreign rites by means of the trade carry'd on between the Phenicians, as well as the Greeks, and Britans; but to adopt or imbibe a few opinions is one thing, and to be indebted for the very being, formation, and fabrick of their whole order, is entirely different. Beſides, the Greek authors who mention the Druids, would not have conceal'd from us a circumſtance, which would have contributed ſo much to the reputation of their influence and learning; if the Druids had been of Greek original, the Greeks would have been fond of recording it, ever ready, as they prove themſelves, to exalt their own antiquity, and pre-eminence over other nations.

'Tis very probable (as it is ſaid before[1]) that the Greeks and Druids, and indeed all other nations, had their ſuperſtition from one and the ſame polluted fountain (all partaking, more or leſs, of the general taints of that falſe religion which obtain'd ſoon after the flood) and for this reaſon muſt have many things alike, as indeed all religions had; but it is no more juſt to infer from thence, that the Druids owed their religion to the Greeks, than that the Greeks owed their religion to the Jews, for their two religions had many the ſame tenets, and ſeveral like ceremonies[m]. If the Druids owed but very little with reſpect to their tenets and religion to the Greeks, much leſs with regard to the eſtabliſhment of their order, and regular Prieſthood. The Greeks had no ſuch Prieſts among them any where; and it would be very abſurd to imagine, that they ſhould ſet up an order in diſtant countries, which they had made no experiment of in their own[n].

Now if the pretenſions of the Greeks are ſo weakly founded, we may ſafely conclude, that no other foreign nation has any right to claim the honour of erecting and eſtabliſhing this ancient order among the Gauls and Britans[o]. Not from any foreign Nation;

---

[1] See chap. I. lib. ii.

[m] As ſacrifices, luſtrations, feſtivals, one ſupreme God, and immortality of the ſoul.

[n] " Non a Græcis igitur (viz. Druidæ) ſed " Britannis." Hoffman. in Dru. pag. 111.

[o] Some will have them to be derived from the Egyptians, becauſe they are ſaid by Dionyſius the African to have celebrated the Orgyes of Bacchus. Warb. Div. Leg. vol. I. pag. 136.

X The

The Druids therefore were a regular order of Priefts, not fetch'd from abroad, but inftituted and form'd at firft either in the countrys of Britain or of Gaul, and peculiar to thofe two nations; an order gradually fafhion'd and fhap'd, partly by their own invention, affifted by the general cuftoms of all the Gentile world, and partly from the adopted precepts of fome philofophers they convers'd with, increafing in learning and authority, age after age, till by its luxuriancy in both it attracted the eyes and admiration of all the curious and the learned; and the next enquiry muft be, which of thefe two nations is intitled to the honour of giving birth to this Order.

CHAP. VI.

That Druidifm had its firft rife in Britain.

AS it appears from reafon and hiftory, that there are no conclufive arguments to prove that Druidifm was a foreign inftitution, nor a rule and difcipline tranfplanted from the more polifh'd nations of the Eaft, 'tis the lefs to be wonder'd at, that it fhould be firft invented and eftablifh'd in Britain, and thence tranflated into Gaul: for if it had been introduced by any foreign philofopher, it would moft probably have been firft taught in Gaul, and next in Britain: if it had been primarily fetched from Greece, it would have paffed from Greece to the Grecian Colony of Marfeilles, thence fpread into Gaul, and from Gaul to Britain; but as it was not a borrowed Order, as is apparent from the foregoing chapter, it is at leaft as likely in the nature of things, that it fhould have had its rife in Britain, as in Gaul; and where things are in their own nature equally poffible and probable, the fuperiour weight of teftimonies, on which hand foever it lies, fhall eftablifh the one and reject the other. Now Cefar is a very exprefs evidence in this matter. " Difciplina, in Britannia " reperta, atque in Galliam tranflata effe exiftimatur."

The French, indeed, are unwilling to own their forefathers indebted fo much to this ifland, but have no arguments on their fide, fufficient to fet afide fo great an authority as that of Cefar, who was too curious to want the beft information that was to be had in fo material a point, and of too noble a mind to record any thing upon light and trivial grounds. 'Tis true, we had our inhabitants from Gaul P, as the neareft part of the continent to

P See Book I. Ch. III.

Britain,

Britain, and with the inhabitants came the Celtic language, but the Druids had no being when this island was peopled, their discipline being invented afterwards [q]; and therefore Britain's having had its inhabitants from Gaul, will by no means prove that they had also the Druids from that country. I must here observe, that none of the ancient authors deny what Cesar advances, Strabo, and Pomponius Mela, in their observations on the Druids, copying him as their best Guide [r], Tacitus in no point contradicting him; and to silence all wonders, how Britans should give an Order of priesthood to their nearest neighbours the Gauls, I must take notice that Pliny [s] (who is more circumstantial in the rites of Druidism than any other) says that the Britans were so excessively devoted to all the mysteries of magic, that they might seem to have taught even the Persians themselves that art [t]. There is another circumstance worthy our notice in what Cesar says, which is, that the institution of the Druids was maintain'd with greater strictness and purity, in Britain than in Gaul; and that when the Gauls were at a loss in any point relating to this discipline, their custom was to go over to Britain for their better information [*]. Does not this in a great measure intimate and confirm that the Gauls were taught this discipline by the Britans, and that when any difficulty occurred, they had recourse to the first fountain of instruction ? These testimonies are too many and particular, to give way to modern jealousies, and national envy; and therefore we have reason to conclude, that Druidism had its first rise in Britain, till the contrary is better supported [u]. And here, before we take our leave of these contested points, it can't but be observ'd how one truth supports another, and how both reason and history (notwithstanding the little cavils against him [w]) unite to confirm and establish every thing that this illustrious author gives us on these heads. Cesar says, the Germans had no Druids; the Germans [x] are loath to own this, but cannot prove they had; and though their religion was really at the bottom the same with that of the Gauls and Britans, yet, with these last, the Priesthood might be more regular, of greater dignity, of higher speculation, more intent on the mysteries of their superstition, classed into societies, and these societies dignified with the particular name of Druid; and this is all Cesar

---

[q] As is plain from the Germans, Danes, Swedes, Russians, who were branches of the Celts, and yet have no Druids. See ch. iii. lib. ii.

[r] See Leland de Sacr. Brit. pag. 3.

[s] Lib. xxx. c. i.

[t] " Britannia hodie eam (viz. Magiam) attonitè celebrat tantis ceremoniis, ut eam Persis dedisse videri possit." Plin. lib. xxx. cap. I.
" Druidæ, ita suos appellant Magos." Ibid. lib. xvi. c. 44. ad finem.

[*] " Et nunc qui diligentius eam rem cognoscere " volunt, illo (viz. Britanniam) discendi causa " proficiscuntur."

[u] The author of La Rel. de Gaulois (supposed Mr. Martin) ingenuously confesses that the Gauls had their Religion from Britain, pag. 13. vol. I.

[w] Cesar.

[x] See Lipsius in Tacit. de M. G. & Schedius, chap. iii. lib. ii.

says

says and intends, in which he is so far from being contradicted by Tacitus, that from the general character which is given in that author of the Germans, and their priests, he is indeed supported and confirmed.

Again, Cesar says, that the institution of these Druids was first invented in Britain. France would not willingly be indebted to her neighbours in a point of such consequence and antiquity ; but this humour of hers will not deprive so great an author as Cesar of the weight, which he must always have with unprejudiced readers, till she can produce testimonies of equal, or superiour authority to refute him.

CHAP. VII.

The Dignity and Power of the Druids.

IF we have so much reason to follow Cesar in the account he gives us of the contested points abovementioned, we can with no sort of justice desert him in things which are less controverted.

Dignity and Privileges. " There were two sorts of nobles in Britain, the one sacred, the " other civil, or rather military ; for most of their civil disputes were " decided by the Druids. The first order of the British nobility was " that of the Druids, the second of the Equites. The presence of " the Druids was necessary in all acts of devotion ;" they were to take care of all publick and private sacrifices, and to explain decisively every thing relating to religion.

Power in times of Peace. The government of youth was under their direction, and none but those who were educated by them were adjudged capable of publick employments. By them, all publick as well as private controversies were decided ; and if any notorious crimes were committed, as murther, or the like ; any dispute concerning lands, or inheritance, by them it was determined ; they conferred proper rewards upon the worthy, and appointed punishments for the guilty, and their judgment was decisive, for if any one was refractory, he was excluded from their sacrifices, which of all other was accounted the most grievous punishment, those who were so excluded, being from that time looked upon as impious and detestable, every one shunning their company as contagious ; nor could such claim any benefit of the law, or succeed to dignities, which might otherwise fall to their share. Besides this, as the Druids had the sole privilege of explaining the appearances of the victim's entrails, and managed all the secrets of augury and divination, they may be reckoned the principal engines, and governours of the state ; and indeed it was not lawful

for

for the King himfelf to refolve, or enter upon any important action, without the concurrence of the Druids [y]. The fame author informs us, that the Druids fat on golden thrones, lived in large palaces, and fared fumptuoufly; and if we credit a modern author [z], the ruins of the Druid palace in the country of the Carnutes (where the annual affembly for the Gaulifh Druids was held) are ftill plainly to be feen, and confiderable in themfelves.

As thefe privileges could not but give them great power in times of peace, they had alfo proportionable weight in times of war: they were indeed by law excufed from attending upon the army, and from all the difficulties and fatigues of war, nor were they burthened with any expence on that account; yet did they frequently attend the military expeditions, as at the battle of Anglefea, praying with great fervency to their Gods with hands lifted up to Heaven [a]; where Tacitus calls the Britans Fanaticum agmen, led on as they were by their Druids. But their prefence was neither improper nor ineffectual in the field; for in the day of battle, their office was to animate their troops by inculcating the immortality of the foul, and affuring them either of victory, or a paffage into a ftate of happinefs; nay, fometimes they prevented bloodfhed, and made peace; for Diod. Sic. informs us [b], that thefe Philofophers, ftepping in between two armies ready to engage, have pacified them as effectually, as if fome wild beafts had been tamed by inchantments. When they had refolved upon a battle, they vowed the booty to Mars [c], the fuperfluous living creatures which they took, they facrificed, the reft they conveyed into one publick repofitory, which was a place of worfhip, and, when once there, no one dared be fo impious, as to take any thing away. As to treaties they held it unlawful to enter into any thing of that kind with foreigners [d].

The Druids had not only thefe general privileges and authority over their countrymen, but they had alfo a fort of government among themfelves. There was one Druid who prefided over all the reft, and with him the chief authority (in all matters relating to the Order) was lodged: when he died, if any one was more noble and famous than the reft, he fucceeded; but if feveral had an equal claim, he was chofen by the fuffrages of the Druids, and fometimes the election has been known to be decided by the force of arms [e]. This is faid by Cefar of the government of the Druids among the Gauls; and as there was this Arch-druid in Gaul to prefide in all cafes of difficulty,

Marginal notes: In times of War. Of the Rule and Government of their Order.

[y] Κελτοι δε ὡς ονομαζωσι Δρυιδας, και τωτως ωερι Μανλικην ὀνlας και την αλλην Σοφιαν, ὡν ανευ, τοις Βασιλευσιν ὠδεν εξην ωρατlειν, ὠδε βωλεωθαι, ὡςε το μεν αληθες εκεινως αρχειν, τως δε βασιλειας αυτων ὑπερητας και διακονως γινεσθαι της γνωμης, εν θρονοις καθημενως, και οικιας μεγαλας οικωνlας, και ωολυlιμως ευωχωμενως. Dion. Chryfoftom. de Recuf. Magiftrat. in Senat. pag. 538. Edit. Paris.
[z] "In agro Carnotenfi extare adhuc veftigia "præclara Palatii Druidum," Bul. in Frick. 145. Rovillard. Hiftor. Carnotenf.
[a] Tacit. Ann. lib. xiv. ch. xxx.
[b] Lib. v.
[c] Cefar, ibid.
[d] Gollut's Axioms of the Druids, Ax. 25.
[e] Cefar, ibid.

Y   importance,

importance, and folemnity; fo doubtlefs in Britain (whence the Gauls had their plan), for the fame reafons, there was lodged the fame, or like authority in one, or more fuperior Druids, it being altogether improbable that peace, difcipline, and a regular adminiftration of Juftice could be preferved in any Order or fociety of men, where there was no fuch proper fubordination.

According to fome accounts [f], the chief authority among the Britifh Druids was lodged in twenty-five Flamens or fuperior Priefts, over which prefided three Arch-flamens, all which Flamens continued in England till the time of King Lucius, A. D. 179, when Chriftianity came in [g]. The truth of this is much to be queftioned, but there was another kind of authority among the Druids, well fupported in hiftory, which confifted in their annual affembly; and this feems to have been the fupreme court, or laft refort for juftice. For the common conveniency of all the nation, the Gauls held this affembly in the country of the Carnutes, as Cefar obferves, the middle fpot of Gaul, lying between the rivers Loire and Seine, where they approach neareft one to the other: here there was a place confe-crated for that purpofe, and at the appointed time, all thofe who had any controverfies which could not be adjufted elfewhere, came and paid entire obedience to the decrees of this affembly: It is not to be imagined that the Britifh Druids were obliged to attend this affembly, in a place chofen for the more commodious refort of the Gauls (but without any regard to the conveniency of Britain), although it is not faid that the Britifh Druids had any court of Judi-cature of this kind; but, as the difcipline of this Order was ftricter in Britain than in Gaul, it is not to be fuppofed that they were with-out a convention, fo neceffary to preferve peace, and finally fettle all difputes of a higher nature, or of more difficult interpretation, and therefore we may reafonably conclude, that for the fame purpofes which induced the Gaulifh Druids to inftitute an affembly of this kind, the Britifh Druids alfo had a court of fovereign appeal, or general annual meeting of the ftates, in a proper place, in their own nation.

---

f Ptolemæus Lucenfis. See Lel. de Scr. Brit. P. 7.

g See Stillingf. Or. Sac. Antiquities of the Britifh Churches, from pag. 36 to 52.

CHAP. VIII.

Of the Druid Diſcipline, the Quality and Admiſſion of their Diſciples, the Privacy, Time, Privileges, and Manner of their Inſtruction, their Correction.

THE great privileges and authority of this Order made people fond of being admitted into it, and parents and guardians thought they could not do better for children of the higheſt birth [h] than ſend them to the Druids to be inſtructed. Some think that the Druids not only kept ſchools for the education of youth (which was their peculiar province), but lived in ſocieties in a conventual manner [i]; and indeed it is not eaſy to imagine, how they could preſerve their Arcana, read lectures in every kind of Philoſophy, and keep up their diſtinction from the vulgar, without ſome kind of collegiate aſſemblies. Their inſtructions were inſtilled into youth in the moſt private manner; ſome Cave, or retired and ſacred Wood [k], or ſome rocky Karn*, being the appointed place of Tuition; in which retirement the ſcholars were gradually introduced into the ſeveral parts of learning, and ſlowly, the education not being compleated in leſs than twenty years †, for one who was to be initiated. No one was capable of publick employments who had not been educated under a Druid [l]. They did not permit parents to intermeddle in the education of their children, it being one of their fixed rules that children were to be brought up at a diſtance from, or out of the preſence of, their parents till they attained to fourteen years [m]. They had this rule alſo among them, that young people (who I ſuppoſe were not to be initiated) were to be diſmiſſed from ſchool when they had the

---

[h] " Nobiliſſimos gentis," Pompon. Mela, Lib. III. cap. ii. See Galtruch P. H. Lib. III. c. iv. Divitiacus, an intimate client of Pompon. Att. and Cicero, and friend to Jul. Cæſar, Prince of the Ædui, was a Druid, and had a principality in Britain as well as in Gaul. See Leland de Scr. Brit. pag. 3. Cicero to Attic.

[i] " Academia ampliſſima exiſtimatur fuiſſe in " ſylva Carnotenſi, eo loco ubi nunc Urbs a " Druidibus nuncupata Gallicè Dreux, et in " Pagis Sylvæ Vicinis (ut Rovillardus) Druid- " arum Domus dicuntur; & non procul ab " Auguſtoduno (ubi Imagines Druidarum de " Montfaucon erutæ ſunt), altera Acad. in " monte Gallicè Montedru." Frick. 147. in Bulæo. " Druides ingeniis celſiores (ut Autho- " ritas Pythagoræ decrevit) ſodalitiis aſtricti " conſortiiſque, Quæſtionibus occultarum rerum " altarumque erecti ſunt, &, deſpectantes hu-

" mana, pronuntiarunt Animas immortales." Ammian. Marc. Lib. XV. Rowl. 234.

[k] " Il faut etre enſeigné dedans les Bocages " Sacreéz." Gollut's Memoirs Ax. 1. " Clam, " in ſpecu, aut abditis ſaltibus." Pompon. Mela. Lib. III. c. ii.

* " In ruinoſis locis, aut ſylveſtribus," viz. in rocky Karns, where the Stones were ſcattered, as in heaps of ruined buildings.

† " Diu, vicenis annis," ibid. " Nonnulli " annos vicenos in Diſciplinâ permanent." Cæſ. Lib. VI. " Non in Urbibus & magnis Civitati- " bus, ſed in lucis & nemoribus veluti Anachore- " tas, a ſtrepitu & turba populari remotas ſedes " habuiſſe." Bul. in Frick. Lucan. Lib. I.

[l] Gatruch. Hiſt. Poet. ibid.

[m] The Parents never ſuffered their ſons to come near them in any publick place, till they could bear arms. Ceſar. Gollut. M. Axi. 28.

courage

courage and resolution to fight for the publick liberty [n]. Under the direction of the Druids the most singular part of instruction was that of learning a great number of verses by heart, for they did not think it lawful to commit what related to their particular discipline to writing [o]. They seem to have pursued the method of teaching their mysteries memoriter for several reasons; because they would not have their mysteries become too familiar to the vulgar, in this, as in many other particulars resembling the Egyptians [p]; nor be divulged and exposed to the caprice of foreign countries; nor their scholars trust too much to the written letter, and neglect to cultivate their memory [q], and, it may be observed, that we find several instances in history of the same custom among the wisest Heathens. "Lycurgus and the Lawgivers of other cities thought it better to imprint their laws in the minds of their citizens, than to engrave them in Tablets, where they might lye neglected and unregarded; and Plutarch informs us, that Numa's sacred books and writings were buried with him by his orders" (perhaps in compliance with the opinion of his friend Pythagoras), "imitating herein the legislators of Greece, who inculcated the contents of their laws so long into the hearts and minds of their Priests, that their understanding became, as it were, living libraries of those sacred volumes, it being esteemed a profanation of such mysteries to commit their secrets unto dead letters [r]." Such was also the opinion of Pythagoras and Socrates, neither of whom left anything behind them committed to writing [s].

When therefore the Disciples of Pythagoras perished in the flames during the Metapontine tumults, the discipline, and science of that Philosopher expired for the most part with them [t]; for their memories were the only repositories in which they had preserved those treasures of knowledge which their great founder had left them. All these therefore were irrecoverably lost, excepting only what some novitiate scholars, who were never admitted into the mysteries, could remember and very badly explain. Socrates disputing with Phedrus in favour of teaching by word of mouth, rather than by written doctrines, says, that written books resemble the works of a Painter where the portrayed animals appear, indeed, as if they had real life, but if you ask them any question, they can give you

[n] Gollut. Ax. 21.

[o] Cef. ibid. This, Sheringham, p. 108, thinks to favour of the customs of the Hebrews, they having been as fond as any nation, of oral tradition.

[p] "Ægyptii sacra sua pollui, si vulgarentur, credentes." Mont. Kempiana XLII.

[q] Cesar, Lib. VI.

[r] Pott. Antiq. Græ. Vol. I. p. 142.

[s] Diog. Laert. indeed, in the Life of Plato, says that Pythagoras composed three Books, and Pliny (Lib. XIV. c. xvii.) quotes a book of Pythagoras; but all supposed spurious. vid. Syntagm. de Druid. p. 160.

[t] Της δὲ συμφορας ουτως κατασχουσης τους ανδρας (says Porphyrius) συνεξελιπε και ἡ επιστημη, αρρητος εν τοις στηθεσιν ετι φυλαχθεισα αχρι τοτε μονων των δυσσυνετων παρα τοις εξω διαμνημονευομενων. Syntag. de Dr. 159.

no

no anfwer. "You may think, adds he, that written difcourfes " might fpeak to you, as if they heard, and underftood what is faid ; " but if, defiring to know the bottom and grounds of things, you " enquire into, and endeavour to examine what they fay, they " fignify but one and the fame thing over and over again ; and, " believe me, as foon as ever a difcourfe is written down, it remains " always the fame ; to the learned it is intelligible, perhaps; to the " vulgar it is not, and never fhall be fo, and it is difficult to fay " what degree of underftanding it will fuit, and what it will not " fuit. When it is wrongfully and injurioufly blamed and ill " treated, it ftands immediately in need of its father's affiftance, for " it can neither revenge itfelf for the injuries it receives, nor clear " itfelf of any mifreprefentations. How much more excellent and " efficacious is the other way of inftruction ? the knowledge, I " mean, which is written and engraved in the mind of him that " teacheth ; who knows what, and before whom, he is to fpeak, " how, and what he is to inculcate, and what he is to conceal. " He fows not his corn in a hot bed, where it fhall foon fprout, " flourifh for a few days, then languifh and decay ; but like a fkilful " hufbandman, fows his field, and waits patiently for a few months " in juft expectation of a plentiful harveft u." In fhort, Socrates allows only of writing, in order to enrich and affift the memory of the teacher, but by no means proper to inftruct the fcholar.

After the example of the ancients (the Chaldeans, Egyptians, and Affyrians), the Druids comprized all the particulars of their re- ligion, and morality in hymns, the number of which, as Mr. Mar- tine w fays, was fo great, that the verfes which compofed them amounted to 20000. In juftification of this part of their difcipline, it muft be obferved, that the fubject matter of verfes is eafier learnt by means of the metre, and more eafily retained, than what is expreffed in profe.

Their Verfe and Metre.

Of the particular forts of verfes which the Bards ufed, there is an account in the ingenious Dr. John David Rhys's Rudiments, &c. of the Britifh language x ; and Mr. E. Lhuyd is there of opinion, " that " the oldeft kind of Britifh verfe is that called by Rhys's Grammar " Englyn Millur," and " that it was in this fort of metre the Druids " taught their Difciples, of which there are fome traditional remains ' to this day in Wales y, Cornwall, and Scotland," and a farther

---

u See Caftlenau's Tranflat. of La Ramée, Cou- tumes de Gaulois.

w La Relig. de Gaul. iii. p. 59.

x See Archæol. Brit. p. 250.

y "At Bala in Merionethfhire an annual meet- ing and feftival of the Bards is celebrated. There affemble together 60 or 70 Harpers, the greateft part of whom compofe extempore verfes, or couplets, in the Welfh tongue, and fet them to their Harps. In all this company of mufical Poets, fcarce fix of them can read or write, and yet fome of them have fuch a poetick genius that their compofitions have both fpirit and in- vention." Letter from the Rev. Dr. Charles Lyttelton, Dean of Exeter, and F. R. S. to the Author.

testimony

testimony the verses themselves bear to this truth, in that they generally contain some divine or moral doctrine [z].

As the Bards (an inferiour class of Druids) were remarkable for an extraordinary talent of memory [a]; this teaching memoriter, and by verse, was likely their office, whilst the superiours of the Order were employed in higher speculations, or the more secret and solemn parts of duty.

Mythology. The Druids used also allegory and fable (as the Orientals did) to convey their doctrines into previously adapted, and well prepared minds, without being at all understood by, or subjected to the refusal, and profanation of the ludicrous and perverse.

Severity. The Druids were exceedingly strict in their discipline, nice and punctual to the last degree in every thing that related to worship, their ordinances [b], and civil duties; and it was one of their maxims [c] that all fathers of families were to be esteemed as Kings in their own houses, and have power of life and death over wives, children, and servants; and in order to give weight and attention to their general public assemblies, and oblige others to the greater punctuality of appearance there, they practised, as it is said, that cruel custom (which Pliny reports of the Cigonii) of cutting in pieces him who came last.

Silence. The Druids were great lovers of silence, insomuch that if any one during their assemblies or sacrifices, was found pratling, they cut off, after the third admonition, a large piece of his robe; and if, after that, he offended a fourth time, they punished him most rigorously [d].

CHAP. IX.

Of the Druidesses, and whether the Germans had any Female Druids.

THE female Druids were some times regulars, consecrated to particular Gods and Temples, bound to observe particular ceremonies, and peculiar forms of discipline as well as the men. They had three sorts of Druidesses (says Mr. Martin Rel. des Gaul. vol. i. p. 206.), of the first class were Virgins during life; the second, though married, saw their husbands but once in the year for to have children, and were obliged to attend the Temples continually; the third sort never separated from their husbands, but governed their families, brought up children, and laboured as much as became their sex and circumstances.

[z] Lhuyd. Ibid. 251.
[a] Galtruchius's Hist. Poetique, Lib. III. chap. iv.
[b] Gollut's Axioms of the Druids, Ax. 38, & 39.
[c] Rowland, p. 61.
[d] Guenebald. p. 29.

The

The third fort of thefe had little different from the common
duties of other women, but the firft and fecond fort of female Druids
may both be difcovered in the accounts we have from Strabo and
Pomponius Mela of the Ifland Sena, and by attending to this diftinction, thefe two Geographers may well be reconciled.   This fmall
Ifland was either on the Britifh or Gaulifh coaft, and confequently
the inhabitants were of the Druid perfuafion.   Strabo fays [e] that
men [f] never landed here, but that the women paffing over in fhips,
and having converfed with their hufbands, returned again to the
ifland, and to their charge, which was to worfhip Bacchus (the God
to whom they were confecrated), with rites and facrifices : that every
year it was their cuftom to unroof their Temple, and to renew the
covering, the fame day, before fun-fet, by the united labours of all
the women ; of whom, if any one dropt or loft the burthen fhe was
carrying to compleat this facred work, fhe was torn in pieces by the
reft (a thing not uncommon during the Orgies [g]), and the feveral
limbs of this unhappy companion they carried round their Temple,
with rejoicings proper to the folemnities of Bacchus [h], untill
their fury abated.   Of this cruel rite, Strabo fays, there always happened fome inftance whenever the annual folemnity of uncovering
their Temple was celebrated.   This ifland is generally fuppofed to
be the fame as the Sena, of which Pompon. Mela [i] gives the following account.   " Sena, fituated in the Britifh fea over-againft the
" land of the Ofifmii (in Gaul), is famous for the oracle of a Gaulifh
" Deity, whofe Prieftefles, devoted to perpetual virginity, are faid to
" be nine in number.   They are called Gallicenæ [k], fuppofed to be
" of great genius, and rare endowments ; capable of raifing ftorms
" by their incantations, of transforming themfelves into what animals
" they pleafe ; of curing ailments, reckoned by others beyond the
" reach of medicine ; quick at difcerning, and able to foretell what
" is to come, but eafy of addrefs only to failors, and thofe who come
" to this ifland on purpofe, to confult them."   Here are two forts
of the Druideffes, both confecrated, one clafs conforting only with
their hufbands once in the year, the other confifting of perpetual
Virgins, and poffibly thefe two Orders might fubfift together on the
fame ifle ; fo far therefore thefe ancient authors do not contradict
each other ; but, as to the fituation of this famous ifland, neither
the ancients nor moderns are eafy to be reconciled ; and I fhall not
carry the reader afide into fuch great, and not material uncertainties.

[e] Lib. IV. p. 303.
[f] Ανδρις, viz. Hufbands.
[g] See the Story of Pentheus, Orpheus and the madnefs of the Bacchanals, in Montf. tom. i. part ii.
[h] Μετ Ευασμυ.
[i] Lib. III. cap. viii.
[k] " Al. Galligenæ quafi a Gallis ortæ, ut " Grajugenæ a Graiis genitæ."

The

The learned Keyſler, p. 378, labours to prove that the Germans had theſe female Druids as well as the Gauls and Britans. I muſt beg the reader's patience whilſt I examine what he advances, becauſe I think it contradicts what ancient hiſtory aſſures us of, I mean, that the Germans had no Druids. It cannot be denied but that the Germans had their Sacræ Fatidicæ, as moſt nations had; but that the ancient Germans ever called theſe Druids, is by no means plain; neither does it at all follow from the Germans having their fortune-tellers, that they had the diſcipline, and order of the Druids among them, any more than that the Egyptians had their Druids, becauſe they had the rites of divining at leaſt as plentifully as the Germans. The Fatidicæ of the Gauls were of Druid parentage, or at leaſt admitted into the Order, and therefore properly called Druids; but the Fatidicæ of the Germans, never had that title. Keyſler goes on, after producing many inſtances of inſcriptions to the Deæ-Matres in Germany (which, however, cannot with any certainty be aſcribed to the ancient Germans, for they might as likely, if not more ſo, have been erected by the Romans diſpers'd over the ſeveral cities of Germany), and tells us p. 446, " Ipſas has mulieres Druides adhuc " ante annos 300, et quod excurrit, apud Bituricenſes fuiſſe indicat " Guil. Pariſienſis;" but the Bituricenſes were indeed a people of ancient Gaul, and that the Gauls had their Druid women no one ever denied. " Quas matres Deas appellant inſcriptiones, eas " mulieres Druides, hoc eſt, Sacerdotes & Divinas nominant " Scriptores." ibid. It is true, antient authors do call the Fatidicæ of the Gauls, Druids, but no other, and the inſtances there produced from p. 447, by the learned author, prove no more; for Diocleſian was among the Tungri in Gaul [l], when he was informed by a female Druid that he ſhould become Emperour. The female Druid who foretold the fatal end of Alexander Severus's expedition, ſpoke to him in the Gauliſh tongue, whence it is to be inferred that ſhe was of Gauliſh birth [m]. When Aurelian was ſolicitous to know whether the purple ſhould continue in his family, he is ſaid, " Gallicanas " conſuluiſſe Dryades.[n]" The following inſcription, " SILVANO SACR. " ET NYMPHIS LOCI, ARETE DRUIS, ANTISTITA SOMNO MONITA D." (Gruter, P. LVIII. 11. 9.) was found at Metz on the Moſelle in Gaul. The Cimbri a branch of the Northern Germans living in, and near the Cimbrica Cherſoneſe, called their Fatidicæ Alyrunæ, or Aliorumnæ, Hellirunæ, Alrunæ, Alirunæ, i. e. Holy Prieſteſſes; (as Keyſler 461. explains thoſe terms [o]). Now it cannot be imagined, that there would have been ſuch particular names (all from one original) for the German Fatidicæ, and ſuch an univerſal ſilence as

---

l Vopiſc. in Numeriano, cap. xiv.
m Æl. Lampridius vit. Al. Sev. cap. lx.
n Vopiſc. in Aurel. cap. xliv.
o Hali ſignifies Sanctus; & Runa Vates.

to the name of Druid, unless the Druids Fatidicæ of the Britans and Gauls had some peculiarities, and such distinguishing marks as could not be justly ascribed to the Fatidicæ of their neighbours : what can we therefore conclude, but that the Germans were sensible that although their Fatidicæ were of the same profession as those of their neighbours, yet that they could not with any propriety call them Druids, because the Druids had not only the Gift of divination and prophecy (as was imagined in those days), but were a particular Sect, Fraternity, Priesthood, and noble Order of the States in which they lived ; looked upon by other nations as a spiritual tyranny, and which they were as unwilling to admit into their countries, as the Druids were tenacious of their influence and dignity in their own ?

Among the other Fatidicæ, the name Thrudur furnishes a third argument that the Germans had Druidesses. " Thrudur etiam in " Dearum numerum relata perhibetur ab Edda, sacerdos sive Druis, " ut ex nomine colligo antea Duri, sive Thori P." But what little stress is to be laid on the fabulous Edda, all the world knows ; and deriving Druis from Thrudur, or Thrudur from Druis q ; Druden's signifying a Witch in Franconia and Helvetia, and Drutner a Magician among the modern Germans, these are foundations too slight and airy to ground history upon. Words will be transplanted, and from short, accidental intercourse, pass from one country to another, and there take root ; but we dispute not about a word or two, but about things ; the question is, whether the Discipline, Order, or Sect of the Druids was established among the Germans, and whether their Priests have been generally, or could properly be called Druids.

There is but one argument more upon which Keysler lays any stress, and this also shall be mentioned. Velleda is by him reckoned among the Druids, p. 473 ; but Tacitus says she was born in the country of the Bructeri (now Westphalia), a part of Germany betwixt the rivers Luppia and Amisia, and she is no where said to be a Druidess r.

C H A P. X.

Of the Druid Learning, Letters, Language, Doctrines, and Tenets.

BY the account we have of the Druids in ancient authors, they must have been very studious and learned for the ages they flourished in, and the countries they inhabited, at such a distance

P Keysler, p. 490.
q " Edda Islandica, Eddam frivolis & ridiculis " figmentis scatere fatetur," Keyslerus, p. 20. Frickius, p. 70. It was compiled by Snorro Sturla,

a lawyer (Nomophylax) of Island in the year 1215. Ibid.
r Vid. Tacit. Hist. Lib. IV. c. lxi. & lxv. & de M. G. c. viii. & Hist. Lib. V. c. xx.

A a   from

from all the affiftances of the Egyptian and Grecian Literature. That they loved and encouraged Learning, appears from their inculcating it as a moft certain truth, that whoever was fkilled in divine things (as they termed every part of their Superftition and Philofophy) was moft agreeable to their Gods, and moft proper to attend their facrifices [s].

Letters and Language. Although the Druids held it unlawful to commit the Myfteries of their Order and Difcipline to writing, yet in all other affairs, either of publick or private concern, they ufed writings, and the Greek letters [t]. It feems however very reafonable to believe, that though they ufed the Greek letter, or character, for ordinary bufinefs, yet that they ufed not the Greek language, but the Celtic or Britifh ; juft as we ufe the Roman letter, and yet write in the Englifh, French, or Spanifh tongue. For this, there are feveral arguments ; Cefar, we find, converfed with the Gauls, and Divitiacus (one of the moft learned of the Druid Order), by an interpreter [u] ; which, had Divitiacus underftood the Greek language, Cefar, who knew Greek as well as his mother-tongue, needed not to have done [w]. Cefar writ in the Greek tongue to Qu. Cicero, then befieged among the Nervii, left the letters being intercepted, his defigns might be known and defeated. In fhort, if the Druids had ufed a foreign language to deliver their myfterious laws in, they might as well have wrote them, for they would have been as much fecrets to the vulgar, if written in Greek, as if intrufted only to the memory of their Novitiates [x].

The learned Selden thinks that the knowledge of the Greek tongue can fcarce be allotted to the Druids ; and, at a diftance from Marfeilles, it is indeed very probable that this piece of learning was rarely to be found : Jof. Scaliger thinks the word, Græcis [y], an interpolation, and indeed the fenfe will very well bear this word's being thrown out, notwithftanding what fome authors [z] alledge to the contrary. Leland [a] feems therefore to be miftaken when he fays, " Druides, quibus & Græca lingua tantùm non familiaris." Lucian (in Hercule Gallico) fays, indeed, that a certain Philofopher of the Gauls (undoubtedly a Druid) explained certain pictures to him in the Greek tongue ; and not unlikely, it being not poffible for the

---

[s] Gollut. ibid. Axiom. 33.

[t] " Non defunt tamen qui prifcos Druidarum " characteras, & elegantes, & Græcis fimiles " fuiffe credant. Xenophonte fiquidem & Archi- " locho teftibus, literarum figuræ, quas in Græ- " ciam e Phœnicia Cadmus intulit, Galaticis " quam Punicis five Phœniciis fimiliores " extitêre." Bucher. Frº. p. 183.
" Afiatici hi Galatæ Gallorum Europæorum, " quibus orti erant, characteras æque ac linguam " retinere potuerint, quam penè Treuerorum

" fuiffe teftatur Hieronymus." Præf. in Ep. ad Galat. ibid.

[u] " Quotidianis interpretibus remotis per C. " Valerium Procillum, cum eo (viz. Divitiaco) " colloquitur." Cæf. Lib. I. Janfon's Edit. p. 12.
[w] Cæf. Lib. I.
[x] Ibid. Lib. V.
[y] Cæf. Lib. VI. de Bell. Gall.
[z] Syntagm. de Druid. p. 66.
[a] Sheringham, p. 390.

Druid

Druid to explain them to a Grecian in the Britifh tongue. This therefore proves only that fome of the Druids underftood Greek, not that it was their common tongue. What Greek the Druids had, came to them, likely from the Greek colony of Marfeilles, which was a fort of academy to the Gauls [b], as well as a Mart to the Britans.

Upon the whole, if we confider what Juftin fays, Hift. Lib. XLIII. of the univerfal influence which the learned colony of Greeks at Marfeilles had upon all Gaul, " Non Græcia in Galliam emigraffe, " fed Gallia in Græciam tranflata effe videretur;" and that as Strabo (Geog. Lib. III. p. 125.) fays, Marfeilles was a fchool to the Gauls, and made them fond of every thing that was Grecian; that Cefar fays, writings in Greek letters were found in the camp of the Helvetii, that in all other affairs than what related to their own Order, they ufed Greek characters: from thefe teftimonies it cannot be doubted but that the Druids in fome parts underftood the Greek tongue, and the moft learned of them did occafionally ufe it; but that it was their common, ufual language, either in things profane or facred, is altogether improbable; for, that the Gauls and Britans had a national language, is true beyond queftion: that the Druids had great concerns with the other Orders, noble and plebeian, is as certain; council, judicial decifions, predictions, devotional exercifes of facrifice, fupplication, and the like, all came from, and through the Druids, and to whom were they directed? Whom did they concern, but their countrymen of Gaul and Britain? Could they therefore be in a language, which, whatever the few learned might do, moft certainly the general body of the people was totally unacquainted with?

The Irifh Druids (if we may credit fome accounts) had a form of Letters very fingular, the alphabet whereof they called Beth, Luis, Nion (from the three firft letters of it, B, L, N,) in which every letter, to the number of twenty-fix, was called by the name of fome tree in the wood [c].

They had a great fondnefs for verfes, as appears by that part of their difcipline, which confifted in making their tyroes to learn by heart vaft numbers for many years together. In verfe they celebrated the praifes of their departed heroes, and feem to have appropriated one third of their whole Order [d] (the Bards) more particu-

Verfes and Rhetorick.

---

[b] Strabo, Lib. III.
[c] Rowland, p. 108. The truth of this is much doubted of, if not unanfwerably confuted in Innes's account of the Caledonians and Picts, a very learned and ingenious work.
[d] " Studia liberalium doctrinarum inchoata " per Bardos Euvates & Druidas." Amm. Marc. Lib. XV.

larly

larly to this ſtudy [e].   They had a kind of rhetorick among them, of which the Druids themſelves were the teachers, and were therefore called Magiſtri Sapientiæ [f].

CHAP. XI.

Of their Phyſical Knowledge.

Aſtronomy.   THAT the Druids applied themſelves to Aſtronomy, Geography, and Phyſicks, Ceſar and Mela aſſure us [g].   They reaſon much (ſay they) and inſtruct their youth in many particulars relating to the Planets and their motion.   Caius Sulpicius, Tribune of ſoldiers in the Macedonian war, a Gaul by nation, foretold an eclipſe of the moon, to the Roman army, upon which Livy adds, that thenceforth " Gallos Romanis militibus ſapientiâ prope divinâ viſos [h]."

Geography.   The extent and limits of the univerſe was another ſubject of their contemplation ; they endeavoured to underſtand the form, and diſpoſition of the ſeveral regions of the earth, and the nature of material ſubſtances.

The Euvates (the third Order of the Druids) ſeem to have had the ſtudy of Nature committed to them [i], as the Bards had Poetry, or the ſtudying and teaching Verſes for their ſhare : but theſe appointments, however, ſeem to be of ſuch ſort, as that the Druids, or ſupreme part of the Order, were not excluded from theſe noble ſtudies, but were at liberty to employ themſelves in every art and ſcience, and alſo to extend their ſearches into the moſt ſublime ſpeculations ; accordingly, to Phyſiology, or the ſtudies of Nature, the Druids added Ethicks, a future ſtate, the immortality of the ſoul, and the will and power of the Gods ; and from theſe profound myſteries, the inferior claſſes of the Order ſeem to have been prohibited.

[e] " Fuere ex hoc hominum genere celebres " aliquot in ipſa etiam Britannici imperii decli- " natione, videlicet Telieſſinus, Mevinus, Mer- " linus." Leland, de Scr. Brit. p. 5.

[f] " Habent tamen & facundiam ſuam, ma- " giſtroſque Sapientiæ Druidas." Pomp. Mela. Lib. III. ch. ii.

[g] Cæſar, Lib. VI. " Multa de ſideribus," &c. et Pomp. Mela, Lib. III. ch. ii.

[h] Liv. Lib. XLIV. cap. xxxvii.

[i] " The Euvates were Prieſts and Phyſi- " ologers." Rowl. 65.
" Vates autem ſacrificiorum naturaliumque " cauſarum curæ dediti." Lel. de Scr. Brit. ex Strabone, Lib. IV.) p. 6.
" Batties vero ſcrutantes ſecreta & ſublimia na- " turæ pandere conabantur." Ibid. ex Amm. Marc.

Diod. Sic. Lib. III. ſpeaking (from Hecateus) of a Northern Iſland, about the extent of Sicily, ſituated over againſt the Celtæ, inhabited by the Hyperboreans, ſays, " it is fruitful, pleaſant, and " dedicated to Apollo, who, for the ſpace of " nineteen years, uſed to come and converſe " with them, and, which is more remarkable, they " could, as if they had the uſe of Teleſcopes, " ſhew the Moon very near them, and diſcover " therein Mountains, &c.   They had a large " Grove and Temple of a Round form, to " which the Prieſts frequently reſorted, with " their Harps, to chaunt the praiſes of " Apollo." Nat. and Civ. Hiſt. of Cork, Vol. I. p. 266. This is a proof of the Druid Aſtronomy, for this Iſland could be no other than one of the Britiſh Iſlands, and the Prieſts no other than Druids, as Rowland, p. 76. thinks in his Mona.

They

They taught alſo that the world had a beginning, and that it Reckoning of Time. would one time have an end, and that by fire[k]. Their computation of time was by nights, not days[l]; the reaſon of which, as Ceſar thinks, was becauſe it had been the conſtant tradition of the Druids, that they were ſprung from Dis, God of the Infernal Shades, or Night. But this does not ſeem to be the reaſon, for it was a tradition generally received among the ancients, that night was before day, or light, and Orpheus calls night the mother of all things. The Hebrews reckoned by the natural day of twenty-four hours, and the night, in this reckoning, was placed before the day; as it was alſo among the Ethiopians[m]. Heſiod alſo makes the day and ether to proceed from night; ſo that their being ſprung from Dis was not, perhaps, the true reaſon of their computing time by nights[n], but was rather a remainder of the ancient tradition, that night or darkneſs was before the world was created, and therefore to be placed, in order and reckoning, before the day[o].

The beginning of their year[p] was July, the moon ſix days old; and an age or generation with them was reckoned to amount to thirty years.

CHAP. XII.

Of their Botany, and Anatomy.

THE Druids ſeem to have been very ſtudious of the virtue of Plants and Herbs, and either from ſome real or imaginary diſcoveries in this branch of knowledge, were led on to that extravagance as to attribute divine power and efficacy to ſeveral vegetables. [q] They were exceſſively fond of the Vervaine; they uſed it in caſting The Vervaine. lots, and foretelling events. Anointing with this, they thought the readieſt way to obtain all that the heart could deſire, to keep off

---

[k] " Conditum mundum credebant & aliquando
" igni periturum."
Αφθαρlὰς λεγᾶσα τας ψυχας, και τον κοσμον, επικρα-
lησειν τε πoῖε πυρ και ὑδωρ. Strabo, Lib. IV. Plato and Cicero held the ſame opinion.
[l] " Nec dierum numerum ut nos, ſed noctium
" computant." Tac. de M. G. Cæſ. Lib. VI.
[m] " Æthiopes diem ordiuntur ab ineunte
" nocte." Joſ. Scaliger, Lib. VII. de Emend.
Temp. p. 677. Syntagm. p. 164.
[n] " Alia proinde & longe prægnantior hujus
" conſuetudinis cauſa fuit quam illa Cæſaris in-
" genio prodita, quæ a fabuloſa Ditis, ſcil. Plu-
" tonis, noctis ac tenebrarum Domini progenie
" repetitur (qua in re nobiſcum conſentit doctiſ.
" H. U. a Lingen. Frickius, 78.) viz. antiquum
" tempora numerandi morem a noctibus reti-

" nuere, illum cujus ipſe Deus auctor erat."
Gen. i. 5. " Ut pluribus oſtendunt Cluverius,
" Schedius, &c." Ibid.
[o] In our common reckonings of time, this cuſtom ſtill obtains in England; for, the ſpace of ſeven days, we ſtill call a ſe'nnight, the ſpace of fourteen days we call a fortnight, or fourteennight; and ſo did the Britans, and the Welſh even to this time. " Hunc morem Cambro-Bri-
" tanni hodie retinent, qui pro ſeptimanâ dicunt
" With-nos, i. e. octo noctes; pro duabus Pym-
" thec-nos, i. e. quindecim noctes, utroque ter-
" mino incluſo." Syntagm. de Druid. p. 163.
[p] Pliny, Lib. XVI. Cap. XLIV. Gollut's
Mem. Axi. 4, 5, 6.
[q] Inſaniunt, ſays Pliny.

fevers,

fevers, to procure friendfhips, to heal all diftempers. That it was to be gathered at the rife of the Dog-ftar, without being looked upon either by fun or moon; in order to which the earth was to be pro- pitiated by a libation of honey, and the honey-comb. The iron inftrument applied to this rite was to defcribe a circle round it, (viz. the plant) and then dig it up; in doing which the left hand was to be ufed, and to wave it aloft after it was feparated from the ground. The leaves, ftalk, aud roots, were to be feparately dried in the fhade; and if their couches were fprinkled with an infufion of it in water, the feafts were thought in a fair way of being much the merrier for fuch a fprinkling. Againft the bite of ferpents they ufed it infufed in wine [r].

Mifletoe.   They deified the Mifletoe, and were not to approach either that, or the Selago, or the Samolus, but in the moft devout and reve- rential manner. When the end of the year approached, they marched with great folemnity to gather the Mifletoe of the oak, in order to prefent it to Jupiter, inviting all the world to affift at this ceremony with thefe words, " The new-year is at hand [s], " gather the Mifletoe."

" The Druids indeed account nothing more facred than the " Oak-Mifletoe, which is however rarely to be found, but when " found is approached with great reverence; and principally when the " moon is fix days old [t], at which time they begin their months and " years, and ages, every 30th year. Then, calling it univerfal re- " medy in their native language, they prepare the facrifices and reli- " gious feafts after their own cuftom, under the tree, and lead forth " two white bulls, never yet yoked, nor their horns till then bound " with ropes; the Prieft cloathed in white afcends the tree, and with " a golden hook cuts off the Mifletoe, which is received in a white " garment, fpread for that purpofe."

This Mifletoe was of a golden colour, an adventitious plant of the Climbing kind, and therefore the golden bough is compared to it by Virgil, Æn. vi. ver. 205.

" Quale folet fylvis brumali frigore Vifcum
" Fronde virere nova, quod non fua feminat Arbos,
" Et croceo fœtu teretes circundare truncos:
" Talis erat fpecies auri frondentis opaca
" Ilice [u]." ———

[r] Plin. Nat. Hift. Lib. XXV. Cap. IX.
[s] " In Aquitania quotannis Prid. Kal. Jan. " pueri atque adolefcentes vicos villafque obeunt, " carmine ftipem petentes, fibique, atque aliis " pro voto, in exordio novi anni acclamantes, " Allguy, L'an neuf." Keyfler 305. fo that the

footfteps of this cuftom ftill remain in fome parts of France.
[t] Pliny, Lib. XVI. Cap. XLIV.
[u] N. B. The Verfe attributed to Ovid, " Ad " Vifcum Druides Druidæ clamare folebant," is fpurious, and not in Ovid. Keyfler, p. 306.

This

This story of the golden bough shews that the Druids were not singular in attributing great magical powers to such scarce and beautiful plants, ritually gathered, and offered to the Gods.

> " Hoc fibi pulchra fuum ferri Proferpina munus
> " Inftituit ; ———
> " Ergo alte veftiga oculis & rite repertum
> " Carpe manu."   Ib. ver. 142.

I muft here alfo obferve, that the Druids in feveral religious particulars had a delicacy fuperiour to moft of the ancients; for in gathering this Mifletoe they ufed only a golden hook, when among other nations a hook of brafs was thought nice enough for like purpofes. "Falcibus et meffæ ad Lunam quæruntur ahenis [w]," and Medea in Sophocles is defcribed gathering her magick herbs with a brazen hook, Χαλχεοισιν ημα δρεπανοις τομας, and afterwards putting their juice into brazen pots [x]. The Sabine Priefts alfo fhaved themfelves with, " ex ære cultris."

Having gathered the Mifletoe they next offer the victims, praying that their deity would profper thofe to whom he had given fo precious a boon. Of the Mifletoe thus gathered they made a potion, which (as they thought) prevented fterility, and was an antidote to all poifon.

With great care alfo and fuperftition did the Druids gather the Selago [y]. Nothing of iron (as too bafe a metal) was to touch or cut it, nor was the bare hand thought worthy of that honour, but a peculiar vefture, or fagus applied by means of the right hand; the vefture muft have been holy, and taken off from fome facred perfon privately, and with the left hand only. The gatherer was to be cloathed in white [z], his feet naked, and wafhed in pure water [a]. He was firft to offer a facrifice of bread and wine, before he proceeded to gather the Selago, which was carried from the place of its nativity, in a clean, new napkin. This was preferved as a charm by the Druids againft all misfortunes, and the fumigation of it was thought exceedingly good againft all defects of the eyes.

The Druids alfo experienced great virtue in, at leaft afcribed it to, the Samolus, and gathered it in a ritual, religious manner [b]: he that was to perform the office of gathering it, was to do it fafting, with the left hand; and whilft he was engaged in this duty, was obliged not to look behind him on any account, nor lay down the herbs

Selago.

Samolus.

---

[w] Scil. Herbæ, Æn. IV. ver. 513.

[x] Macrob. Saturn. Lib. V. Cap. XIX.

[y] A kind of hedge hyffop, refembling the Savin, Pliny, Lib. XXIV. Cap. IX. The Firr-Club-mofs. Hudfon, Flora Anglica, p. 395.

[z] Viz. a Druid whofe garment was white.

[a] " Pureque lotis nudis pedibus." Plin. ibid. Lib. XXIV. Cap. XI. in Marg. Not. ib. pura fubaud. aqua, the pureft of water.

[b] Samolus or Marfhwort, Pliny, Lib. XXIV. Cap. XI. The Round-leaved water Pimpernell. Hudfon, p. 79.

any

any where, but in the cisterns, and chanels, where the swine and bullocks usually drink, and there they were to be bruised for them, and mixed with the water to keep off diseases from them. When Medea gathered her magical herbs, she turned her head back from them, least the pestilential smell might be fatal to her [c]; but here the Druids were obliged not to turn their face from the herbs, to shew, perhaps, the harmless nature and sanative virtue of the plant they gathered.

Anatomy. As the Druids were great admirers of the virtue of vegetables, and therefore studious of Botany in order to guard and restore health, they were sagacious enough to discover that physical remedies, of which they were not ignorant [d] (Pliny calling them physicians, " Sustulit Druidas [e] Gallorum, et hoc genus Vatum, Medicorum- " que,"), could not effectually be applied without a thorough inspection into the several parts of the human body. Accordingly, they encouraged the science of Anatomy to such an excess, and so much beyond all reason and humanity, that one of their doctors called Herophilus, is said to have read lectures on the bodies of more than 700 living men, to shew therein the secrets and wonders of the human fabrick [f].

C H A P. XIII.

Moral and Religious Doctrines.

THE Druids were remarkable for justice [g], moral and religious doctrines, and skill in the laws of their country; for which reason all disputes were referred to their arbitration; and their decision, whether relating to private and domestick, or publick and civil affairs, was final; and the most heavy punishments inflicted on those who should be so obstinate as not to abide by their determination: to do no evil, was one of their general maxims, as to be valiant in battle was another; but the first and chief was, to worship the Gods [h]. The better to inspire their countrymen with a noble ardour to fight their enemies, and to contemn death, they attended the battles; some inculcated the immortality of the soul, others its passage from one body into another, others the certainty of a future life, as doctrines

[c] Macrob. Sat. V. Cap. XIX.
[d] Pliny, Lib. XXX. Cap. I.
[e] Viz. Tiberius Cæs.
[f] Galtruch. Poet. Hist. Lib. III. Cap. IV.
[g] Δικαιοlαloι δε νομιζονlαι, και δια τиlo πιςευοilαι τας τι ιδιωlικας κριςεις, και τας κοινας. Τας τι φοιικας δικας μαλιςα τиloις (viz. Druidis) επιlεlραπlο δικαξειν. Strabo, Lib. IV. p. 146. " Sotion in libro Successionum

" confirmat Druidas Divini Humanique Juris " peritissimos fuisse." Lel. de Scr. Brit. p. 5. Eli. Sched. p. 292. The Manks men ascribe to the Druids those excellent Laws, by which the Isle of **Man** has always been govern'd. See Carte's Hist. of England, p. 46.
[h] Σεβειν Θευς, και μηδεν κακον δραν, και ανδρειαν ασκειν. Diog. Laert. de Druid.

the moſt comfortable and enlivening upon all ſuch dangerous occaſions.   Nor was it only in war that theſe doctrines operated upon
their diſciples, but at all times ; and ſo confident and aſſured of a
future life were the Druids, that they often put off ſettling
their accounts till they met in the other world ; ſome willingly
threw themſelves into the funeral pile of their friends, in order to live
with them after death [i], and others threw letters into the funeral pile,
to be read by the deceaſed in the other world. That they therefore
held the immortality of the ſoul and a future life, I take to be paſt all
doubt ; but from whom they derived, or in what particular ſenſe they
underſtood and taught, theſe doctrines, I do by no means preſume
to affirm ; becauſe we want more circumſtantial and particular lights
from hiſtory as to theſe points ; but we may now enquire whether
they held the tranſmigration, for this is poſitively affirmed by the
ancients, and yet ſeems irreconcileable with the other tenets aſcribed
to them, and is therefore called in queſtion by ſome of the
moderns.

CHAP. XIV.

*Of the Immortality and Tranſmigration of the Soul, and how far
adopted by the Druids.*

CESAR plainly tells us that the Druids not only held the immortality of the ſoul, but its migration after death from one
human body into another [k].   Diod. Sic. Lib. V. tells us, that the
opinion of Pythagoras prevailed among them ; which was, that the
ſouls of men, after a determinate number of years, lived again, the
ſoul entering into another body [l].   According to Valerius Maximus
(Lib. II. c. vi.) it was the ancient cuſtom of the Gauls to lend money
upon condition that it ſhould be repaid them [m] in the next life,
thoroughly perſuaded, as they were, that the ſouls of men were immortal ; in this, ſimple enough (ſays our author, ibid.), and yet they
thought the ſame as the celebrated Pythagoras [n].   Ammian. Marc.
Lib. XV. informs us that the Druids, men of exalted genius, ranged
in regular ſocieties, by the advice of Pythagoras raiſed their minds to
the moſt ſublime enquiries, and, " deſpiſing human and worldly
" affairs, ſtrongly preſſed upon their diſciples the immortality of the

[i] Cæſar, Pomp. Mela. ut ſupra. Diod. Sic.
Lib. V. Cap. II.
[k] " Non interire animas, ſed ab aliis poſt mor-
" tem tranſire ad alios." Lib. VI.
[l] Ενισχυε γαρ παρ αυτοις ὁ Πυθαγορε λογος, ὁτι τας

ψυχας των ανθρωπων ειναι, συνεβηκε και δι᾽ ετων ὡρισμενων
παλιν βιεν, εις ἑτερον σωμα της ψυχης εισδυομενης.
[m] Apud inferos.
[n] " Dicerem ſtultos, niſi idem Bracati ſenſiſ-
" ſent, quod palliatus Pythagoras credidit."

C c   " ſoul."

" foul[o]."   Lucan fays, " that according to the Druid opinion, the
" ghofts of the dead defcended not to Erebus, or the empire of
" Pluto," (there to remain in a ftate of feparation from all body, as
the Greeks and Romans thought) but that the fame foul actuated
another body in another world [p].   Pomp. Mela, Lib. III. c. ii. may
feem to differ from Lucan ; but, indeed, is only relating the fentiments of a portion of the Druid philofophers ; he declares that the
Druids maintained the fouls to be eternal (i. e. without beginning
and without end) that there was another life after this, wherein the
foul exifted amongft other departed ghofts, and that they did for
this reafon burn and interr with the dead, what fuited their rank and
inciinations when they were alive [q].

Objections to the Druid Tranfmigration.   So far the ancients ; from whofe writings it appears, that the
Druids all held the immortality, and fome, the tranfmigration alfo :
but many of the [r] moderns will not allow the latter opinion to be
juftly imputed to the Druids.   Their reafons are thefe ; firft, the
tranfmigration is a tenet erroneous in itfelf, and groundlefs ; not afferted by Ammianus, or Mela, of the Druids ; and inconfiftent with
their other avowed opinions ; and therefore what Cefar and the reft
after him fay, is to be looked upon as the effect of envy, and as a
Anfwered.   moft injurious afperfion.   Now, that the tranfmigration never had
any exiftence, but in the fancy of its whimfical patrons, is readily
allowed ; but this can be no reafon why the Druids fhould not adopt
it ; for in thofe dark ages many abfurdities, as great as this, were
admitted into their fyftem, evidences of which will occur to the
reader from what goes before, fufficient to excufe my not re-entering
into particulars in this place.   It is true, neither P. Mela, nor Amm.
Marcel. do record the tranfmigration, as held by the Druids ; but as
they do not contradict Cefar and the reft, who pofitively affert it,
nothing can be concluded in favour of the moderns, from the mere
filence of thofe authors : neither can it be fuppofed but that Cefar's
fituation in life and knowledge placed him far above envying the
Druids ; for though they were poffeffed of all the efteem which antiquity could give, inftructed in many laudable doctrines, and brought
up to the nobleft contemplations, yet, in the opinion of the Greeks
and Romans, they were far from rivaling them, or moving the leaft
degree of envy.   Monf. Martin [s] has laboured this point with great
zeal for the reputation of his countrymen, in feveral pages, and cannot
allow the tranfmigration to have been held by the Druids, becaufe it

<hr/>

o " Defpectantes humana pronuntiarunt ani-
" mas immortales.
p " Regit idem fpiritus artus.—Orbe alio.—
q " Ils tiennent (dit il, viz. Strabon.) que les
" Ames ne font point fujettes à corruption."
Caftelnau, p. 65.

" Æternas effe animas vitamque alteram ad
" manes, itaque cum mortuis cremant ac defo-
" diunt apta viventibus olim."
r Cluver. Germ. Ant. p. 219. Frickius, p. 71,
&c. Rel. de Gaul. Vol. II. p. 223.
s Rel. de Gaul. Vol. II. p. 223, &c.

is inconfiftent with their other tenets: his arguments may be collected into this narrow fpace; he thinks they could not be fo abfurd, as
to throw letters, accounts, and money-bills into the funeral fires, if
the dead, after death, became different perfons, and even different
creatures from what they were before; neither would flaves or clients
voluntarily die to ferve their mafters in another life [t], or the wife
participate the fate of her hufband, if the fouls of thofe mafters or
hufbands were fuppofed to pafs into the bodies of other men or
beafts.

But in anfwer to this, it muft be obferved, that the Druids never
held the migration of Souls into Brutes. The union of the Soul
after death to another body in another world was never fuppofed to
conftitute a different perfon, the man remained the fame identical
perfon as he was before; in like manner as a man that has changed
his cloaths, or lodgings, continues ftill the fame man; and therefore they imagined that in this new body *(apud inferos)* the man
had all the fame wants, and the fame paffion for horfes, armour,
food, cloaths; the fame rights and claim to money, flaves, and every
other property, which he had in the prefent life. It was in conformity to thefe fentiments (which were no more than what the moft
cultivated parts of the Gentile world held) that the greateft part of
the Druids conveyed fuch things into the grave, urn, or funeral
pile, as the perfon deceafed had, or delighted in when alive, that
they might be of the fame ufe, and preferve the fame relation and
connexion with the dead in another life, which they had been accuftomed to in this [u].

But though this was the general way of thinking, it does not
follow that it was univerfal. Another part of the fame Sect might,
and probably did, diffent from the foregoing opinion, and imagine
with Pythagoras, that the fouls of men when they died, lived continually here upon earth, by paffing into new habitations of the
human form; and it muft be allowed that people of this perfuafion
could not with any propriety or confiftency act as the others are faid
to have done; neither indeed need it be fuppofed [w].

This difpute may be foon ended, if we rightly diftinguifh between
thefe two principles, the Immortality, and Tranfmigration; and
confider that one is effential, and infeparably connected with the

The Im-
mortality
and Tranf-
migration,
diftinct
Principles.

[t] " Animalia, fervi, clientes, juftis funeribus " confectis, una cremabantur." Cefar, Lib. VI. cap. xix.
[u] " Omnia quæ vivis cordi fuiffe arbitrantur " in ignem inferunt." Cef. Lib. VI.
[w] " Ab aliis (fays Cefar) poft mortem tranfire " ad alios (fcilicet homines)." (Joan Brantius and others, in Frick. p. 70.) " Hoc difcriminis effe " ftatuit, quod Pythagoras hominum animas

" etiam ad pecudes tranfire vellet, & rurfum e " pecudibus ad homines revocari, Druides vero " tantum ad alios homines tranfmigrare." To the fame purpofe Keyfler, p. 117. " In eo tamen " a Pythagorica abibat (fcil. Druidum Metemp- " fychofis) quod non in pecorum aliorumque " animantium corpora, fed in fola humana iterum " concedere autumabant.

belief

belief of a future ftate, the other indifferent; and therefore, though all might and did hold the former, that is, the immortality, yet that one fect and party might embrace, and another reject, the tranfmigration, as a point in no fenfe fundamental.

The Im-
mortality an
effential
Principle,

The immortality of the foul is the ancient principle; traces of it may be difcovered in all ages and nations; this was the chief doctrine of Pythagoras [x], and not only the opinion of Pythagoras, but, as Plato informs us, of all the great men and poets who had any thing divine in them, as he expreffes it. But upon this great truth, on which the fpirit of all religion depends, learned men grafted their

but varioufly
built upon,
by the Gen-
tiles.

own fancies, disfiguring truth with fables. Some declared the departed fouls to leave all matter behind them at death, and never afterwards to have any communication with it; fome attributed to them a thin etherial body; fome held that they mixed immediately with the Gods, from whom they were defcended, and of whom they were but detached particles; and others paffed them over the river Styx, and either into the Elyzium Fields if good and virtuous, or into a region of grief and torment, if they had been the fouls of wicked men. This laft was the opinion of the Greeks, borrowed

Pythagoras.

from, or at leaft built upon, an Egyptian plan. But Pythagoras brought with him from the Eaft (where it ftill continues among the fucceffors of the ancient Brachmans [y]) a different doctrine, and added it to his favourite principle, the immortality of the foul; it was this, that after death, the foul having left one earthly habitation, entered into another; from one body decayed and turned to clay, betook itfelf to another frefh and lively, and fit to perform all the offices of animal life. According to him, the fouls of the good paffed into wife, valiant, and virtuous men, and the fouls of thofe who were otherwife, paffed into the bafeft of the fpecies, or were even compelled to animate brutes. This was his literal doctrine, but whether literally to be underftood, and fuch changes really believed to happen, or whether (as is altogether as probable) it was only an allegorical refinement, intending nothing more than that the fouls of good men went into a ftate of happinefs, and thofe of the impious into mifery, is what cannot now be determined with any certainty, the Pythagorean difciples being bound to fecrecy, as their firft and perpetual rule and duty; for which reafon it remains very uncertain, as Porphyrius confeffes, what Pythagoras did communicate to his fcholars [z]. But in what fenfe foever this tranfmigration of Pythagoras is to be underftood, evident it is, that the im-

[x] Μαλιϛα μεν τοι γνωριμα παρα πασιν εγενετο πρωτον μεν ως αθανατον ειναι φησι την ψυχην. Porphyr. Vit. Pythag. p. 188. Δε ψυχης διαμονη και αιδοτης εν τοις μαλιϛα των Πυθαγορικων δογματων, γνωριμον εϛι πασιν και διαϐοητον. Porphyr. apud Stobæum. Syntagma Druid. p. 148.

[y] The Banians, and Chinefe.

[z] Ἁ μεν ϫν ελεγε τοις συνϫσι ϫδε εις εχει φρασαι βεϐαιως, και γαρ ϫδε η τυχϫσα ην παρ αϫτοις σιωπη. Porph. Vit. Pythag. Syntagm. Druid. p. 148.

mortality

mortality of the foul is entirely independent of, and diftinct from it; and therefore Ariftotle held the immortality, but rejected the weak and airy fuperftructure of the tranfmigration [a]: and indeed the immortality was generally held, but philofophers wanting the light of revelation, and not being able to prove the truth, either to themfelves or others, by meer reafon, frequently hefitated, feared, doubted, and at laft remained undetermined; but the tranfmigration was now and then admitted, and as often rejected, being a matter of indifference and fpeculation only; nay, thofe who admitted, did not admit it in the fame fenfe: in the fame fect it was held by fome, and difallowed by others; and this is the reafon, as I apprehend, that the Stoicks are faid by fome [b] to have held this doctrine, and by others [c] to have rejected it. And probably it was the fame thing among the Druids. Some adopted this fancy of the Metempfychofis from Pythagoras; others received it not (at leaft in his fenfe) but rambled into other fables and inventions, more refembling the Grecian fuperftition. No people were more ardent in afferting the immortality, than the Druids; in this they all agreed, but in the fabulous tranfitions they were divided, as the Greeks alfo were. Their firmnefs in the great point does them honour, for in this tenet they were more fteady, than the beft of the Greeks and Romans, whofe fluctuating betwixt hope and defpair is too notorious to be denied [d]; whereas the intrepidity of the Druid fyftem is at all times, and in every particular, the fame, and all owing to this great principle: this was the univerfal fpring of action, it animated the foldier to expofe his life in war, the flave to die with his mafter, the wife to follow her dead hufband, the old and decrepid to precipitate themfelves from rocks, or walk freely and without concern up to their own funeral piles; it reconciled the devoted victim to become a facrifice, the creditor to poftpone his debt till the next life, and the man of bufinefs became thereby contented to throw letters for his correfpondents into the funeral fires to be thence remitted into the next world: all thefe particulars were the natural refult of fuch a principle as the immortality. The immortality was therefore a fpring [e], an engine neceffary to actuate fo warlike, and fo fuperftitious a people; but the tranfmigration had no fuch tendency, it was meer theory, a fpeculative point, and might either be admitted, or not, without injuring the publick, or infeebling the manners of the people: all therefore, in general, held the immortality, and thofe who were content with the plain truth, refted there, whilft thofe

Marginal notes: Ariftotle. — The Tranfmigration held by fome and rejected by others of the fame Sect among the Greeks, and, likely, Druids. — The Druids conftant to the Immortality; — but not unanimous in adopting the Tranfmigration.

[a] Lib. I. de Anima, cap. iii. Syntagm. p. 155.
[b] Gregorius, p. 69. Epiphanius, Epift. Syntagm. p. 155.
[c] Sacritius, ibid.

[d] Hieron. Epift. ad Heliodorum.
[e] ——————— " Inde ruendi
" In ferrum mens prona viris, animæque capaces
" Mortis, & ignavum eft redituræ parcere vitæ."
Lucan.

who

who had a mind to pry further into the ftate of fouls departed, and to reafon out of their depth (which is no little pleafure to fpeculative men), either fell into the opinion of Pythagoras, or into other fables full as abfurd : that fome held the tranfmigration is plain from the united voice of the ancients beforementioned, and that more modern ages had not entirely freed themfelves from the fame groundlefs fancies, we have an inftance from the Edda Iflandica [f]. However, this does not appear to have been any general, fundamental principle among the Druids ; for indeed by the traces of the ancient doctrines which ftill remain (faint as they are, yet perceptible) among the northern nations, it is evident that inftead of the tranfmigration of the foul into another body to live again upon earth ; fome [g] held two ftates of the departed fouls entirely inconfiftent with that opinion ; one ftate was before the general conflagration of the world (which they called the Crepufculum Deorum); the other ftate was in a new and more pleafant world, lately emerged from the fea, and rifen out of the flames of the firft ; in this fecond ftate the good were to enjoy all felicity, the bad to fuffer continual punifhment [h]. In fhort, the immortality was the univerfal doctrine of all the Druid fect, and fhines every where, notwithftanding the fabulous veil now and then thrown upon it ; but fome were bold enough to purfue the foul into its future ftate, whither they had but a dim light to guide

Thofe who held the Tranfmi-gration, did not agree in one fenfe of the Doc-trine.

them ; and therefore it is no wonder they fhould fall into miftakes concerning the manner of its exifting, acting, defiring and loathing ; fome adopting the tranfmigration, and fuppofing the new life in this world, as Pythagoras did, and others adopting the tranfmigration, and fuppofing the new life in another world ; and of thofe Lucan fpeaks, *Regit idem Spiritus artus*—*Orbe alio*—fome thinking that the fouls remained meer fhades or ghofts, whilft others imagined that the dead wanted cloaths, armour, horfes, fervants, and the like appurtenances of the prefent life ; and thefe are they of whom Pomp. Mela writes. Now that fome fhould be more fanciful than others, and that the Theorifts fhould differ one from the other, and even hold inconfiftencies in fuch fpeculative points, is not at all furprizing; in all fuch matters people will think freely, and confequently differently, fometimes contradictorily ; and yet this will not at all affect the reputation any people may have defervedly obtained by means of their eftablifhed and fundamental doctrines ; fo, that what was faid of the ancient Thracians [i], is the worft thing that can be faid of the Druids on this head, and is no more than this, that they held fome tenets concerning the ftate of departed

[f] Keyfler, p. 117.
[g] Ibid. p. 118.
[h] Ibid. p. 122.

[i] Mela, Lib. II. cap. ii. " Alii redituras putant " animas obeuntium, afii, etfi non redeant, non " extingui tamen fed ad beatiora tranfire."

fouls,

souls, not very confiftent and uniform. We may conclude then, that all held the immortality, and a future ftate, and that fome held the tranfmigration ; of whom there were alfo two divifions, fome thought with Pythagoras, and others fomewhat differently. Of the firft of thefe fpeaks Cefar, Diod. Sic. & Val. Max. Of the latter, Lucan and Mela.

C H A P. XV.

Of the Druid Doctrines.

IN teaching their Doctrines, the Druids ufed the ancient Oriental manner of Allegory and Mythology, and moft affuredly for this reafon : left their great and fublime truths, by defcending into the familiar reach of every inattentive and unprepared novice, might fall fhort of the veneration they deferved, and become cheap and contemptible [k]; but left any one fhould think that fuch a manner of inculcating truth was too refined for the Druids, or doubts whether it was their cuftom to deal in fuch emblematick reprefentations, I fhall here produce fome inftances, both from hiftory and monuments, to prove it. Lucian found an odd picture of Hercules Ogmius in Gaul, and has tranfmitted to us the defcription of it in the following manner. * Hercules was there exhibited, and known by his ufual ornaments ; but inftead of the gigantick body, and fierce countenance, given him by others, the Druids painted him, to Lucian's great furprize, aged, bald, decrepid : but to his tongue were faftened chains of gold and amber, which drew along a multitude of perfons, whofe ears appeared to be fixed to the other end of thofe chains. " I find, Lucian, fays one of the Druid Philofophers " to him (as he ftood admiring the ftrangenefs of the fight), you are " full of wonder, at what you fee ; we Gauls do not agree with the " Greeks in making Mercury the God of eloquence ; according to " our fyftem this honour is due only to Hercules, becaufe he fo far " furpaffes Mercury in power ; we paint him advanced in age, " becaufe that eloquence exerts not all her moft animated powers " but in the mouths of the aged : the link, and conftant attach- " ment there is betwixt the tongue of the eloquent, and the ears of " the audience, juftifies the reft of the reprefentation : by under- " ftanding the hiftory of Hercules in this fenfe, we neither " difhonour him, nor depart from truth ; for we hold it indif-

Of their Mythology.

---

[k] Καφρασι τυς μεν Γυμνοσοφιςας και Δρυιδας Αινιγματω- δως φιλοσοφησαι, Diog. Laert. l. c. fegm. 6. " Antiquum Gentium vetuftiffimarum morem in tradenda Philofophia atque Theologia ferva-

" bant Druidæ." Frick. de Druid. p. 52.
* In Hercule Gallico, Tom. X. p. 517. Edit. Salmur.

" putably

" putably true, that he fucceeded in all his noble enterprizes, cap-
" tivated every heart, and fubdued every brutal paffion, not by the
" ftrength of his arms (for that was impoffible) but by the powers
" of wifdom, and the fweetnefs of his perfuafion." Thefe were the
fentiments of the Druid, in which there is fo much true fcience, that
it might do honour to any fchool of Athens, or Rome.   The author
of the Rel. des Gaules, has indeed laboured to prove, in feven long
pages, that it is not Hercules but Mercury in this Picture, and that
Lucian miftook one for the other ; but his arguments are too weak
to fet afide the plain teftimony of fo difcerning an author as Lucian,
and of all thofe other authors (as he confeffes himfelf, p. 307.) who
have writ of Ogmius fince Lucian.   The tenour of the whole fable,
and the fpirit of the picture, confirms every thing that Lucian fays :
the truth contained in the reprefentation is more new, pointed, and
ftriking, than if it had been applied to Mercury : the turn given to
the ftrength of Hercules is the leading beauty of the whole, and
what could not but make fo forcible an impreffion upon the elegant
wit of Lucian, that it was impoffible he fhould forget, or
miftake it.

There is another noble evidence (as it appears to me) of their
fymbolical learning in a bafs relieve, not many years fince difcovered
over the door of the temple of Montmorillon in Poictou [1]; the
plate of it is in Montfaucon's fupplement, tom. ii. p. 221. and in
the Religion des Gaules [m], but in neither of them fatisfactorily
explained ; I think therefore it will explain itfelf, and being fet in
the following light will approve itfelf a moft inftructive monument
of antiquity, as well as a plain inftance of the delicacy of the Druid
learning.

The whole is a lively reprefentation of the feveral ftages of life at
which the Druid Difciples were gradually admitted into the myfteries and truths of the Druid fyftem.   The figures are eight in number ; fix men, and two of the other fex : fome have taken them all
for deities ; the two women do indeed feem to be images of TRUTH,
but the men refemble, in no particular, any fort of divinities hitherto
difcovered, and by the ftripes of their garment, and fome other circumftances which will occur in the explanation, they muft be
Druids : they all ftand in rings, or circles round their feet, of which
figure the Druids were extremely fond [n] ; in the fix men a great
difparity of age is perceivable ; they are divided into two claffes,
each confifting of three perfonages, three on the right are all aged
and bearded, the other groupe of men are all young and beardlefs ;

[1] See Plate IV. p. 53.   [n] See Lib. III. cap. vii.
[m] Vol. I. p. 144. in Frickius, p. 49.

there

there is a manifest gradation of age in both groups; that man next the right-hand woman is very aged and venerable; the next, in front to the eye, is not so old, and the third of this party is somewhat younger still, but barbate, and seemingly of a middle age. In the juvenile triumvirate, there are three stages of youth, each of which has its proper garb. The first (No. 1.), and nearest to the aged group, has a plain Priest's vestment, bound by a surcingle, and distinguished only by the colour, and shape (being without any ornaments), from that of the laity. The next (No. 2.) fronts the eye, and has a sash reaching from the right shoulder cross the body to the bottom of the garment. The third figure (No. 3.) looking towards the left-hand woman, has a broad stream or facing (like a scarf crossed with horizontal stripes), reaching round his neck, and to the bottom of his cloathing, and the garment so edged, is loose, and without a surcingle: it is observable that this last figure, which seems the oldest, most manly, and of most distinction among the youths, looks towards the left-hand woman (No. 7); and that the oldest in the senile cluster looks towards the woman on the right-hand (No. 8.). Such are the figures, habits, and stations, and by them, I think, are plainly pointed out to us, the six different classes through which the Druids were to pass, before they arrived at the summit of their dignity among their brethren, and of their authority in all sacred things. That woman (No. 7.) to whom the youths turn, is cloathed from head to foot[o]. Her hair is plaited in two ringlets which grace each side of her neck; she has shoes on her feet, and gloves on her hands, to shew that knowledge and truth are veiled from youthful eyes, that mysteries are cloathed, and wrapt up in allegory, symbol, and significant rites: at first the young disciples are not permitted to look towards the real truth, but as they grow elder are proportionably brought nearer and nearer unto, and taught the divine secrets, though still enshrined in figure and mythology; but when age has ripened the judgment, and disciplined the passions, the Philosopher is advanced into the assembly of the Seniles. This (N°. 4.) is the first of the aged cluster of Druids, who, though so far advanced, preserves his proper distance, has no ensign of dignity, no distinction, but that of place, and with a reverential awe keeps his face averted from the Goddess (No. 8.). In the next stage of life the Druid (No. 5.) fronts us; he has a large sash depending from his right shoulder cross the body, and the hinder part meets the fore part at the waiste. He is one degree more than the last-mentioned turned towards the female statue on the right-hand: the last figure (No. 6.) is very aged; he turns his face towards the Goddess, (No. 8.)

---

[o] " Ænigmatibus faciem velarent veritati, acsi vetuisset Pudor nudam ostendere populo." Fr. de Druid. 52.

E e   which

which is naked, to fhew, that truth unveils all her myfteries to thofe who by paffing through the feveral ftages of their difcipline, were enlightened, and prepared to receive truth in her moft undifguifed, fimple and natural appearances. Truth, therefore, is here uncovered, her hair waves naturally down her fhoulders, nothing favours of conftraint or art; two ferpents (creatures among all nations the emblems of wifdom) twined round her legs and body, are embraced by both her hands, to fhew the harmony, connexion, and infeparable union betwixt Wifdom and Truth: the heads of both thefe ferpents are applied to the breaft of the Goddefs, to fhew that Wifdom draws all her fupport from Truth; they are clafped faft, and directed to the feat of nourifhment, to fhew that Truth readily yields her choiceft treafures, her moft amiable beauties, to the fearches of the wife and ftudious. The Druids are divided into two groups, as was obferved before, and each group ftands on a femicircular plan, two being in profile, and one in front: Truth is at each end of the bafs-relieve, fignifying, that fhe is to be equally the aim and purfuit of young and old; one group therefore is moving round towards the one fymbol, and the other towards the other fymbol; the young men turn towards the object of their ftudies, bending their courfe from right to left; on the other hand the old men proceed from left to right, ftill approaching to a more direct and intimate view of Truth and Nature.

Cernunnos.   Cernunnos, a deity of the Gauls, lately difcovered at Paris P, is another evidence, how much the Druids were addicted to fymbolical reprefentations; this God is found defcribed in ftone, in the following fingular manner. The face human; old; bearded; of a downcaft thoughtful eye; ears erect, large, and liftening; a ftag's horn, branched, proceeding from each temple; on each horn hangs a ring, or fmall circular fillett, and on the upper margin of the ftone is written C.E.R.N.V.N.N.O.S*. Perhaps the Druids, by uniting the moft confpicuous parts of different animals in one image, might intend to exhibit the feveral attributes of the Supreme Deity, naturally enough to be deduced from thefe emblems; but what ftrikes me more, their defign, I apprehend, was to reprefent the fubordinate divinity, Juftice; not a blind female, as others fancied; but manly, feeing, hearing, and thinking; not unaptly fignifying, that the feat of Power and Princely Rule (of which the horn is an ufual fymbol †) fhould always have its ears open to found counfels, and to both parties, equitably exerting its judicial authority under the checks of fedate age, and deep reflexion. But although

---

P (Viz. A. D. 1711.) See Montfaucon, Tom. II. p. 426. whence the Buft in page 107.

* A name derived from the Horns Hebr. קרן, Kern. a horn; Wallicè, Cornub. & Armor. Corn, & Kern.

† In that fublime defcription of the true Deity given us by Habakkuk, ch. iii. iv. God is faid to have " had horns coming out of his head, and " there was the hiding of his power." viz. *under this fymbol lay couched, and only myftically expreffed, the omnipotence of God.*

the

the learned may not agree in the meaning of a composition seemingly so odd and unnatural; yet it must be allowed by all, that the figure is truely hieroglyphical, and was made so in order to communicate some important piece of knowledge, though what, may be doubtful. Thus much may suffice to prove that the Druids conveyed their tenets by symbols; painting, and engraving their doctrines; and this doubtless they were the more inclined to do, forasmuch as they were prohibited, by a fundamental law, from communicating their erudition in any kind of writing.

PLVI. *p.107.*

from Montfaucon

CHAP. XVI.

Of the Druid Deities and Idols.

ORIGEN on Ezek. iv.[q] says that the Druids taught the Britans to believe that there was but one God; but the meaning of this place in Origen is much disputed; however, some [r] will have it that they acknowledged but one God; yet Abp. Usher [s] thinks otherwise; and indeed Cesar is so express, as well as Pliny, as to their superiour and inferiour Gods, that their Polytheism and Idolatry cannot well be disputed. Mercury was their chief deity, as Cesar informs us, and many images of him they had among them: they esteemed him the inventor of arts, the tutelary God of all travellers and highways, and the sovereign Lord in all matters of gain and merchandize. So far they agreed with the Greeks, who called him Ενοδιος, or Vialis, and Κερδω©-, for the same reasons.

After Mercury they worshiped Apollo [t], whom they called Balenus, and sometimes Belis; by him they meant the Sun, as other nations did. Then Mars, whom they called Hesus [u], and Teutates; then Jupiter, called also Taranys, i. e. the thunderer; and next, Minerva. Their opinion of these Gods was much the same as that of other nations; that is, that Apollo cured diseases, that Minerva taught all works of ingenuity and handycraft; that Jupiter reigned in heaven, and that Mars presided in matters of war. That the Druids, under the names of the sun, the moon, and fire, worshiped the Holy

[q] See Camden's Britannia, LXXXIV. General Descr. Gibson's Ed.
[r] Obad. Walk. Camb. CXVII. Frickius, p. 60.
[s] Prim. Lib. I. cap. i.

[t] Cesar, ibid.
[u] "Æs, vel Æsus, hoc est Deus κατ εξοχην dictus" Keysler, p. 139.

Trinity,

Trinity, was a groundlefs fancy of Cluver, and fome other Germans [w], more zealous for the honour of the Druids, than for the intereft of truth ; but to the great commendation of this fect, it muft be allowed that they acknowledged a Providence [x].

Befides their celeftial Gods, they had their idols, and fymbolical reprefentations of their divinities. A cube was the fymbol of Mercury, who, as the meffenger of the Gods was efteemed the index or emblem of *Truth* always like to itfelf, however you turn it ; as it is with a cube. The Oak, talleft and faireft of the wood, was the fymbol of Jupiter [y].

The manner in which the principal tree in the grove was confe-crated, and ordained to be the fymbol of Jupiter, was as follows [z]. The Druids, with the general confent of the whole Order, and all the neighbourhood, pitched upon the moft beautiful tree, cut off all its fide branches, and then joined two of them to the higheft part of the trunk, fo that they extended themfelves on either fide like the arms of a man, making in the whole the fhape of a crofs ; " Simulacraque mœfta Deorum——Arte carent, cæfifque extant im-" mania Truncis [a]." Above the infertions of thefe branches, and below, they infcribed in the bark of the tree the word Thau, by which they meant God [b]. On the right arm was infcribed Hefus, on the left Belenus, and on the middle of the trunk Tharamis [c].

Under this tree they performed their moft facred rites ; without the very leaves of the Oak firft ftrewed on the altar, no facrifices could be regularly offered ; and to this more than ufual veneration for the Oak, was doubtlefs in a great meafure owing that fubordinate degree of adoration, which they paid to the Oak-mifletoe, thinking it fent from Jupiter, as a kind of inferiour deity [d]. The Druids are alfo faid to have erected in one of their moft retired places of worfhip, a ftatue of Ifis [e]. Of what form this ftatue was, is not faid ; but, if this cuftom really exifted among the ancient Druids, it could not be of the human fhape, for it was contrary to the principles of the Celtic Religion to reprefent any of their Gods by the human figure,

[w] Frick. p. 60.

[x] Λεγεσι δε (viz. Celtæ) και ειναι Θεας, και προνοειν ημων, και προσημαινειν τα μελλονία. Tacitus and Pliny alfo fay the fame thing. Frick. p. 63.

[y] Κελτοι σεβεσι μεν Δια, αγαλμα δε Διὸ· Κελτικον υψηλη Δρυς. Maxim. Tyr. Serm. 38. Camd. xix. The Jews were ftrongly infected with the fame idola-trous veneration for the Oak in the time of Ifaiah. (chap. i. ver. 29.) " They fhall be afhamed of the " Oaks which ye have defired, and ye fhall be " confounded for the gardens that ye have chofen."

[z] Cromer. Lib. xv. Sched. p. 346.

[a] Lucan, Lib. III.

[b] Gr. Θεος, Gal. Dieu. Cornub. Deu. Ir. Dia. Wallicè Duw.

[c] Forfitan pro Taranys. To this ancient way of infcribing names on facred fymbols, St. John may feem to allude, Rev. iii. 12. " Him that over-" cometh I will make a Pillar in the Temple of " my God, and I will write upon him the Name " of my God, and I will write upon him my " new Name ;" and, ibid. xiii. 1. " I faw a Beaft " rife up out of the fea, having feven Heads, and " upon his Heads the Names of Blafphemy, and " upon her Forehead was a Name written —— " Myftery——Babylon the Great." Ib. xvii. 3.

[d] Alex. ab Alex. Vol. II. p. 744.

[e] Eli Sched. p. 237. fed unde non conftat.

juftly

juftly conceiving, according to ancient tradition, that the Divine Power was to be worfhiped, but not feen [f].

Whether the Druids admitted the ferpent into the number of their deities, is rather uncertain, than improbable. The Babylonians, Egyptians, Romans, Jews, and the Perfians alfo, to whofe cuftoms the Druid Ritual is near a-kin, moft certainly paid their adorations to this creature; and if it fhould be allowed that the Druids (as the Guenebald-infcription fuggefts) had groves confecrated to Mithras, a God whofe common fymbol was a ferpent; or fecondly, that they made their temples in a ferpentine form, as the learned Dr. Stukeley in his Abury fuppofed; it will then be paft all doubt, that the Druids worfhiped ferpents; but there are great difficulties attending both thefe fuppofitions [g]: as to the firft, the infcription given us by Guenebald, is ftrongly fufpected to be forged; as is alfo another infcription, in which Mithras is mentioned, viz. Deo-Invicto—MITHR—Secundinus—Dat [h]; and, as to the fecond, notwith-ftanding what is advanced in favour of Dracontia, or ferpentine Temples, it is not altogether clear that the Druids conftructed their Temples on a ferpentine plain. However, from the great value which the Druids placed upon the Anguinum [*], to which they attri-buted fuch wonderful efficacy; it may be conjectured, that thofe muft have had fome veneration for the Serpent, who had confeffedly fuch a regard for, and attributed fuch miracles to, its fuppofititious production. It may alfo be obferved, in favour of the learned Doctor above-mentioned, that there is a mound thrown up on one fide of Karnbrê hill [i] (a place remarkable for Druid monuments of every kind), in a ferpentine form, and in the center of its voluta there are two tall ftones erect ftanding by each other; by which work one would imagine, that if the Druids intended it not as a fymbol of fomething divine (which is not unlikely), yet that a work of fo uncommon an appearance muft have been fome way or other fub-fervient to their fuperftition: this, I fay, one may conjecture; but indeed, whether they worfhiped Serpents, or Mithras, or had fer-pentine Temples, are points much too doubtful, and monuments too few, imperfect, and indecifive, alledged in order to fupport them, for us to affirm or conclude any thing pofitive concerning them.

Among the Gods of the ancient Gauls, and therefore of the Druids, fome reckon the Bull: by this God made of brafs, the Cimbri, Teutones, and Ambrones, fwore to obferve the articles of capitulation granted to the Romans, who defended the Adige againft them: after their defeat, Catulus ordered this Bull to be carried to

---

[f] " Secretum illud quod fola reverentia " vident." Tacit. de M. G. " Non vulgatis " Sacrata figuris — Numina fic metuunt." Lucan, Lib. iii.

[g] See Sepul. of Chyndonax Reveillê, Guenebald.
[h] Rel. de Gaul. Vol. I. p. 418.
[* See Chap. XXI.]
[i] See Map of Karnbr. Plate VII.

F f   his

his own house, there to remain as the most glorious monument of his victory[k]: this God is ranked with Jupiter, Esus, and Vulcan[l], being called Tarvos Trigaranus, from three Cranes perching, one on his head, one on the middle of his back, and the third on his hinder parts[m].

Gildas says that the Druids worshiped mountains, and rivers. Nor unlikely; but that they worshiped rocks, stones, and fountains, and imagined them inhabited and actuated by divine intelligences of a lower rank, is still more evident, and may be plainly inferred, not only from their stone monuments (as we shall see more particularly in the following sheets), but from the prohibitions of several Gallick councils[n]. These inferiour deities the Cornish call Spriggian, or Spirits; they answer to the Genii, and Fairies of the ancients; and of these the vulgar in Cornwall still discourse as of real beings, attribute to them large powers to rule the weather, and to discover hidden treasures, and pay them a kind of veneration.

C H A P. XVII.

Of the Druid Places of Worship.

Groves.

IT was essential to the Druid worship, that it should be performed in a grove[o]; there the Druids lived[p], especially during their ministration in sacred things.—*Nemora alta remotis*—*Incolitis Lucis*—Lucan. Lib. I. de Druid. That we find their places of worship where no groves are at present, is owing to the alterations of time, and no contradiction to the indispensable necessity of groves to the Druid worship. Even Stonhenge itself, where there are no traces to shew that ever a tree grew, stood formerly in a grove according to tradition[q]. Nor would any grove serve the turn, but it was to be a grove of Oaks, of the tallest size, and most venerable antiquity, if to be procured. This custom was owing to the same motive that all ancient idolatrous nations had for chusing such gloomy places to perform their religious rites in; namely, that the shades and solitude might give an air of mystery and devotion to

[k] Plutar. in Mario. Rel. de Gaul. Vol. I. p. 72.

[l] In the square Stone, No. 2. found in Paris Cathedral in the Year 1711, where it has the fourth front of that Stone allotted it.

[m] See Montfaucon, Tom. II. p. 424.

[n] " Cultores Idolorum, Veneratores Lapidum, " accensores facularum, & excolentes sacra Fon- " tium vel Arborum, admonemus ut agnoscant " quod ipsi se spontaneæ morti subjiciunt qui " Diabolo sacrificare videntur." Concil. Turon. A. D. 567. Baluz. Tom. VI. 1234.

[o] El. Sched. in Dedicat. & p. 345.

[p] Cesar Lib. VI. " Consident in Luco conse- " crato" says Casaubon; not in Loco as in the vulgar Edition. Hoffman de Druid.

[q] " Si fides accolis habenda, qui tractum syl- " vestrem in tota illa planitie usque ad Ambres- " buriam fuisse perhibent." Keysler, p. 57. " Nec enim sacra fuit ædes sine Luco, ut auctor " est Callimachus, teste Guenebaldo." Frick. p. 134, ex Petr. Lescalop.

their

their religious fervice, incline the worſhipers to believe the deity was really there, and raiſe a ſullen ſuperſtitious dread of their imaginary divinities.

> *Stat vetus, & multos incidua ſylva per annos,*
> *Credibile eſt illi Numen adeſſe loco.* Ovid Am. Lib. III. El. i.

" If you find, ſays Seneca (Ep. LXI.), a grove thick ſet with " antient Oaks, that have ſhot away up to a vaſt height, the tallneſs " of the wood, the retirement of the place, and the pleaſantneſs of " the ſhade, immediately makes you think it the habitation of ſome " God." And, indeed, without this ſolemn ſcene of ſhade and ſilence, the mind could not be diſpoſed to embrace ſo readily all the fabulous relations of their falſe Gods, much leſs to comply with all the abſurd and deteſtable rites of their idolatrous worſhip. " They " ſacrifice upon the tops of the mountains, and burn incenſe upon " the hills, under oaks, and poplars, and elms ; becauſe the ſhadow " thereof is good." Hoſea IV. 13. Horace, full of that tranſport, which dignifies, and becomes the poet (but is inſufferable madneſs in the Prieſt), having invoked Calliope, and intreated her to deſcend from heaven, fancies her alighted in ſome ſacred grove.

> *Auditis ? an me ludit amabilis*
> *Inſania? Audire, & videor pios*
> > *Errare per lucos, amœnæ*
> > > *Quos & aquæ ſubeunt & auræ.* Lib. III. Od. iv.

Groves being reckoned ſo eſſential to the Druid worſhip, have made ſome think that the woods were their only Temples, and that they had no particular places conſecrated to the more ſolemn rites of Religion, which, as it appears to me to be a great miſtake, I ſhall here examine, and conſider the arguments by which they would ſupport it.

Keyſler [r] thinks the Druids had no temples, founding his opi- *Temples.* nion upon theſe words of Tacitus (Ann. XIV. Cap. xxx.), where he gives an account of the conqueſt of Angleſea : " Præſidium " poſthac impoſitum victis, exciſique Luci ſævis ſuperſtitionibus " ſacri." " Now if there were any Temples, ſays Keyſler, why were " the groves only to be felled, when it was the intention of Sueto- " nius Paulinus, entirely to eradicate all places of that barbarous " Religion [s] ?" If this learned author means that the Druids had no walled or covered Temples, he is right in the general ſuppo- ſition ; but if he denies their having Temples of any ſort, he is very deficient in his proof ; for, though the groves here mentioned were ſacred, there might be one part more ſacred than another,

---

[r] Antiqu. Septent. p. 63.   [s] Keyſler, ibid.

and

and there might be one or more Temples inclosed in this grove (as we shall see hereafter that there really were in the grove at Karnbrê in Cornwall), for any thing that Tacitus says to the contrary; neither does Tacitus say that Suetonius Paulinus cut down the groves, in order to destroy all remembrance of the barbarous religion of the Druids; it is more likely that he thought the groves so many impediments of victory, and destroyed them because they might no longer harbour the rebellious Britans, and their auxiliaries, " Monam Insulam, ut vires rebellibus ministrantem, ag- " gressus" (viz. Suet. Paul. in Tacit.) " Monam Insulam incolis " validam, & receptaculum perfugarum aggredi parat; " (Ibid. Ann. Lib. XIV.) but supposing that Suetonius Paulinus destroyed their groves out of a just abhorrence of the barbarities there committed; yet he might not think it worth his while to throw down their Temples, which consisting only of Stones erected in a circular manner, were much below the indignation of a victorious Roman. This observation of Keysler therefore is very inconclusive. On the other hand there are very strong testimonies, as well from history as monuments, that the Druids had temples, as well as groves.   On occasion of the massacre of the Romans by Boadicea, there were great rejoicings in the British Temples, but chiefly in the wood consecrated to Andate—Dion. in Nerone, Rel. des Gaules, Vol. I. p. 14.   Therefore it is plain that Temples and Woods were two distinct things. Suetonius says of Cesar, " In Gallia, Fana Tem- " plaque Deûm donis referta expilavit; " and Keysler owns, that Tacitus attributes Temples to the Germans (ibid. p. 80.) " Her- " tham Deam, secreta Religione ablutam, Templo fuisse redditam." Lib. de M. G. Tacit. & Annal. Lib. I.   " Tanfanæ Templum " memorat (scil. Tacitus) a Romanis solo æquatum."   To say that " the first Temple means nothing more than a grove, as appears " from all that is said of Hertha by Tacitus," is too much to be granted him; for in the second instance the Temple of Tanfana is particularly named; here therefore recourse must be had to a different reason, and it is alledged that " the Germans borrowed the " manner of erecting this Temple from the neighbouring Romans." The truth is, that all nations professing some, though the false Religion, had sacrifices, and also idols of some kind or other.   For sacrifices they must have had altars, as well as places for their idols; and where these altars were, there generally were the idols, and that place was accounted more holy than the rest, and was separated and distinguished, either simply, and most anciently by mounds, or stones, or more neatly and magnificently by walls and roofs, according to the principles and customs of the nation they belonged to;   and in both cases those places so separated, and distinguished,

may

may with equal juſtice be called Temples; and from Snorro Sturleſon[t], it plainly appears that the antient northern nations (who were a branch of the Celts, and much leſs cultivated than where the Druids were eſtabliſhed) had Temples or fanes. " *Ignis fieri in me-* " *dia Templi area debebat. Vetus tum obtinuerat conſuetudo circa* " *Victimarum mactationes ut ad Fanum ipſum Incolæ convenirent* " *omnes*," ibid. p. 330. " *Stabant autem* (viz. *Majores ſui, ut* " p. 349.) *cum compotationes ſacræ per agerentur circa ignem in medio* " *Templi accenſum.*" ibid. p. 355.

So far were the ancients from having no Temples, that they held one Temple more ſacred than another. " *Spolia Corporis, caputque* " *Ducis præciſum Boii ovantes Templo quod Sanctiſſimum eſt apud eos* " *intulere—poculumque idem Sacerdoti eſſet, ac Templi Antiſtibus*[u]. " *Fridlevus Olai filii fortunam exploraturus nuncupatis ſolenniter* " *votis Deorum ædes precabundus accedit, ubi introſpecto Sacello,* " *ternas ſedes, totidem Nymphis occupari cognoſcit*[w]." This proves Temples among the northern nations ſufficiently, and that caves might be their Temples (as they were, in the Mithraic myſteries), will only prove the manner in which they conſtructed their Temples, and can never prove that they had none.

Mr. Martin[x] endeavours to prove that at Thoulouſe the Gauls had no other Temple than a ſacred lake; but Strabo (as quoted there) ſays only " that the Gauls conſecrated their gold in lakes (by dipping it, perhaps, in lakes before dedicated to ſome particular deity, and incloſing, or being incloſed in, ſome parts of their ſacred woods) and immediately ſubjoins, " that there was a Temple at Thoulouſe " very famous, and immenſely rich in treaſures." Now it is poſſible that this Temple might be ſurrounded by a lake which made it very difficult to get at the treaſure; and if this lake was conſecrated, made it ſtill more heinous to pillage it than otherwiſe it would have been; for they reckoned theſe lakes the ſafeſt aſylum, and repoſitory for their treaſure[y]; but that theſe lakes were their Temples, is quite new, and not tenable; and that they caſt their treaſures into ſuch lakes, there to remain for ever as a dedication, is altogether improbable; nor does Juſtin (whom he quotes) give the leaſt countenance to ſuch a ſuppoſition, but only ſays, that " the Gauls, return- " ing to Thoulouſe, were adviſed by the Prieſts of their own country, " that they ſhould never be freed from the peſtilential diſtemper " then raging amongſt them, till they ſhould throw the gold and " ſilver, got by war and ſacrilege, into the lake of Thoulouſe." It

[t] Keyſler, p. 327.
[u] Liv. Lib. XXIII. cap. xxiv. N. B. The Boii were a People of Gallia Celtica.
[w] Sax. Grammat. Lib. III. Keyſler, p. 396.
[x] Rel. des Gaules, Vol. I. p. 114.
[y] Μαλιϛα δ' αυτοις αι Λιμναι την Αϲυλιαν παρειχον. Strab. ibid.

G g

does

does not appear but any other lake would have done as well; for it is not said *confecrarent*, that they fhould dedicate this gold as to a deity, but *mergerent*, that they fhould drown it, that is, rid themfelves for ever of fuch an accurfed booty [z], in order to propitiate the offended deities: that there was no other Temple at Thouloufe but this lake, is not credible: it is true, the Gauls are faid to have killed, burnt in wicker images, and fhot to death with arrows their human victims, all in their temples; and it muft be owned that thefe cruelties could not be properly or fafely exercifed in fuch covered Temples as the Greeks and Romans had; but does it therefore follow that they (the Gauls) had no Temples at all [a]? far from it. Again; many perfons reforted to a lake (at the foot of the Gevaudan mountain) confecrated to the moon, under the name of Helanus, and thither caft in, fome, the human habits, linen, cloth, and entire fleeces; others caft in cheefe, wax, bread, and other things, every one according to his ability; then facrificed animals, and feafted for three days, p. ibid. 128. I am perfuaded that there is no one, who will not eafily perceive that thefe offerings were made to the Manes of departed friends, fuppofed after death to ftand in need both of food and raiment [*], which was the reafon that their countrymen fent them yearly a frefh fupply, and in a folemn manner attended by facrifice and feaftings. This inftance, therefore, may prove lakes confecrated, and holy, but cannot prove them either to have been divinities, or Temples, as this author contends. It is plain therefore from all the ancients, that the Gauls, and even the Celts, had Temples, as appears by what has been obferved above from Dion Caffius, Livy, Tacitus, and fome modern authors alfo; to which may be added, what Strabo fays of Sena, that the Prieftefes there had a covered Temple, the old covering of which was annually and folemnly taken away, and a new covering immediately laid on it [b].

The learned Dr. Stukeley diftinguifhes the Druid Temples into three claffes [†]: firft, the Rounds or Circles fimply called Temples. Secondly, thofe circles which have the form of a fnake annexed (as that of Abury) which he calls ferpentine Temples, or Dracontia. Thirdly, thofe circles which have the form of wings annexed, by him ftiled Alate, or winged Temples; thefe are all the different kinds which he knows [‡]. Thofe of the firft fort are very numerous in this ifland, and its dependencies, and will be particularly enquired into in book III.; of the other forts I have not met with any; I have indeed feen the famous monument which this author mentions, p. ib. 97. as one of the Alate Temples. It is

[z] Juftin, Lib. XXXII. cap. iii.   [b] See p. 87.
[a] Rel de G. Vol. I. p. 115, 121.   [†] Abury, p. 9.
[*] See before, Chap. XIV.   [‡] Ibid. p. 8.

vulgarly

vulgarly called the Hurlers, in Cornwall, but it confifts only of three circles of ftones-erect, whofe centers are in a ftrait line, and confequently muft belong to the firft clafs.

In placing their Temples Dr. Stukely in his Abury, conjectures " that the Druids ufed a compafs or Magnetick needle, and finds the " works at Stonehenge placed at the variation of between fix and " feven degrees to the Eaft of the North : he finds alfo the variation " at Abury to be about ten degrees the fame way ;" and, from thefe different variations, proceeds to determine the different ages in which thefe two celebrated works were erected; a method of calculation very ingenious, and deferving the higheft praife, provided that this variation of the needle made a conftant uniform progrefs, increafing by equal fpaces in equal portions of time. But, left we fhould attribute more knowledge to the Druids than is their due, this may be well doubted of : it muft be allowed that the ancients knew the attractive power of the Magnet; but whether they ufed, or knew the Polar virtue may be very well queftioned, fince no traces appear of any fuch knowledge among them, or indeed among the moderns till about 500 years fince[c]. The variation of the Magnetick needle from the pole is ftill a later difcovery, not 300 years old ; and although the ancients, by obferving the courfe of the heavenly bodies, might project with great exactnefs a meridian line, (which when croffed at right angles would confequently direct them to the four cardinal points of the heavens) and might regard thofe principal points in placing their buildings; yet, when we find thofe buildings not placed exactly with refpect to thefe points, I apprehend that we fhould attribute this to a miftake, and want of accuracy in aftronomical projections, which, like many Artifts of the moderns (in placing their churches), they did not always carefully attend to, though they had all poffible means of fuch exactnefs within their reach ; this I fhould think a plain and obvious reafon for their buildings deviating from the cardinal points, rather than having recourfe to a variation which they were utterly unacquainted withal ; in the laft place, out of regard to truth, I muft obferve, that there is no fixing of dates from fuch an inconftant and fluctuating index, as the declination of the Needle, which is not only different in different places. but varies alfo at different times in one and the fame place.

Let us haften to more fatisfactory enquiries, and to confider thofe circumftances relating to their places of worfhip which are not liable to fuch difputes.

[c] The Chinefe boaft of this knowledge 1100 years before Chrift ; but the Learned juftly reject the vain Pretences of this people, claiming every Invention, and the remoteft Antiquity upon every occafion.

It

It was a general custom to chuse for their places of worship Woods which stood on the tops of hills, and mountains, as more becoming the dignity and sublime offices of their devotions, and of nearer neighbourhood (as they imagined) to the habitation of their Gods. Thus the devotions and sacrifices of Balaam among the Moabites, and the idolatrous rites of the Canaanites, and the ancient Gentiles in general, were performed in their high places.

The wood was inclosed, sometimes with a fence of pallisades [d], and sometimes the hill was surrounded at bottom by a mound or vallum to keep off the profane, and prevent all abrupt, and rude intrusion upon their mysteries. This mound was also of civil, as well as sacred use, for in these groves were the common publick repositories or treasuries of spoils taken in war. " In many of their cities, " (says Cesar, Lib. VI.) one may see great heaps of such booty laid " up in their places of worship; and it seldom happens that any " one is so impious as to conceal the booty he has made, or to take " it away when it has been once brought into the treasury, that " crime being punished with the utmost severity." The trees of this grove were all consecrated by sprinkling them with the blood of human victims. " *Omnis & humanis lustrata cruoribus Arbos* [*]." Besides the holy Oaks of this grove (which were esteemed by the Druids as much as those oracular ones of Dodona by the Greeks) within the same bounds were inclosed every thing required for performing the several offices of their Religion; circles marked out, and allotted for particular persons, or classes, to officiate in; symbols or memorials of their deities [e]; wells were sometimes inclosed within the sacred limits. Caves for instruction of youth; altars for great and small sacrifices; seats or tribunals of Justice; Cairnes (or Karns) for their holy fires; and on a large hill (which has all these sacred monuments) I find a great number of hollow basons or troughs sunk in the surface of large rocks, which must therefore be looked upon, as having been some way or other subservient to the purposes of the same superstition.

To give the better idea of a place of Druid Worship, it may not be amiss to particularize the several devotional monuments (in the order they offered themselves) upon Karnbrê-hill [f], which has all the evidences that can be desired of having been appropriated to the use of the British Religion.

---

[d] " Prohibetur accessus Lucorum & Fontium " quos autumant pollui Christianorum accessu. " idem scribit Sclavos Quercus coluisse quas am- " biverit Atrium & sepes accuratior ex lignis " constructa." Not. in Tacit. de M. G.
[*] Lucan, ibid.
[e] " Neque illud etiam prætereundum, majores " nostros semper in usu habuisse, ut Aris & Locis·

" sacris eas regiones seligerent quæ Puteum aut " fontem vivum exhiberent abluendis victimis & " auspiciis inde capiendis. Puteus ille septentri- " onalibus populis Blotkelda vel Blotabrum dictus " erat a voce Blot sacrificium cruentum notante." Keysler, p. 47.
[f] Illogan Parish, Cornwall.

This

This Hill is high, and its area on the top is thick set with karns, Karnbrê or groupes of rocks; the spaces between and below were, in the Hill, a Druid memory of the last generation, filled with a grove of Oaks; now Worship, there are no trees, but the places where those trees were charked (or described. burnt into charcoal), are still to be seen.

——————— " Consecrated hills
" Once girt with spreading Oaks, mysterious rows
" Of rude enormous Obelisks that rise
" Orb within Orb, stupenduous monuments
" Of artless Architecture, such as now
" Oftimes amaze the wand'ring traveller
" By the pale Moon discern'd on Sarum's plain ! g"

On a Karn h at the western end (A) i there are artificial basons cut Rock-in the uppermost rocks. On the second groupe (B) there are five of basons. the same kind, two of which have plain and distinct lips or mouths, to discharge whatever was intended to be contained in these vessels; their figure circular, sometimes oblong, and seemingly without any aim at a regular figure: they were all of different dimensions, from three to one foot diameter; from one foot to six inches deep.

After seeing several other basons on the tops of the rocks, as we advanced towards the East, we found a most curious orbicular flat stone (such as in Cornwall are called Quoits from their figure which has pretty much of the Discus form) which was wantonly thrown down from the top of a monstrous rock (F), at the foot of which it now lies. On the surface of this Quoit was an exact circular bason, three foot diameter, one foot deep, and round the edges many little and shallow basons communicating with the great one. Of these basons a particular account will be given in the following book; I will only remark here, that the great difficulty of ascent to the vast rock from whence this Quoit was thrown down, will prevent us from reckoning the rock among the Druid Altars; I rather imagine that it might serve for one of the Gorseddau, or places of elevation, Gorseddau. from whence they used to pronounce their decrees. In some places indeed, these Gorseddau were made of earth, but it was plainly unnecessary to raise hillocks of earth, where so many stately rocks might contribute full as well, to give proper dignity to the seat of judgment; and where rocks were so plenty, it is not to be doubted but decrees and oracles were pronounced from the tops of them k.

g Mr. West's Instit. of the Garter.
h Karn is Cornish for a Ledge or heap of Rocks.

i See the Map of Karnbrê, Plate VII.
k The Delphian Oracle gave forth its answers from a Rock; thus in Sophocles (Oedipus Tyran-

H h   Having

The holy
boundary.

Having attained the fummit of the hill, we croffed fome ftone-heaps at A L.   Thefe heaps are the ruins of a ftone wall which enclofed an area of about an acre of ground.   The enclofure (AM) is called the old Caftle, and appears to have been a fortification, but taken out of the holy ground, as by the map annexed will foon be difcerned from the fhape of the whole plan; and by reafon alfo that there is a mound on the fouth (AK) without any ditch on the outfide, and finking far below the ridge of the hill, which are two proper-ties that no man who fortifies will give to his work.   The fence here was not therefore originally defigned for a military work ; and the many remaining evidences of this hill's being dedicated to the fervice of Religion, makes it plain, that the defign of this low defencelefs mound was to feparate the facred groves from common ufe, to pro-hibit not only cattle, but all perfons profane, and before examination, and on all other but holy days, and on holy purpofes, from entering upon this confecrated ground.   There is a mound of this kind round the ftone circles at Abury [1].   The fame caution was obferved (though for much better reafons) at Mount Sinai.   " Thou fhalt fet " bounds unto the people round about, faying, Take heed unto " yourfelves that ye go not up into the Mount, or touch the border " of it; whofoever toucheth the Mount fhall furely be put to death. " Set bounds unto the Mount, and fanctify it."   Exod. xix. 12. The fame cuftom the Druids certainly ufed ; as Lucan fays, fpeak-ing of their place of worfhip, Lib. III. ver. 400.   *Non illum cu'tu populi propiore frequentant — Sed ceffére Diis.*

Holy Cir-
cles.

There are many bafons on the rocks here at (G), but the moft remarkable I have yet met with any where is at (L), on a large Quoit, which, with the ledge on which it lies, and its bafons, may be feen in the map at (AF), but will hereafter be more at large defcribed. At (I) is the firft circle we meet with, and the others are traced at (N O P Q R S), and figures 1, 2, 3, 4, 5, 6, 8; from 7 to 12 paces (generally) in diameter, the dimenfions to be meafured by the fcale of chains annexed to the map ; they are edged, fome with a mound of earth, others with ftones, forming a kind of walled en-trance from the Eaft ; but the long ftones which formerly dignified thefe circles feem to have been taken away to build the walls of the old Caftle, or rather by the Danes to add to them, for I obferve that the Quoits are fquared, and therefore the fortification feems originally

Stones-erect British, fee Book IV. ch. viii. Paffing from thefe rounds to the South-

---

nus p. 136.), Τις; Οσιν' α Θεσπιεπεια Δελφις ειπε πειρα.
Of thefe feats of Judgement the Reader will find two of different conftruction, one as we advance in this Map of Karnbrê (Z), the Elevation of it AH (of which fort I have met with feveral, efpe-cially in the Scilly Iflands), and the other at Karn Bofcawen in Burien, both which will be particu-

larly defcribed.

[1] " The Druids by throwing outwards the " Earth dug out of the huge circular Ditch, en-" vironing the Town (viz. of Abury), demon-" ftrated to all comers at firft fight, that this " was a Place of Religion, not a Camp or Caftle " of Defence."   Dr. Stukeley, Abury, p. 28.

eaft,

eaſt, we found ten tall ſtones together ſet on end (9), none more than four foot diſtant from each other, ſome contiguous. South-eaſt from this groupe of ten ſtones, there runs a ridge (marked 11.) of earth, in a ſerpentine figure, which in the Voluta of its ſcroll (Nº. 7.), has two very high and large ſtones ſet on end ; the diſtance between them twelve feet. Farther on to the right, we perceived many more ſtones ſet up on end on the top of the mound (AK), and leading the eye to a paſſage or entrance, betwixt two ſtones taller by ſeveral feet than the others (marked Nº. 10.). Turning to the left we found a ſepulchre, whoſe ſides were raiſed with ſtones roughly hewn, and covered with a large flat ſtone ; the drawing of which is marked (AG) in the elevations. Hence keeping due Eaſt, we found at (Z) a natural Karn, which has a flat canopy ſtone, over-hanging, as A in the icon AH. It has alſo a ſtone like a bench at B ; at C there is an area of graſs, which has its outer edge fenced with a row of pillars, fronting what, I think, we may ſafely call this ſeat of Judgement. I have ſeen ſeveral of theſe ſeats, or benches of juſtice, particularly in the iſles of Scilly, but none ſo diſtinct, and ſo manifeſtly pointing out the uſe they were intended for as this. The Caſtle (AC) on this hill is much the moſt modern thing to be ſeen there, and will be deſcribed in another place* ; but I muſt obſerve, that what they call the parlour here (marked in the plan of the Caſtle (AD Nº. 2.) is floored with one rock, and in the ſurface of that rock a very regular elliptical baſon, of the ſame kind as thoſe mentioned before, ten inches by fourteen, which could hardly be ſo exactly delineated, without ſtationing the two focus's of the ellipſis mathematically ; a ſtrong evidence that this baſon was made by the Druids, who underſtood Geometry [m], and may be ſaid to be the only capable men among the ancient Britans of dealing in ſuch regular figures.

A Judge-ment-Seat.

In the weſtern ſide of this hill there is a cave, the bottom of which is now full of water, and there are large ſtones lying croſs its entrance ; there are alſo on this ſide ſeveral long ſtones, which are now proſtrate, but ſeem to have been formerly placed on end : here alſo the flat ſtone of one Cromlêh, with one of its ſupporters, is ſtill to be ſeen, and it is probable there were many Cromlêh's here ; but great devaſtations have been lately made in the monuments of this remarkable hill by ſtone-cutters ; and Cromlêh's conſiſting of broad thin ſtones eaſily cloven for maſonry, were ſome of the firſt that tempted the ignorant to deſtroy them ; this, by the way, is one reaſon why in England we have ſo few Cromlêh's remaining, and none at all near great towns, they having been all cut up for building.

Cromlêh.

* Book IV. ch. viii.   m See Dr. Stukeley's Stonehenge.

In

Druid mo-
numents at
Karnbrê
evidencing
it to have
been a place
of Worſhip.

In this hill of Karnbrê, then, we find rock-baſons, circles, ſtones-erect, remains of Cromlêh's, Karns, a grove of Oaks, a cave, and an encloſure, not of military, but religious ſtructure : and theſe are evidences ſufficient of its having been a place of Druid worſhip ; of which it may be ſome confirmation, that the town about half a mile croſs the brook, which runs at the bottom of this hill, was anciently called Red-drew [n], or more rightly Ryd-drew, i. e. the Druids ford, or croſſing of the brook : and what I have obſerved on theſe points, may give ſome notion of the manner in which ſuch places were marked out, and incloſed, and with what works they were furniſhed within.   It was indeed contrary to the principles of the Celtic Religion, as we have obſerved before, to have any incloſed Temples ; but inſtead of ſuch, they had the moſt ſacred parts of their groves marked out into circles, either by low mounds, or by rude ſtones of the obeliſk form, pitched on end ; and of theſe we find a ſurprizing number near or contiguous to each other, in this hill of Karnbrê ; but ſtill more remarkably ſo in the lands of Botallek in St. Juſt Penwith, as will appear when we come to treat particularly of theſe holy circles.   I will only obſerve, that to have circles, ſo many of one ſort, and ſome monuments of every ſacred, oracular, and judicial kind, in one place, is agreeable to the cuſtom of the Druids, as we find by their remains in other parts of Britain [o].   As the Druids had no incloſed Temples, thinking them inconſiſtent with the majeſty of their Gods, ſo neither had they any carved images to repreſent them, and for the ſame reaſon ; but, inſtead thereof, rude ſtones were erected in their places of worſhip, at ſome myſtick, ſignificant diſtance, and in ſome emblematick number, ſituation, and plan, ſometimes in right lines, ſometimes in ſquares, ſometimes in triangles, ſometimes in both : now ſingle, and 50 paces diſtant or more from the circles ; or, eminently taller than the reſt, in the circular line, and making a part of it, like portals, not only to ſhape the entrance, but alſo to hallow thoſe that entered, it appearing by many monuments, as we ſhall find in the ſequel, that the Druids attributed great virtue to theſe paſſages betwixt rocks.   Sometimes theſe ſtones-erect were placed in the center of the circles, the intent of which will be hereafter inquired into.   Theſe are the reaſons that we find ſo many ſtones-erect in Karnbrê-hill.

[n] As I find by a Grant of the Fairs there to the Baſſets of Tehidy, in the time of Hen. VII.
[o] " The Druids called their Groves Lwyn ; " and in theſe Groves were their Mounts and " Hillocks, which they called Groſeddau, from " their ſitting aloft upon them when they pro- " nounced their Decrees. Here were alſo their " erected Pillars and Idols, or their Heaps and " Carnedde, or their Altars or Cromleche, or in " ſome large and more eminent Grove, many of " theſe all together within one Grove, and En- " cloſement, and in one Place there are the Re- " mainders of all theſe, except the Cromleche's, " in the Verge of one great Grove, as is proba- " ble, though the Wood incloſing them have been " gone theſe many Ages." Rowl. Mon. p. 69.

In

In their facred groves were alfo their Altars, of which, doubtlefs, Druid altars.
they had feveral forts, fuitable to the nature and kind of offering.
That Altar which was for offering human victims muft have been
very different from what they ufed on lefs folemn occafions: there
are many flat large rocks on Karnbrê-hill (efpecially at G, and AN),
which probably might have been appropriated to this horrid rite.
Schedius (p. 356.) fays, that thefe Altars were made of turf, and very
likely, efpecially where no rocks were ; for, at fuch times, it was neceffary that the officiating Druid fhould ftand upon a plain, roomly
area, as thefe victims were oftentimes many in number, and beafts
as well as men were offered up as a burnt offering on a large pile of
wood. Of fuch holocauft Altars, we have fome, I think, remaining
ftill in the higher parts of the parifh of Gullval (Cornwall), built
fome-what like a Barrow, but plain and even on the furface, raifed
about three feet and half from the ground, and about 20 feet
diameter.

The Altars for their libations, and other fmaller offerings, fuch as
their Vifcus[P], devoted fpoils, pecuniary oblations, and the like,
needed not to be fo large. For thefe laft purpofes the Cromlêh
might well ferve, efpecially for all offerings made at the tombs of
the dead ; for that the Cromlêh was, in its original deftination, a
fepulchral monument will appear beyond doubt.

In their facred groves the Germans kept alfo the images of wild Images of
beafts, which in time of war were carried before their troops, think- wild beafts.
ing perhaps that by having been fet up in fuch facred places they
might contract fome divine power and influence, available to victory[q].
The Gauls had the fame cuftom, and their facred Bull which they
brought with their army againft the Romans, was taken from
them[r].

After Chriftianity came in, the dregs of Druidifm had been fettling Places of
for fo many ages, that the veffel was not foon to be cleaned, and worfhip
made wholefome. The fuperftition furvived the lofs of her autho- among the
rity, affluence, and dignity, and the idolatrous places to which the more mo-
Druids of thofe times more particularly reforted to perform their dern Druids.
ordinary fuperftitions, were rocks, ftones-erect (of which fome were
called after the name of one particular God, and fome of another,
ritually deified, and worfhiped [s]), fountains, trees, and crofs-roads.
Thefe are called the " Defignata Loca Gentilium[t]," the ancient
accuftomed places, where the remains of Druidifm were practifed
for many ages by the ignorant and fuperftitious, after Chriftianity

[P] " Non femper homines offerebant fed etiam
" alias res dedicabant, præfertim Vifcum."
Sched. 410.
[q] " Infigne Superftitionis, Formas aprorum
" geftant." Tacit. de M. G. Hiftor. iv. 22.

[r] See of Tarvos Trigaranus, p. 106.
[s] See Lib. III. of the Tolmen, cap. iii.
[t] Baluz. tom. I. p. 518. Concil. Turon.
A. D. 567.

I i   was

was become the national Religion of Gaul : they continued to perform their worſhip either in " Ruinoſis Locis aut Sylveſtribus," that is, either in rocky places or groves [u]. Here they made their vows, paid their devoted offerings, prayed for their own ſafety and ſucceſs, imprecating deſtruction to their enemies [w]. Here they brought their incenſe, their tapers, candles, firſt-fruits and morſels of fleſh [x]. Here they uſed their *Sortes* and incantations [y] ; all this they did with great reverence, lighting their candle or torch with great eſtimation of that light which they took thence [z], as if ſome deity [a] had been really there. Theſe rites were performed oftentimes where two ways croſs (ad Bivia), and indeed it was a very ancient cuſtom among the Gentiles to perform their Religious Rites, at the meeting of Roads. Thus Ezek. xvi. 25. It is objected to the people of Jeruſalem, " Thou haſt built thy high place at every head of the way." Item ibid. v. 31. Ezek. xxi. 21 ; " The King of Babylon ſtood at the part-" ing of the way, at the head of the two ways to uſe Divination. " He made his arrows bright, he conſulted with Images, he looked " in the Liver : at his right hand was the Divination for " Jeruſalem." I muſt obſerve, that part of this ſuperſtition is ſtill remaining ; for the common people in Cornwall will not be perſuaded even at this day, but that there is ſomething more than ordinary at ſuch places ; and their ſtories of apparitions gain greater credit, if the Spirit, Demon, or Hobgoblin, is ſaid to have appeared where four Lanes meet ; there they think apparitions are moſt frequent, and at ſuch places it is common for theſe people travelling in the dark to be moſt afraid. Here the Druids had ſtones-erect, or rude idols, which by the Council of Nantz [b] were to be pulled down and thrown into ſome place, where they might never be found by thoſe who were ſuch fools as to worſhip them.

Why many places of worſhip contiguous, or near to one another.   Before we take our leave of their places of worſhip, it may not be amiſs to obſerve, that it will perhaps ſeem ſurprizing to ſome readers, that many places of devotion, and Altars of the ſame kind, ſhould be found ſo near one the other ; Karns, for inſtance, on adjoining hills, and ſometimes rocks in different parts of the ſame Karns, or ledges of rocks, marked with the ſame traces of the uſe they were deſigned for : but it muſt be remembered, that the ancients were of opinion, that all places were not at all times equally auſpicious, and that the Gods might permit, encourage, or grant in one place, or circle, or on one rock, or altar, what they denied in another : an opinion, firſt ſuggeſted for the furtherance and promoting of error,

---

u Concil. Nantenenſ. Labbé, tom. ix. p. 474.
w Ibidem, Lambard's Laws of Canute.
x Labbé, tom. I. p. 956.
y Lambard, ibid.
z " Veniſti ad aliquem locum, id eſt, ad Fon-" tes, vel ad Lapides, vel ad Arbores, vel ad Bivia, " & ibi aut Candelam, aut Faculam pro venera-

" tione Loci, incendiſti." Burchard Coll. Canon. Keyſler 17.
a " Velut ibi quoddam Numen ſit, quod bonum " aut malum poſſit inferre." Baluz. Lib. II. p. 210.
b Apud Labbeum ut ſupra.

and continued for the private gain of thefe fuperftitious jugglers; for if the appearances of the victim were not favourable in one place, if their divinations, and inchantments were miftaken, and their predictions failed, the fault was not laid to the want of art in the Prieft, or of truth in the fcience, or of power in the idol, but to the innocent place; and the places were changed, till appearances became more fupple and applicable to the purpofes intended. So Balaam viewed the Ifraelites from every fituation, from the top of rocks, from the hills[c], from the high places of Baal, from the top of Pifgah, and when thefe places did not fatisfy, " Come I pray thee, " fays Balaak, I will bring thee unto another place, peradventure " it will pleafe God that thou mayft curfe me them from thence."

C H A P. XVIII.

Of the Druid Worſhip.

HAVING taken notice of every thing remarkable in their places of Worſhip we come now to the Worſhip itſelf.

The principal times of ordinary devotion were either at mid-day, or mid-night.—*Medio cum Phœbus in axe eſt,*—*Aut cœlum nox atra tenet* (Luc. Lib. III). But their more than ordinary aſſemblies ſeem to have been held at their new, and full Moons[d]. Not only men, but women were admitted, and it is ſaid that the Britans brought their wives and daughters-in-law into their Temples naked, and painted with the juice of herbs, there to ſupplicate, and appeaſe the Gods with human victims[e]. Tacitus gives us another reaſon; " the women, ſays he[f], were admitted into their aſſemblies and " councils concerning peace and war, as well as perſonal diſputes, " becauſe it was the opinion of the Celts, that there was in that ſex " ſomething more than ordinarily holy, and clear-ſighted in diſ- " covering what was to come[g]." There may be another reaſon aſſigned for the Druids inſiſting upon the preſence of women at their ſacrifices, which was, to harden their minds by ſuch frequent inſtances of barbarity as their moſt ſacred rites conſiſted of, and ſo

Time of Worſhip.

Women admitted.

---

[c] Numb. xxiii. 9.

[d] " Coeunt certis diebus aut cum inchoatur " Luna, aut impletur, nam agendis rebus hoc " auſpicatiſſimum initium credunt." Tac. de M. G. 10.

[e] Alex. ab. Alex. p. 753.

[f] De M. G. 8.

[g] It is ſaid (Rel. de Gaul. Vol. I. chap. xxiv. p. 198.) that the Gauls carried their complaiſance to a great extream, and conferred the ſupreme Ju-

dicature upon their Wives, before their firſt Expedition into Italy; that the Women enjoyed this Honour when Annibal paſſed the Alps (Plut. de clar. Mulieribus; Polyæn. Stratag. Lib. VII.) and that the Druids by degrees ſupplanted them, and got the Power into their own Hands; Rel. de Gaul. p. 198. but it is by no Means probable that ſuch unlimited Power would be granted to Wives, as ſhould ſet them above their Princes and their Prieſts.

familiarize

familiarize them, even to thofe of the fofter fex, that every one of the other fex, boys as well as men, might be afhamed to hefitate and refufe their attendance, when fuch rites were in hand; but whatever was the reafon, this cuftom was very ancient [h]. The vulgar were to keep at a proper diftance [i]. Whoever among the Germans entered the place of Worfhip, wore (out of reverence to the facred grove) a kind of fetter or fhackle about the leg, to teftify, fays Tacitus, their own fubordination, and the Deity's power; but whether the Druids had this cuftom, does not appear; however, the Priefts themfelves did not approach upon fuch folemn occafions, without a confcious trembling at the bloody rites which were then to be performed.

All with humility and dread.

———— *Pavet ipfe Sacerdos*
Acceffus, dominumque timet deperdere Luci.   Luc. Lib. III.

The Rites.   Before the facred rites began, it was a general cuftom among the ancients to ufe ablutions, fprinklings, or luftrations, in order to purify, as they imagined, and prepare the Priefts, the affembly, the victim, and the facrifical inftruments for what was to enfue.

In the Irifh MSS. according to Mr. Toland [k] (for he produces no proof), " The rites and formalities of the Druids, their Divinity and " Philofophy are very fpecially, though fometimes very figuratively " expreffed." But none of thefe are particularly named. " I find, " that the Priefts firft prayed; then the victim was offered, being " firft ritually devoted; the mola falfa, wine, and frankincenfe at- " tending; then followed the libation [l];" and the victim being dead, prayers fucceeded, the blood of the victim was poured out, and what was to be burnt was placed on the Fire-altar [m]. Sacrifice was never to be performed without a Druid [n]. The Druid was cloathed in white, of which colour they, with many of the ancients, had a great opinion [o]. On their head they had a Diadem or Tiara, which (if the feal found in Anglefea lately, be as ancient as the Druids), may be feen, Pl. IV. Fig. II. and III. They wore a badge of honour on their garments, next in dignity to that of fovereign Princes; " for the Druids had the priviledge of wearing

Druid habit.

---

[h] Alex. ab Alex. ibid.
[i] Lucan, Lib. III. ver. 402.
[k] Of the Druids, p. 46.
[l] Alex. ab Alex. cap. xvii. 4.
[m] Pliny, Lib. XVI. cap. xliv.
[n] Cæfar.—Strabo. Lib. IV. Sched. 335.
[o] They gathered the Mifletoe, and other facred herbs on a white Garment. On the fame coloured Garment they fpread their Lots for Divining. Their Horfes for Divining were white. Pytha-

goras advifed, that Sacrificers fhould addrefs the Gods, not in rich and gaudy Habits, but only in white and clean Robes. Fragm. of Diod. Sicul. The Egyptian Priefts were always cloathed in white Linen. So were the Perfian Magi and Kings. Hyde, p. 20. The Jews had their white Ephod, and the Gauls ufed to carry in Proceffion round their Lands, their Idols covered with white Linen. Rel. des Gaul. p. 104. Sulp. Sever. cap. ix. vit. S[ti]. M[ti].

" fix

" fix colours in their Breacans (or Robes), the King and Queen
" feven, the Nobles five [p]." Their fhoes were of a fingular fhape,
made of wood, of a pentagonal form [q]. The Infigne, or general
diftinction of their Order, was the figure of the Anguinum, or
ferpent's egg [r]. They wore alfo on their garments a Crefcent, becaufe it was at the Neomenia that they gathered their darling Mifletoe.
Selden (and from him Sammes, Rowland, and others [s]), gives us
the Icon of a ftatue found in Wichtelbergue in Germany, by fome,
thought to be a Druid ; but Selden himfelf does not think it to be
fo [*], and indeed, his having a book in his left hand, confirms him
not to be a Druid ; for the Druids taught all without book. Other
images there are [t], faid to be Druid ; but thofe which bid faireft for
being fo, are thofe placed in the beginning of this Book, p. 53. of
which a particular account is given before [u].

The younger Druids are all without beards, the old had very long
ones, and fometimes a wreath of oaken leaves round their temples,
their garments reached down to their heels, and generally their eyes
were fixed upon the ground. The Druideffes are defcribed by Strabo
(who calls them Fatidicæ) to have had white hair, white gowns,
linen cloaks joined together by clafps ; to have been girt with a girdle
of brafs work, and their feet naked [w].

In their hand they carried the magic rod [x], and the Conjurer's
wand is ftill called in the Irifh tongue, Slatnan Druidheacht [y]. The
Magician's rod was reckoned Oracular [z], and they could not regularly
proceed to predict future events without it ; and in the Altar (which
I fhall take particular notice of hereafter) found at Paris A. D. 1711
I think the Magick-Wand is to be found in the hands of the
Druids.

Their victims were of feveral kinds. Sometimes beafts ; as at the Victims
gathering of the Mifletoe, two white bulls [a] ; but efpecially beafts Animal.
taken from their enemies in war ; however, their more folemn facrifices confifted of human victims, and it cannot be diffembled, that the Human.
Druids were extreamly lavifh of human blood. Not only criminals,
captives, and ftrangers, were flain at their facrifices, but their very
Difciples were to be put to death without mercy, if they were will-
fully tardy in coming to their affemblies. No people, however,
could, I think, have wrought themfelves up to fuch a total con-

[p] Tol. Hift. p. 22. Rowl. Mon. p. 107.
In the Portal of Montmorillon (Pl. V. p. 53.
Fig. 3.) the Stripes of the Purple in their white
Robes may be diftinguifhed. See Rel. de Gaul,
Vol. I. p. 142.
  [q] Aventin. Ann. Boi. Lib. I. but fometimes
their Feet are naked.
  [r] See of Divination, cap. xxi. Lib. II.
  [s] See Nat. Difplayed, Engl. Vol. I. p. 211.

[*] Sammes, p. 101.
[t] Frick. Tab. I.
[u] See of the Druid Learning, ch. xv. p. 104.
[w] Strab. Keyfler, p. 375.
[x] Frick. in Bulæo, p. 143.
[y] Toland, ibid. p. 20.
[z] Hofea iv. 12.
[a] Plin. xvi. 44.

tempt

tempt of human life, and the body of man, who had not at the same time the moft elevated notions of the foul, and the moft certain per-fuafion of futurity; but this, inftead of being their excufe, will only fhew us how the greateft Truths may be made the occafion of the moft horrid Sins, where proper notions of the Deity do not obtain, and where Truth, and Reafon, and Philofophy are permitted **Doctrinal** to be built upon by the Father of error. The Druids held feveral **Palliatives** opinions which contributed to confirm them in this dreadful cuftom. **for this in-** **humanity.** For the redemption of the life of Man, they held, that nothing but the life of Man could be accepted by the Gods[b]; and the confe-quence of this was, that thofe who implored fafety from the dangers of war, or the moft defperate diftempers, either immediately facri-ficed fome human creature, or made a vow to do fo, foon after. Their human facrifices generally confifted of fuch criminals as were convicted of theft, or any capital crime; and fome of thefe have been facrificed after an imprifonment of five years[c]; but when fuch malefactors were not at hand, the innocent fupplied their place. They held, that Man was the moft precious, and therefore the moft grateful victim which they could offer to their Gods; and the more dear and beloved was the perfon, the more acceptable they thought the offering of him would be accounted. Hence, not only beauti-ful captives and ftrangers[d]; but Princes and the firft born of their own children, were, upon great and interefting occafions, offered upon their Altars. Nature it feems was filent, and did not fay with the prophet Micah (vi. 7.) " fhall I give my firft-born for my tranf-" greffion, the fruit of my body for the fin of my foul?" In order to fatisfy the fcrupulous of the innocence of fuch barbarous facri-fices, and reconcile the devoted victim to his fate, the Druids held, that the fouls of thofe who ferved as victims to their Gods in this life, were deified, or at leaft tranflated into heaven to be happy there; and the remains of thofe who died in facrifice, were ac-counted moft holy, and honoured before any other dead bodies[e]. **How the** Variety of deaths they had for thofe miferable victims, as if they **Victims** **were killed.** had been afraid that they fhould fall into a loathing, and diflike of fuch facrifices, if they confined themfelves to one particular manner of difpatching them. Some they fhot to death with arrows; others they crucified in their Temples; fome were impaled in honour to their Gods, and then with many others, who had fuffered in a dif-ferent manner, were offered up as a burnt-facrifice. Others were bled to death, and their blood being received in bafons ferved to fprinkle their Altars[f]. Some were ftabbed to the heart, that by the

[b] Cæf. Lib. VI.
[·] Diod. Sic.
[d] Horace, Lib. III. Ode iv.

[e] Rel. de Gaules, Vol. ii. p. 226.
[f] Strabo, Lib. IV. Diod. Sic. Tacit. An-nal. XIV.

direction

direction in which (after the fatal ftroke) the body fell, either to the right or left, forward, or backward, by the convulfion of the limbs, and by the flow of blood, the Druids (fuch erudition there is in butchery!) might foretell what was to come g. One Druid facrifice was ftill more monftrous. They made a huge image of ftraw, the limbs of it were joined together, and fhaped by wicker-work: this fheath, or cafe, they filled with human victims; and Strabo adds, " with wood for fuel and feveral kinds of wild beafts," imagining perhaps, that by a variety of expiring groans and howlings, they might terrify their Gods into a compliance with their folicitations; to this image they fet fire, confuming that, and the inclofed, at one holocauft. In what fhape this image of ftraw was made, Cefar does not fay, but probably it was in that of a bull; for they ufed to facrifice bulls h, and carried to war with them the image of a bull, and the bull is one of the largeft, and moft capacious of the brute kind, and therefore the fitteft for fuch a dreadful office. Whilft they were performing thefe horrid rites, the drums and trumpets founded without intermiffion, that the cries of the miferable victims might not be heard, or diftinguifhed by their friends, it being accounted very ominous, if the lamentations of either children or parents were diftinctly to be heard whilft the victim was burning i. The victim being offered, they prayed moft folemnly to the Gods with uplifted hands, and great zeal; and when the entrails had been properly examined by the Diviners, Pliny thinks that the Druids eat part of the human victim k; what remained was confumed by the laft fire upon the Altar; intemperance in drinking generally clofed the facrificing; and the Altar was always confecrated a-frefh, by ftrewing Oak-leaves on it, before any facrifice could be offered upon it again l.

C H A P. XIX.

Of the fuperftitious Rounds and Turnings of the Body, which the Druids and other Gentiles performed during the Time of Worfhip, and of Luftration.

MANY nations had the cuftom of going a certain round whilft they were worfhiping their Gods, and they thought it of great importance to fix the manner in which the perfon fhould per-

---

g Diod. Sic. Bibl. Lib. V. Cefar, Lib. VI. Strab.

h Plin. xvi. 44.

i Cæl. Rhodig. Sched. 401. Plutar. Δεισιδαι-μονιας.

k Plin. Lib. XXX. cap. i.

l It is faid to have been a part of their worfhip to carry in Proceffion the images of their Deities, or Demons, from one part of the Country to another, veiled over in a white garment (Sulpit.

form

form this round; some contending strenuously, that they ought to proceed from left to right, others insisting that this sacred turn was most prevalent with the Gods when it proceeded from right to left. This custom, as absurd as it may seem, is extremely ancient in foreign countries, as well as this island.   It was the custom of the Romans, during the time that they were performing their more publick devotions, to turn the body quite round from left to right [m], describing, now a small, and at other times a larger circle; a custom founded on a precept of Numa [n].   In the rites of purifying among the Greeks, going round the persons who were to be hallowed, was expressly necessary; and therefore, as Abp. Potter observes [o], most of the terms which relate to any sort of purification, begin with the Preposition Περι (signifying around), as Περιραινειν, Περιματ]εσθαι, Περιθειϵν, Περιαλνιζειν, " to sprinkle about, to wipe all round, to per-" fume, or expiate with sulphur, to lustrate, or ritually purify, all " around;" the vessel also containing the holy water, was called Περιραν]ηριον; to which let me add, that Sorcerers and Exorcists, are stiled in scripture Περιερχομενοι (Acts xix. 13.), and the magical Arts are called Περιεργα (Acts xix. 19.), all from their walking round, to perform the rites of Enchantment and Purification; for which purpose the Greeks were absurd enough now and then to draw a sea onion, and sometimes a dog's whelp round the person to be purified [p].   The Trojans, at the burial of Misenus, were purified by Coryneus's going three times round them with the holy water:

Idem ter socios purâ circumtulit undâ
Spargens rore levi.   Æn. vi. ver. 229.

And Servius on that place observes, that the word *Lustratio* came to signify *purifying*, because the person who performed the rite, was to carry round the person or company a torch, a victim, or (as was the custom in some places) a certain quantity of sulphur, by which means he could not avoid seeing and being seen by the whole company.   In the Temple of Diana, the person who sacrificed, was to go nine times round the Altar, sprinkling the blood of a hind, or doe, and wine [q].   When Medea was performing her incantations, in order to renew the life of Æson, Ovid gives us this picture of her:

Marginal note: This Super-stition how practised among the Greeks and Romans.

Sever. vit. Martini Frick. p. 125.); but their having portable images, was not the pure and ancient, but the mixed Druidism of the more modern ages.

m Ph. " Quo me vortam nescio," Pa. " Si " Deos salutas dextrovorsum censeo." Plaut. Act. i. Sc. i. " Luc. Vitellius primus C. Cæsa-" rem adorari ut Deum instituit, cùm reversus ex " Syria non aliter adire ausus esset quam capite

" velato, *circumvertensque* se, deinde procumbens." Sueton. in Vit. cap. ii. p. 696. Edit. Var.
n " Circumagas te, dum Deos adoras; sedeas, " cum adoraveris." Plutar. in Numâ.
" Atque aliquis modò tunc visâ jam vertitur Arâ."
Ov. Fast. Lib. III.
o Vol. I. p. 221. Greek Antiqu.
p Ibid. Potter, p. 223.
q Pont. Vir. p. 2.

———— *Passis*

——— *Paſſis Medea capillis*
Bacchantum ritu flagrantes circuit aras,
Multifidaſque faces in foſſâ ſanguinis atrâ
Tingit, & infectas geminis accendit in aris ;
Terque ſenem flammâ, ter aquâ, ter ſulphure luſtrat.
Ov. Met. Lib. VII. ch. ii. ver. 258, &c.

The Romans turned, as is before obſerved, from the left to the right, Sun-ways ; but Pliny ſays[r], that the Gauls thought it more conformable to the Religion of the ancients, to turn round the body in *adorando*, from the right to the left; ſo that it may be juſtly How by the inferred, that it was the cuſtom of the Druids to turn round the Druids. body during their prayers, and walk round their aſſemblies, their holy Karns, and their religious fires; and whether they turned to the right or left, or both theſe different ways, at different times, and upon different occaſions, as is moſt likely, we will now examine. The practice of going this myſterious round in worſhip, was very ancient among the Britans, as the multitude of the round monuments, ſtill extant, teſtify ; and, according to Toland[s], " was uſed " 3000 years ago, and God knows how long before;" but the circumambulation, which at preſent remains in ſome places, and is certainly a relick of the Druid cuſtom, proceeds in a contrary direction to what Pliny records of the Gauliſh Druids. Whether the cuſtom has been inverted by the coming in of Chriſtianity (as many cuſtoms of theſe Gentiles have thereby been altered in ſome particulars, and retained in others), or whether the Britiſh Druids in this point held a different opinion from their brethren of Gaul ; certain it is, that the turning round, at preſent in uſe in thoſe places (I mean the iſles of Scotland), where the Druid cuſtoms are not yet wholly extinguiſhed, is Sun-ways, that is, from Eaſt, by South to the Weſt. " In the Scottiſh iſles the vulgar never come to the In the " ancient ſacrificing, and fire-hallowing Karns, but they walk Weſtern Iſlands, i.e. " three times round them, from Eaſt to Weſt, according to the Hebrides. " courſe of the Sun. This ſanctified tour, or Round by the South, " is called Deiſeal, from Deas, or Defs[t], the right hand; and Soil, " or Sul, the Sun; the right hand being ever next the Heap, or Cairn. " The contrary turn from right to left by the North, when the " body faces the Eaſt, was (alſo uſed by the Druids, and) called " Tuaphol, i.e. Siniſtrorſum; the Proteſtants, as well as the Papiſts,

[r] " In adorando dextram ad oſculum referimus, " totumque corpus circumagimus, quod in lævum " feciſſe Galli religioſius credunt." Plin. Lib. XXVIII. cap. ii.
[s] Hiſtory of the Druids, p. 108.
[t] Deſſil, in Martin of the Iſles, p. 117, 140.

L l " are

" are addicted to the Deifol [u]." Of the Tuaphol there are little remains, and we fhall by and by fee the reafon; but the Deifol is
frequently practifed. " When the inhabitants of the Lewis (one
" of the largeft of the weftern Scottifh ifles) go a fowling to the
" Flannan Iflands, to prevent the tranfgreffion of the leaft nicety,
" every novice is always joined with another, who can inftruct him
" in all the punctilios obferved here: when they are got up into
" the Ifland, all of them uncover their heads, and make a turn Sun-
" ways round, thanking God for their fafety. All the crew pray
" three times, in three different places, before they begin fowling,
" the reafon of their going to thefe uninhabited Iflets, being to
" procure a quantity of fowls, eggs, down, feathers, and quills; their
" firft prayer is made as they approach towards the Chapel of St.
" Flannan; the fecond is going round it; the third at or in the
" ruined Chapel. This is their morning fervice, and the Vefpers
" are performed with the fame number of prayers [*]." The fame
author (p. 20. ib.) tells us, that one of the natives of Rona [w], willing
to exprefs the high efteem he had for the perfon of Mr. Morifon, to
whom that Ifland then belonged, would needs make a turn round
about him Sun-ways, and at the fame time blefs him, and wifh him
all happinefs; and when Mr. Morifon refufed that ceremony, the
other inhabitants faid, it was a thing due to his character, as their
Chief and Patron, and they could not, nor would fail to perform
it. In thefe Iflands three times they perform thefe rounds Sun-
ways, about their benefactors, then blefs them, and wifh them good
fuccefs (ib. p. 118.). In the Ifle of Ila the author had this com-
pliment of three turns made round him by an old woman, to whom
he had given alms, after which fhe recommended him to the protection of God, and Mac-Charmig, the tutelary Saint of this Ifland.
This cuftom makes part alfo of the feftival folemnities; for, in the
Ifland of Sena the Druideffes celebrating (as Strabo fays, Lib. IV.
p. 303.) the rites of Bacchus, went round their Temple with rejoicings fuitable to the folemnities of that God, till their fury
abated [†]. In the Ifland of Barray, the inhabitants ftill obferve the
anniverfary of St. Barr on the 27th of September, by a proceffion
on horfeback, which is concluded by three turns round St. Barr's
Church there [x]; and indeed this cuftom was fo generally mixed
with all their rites, that there was fcarce any thing, facred, civil, or
domeftick, undertaken without the performance of the Deffil.

With Fire.   They alfo performed Luftrations by fire, carrying lighted torches,
candles, and fire, in a fuperftitious manner, at certain times, in order

[u] Tol. p. 108.
[*] Mart. ibid. 17.
[w] A fmall weftern Ifland.

[†] See before, ch. ix. Lib. II. p. 84.
[x] Mart. ibid. p. 99.

to drive away evil spirits [y]. In the before-mentioned Island of Lewis, it was an ancient custom to make a fiery circle about the houses, corn, and cattle, belonging to each particular family; a man carried fire in his right hand, and went round. The same Lustration, by carrying of fire, is performed round about women after child-bearing [z], and round about children before they are Christened; as an effectual means to preserve both the mother and infant from the power of evil spirits.

The like custom obtains in water as well as fire, for in the Isle of Skie, after drinking the water of a famous well there (called Loch-siant well, ibid. 140.), they make three Sun-turns round the well, as if some Deity resided in it, to whom they were to pay proper respect before they left it. Weak and simple as these turns may seem, they have been used by the most ancient, and the most polite nations, and in the same number, as now practised by these uncultivated Islanders. The Islanders turn three times round their Karns; round the persons they intended to bless three times; three turns they make round St. Barr's Church, and three turns round the well, so that the number *Three* was a necessary part of the ceremony. _{With Water.} _{Three times very ancient}

It has been before observed, that Corineus went three times round the assembly at Misenus's funeral, to purify them; three times was the effigies of the coy lover to be drawn round the Altar to inspire him with love [a]—*Terque hæc altaria circum——Effigiem duco.*—In the festival called the Ambarvalia, the victim was to be led round the fields three times—*Terque novas circum felix eat hostia fruges* [b]. In the sacrifices of Bacchus the Priestesses were to go round the Altar with dishevelled hair; three times did Medea, in imitation of the Bacchæ, go round the aged Æson with fire, three times with water, and three times with sulphur—*Passis Medea, &c* [*]. And when she was about to invoke all the powers of the Night, her Goddess Hecate, the Moon, the Stars, and all the inferiour Deities resident in the elements of nature, three times she turned herself about. The description of her, the stillness of the night, the propriety of the addresses, and parts of her prayer, are all extremely poetical: _{Among the Romans.} _{Among the Greeks.}

Ter se convertit, ter sumptis flumine crinem
Irroravit aquis, ternis ululatibus ora
Solvit, & in durâ submisso poplite terrâ,
Nox, ait, &c [c]!

---

[y] See Mart. p. 117. And the Laws of the Councils against their lighted Tapers, chap. xx.
[z] Ibid. p. 117.
[a] Virg. Eclog. viii. ver. 74.
" Terna tibi hæc primum triplici diversa colore
" Licia circumdo. ver. 73. ibid.

" Necte tribus nodis ternos, Amarylli, colores;
" Necte, Amarylli, modò, & Veneris dic vincula
" necto." Virg. Ecl. viii. ver. 77.
[b] Geor. I. ver. 345. ibid.
[*] See before, p. 129.
[c] Ovid Met. Lib. VII. from ver. 182 to 190.

But

Different
turns on the
different
occasions
of Curfing,
and Bleffing. But to return.   By thefe odd cuftoms ftill extant in many parts of Britain (evident remainders as they are of the Druid fuperftition, all turning Sun-ways), it looks as if the Druids turned the body Sun-ways in their Worfhip, and not from right to left as Pliny intimates. But indeed, the turning from right to left, contrary to the courfe of the Sun (called Tuaphol), might have been a very ancient cuftom among the Gauls, and reckoned rather more ominous, although not ufed, as Pliny feems to think, in adoring their Gods [d]; and it is very probable that the Druids of Britain ufed the Tuaphol as well as the Deifol, though upon very different occafions. I am apt to think that they turned Sun-ways, in order to blefs one another and worfhip the Gods *, as the Iflanders do in the North ; and that they turned the contrary way when they intended to curfe or deftroy their enemies. The Druids had a rite of curfing (as well as of blefling) as other ancient Idolaters had [e]; and as every thing among them was to be done in a folemn ritual manner, they turned this religious myftick round towards the left, in order to pour out their imprecations the more efficacioufly. " *Druidæque, circum, preces diras fublatis ad* " *cælum manibus, fundentes novitate afpectus perculere milites,*" fays Tacitus [f], of the battle of Anglefea.   Here we have the Druids curfing their enemies not *intercurfantes*, as the women Druids, but *circum*, viz. *euntes*, fe *vertentes*.   The way they turned, indeed, whether to the right or to the left, is not here expreffed; but as the cuftom of blefling was apparently Sun-ways, and ftill remains fo, the rite of curfing muft in all probability have been contrary to it, and may be decided to have been fo, I think, by a paffge in the ftory of Gretterus [g]: " The Inchantrefs, taking a knife, cut the Runick " characters called the Fatales Runæ, on a ftick or piece of wood, " and fmeared it with fome of her own blood [h]; then finging her " Incantations, retrograde [i], fhe went round the inchanted wand, " contrary to the courfe of the Sun, and uttered all her curfings ; " fhe then threw the ftick with obfervation, ritually into the fea, and " prayed—That it might be wafted to the Ifland Drangoa, and " carry every kind of evil to Gretterus [k]." This was the way there-fore, they turned, when they curfed; but when they blefled, and praifed their Gods, imploring their affiftance for themfelves, or friends ; then they turned a different way, even as the Sun proceeds,

---

[d] Mr. Toland thinks that the prefent ufage among the Iflanders does not at all contradict what Pliny fays; but this is certaing his miftake, for the ufage is one way, and what Pliny afferts is the quite contrary turn.
   * See Note [l] p. fequ.
   [e] Numb. xxii. ver. 6.

[f] Annal. Lib. xiv. cap. xxix.
[g] Barthol. Lib. III. cap. ii. p. 661.
[h] " In foffa fanguinis atra—Tingit, & " infectas," &c. fee before, p. 129.
[i] " Contra curfum Solis lignum circuivit, " multafque Diras protulit."
[k] Keyfler, p. 467.

as the Iflanders do at prefent; and as Athenæus obferves[1] (the Druids) anciently did, Τᴇς Θεᴇς προσκυνᴇσι επι τα δεξια ςρεφομενοι.

Sufficient has been faid concerning the manner of thefe religious Turns, and ftrange it may feem to readers unacquainted with the rites of the Ancients (in which every thing was to be myfterious and typical) to what fuch a groundlefs unedifying cuftom as this, could owe its rife. That there was fomething fymbolical in this turning of the body, is very likely; for it is reckoned among the fymbols ufed by the Pythagoreans, προσκυνει περιφερομεν☉, " Turn round whilft " you worfhip[m]". But what the Ancients intended by this circular turn, is very uncertain. Some think it was in conformity to the round figure of the Earth[n]; others to the circular motion of the heavenly bodies[o]; and perhaps one of their reafons might be (for I take it for granted that they had feveral myftical meanings, in one and the fame rite) that in whatever region of the heavens their Deity was then feated, they might, by turning the body quite round, make proper obeifance to him, and their prayers be favourably heard: it may be conjectured alfo, that they intended to teach their Difciples, by this ceremony, that their Deity was not confined to any one fpot of the heavens, and therefore that they needed not to confine them-felves to one pofture or place, but that, wherever their face was turned, there they were fure to meet the afpect of their Deity. If they reckoned all the compafs of Heaven to be their Jupiter, or chief God, as is not unlikely[p], then certainly thefe turns were in honour partly to that extenfive Divinity.

Whence this Rite was derived to the Druids is equally uncertain; as the Pythagoreans had it, it might be among thofe which the Gen-tiles of the Eaft had borrowed from, or rather grounded upon, fome extraordinary incidents of the Jewifh hiftory, communicated to Pythagoras in his travels, and by him imparted to the Druids. Nothing indeed is more apparent, than that the falfe Religion mimicked the true. Heathenifm was as fufceptible of innovation, and as willing to mix with the true Religion (as far as the impurity and error of its principles would allow) as the Jews were to run into the idolatrous Rites of the Heathens. When the Gentiles heard of any manner, in which fome extraordinary event had been produced, they attributed it to the method in which fuch things had been per-formed, and to the external, material inftruments; not, as they fhould have done, to the miraculous interpofition of God. Thus

Likely de-rived from the Jewifh Hiftory.

[1] Lib. IV. cap. xiv. p. 151.
[m] Pithæus, cap. vii. 1.
[n] Elias Sched. p. 370.
[o] " Cæleftis vertiginis quadam imagine."

Not. in Plin. p. 568.
[p] See Chapter xxii. of the Perfian and Druid Conformity.

M m

they

they copied from the facred Hiftory, pouring Libations [q], facrificing upon the tops of Rocks [r], inveftigating Truth by lots [s], and gemms [t], bowing before fire [u], and worfhiping it, ufing the magick wand in imitation of Mofes's rod [w] : hearing that God and his Angels appeared in the human form to Adam, Abraham, Manoah, &c. they made human Images of the Deity, and worfhiped them; finding that Abraham profpered greatly after offering to facrifice his Son Ifaac, they proceeded to facrifice their own children, or were at leaft confirmed in the practice, by thinking they might follow the example of fo good a Man; fo here in this cafe, which we are now treating of, finding that Mofes confecrated, bleffed, and purified the Altar of Burnt-offering, by going round it, as we have it (Levit. viii. 15 [x].); finding that he fprinkled the blood of the Ram (ver. 19.) upon the Altar *round about*; that he did the fame with the blood of the Ram of confecration (ver. 24.); hence they learnt probably the ceremonious part of thefe Rites : neglecting the true God, the Spirit, and the thing typified, they transferred a fimilar worfhip to their Idols, they fprinkled the affembly, they poured the blood of the victim round the bottom of their Altar, they went round the Altar, and confecrated it with fome part of the blood, as Mofes did, in order to perform the emblematical enjoined Purifications of the Levitical law; all thefe Rites are indeed contained (as if copied from the Scriptures) in the paffage before cited, p. 129 *.   Again, it is no improbable fuppofition that the Heathens, finding the facred rounds performed about the city of Jericho, attended with fuccefs, attributed that fuccefs to the religious march (not to the Almighty God, who commanded it), imitated it, and introduced it as a moft effectual Rite of worfhiping, confidently depending upon fuccefs from the forms and fhadows of things, the Spiritual meaning, the real intent and divine author of the injunction, being wholly neglected.

CHAP. XX.

Of the Holy Fires of the Druids.

WE muft not difmifs their Rites of Worfhip without taking fome notice of the Fires, which made a part of the Druid

[q] Judges vi. 20. See the Drink Offerings of the Jews, Exod. xxx. 9.—Ibid. xxix. 12.

[r] Judges vi. 20.—Ibid. xiii. 19.

[s] Jofhua vii. 16, &c.—1 Sam. xiv. 42.—Efther iii. 7.

[t] From the the Urim and Thummim of the Jews.

[u] As Mofes did before the burning Bufh, Ex. iii. out of which God fpake to him, and bid him keep an awful diftance, pronouncing the Ground to be holy.

[w] Exod. iv. 3.

[x] " And Mofes took the Blood (of the Bullock) " and put it upon the Horns of the Altar round " about with his Finger, and purified the Altar, " and poured the Blood at the bottom of the " Altar, and fanctified it."

* —" Flagrantes circuit aras, &c."

Worſhip. Moſt nations of the world had the cuſtom of burning perfumes and ſpices during the times of worſhip, and the Jewiſh Incenſe was enjoined by God[y]; but the Gentiles carried this Rite to an exceſs as unreaſonable and inhuman as it was impious and ido-latrous. " Two Fires were kindled near one another on May-eve in " every village of the Nation; through Gaul, Britain, Ireland, and " the Iſles[z]. One fire was on the Karn," (that is, a Stone-barrow) " the other on the ground adjoining; the men and beaſts to be " ſacrificed, were to paſs through theſe two Fires;" acquiring thereby, I ſuppoſe, a greater degree of Holineſs and Purification. Keyſler adds (p. 356.), that after ſacrifice and banquetting, the Goblets full of wine were to be paſſed through the Fire, as for Puri-fication. The Perſians had their moſt holy Fires perpetually burning in their Temples; but they had alſo occaſional feſtival Fires, on the 9th day of their 9th month[a] (November with the Moderns; March, with the Ancients) and at the winter Solſtice[b], becauſe then the days began to lengthen; and the ſame author there obſerves, that, for the ſame reaſon (at the feaſt of Epiphany) Feſtival Fires are kindled in England (particularly in Shropſhire) upon the hills, for joy that Winter is paſſing away, and the Spring approach-ing. The Druids had alſo their ſolemn Fires on the Eve of Novem-ber, to which the people were obliged to reſort, and re-kindle the private fires in their houſes from theſe conſecrated Fires of the Druids, the domeſtick Fire in every houſe having been, for that purpoſe, firſt carefully extinguiſhed[c]: the Ghavri (of the ancient Perſian Religion) have the ſame cuſtom to this day, as will parti-cularly appear in the ſequel[d]. It is very probable that the Tin-egin or forced Fire, not long ſince uſed in the Iſles, as an antidote againſt the Plague, or Murrain in Cattle, is the remainder of a Druid cuſtom. " All the fires in the pariſh were extinguiſhed, and then " two great planks of wood, were rubbed one againſt the other, till " fire was produced; then a pot full of water is ſet on, and the water " ſprinkled upon the people, or cattle infected with the Plague, and " this they ſay they find ſucceſsful by experience[e]."

Of the Fires we kindle in many parts of England, at ſome ſtated times of the year, we know not certainly the riſe, reaſon, or occaſion; but they may probably be reckoned among the relicks of the fore-mentioned Druid ſuperſtition. In Cornwall, the Feſtival Fires, called Bonfires, are kindled on the Eves of St. John Baptiſt*, and

[y] Exodus xxxi. 1.
[z] Toland, ibid. ut ſupra.
[a] Hyde de Vet. Perſ. Rel. p. 249,
[b] Ibid. p. 225.
[c] Toland, ibid. ut ſupr. p. 71.
[d] Chapter xxii.

[e] Martin of the Iſles, p. 113.
* " The like cuſtom prevails all over Cum-" berland, but the Inhabitants are ignorant of " the Original of it." Right Rev. Dr. Lyttelton, Biſhop of Carliſle, to the Author, 1765.

St.

St. Peter's day; and Midfummer is thence, in the Cornifh tongue, called Goluan, which fignifies both Light, and Rejoicing. At thefe Fires the Cornifh attend with lighted torches, tarred and pitched at the end, and make their perambulations round their Fires, going from village to village and carrying their torches before them; this is certainly the remains of Druid fuperftition; for, *Faces præferre,* to carry lighted torches, was reckoned a kind of Gentilifm, and as fuch particularly prohibited by the Gallick Councils: they were, in the eye of the law, *Accenfores facularum,* and thought to facrifice to the devil [f], and to deferve capital punifhment.

In Cornwall we have Karn-Gollewa [g], that is, the Karn of Lights; and Karn Lefkyz [h] (the Karn of burnings), both called fo probably from the Druid Fires kindled on thofe Karns. Karn Lefkyz has fome things which deferve a particular defcription.—It is a large ridge of rocks, defcending from a very high hill in the tenement of Lechau (St. Juft.) to the fea, and confifting of feveral groups, in the higheft of which there is one fmall bafon, about 18 inches in diameter, its fides about fix inches deep (Plate IV. p. 52. fig. 1. D); about five paces to the left of which, on the fame Karn, whofe furface is planed or flat, is an oblong cavity five feet long (B), and in the fhelving fides of the rocks adjoining on both fides, are feveral little grooves or chanels about two inches wide, and as many deep, cut into the furface, and running by the fide of one another in a vermicular direction (C); they are certainly artificial, but what ufe to affign them I know not, unlefs we fuppofe them the divinatory chanels, into which, as the blood of the unhappy victim flowed, either to the Weft or Eaft, North or South, freely or languidly, into few or many of thefe ducts, fo the fate of the nation, the army, or the facrificing enquirer, was accordingly predicted to be happy or unhappy [i]. There are alfo on the Eaft fide of the oblong cavity before-mentioned, and on the fame Karn, two fmall, exactly round holes funk into the top of the rock; fome others of like kind may be feen intermixed with the little ducts; they are about four inches diameter, and three deep (A A A). I have obferved cut into the rocks at Scilly, in more places than one, fome cavities of the fame fhape, and very little larger than thefe, on rocks, which, in other parts of them, have either furrows, ducts, or bafons worked into them; but what thefe little cup-like cavities were defigned for, it is hard to determine; whether for an holy oil, to hallow the Fire, and the facred inftruments; for wine to fprinkle the facrifice; for Oak leaves dipped in their holy water to purify their Altars afrefh, after

[f] Baluz. tom. vi. p. 1234.
[g] In Sennor parifh.
[h] In St. Juft. parifh.

[i] There are feveral of thefe chaneled Stones to be feen in the Scilly Iflands, particularly at the Giant's Caftle on St. Mary's.

every

every act of sacrificing; or whether they were designed, like the *Acerra* and *Thuribulum* of the Ancients, for holding the frankincense, perfume, or what answered to the *mola salsa*; whether for any of these uses, and for which, is uncertain; but as they are found near, or on these sacred rocks, we may safely conclude, that they were in some shape or other subservient to the Druid superstition. Besides the single bason above-mentioned, I could not perceive one in all these rocks; but in a Karn below, overlooking, and its sides almost perpendicular to the sea, I saw many furrows and clefts crossing the surface of the upper rocks; this lowermost Karn is called in the Cornish tongue Karn-a-wethen, that is, the Tree-Karn, and an Oak-tree (which is singular) growing among the clifts of the rocks is there still to be seen. This whole ridge is called Karn-Leskyz, or, the Rock of burnings, from all which it is natural to conjecture, that these Rocks were appropriated to the Holy Fires of the Druids, that the tops of these rocks were the places where they killed their victims, then burnt them; and that even these Fire-rites, Divination, sacrifice, and worship, could not proceed without some holy water, oil, frankincense, and oak-leaves, nor the rocks be properly prepared for these uses, without several little ducts, and receptacles, such as the bason, the cup-like cavity, and the vermicular chanels.

Sharpy Tor (not far from the church of St. Cleer, Cornwall), is called so from its conick figure, which shoots up a great height from the moors below. This vast Cragg could not but attract and employ the superstition of the Druids: before we came to the highest part of it, on a group of rocks to the right, as we passed, the top rock has three rock-basons in a line communicating with each other, and in the middle of a rock contiguous, but lower, one curious bason; all probably designed for holy water*. But, on the top of all, I found not one rock-bason, which convinces me that the summit of this mountain was dedicated to another Element than what those basons were designed for, I mean that of Fire.

I shall only farther observe, that these Heathen Rites of worshiping by Fire, were common among the Canaanites, and the perverted Jews. Every one knows how they passed their children through the fire to Moloch, and the Prophet Isaiah thus rebukes them for this part of their idolatry: " Behold, all ye that kindle a " fire, that compass yourselves about with sparks. Walk in the light " of your fire, and in the sparks that ye have kindled ᵏ."

---

* See Book III. chap. xi.   ᵏ Chap. l. ver. 11.

N n   CHAP.

C H A P. XXI.

Of their Divination, Charms, and Incantations.

THE Druids were the Magi[1] of the Britans, and had a great number of Rites in common with the Perſians: now, one of the chief funċtions of the Magi of the Eaſt was to Divine, that is, to explain the Will of the Gods, and foretell future events; the term Magus, ſignifying among the Ancients, not a Magician in the modern ſenſe, but a ſuperintendant of Sacred and Natural knowlege[m]. Pomponius Mela tells us, that the Druids profeſſed the ſame art[n], and were ſo remarkable for this pretended piece of knowledge, that ſome derive their name from דרש to conſult, as if it had been their principal ſtudy to conſult, and declare the will and pleaſure of the higher Powers. The Order or Claſs of the Eubates (otherwiſe called Vates) ſeem to have been thoſe, to whom this ſtudy of future events was chiefly allotted[o]. But not only the men-Druids, but the women alſo were very famous for their prediċtions, and often applied to by the Roman Emperours. Gauna (or Ganna) a Celtic Virgin, was accounted by the Germans next in honour to Veleda, who was worſhiped as a Goddeſs[p]. When Alexander Severus, the Roman Emperour, was ſetting out on his laſt expedition, a female Druid cried out to him as he went along, " Go thy way, neither " expeċt viċtory, nor truſt thy ſoldiers[q]." Aurelian is ſaid to have conſulted the Druids, whether the imperial crown ſhould continue in his family; to which the anſwer was, that no name ſhould be more famous in the Republick, than that of the poſterity of Claudius[r]. The ſame author aſſures us, that the Roman Empire *Divining by* was promiſed to Diocleſian, by a woman-Druid[s]. Their moſt *the Entrails.* ſolemn Rite of Divining was, by examining accurately the entrails of their viċtims; an univerſal praċtice among the Gentiles, but a ſcience peculiar to the Prieſts of each nation, who were the ſole judges, whether the appearances (which they thought were ordained purpoſely by the Gods to communicate their Will to the proper obſervers) were favourable or otherwiſe. Beſides the ominous ap-

---

[1] Pliny, Lib. XXIX. cap. i.
[m] Syntagma de Druid. p. 35.
[n] " Quid Dii velint, ſcire ſe (viz. Druidas) " profiteri." Lib. III. cap. i.
[o] " Batties vero ſcrutantes, ſecreta & Sublimia " Naturæ pandere conabantur." Amm. Marc."—— " Vates, qui per auſpicia, & immolationes Futura " prænunciant." Diod. Sic.— " Vates autem

" Sacrificiorum, naturaliumque cauſarum curæ " dediti." Lel. de Scr. Brit. p. 5.—Strabo.
[p] Tacit. de M. G. cap. viii. Dio in Fragm. Not. Lipſ. Var. Edit.
[q] Tacit de M. G. Var. Edit. c. viii. p. 592. in Not. from Lamprid. in Alex.
[r] Vopiſc. in Aureliano, ibid.
[s] Vopiſc. in Numeriano, ibid.

pearances

pearances of the entrails, they had feveral ways of Divining [t]. They divined alfo by Augury, that is, from the obfervations they made on the voices, flying, eating, mirth, or fadnefs, health, or ficknefs, of birds [u]. Thus the Gauls and Britans concerned in the expedition of Brennus, after they had taken and burnt the city of Rome, divided into two parties, one fettled in Italy, the other forced its way into the fea-coafts of Illyricum, led thither by fome ominous flights of birds.

By Augury.

Strabo mentions a fingular kind of Divination practifed by the Druids; by the number of criminal caufes they formed a judgment of the fertility or fcarcenefs of the year, which was to come. They had alfo another way of foretelling plenty, and want; if the facred number of the Druids was found to increafe, a plentiful year was to be expected; if to decreafe, want was to follow [w]. From any re-markable incident, any publick affliction, or misfortune (which the fuperftitious of all ages have been too apt to call a judgment from heaven), they would infer the anger of the Gods; and then confider-ing the fignificancy of names, the relation of perfons and places, and comparing them with the nature of the accident, the Druids would divine what was to enfue [x]. Thus the Roman Capitol being burnt down, in the civil wars between Otho and Vitellius, the Druids prefumed to foretell that the ruin of the Roman Empire was at hand; that the city of Rome had been taken formerly by the Gauls, but the Capitol, the Temple of Jupiter, remained inviolate; but that this remarkable evidence of the indignation of the Gods could portend no lefs than the utter fubverfion of the Roman State, and tranflation of the imperial Power, to the Tranfalpine Gauls.

By the Number of Criminal Caufes,

and of the Druids.

From re-markable Incidents.

The Germans are recorded to have divined by Lots, and the Druids fond of Magick, and abandoned to this foolifh ftudy of Divination, as well as originally of the fame Celtick Religion with the Germans, may with great probability be inferred to have had the fame cuftom. Tacitus's defcription of this method of Divining is this [y]. "They cut "a rod, or twig (taken from a fruit-bearing tree), into little fhort "fticks, or tallies, and having diftinguifhed them one from the other "by certain marks, lay them without any Order, as they chance to "fall, on a white garment [z]. Then comes the Prieft of the State, if

By Lots and Tallies.

---

[t] " The brain of Animals, according to its " different appearances, was fuppofed to prog- " nofticate future Events." Henry's Hift. Ecclef. tom. ix. p. 274.

[u] " Augurandi ftudio Galli præter cæteros va- " lent," Juftin, Lib. XXIV. Λεγυσι δε (viz. Celtæ) και ειναι Θεες, και προνοειν ημων, και προσημαινειν τα μελ-λουfα, και δια Ορνιθων, και δια Συμβολων, και δια Σπλαγ-χνων, και δι αλλων τινων μαθημαfων και διδαγμαfων, Æl. Var. Hift. Lib. II. cap. xxxi.

[w] Strab. Lib. IV.

[x] " Partim auguriis, partim conjectura." Cicero de Divin. Lib. I. cap. xli.

[y] Tacit. de M. G. cap. x.

[z] The Druids were very fond of white Gar-ments (as fee before on the Mifletoe, Selago, and their Habit during the time they officiated): this is the more likely to have been a Druid manner of Divining; and it may be the more probable, be-caufe in the Cornifh, Pren fignifies a Stick, and alfo a Lot.

"the

"the confultation be at the requeft of the publick (but if it be a
"matter of private curiofity, the mafter of the family may ferve
"well enough), and having prayed to the Gods, looking up to
"heaven, he takes up each billet, or ftick, three times, and draws
"his interpretation from the marks before imprinted on them: if
"thefe marks intimate a prohibition to proceed, there is no farther
"enquiry made that day, concerning that particular affair; but if
"they have full authority to go on, they then proceed to the
"Aufpicia, or Divining from Birds."

White
Horfes.

There is another cuftom of the Germans, which may with equal
juftice be inferred, to have been practifed by the Druids. Certain
white horfes were carefully fed in their facred Groves, and never to
be profaned by common labour; thefe were harneffed to a confecrated chariot, and their Prieft attending by their fide, together with
the King, or chief Magiftrate of the State, accompanied their
proceffion, and obferved their neighing, every found they uttered, and
which foot they put foremoft, with other equally important circumftances. Not only the common people, but the Nobles and the
Priefts, placed great dependance on this way of Divining.

By Hydro-
mancy.

From the feveral waves and eddies, which the fea, river, or other
water exhibited, when put into agitation, after a ritual manner, they
pretended to foretell with great certainty the event of battles; a way
of Divining, recorded by Plutarch, in his life of Cefar [a], and ftill
ufual among the vulgar in Cornwall, who go to fome noted Well, on
particular times of the year, and there obferve the bubbles that rife, and
the aptnefs of the water to be troubled, or to remain pure, on their
throwing in Pins or Pebbles, and thence conjecture what fhall, or
fhall not befall them. The Druids alfo (as we have great reafon to
think) pretended to predict future events, not only from holy wells,
and running ftreams, but from the rain, and fnow-water, which
when fettled, and afterwards ftirred, either by Oak-leaf or branch,
or magic wand, might exhibit appearances of great information to
the quick-fighted Druid, or feem fo to do to the credulous Enquirer,
when the Prieft was at full liberty to reprefent the appearances as
he thought moft for his purpofe. The rock-bafons of which we
fhall difcourfe in the next book, will make it evident that the Druids
ufed this fort of Hydromancy.

Convulfions.
of the
Victim.

The Druids Divined alfo, from the fall and convulfion of the
limbs, and from the flow of the blood, immediately after the miferable victim had received the fatal ftroke [b].

---

[a] Ἐπὶ δὲ μᾶλλον αὐτὰς (viz. Γερμανὰς) ἠμβλυνε τα μαν-
τευμάτα των ἱερων γυναικων, αἱ ποταμων δίναις προσβλεπουσαι
και ρευμάτων ελιγμοις και ψοφοις τεκμαιρομεναι προεθεσπιζον.

Hoffman in verb. p. 111.
[b] See Chap. XVIII. and XX. Diod. Sic.
Lib. V. Strabo, Lib. IV.

A re-

A remarkable way of Diving is related of Boadicea Queen of the Britans (in the reign of Nero), and therefore, doubtlefs, ufed by the Druids, who then prefided in all fuch matters.   When fhe had harangued her foldiers, in order to fpirit them up againft the Romans, fhe opened her bofom, and let go a hare which fhe had there concealed, that the Augurs might thence proceed to Divine, concerning the iffue of the intended enterprize.   The frighted animal made fuch turnings and windings in her courfe, as, according to the rules of judging eftablifhed in thofe times, prognofticated happy fuccefs: the joyful multitude made loud huzza's, Boadicea feized the opportunity, approved their ardour, and led them ftraight to their enemies [c]. *By the Running of a Hare.*

Another method of Divining ufed by the Germans, was fingle Duel, which may with great probability alfo be attributed to the Druids, as not only having been very ancient in this Ifland, but as it continued in Britain many ages after Druidifm was extinct, and Chriftianity planted in the room of it.   Curious to know the iffue of any important war, a fingle Combat was appointed, and proclaimed, betwixt one of their Captives, and a chofen Champion of their own people, each accoutered in his own country arms, and as the victory here fell out, fo they judged of the approaching iffue of the war [d]. *Duels.*

Befides the fecret virtues attributed by the Druids to their Mifletoe, Selago, and Samolus, which were looked upon, when ritually gathered and preferved, as fo many powerful charms, to keep off ficknefs and misfortunes; their opinion concerning the *Anguinum* was altogether extravagant.   The *Anguinum*, or Serpent's Egg, was a congeries of fmall Snakes rolled together, and incrufted with a fhell, formed by the faliva, and vifcous gum, froth, or fweat of the Mother Serpent. The Druids fay, that this Egg is toffed into the air by the hiffings of its Dam, and that before it falls again to the earth it fhould be received in the Sagus [e], left it be defiled.   " The perfon who was to " carry off the Egg muft make the beft of his way on horfe-back, " for the Serpent purfues this Ravifher of its young ones, even to " the brink of the next river: they alfo pretend, that this Egg is to " be taken off from its dam, only at one particular time of the " Moon.   The trial whether this Egg was good in its kind, and of " fufficient efficacy, was made, by feeing whether it would fwim " againft the ftream, even though it were fet in gold [f]."   Such abfurdities did they propagate, in order to fet a price and value upon *By the Anguinum.*

[c] Dion in Nerone, Rel. de Gaul. vol. ii. p. 13.
[d] Tacitus, ibid.
[e] A facred white Veftment, in which the Mifletoe, Selago, and Samolus, were folemnly and ritually received from the Prieft that gathered it.
[f] Pliny, Lib. XXIX. cap. iii.

O o

trifles,

trifles, and no doubt to make the credulous multitude purchase them from their own Order only, as by them only regularly and ritually procured, and of full virtue at no other time, or from the hands of any other person than those of a Druid. " I have seen, says " Pliny g, that Egg; it is about the bigness of a moderate Apple, " its shell a cartilaginous incrustation, full of little cavities, such as " are on the legs of the Polypus ; it is the *Infigne*, or badge of " distinction, which all the Druids wear. For getting the better " of their adversaries in any kind of dispute, and introducing them " to the friendship of great men, they think nothing equal to the " *Anguinum* ; and of my own knowledge, I can say, that Claudius " Cesar ordered a Roman Knight, of the Vecontian Family, to be " put to death, for no other reason, but that, when he had a trial at " law before a Judge, he brought into the court in his bosom the " *Anguinum*." This *Anguinum*, is in British, called Glain-neidr, i. e. the Serpent of Glass ; and some remains of that superstitious reverence, formerly paid it by the Britans, is still to be discovered in Cornwall. Mr. Edward Lhwyd h says, " that he had no oppor- " tunity of observing any remains of Druidism among the Armori- " can Britans ; but the Cornish retain variety of Charms and have " still towards the Land's-end, the Amulets of *Maen Magal* and " *Glain-neider*, which latter they call a *Melprev*" (or *Milprev*, i. e. a thousand worms), " and have a charm for the Snake to make it, " when they have found one asleep, and stuck a hazel wand in the " center of her *Spiræ*.

" In most parts of Wales, and throughout all Scotland, and in " Cornwall, we find it a common opinion of the vulgar, that about " Midsummer-Eve (though in the time they do not all agree) it is " usual for Snakes to meet in companies ; and that, by joining heads " together, and hissing, a kind of bubble is formed, which the rest, " by continual hissing, blow on till it passes quite through the body, " and then it immediately hardens, and resembles a glass-ring, which " whoever finds (as some old women and children are persuaded) " shall prosper in all his undertakings. The Rings thus generated, " are called *Gleineu Nadroeth*; in English, Snake-stones*. They are " small glass Amulets, commonly about half as wide as our finger- " Rings, but much thicker, of a green colour usually, though some- " times blue, and waved with red and white." Camden, p. 815.

The opinion of the Cornish is somewhat differently given us by Mr. Carew, " The Country people (in Cornwall) have a persuasion, " that the Snakes here breathing upon a hazel wand, produce a

---

g Lib. XXIX. cap. iii.
h In his Letter, March 10, 1701, to Rowland, p. 342.
* Instead of the Natural one (which surely

must have been very rare), artificial Rings of Stone, Glass, and sometimes baked Clay, were substi- tuted in its room, as of equal validity.

" stone-

" ftone-ring of blue colour, in which there appears the yellow figure
" of a Snake, and that beafts bit and envenomed, being given fome
" water to drink, wherein this ftone has been infufed, will perfectly
" recover of the poifon[i]."

The Druids were alfo wont to confecrate fome particular rocks and *By Fatal*
ftones, and then perfuade their Devotees, that great virtues were to *Stones.*
be attributed to them. Of this kind was the *Fatal-Stone*, called fo,
as fuppofed to contain the fate of the Irifh Royal Family. On this
the fupreme Kings of Ireland ufed to be inaugurated on the hill of
Tarah; and the ancient Irifh had a perfuafion, that in what country
foever this Stone remained, there one of their blood was to reign[k].

The Rocking-ftones, called in Cornwall, *Logan-Stones*, are alfo *By Logan*
thought by fome[l] to be engines of the fame fraud, and the Druids *and other*
might probably have recourfe to them, and pretend that nothing, *confecrated*
but the holy hands of a Druid, could move them, when they wanted *Stones.*
to confirm their authority, and judicial decifions by any fuch fpecious
miracle.

Wafhing the *Blue-Stones* in order to prcure a favourable
wind, applying it to the part affected to cure ftitches and pains, and
fwearing folemnly upon it[m], as alfo the virtues of Molingus's
ftone-globe[n], feem remainders of thefe Druid fuperftitions.

Another Relick of fuch Druid fancies and incantations, is doubtlefs the cuftom of fleeping on ftones, on a particular night, in order
to be cured of lamenefs; drawing children through a round hole
made in flat rocks, to cure the Rickets, with fome other obfolete
ufages of the fame ftamp, which will occur in the explication of
particular monuments.

By the prohibitions of Councils[o], we find the weftern Heathens, *And the*
not only divined by Augury, but defcended to ftill more trifling, *moft abfurd*
and abfurd examinations[p]. In fhort, nothing is fo groundlefs or *Speculations*
extravagant, but that fuperftition lays hold of it, and grafts it into
the body of its airy fcience; as if what the fupreme Power had
concealed induftrioufly from the fubtil Spirit of Man, he had
wantonly difperfed the criterions of, in the whole conduct of Birds,
in Stones and Gems, Lots and Waters, and in all the feveral
parts of the Victim, the Horfe, the Ox, and what not?

---

[i] Carew, p. 22, who had one given him of this
kind; and the Giver avowed to have feen a part
of the Stick fticking in it; but, *penes Authorem*
fit fides, says he.

[k] " This Stone was fent into Scotland, where
" it continued as the Coronation Seat of the
" Scotifh Kings till, in the Year 1300, Edward
" the Firft of England brought it from Scone,
" placing it under the Coronation Chair at

" Weftminfter. The Irifh pretend to have
" Memoirs concerning it for above 2000 Years."
Tol. p. 103.
[l] Toland, ibid.
[m] Martin, p. 167.
[n] Ibid. p. 225.
[o] Concil. Liptinenf. &c.
[p] " Du fiente et l'eternuement des chevaux,
" ou des boeufs."

CHAP.

CHAP. XXII.

*Of the great Resemblance betwixt the Druid and Persian Superstition,
and the Cause of it enquired into.*

AMONG all the Eastern Nations no superstition was so extensive, and famous, as that of the Persians; and it is very well worth our notice, that there was a remarkable conformity betwixt them and the Druids, as to Temples, Priests, Worship, and Doctrines.

By all the Monuments which we have left of the Druids, we cannot find that they ever admitted of covered Temples for worshiping their Gods *; and we find that the ancient Persians held the same opinion q, and performed all the offices of their Religion in the open air r; and Cicero tells us, that " in the expedition of Xerxes into " Greece, all the Grecian Temples were burnt at the instigation of " the Magi, because the Grecians were so impious as to inclose those " Gods within walls, who ought to have all things round them open, " and free, their Temple being the universal world s." This was perhaps one and the principal reason of these Temples being demolished; but the Persians had another objection to the Grecian Temples, equally conformable to the Druid principles (viz. their containing so many statues) which will be taken further notice of in the two following pages.

A great conformity there was betwixt the Druids and the Persian Priests, called the Magi, which is the reason that Pliny calls the Druids, the Magi of the Gauls and Britans. As the Druids were divided into three classes, viz. Druids, Bards, and Euvates, so were the Persians into Priests, Presuls, and Superintendants, that is, Archpresuls, or High Priests t. The Druids also had their Arch-druid, or sovereign of their Order, as the Persians had their Archimagus.

The Druid Priest was cloathed in white, the holy vesture (called the Sagus) was white; the bull for sacrificing, white, their oracular horses white; and the Persians were altogether as fond of the white colour; the Persian *Magus* was cloathed in white u; the horses of

---

* The Temple in the Island of Sena, mentioned p. 87, may seem to be an exception to this general rule; but was probably a slight and and small Covering only of a corner of the Temple, for an Idol, for Fire, or the Priestess to shelter herself in; for this Covering was to be taken off annually, and renewed the same day before Sun-set.

q Prideaux, Conn. part i. book i. Hyde de V. R. P. chap. viii. 29.

r " Zoroastres was the first who introduced " into the Persian Religion covered Temples, in " the Time of Darius Hystaspis, Father of " Xerxes, in order the better to preserve the

" sacred Fire from being extinguished, and that " the sacred Offices might proceed with less " Interruption from the Weather; but in these " covered Temples introduced by Zoroastres, " they had no Deities or Images; and before him " they had no covered Temples at all." See Prid. vol. i. p. 216.

s Cic. de Leg. Lib. II. cap. ii.

t Sacerdotes, Præsules, Archipræsules. Hyde, chap. xxviii. and xxx. p. 380.

u " Veste alba induti super albis equis equi-" tantes." Hyde, p. 253.

the

the *Magi* were white; the King's robes[w], and his horse-trappings [In Habit.] of the fame colour. The Druids wore Sandals, the Perfians did the fame[x]. Zoroaftres, chief *Magus* of the Perfians, lived and taught in a Cave; in the fame place did the Druids chufe principally to inftruct their Difciples[y].

Both the Druids and Perfian *Magi* were of the nobleft Order in [In Dignity.] the State, and the Kings were ranked both with the Druids and the *Magi:* Divitiacus, a King of the Gauls, and alfo of part of Britain, was of the Druid Order; and the Kings of Perfia were always ranked in the Sacerdotal Tribe[z].

No Sacrifice of the Gauls or Britans was to be performed without a Druid[a]; and among the Perfians it was reckoned a high crime to approach the Altar, or touch the Victim, before the *Magus* had made the ufual prayers, and gone through the preparatory atonements[b].

The Druids excluded from their Sacrifices (as one of the moft grievous punifhments they could inflict) all thofe who were contumacious; the Perfians had the fame cuftom, and excommunicated the impenitent and abandoned in like manner[c].

Not lefs furprizing is the conformity betwixt the Druid and the [In Worfhip.] Perfian Worfhip. Some think the Perfians worfhiped the Serpent; this creature being the fymbol of their God Mithras, or the Sun; and we have as much reafon to believe the fame of the Druids; for it muft be confeffed, that the veneration which they had for the *Anguinum*, or Snake-Egg; the portrait of the two Serpents found in the Bafs-relieve at the Temple of Montmorillon (not to infift upon the fuppofition, that fome of their Temples are founded on a ferpentine plan), give us great reafon to think, that the Druids paid a veneration to the Serpent, very little fhort of divine Worfhip.

The Perfians held that their chief God Mithras was born from a Rock, that he was married to a Rock, and of that Rock begot a Son, called Diorphus[d]; and the Druids imagined that fome divine intelligences dwelt in Rocks; hence their oracular, or fpeaking-Rocks; their Logan-Stones, their Rock-Idols, Bafons, and Rock-Worfhip.

Whatever innovations the more modern Druids adopted from the Greeks and Romans; we muft conclude, that the ancient fyftem of this Order admitted of no Statue-Worfhip, it being one of the fun-

[w] " Rex albis veftibus indutus fuper albo " ftragulo fedebat." Ibid. p. 254.

[x] Hyde, p. 20, 356. " Pedibus gerunt San- " dalos, nam nudis pedibus terram contingere " nefas." Hyde, p. 370.

[y] Cæf. Lib. VI.

[z] Prid. vol. i. p. 222.

[a] Diod. Sic. v.—Cæfar, Lib. VI.

[b] " Erat piaculum Aras adire, vel hoftiam " contrectare, antequam Magus conceptis preca- " tionibus litamenta diffunderet præcurforia." Hyde, p. 356.

[c] Hyde, p. 406.

[d] See Montfauc. tom. i. p. 368.

damental

damental principles of the Celtick Religion[e] (and all these principles the Druids certainly held), that the Gods were not to be represented by any human figure[f]; and we know, that though the sect of the Sabians would have introduced Image-worship into Persia; yet, that the Magians (before, and after Zoroastres), never admitted any Statues into their Temples (which was indeed the most ancient and justifiable principle), and the Grecian Temples being so full of Statues, was one reason, likely, that the Magi insisted upon their utter destruction, when they attended Xerxes in his western expedition.

The Druids worshiped the whole expanse of heaven, and therefore had open Temples, and turned round the body during the performance of their Religious Offices[g], and took the circle for one of the Ensigns of their Order[h], as well as for the plan of their Temples[i]; and Dr. Hyde informs us, that the Persians held, that the whole circuit of Heaven was their Jupiter[k].

It is plain from Chapter XVIII. that the Druids performed the several acts of their Religion on the tops of hills; the Persians also did the same, worshiping their God on the highest parts of mountains, according to the manner of the Ancients[l].

In Ritual Purifications. The Persians used Ritual Washings and Purifications[m], and with the purest water, being obliged to use all the Elements in their utmost purity[n]; they washed their heads and their body, and then held themselves pure, and fit to approach the Altar, and the sacred Fire in their Temples[o]; they had also a particular prayer in their Formulary to be said in the morning, at the washing of their hands[p]. In like manner, the Druids had also their pure Holy-water, and, by the multitude of Rock-basons[q], must have had many Rites of Washings and Purifications.

In Sorcery. The Persians were remarkable for Magick and Witchcraft[r], and the British Druids went such lengths in that diabolical art (as has been already observed), that Pliny says, they seemed to him to have exceeded the very Persians themselves, and the latter to have been only scholars of the former.

---

[e] Lucan, Lib. III.—" Simulachraque mœsta " Deorum—Arte carent, cæsisque extant im- " mania truncis."—

[f] See Chap. XVI. Lib. ii.

[g] Chap. XIX. book ii.

[h] Altar in Tiberius's time, at the end of this Book.

[i] See of the Circles, Lib. III. cap. vii.

[k] " Totum cæli gyrum, Jovem existimantes." Hyde, cap. vi. p. 137. Τον κυκλον παντα τε ερανε Δια καλεοντες. Herod. in Clio.

[l] " In summis montium jugis, antiquissimo

" more, Deum colebant." Hyde, p. 17.

[m] " Aqua munda vos lavate, et Deo gratias " agite." Hyde, p. 236.

[n] " Elementa enim omnia tenentur servare " pura." Ibid. 406.

[o] Ibid. p. 357.

[p] Ibid. p. 371.

[q] See Chapter of the Rock-basons, cap. xi. Lib. III.

[r] " Sine dubio illic orta (viz. Ars Magica) " in Perside a Zoroastre, ut inter autores conve- " nit." Plin. Lib. XXX. cap. i.

The

The Druids facrificed human Victims, and fo did the Perfians [s]. In Holy Fires.
The Perfians had their Holy Fires, before which they always worfhiped; the Druids alfo had their Holy Fires [t], to which the people
were obliged to come and carry off fome portion (for which they
doubtlefs payed according to their abilities) to kindle the fire in their
own houfes; and, at prefent, the Perfians have the fame cuftom, for
the day after their feaft, which is kept on the 24th of April, they
extinguifh all their domeftick fires, and, to rekindle them, go to the
Prieft's houfe, and there light a candle, paying the Prieft his fee of
fix fhillings and three pence, Englifh money [u].

The Perfians thought that this Holy Fire was the caufe of domeftic
plenty, and placed the fick before it, thinking it of great and healing
virtue [w]; and the Druids had probably the fame opinion of it, for
they ufed a Holy Fire, as an antidote againft the Plague, or the
Murrain in Cattle [x].

The Druids had their Feftival Fires, of which we have inftances
ftill remaining in Cornwall; fo had the Perfians at the Winter Sol-
ftice [y], and on the 9th of March [z].

The fcrupulous, awful regard which the Druids payed to a few In venerat-
plants (as the Mifletoe, Samolus, and Selago) which they accounted ing Plants.
facred, and the extravagant opinion they had of their virtues, may
be reckoned among the greateft abfurdities of their fyftem; yet in
this they have the Perfians to keep them in countenance, for the
Perfians and Maffagetes thought the Mifletoe fomething Divine as
well as the Druids [a].

The Druids thought it unlawful to cut the Mifletoe, with any
other than a golden hook; and the Perfians were altogether as fuperftitious: they were to cut the facred twigs of *Ghez* or *Haulm*, called
Berfam, with one peculiar fort of knife only, which had an iron
handle, was firft carefully to be wafhed, then bleffed by a few
words muttered over it, in praife of God and Fire [b]. The Druids
thought their Mifletoe a general antidote againft all poifons whatfoever; their Selago was preferved as a charm againft all misfortunes;
and the prefent Perfians on the 24th of December, or (according
to their more ancient way of reckoning) April, eat flefh, boiled with
Garlick, and fome other herbs, as a fure prefervative againft all the
ill influences of Demons; they have alfo a notion, that whoever on
this fame day eats Annice, or (as fome think it fhould be read)
Apples, and fmells to a Narciffus-flower, fhall for the whole enfuing
year be eafy in his mind, and healthy as to his body. Another

[s] Alex. ab Al. vol. II. p. 750.
[t] See Chap. xx. p. 135.
[u] Hyde, ibid. p. 351
[w] Hyde, p. 546.
[x] Martin of the Ifles, p. 113.
[y] See Chap. xx. p. 135.
[z] Hyde, p. 255, 249.
[a] Alex. ab Al. Vol. II. p. 744.
[b] Hyde, p. 345.

fancy

fancy the Perſians ſtill have of like kind, which is, that by ſmoking, or burning the Iris or its root, they are to be preſerved from hunger and poverty all the year after [c].

Tranſmi-gration. In the xvɪɪth Chapter, Book II, the Druids are ſhewn to have held the Trnſmigration of the Soul; and the Perſians held the ſame doctrine, as the myſteries of Mithras ſufficiently intimate [d].

Divination. The Druids were very much given to Divination [e], and no people more notoriouſly addicted that way than the Perſians [f]. The Druids divined from incidents, perſonal diſappointments, and remarkable afflictions; and the Perſians had the ſame way of Divining, for when Haman was diſappointed in his deſigns againſt Mordecai, and inſtead of hanging him on the gallows which he had prepared, was con-ſtrained, contrary to all expectation, to attend upon him in pro-ceſſion, as an inferiour, after cloathing and crowning him as King of Perſia; his *Magi* preſently concluded that this extraordinary incident, ſo much the reverſe of Haman's ſcheme, portended no leſs than that Haman, inſtead of prevailing againſt Mordecai, was but haſtening on his own fall [g].

It is intimated, that the Druids had their white oracular horſes, by obſerving the neighing of which, and ſome other circumſtances in their going, feeding, and the like, they prognoſticated what was to come. Cyrus, King of Perſia, had alſo his white and ſacred horſes [h]; and not long after him the neighing of horſes was pitched upon for determining, who ſhould have the vacant imperial throne, and it was accordingly given to Darius Hyſtaſpis, becauſe his horſe neighed firſt.

One of the virtues of the fatal Stone [i] was to diſtinguiſh the right-ful owner of the throne from an Uſurper; and the Perſians too had their fatal Stone; the Artizoe with them was to point out the moſt deſerving candidate for the crown of Perſia [k].

Whence this Reſem-blance pro-ceeded. In theſe, as well as other particulars, common to theſe two nations with the other Gentiles (which I here induſtriouſly omit), did the Druids reſemble the ancient Perſians; but whence this ſurprizing conformity in Temples, Prieſts, Worſhip, Doctrines, and Divination, betwixt two ſuch diſtant nations did proceed, it is very difficult to ſay: there never appears to have been the leaſt migration, any acci-dental or meditated intercourſe betwixt them, after the one people was ſettled in Perſia, and the other in Gaul and Britain; and whe-ther the Celts (much leſs the Gauls and Britans) can ever be proved

---

[c] Hyde, ibid. p. 254.
[d] " Decretum enim apud primos habetur de " Animarum in diverſa corpora Tranſmigratione, " id quod etiam in Mithræ myſteriis videtur " ſignificari." Ibid.
[e] See foregoing Chapter of Divination.

[f] Pliny, Lib. XXX. cap. i.
[g] Eſther, vi. 13.
[h] Xenophon Cyropæd.
[i] See Chap. v. book III.
[k] Ibid.

to

to have been one and the fame people with the Perfians, fince the general difperfion (which is a time too early to produce fuch a minute conformity) is much to be queftioned.

This ftrict agreement betwixt the Perfians and the weftern nations of Europe was too obvious to efcape the notice of the judicious and learned Pelloutier in his hiftory of the Celts; therefore he takes it for granted, that the Celts and Perfians were one and the fame people[1], and feems to ground his opinion upon the little difference there is betwixt the Language, Cuftoms, and Religion of the two nations[m]: but this Union, I am afraid, muft have been fo early (for we have no tracks of it in hiftory) that it can only account for an agreement in the effentials of Religion, which in the firft ages of the world were few, fimple and unadorned, and fpread into all parts, and there continued in great meafure the fame as at firft. Such were the effentials of both the true and falfe Religion in the beginning of the world after the Flood, and the principles of the true Religion continued ftill to be few, and always the fame; but falfe Religion grows, contracts a multiplicity of Doctrines, adopts new Deities and Rites, according as the invention of its own country, or the contagious commerce which it carries on with foreign countries prevails.

I am fenfible that Dion. Halicarn. VII. 474. denies, that either the Egyptians, Africans, Celts, Indians, or indeed any other of the Barbarians, in the courfe of fo many ages down to his time, ever deferted their country Rites of Worfhip, or changed any thing even fo much as in the ceremonies of their Religion, unlefs compelled thereto by their Conquerours; but, whoever confiders the variable tempers of mankind, their thirft of novelty, the luxuriancy of human invention, and the infectious nature of Superftition equally calculated to profelyte the Jew and Gentile, cannot but differ from this learned Hiftorian in this point: we may indeed allow, that the lefs intercourfe thefe nations had with the other parts of the world, the more tenacious they were of their old ways of worfhip; the lefs learning and commerce, the more fimple their Rites, and more the fame (as before) they continued; but that fuch large portions of mankind, who had fuch a multitude of Gods and ceremonies, could have them all from the very beginning of their nation, and retain them all without adding to, or retrenching any thing from what they had at firft, is inconceivable, contrary to the temper of mankind, and repugnant to the very nature and defign of their Religion.

Idolatry and Gentilifm offering us, every now and then, new Gods, tempt us at the fame time with new enfnaring Rites of worfhiping

Margin notes:

Celts and Perfians, not one People fince the Difperfion.

Idolatry and Superftition, infectious and fpreading.

---

[1] " A l'egard de Perfes, Je ne doute point du " tout qu'ils ne fuffent le meme peuple que les " Celtes. Ni la langue des Perfes, ni leurs cou- " tumes ni leur Religion ne differoient pas " anciennement de celle des Celtes." Ib. p. 19.

[m] Vol. I. p. 18.

Q q   them,

them, and run us deeper still into the abyss of vice and errour. Whence had the Gentiles the Rite of Circumcision, did they not borrow it from the true believers? did not the Egyptians borrow this Rite from the Jews [n], as the Jews contracted from their intercourse with them a propensity to make to themselves a golden Calf? Can it be denied, that Zoroastres copied a great deal from the Mosaick Institutions? Dr. Prideaux, in his Connexion (part I. book IV.), hath placed this beyond all doubt [o]. Let these two instances (to which many more spread through these papers might here be added) suffice to shew, how bold, and untenable the assertion of Dion. Halicarn. is, and that the Religion of the Heathens has always been in a fluctuating condition, sometimes losing in one part, but generally increasing, and altering in more [p].

The great question is, whether the Persians and Celts could be one nation, late enough in time to have had such a variety of Customs, Rites, and Doctrines of the same cast and turn among them, when one People; so as that when they separated and settled, some in Persia, and the others in Europe, they carried these Rites, Customs, and Doctrines with them into their several departments, whence a constant visible conformity ensued. This is a difficulty not easily solved. I shall therefore examine this matter a little more narrowly, and, by distinguishing between the several parts of Gentilism, endeavour to shew whence they did severally proceed.

Whence the Principles, Doctrines, Rites. Some Principles and Rites they had in common with the true believers, Principles which began with mankind, and still continued with them, though obscured, and almost defaced by fable. Others sprung from the seeds of the first Idolatry, and were the same in all the Gentile world; but a third sort of Religious Customs and Opinions, were the peculiar growth of particular climates, inventions of later ages, or the product of imitation. Their having open Temples, for instance, worshiping in high places, not worshiping Statues, holding the immortality of the Soul, and the necessity of Sacrifices; these are what they may well be supposed to have had in common with the rest of mankind, when united in one nation, and as yet incorrupted; other Rites and Superstitions they had in common with all other Heathens, derived from the fundamental errours of Idolatry [q], which proceeding from one author, and one general design, was

[n] Herodotus thinks the Jews had this Rite from the Egyptians; but the Scripture Original of this Rite will prevail with all impartial Readers.

[o] See Prid. Connex. p. 216, and 219, first Edit.

[p] The Persian Religion was first Magian entirely; then came in Sabianism with all the Additions of Image-worship, and at one time, had got a greater multitude of followers than the Magians; then came Zoroastres, and his Reformations of Magianism, and set aside the Sabians; and lastly, Mahometanism jostled them out both. The Phenicians anciently worshiped only the Sun and Moon, under the Names of Baal, or Belus, and Astarte, "prorepente autem Idolatria Hercules Phœnix, aliique Deorum numerum auxerunt." Wise, Bodlei. Med. p. 218.

[q] See Lib. II. cap. i.

originally

originally tainted fo ftrongly, as to fome particulars, that it never loft the venom. Of this kind was Polytheifm, human Sacrifices, Witch-craft, Necromancy, Proftitution, and Debauch after Sacrifice, thefe, being corruptions at the fountain head, fpread wherever the waters flowed, and as they are common to all Idolaters, need no migration, nor union of nations, to account for their being alike in all countries. But the remaining part of this likenefs remains ftill to be accounted for. The Tranfmigration of the Soul was a fancy added to the old Doctrine of the immortality, of Eaftern growth, where it ftill conti-nues, the Bannians and Chinefe making it at this time a fundamental principle of their perfuafion, received, as they fay, from the ancient Brachmans. Magick, with all its horrid erudition, aftrology, com-merce with Demons, examining the entrails of human victims, and fuch a multitude of ceremonies wherewith the Britans, to the aftonifhment of all beholders, exercifed the arts of Divination, could never have exifted early enough to have been ufed by the Celts and Perfians, when one people; the fame may be faid of worfhiping the Serpent, and always before Fire, which were both borrowed by the Perfians from the Jewifh Hiftory, after the migration of the Jews from Egypt. The Druids were a Sect which had its rife among the Britans, after the Celts were broke into Germans, Gauls, and Britans, &c. fince which time it is impoffible that the Perfians and Celts fhould have been one people without our knowing it; and the great refemblance betwixt the Druids and the Magi, as to their eminent Power and Dignity in their own nations, their fkill in Magick, the colour of their habit, the fame degrees in the Prieft-hood, their like ways of Divining; all thefe, as much too modern for the time when the two nations of Celts and Perfians were united in one community, muft be fetched from another chanel.

It has been hinted before, that the Druids were probably obliged to Pythagoras for the Doctrine of the Tranfmigration, and fome other particulars; and as that great Philofopher had been a Difciple, either of Zoroaftres, or fome of that Perfian's immediate fucceffors, there can be no doubt but he was learned in all the Magian Religion, which Zoroaftres prefided over, regulated and eftablifhed in Perfia: it was with this Magian Religion that the Druids maintained fo great an uni-formity; and as Pythagoras is juftly thought to have converfed with the Druids, after he had returned full fraught with, and eager to impart, his oriental Learning, it is not improbable, but the Druids might have drawn by his hands out of the Perfian fountains. *Partly from Pythagoras.*

It may be obferved in the next place, that the Phenicians were very converfant with the Perfians for the fake of the Eaftern Trade, of which Tyre and Sidon were the principal Marts for many years, and nothing is more likely than that the Phenicians, and after them *Partly from the Pheni-cians and Greeks.*

the

the Greeks, finding the Druids devoted beyond all others to superstition [r], should make their court to that powerful Order, by bringing them continual notices of the oriental Superstitions, in order to promote and engross the lucrative trade, which they carried on in Britain for so many ages. What makes this the more likely, is, the general character of the Druids, who were glad to catch at every thing they could lay hold of to enrich their superstition. It may not be amiss here to observe, that the same chanel which imported the Persian, might also introduce some of the Jewish and Egyptian Rites: the Phenicians traded much with Egypt, and had Judea at their own doors, and from the Phenicians the Druids might learn some few Egyptian and Jewish Rites, and interweave them among their own; this is much more probable, than that the Druids should have had their whole Religion from Egypt, as some think, or from the Jews, as others with as little reason contend.

CHAP. XXIII.

The Declension and Expiration of Druidism.

A Great deal may be said in favour of the strictness of the Druid Discipline, and the extensiveness of their learning; and the veneration paid to their Morality and Justice in civil matters must be acknowledged their due; but it must be surprizing to all the world, that a system of so much barbarity in the chief part of worship (I mean their Sacrifices) such fanciful Rites in some particulars, and such groundless speculations relating to others, a sect which contributed so little to the exigencies of the community, and yet appropriated to its self the most invidious superiority over its fellow subjects, should maintain its elevation from the most remote antiquity down through so many ages. The great reason was, the Judicial and absolutely decisive power in all causes, civil, military, and religious, which they had the artifice to procure for, and appropriate to their own Order: this preserved the Druids as long as the Gauls and Britans preserved their independency; but as soon as these nations were forced to stoop to foreign Masters, and became no more than so many Provinces of the Roman Empire, all the authority of the Druids was subject to the controll of a higher jurisdiction, and the Romans were so far from shewing them the respect and veneration which they had held among their own people for so many generations, that they utterly detested their most solemn Rites as shocking to human nature. This was the first blow to Druidism, and particular laws were soon after made against their human Sacrifices. Augustus forbad the Roman

Druidism in Gaul condemned and prohibited by the first Roman Emperours.

[r] "Natio est omnis Gallorum admodùm dedita Religionibus." Cæs. Lib. VI. p. 16.

citizens

citizens from practifing any part of the Religion of the Druids [s];
but Tiberius Cefar carried this matter farther, and ftrictly forbad
the celebration of the Druid Rites in the city of Rome, and the
adjoining Provinces, if he did not utterly abolifh the whole Druid
Order in the Gaulifh Nation, as Pliny feems to intimate [t].

There was an Altar found in the Cathedral of Paris, in the year
1711, which was dedicated to Jupiter, in the time of Tiberius, and
very probably on account of that Emperor's proceeding to abolifh
Druidifm. The Infcription takes up one front of the Altar (A)
Pl. VIII. p. 157. the other three fronts have ftill remaining in them
plain figns of the Druids giving way to the imperial Edict. Whether
in that part of front the fecond (B), which is defaced (for the two
armed youths (a, b,) here take up but half the bafs relief) there might
not have been fome fymbol of the Emperor's Profcription (as a whip,
or lafh), is what cannot now be determined, but from the contents
of the other bafs relieves, is very likely. The figures are haftening
forwards; if they are Soldiers putting in execution Tiberius's law,
what the fecond (b) holds in his hand may be a drawn fword, a pike,
or *flagellum*. In the third front (C) there are two perfons bearded
and old, and one in the middle not bearded. The right hand old
man (a) has the Virga divinatoria, perhaps, in his hand, the fecond
and middle figure (b) feems to be young and beardlefs, perhaps fhe is
a Druidefs, and the torch in her right hand, a fymbol of their holy
fires. The third (c) is old, bearded, and in his right hand carries the
Magick circle (d) of which figure the Druids were extreamly fond:
they have all three in their left hand an octangular kind of plate [u] (e),
but by no means like the fhields of the front before this, as Mr.
Martin thinks [w]; neither are thefe figures helmeted, but have loofe
caps, or turbants on their heads. By their tunick, cap, and circle,
I take it for granted, that they are Druids; what they carry in their
left hand therefore, cannnot be fhields, the Druids being privileged
againft carrying arms; befides that the left hand feems not to be on
the infide as in carrying fhields it ought always to be; thefe things
therefore are not born as arms of defence, but may rather be fome
mufical inftrument of the Bards, or perhaps fome tablet on which they
were ufed to caft their *Sortes*, or lots of Divination: the figures are
all upon the march, and feem to reprefent the Exit of the Druid
Rites, Holy Fires, and Magical Incantations. The fourth front
of this Altar (D) as Martin juftly obferves (p. 64.) fhews us the
departing Druids, and, I doubt not, had different Symbols to exprefs
the other Druid Superftitions; but this front of the ftone is unhappily defaced, and one head only has the appearance of a Diadem.

[s] Suetonius in Claudio.
[t] "Tiberii Cæfaris principatus fuftulit Druidas
"eorum." viz. Gallorum. Lib. XXX. cap. i.

[u] Montfaucon, tom. II. p. 423. is miftaken in
calling them Hexagonal. See the Icon.
[w] Rel. de Gaul. vol. II. p. 60.

R r   Montfaucon

Montfaucon[x] thinks, " that thefe Bafs-relieves do reprefent the " confecration of this Altar, that it is hard to guefs for what reafon " the Circle is here inferted; but concludes, that it muft have born " its fhare in the ceremony of this Proceffion." In what ceremony then more likely, than in one relating to the Gaulifh Superftition?

Notwithftanding what Tiberius did, it was thought neceffary to proceed againft the Druids with more feverity in the reign of Claudius Cefar, and therefore Suetonius attributes the honour of fuppreffing the Gaulifh Druids to Claudius[y], and his zeal againft them is apparent enough from his putting to death a Roman of the Equeftrian Order, for carrying the *Anguinum* (that Druid charm) in his bofom[z]. But notwithftanding thefe imperial Edicts it is not to be imagined that the whole Druid Order and Difcipline in Gaul immediately and abfolutely ceafed; their cruel Sacrifices of human Victims were doubtlefs expreffly forbidden, as well as the more fraudulent parts of their Magick and Incantations, under the moft fevere penalties; however, it is by no means to be queftioned, but that they retained and publickly exercifed, their other more innocent Rites of worfhip; nay, in private, it is very much to be fufpected, that they continued alfo their ancient bloody cuftoms[a] even till Chriftianity itfelf appeared, and corrected the heart, their hands only having been reftrained by the laws of the Empire. And yet indeed, after Chriftianity (which is moft to be wondered at), their fondnefs for human Victims continued, though perhaps in few places; for Procopius, who lived about the middle of the fixth century, fays [b], " *Francos etfi Chriftum jam colerent, humanis tamen ad fuum ævum* " *hoftiis ufos.*" Some other of their Rites feem alfo to have reached down far below the date of their converfion to Chriftianity.

Though Druidifm in Gaul was ftrictly prohibited as early as Tiberius and Claudius; yet in Britain it was practifed a long while after with impunity, and all its moft dreadful Rites, fo religioufly, and with that diligence, pomp, and exactnefs perfifted in, as made Pliny fay, that the Britans out did the very Perfians.

Druidifm in Britain yields to Chriftianity   The Druids continued authorized in Britain, as Arch-bifhop Ufher[c], and Leland[d] think, with all their Rites in as full force, as the Roman powers here would permit, till the reign of King Lucius (A. D. 177.) when Chriftianity being embraced by the King[e] and Princes of the Ifland, Bifhops were ordained, and fupported by the Civil Power, in preaching to, and converting the people. This change

[x] Tom. II. p. 423.
[y] " Druidarum Religionem apud Gallos diræ " immanitatis & tantum civibus fub Augufto in- " terdictam penitus abolevit, viz. Claudius." Sueton. in Claud. chap. xxv.
[z] See Chapter xxi. p. 142.
[a] Gronovius in Tac. Ann. Var. p. 592.

[b] Lib. II. de Bello Gothico. Lipfii not. in Tac. de M. G. cap. ix.
[c] Prim. pages 57, 58, 59.
[d] De Scr. Brit. p. 4.
[e] See of Lucius, in the Catalogue of the Kings of Britain, at the end of this work.

took

took away from the Druids the eftablifhment, and countenance of the
Civil Government; but notwithftanding this (as Superftition takes
deep root, and in more places than can prefently be attended, admi-
niftered unto, and effectually cured by the moft diligent Paftors) it
doubtlefs required time to introduce a thorough change in the people:
however, from the time of the Gofpel's taking place, Druidifm certainly began to dwindle, as having loft that Power which was the
principal fupport of their whole fyftem [f]; Druidifm continued in
Mona, till Crathlintus, King of Scotland [g], expelled the Druids, and
fettled a Bifhop there [h].

But the laft place we read of them in the Britifh dominions, is Ireland, where they continued in full poffeffion of all their ancient power
till the year 432 after Chrift, when St. Patrick undertook the converfion of that Ifland. The Druids, or Irifh Magi, are faid to have
foretold the coming of St. Patrick, and that it was to happen in the
year abovementioned; they are alfo faid to have difputed with him in
prefence of Leogarius, King of Ireland, this fame year [i]; and from
the great progrefs which St. Patrick and his Difciples made in converting the Druids, and the people of that Ifland to Chriftianity, he
has ever fince been accounted the Apoftle and Tutelary Saint of the
Irifh Nation [k]. After the Druids were entirely abolifhed, and no Prieft
of that Order fuffered to officiate, many of the Druid fuperftitious
Cuftoms, of the lefs enormous kind, remained, and may be manifeftly
traced, even to this day, in Ireland, in the Scotifh Ifles, and in Cornwall.

A Priefthood of fuch antiquity and eminence, could not but leave
many Monuments behind them.

As Priefts, dedicated to the facred offices of their Religion, the
Druids muft have had in all their places of worfhip, Idols, Temples,
Groves, Altars, Lavacra (or holy Baths): as Men they muft have
had houfes, and doubtlefs, habitations of the better fort; as they were
abfolute Judges in every cafe of importance, they had their Forums,
or appropriated courts of judicature; as the firft clafs of the Nobility,
they were certainly buried (efpecially the chief Flamens) with fome
diftinction, and confequently muft have had fepulchres, the moft remarkable which the times they lived in afforded: now, as all thefe
things were intended for the ufe of pofterity, as well as of the age
that erected them, it is no wonder that many of them fhould furvive
the fate of their Superftition. But as the country became more cul-

In Ireland exifted till the year 432.

Some Re-mains ftill to be traced of the Mo-numents they left be-hind them.

[f] It is recorded of Elvanus, immediate Succef-for to Theanus (the firft Arch-bifhop of London, appointed by King Lucius), that he converted many Druids to the Chriftian Faith. Ufher, Prim. p. 67.
[g] Ibid.
[h] This Mona was at that Time under the Dominion of the King of Scotland, and therefore, as Ufher obferves (ibid. ut fupra), more likely to be the Ifle of Man, than that of Anglefea: to

which I cannot but add, that Cefar calls the Ifle of Man, Mona, and fays it was in the Middle of the Sea, betwixt Britain and Ireland. The Britifh Hiftorians, however, endeavour to appropriate this Name to the Ifle of Anglefea.
[i] " Apud Probum, & Jocelinum," c. liii. Ufher, ibid. p. 852. Ind. Chron. ibid. p. 430.
[k] Flaherty and Matt. Kennedy, p. 19 Rowland, p. 107.

tivated,

tivated, people and trade increaſed, towns built, and cities, churches, monaſteries, and palaces erected, many of theſe ancient monuments were, doubtleſs, applied to the uſes of building, for which reaſon very few or none of them are to be found near great cities and towns. However, in more retired ſituations, particularly on rocky hills, and mountains of difficult acceſs, as well as on deſert plains, there are ſome of every ſort abovementioned, ſtill remaining.

Groves.   Of their Groves it cannot be expected that many ſhould remain, tillage and cultivation having made more than bare amends for their ſhade and beauty; but Tradition unqueſtionably aſſures us, that there were formerly many woods and groves, where now there is not a tree to be ſeen; and though we find the Druid monuments at this time naked and uncovered, yet there is great reaſon to believe, that anciently they all ſtood under their proper coverture of ſacred trees.

Caves.   Their Caves were all as rude as nature formed them, or ſo little altered from nature, that nothing of art might appear, the Druids imagining (as it appears from moſt of their monuments) that it was beneath the antiquity of their Order, as well as the majeſty of the Gods, to make uſe of the modern delicacies of art, or carving. Their Houſes alſo (or at leaſt thoſe what Tradition call ſo) many of which are ſtill to be ſeen in the Scotch Iſles (called *Tig-the-nan-Druidh*) have little art, being capable only of holding one perſon (as fitter for contemplation), without lime or mortar, and of as few and unwrought Stones as poſſible. But it muſt be obſerved, that theſe little houſes were their Sacella (ſacred Cells), to which the people were to have recourſe for Divining, or deciding controverſies, or for prayers; but not their family-ſeats, or uſual habitations, which were neceſſarily to be of a different ſize and ſhape, and were ſurely as convenient and noble as were cuſtomary in that age.

There is no room to doubt, but as judicial Arbitrators of all diſputes, Civil and Religious, the Druids had their Forums, or proper places allotted them, ſuch as might beſt anſwer the exigencies of their function, and of theſe ſome muſt remain.

Gorſedaus.   Gorſedaus, we have many in Cornwall; whether they were ſome conſecrated Rocks, elevated above the the reſt, or whether they were ſtone-heaps, ſerving to pronounce their judicial decrees from, as being the encloſures of their anceſtors aſhes, which they would not by any means violate by unjuſt deciſions. Of which ſoever kind the Gorſedaus were, there are a great number in the weſtern parts of Cornwall.

Stone-heaps   Stone-heaps, with a rough Pillar erected in the middle of them, are, doubtleſs, Druid monuments, traces of ſuch being found in the hiſtory of the moſt ancient Eaſtern nations, applied to like Superſtition.

Sepulchres.   What kind of Sepulchres the Druids made uſe of may be perhaps diſputed, but as they unqueſtionably burnt their dead, it is very reaſonable

fonable to fuppofe, that their principal Priefts, and great Men, had their afhes collected into an Urn, and fometimes had the Urn placed in a grave, ftone-vault (or *Kift-vaen*[l]), near fome place of worfhip, where they officiated; or near their dwelling; without any other note, or mark of dignity, infcriptions being a tranfgreffion againft the general prohibition of committing any thing to writing. At other times, when leifure permitted, and the defires or dignity of the departed Druid were properly confidered; they erected Barrows over the Urn, there being no country of any efpecial note in hiftory, in which this general kind of Sepulchre (I mean the Barrow) is not to be found; and there is the more reafon to think the Barrow-burial ufed by the Druids, becaufe fometimes, upon thefe Barrows, and fometimes at the bottom, and near them, the Druids burnt fome of their holy and feftival Fires[m]; all nations paying great honours to the tombs of their anceftors, and annually facrificing, feafting, and appointing games at thofe very places, as doing honour to the dead, and giving pleafure, and entertainment at the fame time to the living.

We have great plenty of thefe Barrows every where; and indeed, by their plain and fimple figure, they are to laft as long as they continue free from the hands of violence.

All the remains of the Druids, befides what has been hinted at above, are few and inconfiderable. In fome places they left their names to towns and houfes, hills and brooks, which ftill continue; and all names that have Drudau, Dru, Druwydd, Drudion, Derwyddon, Derw, and Dâr, may be reckoned of Druid original[n].

[l] i. e. Stone Cheft.

[m] Chap. xx.

[n] Bod-Drudau, viz. Druids Houfe in Anglefea, Rowland, p. 245. — Boddryddau in Difert Parifh, Flintfhire, Druids Houfe. — Bod-druden (vulgo Bod-drugan in Cornwall) of the fame Derivation. Boddrugy in Philak. — Rhied-Druith (vulg. Red-Druth), i. e. Nobilium Druidarum vadum, vel Statio. Goon-Derw (vulg. Conderow) the Druids Downs. Tin-Derw (vulg. Tinderow), in St. Anthony Meneague, Druids Hill.

 END OF THE SECOND BOOK.

PL.VIII.

A

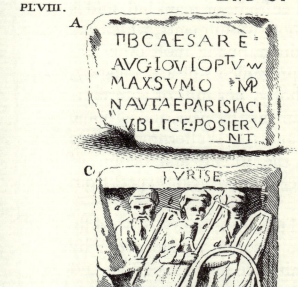

C

B

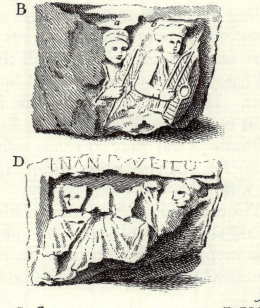

p. 157.

See p. 153.

S f   RUDE

RUDE STONE-MONUMENTS.

BOOK III.

CHAP. I.

Of Rude Stone-Monuments in general.

SOME things are remarkable and curious for their elegance, richnefs, fhape, and magnificence, and fome others for their fimplicity, and remote Antiquity. If the Reader is of that turn, as to be delighted only with the former kind of Monuments, I can promife him but little pleafure in the enfuing Treatife; but if he has a juft regard for the firft ages and cuftoms of mankind, and is willing to enquire into the original of thofe Monuments, which are difperfed not only in thofe Iflands of Britain, but in moft other nations, and certainly preceded all the improvements of art, imagery, and fancy, he may not lofe his labour wholly, nor mifs of entertainment. He may here fee the fame Monuments in Afia, and at home at his own doors; the fame in Egypt, and the Wefternmoft parts of Britain; and may perhaps difcover the intent and defign of them, fet forth in other hiftories, better than we can expect from the hiftory of our own country.

The precarioufnefs of human life, and the uncertainty of worldly affairs, taught people very foon after the Creation to endeavour by fome memorials to perpetuate the remembrance of thofe perfons and events, which had been of importance in their time.

Religion

Religion did also prompt them very early to mark out particular places for worſhip; and there is no room to doubt, but that theſe Monuments were at firſt of the moſt ſimple kind, rude, without Art, or Inſcription, the Authors of them regarding more the thing to be remembered, than the materials or faſhion of the Memorial, and conſulting their preſent exigencies, without any view of ſatisfying the curioſity of after-ages, by affixing dates and names upon their works: they therefore choſe ſuch kind of Monuments as offered moſt readily, and required only the good-will, labour, and aſſiſtance of that multitude, from whom they could expect no elegance, invention, or beauty: of this moſt ancient ſort of Monuments muſt thoſe be reckoned, which conſiſt of rude unhewn Stones, as offering themſelves in moſt, or all countries, on the higheſt hills (ſuch as the Ancients generally choſe, for their eminency, to erect their memorials upon), and promiſing a longer duration, than Monuments of a more compounded nature.

Theſe ſtones were erected in different number, and figure, and upon different occaſions.

In Cornwall, they are ſometimes found ſingle, as Obeliſks, ſometimes two, three, or more, compoſing one Monument, ſometimes diſpoſed in a lineal, ſtraight direction, ſometimes in a circle; often in heaps, or Barrows, and now and then, three or four large flags, or thin ſtones, capped with a much larger one, which go by the Britiſh name of Cromlêhs.

It appears from hiſtory, that ſome of theſe Monuments were of a truly Religious Inſtitution, erected by particular perſons, either as Monuments of their gratitude for ſome extraordinary bleſſing, or to be a ſymbol to poſterity of a Religious Covenant, either with God, or with one another: others were ſepulchral, and both theſe ſorts of Monuments became afterwards, with the true believers, places of publick national Worſhip; but with the Heathens they became Idols, Altars, or Temples, ſubſervient to the purpoſes of Idolatry; and with both true Believers and Gentiles, the places where theſe Rude Stones were erected, became the ſeats of Judicature, of Inauguration, and national Councils. Some of theſe Rude Stones were memorials of civil contracts, or military exploits. Others were boundaries of lands and countries, and ſometimes goals of *ſtadia*, the termination of courſes; others, according to the voice of Superſtition, were of miraculous, healing, and ſacred virtue. Let us paſs on to treat of each ſort particularly, following the Order in which they may be ſuppoſed to have had their beginning; and from theſe Monuments ſee what lights we can ſtrike out in ancient hiſtory; for as the Author of the Religion of the ancient Gauls ſays, " Monuments

" are

" are oftentimes more fure guides to truth, than Hiftorians themfelves[o].

<h1 style="text-align:center">C H A P. II.</h1>

Of fingle Stones-Erect, or rude Pillars.

THE moft ancient Monument of this kind, which hiftory affords us (if Jofephus is to be credited), is that which Seth erected : this Patriarch, fearing (as the Jewifh Hiftorian fays) the deftruction of mankind, becaufe of their abominable wickednefs, but not forefeeing whether this defolation was to be executed by Fire or Water, fet up two Pillars, the one of Stone, the other of Brick ; that by their different conftructions, one of them might be proof againft that Element (which foever it was) which fhould accomplifh the divine judgement [p]. There is alfo a Stone mentioned (1 Sam. vi. 18.), which bore the name of Abel, but whether a fepulchral Monument, or any memorial of Seth's elder brother, hiftory is filent [q]. But let us pafs on to what is more authentick.

SECT. I.
Single Stones Reli-ligious.

Jacob erected feveral of thefe Monuments, and upon different occafions: the firft we read of, is that which he erected at Luz, afterwards by him named Bethel. It was a Religious Monument, which Jacob (at once full of holy dread, at the vifion of God and his Angels, and infpired with the moft grateful fenfe of the Divine Goodnefs, fo plainly declared to him in this gracious Vifion) thought he could not do lefs than mark the place withall, where he had been fo favoured by Heaven.   [r] " And Jacob rofe up early in the morning, and took " the Stone which he had put for his pillow, and fet it up for a " Pillar (Matzebah) and poured oil upon the top of it[s], and called " the name of that place Beth-el," vowed to worfhip the true God only, and that the place where he had fet up this Stone fhould be the

[o] " Les Monuments font fouvent des guides " plus fûrs que les Hiftoriens. De quelque ex-" actitude qu'ils fe foient piquez, non feulement " il leur a echappé une infinité des chofes impor-" tantes, mais même ils font tombez dans erreurs " groffiers, qui pafferoient pour des veritez con-" ftantes fans le fecours de Monuments." Monf. Martin, Rel. de Gaules, vol. ii. p. 332.

[p] Jofephus (Jewifh Antiq.) fays, that one, or both of thefe Pillars, were to be feen in his time. viz. in the Reign of Vefpafian ; but it is indeed very unlikely, that any fuch Pillars fhould have been erected. See Stillingfl. Orig. Sacr. Lib. I. cap. ii.

[q] It is very likely, that what is in our Hebrew Text here, Abel, is a falfe Reading, and ought to be Aben, a Stone, as it is in our marginal Reference in the Englifh Bible.

[r] Gen. xxviii. 18.

[s] From this ancient Rite of pouring Oil on Stones (not begun by Jacob, but received from his Predeceffors) came among the Heathens the Cuftoms, of confecrating Stones into Idols in this fame Manner, and making frequent Libations of Oil upon the top of them ; which Stones whenever they faw marked with thefe Inftances of Devotion, they worfhiped as the Cafe, and Shrine of fome Divinity: Clem. Alex. Strom. vii. 1.—Apuleius — Arnob. Lib. I. " Si quando confpexeram " lubricatum lapidem, et ex Olivi unguine ordi-" natum, tanquam ineffet Vis præfens, adulabar." At Delphi there was a Stone on which they daily poured a certain Quantity of Oil. Paufan. Phocic. de Delphis. Many have a cavity on the top capable of a Pint, with a Groove, about an inch deep reaching to the Ground. Camd. — Toland, p. 101.

houfe

houſe of God. As Jacob was at this time young in years, and had never yet lived from his parents, it may be reaſonably inferred, that in this ceremony of marking out, conſecrating, and new-naming this place, he inſtituted nothing new (as being alone, and intent upon other things, viz. the length, danger, and iſſue of his journey) but followed the cuſtoms of his Anceſtors, ſo that Antiquities of the kind we are now diſcourſing, may be juſtly concluded older than the times of this Patriarch [t].

As Jacob erected this Religious Memorial at Beth-el, Joſhua ſet up another of the ſame kind, and upon a Religious occaſion. He had called all the tribes to Shechem, and after reciting the meſſage to them, which he had in charge from God, he exhorted them to ſerve God only, and they covenanted ſo to do. " And Joſhua took " a great Stone, and ſet it up there under an Oak, that was by the " ſanctuary of the Lord; and Joſhua ſaid unto all the people, " Behold this Stone ſhall be a witneſs unto us, for it hath heard all " the words of the Lord which he ſpake unto us, it ſhall be there- " fore a witneſs unto you leſt ye deny your God [u]."

Theſe are the firſt ſimple Memorials erected by true Believers, on a Religious Account. As for the Gentiles, they ſet up Pillars of the ſame kind in every country, but with very different ends from thoſe of Jacob and Joſhua; for, as, afterwards, when Arts were invented, and became applied to the purpoſes of Superſtition, in making images, adorning Altars, and conſtructing Temples, they worſhiped Statues, and Images; ſo before Arts they worſhiped thoſe Rude Stones [w]. Some think that God's appearing in a pillar of fire by night, and of a cloud by day, ſuggeſted to the Gentiles the contrivance of ſetting up Stone Pillars, and worſhiping them, as the reſemblance of that form in which the Deity had choſen to appear [x]. But it is evident, that the Heathens had this cuſtom of worſhiping Stone Pillars, before the migration of Iſrael out of Egypt; for the children of Iſrael, before they came into Canaan, are expreſsly prohibited from worſhiping theſe Idols, common at that time in Canaan, and therefore not borrowed from any appearances in the Peregrination. That the Canaanites worſhiped them as Gods, we learn from the expreſs prohibitions given to the Iſraelites. " Ye ſhall " make you no Idols, nor graven Image, neither rear you up a " ſtanding Image (מצבה a Pillar [y]), neither ſhall ye ſet up any Image

SECT. II.

Single Stones Idolatrous.

---

[t] It is ſuppoſed by ſome, that from this important Incident in the Hiſtory of Jacob, communicated by Tradition to the Gentile World, the Gentiles called their Stone-Deities Βαιλυλια. Seld. de Diis Syris. Phil. Bybli.
[u] Joſhua xxiv. 14, 26, 27.
[w] " Antequam accuratè tenerentur Imaginum

" habitus, Veteres, columnas, erigentes, eas cole- " bant tanquam Statuas." Clem. Alex. Strom. Lib. I. Rowland, p. 224. " Nec pietas ulla eſt, ve- " latum ſæpe videri—Vertier ad Lapidem."— Lucret. Lib. V.
[x] Rowland, p. 229.
[y] Gen. xxviii. 18.

T t

" of

" of Stone in your land to bow down unto it[z]." And what we read in facred Writ we find confirmed alfo by other hiftories.

Semiramis is faid to have erected an Obelifk 125 feet high, and five foot wide[a]. All the world knows, and ftill admires, the work-manfhip of the Egyptian Obelifks; they were generally dedicated to the Sun, and worfhiped[b]. The Paphians worfhiped their Venus, under the form, nearly, of a white Pyramid[c]; and the Brachmans worfhiped the great God, under the figure of a little column of Stone[d]. The Symbol of Jupiter Ammon, was a conick Stone[e] in his Egyptian Temple; and in Africa Apollo's Image was a kind of Erect-ftone, like a Pyramid[f]. A fquare Stone was the Image of Mercury, as a pillar was that of Bacchus[g]. The Jews alfo were carried away by this ftrong current of Idolatry, and they fet up pillars in every high hill, and under every green tree[h]; fo that this Idolatry of worfhiping Rude Stones-Erect may be reckoned to have infected much the greateft part of the world, efpecially thofe parts which had any communication with Syria, Egypt, or Greece, and may with equal reafon be fuppofed to have occafioned the erecting many of thofe large Stones which are to be found in Britain, where the ancient Phenicians and Grecians had frequent reforts.

In Cornwall there is a great number of high Stones (probably fome of the ancient Idols) ftill ftanding[i] in many places. Many have been carried off for building, as has been mentioned in the defcription of Karn-brê, and many ftill remain where they fell from their erect pofition. In a village called Mên-Perhen in Conftantine Parifh, there ftood about five years fince a large Pyramidal Stone, twenty foot above the ground, and four foot in the ground; it made above twenty Stone Pofts for gates, when it was clove up by the Farmer, who gave me this account. In the fides of Sharpy-tor (mentioned chap. xx. Lib. II.) and Wringcheefe in the parifh of St. Cleer, I obferved many large Stones of a rude Columnar fhape, now lying proftrate; but formerly, without doubt, Erect, confecrated to Super-ftition, and by their tallnefs ferving, to make thefe Craggs (fo rough by nature) ftill more forked and briftly.

After Chriftianity took place, many continued to worfhip thefe Stones, to pay their vows, and devote their offerings, at the places where thefe Stones were erected, coming thither with lighted torches, and praying for fafety and fuccefs; and this cuftom we can trace

[z] Lev. xxvi. 1.
[a] Diod. Sic. Lib. II. cap. i.
[b] On the Pedeftal of the famous Obelifk, erected by Theodofius the Emperor, in the Hippodrome at Conftantinople, the People are juftly repre-fented in Bafs-relieve proftrate, and adoring thefe Obelifks, Spon. vol. i. p. 139.

[c] Max. Tyr. Serm. 38.
[d] Plott's Oxford (from De la Valle) p. 352.
[e] Qu. Curtius Var. p. 185.
[f] Paufan. Lib. I.
[g] Toland 101.
[h] 2 Kings xvii. 10.
[i] See Plate X. Figures I. II.

through

through the fifth and sixth centuries, even into the seventh, as will appear from the prohibitions of several Councils.

In Ireland some of these Stones-erect have crosses cut on them, which are supposed to have been done by Christians, out of compliance with the Druid prejudices; that when Druidism fell before the Gospel, the common people, who were not easily to be got off from their superstitious Reverence for these Stones, might pay a kind of justifiable adoration to them when thus appropriated to the uses of Christian Memorials, by the sign of the Cross.   There are still some remains of Adoration paid to such Stones in the Scottish Western Isles even by the Christians.   They call them Bowing-stones from the reverence shewn them, as it seems to me; for the *Even Maschith*, which the Jews were forbad to worship [k], signifies really a Bowing-stone [l], and was doubtless so called, because worshiped by the Canaanites [m].   In the Isle of Barray there is one Stone, about seven foot high, and when the inhabitants come near it, they take a religious turn round, according to the ancient Druid custom [n].

The abovementioned Patriarch, Jacob, seems to have been desirous SECT. III. above any of his Ancestors, of leaving some traces of his adventures Memorials to posterity, by something more than bare Tradition; accordingly, of Civil when Laban had overtaken him in his return to his native country, Contracts. and desired to enter into a solemn contract of amity with him, Jacob took a Stone, and set it up for a Pillar [o]; and his kinsmen who attended upon Laban took Stones, and made an heap, to intimate, that they did thereby become parties in, or guardians of the treaty, as well as witnesses to the execution of it by the principal persons concerned, Laban, and Jacob. There is one other circumstance here observable, which is, that when any thing, or place, was by consent appropriated to a particular use, it was the custom to give it a new, and expressive name; thus Luz was called Beth-el, or the house of God, and this second monument was called Galeed, or heap of witness. It was also called Mizpah, or Mitzpah, i. e. a high place of Observation. Where, therefore, we find a small heap of Stones, and a Pillar erected among them, there are some grounds to think, that it is a monument of the same design as that of Jacob at Galeed, for as much as it is of the same structure.   The Stone (Plate X. fig. III.) and little Barrow at the bottom was either a Monument of such a civil contract as Galeed, or a Sepulchre; for that the Ancients buried thus we shall see soon.

[k] Lev. chap. xxvi. 1.
[l] See State of Downe, p. 209.
[m] Mr. Martin of the Isles, p. 88, and 229. thinks them called Bowing-stones, because the Christians had there the first View of their Church, at which place, therefore, they first bowed themselves; but this Custom is much more ancient than Christianity.
[n] Martin, ibid.
[o] Gen. xxxi. 45.

The

The Monument of Galeed was firſt erected upon account of a civil compact, or treaty of friendſhip, confirmed by ſolemn Oaths and Imprecations, and to be tranſmitted to Poſterity by the proper Memorials of a Pillar, and a heap. This ſame Monument in after-ages drew the attention of the People to it ſo much, as to make the place become the great place of worſhip for the twelve tribes [q]; ſo that this ſort of Stone-monuments, originally only intended as Memorials of private family-leagues (though theſe leagues were attended by ſome religious Oaths and Rites), becoming famous on account of the Authors of them, and places of great reſort, were ſoon afterwards appointed to be places of worſhip for the whole nation ; and hence proceeded the cuſtom (which afterwards obtained much among the Ancients) of marking out places of worſhip, by theſe Stones-erect.

First then, where theſe Stones were erected, places of worſhip were eſtabliſhed out of reſpect to the moral and religious Character of their Author. Bethel[r] became a place of worſhip, becauſe of Jacob's Pillar; Gilgal alſo [s], for like reaſon, becauſe of the Pillars erected by Joſhua, at the paſſing of Jordan ; Gilead, Galeed, or Mizpah, became alſo in after-ages a place of worſhip[t], and of idolatry[u], as the reſt.

Theſe places having been conſecrated to the purpoſes of Religion were ſoon after juſtly thought worthy of being the ſcenes of all the moſt important affairs of the nation, ſo that no ties, or covenants, were thought ſo obligatory, as thoſe which were contracted in theſe ſacred places. Samuel made Bethel and Gilgal the annual ſeats of Judgment[w]. At Gilgal, Saul was confirmed King, and the allegiance of his people renewed, with Sacrifices, and great Feſtival Joy[x]. At Mizpah, Jephtha was ſolemnly inveſted with the Government of Gilead[y], and the general council againſt eBnjamin ſeems to have been held here[z]. At the Stone of Shechem, erected by Joſhua[a], Abimelech was made King[b]. Adonijah by the Stone of Zoheleth[c]. Jehoaſh was " crowned King ſtanding by a Pillar, as the manner was[d];" and Joſiah " ſtood by a Pillar" when he was making a ſolemn covenant with God[e]. There was ſomething emblematical in their chuſing

---

[q] Judges xxi. 1. 1 Sam. vii. 5, 6, &c.
[r] Amos vii. 13.—Gen. xxxv. 1.—1 Sam. x. 3.
1 Kings xii. 33.
[s] Hoſ. ix. 15. xii. 11.—Amos iv. 4.—1 Sam. xi. 15.
[t] Judges xi. 11.
[u] Hoſea v. 1.
[w] 1 Sam. vii. 16.
[x] 1 Sam. xi. 14.
[y] Judges xi. 11.

[z] Judges xx. 1, 3.
[a] Joſh. xxiv. 26.
[b] In the Engliſh Tranſlation it is ſaid, that Abimelech was made King, " by the Plain of " the Pillar that was in Shechem;" but it ſhould be " by the Oak of the Pillar," for under an Oak this Pillar was erected. Joſh. xxiv. 26.
[c] 1 Kings i. 9.
[d] 2 Kings xi. 14.
[e] 2 Kings xxiii. 3.

thus

Fig. VI p. 187.
Monumental Stones at Drift in Sancred

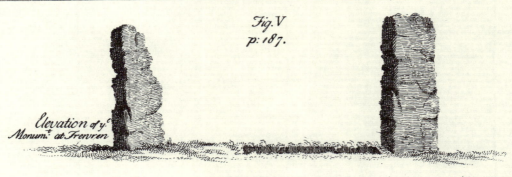

Fig. V
p: 187.

Elevation of y.
Monum.t at Trenven

Fig IV

Plan.

Sepulchral Monument at Trenven in Maddern

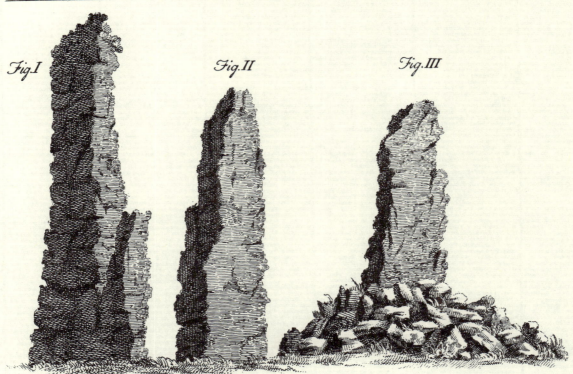

Fig. I   Fig. II   Fig. III

Two Stones erect at Bolleit in S.t
Beryan. about a furlong asunder
explain'd p: 162.

Long Stone in Boswens Croft Sancred
see p: 163.

3   6   9   12 Feet

PL X.
p. 164.

thus to ſtand by erected Stones or Pillars, when they were employed in affairs of ſuch ſolemnity ; and doubtleſs, it was their intent to intimate, that their engagements entered into in ſuch places ought to be as firm and laſting, and their deciſions as impartial and upright, as the ſymbolical Pillar that ſtood before their eyes.

But of theſe rude Stone Monuments, ſome were originally Sepul- **SECT. VI.** chral, and did neither owe their beginning to the true, or falſe Sepulchral. Religion, however afterwards applied.

We are obliged to Jacob for the firſt recorded Monument of this kind ; for when his beloved Rachel died, he did not bury her under an Oak, as Deborah the nurſe of Rebeccah was buried [f], leſt her grave might not be enough diſtinguiſhed, but " ſet a Pillar upon " her Grave [g]." Bohan the ſon of Reuben ſeems to have been buried alſo in the ſame manner, his Stone Monument becoming afterwards one of the boundaries of the Realm of Judah [h], and indeed this was reckoned a very honourable way of burying among the ancients.

To make the grave and pillar more conſpicuous, moſt countries ſoon adopted the manner of placing the latter on a heap of ſtones or earth. Ilus the ſon of Dardanus King of Troy, was buried in this manner in the plain before that city [i]. When Sarpedon was killed in battle, Jupiter deſired Apollo, to ſend his wounded body, waſhed, anointed with ambroſia, and cloathed with never-fading veſtures, to his native country, there with due honours to be depoſited by his friends and relations [k] Τυμϐῳ τε Σ]ηλη τε, το γαρ γερας εςι θανον]ων; an evident ſign that this was the moſt honourable way of burying, as being what Jupiter himſelf ordered for his favourite ſon. Abradates king of Suſa and his wife Panthea had alſo a pillar erected on their grave by Cyrus [l], and their State Officers or Eunuchs had a pillar for each on their graves [m].

It is likely that in Greece they launched out into ſome extravagancy in the erected-Stones of Sepulchral inſtitution; for Plato is ſaid to have forbidden any larger Stone to be fixed on the grave, than what would contain the Eulogy of the interred: " Plato vetabat" (Cic.ii. de Leg.) " ne ſit ſepulchrum altius quàm quod quinque homines " diebus quinque abſolverent, nec e Lapide excitari plus, nec imponi, " quàm quod capiat laudem mortui inciſam, nec plus quatuor herois " verſibus quos Longos appellat Ennius." Demetrius Phalereus alſo ordered at Athens, that no perſon for the future ſhould have a Stone on their *Tumulus* higher than three Cubits.

---

[f] Gen. xxxv. 8.
[g] Ibid. xxxv. 20.
[h] Joſh. xv. 6.
[i] Paris taking the advantage of this Pillar, wounded Diomed. Il. xi. 317.

Στηλη κεκλιμεν©· ανδροκμητῳ επι τυμβῳ
Ιλυ Δαρδανιδαο παλαιυ δημογερον]©·.
[k] Il. xvi. 667.
[l] Xenoph. Lib. VII.
[m] See Of Barrows, chap. viii.

U u

There are many of these rude Obelisks in Denmark and Sweden, which are generally supposed by the natives of these countries to be sepulchral [n]; and Olaus Magnus tells us [o], that it was one of Woden's laws to erect high Stones on the graves of famous men. In Scotland there are many, and King Reutha is said by Boethius to have invented this way of honouring the memory of valiant men [p]. In Ireland there are many of the same kind still to be seen, near which ashes and bones being found, make it justly believed that they are Sepulchral Monuments [q].

The Pillar said to be erected to the memory of Pompey, the Trajan and Antonine Columns (all Sepulchral Memorials), are but imitations of this ancient custom, the magnificence of after ages getting the better of ancient simplicity, and altering the construction of these Monuments, without rejecting or totally obscuring the custom of their predecessors.

These Sepulchral Monuments became afterwards famous for the Annual Sacrifices, Feasts and Games celebrated in honour of the departed Heroes, there interred.

SECT. VII. **Military Memorials.** Some of these rude single Stones were also of Military Extraction, and were erected as Memorials of single Combats, Battles, and considerable Victories. The most ancient Trophy we read of is that erected by the Prophet Samuel, betwixt Mizpeh and Shen, in commemoration of a signal and miraculous overthrow of the Philistines: it was called Ebenezer, or the Stone of Help, that holy leader ascribing all (without allowing any share to his own conduct, or to the valour of the Israelites) to the divine assistance [r]. The Swedes [s] and Danes have many of these single Stones, as has been before observed, and, among other uses assigned them, tradition has there preserved the names of the heroes, and the warlike occasion upon the account of which they were erected [t]; and in Scotland, in the shire of Murray, there is a single Stone set up as a Monument of the fight betwixt King Malcolm son of Keneth [u] and Sueno the Dane.

Trophies. In other parts of Scotland more Monuments of the same kind, are attributed to the same use [w]. In process of time, as mankind became more fond of ornament, the Spoils and Armour of the conquer'd were employ'd to dress up the naked Stone; afterwards the Stock of a Tree was found to be better adapted to exhibit the signals of Victory in a proper figure, than the rude Stone: Art and Ingenuity afterwards carved all the proper emblems out of the Marble,

---

[n] Wormius, p. 64, 65. Ol. Mag. Lib. I. p. 8.
[o] Lib. I. cap. vii.
[p] Camden, p. 1480.
[q] Toland, p. 84. Other instances may be seen in Camden, p. 1256; Martin of the Isles, p. 59, and 388.

[r] 1 Sam. vii. 12.
[s] Ola. Mag. Lib. I. p. 8.
[t] See Wormius, Mon. Danica, p. 62. and ibid. p. 118.
[u] Camden, p. 1268.
[w] Wallace, of the Orkn. p. 54.

the

the Porphyry, or the Granite, erected them with grandeur, and difpofed the arms with more elegance and unity in fculpture, than the realities would admit of.

Some of thefe Stones were alfo erected by the Ancients as Boundaries either national, or patrimonial. Laban and Jacob's Monument beforementioned, was partly of the patrimonial kind. " This " Heap be witnefs, and this Pillar be witnefs, that I will not pafs " over this Heap to thee, and that thou fhalt not pafs over this " Heap and this Pillar unto me for harm [x]." So was the Stone which Minerva wounded Mars withal [y]. As to national Boundaries, the Ifraélites, where no city, fea, lake, or hill, offered itfelf, made a Stone their boundary, as in the limits of the kingdom of Judah [z].

SECT. VIII.
Boundaries

But thefe Monuments were not always the works of War, or Compact, or of Law, Religion, or Sepulture, but fometimes of Execration, and Witchcraft.

Scopelifmus

The Arabians are faid to have had a cuftom of placing Stones upon the field, or farm, of the man they hated, as a denunciation of utter deftruction to any one who fhould afterwards attempt to occupy or cultivate the ground on which they were erected, and fuch terrour attended this malevolent interdiction, called Scopelifmus [a], that no one ventured to come near fuch ground.

In the rage of War and Victory, when the Enemy and every thing he had was devoted to utter deftruction, it was ufual to mar and defolate his beft lands of corn and pafture by ftrewing them with ftones, thereby rendering them fterile and ufelefs to the unhappy vanquifhed. 2 Kings iii. 19. 25. Some have thought this act to have been a kind of Scopelifmus, but the Arabian cuftom was differently grounded, and with more extenfive malice and cruelty. The former was the violence of open war, which laid no penalty on thofe who came afterwards and endeavoured to cultivate the fpoiled lands; the latter was an interdiction of every kind of cultivation, in times of peace as well as war, an interdiction ratified probably, and made irreverfible, by ritual Magical execrations, fubjecting the lawful poffeffor to the moft treacherous murder, only for undertaking to improve his barren and rocky grounds.

The account given of this Arabian cuftom by Ulpian is as follows [b], " Sunt quædam quæ more Provinciarum coercitionem

[x] Gen. xxxi. 52.
[y] —————— Λιθον ειλιλο χειρι παχειη,
Κειμενον εν πεδιω, μαλακα, τρηχυν τε μεγαλε,
Τον ρ' ανδρες προτεροι θεσαν εμμεναι ουρον αρουρης.
                                    Il. xxi. ver. 403.
[z] Jofhua xv. 6. xviii. 17. The Northern Nations had alfo the fame way of marking out the Boundaries of Diftricts. Ol. Mag. p. 11.
[a] Scopelifmus, à σκοπελιζειν, to threaten or endeavour the death of any one; from a cuftom

among the Arabians of erecting Stones upon the land of the perfon with whom they were angry. Wood's Civil Law, p. 322. D. 47, 11, 9, and 39, 2, 11.
[b] Ulpian, de officio Proconfulis, p. 1673. Lugduni, 1585, 4to. 4 vol. For the firft notice of this paffage in Ulpian, I was indebted to the Right Rev. Dr. Lyttelton, Bifhop of Carlifle, in the year 1762.

" folent

" ſolent admittere : ut putà in Provincia Arabiæ Σχοπελισμον, Lapi-
" dum poſitionem, crimen appellant ; cujus rei admiſſum tale eſt.
" Plerique inimicorum ſolent prædium inimici σχοπελιζειν, i. e. Lapi-
" des ponere, indicio futuros, quod ſi quis eum agrum coluiſſet malo
" letho periturus eſſet inſidiis eorum qui ſcopulos poſuiſſent : quæ
" res tantum timorem habet, ut nemo ad eum agrum accedere audeat,
" crudelitatem timens eorum qui Scopeliſmon fecerunt.   Hanc rem
" Præſides exequi ſolent graviter uſque ad pœnam capitis, quia et
" ipſa res mortem comminatur."   Zieritzius [c] (in his comment on
this paſſage) obſerves, that as the province of Arabia and the neighbouring countries have been from all Antiquity remarkable for incantatorial herbs and animals, and alſo for Superſtition and Witchcraft (as appears from the Holy Scriptures, Joſephus, Pliny, Mela,
and others), it is moſt likely that the Arabs either placed ſome magical inſtruments of their diabolical commerce under theſe Stones, or
perpetrated at or near them ſome infernal rites of Execration and
Darkneſs [d].

To this may be added, that theſe Stones muſt have been of ſuch a
ſize, and placed in ſuch a particular order, as might exhibit in
ſome degree the intention of thoſe that placed them*, (for if
there was no indication, there could be no tranſgreſſion) yet
left in ſuch a myſtical arrangement as might ſubject the innocent to
miſtake, and incite the raſh and cruel to renew hoſtilities, and to
ſhed blood on the ſlighteſt pretences.   The Roman Governours
therefore, juſtly made it a capital crime to devote Lands in ſuch
a deteſtable manner to deſolation, preventing at once the
deſirable cultivation of lands in ſo deſart and rocky a Province
as Arabia, and equally expoſing the lives of the Romans, and their
induſtrious provincial ſubjects, to the revenge of the inſidious and
aſſaſſin.

C H A P. III.

Of Rock-Idols, their ſeveral Shapes, and the high Opinion which the Ancients entertained of them.

Phenicians.

Syrians.

BESIDES tall Stones-erect, the Ancients had Stone-Deities of
various ſhapes.   The Phenicians made the Image of the Sun of
one black Stone, round at the bottom, its top ending, either in the
ſhape of a cone, or a wedge [e].   Their neighbours the Syrians had the

---

[c] In the Bodleian Library, Oxford.
[d] Nox, & Diana quæ Silentium regis,
    Arcana cum fiant Sacra,

Nunc, nunc adeſte, nunc in hoſtiles domos
Iram atque Numen vertite.
                    Hor. Canidia, Epod. V.
* " Indicio futuros," Up. ibid.
[e] Herodian, Lib. V.—Alex. ab Alex. Lib. IV.
    p. 1026.

                                              ſame

same cuſtom, and worſhiped a Rude Image of the Sun[f]. " The " Arabians, ſays Maximus Tyrius[g], worſhip ſuch a God as I have not   Arabians. " before met with ; the form of the Idol is a Quadrangular Stone," likely dedicated to Mercury. Arnobius[h] calls the Arabian Deity *(Informem Lapidem)* a ſhapeleſs Stone[i]. Among the ſeveral Demigods that went by the name of Hercules, I find one called Hercules Saxanus, who was worſhiped, more eſpecially in Rocks, or in rocky   Grecians. Places[k]. The Statue of the Theſpian Cupid, was a rough Stone untouched by a Tool[l]; and the Grecians in general, in their more ancient times, worſhiped Rude Stones inſtead of Images[m]. The Canaanites, whoſe chief God was Saturn[n], had this cuſtom of wor-   Canaanites. ſhiping Rocks very anciently ; for Moſes (in his Song, Deut. xxxii.) cautioning the Jews againſt Apoſtacy, alludes ſeveral times to the corruptions of Rock-Worſhip, to which he foreſaw they would be drawn aſide by their neighbours. " How ſhould one chaſe a thou- " ſand, and two put ten thouſand to flight, except their Rock (meaning their true God) " had ſold them, and the Lord had ſhut " them up: for their *Rock* (meaning their falſe God of Stone) is not " as our Rock, even our enemies themſelves being Judges" (ver. 30.) And again, ver. 37. " Where are theſe Gods, their *Rock*, in whom " they truſted, which did eat the fat of their Sacrifices, and drink " the wine of their Drink-offerings? Let them riſe up, and help " you, and be your protection[o]." The Italians had anciently this   Italians. cuſtom, and their Rocks and high hills were generally dedicated to, and called after, the name of Saturn[p]. By this it appears, that ſuch conſecrated Rocks were called anciently by the name of ſome God, that is, named, ritually dedicated, and advanced into Divinities. After theſe Rocks had been conſecrated, the Ancients paid them all manner of reverence, imagined, that thenceforth ſome ſpiritual intelligences reſided within them, and that whatever touched them was ſacred, and derived great virtue and power from them. Hence aroſe a Cuſtom, which continues to this day, of lying down, and ſleeping upon Rocks, in order to be cured of lameneſs; and the very rain that fell from their ſides, or was contained in their hollows, was accounted holy, of great uſe to purification, to cure diſtempers, and foretell future events[q]. Nay, they went ſo far in the madneſs of this kind of Idolatry, as to imagine, that they heard

---

[f] Αντγϱαϛον Ηλιϗ εικονα. Herod. in Heliogab. —
Sched. 342.
   [g] Sermo 38.
   [h] Contra Gent.
   [i] " The oldeſt Idol of the Arabs was called " Manah, a Goddeſs like Venus, and Fate, wor- " ſhiped under the form of a great unhewn Stone." Letters of Mythology, p. 374. See Sale's Alcoran.
   [k] Keyſler, p. 195.

[l] Pauſan. in Ach.
[m] Pauſan. ibid. p. 579.
[n] See p. 64. Note [l].
[o] See Iſaiah lvii. 5, 6.
[p] " Multa etiam Loca (viz. in Italia) hujus " Dei (viz. Saturni) nomen habent, et præcipuè " Scopuli et colles excelſi." Dion. Halic. Lib. I. cap. iv. p. 27.
[q] See Chapter xi. Book. III.

ſignificant

significant noiſes, and even diſtinct oracular Predictions, proceed out of theſe Rocks. The Statue of Memnon, in Upper Egypt was likely the Deity of that country; it conſiſted of one immenſe ſtone, and at Sun-riſing was imagined to utter Sounds, and as Pliloſtratus ſays, to ſpeak; and the probable Remains of this Statue are ſtill full of Inſcriptions, placed there by Greek and Latin travellers, credulous enough to leave their names and teſtimonies (ſuch as they are) of their having heard the miraculous effuſions of this Vocal Statue[r]. There is a remarkable Story in Giraldus Cam-

brenſis[s], which ſhews, that the common people in his days attributed the power both of ſpeaking and protecting to theſe ſacred Rocks. There was a large flat Stone, ten feet long, ſix wide, and one foot thick, which in his time ſerved as a bridge over the river Alun, at St. David's, in Pembrokeſhire. It was called in Britiſh *Léch Lavar*, that is, the Speaking-ſtone, and the vulgar Tradition was, that when a dead body was, on a time, carrying over, this Stone ſpoke, and with the ſtruggle of the voice cracked in the middle, and the chink, from which the voice iſſued, was then to be ſeen. In this ſimple ſtory the remains of that part of the Druid ſuperſtition, of which we are treating, are clearly to be perceived. There is no doubt but this *Léch Lavar* was the top Stone of a Cromlêch (the Dimenſions ſhew it), which being at firſt no more than a Tomb-ſtone for the dead, became afterwards an Altar, and by degrees had a kind of worſhip paid to it, and was reckoned to give forth oracular ſounds, whence it had the name of *Léch Lavar*, and being of ſo holy a nature, it was thought to be profaned and incenſed by the touch of a dead body[t]; and therefore, even to the middle of the 12th century, the people could never be perſuaded to carry dead bodies over it; and that they attributed more than ordinary power and virtue to this Stone is plain from what the ſame Author ſays in the ſame place, that a woman having made ſome complaints to Henry II. (then juſt arrived at St. David's from Ireland) and not immediately receiving a favourable anſwer, cried out with a loud voice to *Léch Lavar* for redreſs: being checked by the ſtanders-by for her unſeemly behaviour, ſhe cried out ſo much the more violently,

" *O Léch Lavar*, revenge our Injuries!" The Iriſh had the ſame Superſtition; " in an adjacent brook to the Weſt of Bally-caroge, the " country people ſhew a large Rock, as big as an ordinary houſe, " which they call *Cloughlowriſh*, i. e. the Speaking Stone, and relate " a Fabulous account of its ſpeaking at a certain time in contradic- " tion to a perſon who ſwore by it in a lye. The Stone is remakably

[r] See Pocock's Travels, Vol. I. p. 103.
[s] Itinerar. Cambr. Lib. II. cap. i.
[t] See 2 Kings xxiii. 14.

" ſplit

" split from top to bottom, which they tell you was done at the
" time of taking the above-mentioned Oath[u]." We have a Karn
in the parish of St. Juft, Cornwall, named Karn-idzek, or the Hooting-
Karn, called so probably from the prophetick sounds, which confecrated Rocks were suppofed occasionally to send forth.

The learned Keyfler (p. 22.) setting before us the superftition
and credulity of people in this point gives us an inftance of what
the Northern Nations thought on this head. " They believed that
" a kind of Fairies or Demons refided within their Stone-Deities.
" For which reafon it was not very difficult or unnatural for them
" to proceed to that degree of infatuation as to perfuade themfelves
" that they really heard diftinct and prophetick voices proceeding out
" of fuch Stones," of which he then produces the following inftance
from the Holmveria faga of Norway. Indridus, going out of his houfe,
lay in wait for his enemy Thorftenus, who was wont to go to the
Temple of his God at fuch a particular time. Thorftenus came,
and entering the Temple, before Sun-rife, proftrated himfelf before
his Stone-Deity, and offered his Devotions. Indridus ftanding without, heard (or fancied) the Stone to fpeak, and pronounce Thorftenus's doom in the following words:

Northern Nations.

" *Tu huc,*	Heedlefs of thy approaching fate
" *Ultima vice,*	Thou tread'ft this holy ground:
" *Morti vicinis pedibus*	Laft ftep of life! thy guilty breaft,
" *Terram calcafti:*	Ere Phœbus gilds the ruddy Eaft,
" *Certè enim antequam*	Muft expiate
" *Sol fplendeat,*	Thy murderous hate,
" *Animofus Indridus*	Deep pierc'd with crimfon wound.
" *Odium tibi rependet.*	

This is a fufficient proof, as Keyfler well obferves[w], that the ancients
believed not only that Rocks and Stones contained fomething divine
within them, but had a power alfo of difclofing the fecrets of futurity.

The Druids held thefe confecrated Rocks in fuch eftimation, that,
if we may credit the account we have from Ireland[x], they covered
the famous Stone of Clogher (which was a kind of Pedeftal to Ker-
mand Kelftack, the Mercurius Celticus) all over with gold[y].

We have in Cornwall Rocks of that grandeur, remarkable fhape,
and furprizing pofition, as can leave us in no doubt but that they
muft have been the Deities of people addicted fo much to the fuperftition of worfhiping Rocks.

Cornifh.

---

[u] Hift. of Waterford, p. 93.
[w] Keyfler, p. 23.

[x] Toland, p. 100.
[y] See Crum Cruach. chap. ix.

Why Rocks worfhiped. Rocks were firft chofen, as it feems to me, to reprefent the Gods from the firmnefs of their fubftance, continuing ftill the fame, neither difappearing foon, as Fire; nor ruffled, and by drought diffipated, like Water; nor wafting away like Earth; and therefore proper emblems of Strength, Shelter, Shade, and Defence[z]. After Rocks became Symbols, they were occafionally varied and fhaped for feveral fuperftitious reafons; to avoid which, God ordered that the Stones ufed in his Worfhip fhould continue as nature left them. But Gentiles, in this, as well as all other inftances of Simplicity, could not but depart from the true Religion. Accordingly our Rocks in Cornwall have in fome inftances been cleared of their wildeft excrefcences, by art, in others evidently fhaped and fitted by tools, and this could not be done without fome aim or defign; and no defign fo likely, as that fome, by fhewing themfelves to greater advantage (being feparated from the adjoining rocks), might by their vaftnefs more eafily procure the adoration of the beholder; that others, by being fhaped in a particular manner might be more fignificant fymbols of that Deity, or Attribute, which they were defigned to reprefent; and that a third fort might be fo carved as to become moveable to a certain point, or furnifhed with Rock-Bafons (both which are often met with in one Monument) to promote the delufion of the people, and gain of the Priefts. Thefe Rocks have loft the names of the Deities to which they were dedicated; and therefore I fhall content myfelf with calling them by their common names, though no ways expreffive of that Divinity formerly afcribed to them. We have, however, fome reafon to think them dedicated to Saturn, Mars, or Mercury; for we have many places in Cornwall called Trefadarn[a], that is, the town or houfe of Saturn; and we have Nanfadarn, or the Valley of Saturn: and as Saturn was the God that chiefly delighted in Human Sacrifices[b], as the Druid age confifted of thirty years, and was probably taken from one Revolution of the Planet Saturn; as Saturn was worfhiped in Italy, in Rocks and in fuch rocky Places where we find thefe Stones fet up, the Druids may well be fuppofed to have worfhiped Saturn principally in and among thefe Rocks. The Fable of Saturn adds confirmation to the forementioned opinions. His delight in Human Sacrifices, and even offering his own fons, is well expreffed in his cuftom of devouring his own children; his lying hid in Latium [derived *a Latendo*] expreffes his fondnefs for defart rocky places; and his receiving a Stone to devour, inftead of Jupiter, reprefents his having Stones offered and dedicated to him. We have alfo places called after the

And Moftly dedicated to Saturn.

---

[z] " The Lord is my Stony Rock," Pfalm xviii. 1. alibique paffim. " As the Shadow of a " great Rock," Ifaiah xxxii. 2.

[a] In the parifhes of St. Columb, Ruan-Major, Red-druth Guenap, &c.
[b] See p. 64.

name

PL.XI. p.173.

Great Stone in Scilly
Fig.II. p.173

Great Stone in Mên
Fig.I. p.173

Karn Qwoit.
Fig.III. p.180 & 241

Fig.IV. The Logan Stone in S.t Agnes Isl.d Scilly p.182

Fig.V. The Logan Stone in Sithney
call'd Mencomber p.182

Green Sculp.t

To S.r Richard Vyvyan of Trelowarren in Cornwall Bar.t   This Plate is with great respect inscrib'd by Wm. Borlase.

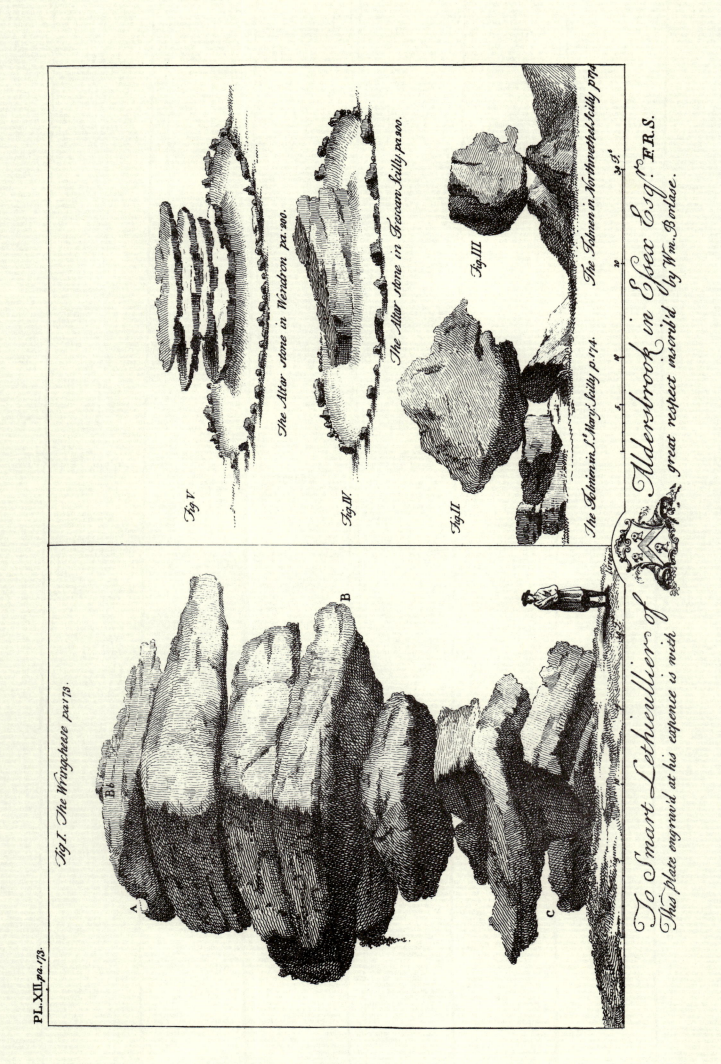

PL. XII. pa. 173.

Fig. I. The Wringcheese pa. 173.

Fig. V.

The Altar stone in Wendron pa. 200.

Fig. IV.

The Altar stone in Trevean Scilly pa. 200.

Fig. III.

The Tolmen in Northwethel Scilly p. 174.

The Tolmen in St. Mary: Scilly p. 174.

To Smart Lethieullier of Aldersbrook in Essex Esqr. F.R.S.
This plate engrav'd at his expence is with great respect inscrib'd by Wm. Borlase.

name of Mars, as Tremêr, the town of Mars; and after the name of Mercury, as Gun Mar'r, and Kelli Mar'r; *i. e.* the Downs, and Grove of Mercury: and to thefe Gods too, it is moſt likely that the Druids ſometimes dedicated in a formal manner theſe Rock-Idols; and, that Rock-worſhip was univerſally ſpread throughout the Druids, in whatever parts of the iſland they reſided, will appear plainly, becauſe in ſuch rocky places moſt of the Druid Monuments of every kind were erected, and are at preſent to be found.

In the pariſh of Conſtantine, Cornwall, in a village called Mên, I obſerved a Stone (Plate XI. Fig. I.) in a very uncommon ſhape; it is like the Greek letter Omega, ſomewhat reſembling a Cap. In the Impoſt upon the Plint (A. A.) it is thirty feet in girt, eleven feet high from B to C. The ground about it is uneven, as if there had been walls or houſes near it; and ſome other rocks adjoining had plain ſigns of workmanſhip near the baſe, as if they had been begun to be formed after the model of the other. In the iſland of St. Mary, Scilly, on the edge of a moſt remarkable circular Temple[c], there is a vaſt ſtone (Fig. II. Plate XI.) which is cut much in the ſame form with Fig. I. but whereas Fig. I. has no Rock-baſon, this at Scilly has thirteen perfect Baſons cut on the ſurface. As theſe Stones are evidently ſhaped by art, and for no conceivable purpoſe, either civil, military or domeſtick, I conclude them Stone-Deities; their Plint (DD, Fig. I.) deſigned perhaps to expreſs the ſtability of their God; and the roundneſs of the upper part his Eternity.

The Rock now called Wringcheeſe[d], is a groupe of Rocks that attracts the admiration of all Travellers. It is beſt apprehended by its Icon (Plate XII. Fig. I.); on the Top-ſtone B were two regular Baſons; part of one of them has been broken off, as may be ſeen at (A). The upper ſtone B was, as I have been informed, a Logan, or Rocking-ſtone, and might when it was entire be eaſily moved with a pole, but now great part of that weight which kept it on a poiſe is taken away. The whole heap of Stone is 32 feet high; the great weight of the upper part from A to B, and the ſlenderneſs of the under part from B to C, makes every one wonder how ſuch an ill-grounded Pile could reſiſt for ſo many ages the ſtorms of ſuch an expoſed ſituation. It may ſeem to ſome that this is an artificial building of flat Stones layed carefully on one another, and raiſed to this height by human ſkill and labour; but as there are ſeveral heaps of Stones on the ſame hill, and alſo on a hill about a mile diſtant, called Kell-mar'r, of like fabrick too, though not near ſo high as this, I ſhould think it a natural Cragg, and that what Stones

[c] See Chap. vii. Lib. III. Sect. iii.
[d] In the Pariſh of St. Clare, near Liſkerd, Cornwall.

Y y   ſurrounded

furrounded it, and hid its grandeur, were removed by the Druids. From its having Rock-bafons, from the uppermoft Stone's being a Rocking-ftone, from the well-poifed ftructure and the great elevation of this groupe, I think we may truely reckon it among the Rock-Deities, and that its tallnefs and juft balance might probably be intended to exprefs the ftatelinefs and juftice of the Supreme Being. Secondly, as the Rock-bafons fhew that it was ufual to get upon the top of this Karn, it might probably ferve for the Druid to harangue the Audience, pronounce decifions, and foretell future Events.

Of the Tol-mên,

There is another kind of Stone-Deity, which has never been taken notice of by any Author that I have heard of. Its common name in Cornwall and Scilly, is Tolmên; that is, the Hole of Stone. It confifts of a large Orbicular Stone, fupported by two Stones, betwixt which there is a paffage. There are two of thefe in the Scilly Iflands, one on St. Mary's Ifland, at the bottom of Salakee Downs; the top Stone 45 foot in girt, horizontally meafured (Plate XII. Fig. II.); the other in the little Ifland of Northwethel (Plate XII. Fig. III.) 33 feet in girt horizontal, by 24 perpendicular meafurement. They are both in the decline of hills, beneath a large Karn of Rocks, ftanding on two natural fupporters; the firft has one exactly round Bafon on it; the fecond has none, neither are there any Bafons on the Rocks below or near it; but elfewhere on the Ifland there are feveral. Both thefe are probably erected by Art; and the Top-ftones, large as they are, brought from the Karns above, and placed by human ftrength where we fee them. But the moft aftonifhing Monument of this kind, is in the Tenement of Mên, in the Parifh of Conftantine, Cornwall (Plate XIII.). It is one vaft egg-like ftone, placed on the points of two natural Rocks, fo that a man may creep under the great one, and between its fupporters, through a paffage about three feet wide, and as much high. The longeft diameter of this Stone is 33 foot from C to D, pointing due North and South; from A to B, is 14 feet 6 deep; and the breadth in the middle of the furface, where wideft, was 18 feet 6 wide from Eaft to Weft. I meafured one half of the circumference, and found it, according to my computation, 48 feet and half, fo that this Stone is 97 feet in circumference, about 60 feet crofs the middle, and, by the beft informations I can get, contains at leaft 750 ton of Stone. Getting up by a ladder to view the top of it, we found the whole furface worked, like an imperfect, or mutilated Honey-comb, into Bafons*; one, much larger than the reft (bb), was at the South-end, about feven foot long; another at the North (cc), about five; the reft fmaller,

* See the Plan of it, Plate. XX. Fig. IX.

feldom

Pl. XIII. pa. 174.

To the Rev.ᵈ Charles Lyttelton LLD. Dean of Exeter This Tolmen in Constantine Parish in Cornwall is most gratefully inscrib'd by Wm: Borlase.

I. Green sculp Oxon.

feldom more than one foot, oftentimes not fo much, the fides and fhape irregular. Moft of thefe Bafons difcharge into the two principal ones (which lie in the middle of the furface), thofe only excepted which are near the brim of the Stone, and they have little lips or chanels (marked in Plate XIII. 1, 2, 3, 4, 5.), which difcharge the Water they collect over the fides of the Tolmên, and the flat Rocks which lie underneath receive the droppings in Bafons cut into their furfaces. This Stone is no lefs wonderful for its pofition, than for its fize; for although the underpart is nearly femi-circular, yet it refts on the two large Rocks E, F; and fo light, and detached, does it ftand, that it touches the two under ftones but as it were on their points, and all the Sky appears at G.[f]. The two Tolmêns at Scilly are Monuments evidently of the fame kind with this, and of the fame name, and thefe, with all of like ftructure, may with great probability, I think, though of fuch ftupendous weight, be afferted to be the works of Art, the under ftones in fome inftances appearing to have been fitted to receive and fupport the upper one. It is alfo plain, from their works at Stonehenge, and fome of their other Monuments[g], that the Druids had fkill enough in the mechanical Powers to lift vaft weights; and the Ancients, we know, in thefe rude works, fpared no labour to accomplifh their defign; Haraldus, at one time (as Wormius informs us[h]) employing his whole Army, and a great number of Cattle, to bring one fingle Stone to the place intended. Notwithftanding all this, I have fome doubts whether ever this Stone (fo vaft it is) was ever moved, fince it was firft formed, and whether it might not have been only cleared from the reft of the Karn, and fhaped fomewhat to keep it in proper poife, fo as it might fhew itfelf to that advantage which it now does moft furprizingly at fome miles diftance. But yet I am far from thinking it impoffible that this Rock might be brought where we fee it by Human force. The Ancients had powers of moving vaft Weights, of which we have now no idea; and in fome of their works we find bodies even heavier and larger than this Tolmên. In the Ruins of Balbeck (the ancient Heliopolis of Syria), there are three ftones lying end to end, in the fame row extending fixty one yards, and one of them is fixty three feet long, the other two fixty each. Their depth is twelve feet, and their breadth the fame, and, what adds to the wonder, they are raifed up into the Wall above twenty feet from the ground[i].

[f] In Ireland there are Monuments of the fame kind. One mentioned in the Hiftory of the county of Waterford, p. 70, is called St. Declan's Stone: "It lies fhelving upon the point "of a Rock, and on the Patron-day of this "Saint, great numbers creep under this Stone "three times, in order, as they pretend, to cure "and prevent pains in the back. This Stone, "they tell you, fwam miraculoufly from Rome "conveying upon it St. Declan's Bell and "Veftments."

[g] See the following Chapter, of the Logan-Stones.

[h] Mont. Dan. p. 39.

[i] Maundrell's Travels.

And,

And near the city of Alexandria ſtands what is vulgarly called Pompey's Pillar (but erected by one of the Ptolemies), the ſhaft of which conſiſts of one ſolid granate ſtone, 90 feet high and 38 in compaſs. Le Bruyn's Voyage, p. 171. Both theſe Weights are greatly ſuperiour to that of this Tolmên.

In the Area below this Stone there are many great Rocks, which have certainly been divided and ſplit, but whether thrown down from the ſides of the Tolmen, for the purpoſes abovementioned, I will not pretend to determine. One thing is remarkable, which is, that theſe Tolmens reſt on ſupporters, and do not touch the Earth, agreeably to an eſtabliſhed principle of the Druids, who thought every thing that was ſacred, would be profaned by touching the ground[1]; and therefore, as I imagine, ordered it ſo, as that theſe Deities ſhould reſt upon the pure Rock, and not be defiled by touching the common Earth. Another thing is worthy our notice in this kind of Monuments, which is, that, underneath theſe vaſt ſtones, there is a hole, or paſſage, between the Rocks[k]. What uſe the Ancients made of theſe paſſages, we can only gueſs; but we have reaſon to think, that when Stones were once ritually conſecrated, they attributed great and miraculous Virtues to every part of them, and imagined, that whatever touched, lay down upon, was ſurrounded by, or paſſed through, or under theſe Stones, acquired thereby a kind of Holineſs, and became more acceptable to the Gods. This paſſage might alſo be a ſanctuary for the offender to fly to, and ſhelter himſelf from the purſuer; but I imagine it chiefly to have been intended, and uſed for introducing Proſelytes, or Novices, people under Vows, or about to ſacrifice, into their more ſublime Myſteries: for the ſame reaſon, I am apt to think, the vaſt Architraves, or Croſs-ſtones, reſting upon the uprights at Stonehenge, were erected; namely, with an intent to conſecrate and prepare the worſhipers, by paſſing through thoſe holy Rocks, for the better entering upon the offices which were to be performed in their *Penetralia*, the moſt ſacred part of the Temple. The Druid Throne at Boſcawen Rôs[l] might alſo ſerve at particular times for the like preparatory Rites, and might be thought to inſtill a greater degree of ſanctity into the preſiding Judge, the ſeat being ſurrounded ſo on every ſide by Rocks. Nor had Rocks only the privilege of conferring this imaginary exaltation and purity; whatever had the ſtamp of ſacred and divine imprinted on it, was thought to be endowed with the ſame power upon the

[1] This was the reaſon that they gathered the Miſletoe, Selago, and Samolus, and took ſuch care to catch the Anguinum, before it touched the Ground. See Cap. xii. Lib. II. and Cap. xxi. Ibid.

[k] From this Hole they have the Name of Tolmen.
[l] See Plate XIV. fig. III. and chap. vi. ſect. iii.

people's

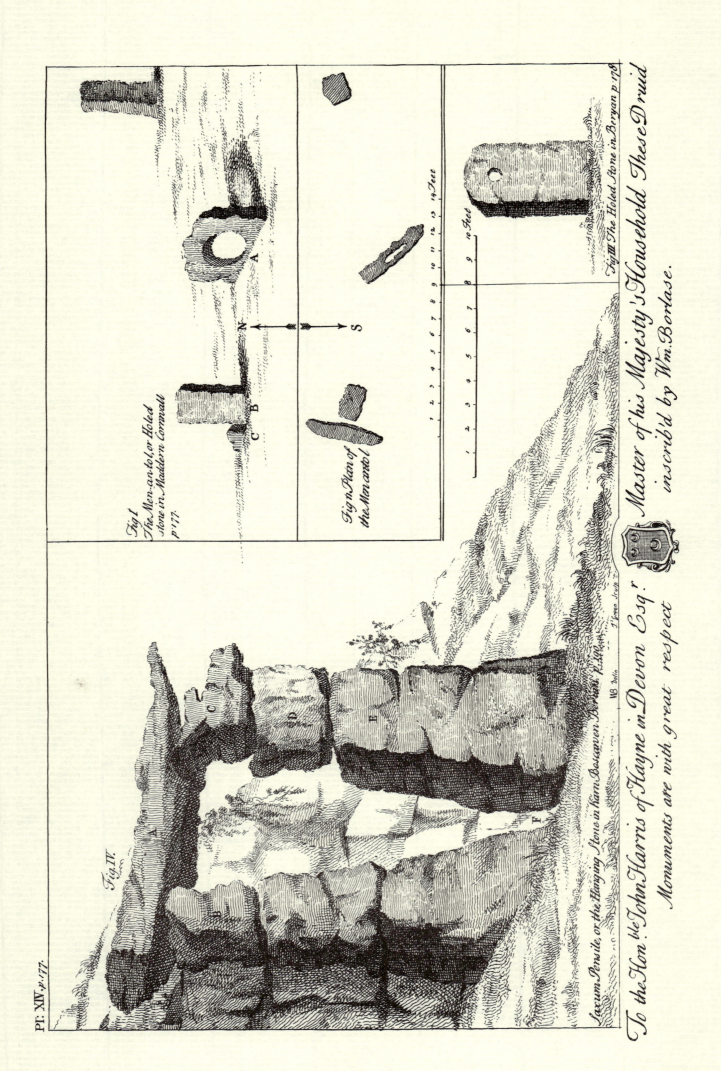

Pl. XIV. p. 177.

Fig. IV.

Fig. I.
The Men-an-tol, or Holed
Stone in Madern Cornwall
p. 177.

Fig. II. Plan of
the Men an tol.

1 2 3 4 5 6 7 8 9 10 11 12 13 14 Feet

10 Feet

1 2 3 4 5 6 7 8 9

Fig. III. The Holed Stone in Boryan p. 178.

Saxum-Pensile, or the Hanging Stones in Karn-Bosaven Borowh p. 176.   W.B. delin   J. Green sculp.

To the Hon.ble John Harris of Hayne in Devon Esq.r   Master of his Majesty's Household   These Druid
Monuments are with great respect   inscrib'd by Wm. Borlase.

people's complying with the fame rites. The ancient Idolaters made their Children pafs through their confecrated Fires, a Luftration, which ever afterwards made the Gentiles think, that thofe who had gone through, had acquired thereby a greater degree of Purity than any others ; and as Maimonides informs us [m], the Canaanites believed that fuch Children fhould not die before their time.

One of the abominations objected to the Jews (Jeremiah xxxiv. 18, 19.) is this, that " they cut the Calf" (after being ritually killed as a Victim) " in twain, and *paffed* between the parts thereof," by fuch a paffage devoting themfelves more religioufly, as they thought, to the worfhip of their Idols, and acquiring a greater degree of Purification.   This cuftom (like many other of the Gentile Rites) may be traced in the writings of Mofes, particularly in the facrifice made by Abraham (Gen. xv. 10.) in obedience to the command of God ; which command is alfo thought to be in compliance with the then cuftom of facrificing, in order to confirm Covenants, and yet it was hallowed by a miraculous Lamp of fire, paffing between and confuming the pieces, (ibid. ver. 17.)   The fame Cuftom is very vifible among the ancient Gentiles. " Peleus having killed the Wife " of Acaftus, divided the Limbs and paffed the army through them." Apollodorus. Livy tells us, Lib. XXIX. that a Bitch being facrificed, and the head divided into two equal parts, the Army paffed between them.   Why they did fo, we learn from Plutarch in his Roman Queftions, viz. That it was the common method of Purification among the Beotians to pafs between the parts of a Dog when they were divided into two parcels.   The Sacred Oak, when it was cleft, and the Earth (by many nations counted divine) were thought to be endowed with equal and ftrong powers of Luftration [n].   Surely the fame Superftition which made people defirous of purifying themfelves by paffing between the parts of the Victim, the Oak, the Earth, the Fire, might alfo prompt them to feek for the like delufive Purification, by paffing through the confecrated parts of their Rock-idols, Temples, and Altar [o].

Since we are now confidering thefe Stone-monuments, there is a very fingular Monument in the Parifh of Madern (Cornwall) which in this place, will naturally offer itfelf to our enquiry. In the Tenement of Lanyon ftand three Stones-erect on a triangular Plan. The fhape, fize, diftance, and bearing, will beft be difcerned from the plan and elevation of them (Plate XIV. Fig. I. and II.) The middle Stone (A) is thin and flat, fixed in the ground, on its edge, and in the middle has a large hole one foot two inches diameter, whence it

---

[m] Pol. Synopf. Deut. xviii.

[n] " Qu'on ne faffe point paffer le Betail par un " arbre creux, ou par un trou de la terre." In-

junctions of St. Eloi, Rel. de Gaules, p. 71.

[o] See Note * p. 178.

is called the Mên an Tol (in Cornifh the holed Stone); on each fide
is a rude Pillar, about four foot high; and one of thefe Pillars (B)
has a long Stone lying without it (C), like a cufhion, or pillow, as
if to kneel upon.   This Monument as is plain from its ftructure,
could be of no ufe, but to fuperftition. But to what particular fuperftitious Rite it was appropriated is uncertain P, though not unworthy
of a fhort enquiry.

The inhabitants of Shetland, and the Ifles (as Mr. Martin informs
us, p. 391.) ufed, very lately, to pour Libations of milk or beer q,
through a holed Stone, in honour to the Spirit Browny r, which is
therefore called Browny's Stone. Now whether the Cornifh Druids
applied this Stone to the ufe of fuch Offerings, I cannot fay; but the
Cornifh to this day invoke the Spirit Browny, when their Bees
fwarm, and think that their crying Browny, Browny, will prevent
their returning into their former hive, and make them pitch, fo as to
form a new colony.   It is not improbable, but this holed Stone
(confecrated, as by its ftructure and prefent ufes it feems to have
been) might have ferved feveral delufive purpofes. I apprehend that
it ferved for Libations, ferved to initiate, and dedicate Children to
the Offices of Rock-Worfhip, by drawing them through this hole,
and alfo to purify the Victim before it was facrificed s; and confidering the many lucrative juggles of the Druids (which are confirmed
by their Monuments) it is not wholly improbable, that fome
miraculous Reftoration of health, might be promifed to the people
for themfelves and children, upon proper pecuniary gratifications,
provided that, at a certain feafon of the Moon, and whilft a Prieft
officiated at one of the Stones adjoining, with prayers adapted to the
occafion, they would draw their infirm children through this hole.
It is not improbable, but this Stone might be alfo of the oracular
kind; all which may, in fome meafure, be confirmed by the prefent,
though very fimple, ufes, to which it is applied by the common
people.   When I was laft at this Monument, in the year 1749, a
very intelligent farmer of the neighbourhood affured me, that he had
known many perfons who had crept through this holed Stone for
pains in their back and limbs; and that fanciful parents, at certain
times of the year, do cuftomarily draw their young Children through,
in order to cure them of the Rickets. He fhewed me alfo two brafs pins,

P " Maen Tol, or the Stone with a hole, on " Agnidal downs in Madern, famous for curing " pains in the back by going through the hole, " three, five, or nine times." T. T. MS. H.

q To pour Libations of Beer to Othinus, or Woden chief God of the Northern Nations, was a common Cuftom. Keyfler, p. 155.

r The Spirit Browny was a kind of Hob-gob-lin, fuppofed to haunt the moft fubftantial Fami-lies of the Iflands. Martin, ibid.

s " Fabula fert Paganos quondam Humanis

" Hoftiis litare folitos, ea per Foramina mactan-dos homines tranfire coegiffe. — Conftitutofque " ad aras immolaffe. — Eum Ritum ad Bonifacii " Epifcopi Ultrajectini tempora duraffe." Ol. Worm, ex Ubb. Emm. p. 9. The fame Cuftom the Jews feem to have had in the time of Ifaiah, when " they inflamed themfelves with Idols " among the Oaks, and flew the Children in the " Valleys, under the Clifts of the Rocks." If. lvii. 5.

carefully

carefully layed a-crofs each other, on the top-edge of the holed Stone. This is the way of the Over-curious, even at this time; and by recurring to thefe Pins, and obferving their direction to be the fame, or different from what they left them in, or by their being loft or gone, they are informed of fome material incident of Love or Fortune, which they could not know foon enough in a natural way, and immediately take fuch refolutions as their informations from thefe prophetical Stones fuggeft.

Of the fame kind, and appropriated to the fame ufes as that I have here explained, I look upon all thin Stones which have a large hole in the middle[t]; but, before I clofe this Chapter of the holed Stones, I muft juft mention fome of another fhape, many of which I have feen; but the figure of one will fufficiently explain the whole, and may be feen Plate XIV. Fig. III. About 65 paces exactly North of Rofmodreuy Circle in Burien, Cornwall, is a flat Stone, fix inches thick at a medium, two foot fix wide, and five foot high; 15 inches below the top, it has a hole fix inches diameter, quite through. In the adjoining hedge I perceived another, holed in the fame manner; and in one wall of the village, near by, a third of like make. By fome large Stones ftanding in thefe fields, I judge there have been feveral Circles of Stones-erect, befides that which is now here to be feen entire; and that thefe belonged to thofe Circles, and were the detached Stones, to which the Ancients were wont to tye their Victims, whilft the Priefts were going through their preparatory Ceremonies, and making Supplications to the Gods to accept the enfuing Sacrifice.

CHAP. IV.

Of the Logan, Lágan or Rocking Stones.

AMONG the curious Rude Stone Monuments, confifting of fingle Stones, we may take fome notice of the Gygonian, Rocking, or Logan Stones, and confider what ufes they might probably have been applied to by the Druids.

Of thefe Stones the Ancients give us fome account. Pliny tells us, that there was to be feen at Harpafa, a town of Afia, " a Rock " of a wonderful nature: Lay one finger to it, and it will ftir, but " thruft at it with your whole body and it will not move[u]."

---

[t] As that at Conftantine, above a mile Weft of the Church, and others in Cornwall, and the two Stones in one of the Orkneys, mentioned by Toland, Hift. of the Druids, p. 91, and 92.

[u] " Cautes horrenda uno digito mobilis, " eadem fi toto corpore impellatur refiftens." Plin. Lib. II. cap. lxix.

Ptolemy

Ptolemy Hepheftion[w] mentions the Gygonian Stone, near the ocean, which may be moved with the ftalk of an Afphodel, but cannot be removed by any force. " It feems this word Gygonius " is purely Celtick, for Gwingog fignifies *Motitans*, the Rocking " ftone[x]." In Wales they call it Y Maen figl, that is, the Shaking Stone. In Cornwall we call it the Logan Stone, the meaning of which I do not underftand[y]. Logan, in the Guidhelian Britifh, fignifies a Pit, or hollow of the Hand[z], and Leagan a high Rock, and thence I fhould think it moft reafonable to derive it, although the Welfh word Kloguin, a great Stone or Rock (fee Lhuyd in Saxum) comes very near it; but whether the word Logan be thence derived, or may poffibly be a corruption of the Britifh Llygadtyn, in Welfh fignifying Bewitching (forafmuch as the fingular property of this Stone may feem the effect of Witchcraft), I fhall not take upon me to decide.

Some Authors[a] take thefe Stones to be placed in their prefent pofition by human Art; but there are two forts of them, fome natural, fome artificial. In the Parifh of St. Levin, Cornwall, there is a promontory, called Caftle Treryn[b]. This Cape confifts of three diftinct groupes of Rocks. On the Weftern fide of the middle groupe near the top lies a very large Stone (marked A), fo evenly poifed, that any hand may move it to and fro; but the extremities of its bafe are at fuch a diftance from each other, and fo well fecured by their nearnefs to the Stone, which it ftretches itfelf upon, that it is morally impoffible that any lever, or indeed any force (however applied in a mechanical way), can remove it from its prefent fituation. It is called the Logan Stone, and at fuch a great height from the ground, that no one who fees it can conceive that it has been lifted into the place we fee it in. It is alfo much of the fame fhape as the Rocks which lie under it, and makes a natural part of the Cragg on which it ftands at prefent, and to which it feems always to have belonged. There is alfo a natural Logan Stone in the large heap of Rocks, called Bofworlas Lehau[c]. Although thefe Stones fhew, by their fituation, that they were never placed there by Art, yet fome Stones are fo fhaped, and placed, as that there is great reafon to believe they were erected by human force. Of this kind I take the great Quoit on Karn-lehau in the Parifh of Tywidnek to be. It may be feen Plate XI. Fig. III. it meafures in girt 39 feet, is four feet thick at

[w] Lib. III. chap. iii.
[x] Stukeley's Stonehenge, p. 50.
[y] In Belgic, Saxon, and German, *Leogan* fignifies mentiri, *Logen*, mendacium; and from the impoftures and falfities, propagated by the Druids from the top of fuch rocks of prodigy, it is not impoffible but the Stones might, after the expiration of the Druid Syftem, obtain the names of the Lying-Stones. See Junius in voce Lic, or Lyc, laft Edit.
[z] Lhuyd's Arch. Ir. Engl. Vocab.
[a] Toland, p. 103. Hift. Druid.
[b] See Plate XXVI. ad fin. Lib. III.
[c] Parifh of St. Juft, Penwith.

a media medium; it lies on one single Stone as well poised as if placed there by the moſt ſkilful Artiſt.

There is a very remarkable Stone of this kind on the Iſland of St. Agnes in Scilly. The under Rock, A (Plate XI. Fig. IV.) is ten foot ſix high, and 47 feet in circumference round the middle, and touches the ground with no more than half its baſe. The upper Rock, C, reſts on one point only, ſo nice, that two or three men, with a Pole, can move it; it is eight feet ſix high, and 47 in girt. On the top is a large Baſon, D, three feet eleven in diameter (at a medium), at the brim wider, and three foot deep: by the globular ſhape of this upper Stone, I gueſs that it has been rounded by art at leaſt, if it was not placed on the hollow ſurface of the Rock it reſts upon by human force, which to me appears not unlikely [d]. In the Pariſh of Sithney, ſtood the famous Logan Stone, commonly called Mên amber (Plate XI. Fig. V.) It is eleven foot long from Eaſt to Weſt, four foot deep from E to F, wide ſix foot from C to D. There is no Baſon on the ſurface of A; but on the Stone B, there is one plain one. This Top-ſtone, A, was ſo nicely poiſed on the Stone, B, that " a little Child (as Mr. Scawen in his MS. ſays) could inſtantly move " it, and all Travellers that came this way deſired to behold it; but " in the time of Cromwell, when all monumental things became " deſpicable, one Shrubſall then Governour of Pendennis, by much " ado, cauſed it to be undermined, and thrown down, to the great " grief of the country." There are ſome marks of the tool upon this Stone, the ſurface C D, being wrought into a wavy plane, as in the Icon; and by its quadrangular ſhape, I ſhould judge it to have been dedicated to Mercury, as, by a Baſon cut in the under Stone, B (which I conclude from other works of this kind muſt have been done when this Stone B was without any covering, and entirely ex-poſed to the Heavens (ſee Chap. IX. of this Book), I judge the Stone A, to be placed on the top of this Karn by human Art. However that be, certain it is, that the vulgar uſed to reſort to this place at particular times of the year, and payed to this Stone more reſpect than was thought becoming good Chriſtians, which was the reaſon, that, by cleaving off part of the Stone, B, the Top-ſtone, A, was layed along in its preſent reclining poſture, and its wonder-ful property of moving eaſily to a certain point, deſtroyed. It was the Top-ſtone therefore of this Cragg which drew the common people together, and raiſed their admiration; and I find that in the Corniſh Language Mên-an-bar ſignifies the Top-ſtone; and I do not at all doubt, but that Mên-amber is a corruption of Mên-an-bar,

[d] I did not ſee this Monument, but its Draw-ing and Meaſurement was taken by a Friend, and ſent to me; and I have no Reaſon to think but that it is exact.

A a a   and

and fignifies nothing, either relating to Ambrofius Aurelius King of Britain, or to the Petræ Ambrofiæ of the Ancients, as fome learned Men have thought. This Stone Mr. Carew, placing it among the wonders of Cornwall, thus addreffes, p. 152.

> " Be thou thy mother Nature's work,
>   Or proof of Giants might,
> Worthlefs and ragged though thou fhew,
>   Yet art thou worth the fight.
> This hugy Rock one finger's force
>   Apparently will move,
> But to remove it many ftrengths
>   Shall all·like feeble prove."

There are fome of thefe Logan Stones in Ireland [e], and in Wales; and in Derbyfhire, I have been informed of three; one near Byrchover four yards high, and twelve round; and two at Rowtor, the largeft of which is computed to weigh, at leaft, twenty ton, on a Karn, twenty feet high.

That thefe are Monuments of the Druids cannot, be doubted; but what particular ufe they applied them to, is not fo certain. Mr. Toland [f] thinks, " that the Druids made the people believe that " they only could move them, and that by a Miracle; by which " pretended Miracle, they condemned, or acquitted the accufed, " and often brought Criminals to confefs what could in no other " way be extorted from them:" and I muft own that it is not at all improbable, that the Druids, fo well verfed in all the Arts of Magick (the fole bufinefs of which is to deceive), obferving this uncommon property in the natural Logan Stones, foon learned to make ufe of it, as an occafional miracle; and, where they had no natural ones, made artificial ones, and confecrated them. They then imagined Spirits to inhabit them; and this motion, likely, they infifted upon as a proof of thofe Spirits refiding within them, and fo they became Idols. As to the pits or bafons which we find funk into the tops of thefe Logan ftones, Plate XI. Fig. III. and IV. I will only obferve here, that it can fcarce be doubted but they had their part to act in thefe juggles, and by the ruffling or reft of the water, which after every fhower of rain they muft have contained, were to declare the wrath or pleafure of the God confulted, and fome way or other to confirm the decifion of the Druid, as we fhall fee when we come to treat of them more circumftantially.

• Camden, p. 762.　　　　　f Hift. of the Druids, p. 103.

CHAP.

CHAP. V.

Of the great Virtues attributed by the Ancients in Foreign Parts, and the Druids here, to particular Stones, and Gems.

AMONG the several superstitions of the Ancients, which claim a place here, we must not pass by the great virtue attributed to certain Stones and Gems. It has been before observed g, that when the Gentiles were informed of any extraordinary incident's being foretold, or any miraculous event produced by the Divine Power among the Jews, they attributed all this to the visible means, the order, ceremony, or symbol, substituted, and enjoined by God (and therefore, used by the Jews), and not to the Divine Power operating through its own appointed *medium*, without which all the rest was but dumb, inactive matter, impotence and shew.

Among the rest of the observations they made upon the history of the Jews, they found that the Divine Will was to be discovered by means of certain appearances in Gems. The Magi of the East, either really thinking, or at least making the vulgar believe, that these discoveries made by the Urim and Thummim of the Jews h, were owing to some innate Virtue in the Stone, made it a part of their magical system: immediately after, it became the profession of persons properly appointed to explain, and interpret, the various shades and coruscations, the different colours, dews, clouds, and images, which these Gems differently exposed to the Sun, Moon, Stars, Fire, or Air, at particular times inspected by proper persons, did exhibit: after these Stones were ritually blessed and consecrated, they assumed in the next place a medicinal influence, and their power was pretended to be very great, as a Charm, or Amulet, against misfortunes.

Zoroaster i is said to have celebrated the wonderful efficacy of the *Astroite* in all the Arts of Magick, as he did also of the *Daphnias* k. Democritus thought the *Erotylos* of great virtue in Divination l. Zachalias the Babylonian, in his books dedicated to King Mithridates, thinks the destiny of Man may be foreknown, accelerated, or

---

g Page 133.
h The Urim and Thummim (viz. Lights and Perfections) were precious Stones in the Breast-Plate of the High Priest, by the particular Appointment of God, Oracular, and under some Restrictions, Declarative of the Divine Will. Ex. xxviii. 30. Numb. xxvii. 21. " The same " of a thing so surprizing could not but pass

" abroad to the neighbouring Oriental Nations, " and it is not wholly improbable, that the Zoro- " astrian, and other like Gems were made in Imi- " tation of this, and took their Rise from it." Woodw. Method. Foss. Part II. p. 36.
i Pliny Lib. XXXVII. cap. ix.
k Ibid. cap. x.
l Ibid.

reversed,

reverſed by Gems [m]; and not content to attribute medicinal Virtues to the *Hematites*, or Blood-ſtone, recommends it as neceſſary to make applications to great men ſuccefsful, of great power in Law-ſuits [n], and very effectual in the day of battle towards procuring Victory.

The *Agate* was good to allay Tempeſts, as the Perſians thought, and the *Artizoe* [o] to inſpire them with proper diſcernment to chuſe a King. The *Cinœdiæ*, as they were clear or troubled, were ſuppoſed to foretell fair or foul weather at ſea; the *Chelonitides* to appeaſe ſtorms; the *Heliotropium* to render people inviſible [p]; the *Cornu Ammonis* is ſaid to prepare the mind to foreſee things to come in Dreams; the *Siderites* to create or continue Diſſention. The *Zoraniſcos* is ſtyled the Magicians Gem, by way of eminence; becauſe, perhaps, it was a chief favourite of that Order, and generally carried about them. Doubtleſs, the Magicians found their account in pro-pagating ſuch extravagancies; and as there was a remarkable confor-mity between the Magick of the Eaſtern Impoſtors, and that of the Druids, it is not to be imagined, that the latter would neglect an Art, which might be ſo much the more eaſily converted to their private gain, as it was entirely groundleſs, and exhibited wonders, *Spectra, & Predictions*, which none but themſelves could ſee, and none but themſelves were to explain [q]. There are ſeveral remainders of this ſuperſtitious foolery ſtill ſubſiſting, eſpecially in thoſe parts where Druidiſm impreſſed her laſt footſteps when ſhe took her leave. " In a little Iſle [r], near the Skie, in a chapel dedicated to " St. Columbus, on an Altar, is a blue Stone, of a round form, " always moiſt : Fiſhermen, detained by contrary winds, waſh this " Stone with water, expecting thereby to procure a favourable wind, " which, the credulous ſay, never fails : it is likewiſe applied to the " ſide of people, troubled with ſtitches ; and ſo great is the regard " they have for this Stone that they ſwear deciſive Oaths upon it. " Baul Muly [s] is a green Stone, like a Globe in figure, big as a " gooſe-egg, the virtue of it is to remove ſtitches, and to ſwear upon; " the credulous firmly believe, that if this Stone is caſt among the " front of an Enemy, they will all run away. Joachim Camera-

---

[m] " Humana gemmis attribuit Fata." Plin. ib.
[n] The ſame Power was attributed by the Druids to the Anguinum.
[o] See Pliny, laſt Edit.
[p] " Magorum impudentiæ vel manifeſtum in " hoc quoque exemplum eſt." Plin. ibid.
[q] That the Druids profeſſed this Part of Magick is plain, from the great Powers they at-tributed to the Anguinum. Dr. Woodward, Method. Foſſilium, Part II. p. 30. ſpeaking of Gems, ſays, " Mr. Aubrey, who much ſtudied " the Antiquities of this Iſland, contends, that

" they were uſed in Magick by the Druids." And in his Miſcellanies, 8vo. Lond. p. 128. he takes notice of " a Cryſtal Sphere, or Mineral " Pearl, uſed by Magicians, and to be inſpected " by a Boy."
[r] Martin of the Weſt-Iſles, p. 167.
[s] That is Molingus's Globe. " This Molin-" gus was Chaplain to Macdonald, King of the " Iſles. The Stone is carefully kept by the " Mackintoſhes of the Iſle of Arran in Scotland, " who have that Priviledge." Mart. p. 225.

" rius

" rius [t] mentions a round Cryftallin Gem, into which a chaft boy
" looking, difcerned an Apparition, that fhewed him any thing that
" he required.   Paracelfus avers [u], that in thefe *Specula* [w], are feen
" things paft, prefent, and to come.   Of this fort were the Cry-
" ftallin Stones made ufe of by Dr. Dee, and Mr. Kelly in their
" myfterious Vifions and Operations.   One, round, pretty big, and
" of Cryftal, they call the Shew-ftone, and holy Stone [x].   The Irifh
" had the fame fuperftition.   A folid Globe of Glafs or Cryftal has
" been time out of mind in the family of Tyrone, and is faid to cure
" the Murrain in cattle by putting it into a veffel of Water, or even
" a Rivulet, and giving that Water to the cattle to drink [y]."

Every one is fenfible, that though the Hematites has been divefted
of fome of its wonder-working properties [z], yet, that it is ftill
reckoned of great ufe, to prevent unufual and too frequent
bleedings.

The political property, attributed to the *Fatal Stone*, has been
already mentioned, p. 143.   It was enclofed in a wooden chair,
and thought to emit a found under the rightful King, but to be
mute under one of a bad Title.

The Druid Oracle concerning it is in verfe, and in thefe words,

" *Cioniodh fcuit faor an fine*   " The Lowland Scots have rim'd
                                         " it thus,
" *Man ha breag an Fais dine*   " Except old Saws do feign,
" *Mar a bh fuighid an Lia fail*   " And Wizards wits be blind,
" *Dlighid flaitheas do ghabhail* [a]. " The Scots in place muft reign,
                                         " Where they this Stone fhall find [b]".

By this means the Druids (who were always Interpreters of Prodigies, and Oracular Emiffions) had it in their power of chufing a
King, whom they thought moft likely to favour their Order; and
could perfuade the credulous people, that the Stone affented, or was
filent, as fuited beft their purpofe.

[t] Martin, ibid.
[u] Explicat. Aftron.
[w] The Gems, which are to be infpected, were
called *Specula*, and the Appearances in them
Spectra.
[x] Woodward, Meth. Foff. Part II. p. 30.
[y] Hift. of Waterford (Ireland), p. 107.
[z] Page 183.

[a] N. B. This is the fame Metre as the Britifh
Verfe, called by J. Dav. Rhys's Grammar, the
Englyn Milur, and in which Mr. Edward Lhwyd
thinks the Druids delivered their Doctrines. See
Archæol. Br. p. 250, 251 ; and therefore thefe
lines are not improbably of Druid original. See
p. 85.
[b] Toland, Hift. Druids, p. 103.

B b b   CHAP.

CHAP. VI.

Of Monuments, consisting of Two, Three, or several Stones, their Description, and Original Design enquired into.

TO convey the memory of any material Incident to Posterity, in a more lasting manner than Tradition seemed to be capable of the Ancients made use at first of rude and single Stones; afterages added more in number, and assembled them together in several figures the better to preserve a distinction as well as remembrance, which through the fewness of such Monuments among the more Ancient was not altogether so necessary.

SECT. I.
Of Two-stone Monuments.

To the first manner of erecting one single Stone Pillar, another was added, either out of equal respect to two Divinities, as Apollo and Diana (Sun and Moon) Jupiter and Juno, or the like; or to make the Monument more conspicuous, and distinguish it from other Monuments of one Stone only. It is not at all strange, that two allied Divinities should seem worthy of equal honours; and as the erecting one Stone only by the ancient Patriarchs might be intended to express and imply the Unity of the Godhead, so, after Polytheism, Theogony, and Idolatry took place, the first simple Unity of the Memorials was also laid aside, and the Stones and Pillars multiplied together with their false Gods and Idols.

The first we read of, I think, are the Pillars of Hercules, erected at the ancient Gades, as Terminations of his Western Travels. The memory of these two Pillars seems to be still preserved in Medals[c] for in the Coins of old Tyre, are erected two Stones with a Tyrian Hercules, sacrificing by them; they were called Αμβροσιαι πετραι, because, as some think, they were dedicated to Divine purposes by pouring on them Oil of Roses[d].

Homer intimates to us two different ends, for which the Ancients erected Monuments of this kind. The Goal, or Termination of Horse and Chariot Courses was often anciently marked out, by two erected Stones[e]; and for this purpose, probably, that the *Meta* might be more distinctly seen and observed by the Racers, than if there had been but one Stone. But the most obvious end of this kind of Monument was to distinguish the Graves of considerable persons, by placing an erected Stone at each end of the body interred[f]. There

---

[c] Some Authors, however, treat this Story of Hercules as a Poetical Fable. See ver. 1. Juvenal Sat. x. Not. Var.
[d] Stukeley's Stonehenge, p. 50.

[e] Η τογε Νυσσα τετυκτο επι προτερων ανθρωπων. Il. xxiii. ver. 332.
[f] Η τευ σημα βροτοιο παλαι καταλεθνειωτ. Ibid. ver. 331.

is fuch a Monument in the Tenement of Dryft in Sancred, Cornwall; one of the Stones ftands nine foot high out of the Earth, the other fomewhat more than feven; they are eighteen feet diftant, the line in which they ftand pointing North-weft. Another of the fame fort in the Tenement of Trewren Madern, the diftance ten feet, the line of their plan lying E. N. E. Upon fearching the ground between thefe two Stones (October 21, 1752). the diggers prefently found a pit fix feet fix long, two feet nine wide, and four feet fix deep; near the bottom it was full of black greazy Earth, but no bone to be feen. This grave came clofe to the Weftermoft and largeft Stone, next to which, I imagine, the head of the interred lay. The dimenfions and plan of this Monument, are exhibited (Plate X. fig. IV. V. and VI.) The Chriftians in fome parts buried in this manner, but in compliance, as it is to be imagined, with a more ancient Pagan cuftom g. The victorious King Arthur was buried in the Church-yard of Glaftonbury, betwixt two Pyramids, as the Welfh Bard fung to King Henry II; and as their refearches in that place afterwards are fuppofed by fome to have put beyond doubt h.

In fome ancient Monuments we find three Stones fo placed as to conftitute one Monument; this was fometimes to record the number of perfons interred. Xenophon takes notice that where the three Eunuchs of Abradates were buried, there were three Pillars i erected.

SECT. II.
Of Three-
ftone Mo-
numents.

The Number Three had alfo refpect unto the three Primary Idols k. One of the Idols, or erected Symbols of the God Mercury confifted of three Stones; two large Stones were pitched on end, over which another Stone was laid, which covered the reft, bearing with its middle upon the Stones underneath. At thefe three Stones, fo difpofed, it was a piece of Religion among the Heathens to throw certain other fmall Stones, as a kind of Offering to the Idol l.

Strabo, in his Travels through Upper Egypt, defcribes feveral Stone-Heaps or Parcels, confifting of three circular Stones piled one on the other, the largeft underneath, and twelve feet diameter; the other two fmaller in proportion, but the fmalleft exceeding fix feet diameter. He calls them *Hermæa*, thinking them neareft in

g "The Monk, O Gorgon, is buried near to "this Chapel, and there is a Stone five Foot high "at each End of this Grave." Martin, of St. Columbus's Chapel in an Iflet near the Skie, p. 167.
h Speed, Chron. p. 272. &c. "The late "learned Dr. Ward of Grefham College, and "the late ingenious Smart Lethieullier, Efq; "F. R. S. were both of opinion that the whole "account in Gyraldus Cambrenfis, of Arthur's "Sepulchre being difcovered at Glaftonbury, "was an impofition upon him, and Lord Lyttel-

"ton in his Hiftory abfolutely rejects it." Lord Bifhop of Carlifle to the Author.
i This feems to be the moft obvious and natural reafon for erecting Stones in this Number; and of this kind probably may be the three huge upright Stones called the Devil's Quoits, in a ploughed field near Kennett in Oxfordfhire, which Dr. Plott thinks Britifh Deities. Hift. Oxf. ch. x.
k Worm. p. 8.
l Buxt. Lexic. Talm. in voce MARCOLIS.

refemblance

resemblance to the Heaps near the Highways erected to the honour of Mercury [m].

Strabo (Lib. III. p. 202.) takes notice of three or four Stones placed together (but he mentions no Ichnography) in a sacred piece of ground near Hercules's Temple [n].

SECT. III.
Of Several-
stone Mo-
numents,
and why of
different
Numbers.

When the Ancients erected Stones in order to compose any Memorial, there was something expressive either in the number of the Stones of which the Monument did consist, or in the shape of the Stones themselves, or in the Order and figure in which they were disposed.

Of the first kind were the Monuments of Mount Sinai [o], and that at Gilgal, erected by Joshua upon the banks of Jordan; they consisted of twelve Stones each, because the people of Israel (for whose sake the Altar was built, and the streams of Jordan dividing themselves, opened a miraculous passage for the whole nation) were principally classed into twelve tribes [p]. The same number of Stones, and for the same reason, were set up in the midst of Jordan, where the Ark had rested [q].

The Altar also which Elijah built [r], was composed of twelve Stones only, according to the number of the twelve Tribes of Israel; intimating thereby, that this Altar was dedicated to the God of Israel, who had chosen those twelve Tribes for his peculiar people, and, by a long series of miracles and revelations, had proved himself to them not to be a dead Idol, but a living God.

There is a very singular Monument recorded by Wormius [s]; and as the Stones are neither shaped by Art, nor placed in any regular emblematick figure, it may be supposed that the number was expressive of what Tradition is now silent. Six large tall Stones are the principal parts of this Monument [t]; four of them have two small circles, or ringlets, of Stones round the base of each; the other two have a few small Stones heaped round their bottom. Between the principal Stones, are six little piles of Stones interspersed: the neighbours relate, that it is a monument of a battle fought there.

Perhaps it was the Memorial of an appointed Duel betwixt six persons of each side (as that of the *Horatii* and *Curiatii* was of three). The little heaps (which are generally construed to be sepuchral) being intended as Memorials of the conquered and slain, the erect Stones emblems of the victorious, whereof four survived the Combat,

---

[m] Strabo, Lib. XVII. p. 1173. Univers. Hist. English, Vol. I. folio, p. 217.

[n] Of which Keysler, p. 189, thus, " *Apud* " *Strabonem*, quidam, de fano Herculis ad occi- " dentem sito mentionem faciens, neque aram " ibi esse ait, neque ullius Deorum [scilicet " templum] sed Lapides multis in locis Ternos " aut Quaternos compositos. Fas ibi non esse " sacrificare, neque nocte eum locum adire,

" quòd ferunt eum nocturno tempore a Diis " teneri."

[o] Exod. xxiv. 4.

[p] Josh. iv. 8.

[q] Ibid. ver. 9.

[r] 1 Kings xviii. 31.

[s] Mon. Dan. p. 63.

[t] See the Monument at the End of Chap. VII. copied from Wormius.

and were invested with Garlands, or Ringlets of Stones, as tokens of Victory; the other two fell in the action, and have therefore little heaps round their bafe; but, being entitled to a fhare of the Conquerour's Glory, they have therefore the honour of a Στηλη, or column, erected to their Memory.

Some of the Ancients were wont to place as many Obelifks, or Stones-erect, at the Grave, as the departed Warriour had flain of the Enemy [u]. In the number of Stones of which they compofed their circular Temples, they fometimes had regard to the divifions of time into Days, Weeks, and Months. There is alfo reafon to believe, that when any new Circle of Stones was formed for the more folemnly electing a King, or Chief, as many Stones went to compofe the Circles, as there were Electors who had a right to vote at the Election, one Stone for each, and no more.

Sometimes, by the particular fimilar fhape of many Stones erected, they expreffed their reverence for their principal Deity, by conforming all the Symbols to that figure in which he was ufually reprefented. Thus the Phareans [w] round their *Mercurius Agoræus*, which held the middle and moft honourable place of their *Forum*, erected 30 Cubes of Stone, out of refpect to their chief God, Mercury (whofe Symbol was a Cube), each of which they worfhiped under the name of fome particular Deity. *Why of different Shapes and Plans.*

Some Authors think that erected Stones, placed in a ftraight line, are Memorials of Battles, or Combats [x]. In Weftmoreland, is a row, or range, of ftones erect, fome nine foot high, pyramidal, placed almoft in a direct line, and at equal diftances for a mile together. They feem erected, fays the learned Annotator, in memory of fome great action [y]. With as much reafon, at leaft, it may, from the extent of thefe Monuments, be prefumed, that they were boundaries of patrimonial Lands, or thofe little Territories, into which moft countries anciently were divided; for " in Anglefea there are many " lines of fingle Stones-erect, which are ftill called *Terfyne*, or " *Terfyneau*, that is, terminations of Lands [z]." *Rectilinear.*

On the Downs leading from Wadebridge to St. Columb, and about two miles diftant from it, is fuch a line of Stones (Pl. XVII. fig. I.) bearing N. E. and S. W. This Monument is generally called the Nine Maids.

Olaus Magnus [a] tells us, that Stones difperfed in a triangular figure, denote a Victory obtained by a body of horfe; that by a fquare *Triangular.*

[u] " Iberi pro hoftium interfectorum numero, " tot Obelifcos apponunt, hoc infigne teftimo- " nium virtutis, & expertiffimum decus arbi- " trati." Al. ab Al. vol. I. p. 558. Lib. III.
[w] Paufan. Acha. Lib. VII. cap. xxii.
[x] Wormius, Mon. Dan. p. 62.—Olaus Mag.

Lib. I. cap. xxxix.—Plott's Staffordfhire, p. 398, of the four Pyramidal Stones near Burrow-Bridge, Yorkfhire.
[y] Camden, p. 996. Britan. Ed. Gibfon.
[z] Rowland, chap. xxvi. p. 5.
[a] Lib. I. cap. xxix.

figure,

figure, the place where armies (or rather, champions for single Duels) met and engaged, is signified; by a round, family-burial-places [b].

Penfile.   Sometimes we find Stones erected, and others lying horizontally on the tops of them, making, as at Stonehenge, &c. so many Portals; and in this fashion we find the Ancients sometimes erected their Trophies to perpetuate the Memory of some important Victory.

The Victory gained by Regnerus over the Kings of the Biarmi, and the Finni, was transmitted to posterity by a Trophy of this kind [c].

Some Stones placed in this latter manner were (as I conjecture) seats of Judgement; of Instruction, of Ritual Admission of Disciples, and giving Audience to persons of superiour note [d].

There is a Monument of this penfile kind in Karn Boscawen [e]; it consists of one large flat Stone (A), one end of which rests upon the natural Karn (B); the other end on three large Stones (CDE) placed on one another, in order to raise a proper support for the weight above (Plate XIV. fig. IV. p. 177.) Between this Canopy-stone, and its supporters, there is an opening, wide at the top seven feet, but the Chasm closes into a sharp point at the bottom (F). This Canopy is too nicely supported to be the work of nature, and one must check one's imagination very much not to conjecture, that the opening, underneath it, was designed for the seat of some consider-able person; from which he might give out his Edicts, and Decisions, his Predictions, and Admissions to Noviciates. The mind can hardly frame to itself a scene more striking and awful than this must be to all persons, who came hither for judgement, or instruction; nothing can be more suitable to the superstition of the Druids, nor more likely to promote the delusion of all that were to be initiated into the mysteries, or introduced into the presence of the Chief Priest: we may fancy, with some probability, that, when any person of more than ordinary figure was to be admitted, he was to be con-ducted first round the holy Circle (of which the remains are still to be seen on the brow of the hill above); that, as he descended, he was to be sprinkled and purified at proper pauses, and stations, by the heavenly waters which the Rock-basons (very numerous here) contained: as he descended farther, passing along between the sacred Obelisks (of which some are still to be seen) he loses sight of every thing, but of vast Rocks on either side, above, and below, and the immense ocean before him, till being got about half way down this

[b] Wormius, however, a more cautious Writer, p. 67. doubts, whether these Characteristicks are always infallible. " J. Speed, in Descriptione " Devon. ad Exmore, Saxa in triangulum, alia " in orbem erecta. Trophæa certè victoriarum " quas Romani, Saxones, vel Dani obtinuerunt, " ac Danicis literis unum inscribi refert." Worm. p. 67.

[c] Worm. p. 96.

[d] See pages 176, 178.

[e] In the Parish of St. Burien, Cornwall.

steep and craggy Cliff, doubtful whither he was to be led, he is surprized with this Throne, which has something so truely grand and simple in its supporters and Canopy, that it almost leaves us uncertain, whether it be the work of Nature, or of Art. Between the supporters sits the venerable Chief Druid, his Tiara on his head, his holy vestments on, his Scepter in his hand, all these decorated with the *Insignia* of his Order, and every where round him the most stupendous Rocks.—A few paces below this Throne is an Area of about twelve feet diameter, cleared of the Rocks, from whence the person introduced, with his attendants, might well hear the Precepts of the Druid without violating his Dignity by too familiar an approach.

CHAP. VII.

Of Circular Monuments, the Use and Design of them among the Ancients in foreign Countries, and the Druids in this.

AMONG the most ancient British Monuments, the Circles of Stones-erect may justly claim a place; we come therefore to discourse of them particularly, for as much as, by their simplicity, they appear to be next in date to the Monuments which go before.

We find the number of Stones erected on a circular plan various; SECT. I. some Circles consisting of twelve, others of more, the most which have Number of reached my notice, seventy-seven. This difference in number was Stones. not owing to chance, but either to some established Rules observed in the construction of these Monuments, or referring to, and expressive of, the Erudition of those ages. In some places we find them oftner of the number *Twelve* than of any other number, either in honour to the twelve superiour Deities, or to some national Custom of twelve Persons of Authority meeting there in Council upon important affairs[e]; or alluding to the twelve months of the year. There are four Circles[f] in the hundred of Penwith, Cornwall (the most distant two of which are not eight miles asunder), which have nineteen Stones each, a surprizing uniformity, expressing, perhaps, the two principal divisions of the year, the twelve months, and the seven days of the week. This conjecture will not seem strange and groundless, when we reflect that the Priests were the only Chrono-

[e] The Monument of Sinai, p. 188. and of Gilgal, ibid. (which were both probably of the circular kind) had twelve Stones each, because such was the Number of the Tribes. "Reperi- "untur in his oris loca quædam in quibus Reges "olim solenni creabantur pompa, quæ cincta "adhuc grandibus saxis *(ut plurimum duodecim)* "conspiciuntur." Worm. M. D. p. 87.
[f] Boscawen'uun, Rosmodereuy, Tregaseal, Boskednan.

logers

logers and Regifters of Time; and it is no wonder that they (forbidden as they were either to teach by Letters, or commit their Myfteries to writing) fhould endeavour to perpetuate the memory of their Learning, and Aftronomical Computations, in fuch Characters as were moft likely to defcend through all ages of their Pofterity, without tranfgreffing the laws of their Order. But whatever was the reafon, the number of thefe Stones in other places is different, and where the defign of the Circle was for electing; Governours, or holding Councils, muft needs have been fo, becaufe the number of Nobles there affembled could not but be frequently different, and each Noble, fo convened, had a right to his Pillar, at which he was to take his ftand; again, when the Authors of fuch Monuments were eminent for family, fortune, or learning, they might probably chufe to record fome difcovery in Science, the number of their famous Anceftors, or of the Principalities they inherited, in thefe their works.

Diftance of thefe Stones.

The diftance of the Stones from each other is alfo different in different Circles, but was likely the fame, or nearly fo, at firft, in one and the fame Circle, fo that, by the diftance of what remain ftanding, or otherwife, may in a great meafure be afcertained the number of Stones of which the Circle formerly confifted. Whether they were very exact in fuiting thefe diftances according to the fize of the Stones, and obferved a regular gradation from the fmaller to the great, and again a gradual declenfion from the greater to the fmall, is what I cannot affert; but is imagined fo to be by fome of the learned, as well as that they meafured thofe diftances by Cubits in whole numbers, not by the foot or yard[g].

It was not in any indifferent or common place that thefe Circles were erected; but the Rites of Augury, and the opinion of the Magi (or Philofophers of the Country) were firft confulted, efpecially if Religion, or the Election of Princes, was upon the carpet[h]; but if Victory, the place where it was won was to be honoured with the Trophy.

Plans.

The figure of thefe Monuments is either fimple, or compounded. Of the firft kind are exact Circles, elliptical or femicircular. The conftruction of thefe is not always the fame, fome having their circumference marked with large feparate Stones only; others having ridges of fmall Stones intermixed, and fometimes Walls and Seats, ferving to render the inclofure more compleat. Other circular Monuments have their figure more complex and varied, confifting, not

---

[g] Dr. Stukeley's Abury, p. 21.
[h] " Augures vero eadem ferme Tefqua quæ & " Templa, vocabant; Loca *Auguriis* defignata, " quorúm termini, cum fere rupibus, fylvifque ac " montibus finirentur." Not. Var. Hor. Epift.

Lib. I. p. 14. ver. 19. " No Place was called " a Temple, but what had been marked out, that " is, confecrated, by the Augurs." Scal. de Lin. Lat. Lib. V. p. 54. Moyle, P. Works, vol. I. p. 390.

only

only of a Circle, but of fome other diftinguifhing Properties[i]. In, or near the center of fome, ftands a Stone taller than the reft[k]; in the middle of others a Kift-vaen, that is, a Stone-fepulchral-cheft, or Cavity. A Cromlêh (or Altar-tomb of rough Stone) diftinguifhes the center of fome circles[l]; and one remarkable Rock that of others; fome have only one line of Stones in their circumference, and fome have two; fome Circles are adjacent, fome contiguous, and fome include, and fome interfect each other. Sometimes Urns are found in or near them; and thefe Circles are of very different dimenfions, as will be feen in the Icons. Some are curioufly erected on geometrical Plans, the chief entrances facing the cardinal points of the Heavens; fome have avenues leading to them, placed exactly North and South, with detached Stones, fometimes in ftreight lines to the Eaft and Weft, fometimes triangular; all evidences of more than common exactnefs and defign: of all thefe we fhall produce inftances in their proper place.

Thefe Monuments are found in many foreign Countries[m], as well as in all the Ifles dependant upon Britain[n], and in moft parts of Britain itfelf[o].

They go by feveral names in different places. In the Highlands of Scotland they call them Temples; and from two or three of them in the Parifh of Strathawen, there is a place adjoining called Temple-Town; and, where two Circles are called the Temple Stones, in Auchincochtie, there, as Tradition fays, Pagan Priefts had formerly their Habitation. In Scotland fometimes they are alfo called Chapels; and from one of them in Bamffhire, a Place is called Leachell Beandic, or Bleffed Chapel[p].

In the Weftern Ifles (where there are many) they are called by the common people Druin Crunny[q], that is, Druid Circles. In Denbighfhire, there is one Circle called Kerig y Drudion, or the Druid Stones[r]. Another name (though foreign) may be here taken notice of, which is, that Stone-Circles in Denmark, and in the Ifles of Ifland, Shetland, and Man, are called Ting, that is, a Seat of Juftice, a *Forum*[s]; and the hill on which the King of the Ifle of Man was

SECT. II.
How named.

---

[i] One Circle at Abury has a work in the Center, which the old Britans called a *Cove* (as Dr. Stukeley fays, ibid.), confifting of three Stones making an obtufe Angle toward each other; this was the Kibla, or point, to which they turned their Faces during the time of Worfhip.

[k] See the Circle of Bofcawen-ûun (Plate XV. Fig. III. p. 198.) this is alfo called the Kibla by Dr. Stukeley. See his Abury, p. 24.

[l] See Karn Lechart in Glamorganfhire, Camden, p. 739.

[m] Ifland, Sweden, Denmark, in the Marquifate of Brandenburg, the Dutchy of Brunfwick Lunenburgh, and other Parts of Germany.

[n] The Orkneys, Weftern Ifles, Jerfey, Ireland,

and the Ifle of Man.

[o] Scotland, Cumberland, Wales, Oxfordfhire, Wiltfhire, and in Cornwall many, and very entire.

[p] Camden.

[q] Rowl. Mona, p. 112.

[r] Lhuyd's Letter to Mr. Paynter, in Moyle, p. 239. And his Letter to the Bifhop of Carlifle. Baxt. Gloff. p. 272.

[s] Worm. Mon. Dan. p. 68. — "Ding, Judi- "cium, Dingftuhl, Sedes Scabinalis (or Sheriffs "Seat), Dingdach, Dies Juridicus. — Huftin- "gum & Huftingian, Anglo Saxones pro Curia "ufurpabant." Keyfler, p. 78.

D d d   formerly

formerly inaugurated, ftanding in the Center of a Circle (his Nobles
round him, and the Commons without the Circle) is called the
Tinwald-hill.

In Cornwall there is a great number of thefe Circles (and of moft
forts that have been mentioned) and the name they go by moft commonly is, that of Dawns-mên, that is, the Stone-Dance, " fo called
" of the common people on no other account, than that they are
" placed in a circular Order, and fo make an Area for Dancing[t]."
This is the true reafon of that name, and not a corruption of Danif-
mên (as fome have imagined), as if thefe Monuments had been of
Danifh erection ; the traditions of the common people feldom fixing
upon, and being conftant to, points of hiftory, but rather taking their
rife from fome obvious property that ftrikes the fenfes, and refembles
the Cuftoms of their Country.   To confirm Mr. Lhuyd's opinion, I
muft obferve, that thefe Circles are found where the Danes never
were ; that, Dawnfe in Cornifh, fignifies a Dance, and that in the
circular Figure (of which we are now treating) there is a very ancient Dance, or play[u], ftill practifed among the Cornifh.   For the
fame reafon, as I fuppofe (namely, becaufe thefe circular Stones-erect
feem to have thrown themfelves into a Ring towards a Merry-
making) about eight miles Weft of Bath, a Monument of this kind
is called the Wedding ; and I cannot but obferve, that the Greeks
had fuch a Dance at their hymeneal folemnities, as appears by the
Nuptials engraved on the fhield of Achilles, where the young men
are faid to run round, or dance in a Ring.

——Πολυς δ' Ὑμεναιῷ ορωρει —— The Hymeneals far refound,
Κȣροι δ' ωρχηϛηρες εδινεον.—— And Youths in myftic Mazes whirl[w].——
                                            Hom. Il. Lib. XVIII. ver. 493.

SECT. III.   The feveral names by which thefe Monuments are diftinguifhed in
Of the in- different parts of the world, confidered jointly with the other before-
tent and ufe
of thefe   mentioned properties of Size, Figure, Number, and fome Pecu-
Circles.   liarities belonging to particular Circles, will contribute to difcover in
a great meafure by whom they were erected, and for what ufes they
were intended ; and our conjectures formed upon thefe, we muft be
contented to fortify as well as we can by Tradition, and fuch hifto-
rical Records as offer in other Countries as well as in our own.

Some Reli- Firft, it is highly probable that fome of thefe Monuments were of
gious.   Religious Inftitution, and defigned originally and principally for the
Rites of Worfhip.   " And Mofes rofe up early in the Morning, and

[t] Lhuyd : Moyle's Posthum. Works, vol. I.   [w] " Adolefcentes autem Saltatores in orbem
p. 239.   " agebant fe." Cler. Hom. ibid. ιʋ δ' αρα, viz.
[u] It is called Trematheeves.   ut fieri folebat.

                                                          " builded

" builded an Altar under the hill, and twelve Pillars according to
" the twelve Tribes of Israel[x]." Certainly this was a Religious
Monument; the Altar for Sacrifice, and the twelve Pillars for a
Prince of each Tribe to stand by, to partake of the Sacrifice, to
covenant in the name of his Tribe, and to seal that covenant which
he made with God, by receiving the Blood with which Moses besprinkled these Delegates of the people, as they stood round about
the Altar[y]. If it be said, that the Scripture leaves us in the dark as to
the plan and form of this Monument; yet it must be observed, that the
ceremonial circumstances make it clear, that it was of the circular
Figure. I would only ask, in what form these Pillars would be
erected by any person who was to perform the like ceremonies; I
fancy it would be answered, without any hesitation, in the circular
form, as liable to less exceptions, with regard to the Princes, and
most convenient for the officiating Prophet.

In obedience to the Divine Command, there was a Monument set
up by Joshua at Gilgal, which consisted of twelve Stones fixed in the
Earth. The design of it was to make the Israelites constantly adhere
to the worship of the true God, by remembering their miraculous
passage (dry shod) over the river Jordan, from the chanel of which
these twelve Stones were taken[z]. In what figure these Stones were
disposed, the Scriptures do not say; but from the resemblance which
Monuments did usually bear to some of the principal incidents they
were designed to commemorate, as well as also from the name of
Gilgal[a]; it is most probable that this Monument was round. It must
here also be noted, that there was not only twelve Stones erected
upon the banks of Jordan, but the same number also in the chanel
of the River, exactly " in the place where the feet of the Priests,
" which bare the Ark of the Covenant, stood[b]." Now as the Priests
stood round about the Ark, to prevent the approach of every thing
that was unholy; it is more likely that the Stones in the Water were
erected with a conformity to the Order in which the Priests stood,
whilst the people were passing over, than in any other manner.
This Gilgal was first a place of worship[c], then of national Council[d],
and Inauguration[e], and when the Israelites had degenerated into
Paganism, it became a place of Idolatrous Worship[f]; as suiting the
principles of the Eastern Superstition: for, as it was their Custom

[x] Exod. xxiv. 4.
[y] Ibid. 7, 8.
[z] Joshua iv. 21, 22, and 24.
[a] Which signifies Rolling, surrounding, Roundness, a wheel, and the like. See Buxtorf's Lex. Heb. Leigh's Crit. Sacr. p. 40. and Paul. Fag. ibid. so that, besides rolling away the Re-proach of Egypt (mentioned Josh. v. 9.), there seems to be in Gilgal a mutual Relation and

Agreement between the Name and the Figure of the Monument; and therefore Dr. Stukeley in his Abury thinks Gilgal a Circular Monument.
[b] Josh. iv. 9.
[c] Ibid. v. 10.
[d] 1 Sam. vii. 16.
[e] Ibid. xi. 15.
[f] Hosea iv. 15, and xii. 11.

to confecrate places to Religion, fo it was equally their principle to take care, that thofe places fhould be open, and nothing like confinement in their Temples, left it fhould look like *Limiting, Inclofing*, or *Imprifoning*, an infinite, ubiquitarious being. The Images of the Sun were to be open to the Heavens, and were therefore called חמנים g, that is, *Subdiales*, or Statues in the open air; and the Phenician Hercules (or the Sun) was wont to be adored in an open Temple [h]; and their Sacrifices, and publick Devotions were always, *fub dio*, on the tops of Rocks and Mountains, or in the midft of Groves, but never under covert. Now thefe two principles of dedicating particular places to worfhip, and at the fame time keeping them open and unconfined, were thoroughly reconciled in Monuments of this circular kind. The places were marked out fufficiently to preferve them from rude, profane abufe, and yet by Stones placed at fome diftance from each other on their ends, there was no abfolute, compleat inclofure. That the Druids held, the firft of the above-mentioned Principles, and had places appropriated to facred ufe, has been fhewn before [i]; and that they alfo maintained the fecond principle, namely, that the Gods were not to be confined within walls, is not to be doubted, it being one of the fundamentals of the Celtic Religion [k], from which we have no reafon to think that the Druids ever departed, if we judge from their Monuments, which are the beft vouchers for their opinions. Befides, the multitude and nature of their Sacrifices required fuch Fires as could not admit of Roof or Coverture. Again, the Druids were extreamly addicted to Magick, in which Art the Circle was efteemed effentially neceffary, to carry on all the nefarious Rites of Witchcraft, and Necromancy; and the vulgar opinion that Conjurers have no power to call forth the Demon to foretell future events, or difcover what is concealed from others, unlefs he draws a Circle round him, feems to be a remaining part of this Druid Superftition. It has been already obferved [l], that the Druids had a furprizing refemblance to the Perfians, who took in all the whole compafs of Heaven into their Idea of Jupiter [m]; and it muft be owned, that the Druids had the fame Deity, and that they could not erect their Temples more analogous to, and expreffive of, that God, nor better adapted to perform their adorations to every Region of the Heavens, than in the Circular Figure [n]. Again, we find in the middle of fuch Circles, fometimes a tall Pillar, fuch as formerly were worfhiped as Idols; at other times a Rock, or

g Ifaiah xxvii. 9. Buxtorf. in voc.
h Maundrel's Travels, p. 21.
i Cap. xvii. Lib. II.
k Tacitus, de M. G. Sched. p. 340.
l Cap. xxii. Lib. II.
m Herodot. in Clio. Hyde, Cap. VI. p. 137.

n In the Symbols of their Deities there was fomething in the Figure which expreffed the principal Attribute of their God (fee p. 108.), fo alfo in their Temples; the Temple of Vefta was round, becaufe Vefta was the Earth.

Cromlêh,

Cromlêh, which have all the appearances of having ferved on fome occafions for Altars; and therefore nothing can be fo probable, as that the ring of Stones ferved to mark out the limits of the Temple, where facred Offices were performed to fuch Idols, and upon fuch Altars. The Circular Figure (as every one muft allow) was moft convenient of any for the audience to fee, and hear, and enter into their parts of the facrifical Rites; and therefore could not but fuggeft itfelf, from the moft remote Antiquity, to all Idolaters that placed their whole ftrefs upon the outfide of Religion. Let me obferve farther, that fome of thefe Monuments are of aftonifhing Grandeur and Magnificence°, much exceeding every other end, and occafion, than that of Religion. I am aware that fome attribute the Circle of Stonehenge to the Romans, and not to the Druids; but there is fuch a wildnefs in this grand Structure, that to imagine it of Roman erection after Julius Cefar's time, is too groundlefs a fuppofition to be worth confuting. However, to add a word or two to this difpute, let it be only confidered, that the Roman ways crofs and mangle thefe Circles (as fee Tab. IV. of Dr. Stukeley's Stonehenge); and it can never be true, that the Romans would erect and disfigure the fame, and their own works. It is alfo evident, that fuch Monuments were prior to the Roman ways, for the Druids would never be fuffered to impede the Highways of their Lords and Mafters; therefore, thefe muft have been built before the Roman ways were made, which will naturally lead us to another conclufion equally evident, which is, that as they could not be Roman works, becaufe prior to the Roman ways; fo neither, for the laft mentioned reafon, could they be of the Saxon or Danifh age and conftruction, and therefore can juftly be afcribed to none but the Druids.

That thefe Temples are of different fizes, and fome exceeding fmall, no more than twelve feet diameter, muft be confeffed; and yet this will not hinder but that all might be places of worfhip: that fome are of larger dimenfions than others, may probably be owing either to the different quality of the Founders and Priefts, or the different end for which they were defigned; the larger for more noble and general affemblies, the fmaller for more private, and, perhaps, family ufes: the large for Sacrifices and feftival Solemnities, the fmall for particular Interceffions, Predictions, and perhaps Sepulchres of Priefts and Worthies. — In fhort, thefe Circles were of different fize, either becaufe thereby they were better proportioned to the different kind of Superftition therein to be performed, or to the different ranks and claffes of the Druids; if the riches or power of the perfons who erected them was great, fo was

---

° See Dr. Stukeley's Stonehenge and Abury.

E e e

their

their work; if their ability was fmall, the Circles they erected were in proportion.

Of thefe Monuments that kind was moft ancient which was moft fimple, and confifted only of a Circle of Stones-erect. Of this fort we have a great number in Cornwall, which differ not materially from one another: Bofkednan Circle therefore (Plate XV. Fig. II.) may reprefent the whole.—In the tenement of Kerris P there is an oval Inclofure, which may be feen Plate XVII. Fig. II. It is about 52 paces from North to South, and 34 wide, from Eaft to Weft: At the Southern Termination A, ftand four rude Pillars about eight feet high, at the foot of which lie fome large long ftones, which I am apt to think did formerly reft upon thefe Pillars. The Plan on which thefe Pillars ftand q is eighteen feet from North to South, and eleven feet wide. I am inclined to think that this was a place of Worfhip, that thefe Stones-erect were defigned to diftinguifh and dignify the Entrance, and were the Kibla of the Place (as the learned Dr. Stukeley calls the Cove of one of his Abury Circles), and that they were erected like fome of the Stones at Stone-henge in the fhape of two rude Portals, to infpire thofe that entered this enclofure with double Sanctity r. It is at prefent called the Roundago, which name (though Englifh) it may have acquired poffibly from the fuperftitious Rounds ufed in the Druid Worfhip.

On a Karn adjoining to the Giant's Caftle in St. Mary's Scilly, we found the back of the Rock cleared, as it feemed, of all uneven-nefs, and making one plane of Rock. This Area is of a circular figure, 172 feet from North to South, and 138 feet from Eaft to Weft; on the edges of it are nine vaft ftones ftill remaining, planted in a circular line; feveral others perfected the round, but from time to time have been removed, and fome of them within thefe few years. There is no uniformity in the fhape of the Stones that remain, neither do they feem to have ever been placed at any calculated, equal diftances. The Stone (Plate XI. fig. II.) placed among the Rock-idols s makes one of the ring; the front of it, towards the center, is 20 foot long; a rude Pillar fallen down lies before it, about five paces diftant, inwards. This Rock ftands Eaft of the Central Point; and in a line from it fomewhat to the North of the Weft, are three large flat Stones, which have Bafons on the top of them, but pieces of them are broke and carried off. This was a great work of its kind, the floor of one Rock, and the Stones round the edges of an extraordinary fize.

Some Circles are near one the other, and their Centers in a line, to fignify, perhaps, that they were intended for, and directed to, one

---

P Parifh of Paul, Cornwall.   r Chap. iii. p. 176.
q See the Entrance, or Portal, Pl.XVII.fig.III.   s Ibid. p. 173.

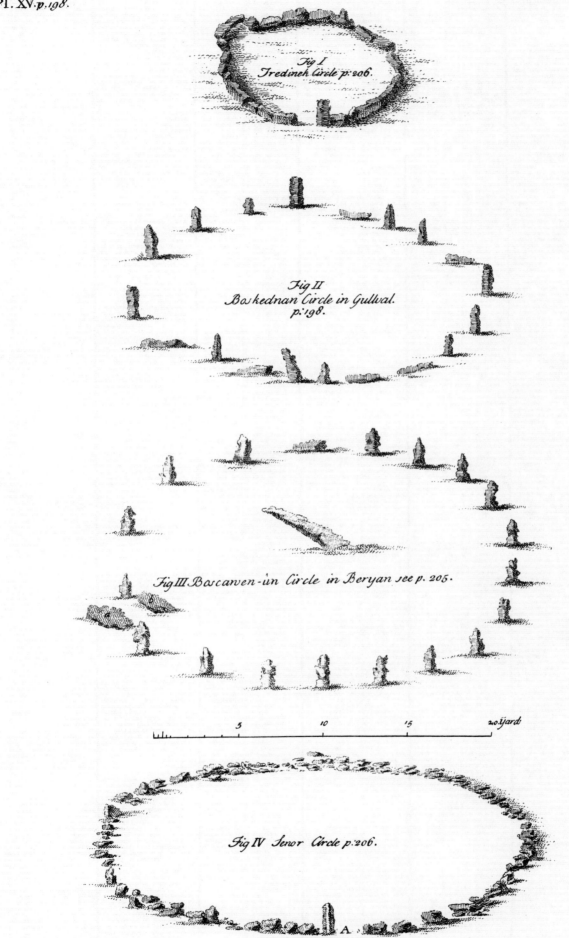

Pl: XV. p. 198.

Fig I
Tredineh Circle p: 206.

Fig II
Boskednan Circle in Gulval.
p: 198.

Fig III Boscawen-un Circle in Beryan see p. 205.

5   10   15   20 ¼ yards

Fig IV Senor Circle p: 206.

A

To Christopher Hawkins of Trevinard in Cornwall Esqr
This plate is with great respect inscrib'd by Wm. Borlase.

Botallek Circles in S.ᵗ Just

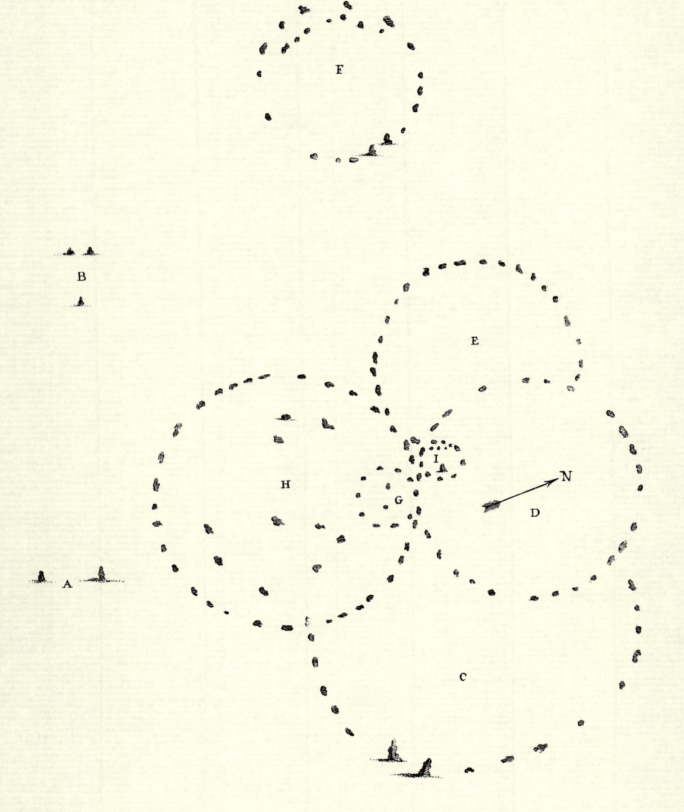

To the Rev. Jeremiah Milles D.D. *Precentor of the Church of Exeter*

This Plate is with great *respect inscrib'd by Wm.Borlase.*

ufe.   Of this kind is the Monument called the Hurlers, in the Parifh
St. Clare, Cornwall; the Stones of which, by the vulgar, are fuppofed
to have been once Men, and thus transformed, as a punifhment for
their hurling[t] upon the Lord's Day.   This Monument[u] confifted of
three Circles from which many Stones are now carried off; what
remain, and their diftances, may be feen (Plate XVII. p. 215.
fig. VI.)   Again, fome of thefe Circles include, and interfect one
the other, as in the curious clufter of Circles at Botallek (Plate
XVI.), in the feeming confufion of which, I cannot but think that
there was fome myftical meaning, or, at leaft, diftinct allotment to
particular ufes.   Some of thefe might be employed for the Sacrifice,
and to prepare, kill, examine, and burn the Victim, others allotted
to Prayer, others to the Feafting of the Priefts, others for the ftation
of thofe who devoted the Victims: whilft one Druid was preparing
the Victim in one Place, another was adoring in another, and defcribing the limits of his Temple: a third was going his round at
the extremity of another Circle of Stones; and, likely, many Druids
were to follow one the other in thefe myfterious Rounds: others
were bufy in the Rights of Augury[w], that fo all the Rites, each
in its proper place, might proceed at one and the fame time, and
under the infpection of the High-Priefts; who, by comparing and
obferving the indications of the whole, might judge of the Will of
the Gods with the greater certainty: laftly, that thefe Circles inter-
fected each other in fo remarkable a manner as we find them in this
Monument, might be, to intimate that each of thefe Holy Rites,
though exercifed in different Circles, and their own proper com-
partments, were but fo many Rings, or Links, of one and the fame
chain; and that there was a conftant dependance and connexion
betwixt Sacrifice, Prayer, Holy-Feafting, and all the feveral parts of
their Worfhip. It is farther to be noted, that near moft of thefe Circular Monuments we find detached Stones, as particularly on the
South-Weft fide of thefe circles at (A) and (B), which are placed fo
orderly, that there can be no doubt of their having had fome fhare
allotted them of the fuperftitious Rites.——At thefe Stones, probably, the High Prieft had his Officers to keep filence, and the officiating Priefts their Affiftants to prompt them, left any material
words might be left out, or what were diforderly inferted; for the
Ancients were fcrupuloufly nice in every thing faid, or done, upon
fuch folemn occafions, and were not only allowed their Prompter[x],
but a fecond perfon alfo at hand to mark that no Ceremony or Cir-

---

[t] Hurling, is playing with a Ball, and endea-
vouring to get at the Goal with it before one's
Antagonift;   an ancient trial of Strength and
Swiftnefs among the Cornifh.   See the Nat.
Hift. of Cornwall, firft Edit. p. 300.

[u] The Circles DEF (Plate XVI.) are alfo
in a Line.
[w] See Lib. II. Cap. xix.
[x] Plin. Lib. XXVIII. Cap. ii.

cumftance

cumftance fhould be omitted; let me farther obferve, that, where thefe detached Stones are found at too great a diftance for the before-mentioned purpofes, inferiour Priefts might be ftationed to prevent or regulate any diforderly behaviour on the out-fkirts of the congre-gation, and might attentively obferve the flying of Birds, or any other ominous appearances, during the time of thefe folemnities. I have only farther to remark, that the Circles, F, H, I, in this fingular Monument of Botallek, appear to have been edged with two rows of Stones. It need not be here added, that in whatfoever Circles we find Afhes and Altars, they want no arguments to prove that they were places of facrifice and worfhip[y].

Circles with Altars at Trefcaw, Wendron, and the Ifle of Arran.
Of that kind of Circle, which has altars within it, I fhall take notice of three only. The firft of them is on the Ifland of Trefcaw in Scilly. It is one rude Stone, nineteen feet long, fhelving on the top, round the bottom of which there is a hollow circular trench 36 feet in diameter, the brim of which trench is edged with a line of rude and unequal Stones (Pl. XII. fig. IV. p. 173.) The other (Pl. XII. fig. V. ibid.) is in the Wilds of Wendron Parifh, Cornwall, on a high hill called Karn-Menelez; it confifts of four flat thin Stones, by nature placed on each other; the upper Stone is circular, and meafures juft nineteen feet long, as the Rock abovementioned; but, what is more remarkable, the circular Trench at the bottom of it is in fhape and cavity like to that of the former, and meafures 35 feet and half diameter, which is within half a foot as long as the former; and that fmall difference may be owing to the inaccuracy of my meafurement, rather than to any real difference betwixt the things themfelves. I leave the Reader to make his remarks on this conformity; but I cannot help mentioning, " that in the Ifle of " Arran (Scotland) there is a Circle of big Stones, the Area of which " is about twelve paces. In the middle of this Circle, there is a " broad thin Stone fupported by three leffer Stones; the ancient " Inhabitants are reported to have burnt their Sacrifices on the " broad Stone in the time of the Heathens [z]." See there, the fame dimenfions of the Circle as thofe of the two before mentioned, the Stone in the middle alfo; and I fee no reafon to queftion the truth of the Tradition, as to the ufe of the latter, which may therefore point out to us the ufe and intent of the two former.

[y] " In medio Fani Focum inftruebant coquen-" dis hoftiis deftinatum." Worm. p. 28. " Some perfons who are yet alive declare, that " many years fince they did fee afhes of fome " burnt matter digged out of the bottom of a " little circle fet about with Stones, ftanding " clofe together in the center of one of thofe " Monuments, which is yet ftanding near the " church of Keig in the Shire of Aberdeen." Dr. James Garden's letter, dated June 15, 1692, to John Aubrey, F. R. S. of Eafton Pierce in Wiltfhire, Efq; communicated by the Right Rev. Dr. Lyttelton, Bifhop of Carlifle.
[z] Martin, ibid. ut fupra, p. 220.

We

We see how easy it is to reconcile all the different appearances of these Circles to the Rites of Worship; and I must observe in the last place, that Tradition, and the opinion of the learned, confirm the arguments above, which are drawn from the Structure of the Monuments, and the Customs of ancient ages. Boethius, in his life of Mainus, King of Scots, intimates that some of these Circles were erected by him, and appropriated to the Worship of the Gods [b]. In the Western parts of Island, in the province of Thornesthing, there was a Cirque, in which Men were sacrificed, after they had been killed, at a vast Stone placed therein [b]. In the Mainland (one of the Orkneys) they worshiped the Sun in a Circle, as they did the Moon in a Semi-circle [c]. "The Grave of Gealcossa, a Druidess, is " in Inisoen in the County of Donegall (Ireland), and hard by is her " Temple, being a sort of a diminutive Stonehenge, which many of " the old Irish dare not even at this day any way profane [d]."

The Temple at Classerniss is the most regular example of this kind that I have met with; and therefore I have inserted the plan of it (Plate XVII. fig. V. p. 206.) It is in the Island of Lewis near Classerniss, and called a Heathen Temple [e]. It consists of an avenue, which has nineteen Stones on each side, from F to E, and one at F; this leads you to a Circle of twelve Stones, with one in the center, A; from the circumference of which Circle, and in a line with the center, run a line of four Stones to B, four to D, and four to C. " I enquired (says Mr. Martin [f]) of the inhabitants what Tradition " they had concerning these Stones; and they told me, it was a place " appointed for worship in the time of Heathenism; and that the " chief Druid stood near the big Stone in the center, from whence he " addressed himself to the people that surrounded him." One observation occurs to me relating to this curious Monument, which is, that the number of Stones in the Avenue is 39, and the Circle 13, in all 52, and the detached Stones to the South, East, and West, twelve; whether these numbers happened to be so compleat by accident, or whether (as I rather imagine) they were intended to express the number of weeks and months in one whole year, I submit to the

Temple at Classerniss.

[a] Camd. Wallace of the Orcades, p. 54.
[b] Arngrim. ex Eyrbyggia, Worm. Mon. Dan. p. 27.
[c] Martin, p. 365.
[d] Toland, ibid. ut supra, p. 23. — "Temples " of the Druids Circles of Obelisks." Ib. p. 87. " I conjecture, says the late learned Mr. Lhuyd, " that they (viz. those Circles) were Places of " Sacrifice, and other Religious Rites, in the " times of Paganism." Lett. concerning the Dawnf-mên, Moyle's Works, vol. I. p. 239. " The Reason why we use Lhan for a Church, " was, as I conjecture, that before Christianity " the Druids sacrificed, and buried their dead, in " a Circle of Stones." Ibid. Baxt. Gloss. p 272. Wallace, ibid. ut supr. p. 53. is of like Opinion.

[e] In copying this Monument, I have followed the description of it given us in Mr. Martin's own Words (p. 9.), as being likely taken on the Spot, and therefore true, and not the Copper Plate (ibid.) which does not at all agree (in Number of Stones, or largeness of the Circle) with the verbal Description; being committed, as I suppose, to the Hands of some inaccurate Engraver.
[f] Of the Isles, p. 9.

F f f　　　　　　　　　　　　　　learned

learned g.   The Rev. Dr. Stukeley has given us some extraordinary
instances of exactness in works of this kind in his plans of Abury
and Stonehenge, which, being in every one's hands, I shall not detain
the Reader withall.

Of Reli-
gious Use
originally.   To have done with this first Class of Circular Monuments.
When it is remembered that Stones-erect were the Idols of those ages
(p. 161) what is more likely than that they were set round about
their altars to put those who were engaged in the religious rites in
mind, that what they said and did at such times was in presence of
their Deities? " Among their Idols, round about their altars, upon
" every high hill, in all the tops of the mountains, and under every
" green tree, and under every thick Oak, the place where they did
" offer sweet savour to all their Idols." Ezek. vi. 13.   I take every
thing indeed of this figure, that is either magnificent, greatly
expensive, regular, or laborious, to have been erected for Religious
use : in this number, therefore, I reckon, all the great works we
have of this plan, the Circles of Main-land, Abury, Stonehenge, the
Circles of vast Stones on Salakee Downs in St. Mary's, Scilly,
Rollrich h, in Oxfordshire, and in other places wherever they appear.
The intent of them, Wormius i attributes to a different reason ; but
what he says is too vague to be convincing.   I take them (says he k)
for Altars, or for Courts of Judicature ; and then speaking particularly of Rollrich, Stiperstons, and Stonehenge (undoubtedly the
noblest Monument of its kind),   " All these are no more than
" Monuments, and Trophies of Danish Victories."   Here we have
Stonehenge declared to be an Altar, a *Forum*, a Trophy.   The
same perplexed account of these things we have from Speed l :
" Trophies most certainly (says he) of Victories here obtained, either
" by the Romans, Saxons, or Danes."   Now, can any one suppose
that the Romans, at the time they lived in Britain, erected Trophies
in the same taste as the Saxons and Danes did afterwards? or will
any one believe that the stupendous Fabrick of Stonehenge was
erected by an army intent on action and conquest?   The grandeur
of the design, the distance of the materials, the tediousness with
which all such massy works are necessarily attended, all shew that
such designs were the fruits of Peace and Religion ; that they must
have been chimerical and impossible, during the busy scenes of war.

g Since my writing the Observation above, I
find Mr. Carte (English Hist. vol. I. p. 55.)
thinks there is something emblematical in the
number of Stones (xix.) on each side the Avenue, which he refers to the great Year or Circle
of xix years; and the xii Pillars, composing the
Body of the Temple, he thinks an Emblem of
the Zodiac.

h Al Roll-dricht, or Roll-druicht, i. e. the
Druid-round, as the ingenious Sanderson Miller,
Esq; of Radway, Warwickshire, has lately
informed me.
i Mon. Dan. p. 67.
k Ibid.
l Wormius, ibid.

Trophies

Trophies are fuggefted by the fudden tranfport of victory; but when the mind cools, and national or perfonal animofities fubfide, they are the evidences of a vain-glorious prefumption, and rather infults upon the vanquifhed and unhappy, than Monuments of any real honour to the victor[m].

To imagine that Stonehenge is only a Sepulchral Monument[n], is equally incongruous both to the fhape and vaftnefs of the building; that it might, after it was built and confecrated, be applied to fuch purpofes, for the greateft Princes or Priefts, is very likely; for though thefe Circles were originally of Religious Inftitution, yet that they became afterwards applied to other ufes, we fhall fee in the next Section.

Next to Religion, Government muft be fuppofed to have claimed the attention, and employed the labour and arts, of mankind; and in order to give weight to the moft folemn Acts of the Society, where could Affemblies be held more properly than in places confecrated to Religion, already reverenced equally by the Nobles and the Commonalty, and therefore likely to influence thofe who were to make Laws and govern, as well as awe thofe who were to follow them, and obey? Accordingly when any place had firft been diftinguifhed by the Rites of Worfhip, and was looked upon with a kind of facred dread, as the habitation of the Deity (where he was moft efpecially and always prefent); this place naturally fuggefted itfelf to all ranks, as moft likely to infpire the Rulers with juftice and knowledge, and the people with fubmiffion: the Laws made here were reckoned to partake of the facrednefs of the place; the Oaths fworn here were of higheft obligation, and double impiety it was accounted to violate any compact, or difturb any friendfhip, here contracted: befides, as the Ancients took care that all civil Treaties, Laws, and Elections fhould be attended by Sacrifices, no place could ferve fo commodioufly for ratifying thofe Acts of the Community, as where they could fo eafily have all the means of the moft facred atteftations, fuch as Priefts, Altars, and Victims, to confirm them.

SECT. IV.

Places of Council and Judgment.

The Monument of Gilgal was firft dignified by Religious Rites there performed: here the whole nation, by God's particular appointment, was circumcifed; here they kept a folemn paffover (which, fince their departure from Mount Sinai they had entirely omitted[o]), confequently, the Ark and Tabernacle remained here for fome time, and where they were, there were their ftated conftant

---

[m] Wormius himfelf, ibid. p. 90, thinks fuch Circles more likely to be Places of Election, than Trophies.

[n] As Keyfler, p. 109.

[o] The firft Paffover was held on the Day they came out of Egypt, Exod. xii. 2. The fecond the Year after, upon their receiving the Law, and fetting up the Tabernacle in Sinai, Numb. ix. 2. The third was this at Gilgal.

Sacrifices,

Sacrifices, and devotional Oblations, publick prayers and interceffions. This Monument became afterwards the Seat of Juſtice and National Councils; but we do not read of its being uſed as ſuch, till the time of Samuel, which was ſome centuries after its firſt erection by Joſhua; and then, out of regard to the holineſs of the place, and from a perſuaſion that God was preſent there in an eminent and peculiar manner, by his power and goodneſs: for whatever was done there, was ſaid to be tranſacted " *before the Lord,*" that is, in the moſt ſolemn manner, in the moſt holy place, and with the additional corroboration of Sacrifice and Devotion P.

There is no doubt but the ancient Monuments of Stones erect, and particularly theſe Circles, underwent the ſame alterations in other countries; and for the ſame reaſon became, in ſucceeding ages, the common places of aſſembling upon any emergent and more than ordinarily intereſting occaſion. In the ſame place was the *Forum* (viz. Court of Judicature), and the Altars of the Gods, ſo as that the *Fora* might at once ſerve for Worſhip, Law, and Juſtice: ſo Homer, Il. xi. ver. 805.

— — — — — Ινα σφ᾽ Αγορη τε, Θεμις τε
Ηεν, τη δη και σφι Θεων ἐ[ε]ευχα[ο Βωμοι.

So alſo Virgil, deſcribing the Grove and ancient palace of Picus q, ſays, that it ſerved for the inauguration of the Latin Kings, and for Religion too:

Hinc ſceptra accipere, & primos attollere faſces
Regibus omen erat; hoc illis curia, Templum,
Hæ ſacris ſedes epulis; — — — — —

Inſtead therefore of detaining the reader with a diſpute whether they were places of Worſhip, or Council, it may with great probability be aſſerted that they were uſed to both purpoſes; and having for the moſt part been firſt dedicated to Religion, naturally became afterwards the *Curiæ* and *Fora* of the ſame Community.

SECT. V.
Stones to
ſtand by.

When theſe Circles paſſed into Courts of Council, Judicature, and Election, they probably underwent ſuch alteration as the national cuſtoms upon thoſe occaſions did require; for, when the aſſembly was convened, it was the cuſtom either to ſtand by, or to ſtand upon, or thirdly to ſit upon theſe ſtones; and each of theſe different poſitions of the body required a peculiar arrange-

P 1 Sam. ii. 14. xv. 31.——xv. 33.   q Æn. vii. ver. 174.

ment

ment of the ftones [r]. In the firft cafe, whilft any election or decree was depending, or any folemn compact to be confirmed ; the principal perfons concerned ftood each by his pillar; and where a Middle Stone was erected in the Circle, there ftood the Prince, or General elect. This feems to be a very ancient cuftom, and is fpoken of as fuch, before the Babylonifh Captivity [s]. A Monument of this kind I take the circle of Bofcawen-ûn to be (Plate XV. Pag. 198. Fig. III.), as having a Middle Pillar erected near the centre of the Circle, probably at the Election of fome confiderable Prince, or at the eftablifhment of fome new Decree ; each Elector, or Legiflator, ftanding by his Pillar in the circumference, as the Prince did by that in the middle.

Bofcawen-ûn Circle.

It was alfo the cuftom to ftand upon Stones, placed in a circular manner, and fhaped for that purpofe, as fo many pedeftals to elevate the Nobles above the level of the reft ; confequently, fuch Stones (however rude) were of different fhape, and are therefore carefully to be diftinguifhed from the abovementioned Columnar Stones erect, by the fide of which the Kings ftood, and *upon* which it cannot be fuppofed that any one ever intended to ftand. Where we find Stones of this Kind and Order, we may pronounce them merely elective, confultory, and judicial, as never intended for the Rites of Worfhip [t]. This cuftom of chufing Princes, by Nobles ftanding in a Circle upon Rocks, is faid to have remained among the Northern Nations, 'till the Reign of Charles IV. and the Golden Bull, A. D. 1356 [u]. Some of thefe Circles have a large Stone in the middle, as the Monument near Upfal in Sweden, called Moraften, of which Olaus Magnus gives us both the defcription and ufe [w]. On this Moraften, Ericus was made King of Sweden, no longer fince than the year 1396 [x]. In Denmark alfo there are Monuments of this kind [y] ; and Macdonald was crowned King of the ifles, in the ifle of Yfla, ftanding upon a Stone with a deep impreffion on the top of it, made on purpofe to receive his feet [z].

SECT. VI.

Stones to ftand upon.

[r] Wormius, p. 87. feems to make no diftinction betwixt thefe Monuments ; whereas, whoever confiders the fhape of the Stones which compofe them, muft immediately perceive that the tall Columnar Stones erect could neither be for fitting or ftanding upon, as the Moraften and Kongftolen kind evidently were.

[s] See p. 164.

[t] " Lecturi Regem, veteres, affixis humo faxis " infiftere, fuffragiaque promere confueverunt " fubjectorum lapidum firmitate facti conftan-" tiam ominaturi. Quo ritu Humblus, dece-" dente patre, novo Patriæ beneficio Rex cre-" atus." Sax. Gr. in Worm. p. 88.

[u] Worm. ibid.

[w] " Eft etiam Lapis ingens & rotundus, cir-" cum circa duodecim minores adjacentes ha-" bens, cuneatis petris paululum e terra eleva-" tus, non procul a Metropoli Upfalenfi Mo-" raftên dictus, fuper quem novus Rex eligen-" dus, infinita populi multitudine præfente fuf-" cipitur." Lib. I. p. 11.

[x] Worm. p. 90.

[y] Ibid. p. 87.

[z] Martin of the Ifles, p. 241. Of this kind I have not yet met with any in Cornwall, unlefs it fhould pleafe the Reader to reckon the great Stone on the Ifland of Trefcaw, Scilly (Plate XI. Fig. IV.), in that number, which by the hollownefs of the Ground round it, I have judged rather to be an Altar, p. 200.

Ggg

It

SECT.VII.   It was alfo a cuftom to fit on Stones, placed in the fame Circu-
Stones to lar manner, during the time of Council, Law, or Election; and
fit on.
the feat where the King fat, is ftill in Denmark, called Kongftolen,
or King's feat, as that whereon the Queen was crowned, is called
Droning-ftolen.   In the Holm, as they call it, in Shetland (i. e.
the Law-Ting), " there are four great Stones, upon which fat the
" Judge, Clerk, and other Officers of the Court [a]."

Tredineck   Of this kind of Circular Monuments for the principal of the
Circle.
Affembly to ftand, or to fit on, I take our Circle of Tredinek in
Gullval (Cornwall), to be: the drawing of which will beft fup-
port the conjecture (Plate XV. Fig. I.).

Bodinar   Of the fame kind, I take the following fingular Monument,
Crellas.
called the Crellas [b], to be.   Its plan is very regular (Plate XVII.
Fig. IV.).   It confifts of two low walls, the outermoft forms two
Circles, one of which, B, is but 18 feet diameter, the other, C,
is 55 feet diameter by 50; and inclofes within it another circular
wall, which makes an Area within, 41 feet from North to South,
and 36 from Eaft to Weft; between each wall of the great inclofure, is a ditch four feet wide.   The larger Circle has two
entrances from the adjoining grounds at E and F, and one into
the fmaller Circle at G; thefe entrances have tall Stones on each
fide: I conjecture, that the little Circle might be for the Prince,
with thofe of higher rank, to fit, or ftand upon, and the other two
Circles, for the inferiour part of the Council.

Senor Cir-   In the Parifh of Senor, I met with a remarkable Cirque (Plate
cle.
XV. Fig. IV.), formed by fmall Stones thrown loofely together in
a circular Ridge.   At the entrance A, there is one tall pillar.
The dimenfions of it may be found by the fcale annexed.   I
judge this to have been an elective Circle; but why this Round
fhould confift of fuch a number of fmall Stones heaped together,
and the reft of a few, and fo much larger, I cannot guefs; unlefs
that in the latter, fuch as Bofcawen-ûn, &c. where the Stones are
few, great, and erect, the Election was made by a few Leaders, or
Nobles; and here, where the Stones are fmall and numerous, the
Election was was more popular, and determined by the Voices of
the common people.

This Cuftom of fitting on Stones in Council, was very ancient
among the more Eaftern Nations; for, in the feveral fculptures,
which the fruitful imagination of Homer beftows fo liberally on
the fhield of Achilles, one of them is of the Elders of the community, met together to decide a matter in difference, fitting
on Stones properly adapted to receive them, and in a facred
Circle:

---

[a] Martin of the Ifles.   [b] In the Tenement of Bodinar, Sancred, Cornwall.

— Ot

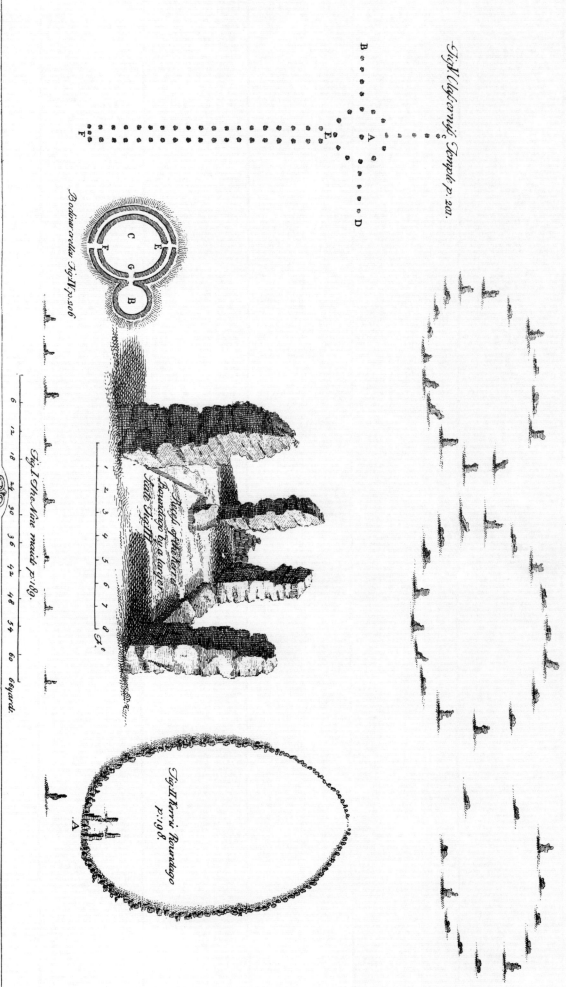

Fig. VI. Uny's corni, Temple p. 201.

B
F
E A
C
D

Bodinar circles Fig. IV. p. 206.

C E
F G
B

Fig. VII. The Hurlers p. 199.

Fig. I. The Nine maids p. 169.

Angle of Shelter & Boundage by a larger Scale Fig. III.

1 2 3 4 5 6 7 8 9 feet

6 12 18 24 30 36 42 48 54 60 69 yards

Fig. II. Kern's Roundago p. 198.

A

To Thomas Hawkins of TREWITHEN in ——— Cornwall Esq.r Member of Parliament

This Plate is with great ——— respect inscrib'd by W.m Borlase.

——— — — — — Οι δε γερον]ες
Ειατ' επι ξεϛοισι Λιθοις ΙΕΡΩ ΕΝΙ ΚΥΚΛΩ[c].

On rough-hewn Stones, within the sacred Cirque,
Convok'd, the Hoary Sages sat. —— — — —

We must not think, however, that all the Monuments of the **SECT. VIII.** *Some Thea-* Circular kind had no other use, but those before mentioned, of *tres, and* Religion, Law, and Election. The names which some of them *Amphi-the-atres.* are still called by, and the singular construction of others, as well as particular Customs, recorded in history of the Ancients, will suggest some other very different uses, to which Monuments of this Figure were applied.

Where these Stone inclosures are semi-circular, and distinguished **For Plays.** by seats and benches of like materials; there is no doubt but they were constructed in that form, out of regard to and for the convenience of the spectators[d], at plays, games, and festivals. There is a Theatre of this kind in Anglesea, resembling a horse-shoe, including an Area of 22 paces diameter, called Bryngwyn (or supreme Court[e]), with its opening to the West: it lies in a place called Tre'r Drew (or Druids town), from whence it may be reasonably conjectured, that this kind of structure was used by the Druids.

There is also one in Main-land (Orkney), from its theatrical or crescent-like form, supposed to have been dedicated to the worship of the Moon; but perhaps nothing more than one of these ancient Theatres.

But though the theatrical form is best adapted for the instruction and information of the Audience, yet (as men cannot be supposed in those illiterate times to have consulted the delight and instruction of the Ear, as much as the pleasure and entertainment of the Eye) it is not so commonly met with among the Ancients, as the Amphitheatrical, which, being more capacious, had generally the preference to the former. In these continued Rounds, or Amphitheatres of stone (not broken as the Cirque of Stones erect), the Britans did usually assemble, to hear plays acted, to see the Sports and Games, which upon particular occasions were intended to amuse the people, to quiet and delight them; an institution (among other Engines of State) very necessary in all Civil Societies: these are called with us in Cornwall (where we have great numbers of them) *Plán an guare*; viz. the level place, or Plain of sport and pastime. The benches round were generally of Turf, as Ovid, talking of those ancient places of sport, observes[f]:

[c] Il. xviii. ver. 504.
[d] The Reason why Theatres are built in, or nearly in, a semicircular Figure, is this. The Right Line is for the Actors and Speakers, and the Curve better distributes the Hearers than any Figure.
[e] Rowland's Mon. Ill. 84.
[f] De Arte Amat. Lib. I.

In

In gradibus ſedit populus de ceſpite factis,
Qualibet hirſuta fronde tegente comas.

We have one whoſe benches are of Stone, and the moſt re-markable Monument of this kind which I have yet ſeen; it is near the church of St. Juſt, Penwith, now ſomewhat disfigured by the injudicious repairs of late years; but by the remains it ſeems to have been a work of more than uſual labour and cor-rectneſs (See Plate XVIII. Fig. I. and II.). It was an exact Circle, of 126 feet diameter; the perpendicular height of the bank, from the area within, now ſeven feet; but the height from the bot-tom of the ditch without, ten feet at preſent, formerly more. The ſeats conſiſt of ſix ſteps, fourteen inches wide, and one foot high, with one on the top of all, where the Rampart is about ſeven feet wide. The Plays they acted in theſe Amphithea-tres were in the Corniſh language; the Subjects taken from Scripture Hiſtory, and " called Guirimir, which Mr. Llhuyd " ſuppoſes a corruption of Guari-mirkl, and in the Corniſh dialect, " to ſignify a miraculous Play, or Interlude. They were com-" poſed, for begetting in the common people a right notion of " the Scriptures, and were acted in the memory of ſome not long " ſince deceaſed g."

In theſe ſame Cirques alſo were performed all their Athletary Exerciſes, for which the Corniſh Britans are ſtill ſo remarkable; and when any ſingle combat was to be fought on foot, to decide any rivalry of Strength or Valour, any diſputed Property, or any Accuſation exhibited by Martial Challenge; no place was thought ſo proper as theſe incloſed Cirques h. When a ſudden Challenge and Rencounter happened, and the Champions were to fight it out on the ſpot, the area was marked out immediately with ſuch ſtones as were at hand i; and indeed it muſt be obſerved, in favour of theſe rude cuſtoms, that the marking out the place of battle muſt have prevented much cruelty, and ſaved many innocent lives; for if either combatant was, by any accident, forced out of the deſcribed Gyrus or Cirque, he was to loſe his cauſe, and to pay three marks of pure ſilver as a redemption of his life k. Frotho the great, King of Denmark (cotemporary with our Saviour) is reported l to have firſt ordered, m that all controverſies ſhould be decided by the ſword; for which law he had doubtleſs this reaſon of ſtate, viz. That all his ſubjects might ſtudy and practiſe the

---

g Biſhop Nicholſon's Letter to Dr. Charlett, Nov. 14, 1700. pen. Mr. Ballard, of Magdalen College, Oxford.
h " Quædam (viz. Saxa) Circos claudebant in " quibus Gigantes & pugiles duello ſtrenue de-" certabant." Worm. p. 62.

i " Nec mora (ſays Sax. Gr. Worm. p. 65.) " circuatur campus, milite circus ſtipatur con-" currunt pugiles."
k Worm. p. 68, 69. l Sax. Gr. Lib. V.
m " Ut de qualibet controverſia ferro decerne-" retur." Worm. p. 68.

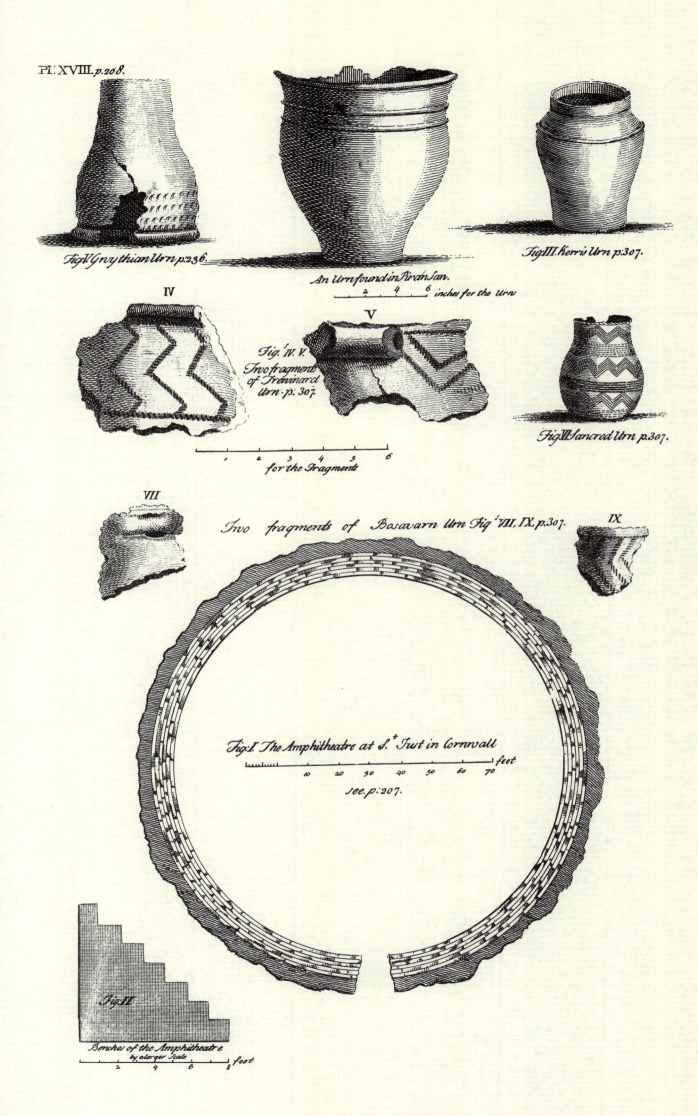

Pl: XVIII. p. 208.

Fig. VI Gwythian Urn p. 236.

An Urn found in Pirdn San.

2 4 6 inches for the Urn

Fig. III. kerris Urn p. 307.

IV

V

Fig. IV. V.
Two fragments
of Trewinard
Urn p: 307.

1 2 3 4 5 6
for the Fragments

Fig. VI Sancred Urn p. 307.

VII

Two fragments of Bosavarn Urn Fig.s VII. IX. p. 307.

IX

Fig. I. The Amphitheatre at S.t Just in Cornwall

10 20 30 40 50 60 70 feet

see. p: 207.

Fig. II

Benches of the Amphitheatre
by a larger Scale

2 4 6 8 feet

uſe of Arms ; for upon any diſpute whatſoever, if a man could not vindicate his own right, he muſt give up the Cauſe, and bear the Inſult, as if he had been actually overcome in a Duel [n]. This warlike, but unjuſt manner of trial obtained in Denmark, 'till the year 987, when it was aboliſhed for a ſtill more whimſical deciſion (Ordeal) to take its place. It was not prohibited in England 'till the Reign of Edward III [o]; who better underſtood the true nature of Military Glory, than to ſuffer Duelling any longer [p].

The Cirques, whether open or encloſed, were alſo often Sepulchral. For in, or adjoining to the edge of theſe Circular Monuments, we find Kiſt-vaen's (or Stone Cheſts) ſometimes Cromlêhs [q], and at other times Sepulchral Urns, or Barrows [r], all evident ſigns of burial ; and, doubtleſs, of the burial of perſons, the moſt illuſtrious in their country for Knowledge, Virtue, or Power. It muſt therefore be obſerved, that theſe Cirques were never the ordinary, common places of burial, it being very ſeldom that more than one Kiſtvaen, Barrow, or Cromlêh, is found in or near them, ſcarce ever more than two, and very few Urns. And, indeed, it is no wonder that their friends ſhould deſire, and the general voice conſent, that thoſe (and thoſe only) who were at the head of the Religion and Laws of their Country, might be interred, when dead, in thoſe ſacred places, where they had preſided with ſo much eminence whilſt they were alive. Thales the Mileſian (being preſſed probably by his friends to declare in what *Forum*, or what part of the *Forum* he would be buried) commanded them to bury him in an obſcure and contemptible part of Miletus, ſaying, " That place would in after- " times become the *Forum* of the Mileſians [s]," as if the *Forum* was not ſo able to do honour to his remains, as his remains to erect a new *Forum*.

A late diſcovery in Ireland has placed it beyond all doubt, that perſons were ſometimes buried in thoſe Circles ; for the account of it I am obliged to Mr. Wright in his Louthiania (Plate II. book III.). " The center of two Circles he procured to be opened, and in both " of them were found ſeveral decayed human bones. In one the broken " parts of two or three different Urns were taken up, one of which was " filled with burnt bones, and pieces of charcoal, but the reſt were " almoſt quite decayed, and turned to a black grey ſubſtance. Two " ſuch Circles of Stones, not long ſince, were, by accident, laid open

---

[n] Worm. p. 69.   [o] Camd. vol. I. p. 349.

[p] Notwithſtanding this Prohibition, and of ſo great a King, ſome remainders of the inveterate old Cuſtom remained 'till " the beginning of " Elizabeth, when a Duel was appointed, and all " the Apparatus ſettled, but when the Champions " had entered the Liſts, the Queen interpoſed " and made up the difference."

[q] There is part of a Cromlêh to be ſeen on the Skirts of Boſcawen-ûn Circle (Pl. XV. Fig. III.) marked there B. On the outſide edge of the Roundago at Kerris, there is alſo a Kiſtvaen, or Sepulchral Stone Cavity. At Killimille, near Dungannon, Ireland, within a Circle of Stones on the top of aHill, have been found Urns. Philoſ. Tranſ. 1713, p. 254.

[r] Camd. Annot. 1396.

[s] Plut. in Solone.

H h h   upon

" upon Mr. Kaux's Eftate near Dungannon [t], and three fuch Urns were
" difcovered, but the Urns were broke [u]." But either all Circles have
not been ufed for this purpofe of burial, or all people have not been
alike fuccefsful in their refearches, for " Ralph Sheldon, Efq; [w] digging
" in the middle of Rollrich Circle [x], (Oxfordfhire) found nothing [y]."

SECT. X.
Little Circles originally fepulchral.

We muft not difmifs this fubject, before we have obferved, that
there are many little Cirques, fometimes of a low bank of Earth [z],
fometimes of Stones erect [a], fometimes of loofe fmall Stones thrown
together in a circular form, inclofing an Area about three yards [b],
without any larger Circles round them.

Now as the firft are found in the Area of a Fortification, and the fecond intermixed with the Circles of Worfhip, I fhould be apt to think
them, in both, places of Burial; in the firft inftance, Monuments of the
leaders of the Garrifon of Bartinè, who fell during the Garrifon's lodging there, and were brought off from the Enemy (it being accounted
moft difhonourable of all things to the engaged party, to leave behind
them their flain commander [c]); and in the fecond inftance the Sepulchres of fome principal Druids buried there. Thirdly, the little Circles
on the Moors of Altarnun are about three yards diameter, more or lefs
fomewhat; about four or five in the Botallek Monument; and the
three in Bartinè Caftle are fix and half, 7, and 9 yards diameter;
all much too fmall for fortification, or duel, attended with no veftiges
which can make us fuppofe them habitations, and much below the
general fize of the other Circles (mentioned in fect. III.) and therefore intended I fhould think originally for Sepulchres.

[t] In the County of Tyrone in Ireland.
[u] Nat. Hift. of Ireland by Molyneux, p. 184.
Wright's Louth. p. 8, 9.
[w] Stukeley's Abury, p. 12.
[x] Rollrich is fuppofed Sepulchral by Sir Tho.
Brown, Hydriot. p. 28, but a Temple by Dr.
Stukeley in his Abury; both likely right.
[y] That the Druids ufed fuch Places for Burial,
fee Camd. p. 739. and that thefe Circles continue to this Day in Scotland, applied to the fame
Ufe, fee ibid. 1270.
[z] As at Bartinè Caftle (Pl. XXIX. Fig. I. *a,
b, c.*).
[a] Among Botalleck Circles (Pl. XVI. *a, b, c.*).
[b] In the wilds of Altarnun Parifh near Lancefton.
[c] See Homer's Iliad. The long Difpute
about the Body of Patroclus.

Pl. XIX. *pa.* 210.

A Singular Monum. *from Wormius, p. 63.* *Expl.* *p. 188.*

CHAP. VII.

Of Barrows.

IN Cornwall there are difperfed on every plain (almoft) as well as tops of hills, great numbers of thofe artificial heaps of earth or ftone, which are at prefent called Barrows [d]. A kind of Monument this, found, in moft countries, of the remoteft Antiquity, oftentimes of the higheft Dignity, of various name and conftruction, but for one ufe only, forafmuch as all of them feem primarily intended for the more fecurely protecting the remains of the dead, though afterwards transferred to other ufes.

The moft ancient Barrow we read of, is that of Ninus founder of SECT. I. the Affyrian Empire[e]: Semiramis, as it is related, wife of Ninus, *Found in moft Countries.* buried her hufband in the Royal Palace, and raifed over him a Mount of Earth.

In Perfia the fame manner of burying obtained[f]; though, generally fpeaking, none but princes were fo buried.

Achang, after his body had been burnt (he, and his children, and cattle being firft ftoned), was buried under a Stone Barrow, during the time of Jofhua's command; and the King of Ai was buried in the fame manner. In the 2 Sam. xviii. 17. it is faid that " they took " Abfalom and caft him into a great pit in the Wood, where they " laid a very great heap of Stones upon him." But it may be well queftioned whether this was properly Barrow-burial; and not rather burying a King's fon (whofe life had been taken away fo ex- prefily contrary to the royal command) in as expeditious a manner as poffible; and in a Stone quarry, perhaps, where rubbifh for covering the body was at hand. However, by the above inftances, it feems that this way of burying was not always intended to do honour to the dead, but fometimes to create an abhorrence of their crimes. In general they were Sepulchres of Dignity; Alyattes the Father of Crefus, and King of Lydia[h], was buried under a Barrow.

The fame method obtained among the Grecians. The Monument of Laius father of Oedipus is yet extant in the middle of the way *(Trivium)* where he and his fervants were buried, " collected Stones"

---

[d] I call them Barrows, becaufe that Name is commonly ufed; but in Cornwall, we call them, much more properly, Burrows; for Barrow figni- fies a Place of Defence (Dugdale's Warwickfhire p. 782.), but Burrow is from Byrig, to hide or bury; and fignifies a Sepulchre, as what we call

Barrows moft certainly were.
[e] Diod. Sic. Lib. II. cap. i.
[f] Xenophon, Lib. VII. — Hyde, cap. xxxiv. p. 410.
[g] Jofh. vii. 26. viii. 29.
[h] Herodotus.

being

being thrown over them [i].   Tydeus, the father of Diomed, slain in
the Theban War, was buried in that country under an Earthen
Barrow [k]; and it seems to have been the universal custom of Greeks
and Trojans, to bury both the Soldiers and Generals in the same
manner during the siege of Troy [l].   " The Monument of Lycus
" near Sicyone, was an Earthen Barrow, and the Sicyonians generally
" buried in that manner [m]."   Alexander intombed his friend
Hepheſtion in a Barrow [n].

As we come farther Weſt, in Sicily we find vaſt numbers of theſe
Monuments. The Romans had the same cuſtom, some think as anciently as Remus and Numa ; and Virgil [o] makes it ſtill more ancient.   From Livy [p], it appears, that Claudius Nero buried his own
Soldiers after this manner, in the second Carthaginian War ; and
Cefar Germanicus brought the firſt Turf himself, to raiſe the Barrow
over the Remains of Varius's unfortunate army [q].

In Germany there was the same way of interring [r]; and in the
moſt Northern Kingdoms there are ſtill many Barrows of great
Note and Extent.

In Britain, and the Britiſh Iſles, they are without number, for
the Druids burnt and then buried their Dead.

Mr. Martin (Rel. de Gauls, Vol. II. p. 345.) denies the Druids
to have had either Barrows or Urns ; but as the Gauls burnt their
Bodies, and uſed Urns, at leaſt for their Victims, as this Author
confeſſes (ibid.), can it be imagined that they uſed not the same
way of interring their Prieſts, Generals, and Princes ? Who could
be the Authors of the numerous Barrows in Britain, but the Britans
themſelves ? How could it ſurprize this Author that Aſhes ſhould
be mixed in theſe Barrows, when the Heap was formed from the
neighbouring Ground, upon which the Funeral Pile had been burnt ?
That the Gauls honoured the Remains of their human Victims is
true ; but that they could not but reſpect the Remains of the moſt
conſiderable men among them, muſt alſo be as true.

SECT. II.   Theſe Monuments are differently named, according to their obvi-
Name.   ous and moſt diſtinguiſhed properties.   From the Stone Materials
of which some are built, they are, in Scotland, in the Iſle of Man,
Ireland, and in Cornwall, as well as in other parts of England,
called Kairnes or Karns ; but when among the Grecians they con-
ſiſted of Earth ($\chi \upsilon \eta$ $\gamma \alpha \iota \alpha$ [s]), they were then called $\gamma \eta \lambda o \varphi o \iota$, or $\gamma \varepsilon \omega \lambda o \varphi o \iota$,

[i] Pauſanias in Phocicis, cap. v. p. 808.
Αιθοι λογαδες.   " A little below the City (viz. of
" Orchomenos) are some heaps of Stones some-
" what diſtant from each other, erected to the ho-
" nour of Men that had fallen in Battle." Ib.
Arcad. p. 626.
    [k] Iliad. xiv. ver. 119.
    [l] Il. vii. ver. 336. Il. xxiii. ver. 247. Il. xxiv.
ver. 795.

[m] Pauſan. p. 126.
    [n] " Tumulumque ei xii mill. Talentorum fe-
" cit." Juſtin, Lib. XII. cap. xii.
    [o] Æn. xi. ver. 207, &c.
    [p] Lib. XXVII. cap. xlii.
    [q] Worm. p. 34.
    [r] " Sepulchrum cefpes erigit." Tacit. de M. G.
    [s] Il. x. ver. 799. and ver. 801.

or

or *Tumuli* of Earth [t]; fometimes Ἑρμαῖα, from being near the Highways, where the Symbols of Mercury ufed frequently to ftand. From the circular plan on which they were erected, in Cornwall they are often called Crigs, or Crugs (in Britifh, round Heaps), and by the Vulgar oftentimes Crig an Bargus, or the Kite's round Hill; it being no uncommon thing for a bird of that kind to perch upon fuch Habitations of the Dead.

From their being intended for Sepulchres, they are called Lows in Staffordfhire [u], &c. and Lawes in Ireland; in Wales they are called Tommens, or Hillocks; in Oxfordfhire and Northamptonfhire, Cops [w]; in Teutonick Broghs, in Saxon Byrighs (whence comes our Englifh word); and Burrows they are ftill called in Cornwall. Becaufe they confift of Earth or Stones gathered into a Heap, Quintilian calls the manner of burying Sepultura Collatitia: in Denmark and the Northern Kingdoms, they have their names from the Kings and Generals interred under them.

When the Funeral Pile was exceeding large, or the number of the Perfons burnt great, the fire was not fuppofed to be extinguifhed till the third day, when they proceeded to collect the Bones and make the Barrows.

SECT. III. Conftruction of plain Barrows.

Tertia lux gelidam cœlo dimoverat umbram,
Mœrentes altum cinerem, & confufa ruebant
Offa focis, tepidoque onerabant aggere terræ [x]:

The materials, of which the Barrows confift, are either a multitude of fmall or great Stones, or fecondly Earth; or Stones and Earth mixed together, collected (as they feem to me) by many hands, from the neighbouring neareft ground, and heaped together till they make a little Hill, or *Tumulus*. It is fuggefted [y] that " fome Barrows are " compofed of foreign, adventitious Earth, of a yellow colour, " known to be the natural foil of a hill a mile diftant from them;" but whether the Sun, Rain, and Air, together with the admixtures of Clay, Turf, Earth, and Sands (moft of them entering jointly into the compofition of fuch Monuments) may not have contributed to alter the original colour of the compoft; and why the Ancients fhould go a mile for Earth, when fo much eafier to be procured in the adjacent Plains, are queftions not fo eafy to be anfwered. If it be faid with this Author, that the more trouble the Ancients took in erecting thefe Monuments, the more refpectful (as they thought) they fhewed themfelves to the memory of the deceafed; it fhould alfo

[t] Paufan. p. 126. in Corint. calls the Tumulus of Lycus, χῶμα γῆς, a Heap of Earth.
[u] Plot, Staff. p. 402. Low fignifies a Sepulchre, as Kow-low, regale Sepulchrum.
[w] Morton, Northamptonfh. p. 530.
[x] Æn. xi. ver. 210.
[y] Dr. Williams's Differtation on the St. Auftle Barrows. Philof. Tranfact. 1740.

I i i   follow,

follow, that in erecting Stone Barrows, they fetched the Stones from far, and neglected the Stones near at hand, and equally for their purpose; but this does not appear to be the case: it is true, the Ancients thought, that the larger they made these Monuments, and the vaster the Stones with which they sometimes adorned them, the greater honour they did to their departed friends; but to chuse one Earth before another, purely because at a greater distance, contributed nothing to the grandeur of the work; the colour, richness, or distance of the Mould, were things too minute to have any place in designs of such simplicity, and hasty erection.

In a field at Trelowarren [z], there was opened in July 1751, an Earthen Barrow, very wide in circumference, but not five feet high. As the Workmen came to the middle of the Barrow, they found a parcel of Stones set in some order, which being removed, discovered a Cavity about two feet diameter, and of equal height. It was surrounded and covered with Stones, and inclosed Bones of all sorts, Legs, Arms, Ribs, &c. and intermixed with them some Wood-ashes; there was no Urn here; but at the distance of a few feet from the central cavity, there were found two Urns, one on each side, with their mouths turned downwards, and small bones and ashes inclosed. All the black vegetable mould which covered the place where the Urns were found, was industriously cleared off, and the Urns, inverted, placed on the clean yellow clay (which in this field lies under the soil); then the black vegetable mould was placed round about the Urns; and throughout the whole composition of the Barrow, I observed afterwards the same materials, clay, mould, wood-ashes, and rubble-stone, mixed very disorderly, so that there can be no doubt, but that the people who formed this Barrow took indifferently of the mould and clay that lay nearest at hand. Three thin bits of brass found near the middle, just before I came there, were given me by the Workmen; they were covered with *ærugo*, neither inclosed in the cavity nor in the Urns, by which I conjecture, that they were pieces of a sword, or some other instrument of war, which, after having been inserted in the funeral pile, and broke, were thrown into the Barrow among the Earth and other materials that were heaped together.

All the materials, therefore, were in this instance (as I believe they were in most others) fetched from the adjacent and most convenient grounds, gathered from the surface nearest to the funeral pile, not dug very deep for, but the surface skimmed and stripped of its glebes [a], which lying more dispersed, and open to numbers of Workmen, were easier raised, and lighter to carry, than if the more solid parts which lie under the Glebe were first dug and broke, and

---

[z] The Seat of Sir R. Vyvyan, Bart. in Cornwall.

[a] Dugdale, on the Lowes in Warwickshire, is of the same Opinion.

then

then carried; the chief point was for many to work at a time, and for each party to bring their share of Earth, Stone, and Turf, in such regularity and succession as might create no confusion, or any way retard the work in hand, about which such a number of workmen were to be constantly employed: that they skimmed the surface in this manner, needs no other proof than that no hollows (generally speaking), trenches, or pits, appear in the neighourhood of these Monuments from which the Earth might possibly have been dug. The Earth was brought, and poured out of the Helmets [b].   The Stones, were brought from as far as conveniently might be, on the shoulders of the Soldiers, and so the Monument was soon compleated; especially if plain, and not immoderately great, neither adorned with Circles, or Pillars of Stone, nor crowned with large flat Stones; which Stones in some Monuments are indeed of astonishing magnitude, must have been far fetched, and brought with considerable labour, to bear a part in these works.   In places where Stones were more plentiful, and easier to be collected than the Earth, these Barrows were composed of Stones, seldom larger than what might be carried easily by one Soldier, but oftentimes less.   In places where Stones were not to be had, the Barrows were formed of the Earth, or such a mixture of Earth, Sand, or Stone, as the soil presented [c]; and this the Ancients seem to have done, not out of any preference which they gave to either of these materials (unless the Stones were large, and thereby became more suitable to the magnificence of the design), but purely directed by the nature of the place, and their own conveniency; indifferent, whether the remains of the dead were to be covered by heaps of Stone or Earth, they contented themselves with answering the principal intention of the monument, which was, that persons of distinguished merit should have the honour of being interred by the united labours of so many of their own countrymen, of which the Barrow was to be a perpetual (Σημα, or) Memorandum.   Some think that Earthen Barrows denote an inferiour quality of the person interred [d]; but we find them erected (as well as the others) for persons of the highest quality.   King Dercennus's in Italy was of Earth (Virg. Æn.) so was that of Abradates in Lydia; so was Patroclus's; the King of Ai's Monument of Stones; so was Achan's; so was that of Laius; Hector's was of Stone and Earth; so was that of

[b] 'Ριμφα δε σημ'εχεαν. Il. xxiv. ver. 795.
   There is a passage in Homer which very happily (though no where, as I remember, taken notice of by Commentators) expresses the diligence and expedition with which they worked on such Sepulchres:
——————— ειθαρ δε χυλην επι γαιαν εχευαν,
Χευαιλες δε το σημα παλιν κιον. Il. xxii. ver. 256, 7.
Where χυλην, εχευαν, & χευαιλες — come so thick on the back of one the other, on purpose to express

the quickness and activity with which the Soldiers poured out their Helmets full of Earth one upon the other, in order to compleat the Barrow as soon as possible.
   [c] That some of the Stone Barrows are earthen ones petrified (as Dr. Plot imagines, Staffordshire, p. 414) is very unlikely, to say no more on't.
   [d] As Pet. Lindeberg. & Joh. Cypræus, in Worm. p. 33, 34, 38.

Alyattes

Alyattes King of Lydia. To thefe materials of Earth (as is thought)
fome added a covering of green fod, as more pleafant for the eyes
of thofe that paffed by[e]; but as likely, perhaps, to keep the Barrow
in fhape, and give it an air of neatnefs.

This was the conftruction of plain Barrows, or *Tumuli*; nothing
more was requifite than heaping together the materials till they
made a hillock, over the dead body, of a Conic fhape: that fome
of them are now become of a more depreffed and hemifpherical
figure, is owing to the rage of winds and rain, the firft original
defign being to heap up the Earth, or Stones, as high as
the Bafe would bear. This was a fhape (I mean the Conoeid)
of the greateft fimplicity, and therefore moft ancient; lefs
fubject than any other form to the injuries of Time, nor likely
to be violated by the fury of Enemies, and therefore the moft
lafting; indeed, the Egyptian Pyramids themfelves are but improvements of this firft Plan, they are but fo many Conic *Tumuli*
of Mafonry (if I may call them fo), hollowed into Galleries
and Chambers, to preferve the fucceffive Remains of Egyptian
Princes. Barrows therefore, and Pyramids (folids the moft fimple,
next to Barrows) bid fair to laft as long as the world: for fmall
ones efcape the attention and envy of the deftroyer, and little labour will not deface the large ones; no one but a Cambyfes[f] can
be found in hiftory barbarous or mad enough to ufe much labour
in order to deface fuch venerable inftances of the magnificence of
former ages. By the Laws of Solon, there was a Penalty laid
upon the violation of all fuch Monuments[g].

SECT. IV.   Befides thefe plain Barrows, there are others which fhew greater
Barrows lefs art and exactnefs. Some are furrounded with a fingle row of Stones
fimple, how which form the Bafe; others with a ring or foffe of Earth. Some
orna-   have a large flat Stone on the top, and fome a Pillar, now and
mented.   then with, but oftner without, Infcription[h]. Some have a circle
round the bottom, and round the top alfo; and where this cuftom
prevailed, and no Stones offered for the purpofe; there Trees were
planted[i], Oak or Beech, to fupply the want of high Stones:

[e] Wormius, p. 41.
[f] Son of Cyrus the Great, who, when he conquered Egypt, employed his army to deftroy one
of the greateft Pyramids; but the Officer who
had the direction, after much time and labour
expended in making a Breach or two (ftill to
be feen), gave over the defign, as equally im-
practicable and ridiculous.
[g] " Pœna eft fi quis, *Buftum* (nam id puto ap-
" pellari *Tymbon*) aut Monumentum, aut Colum-
" nam, violarit, dejecerit, fregerit." Cic. de Leg.
lib. II.

[h] " The Barrows with Pilars are pretty fre-
" quent in Ireland; in the county of Waterford
" the Heap of Stones has in the middle a long
" Stone about fix feet high, ftuck in the ground:
" Thefe we fuppofe to be Monuments of per-
" fons of great diftinction. Under the Stones of
" fuch Karns they have found a fort of a coffin
" made with rough ftones." See p. 163, and
165.
[i] Wormius, p. 38.

                                                  —— *Fuit*

——— ——— ——— *Fuit ingens monte sub alto*
Regis Dercenni terreno ex aggere Buſtum
Antiqui Laurentis, opacaque ilice teĉtum.   Æn. XI.

When theſe Barrows were not very large; that is, when they were intended for private perſons, they were either placed near public roads to put travellers in mind of their common deſtiny, or, like Joſhua's Sepulchre, in the borders of their patrimony; moſt people deſiring to reſt in peace where they had uſually lived with content and reputation [k]. Plato enjoined, that no arable or cultivated, but only coarſe and barren land ſhould be allotted for Sepulchres, leſt that ſhould be taken up to no purpoſe by the dead, which ought to feed the living [l]. If they were the Sepulchres of common Soldiers, they were thrown up generally on the Field of Battle, where the Soldiers fell, and are ſtill to be known in ſome places, by being found in ſtraight lines ſtretched along the plains, which have been the Scenes of great Aĉtions, as regularly as the Front of an Army. On Saint Auſtle Downs in Cornwall, the Barrows " lie ſometimes two, three, even ſeven in a ſtrait " line [m]." It was indeed reckoned ſo honourable to be interred on the Field of Battle, that not only the Athenian and Platæan Soldiers, who fell in the Plains of Marathon were there interred [n], but Miltiades alſo (who commanded in and ſurvived that great Aĉtion) choſe to be buried in the ſame place, leaving there his mortal Remains, where he had gained immortal Glory. This General's Sepulchre was apart, at a diſtance from thoſe of the common Soldiers [o]. Sometimes Barrows are found in Valleys, but generally, and much oftner, on the tops of Hills and Plains, where Engagements for the moſt part, as well as Encampments, happen, and where ſuch works may have the advantage of being more conſpicuous than if they were lower placed.

SECT. V.
Place.

The Size of theſe Sepulchral Monuments is various, but generally large in proportion to the Quality of the deceaſed, or the Vanity, Affeĉtion, and Power of the Survivors. That of Ninus, according to Cteſias, was of a wonderful bigneſs, nine furlongs in height [p], and ten in breadth [q]; ſo that the City ſtanding in a Plain near the river Tigris, the *Tumulus* looked like a ſtately Citadel at a diſtance; and it is ſaid that it continues to this day, though

SECT. VI.
Of the Size of theſe Mo-
numents.

---

[k] Joſhua, xxiv. 30.   [l] Cic. de LL.   [o] Ibid.
[m] Philoſ. Tranſ. 1740.   [p] This Height muſt be reckoned by the ſlant
[n] Under *Tumuli* with Stones on the top, in-   line, not the perpendicular.
ſcribed with the names and tribes of the Slain.   [q] Diod Sic. Lib. II. cap. 1.
Pauſan. in Attic is, p. 79.

K k k   Nineveh

Niniveh (where it was erected) was destroyed by the Medes when they conquered the Assyrian Empire.

The Barrow erected by Achilles, over his friend Patroclus, was reckoned but a very moderate one[r], though it exceeded 100 feet in diameter[s]. But this was owing to the particular order of Achilles, who commanded that it should be made no larger until he himself came to lie down with his friend in the same Sepulchre; for then it was to be made higher and wider[t]. The Barrow of Alyattes King of Lydia was more than a quarter of a league in circuit, and 1560 Italian feet wide. It is indeed certain that, where time and power permitted, persons of rank were not interred in small Barrows.

When Abradates (of Princely Dignity) was killed fighting under Cyrus, against Cresus King of Lydia; his Eunuchs and Servants dug a private grave for him in a rising ground. Cyrus thinking this too mean a setting for such a Jewel, went to visit his widow, Panthea, and to assure her of a more honourable Sepulchre for her husband. He found her sitting on the ground, Abradates her dead husband lying by her with his head on her knees: Cyrus in a friendly manner taking the dead by his hand, and the hand (cut off in Battle) following on the touch, Panthea adjusted it again to its place; it seems she had been before employed in the mournful office of collecting and disposing his other dispersed and mangled limbs. Cyrus, moved with compassion, endeavours to comfort her (though in vain) with a promise that a great number of Soldiers should come and raise a Monument (χωσυσι το μνημα, i. e. *heap up a Barrow)* worthy of his dignity. Panthea killing herself that she might be buried in the same grave with her husband, Cyrus took care that their burial should be performed with proper honours; a very large Barrow was erected, and on the top of the Barrow a high stone, was placed with the names of the Princes, there buried, inscribed in the Syriac language [u].

The *Tumulus* erected by Alexander the Great over his friend Hepheftion, was so large that it cost 1200 Talents [w]: the Greeks, seem about the time of Alexander, to be launching out into great extravagance in this particular; and, therefore, Plato proposes a regulation, which no one ought to exceed in erecting such Monuments, viz. that no one Sepulchre should be larger than what five men could compleat in five days; nor a Pillar larger than what

---

[r] Iliad xxiii. 246. Ου μαλα πολλον—Αλλ' επιεικεα τοιον.

[s] It was erected round the Funeral Pile, which was 100 Feet each way. Ib. ver. 164.

[t] Ευρυν, τ' υψηλον τε τιθημεναι, Ib. ver. 247.

[u] Xenophon, Lib. VII. Cyroped.

[w] Justin. Lib. XII. cap. xii. Curt. X. iv. 25.

would

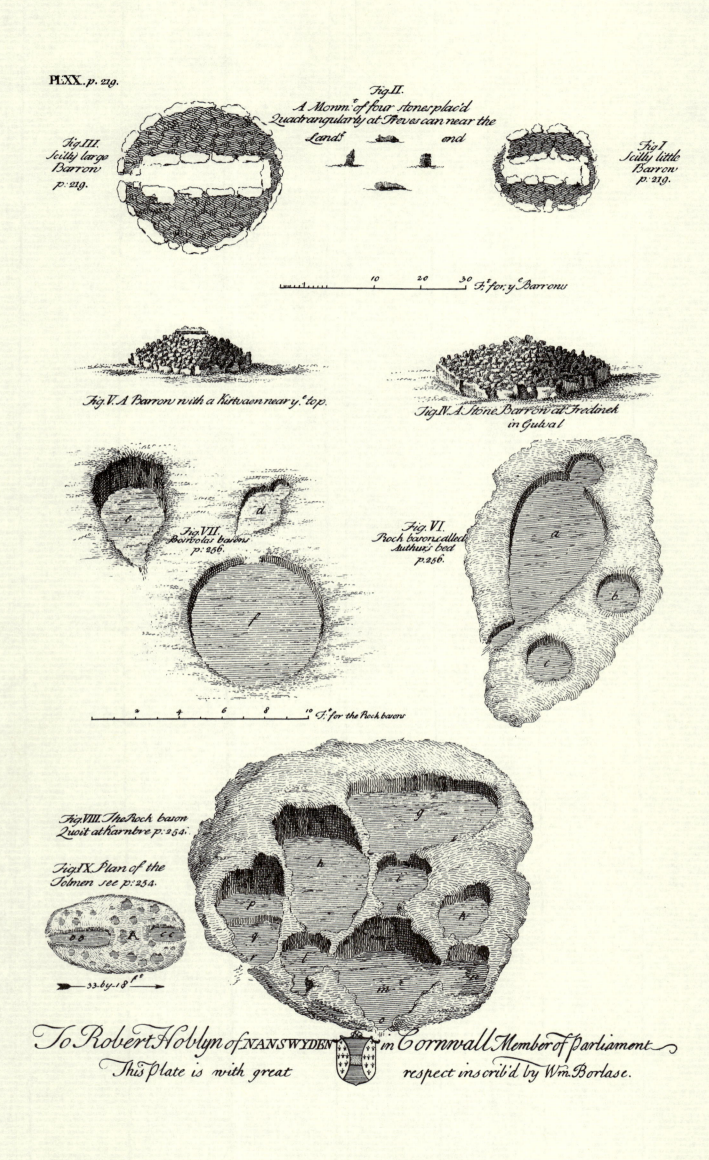

PL.XX. *p. 219.*

Fig.II.
A Monm.^t of four stones plac'd
Quadrangularly at Trevescan near the
Land's   end

Fig.III.
Scilly large
Barron
p: 219.

Fig.I
Scilly little
Barron
p: 219.

10   20   30   F.^t for ye Barrons

Fig.V. A Barron with a Kistvaen near ye top.

Fig.IV. A Stone Barron at Tredineh
in Gulval

Fig.VII.
Bosholas basons
p: 256.

Fig.VI.
Rock baron called
Authur's bed
p. 256.

2   4   6   8   10 F.^t for the Rock basons

Fig.VIII. The Rock bason
Quoit at Carnbre p: 254.

Fig.IX. Plan of the
Tolmen see p: 254.

33. by. 18 f.^t

To Robert Hoblyn of NANSWYDEN in Cornwall Member of Parliament
This plate is with great   respect inscrib'd by Wm Borlase.

would contain four Heroic Verfes[x].   In the Northern Kingdoms, the cuftom was to deny the honour of being buried under Barrows to Tyrants, Parricides, and other Criminals ; but to grudge no labour or expence in erecting Barrows to their truly great and worthy Princes.   The carcafe of Fengo was to have neither Urn nor *Tumulus,* but only to be burnt by the common Soldiers, and the afhes fcattered into the air[y].   On the other hand, the Barrows of good Princes, and brave Generals, were exceedingly large in themfelves, or adorned with immenfe Stones ; fometimes one *Tumulus* took up three years in the making[z] ; the Monument of Haco was *Collis fpectatæ magnitudinis*[a] ; Haraldus employed his whole Army, and a great number of Oxen, in drawing one vaft Stone to adorn the *Tumulus* of his Mother[b] ; and it is to be obferved, that where Stones of fufficient Magnitude to do honour to the dead were not to be procured, there the Earth-barrows were made fo much the larger, and were heaped up into little Mountains, that by their aftonifhing fize they might excite the wonder and curiofity of the living, and thereby perpetuate the dignity and merit of the dead.

Silbury Hill in Wiltfhire is an evidence of the labour and time which the ancient Britans did fometimes beftow on fuch Works. The diameter on the top is 105 feet[c], at the bottom fomewhat more than 500 feet ; its perpendicular height 170 feet.   On the top of it the workmen planting trees dug up a Human Body.   " In Ireland " their Barrows are alfo fo very large, that, during their Civil Wars, " they erected Caftles and Fortifications on their tops[d]."   In Cornwall, we have them from 30 feet high and under, down to four feet, and from 15 to 130 feet wide ; where Stones are plenty, of Stones ; in champain countries and Plains, moftly of Earth : fome have *Crypta,* or hollows, in the top ; fome a pillar[e].

There is a very fingular kind of Barrow which obtains throughout all the Scilly Iflands ; they are edged with large Stones, which form the outward Ring (as Fig. I. and Fig. III. Pl. XX.) ; in the middle they have a Cavity walled on each fide, and covered with large flat Stones, and over all is a *Tumulus* of fmall Stones and Earth, in fome more of Earth than Stones, in others *vice verfa*.   Upon opening it (Fig. III.), in the middle of the Barrow we found a large Cavity, as reprefented in the Plan, full of Earth ; there was a paffage into it at the Eaftern end, one foot eight inches wide, between two Stones fet

SECT. VII.

Remarkable Barrows at Scilly.

x Several laws were made at Athens to reftrain this Vanity.   Cic. de LL. Lib. II.
  y " Non Urna, non Tumulus, nefandas offium " reliquias claudat, nullum Parricidii veftigium " maneat" (fays Amletus to the Soldiers in Sax. Gramm.)   " His exequiis profequendus tyran- " nus."   Wormius, p. 39, &c.
  z Worm. Mon. D. p. 39.

a Ibid. p. 33.
  b See before, p. 175.——Sax. Gram. Lib. X. Worm. p. 39.
  c Stukeley's Abury, p. 43.
  d As fee the Louthiana, paffim.
  e As at Bofwens, in the parifh of Sancred, Cornwall.

on end.   In the middle it was four feet eight inches wide, the length of it 22 feet.   It was walled on each fide with Mafonry and Mortar, the fides four feet ten inches high ;   at the Weftern end, it had a large flat Stone, which terminated the Cavity ; its length bore E. and by N. and it was covered from end to end with large flat Stones, feveral of which we removed in order to get the exact dimenfions of the Cavity, and others had been carried off for building.   Forty-two feet diftant, to the N. E. we opened another Barrow of the fame kind.   The Cave was lefs in all refpects, but of the fame fhape ; the length bore N. E. by E. 14 feet, the walled fides two feet high ; where the Cavity was narroweft, it was but one foot eight inches, in the middle four foot, and at the S. W. end two feet wide in the bottom.   On one fide, in the floor, was a fmall round Cavity, dug deeper than the reft.   It was covered with flat Rocks as the former. In both thefe we found neither Bone nor Urn, but fome ftrong unctuous Earth, which fmelt cadaverous, and was of a different colour from the natural.   The reafon why thefe Cavities were made fo much beyond the dimenfions of the human body, was probably that they might contain the Remains not of one perfon only, but of whole families, it being ufual among the ancients for particular families to have feparate Burying-places.   The vulgar, however, are not eafily perfuaded, but that thefe Graves were made according to the Size of the Body there interred, and they are ftill called in thefe Iflands, *Giants Graves* [f].

In moft of thofe Barrows which have been examined by the Curious, they have found Urns, of which we fhall difcourfe at large, as foon as we have gone through the Monuments that in-clofe them.

In fome Barrows there are no Urns ; but in or near the centre there are either round or fquare Pits [g], which, by their containing black greafy Earth, fhew that they were defigned to ferve the office of Urns ; but the moifture of the furrounding Earth, in this kind of burying, foon confumes the Bones.   In fome Barrows again, there are neither Urns, nor little Repofitories inftead of them, but Human Skeletons without any Sign of their having paffed through the Fire.   Whofe Sepulchres thefe were, we fhall prefently confider.

SECT. VIII.   It muft be obferved, that this way of burying under *Tumuli* was
To what   fo univerfal, that it is no eafy matter to decide by what Nation any
Nation the   Barrows were erected, unlefs fome criterion, found within, affift us to
Barrows in
Britain are
to be
affigned.

f " In hifce vulgus Gigantes fepultos credit."
Wormius.
   g Dr. Williams, ibid. ut fupra, N°. 2, 3, 4.
Plot's Staffordfhire, p. 405.
   " On opening one of the Barrows on Clent

" Heath, mentioned by Plot in his Nat. Hift. of
" Staffordfhire, there was found, at the depth of
" ten feet, a quantity of black greafy earth, and
" fome half-burnt fticks and afhes." Letter, 1744.

form

form our judgment. Thus, by the Materials and Workmanſhip of the Urn, the Cell that contains it, Coins perhaps, and Inſtruments of War, or Domeſtick life, which may accompany the Bones, we may diſcover to what Nation we are to aſſign ſuch Sepulchres; but where theſe Indications are wanting, we muſt reſt contented in our uncertainty. If indeed it be true " that the Saxons and " the Danes, though they continued to bury their dead under " Earthen Hillocks, had left off burning them, at or before their " arrival and ſettlement in this Iſland;" as Morton [h] conjectures from Wormius (Mon. Danica, Lib. I. cap. vi. and vii.), then all our Barrows in Cornwall with Urns or Aſhes muſt be either Britiſh or Roman (few, if any, being to be attributed to the Traders of Phenicia and Greece, as being too diſtant from the Sea Shore): but I doubt whether ſo much can be clearly concluded from Wormius. That the Danes and Swedes ſometimes burnt their dead bodies (eſpecially thoſe of their principal men) and ſometimes interred without burning, is to be gathered from Sax. Gram. [i] (p. 50. ibid. Wormius, p. 51.) but no more. Thus far, then, we may proceed upon ſure grounds in aſſigning theſe Monuments to their proper Authors, that where there are no Coins or Pavements underneath, or elegance in the Workmanſhip of the Urns, or choice in the Materials of which the Urns are made, or Roman Camp or Way near or in a line with theſe Barrows, we may ſafely conclude, that ſuch Barrows are not Roman, and *vice verſa*. But we cannot determine all the reſt to be Britiſh, nor indeed diſtinguiſh the Saxon, Daniſh, and Britiſh, one from another; arts being at much the ſame height with them all, and their cuſtoms very like, eſpecially in the ancient ſimple manner of beſtowing their dead; the Saxons, and Danes, likely, when they had leiſure, were as willing to honour their Generals with funeral Piles, as the Britans were their Princes and Prieſts: but it muſt be allowed, that where Barrows have neither Urns, nor little repoſitories inſtead of them, but human Skeletons, without any ſign of their having paſſed through the fire; theſe are more likely to have been the Sepulchres of ſuch unſettled ſtrangers as the Saxons were (whilſt they infeſted Cornwall before the time of Vortigern), and the Danes after them, who were perpetually engaged in in-roads, and all the hurry of wandering parties, than of the fixed natives.

[h] Northamptonſh. p. 531.
[i] The Danes buried the body of Hubba, in the year 878, in Devonſhire. Hearne's Nòte on the Life of Alfred, p. 60. The Stones are ſwept away by the Sea's encreaſing, yet the name ſtill remains on the Strand near Appledore in the North of Devon, and to this day the place is commonly known by the name of Whibble Stow. Iſ. Mem. of Ex. p. 8. but ſometimes they alſo burnt their Dead. See Worm. and Nich. Hiſtor. Lib. p. 52.

By the contents of all Barrows which have been examined elſe-where as well as in this Iſland, it appears that the principal cauſe of their erection was to encloſe either the Aſhes, or the Bodies (unburnt), of the dead: however, the Sepulchres of the Ancients being always looked upon with a kind of veneration, they became afterwards applied to the ſolemnization of their higheſt Rites of Religion and Feſtivity. No ſooner was Alexander arrived upon the Plains before Troy, but he performed Sacrifices and other uſual Rites at the *Tumulus* of Achilles; and this is recorded of him not as any thing new, or inſtituted by him; we are therefore only to conſider him here, as complying with the already eſtabliſhed cuſtoms of his country. Again, as the Druids burnt, and afterwards buried their dead[k], there is no doubt but they had Barrows for their Sepulchres as well as other nations, and this was the original uſe of them, but they were afterwards otherwiſe applied; for, on the Stone Barrows, the Druids kindled their annual fires, eſpecially where there is a large flat Stone on the top[l]. Where the Earth-Barrows are incloſed, or ſhaped by a Circle of Stones erect, they may ſafely be preſumed to have ſerved as Altars for Sacrifice. Theſe Heaps were alſo, probably, at times, places of Inauguration, the Chieftain elect ſtanding on the top expoſed to view, and the Druid officiating cloſe to the edge below[m]. On the ſame Hillocks (likely) judgment was frequently pronounced, and the moſt important deciſions made, as from a ſacred eminence; and where theſe were not at hand, ſomething of like kind[n] was erected, for the Judge to ſtand or ſit upon, and give forth his Decrees with proper advantage.

In the Scotch Iſles they reſt their Corpſes (as they are carried to burial) at ſome little Barrows, oblige themſelves to make a religious tour, ſun-ways, round ſome heaps of Stones; and, that they might retain this very ancient, but Druid Cuſtom (though Chriſtians), maintain a Tradition among them, that one Barrow was conſecrated to St. Martin, and another to the Virgin Mary.

The firſt Miſſionaries in Ireland (in order to prevail in greater points) were forced to connive at ſome of the Druid Superſtitions, and, inſtead of aboliſhing them quite, thought it beſt to give them only another, and a Chriſtian turn. Not being able to withdraw the people from paying a kind of Adoration to Erected ſtones, they cut Croſſes on them, and then permitted that Superſtition. So here,

[k] Pomp. Mela, Lib. III. cap. ii.
[l] See Book II. chap. xx. p. 135.
[m] Martin of the Iſles, p. 365.
[n] " When an aſſembly met together for the " title of lands, the King, or his Deputy, came " upon the land, and with the contending " parties and their friends, and a champion for " each, viewed the controverted lands; then " cauſed a round Mount to be caſt up, and upon " the ſame was the Judgment-ſeat placed, having " his Back towards the Sun or the Weather. " Some of theſe Mounts were made ſquare, ſome " round, and both ſorts bore the name of " Gorſeddevy dadle, that is, the Mount of " Pleading." Jones's Anſwers in Toland of the Druids, p. 94.

their

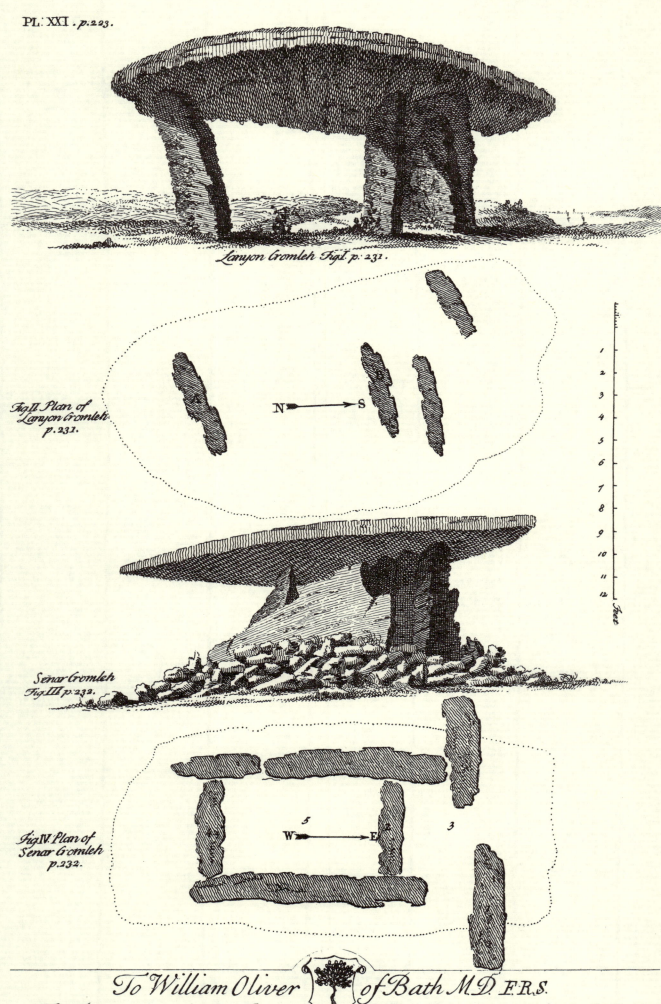

PL: XXI . p.223.

Lanyon Cromleh Fig.I. p. 231.

Fig.II. Plan of Lanyon Cromleh p. 231.

N → S

Senar Cromleh Fig.III p.232.

Fig.IV. Plan of Senar Cromleh p.232.

W → E

5   3

To William Oliver of Bath M.D. F.R.S.
This Plate, engrav'd at his Expence, is with great respect inscrib'd by Wm. Borlase.

their Miffionaries, fent to convert thefe ignorant Iflanders, feeing the profound veneration they had for Barrows, dedicated them to Chriftian Saints, and then allowed of the religious turn, refting the Corps, and the like fanciful abfurdities.

CHAP. IX.

Of the Cromléh.

IN feveral parts of Cornwall we find a large flat Stone in a horizontal pofition (or near it) fupported by other flat Stones fixed on their edges, and faftned in the ground, on purpofe to bear the weight of that Stone, which refts upon, over-fhadows them, and, by reafon of its extended furface, and its elevation of fix or eight feet or more from the ground, makes the principal figure in this kind of Monument. The fituation, which is generally chofen for SECT. I. this Monument, is the very fummit of the hill; and nothing can be Place of the more exact than the placing fome of them, which fhews, that thofe Cromléh. who erected them were very folicitous to place them as confpicuoufly as poffible. Sometimes this flat Stone, and its fupporters, ftand upon the plain natural foil, and common level of the ground; but at other times it is mounted on a Barrow made either of Stone or Earth; it is fometimes placed in the middle of a Circle of Stones-erect [o], and, when it has a place of that dignity, muft be fuppofed to be erected on fome extraordinary occafion; but when a Circle has a tall Stone in the middle, it feems to have been unlawful to remove that middle Stone, and therefore we find this Monument of which we are fpeaking, fometimes placed on the edge of fuch a Circle [p]. But we find fome Cromléhs erected on fuch rocky fituations, and fo diftant from houfes (where no Stones-erect do ftand, or appear to have ftood), that we may conclude, they were often erected in places where there were no fuch Circles. Some of thefe Monuments are quite inclofed, and buried, as it it were, in the Barrow; as that of Senor in Cornwall (Plate XXI. Fig. III.) and that at Chûn (Plate XXIV. Fig. X.) and that mentioned by Wormius, p. 4. Mon. Dan [q].

[o] As at Carig a fouky in the County of Cork, Ireland, Hift. of Cork, vol. i. p. 190. where the Caftle adjoining feems to have taken its name from the vulgar notion of this Monument being erected by the Fairies; Carig a fouky fignifying in Irifh the Fairy rock.

[p] See Pl. XV. Fig. III. *a*, and *b*, in Bofcawen-ûn: from which we may draw this confequence; that the Cromléh was pofteriour in date to the Circle, and the former erected there for the fake of the latter.

[q] One only which I have yet heard of, has its Supporters, or Side-ftones, fixed on a folid Rock. State of Downe, p. 199.

I find

I find the number of fupporters, in all the Monuments of this kind which I have feen, to be no more than three, the reafon of which I take to be this; they found it much eafier to place and fix fecurely any incumbent weight on three fupporters than on four, or more; becaufe, in the latter cafe, all the fupporters muft be exactly level on the top, and the under furface alfo of the covering Stone be planed and true, in order to bring the weight to bear equally on every fupporter; whereas, three fupporters have no occafion for fuch nicety; the incumbent weight eafily inclining itfelf, and refting on any three props (though not of one level on the top); and accordingly, we find the Covering Stones, not horizontal, but always more or lefs fhelving, the weight naturally fubfiding where the loweft fupporter is found, and fupporters of unequal height being eafier found than thofe of one and the fame[r].

The Supporters mark out, and inclofe an area, generally, fix feet long, or fomewhat more, and about four feet wide, in the form of a ftone Cheft or Cell[s]; on thefe Supporters refts a very large flat, or gibbous ftone[t]. In what manner they proceeded to erect thefe Monuments, whether by heaping occafional Mounds, or Hillocks of Earth, round the Supporters, in order to get the Covering Stone the eafier into its place, or by what Engines, it is in vain for us to enquire; but what is moft furprizing is, that this rude Monument of four or five Stones is fo artfully made, and the huge incumbent Stone fo geometrically placed, that though thefe Monuments greatly exceed the Chriftian æra (in all probability), yet it is very rare to find them give way to Time, Storm, or Weight; nay, we find the covering Stone often gone, that is, taken down for building, and yet the Supporters ftill keeping their proper ftation.

From the oblate and fpreading form of the upper Stone (refembling a *Difcus*) this Monument is in Cornwall called by the name of Quoit. In Merionidfhire (Wales) alfo there is one called Koeten-Arthur, or Quoit of Arthur; and another in Carnarvonfhire, called Bryn y Goeten, or the Quoit Hillock. The Cromlêh in Kent (Pl. XXII.) is called Kitt's Cotty-houfe (or rather, with Camden Keith, Coty-houfe), a corruption likely of the Britifh Koäten, or Goäten, a Quoit. In the Ifle of Jerfey (where there are many) they are called Pouqueleys[u]. There is a Cromlêh near Cloyne in Ireland, named Carig

---

[r] In Denmark alfo, Wormius fays, the Supporters are but three.

[s] " Sub hac Mole, Cavitas vifitur in quibuf-" dam vafta fatis, in aliis terrâ ac lapidibus repleta, " quæ fanguini victimarum recipiendo deputata " creditur." Worm. p. 7. How right he is in the ufe affigned for this Cavity, will be feen hereafter.

[t] One in Wales at Bodofwyr (Camd. p. 810.) is faid to be neatly wrought and pointed into

feveral Angles, which, if not the effect of fome modern Fancy, and love of Alteration, is very rare in Monuments of this kind. Thofe five which I have exhibited here from Cornwall in Pl. XXI. and XXIV. and others which I have feen, are more more artlefs.

[u] This feems to be a Britifh Compound word; for in Cornwall we ftill call a Heap a Pook (as a Pook of Turves, a Pook of Hay, i. e. a heap of Turves, a Haycock); and Ley is nothing but

Croith

Pl. XXII. p. 224.

Two Views of Kitts Cotty House in Kent.

E. Front

W. Front

" *Kitts Cotty House stands on the brow of a Hill about 1 Mile & ½ from Aylesford*
" *¼ Mile to the right of the great Road from Rochester to Maidstone & is compos'd of 4*
" *vast Stones call'd Kentish Ragg. The dimensions of the Stones, That on the S. side is*
" *8 f.ᵗ high by 7 ½ broad & 2 f.ᵗ thick weight about 8 ton. That on the N. 8 f.ᵗ by 8 & 2*
" *thick weight 8 ton 10 hundᵈ. the end Stone 5.6. high by 5 broad thickneſs 14 inchᵗ.*
" *weight 2 ton 8 ¼. The transverse or impost 11 f.ᵗ long by 8 broad & 2 thᵈck wᵗ. 10 ton*
" *7 hundᵈ. According to Camden & others it is erected over the burial place of Catigern*
" *brother of Vortimer King of the Britans slain in a battle near Aylesford betwixt*
" *the Britans & Saxons. — N.3. The nearest Quarry is six Miles distant*
    For this Monument (the Author having never seen it) the present Edition is indebted to the Genˡ. Mag. May, 1763. pa. 248.
N.3. *'Tis not by the same Scale as the Cornish Gomlehs, but is evidently of the same construction.*

Croith[w], i. e. the Sun's rock, as if it were dedicated to the Sun, which the Irish certainly worshiped: but the general name by which they are known among the learned is that of Cromlêh[p] (or crooked Stone), the upper stone being generally of a convex or swelling surface, and resting in an inclined or crooked position.

What Nation, Sect, or Religion, this kind of Monument may be said properly to belong to, or had its rise from, is a point not easily to be adjusted, seeing we find them in Denmark, France, Germany, and in the Isles of the Mediterranean Sea, adjacent to the Coasts of Spain and France, in Jersey, Ireland, Britain, and the British Isles; and perhaps in many other countries they will occur, especially the Northern Kingdoms, by which they should seem to have been Celtick Monuments, and with that numerous people carried into all their Settlements.

SECT. III.
What Nation to be ascribed to.

That the Druids erected Monuments of this kind, I think is more than probable, for there are remains of several in the Isle of Anglesea, and in places denominated from the ancient Druids[y]. There are also many Cromlêhs still entire in the West of Cornwall, where, by the number still remaining of their Monuments, the Druids must have been long fixed. For which reasons I conclude (as well as for that the Christians never erected such Monuments), that the Druids were accustomed to erect Monuments of this kind. To whom else can we attribute them? If it be said, to the Danes; some of them would likely have been inscribed, if that were the case, among such a number as we meet with in Cornwall; for inscribed, some of them are, in Denmark, as Wormius informs us: besides, we find them in places where the Danes never were, and therefore they cannot all be Danish; neither do they appear to be such as Sojourners, and generally in an Enemy's Country, would have leisure and security enough to erect. But as they are not likely to be Danish, so neither can they be said to be peculiar to the Druids; for we find them also in many foreign parts, where the Druid Priesthood never took footing.

Doubtless they are very ancient, as appears by their simplicity, the grandeur and fewness of the Materials. The Irish Historians

---

Lêh, in Armorick and Cornish signifying a flat Stone; so that Pookleh (Gallicè Pouqueley) means a heap of Stone.

[w] Nat. and Civil Hist. of Cork, p. 148.

[x] In Welsh, Cromlech; but the Cornish (instead of pronouncing the Greek X as ch), only accent the Vowel before the H, and drop the C; thus, instead of Lech a flat Stone, they say Lêh, plur. Lêhou. Crom, or Crum (Armorice Crewm), is crooked, and a Word still in use among the Cornish, in that sense. From Crom or Crûm, comes Crymmy, bending, bowing;

whence some (viz. Toland, and the State of Down, &c.) conjecture that these Stones were called Cromlech, from the Reverence and Adoration, which Persons bowing paid to them. It the Reader chuses to derive Cromlech from the Hebrew with Rowland, p. 47, 214. חרם לוח will signify a devoted, consecrated Stone.

[y] As Tre'r baird, and Bodofwyr; and Monuments of the same nature, viz. Kistvaens (or Stone-chests) covered, are called in Denbighshire, Kerig y Drudion, that is, Druid Stones.

say

say that Tigernmas King of Ireland, firſt Author of Idolatry there, died *anno mundi* 3034, in the Plains of Magh Sleachd (i. e. the field of worſhip) with a great number of his ſubjects, whilſt they were ſacrificing there to Crom Cruach [z]. The largeſt Cromlêh in Angleſea, is ſaid to be the Sepulchral Monument of Bronwen, Daughter of King Leirus, who by the Welſh Traditions began his Reign, A. M. 3205 [a]. The Supporters, indeed, are found marked with Croſſes in a Monument of this kind called Ty Iltud [b] in Wales; but the Croſſes and the Saint's name muſt have been given it after Chriſtianity came in, if this be a true Cromlêh, for it is difficult to prove that the Chriſtians ever erected Structures of this kind [c].

SECT. IV.
The intent and uſe of theſe Monuments.

Some have been fanciful enough to imagine that the Cromlêh was intended for a federal teſtimony [d]; ſome, from the Sacrifice and other ſacred Ceremonies performed near it, ſeem to have miſtaken the Cromlêh, for the Idol to which divine honours were paid, as at Crom Cruach abovementioned; others have been ſo weak as to think them Priſons, becauſe one of them goes by the name of Kenricus's Priſon in Wales, and might poſſibly be converted to that uſe; but the moſt prevailing opinion is, that they were Druid Altars [e]; which, becauſe eſpouſed by ſeveral learned men, we will now proceed to examine, by conſidering their ſtructure, and fitneſs, or unfitneſs, for ſuch an uſe.

Not Altars originally.

It is very unlikely, if not impoſſible, that ever the Cromlêh ſhould have been an Altar for Sacrifice, for the top of it is not eaſily to be got upon, much leſs a fire to be kindled on it, ſufficient to conſume the Victim, without ſcorching the Prieſt that officiated; not to mention the horrid Rites with which the Druid Sacrifice was attended, and which there is not proper room, or footing, to

---

[z] This Crom-Cruach (i. e. a heap of crooked, unwrought Stones) was the moſt famous Idol of all Ireland; it ſtands in the middle of a Circle of twelve Obeliſks on a hill in Brefin, in the County of Cavan; and by the Iriſh Writers (State of Down, p. 20. Tol. Hiſt. Druids, p. 100) is ſaid to have been covered with Gold and Silver: I ſuppoſe they mean when it was at the moſt celebrated point of Glory; for Idols riſe and fall in value, and have greater, or leſs reſort, according as the fits of Superſtition are more or leſs inflamed.

[a] Camd. p. 810.

[b] i. e. Houſe of St. Iltut.

[e] Keith Coty-houſe near Ayleſford in Kent (which is plainly a Cromlêh, as ſee Plate XXII. p. 224.) is thought by ſome (Camden, laſt Edit. p. 230.) the Sepulchre of Catigern, brother of Vortimer King of the Britans, who invited the Saxons into Britain. If this Tradition is true, Catigern (it may be ſaid) was likely a Chriſtian, and the people who erected his Monument

Chriſtians (Britain having before this received the Chriſtian Religion); but it muſt be conſidered, that the Chriſtianity then among the Britans, particularly thoſe of Cornwall (from whence Vortimer came, and ſucceeded his father Vortigern, who was advanced from that Earldom to be the general King of Britain) was ſo deeply tainted with Druidiſm, and exerciſed the great abilities of the Iriſh Saints ſo long after as well as before this period, that it is difficult to determine whether we are to look upon Keith Coty-houſe as a Druid or as a Chriſtian Monument: even though allowed to be of the date Camden gives it.

[d] See the Louthiana, Book III. p. 12.

[e] " Ego ejuſmodi (viz. Tumulos) integris " etiam familiis deſtinatos puto, unde et (in his " Aræ, viz. Cromlehs) quæ communia ſacrificia " pro totius gentis incolumitate immolata ex- " cipiant." Worm. p. 35. See Rowland, p. 47. 215.

perform

perform in fo perilous a ftation[e]. Molfra and Senar Quoits are fo very thin, that the intenfenefs of the Sacrifical Fire muft have cracked and foon broke the Quoits, which are all of Moor-Stone[f], and can, therefore, refift the fire but very indifferently, the ftrongeft and moft compact ftone eafily fplitting on being roafted. But what is almoft decifive in this difpute is, that the Table Stone of the Cromlêh at Ch'ûn, in Morvah, Cornwall (Plate XXIV. Fig. X.), is fo very gibbous, that no Prieft could ftand on it, either to tend the Fire, or overfee the confumption of the Victim. There is alfo one in Pembrokefhire, of which the middle, or covering Stone, is eighteen feet high, and nine feet broad towards the Bafe[g]; now what kind of Altar could this be? I know that it is confidently affirmed that all Cromlêhs were Places of Worfhip[h]; but this is a hafty, vague expreffion, and it was not at all confidered by the Author how improper the dimenfions and parts of a Cromlêh were for a Place of Worfhip. That part of it which lies directly under the Quoit, and may be termed the Kift-vaen[i] of this Monument, is in fome fo clofe (as particularly at Senar and Ch'ûn) that 'tis with great difficulty any man can get into it; and where the Kift-vaen is not fo regularly marked out, and enclofed on every fide (as at Lanyon and Molfra it is not), there is great reafon to believe that fome of the conftituent parts have been removed: befides, many are erected on Stone Barrows, viz. Heaps of loofe fmall Stones; a very uneafy ftation for people to perform their Devotions upon. The Top-ftone is alfo too high for the Prieft to pour out his Libations upon; fo that it could in no fenfe ferve the purpofe of any Altar, but only (which is not improbable) of fuch an Altar as was to receive the Oblations and Prefents of the Affembly, in honour of the deceafed.

That the ancients might facrifice near the Cromlêh, is not unlikely; whence it comes to pafs that great quantities of Afhes may be found near thefe Monuments, as in Jerfey; but that the Cromlêh itfelf was an Altar for Fire, will by no means follow: it is incongruous both to the Structure and the Materials, the nature of which laft, as well as the fhape and dimenfions of the former, are more invariable rules to judge by, than any other now to be difcovered or expected.

As the whole frame of the Cromlêh fhews itfelf unfit for an Altar of Burnt offerings, fo I think it points out evidently to us But Sepulchral.

---

[e] Of this opinion I have the pleafure to find the judicious Keyfler (p. 46.) fpeaking of the Cromlêh Monuments, "Quod enim alia hujuf-modi monumenta in Drenthia & Septentrione attinet, conftat fuperiores eorum lapides planè rudes, gibbofos atque ad facrificia fuiffe ineptos: Accedit quod nulli in ullis appareant gradus, "quibus facerdos facra peracturus afcendere & "in fumma eniti potuerit."

[f] A Stone of a large grain or gritt, a kind of Granite eafily clove, and fometimes free enough to yield to a chizzel.

[g] Toland, p. 98.

[h] Ibid. p. 97.   [i] See note [k], p. fequ.

feveral

several reasons to conclude that it is a Sepulchral Monument. The area inclosed underneath the Quoit is about six feet and a half long, and four wide, so very near is this space to the dimensions of the human body, and every kind of *Sarcophagus* of the ancients.

In Cornwall, and elsewhere, we find Kist-vaens[k] (of an area equal to the size of the human body), consisting of Side Stones pitched on end, without any Covering Stone; these certainly once inclosed the Bones of the Dead, though now generally dug up to search for money; and what else is our Cromleh but a Kist-vaen consisting of larger Side Stones, covered with a still larger and flat one on the top?

The Supporters, therefore, as well as Covering Stone, are no more than the suggestion of the common universal sense of mankind; which was, first, on every side to fence and surround the dead body from the Violences of weather, and from the rage of enemies, and in the next place, by the grandeur of its construction, to do honour to the memory of the Dead. Our Altar-tombs at this day are but a more diminutive and regular Cromlêh, and called Altar-tombs (as I apprehend) not from any divine service or sacrifice ever intended to be performed upon them, but rather because they are raised from the Earth as Altars are, near the height, and near their figure: I leave it to be considered, whether the Cromlêh might not obtain the name of the Altar from the same resemblance[l]. If it be objected, that the Covering-stone of this Monument is usually so large, that it is very unlikely people should combine to call it an Altar, unless tradition had constantly and justly asserted that it was really so: I answer, that the generality and vulgar part of mankind have always thought with the Fabulous, that our Forefathers much exceeded in proportion the present race of mankind, and therefore had seats or chairs (as we find the Giant's chair almost in every country), Altars, Tombs, and Weapons, proportionably larger, than what the dwindled present generation have any occasion for. Next, let it be observed, that the Cromlêhs are sometimes found on, and often surrounded with Barrows. Now the Barrow was one of the most ancient and most general way of interring the dead; and, therefore, its lying sometimes under, and at other times round this Monument is no weak reason for the Cromlêh to have been a place of Sepulture. Again, it is justly observed[m], that a small brook near this kind of Monument, is called Rhyd y Bedheu, or the ford of the Graves. In the same page it is said, that hu-

---

[k] i. e. Chests made of Stone.
[l] " Ea dispositio est" (says Emmius in

Wormio, p. 9.) " ut aras referre videantur."
[m] Annot. on Camden, p. 810.

man

man bones and afhes have been found near them. The names alfo of fome perfons interred in them are recorded, as that of Haraldus, (in Wormius, p. 22.[n]) and that of Bronwen in Wales. Wormius mentions a *Crypta* and a Cromlêh together on one Barrow (p. 44.), but, for want of an accurate drawing of both, his defcription is not fufficiently diftinct; out of the firft were taken a great many human bones, from which he concludes it to have been the burying place of fome remarkable family.

It is very probable, therefore, that the ufe and intent of the Cromlêh was primarily to diftinguifh, and do honour to the dead, and alfo to inclofe the dead body, by placing the fupporters, and Covering-ftone, fo as they fhould fecure it on all fides.

When this Monument is found in the middle of a facred Circus, it was probably the Sepulchre of one of the Chief Priefts or Druids, who prefided in that diftrict, or of fome Prince, a favourite of that Order. When the middle of the Circus was already taken up by a fingle Obelifk, which was always regarded as a Symbol of fomething divine, and generally worfhiped[o], then was the Cromlêh placed on the edge of that Circle, and perhaps refpecting a particular region of the Heavens. Princes and great Commanders were not only interred in a Barrow, but had their Sepulchres farther dignified by a Cromlêh erected over them. Laftly, it was the defire of many in former times, as it ftill is, to be buried near the remains of an illuftrious Anceftor, or Predeceffor in Office; and hence it is, that fome Vaults are difcovered near thefe Cromlêhs; hence, in the large Crypta, above-mentioned from Wormius, fome bones, afhes, and the Enfigns of military command, as fpears, helmets, and the like; the principal body remaining (as I fufpect) undifturbed by the after-interments in the Kiftvaen of the Cromlêh; but either through age and moifture decayed, or diffipated by the foolifh, in hopes of finding treafure.

That thefe places of burial became afterwards the fcenes of the Parentalia, or where divine honours were payed, and facrifices performed to the Manes of the dead, is very reafonable to believe; but thefe Rites muft have been tranfacted at fome diftance from the Cromlêh, which (as I think has been fhewn) could never ferve for facrifice. " *Uncia ubi vifitur* (viz. *Ara*, i. e. the Cromlêh) " *maximâ ex parte Sepulchro impofita effe folet, eo fine, ut ibidem* " *in memoriam defuncti quotannis facra peragantur*[p]." By which

---

[n] Snorro (in his Hiftory of King Harald, ch. 45.) defcribes his Tomb fo, that it muft needs have been of the Cromlêh kind. " In " medio Tumuli (viz. Barrow) fepultus eft Rex " Haraldus, difpofito utrinque Lapide juxta " caput, pedefque, ac fuperimpofita *Sepulchrali*

" *Petra*, aggeftis etiam ad latera lapidibus mino- "-ribus." Keyfler, from Snorro, p. 101.
[o] See before on fingle Stones erect, Book III. chap. ii. p. 160.
[p] Worm. p. 8..

N n n   words,

words, if he means, that there, in that place, near by, that is, round about the Barrow and Cromlêh, facrifices were performed, his opinion is juft, and the Cromlêh might be, as it were, the facred Kibla, to mark the place of affembling, and to which they were to direct their devotions.

I muft not difmifs this Article without proper Examples and Figures given of fome of thofe Monuments in Cornwall.

SECT. V. *Examples.* Five Elevations I have chofen to exhibit here, and four plans, which, as there are fome peculiarities in each, may, perhaps, afford fome light and confirmation to what goes before, or, paffing into more fkilful hands, may prove the means of explaining the ufe and intent of this Monument in a ftill more fatisfactory manner.

Môlfra Cromlêh defcribed. In the Parifh of Madern (Cornwall), there are two Cromlêhs; one at Môlfra (Plate XXIV. Fig. XI.) the other at Lanyon (Plate XXI. Fig. I.) The former is placed exactly on the fummit of a round bald hill, as the word fignifies in the Cornu-britifh. The Cover-ftone is nine feet eight by fourteen feet three inches, reckoning a piece evidently clove, or broke off from it, and lying near it. The fupporters are three, five feet high, inclofing an Area fix feet eight from Eaft to Weft, and four feet wide, fo that the length bears due Eaft and Weft, has a fide Stone to the North, but is open to the South, that Stone being probably removed, or broken into pieces. This Quoit was evidently brought from a Karn or Ledge of Rocks below, about a furlong to the North Weft, in which Karn may be feen feveral very large flat Stones lying on one another horizontally; and fome thin ones, near the top, feem by their parallel edges to have been raifed or clove off from the Rock underneath by art, as if on purpofe to form more Cromlêhs; thofe that did not rife well ferving for Supporters, and the more entire for Quoits, or Covering Stones. The Stone-Barrow with which this Cromlêh is furrounded is about two feet high from the general furface, and 37 feet three inches in diameter.

As this Quoit is off from its ancient fituation with one edge refting on the ground, I thought it might permit us fafely to fearch the inclofed area. In digging, one foot was very black, the natural upper foil; we then came to a whitifh, cinereous-coloured ftiff clay, two inches in depth, then a thin ftratum of yellow clay mixed with gravel, four inches deep; then a flat, black, greafy loam, mixed in and throughout, more or lefs, with the yellow natural clay ten inches in depth, under which appeared the hard, natural, ftony, ftratum which lies on the Karn, not moved fince the deluge. The pit was 20 inches deep under the natural hill. Although here is not all the difcovery that might be wifhed, yet the following truths may be deduced from this digging: by the black greafy loam being

got

got down under the two layers of yellow and cinereous clay, it appears that a pit was dug in the area of the Kiſt-vaen; that ſomething which either was originally, or has ſince turned black, was placed in the bottom of the pit.

The length of the area deſcribed by the ſupporters of Lanyon Quoit is ſeven feet; but it does not ſtand Eaſt and Weſt, as at Môlfra, but North and South, as that Monument of Haraldus mentioned by Wormius, p. 22. There is no Kiſt-vaen, that is, no area marked out by Side Stones, under this Quoit, which is more than 47 feet in girt, nineteen feet long; its thickneſs in the middle, on the Eaſtern edge, is ſixteen inches, at each end not ſo much, but at the Weſtern edge this Quoit is two feet thick. The two chief ſupporters (A and B [q]) do not ſtand at right angles with the front line, as in other Cromlêhs, but obliquely, being forced from their original poſition, as I imagine, by the weight of this Quoit, which is alſo ſo high that a man can ſit on horſeback under it. Under this Quoit I cauſed to be ſunk a pit of four feet and half deep, and found it all black earth that had been moved, and ſhould have ſunk ſtill deeper, but that the Gentleman in whoſe ground it is, told me, that a few years before, the whole cavity had been opened (on account of ſome dream) to the full depth of ſix feet, and then the faſt [r] appeared, and they dug no deeper; that the cavity was in the ſhape of a grave, and had been rifled more than once, but that nothing was found more than ordinary. This Cromlêh ſtands on a low bank of earth, not two feet higher than the adjacent ſoil, about 20 feet wide, and 70 long, running North and South: at the South end has many rough Stones, ſome pitched on end, in no order; yet not the natural furniture of the ſurface, but deſignedly put there; though, by the remains, it is difficult to ſay what their original poſition was. Weſt N. W. there is a high ſtone about 80 yards diſtance. By the black earth thrown up in digging here, nothing is to be abſolutely concluded, there having happened ſo many diſturbances. By the pit being in the ſhape of a grave, and ſix feet deep, it is not improbable that a human body was interred here, and by the length of the bank, and the many diſorderly ſtones at the South end, this ſhould ſeem to have been a burial place for more than one perſon.

On the top of a high hill about half a mile to the Eaſt of Senar Church-town ſtands a very large handſome Cromlêh; the area incloſed by the ſupporters is exactly of the ſame dimenſions as that at Molfra, viz. ſix feet eight inches by four feet, and points the ſame way, running Eaſt and Weſt (Plate XXI. Fig. III. and IV.) The

Lanyon Cromlêh.

Senar Cromlêh.

q See Pl. XXI. Fig. I. and II.
r The Ground which has not been moved is called in Cornwall the Faſt.

Kiſt-

Kift-vaen (Fig. IV. N°. 5.) is neatly formed, and fenced every way, and the fupporter marked N°. 2. in the Plan, is eight feet ten inches high, from the furface of the earth in the Kift-vaen, to the under face of the Quoit. The fide Stones of the Kift-vaen running on beyond the end Stone (N°. 2.) form a little Cell (N°. 3.) to the Eaft, by means of two ftones terminating them at right angles. The great depth of this Kift-vaen, which is about eight feet, at a medium under the plane of the Quoit, is remarkable; there is no ftone in it, and the Stone-barrow fourteen yards diameter was heaped round about it, and almoft reached the edge of the Quoit, but care taken that no ftone fhould get into the Repofitory. This Quoit was brought from a Karn about a furlong off, which ftands a little higher than the fpot on which this Cromlêh is erected; and near this Karn is another Cromlêh, not fo large as that here defcribed, in other refpects not materially different.

Chûn Cromlêh. About 500 yards to the South Weft of Ch'ûn Caftle, in the parifh of Morvah (Cornwall) ftands a Cromlêh, the Covering-ftone of which, being twelve feet and a half long, and eleven wide, is fupported by three ftones pitched on edge, which with a fourth form a pretty regular Kift-vaen.

The top of the Quoit is very convex; it has a low Barrow, or Heap of Stones, round it as at Môlfra, Plate XXIV. Fig. X.

Carwynen Cromlêh. In a tenement called Carwynen, in the parifh of Camborn (Cornwall), ftands a very entire, and plain Cromlêh; it is called the Giant's Quoit: the three fupporters inclofe an area five feet three inches wide, and feven feet long: the Covering-ftone is twelve feet three inches long, by eleven feet fix wide, and no more than one foot thick at a medium, Plate XXIV. Fig. IX.

Though, in fearching thefe Monuments, I was not fortunate enough to find any Bones, or Urns, yet thofe who have lately been employed in the fame enquiries have had better fuccefs, and, as their difcoveries plainly confirmed the ufe affigned to thefe Monuments in the foregoing papers, I beg leave to tranfcribe a paragraph or two from Mr. Wright's Louthiana.

" I chanced one day to meet with a fallen one (viz. Cromlêh)
" upon Lord Limerick's ground about two miles from this, by the
" fide of a River, exactly between the two Druids groves before
" defcribed: two of the fupporters were broke down with the fall
" of the incumbent load, the other ftanding. This (viz. the cavity
" between the Stones) his Lordfhip immediately ordered to be
" carefully dug into, and in the middle, about two feet deep,
" covered, and inclofed within broad flat Stones, great part of the
" Skeleton of a human figure was found, all crowded together
" within a bed of black greafy earth, as if originally inclofed within

" an

" an Urn. Mixed with the bones, were found some pieces of clay
" about the thickness of my little finger quite solid, and round, as if
" part of a Rod broke to pieces, which, if really so, probably may
" have been the *insignia* of the high office of the person here
" interred. Since my return from Ireland, I received this farther
" account from a friend upon the place. "" Yesterday I went with
""" Lord and Lady Limerick to the great Cromleche at Bullrichan
""" (near Dundalk, Louth) where you found the human bones :
""" the country people had sunk above a yard deeper in quest, I
""" believe, of treasure, and we found them still at work ; they had
""" got under, and were trying to pull up the large square Stone
""" which stood on one edge ; they came to another flat Stone, under
""" which they found many large Bones, but we do not yet know
""" whether they be human[s] : they raised also many regular Stones
""" of a considerable length, and the whole place seems to have been
""" built up regularly, as well to strengthen the three great props, as
""" to contain a proper Repository for Bones, or whatever was to be
""" laid there[t].""

C H A P. X.

Of Urn-Burial ; and some remarkable Urns found in Cornwall.

THAT the Britans burnt their dead, and then interred the
Remains in Urns, cannot but appear from the number of
Barrows and Urns found every where, and Ashes mixed with the
Earth of the Barrows ; that the Gauls did the same, we are well
assured[u] ; let us therefore proceed to take notice of the most
remarkable circumstances relating to Urn-Burial in general, and
Urns found in Cornwall in particular.

The Urns designed to contain Human Bones were sometimes of
Gold[w], Silver, Brass, Marble, or Glass, but are generally of Pottery
Ware ; among the *barbarous* nations, of rude fashion, coarse clay,
and rather smoked than burnt ; but those of the Romans easily
distinguished by their elegant shape, materials, and ornaments.
Among the politer Ancients, when the Urns were carried to be
intombed in the Barrows prepared for them, they were sometimes
decked with flowers, ribbons, or other gay attire ; but the stern

---

[s] If they were not human, why buried with that care and labour, and the same sort of covering over them as where human bones were found by Mr. Wright ?
[t] Wright's Louthiana, Book III. p. 12.

[u] See Montfaucon, tom. V. p. 194.
[w] Patroclus's was of Gold, Ii. xxiii. ver. 253. Corineus's of Brass, Æn. vi. ver. 226. A Glass one, see Kenn. Par. Ant. p. 12.

O o o   Lycurgus

Lycurgus confined the Spartan Urns to the more fober drefs of Olive and Myrtle[x].   If the Barrow could not be immediately erected, the Urn, with the Bones in it, was fecurely laid by, covered with tranfparent linen or filk, till the Sepulchre was ready.

The place where we generally find them is the middle of the Barrow, but there are fome which are found near the outward edge[y]; the reafon of which different pofition feems to be this: the Urn, which the Barrow was purpofely erected to inclofe, lies in the middle of it; but, if any perfon had a defire afterwards to be intombed in the fame Barrow, a fkirt of it only was opened near the extremity of the circumference, or a little trench dug that reached not to the middle, and there the fecond Urn was made partaker of the fame Monument, but in fuch a manner that no violence might be offered to the Remains firft interred.

It was common among the Ancients, where there had been great intimacy and friendfhip, for the Survivers to defire to be interred near the perfon that died firft.

— — — — — Και νυν ποθω
Του σου θανουσα μη 'πολειπεσθαι Ταφου.

— — — — — And now my laft requeft,
Grant me, ye Gods! with thee intomb'd to reft.

Says Electra, lamenting over the fuppofed Urn of her brother Oreftes[z].

Sometimes not only one, but two (or more) Urns were depofited round the central Sepulchre, and fometimes a whole family chofe to be buried in the fame Barrow, and then we find many Urns placed clofe one to another; the moft remarkable Monument of which kind that I have yet heard of in Cornwall, was that opened by Ralph Williams, yeoman, in the tenement of Chikarn (St. Juft, Penwith) where (A. D. 1733.) in removing a Barrow was difcovered a great number of Urns; and as they approached nearer the center, a ftone fquare cheft, or cell, paved underfoot[a], in which was alfo found an Urn, finely carved, and full of human Bones. As well as could be remembered (at the time when I had this relation from him, which was four years after the difcovery), there were about 50 Urns which furrounded the central and principal one, which alone, becaufe it appeared to be neatly carved, he carried home to his

---

x Brown, p. 37. Hydriotaphia.
y Dr. Williams, Philof. Tranf. 1740. of the St. Auftle Barrows, Cornwall.
z Sophocles, Electra, Act. iv. Scene i.

a As I have been informed (fince the Death of R. W.) by his Daughter, who faw the Urn, which her Father brought from the Field into his Houfe.

Houfe,

Houfe, the reſt (all which had ſome remains of Bones and Earth in them) were thrown away and broke, as of no conſequence.

Farther particulars have been diſcovered, by ſearching three Barrows lying in a line nearly S E, and N W, in the tenement of Boſavern Rôs, in the ſame pariſh, about a mile diſtant from the foregoing. In the eaſternmoſt Barrow, about the year 1748, there was found the carcaſe of a man laid at full length; a long ſtone on each ſide, and one at each end on their edge, the cavity like a grave, the bones large ſized, no ſtone covering the body; the middle Barrow was opened afterwards, and bones in it, but not regularly placed; the Barrow ſeemed to have been ſearched before. On the 29th of May 1754, I got the weſternmoſt Barrow to be opened; there was a kind of cave or door-vault which led into this Barrow with a tall ſtone on each ſide and a covering ſtone acroſs, but fallen inſide; the floor was ridded clear to the rabman [b], on which there was about three inches depth of ſea-ſhore gravel, the biggeſt of the gravel about three quarters of an inch diameter, then ſome bones ſcattered on the gravel, then an Urn of the contents of three quarts (beer meaſure) full of bones, and a little partition beyond it fixed on the gravel; about a foot farther, ſome walling, which being removed, a little Urn of about a pint full of bones appeared in a cell of ſtone work (the cell about two feet eight inches long, and one foot ſix inches wide, with a covering flat ſtone), placed upon the rabman (no beach, or gravel under the Urn); when this little Urn was taken out, at about a foot diſtance appeared the ſide of a tall great Urn one foot three inches high, the bottom eight inches wide, of the contents of three gallons and half, full of bones to within three inches of the top; ſome bones eight inches long, and with the bones ſeveral pieces of burnt ſticks. About four inches diſtant from the great Urn ſtood two other Urns of about two quarts each, which, with the little one abovementioned, ſtood triangularly round the great one which ſtood in the middle. Matted grafs had forced its roots in among the bones. The Northern and Eaſtern parts of this Barrow conſiſted of natural rock and ground, not moved ſince the flood; the reſt was artificial, with a ring of rocks forming the outer edge: that part which incloſed the Urns was faƈtitious, had a wall doubled (i. e. faced within and without) of large ſtones for the ſpace of fifteen yards, about five feet high; the whole Barrow about fifteen feet high, thirty-ſix feet diameter. Several ſhreds of Urns were found before they came to the bottom; Urns, by which it may be juſtly conjeƈtured that there were more ſtages of Urns than one, ſome likely placed above the lowermoſt, when the undermoſt area was filled.

[b] A Corniſh word, ſignifying a ſtratum of ſtone not quite ſolid, but next in conſiſtence to the ſolid rock.

That

How guard-ed and placed.

That thefe Urns might be guarded from the weight above and round them, they are generally found in fuch little Cells of Stone-work; but fometimes they are inclofed with greater neatnefs and fecurity, efpecially when depofited by the more cultivated nations[b].

Urns are generally found ftanding erect on their bottom, and covered with a flat Stone, or Tile; but fometimes they are themfelves a covering to what they contain, being found placed with their mouths downwards, as were the Urns at Trelowarren (Chap. viii. p. 214.) and a remarkable one (Pl. XVIII. Fig. V. p. 208.) found in Gwythian Parifh, Cornwall, where, in May 1741, about half a mile to the South Weft of the Church-town, the fea having wafhed away a piece of the Cliff, difcovered about three feet under the common furface of the Land a fmall cavity about 20 inches wide, and as much high, faced and covered with Stone; the bottom was of one flat Stone, and upon it was placed an Urn with its mouth downwards, full of human bones, of which the *vertebræ* were very diftinct. Round about the Urn was found a quantity of fmall Duft or Earth, which had all the appearances of *human* Afhes, and filled the lower part of the cavity about four inches high from the bottom. This Monument will fhew, that the Ancients took different ways to fecure the remains of their friends. Here, the bones being placed in the Urn, and fecured therein with clay, earth, or fat[c]; the Urn was inverted, and placed in its cell with its mouth downwards, a method of proceeding which they thought might prevent the moifture of the ground above from fuddenly rotting the bones, and, in cafe of any accidental failing of the coverture, might refift the weight with greater ftrength, than if the Urn was placed on its bottom; but there was here another caution obferved, which is, that when the Urn was thus placed on its mouth, the afhes of the human body feem to have been collected and placed round the Urn, filling the cavity to fuch an height, that the mouth of the Urn ftood about four inches deep in thefe afhes. This body was well burnt, which is a mark of dignity in the deceafed, as we fhall fee by and by; and, as the bones of fome bodies which have not undergone fo much fire are found round the Urn in fome Sepulchres, fo here the afhes were laid round the Urn which inclofes the bones, for the fame reafon, namely, becaufe both the bones and afhes belonged to the fame perfon.

SECT. II. Bones how difpofed.

In thefe Urns the friends or relations of the deceafed thought it their duty to lay up the collected bones as free from filth and

b Such a one was the Urn found at Kerris, and the Urn found in Golhadnek Barrow, of both which there will be a particular account given hereafter, Lib. IV. cap. ii.
c See Hom. Iliad, paffim.

pollution

pollution as the nature of mortality will permit. The larger bones of the body were burnt again and again, till they were reduced to the smallest shreds, and till all the bones, both great and small, could easily be crowded into so narrow a compass as that of an Urn: this was the general way of proceeding, for human bones are seldom found scattered, in the Barrows: when the bones were thus reduced, they were laid in the Urn, and the ashes which the Urn would not contain were spread about it, and covered by the Barrow. But we find that the fires were not always so well attended, nor continued long enough to consume the greater bones, for in a Cell in the middle of the Barrow at Trelowarren (mentioned, p. 214. before), we find bones of all kinds and sizes, which seems to have been the reason that they were placed in a Cell, as being too large for an Urn; but adjoining to this Cell we find two Urns (one on either side) full of bones, which being certainly laid there after the Cell was made, in the middle, shew that the bones of them were better burnt, and reduced small enough to be inclosed in Urns.

Sometimes they inclosed what was well burnt in an Urn, and what was not so, in a Cell round the Urn; for in the year 1716, a farmer of the village of Mên, near the Land's End, Cornwall, having removed (in order to cleave it for building) a flat Stone seven feet long, and six wide, discovered a cavity underneath it, at each end of which was a Stone two feet long, and on each side a Stone four feet long. In the middle of this square cavity, was an Urn full of black Earth, and round the Urn very large human bones, not placed in their natual Order, but irregularly mixed. In these instances it appears that the ancient Cornish-Britans either wanted time, or were not always so religiously punctual in consuming the larger bones of the body as others of the Ancients thought themselves obliged to be.

Whilst we are treating of the disposal of the bones, it may not be amiss to observe, that in some Sepulchres are found bones much larger than those of the human body, which are therefore by the vulgar thought to be the Remains of Giants; but they are more likely the bones of horses, which, as well as arms, were thrown into the funeral pile, and thought as absolutely necessary (for those who were Soldiers) in the next life, as they had been in this; and so honourable was it accounted to have the horse interred with them, that (as Keysler observes, p. 169.) none but the *Equites* had a right to this honour, the Foot-Soldiers were not allowed it.

The bones being laid in the Urn were covered sometimes with earth pressed in close, whence it comes to pass, that in some Urns we find the roots of grass; in other Urns, the bones seem to have been cemented by strong mortar, to prevent any impure mixture, and keep out the air and moisture; but the most ancient and

P p p
effectual

effectual way was to cover the bones with the fat of beasts, the oil of which, the bones, hot from the embers strongly imbibed, and became thereby much better guarded against successive drought and moisture, than by any other method then known. Achilles therefore, out of his tenderness for the remains of his friend, orders his attendants to cover the bones of Patroclus with a double coat of fat [d].

SECT. III. Various Contents of Urns.

Besides human bones, it was usual among the politer nations to inclose in the same, Urn, lamps, lacrymatories such (small vials as were filled with purchased tears) and other utensils of mourning, which had attended the funeral. Sometimes the furniture of the toilet accompanied the Matron to her grave; combs, inlaid boxes, nippers, some favourite jewel or bracelet [e], were thrown into the Urn, as of no farther use when the lady was to dress no more; others chose to throw in a little deity, in Agate, Amber [f], or Crystal. In some Urns are found Coins, kindly inserted for the satisfaction of posterity, being of the age nearly in which the body was interred. In others are found vessels of oil, aromatick liquors, or vinous spirits [g]. The Helmet, Sword, or Spear, were usually thrown into the funeral pile of the Soldier. It was a very ancient custom for a Soldier to be thus accompanied, whether the body was interred without burning, or burnt, and the ashes placed in an Urn. If the body was not burnt, the sword is found entire, and was usually placed under the head, a custom recorded by the Prophet Ezekiel, chap. xxiii. 27. "They shall not lye with the mighty that are "fallen of the uncircumcised, who are gone down to hell with "their weapons of war, and have laid their swords under their "heads." But if the body was burnt, we cannot expect to find the Sword, Helmet, or Javelin, entire; they were either melted, or crushed, and broke in the fallings of the funeral fabrick, undermined by the fire, or purposely broke before thrown into the funeral pile; the reason of the latter was either that some piece, after it had gone through the same fire with its master, might be inserted in the Urn, or that the pieces might be strewed round about it in the Barrow, to give notice to all who should dig, that the remains of a soldier lay there, and were not to be violated; these seem to me to be the reasons that we find only small pieces of these weapons in Sepulchres where the bodies had been burnt. Several bits of brass were found among the bones in the Mên Sepulchre [h], and the person who found the Urn, shewed

---

[d] Il. XXIII. ver. 243.

[e] A beautiful bracelet of gold, about three inches broad, but excessively thin, was lately found in a brown earthen Urn under a Stone Barrow in Ireland. By the size it should be a lady's bracelet, for it will hardly come on a man's hand: the gold was of the finest sort.

Letter from the Rev. Dr. Mills, to the Right Rev. Dr. Lyttelton, Bishop of Carlisle.

[f] Brown, of the Farnese Urn. Hydriot. p. 23.

[g] Brown, ibid. 33. Kenn. Paroch. Antiquit. p. 23.

[h] Page preced.

me

me the point of a sword of brass found at the same time and place: some thin bits of brass I had also out of the Trelowarren Barrow, which I take to have been parts of a sword.

In some Urns have been discovered thin plates of brass, remainders, either of swords, or some neat implements belonging to a deceased Artist, and these, which is very remarkable, are half-melted; which last circumstance seeming to be an evidence, that such Urns contained the remains of some person of quality[i]; we will examine a little into, especially as we had reason, in the foregoing page, 238, to take notice of the different degrees of burning which our Cornish remains of mortality have undergone.

There is no doubt, but that the funeral piles of persons of rank and character were better contrived, the materials greater in quantity, and of the most combustible kind, the fires better tended, and consequently more vigorous, than when persons of lower circumstances, or impious lives, were to be burnt. It is no wonder, then, that the bones of the vulgar, of detested Tyrants, such as Tiberius (whose body was to be but half burnt[k]), or of those who died by pestilence, whose piles were erected in haste, and but little care taken whether their burnings were properly compleated or not; it is no wonder, I say, that their Relicks should be but half burnt, and exposed to putrefaction, the most dreaded of all catastrophes; a fate, of which Nero was more afraid than of death itself[l]. But it was otherwise, where the quality of the deceased, and the love of their surviving friends, called jointly for all the ritual Obsequies to be most minutely performed; here all imaginable care was taken by the friends, that the Fire should be kept in full force, till the flesh was quite consumed, and the bones blanched fair[m], and few, fit to take their place in the appointed Urn. The fierceness of such strong Fires melted the Sword Blades, Spear-Heads, Spurs, and other Ensigns of War or Art; and therefore, where these evidences of such intense Fires are found, it may be fairly concluded, that the intombed remains were those of some considerable person. On the other hand, if a great quantity of Bones remained unconsumed, it may be inferred, either that the person interred was of common ordinary circumstance, or, what may have been more probably the case, that the funeral was performed in haste, during the alarms of war, when they had not sufficient time to superintend the burning; for by the bits of Brass, and piece of a Sword, found at Trelowarren, and also at Mên, there must have been Soldiers buried in both Sepulchres, though so many Bones remained entire.

SECT. IV.

Some Bones more burnt than others, and why.

[i] As Sir T. Brown very judiciously supposes, ibid. p. 37. To whom assents Keysler, p. 517.
[k] " Et in amphitheatro semiustulandum."
Sueton. in Tiber. not. Casaubon.
[l] Sueton. Brown, p. 38.
[m] Λευκεα οστεα. Hom.

However,

However, in all countries, where burning of the dead obtained, it was accounted very unhappy for the deceased, not to have every part of his body (except a few Bones, which, becaufe they were fo much burnt, were generally called afhes) conveyed into the etherial Regions by the flame; and it is this general fentiment of the Ancients, to wit, that the body fhould be thoroughly confumed by the funeral Fires, which is conveyed to us by Homer in the following beautiful Epifode.

The body of Patroclus being placed on the funeral pile, and the fires lighted[n], Achilles, intent upon the laft offices of friendfhip, perceived, with concern, the Fire to burn faint and languid; immediately he fufpends his addreffes to the *Manes* of his departed friend, retired a little from the pile; from an exulting Hero became a fubmiffive fupplicant; offered up his Prayers, and poured his libaticns to Boreas and Zephyr; having then vowed proper Sacrifices, he befeeches them to come without delay, to roufe and fan the Fire, that it might confume the dead body of his dear Patroclus: in fine, left the prayers of a mortal fhould prove ineffectual in an affair fo effential to the honour and happinefs of the deceafed, Iris, from the Gods, feeing the diftrefs of Achilles, haftes away to folicit the Winds; they come, and blow the fire, and the body is burnt.

C H A P. XI.

Of the Rock-Bafons.

IN Cornwall there are Monuments of a very fingular kind, which have hitherto efcaped the notice of Travellers; and, though elfewhere in Britain, doubtlefs, as well as here, in like fituations, have never been remarked upon (as far as I can learn) by any Writer; they are Hollows, or artificial Bafons, funk into the furface of the Rocks.

SECT. I.

In feveral Parts of Cornwall, &c.

The firft which I met with of this kind were thofe cut into a Karn, or large groupe of Rocks, in the tenement of Bofworlas, in the Parifh of St. Juft, Penwith, in the year 1737. Three of them may be feen, Plate XX. Fig. VII. *d, e, f,* p. 219.

There are many more Hollows of the fame kind on this Karn; and in the tops of feveral feparate large Rocks, which are fcattered in the Valley beneath, there are more, and fome have one fingle Bafon on their higheft part.

---

[a] Iliad XXIII. ver. 192, &c.

In

In the higher part of a Tenement called Karn-Lêhou, in the parifh of Tiwidnek, are many large flat Rocks. Many Bafons there are cut into the tops of thefe Rocks, which have no communication with one another (as before at Bofworlas) nor any chanel to difcharge whatever it was that they were defigned to contain: thefe are of feveral fizes, but of no particular Figure.

On the top of a large Quoit here (Pl. XI. Fig. III. p. 173.) is one Bafon, which has feveral little ones round it, communicating what moifture they collect to this principal Refervoir, which is triangular, about three feet feven long, is funk on the extremity of the Rock, having only a brim left round the edge to confine the contents, and oblige it to difcharge them through one lip, lying to the South.

Round Arthur's Bed, on a rocky Tor in the parifh of North-hill, there are many, which the country people call Arthur's Troughs, in which he ufed to feed his Dogs. Near by alfo, is Arthur's Hall; and whatever is great, and the ufe and Author unknown, is in Cornwall, for the moft part, attributed to king Arthur; the dimenfions, fhape, and diftance of thefe Rock-bafons, may be feen Plate XX. Fig. VI. a, b, c, p. 219.

I have an account of fome of the fame kind found in Wales, where I doubt not but, upon proper enquiry, more will appear; and I think we muft underftand a paffage of Leland's Itin. (Vol. V. p. 59.) to relate to works of the fame kind º. I have obferved fo many of thefe Bafons in other Karns here in Cornwall, that I may venture to fay, there was hardly any confiderable groupe of Rocks in thefe Weftern parts which had not more or lefs of them; but no where perhaps are they to be found in greater number, or variety of fhape, fize, and fituation, than on the top of Karn-brê-hill in the Parifh of Illogan.

Since no author has mentioned, and attempted to explain, thefe Monuments; let us fee what light and affiftance their fhape and ftructure, expofition, number, and place, confidered together with the cuftoms and known Rites of Antiquity may afford us in this untroden path.

Of thefe Bafons there are two forts; fome have lips or chanels SECT. II. to them, others have none: and therefore as thofe lips are manifeftly Properties the works of defign, not of accident, thofe that have fo material a obfervable. difference muft needs have been intended for a different ufe; and

---

º "On the farther ripe of Elwy, a three or "four miles above St. Afaphes, is a ftony rock "caullid Kereg the tylluaine, i. e. the Rok with "hole Stones, &c. There is in the Paroch "of Llanfannan in the fide of a ftony hille a "place wher ther be 24 hole ftones or places in "a roundel for men to fitte in, but fum leffe and

"fum bigger, cutte oute of the mayne Rok by "manne's hand, and there children and young "men cumming to feek their catelle ufe to fitte "and play. Sum call it the rounde table. Kiddes "ufe ther communely to play and fkip from fete "to fete."

Two Sorts, some have Lips, some none. yet both these sorts seem to be the works of the same people, for there is a multitude of these Basons which have no lips or outlets, as well as those which have, to be seen in Karn-brê-hill, and elsewhere, on contiguous rocks.

Where found. These Basons are generally found on the highest hills, spread on the tops of the most conspicuous Karns, very numerous in some places; and where we find few of them, and perhaps none at all, it is owing, in all likelihood, to the many rocks which have been clove and carried off for building P.

On some single rocks, as we descend the hill at Bosworlas, we find a few single Basons, but they are small.

They are never on the sides of Rocks (unless displaced by violence) but always on the top, their openings horizontally facing the Heavens.

They are often found on the tops of Logan, or Rocking Stones; wherefore they, as well as those, should seem to have some affinity to, and to be in their several kinds subservient (on different occasions) to the same superstition.

Some are found sunk into thin flat stones, but they are oftner worked into more substantial and massive Rocks.

Their Shape. The shape of these Basons is not uniform; some are quite irregular, some oval, and some are exactly circular: one I measured at Karn-brê is a very regular Ellipsis, and is already taken notice of, p. 119.

Their openings, do not converge in the top as a jar or hogshead, but rather spread and widen, as if to expose the hollow as much as possible to the skies.

Some have little falls into a larger Bason, which receives their tribute, and detains it, having no Outlet.

Other large ones intermixed with little ones have passages from one to another, and by successive falls uniting, transmit what they receive into one common Bason, which has a drain to it, that serves itself and all the Basons above it.

The floor of these Basons (if I may so call it) is generally sunk to a horizontal level, or at least shelving, so as that whatever falls into it, may run off into the next Bason, then into a third, and so on; this I have observed, more especially in the works of this kind which have most art, and are most finished; but in others which favour less of workmanship, the bottom is not so exactly leveled.

The Lips do not all point in the same direction, some tending to the South, some to the West, others to the North, and others again to the intermediate points of the Compass, by which it seems as if

P As is apparently the case at St. Michael's Mount, where, and at Boscawen Rôs, and elsewhere, some fragments of them, but not many in proportion to the still remaining Karns, are found.

the

the Makers had been determined in this particular, not by any mystical veneration for one region of the Heavens more than another, but by the shape and inclination of the Rock, and for the most easy, and convenient Outlet.

The size of them is as different as their shape, they are formed *Size.* from six feet to a few inches diameter : in Bosworlas the vulgar call the largest, which is circular, and six feet diameter, the Giant's Chair (Plate XX. Fig. VII. *f.* p. 219.); and in the great Rock at Bossavarn just by, there is another of the same kind, which goes by the same name; the common people here attributing all those works which have something vast in them, as they do in other countries, either to Giants in general, or to their own national heroes in particular.

Many uses may suggest themselves to the imaginations of the *SECT. III.* curious from the description of these new, and hitherto scarce *For what* mentioned Monuments; in order therefore to obviate some *Use* prepossessions, and prevent the mind from resting so far on groundless suppositions as may make it more difficult to embrace the truth, I shall first consider (by comparing and recurring to the foregoing properties of these Basons)

What, in all probability, *cannot* have been the design of them, *they are* and then submit to the reader a conjecture or two relating to the *not fit.* intended use of them, drawn from their shape, structure, number, and situation, and conformable to some universal principles and tenets of the ancients.

Some may perhaps imagine that they were designed to prepare and dry salt in for human use [p] (because, on the sea shore in Cornwall, we find little hollows in the rocks spread with the whitest sea salt); but these Basons are found in great plenty many miles distant from the sea [q].

Diodorus Sic. (Lib. III. cap. i.) informs us, that the men employed about the gold mines in Ethiopia take a piece of the Rock (viz. of the Ore broke out of the Mine with its *pabulum)* of such a certain quantity, and pound it in a stone mortar till it be as small as vetch : and the ancient Tinners had certainly the same custom of pounding in Stone-troughs their Tin-ore, before stamping-mills were found out : it may therefore be imagined, that these Basons were intended for so many troughs to pound their Tin-ore in, especially if no such Monument occurs in other parts of this island; but there are many objections to this use of these Basons. First, these Basons

[p] Rev. Francis Wise, late B. D. Radcliff Librarian, Oxford.

[q] The reader might justly think me too minute and circumstantial in the description of these, seemingly so trifling, peculiarities ; but he is desired to consider, that, in case the Author should be mistaken in the use and application which he has made of these several properties, yet, being so particularly described, they may one time or other lead some one (more happy in his conjectures) to discover the true and real use of these Monuments.

are

are on the tops of hills, whereas the ancient workings for Tin were altogether in valleys by way of ftream-work, or wafhing (by the help of adjacent rivers) the Tin brought down from the hills by the deluge, and violent rains. Thefe bafons are generally far from water, which every one knows is of abfolute neceffity to promote the pulverizing any ftubborn, obdurate ftones, as our Tin-ores generally are. In the next place, it may be obferved, that if thefe Bafons had been much ufed in pounding Tin, they would be all concave at the bottom; but what is more convincing ftill, is, that many of the Bafons are found on fuch high, and almoft inacceffible Rocks, that people muft have been very fimple indeed to have made them there, when they had fo weighty a fubftance to manufacture by their means, and muft have lifted up and let down both the Tin and themfelves with fuch inconveniency.

It may with more reafon be thought that thefe Monuments were intended fome way or other for the purpofes of Religion, rather than of Mechanicks; and according to our propofed method we will firft fhew what religious Ufe they feem not to have been intended for. Firft, they are evidently too fhallow and irregular, and too clofe together, to have received Obelifks, or Stone Deities erected in them.

Neither do they feem to have been defigned for Altars, either of Sacrifice, of Libation, or Holy Fires.

The Ancients indeed facrificed on Rocks[r]; but the Rocks of which we are difcourfing, have their furfaces fcooped out in fuch a manner as no Altar extant, or on record, ever fhewed the like: Altars of 20 feet high, and more (for fo high are fome of our Rock-Bafons) without any eafier accefs than climbing from Rock to Rock, are no where to be found. If they were defigned for a whole Burnt-Sacrifice, how fhould the Victim, or the neceffary fuel, without great labour be drawn up to the top of the Altar? How fhould the Fire be properly attended, nourifhed, and continued in fo high a fituation as that of the Mountainous Rock at Karn-brê[s]? To what purpofe the fmall Bafons round that capacious Urn, which ftood on the top of this Rock, of three feet diameter, and one foot deep, beforementioned, p. 117.

See Pl. XX.
Fig. VIII.

If they were for Altars, why fuch communications, as if to drain away through one common paffage, fomething not commonly found in the Element of Fire? Why fuch thin and artful partitions, as we fee in fome of them, betwixt the feveral Bafons? If thefe were all for Altars, and offerings made by Fire, why fhould they not be all of one ftructure? Why have fome Lips, and others never defigned

[r] As Balaam, Numb. xxiii. 9.—Gideon, Judg. vi. 20.—Manoah, ibid. xiii. 19.
[s] Map, Pl. VII. Fig. F. p. 117.

to

to have any? Or, indeed, for the ufes of Fire, what needed the furface of Rocks to be any more than meerly planed and leveled? Why fuch hollows at the bottom of the Fire-place, as muft have been retentive of water, and therefore in a great meafure weaken, if not wholly defeat, all Ignition? This would evidently be the cafe with thofe Bafons which had no Lips; and thofe which had, would pafs away the holy afhes upon every fhower. In the laft place, it may be obferved, that fome of thefe Bafons are funk into thin flat Stones, fome not ten inches thick [t]; which Stones could not long refift the fretting power of Fire, but muft crack and fly to pieces with intenfe heat. If it be furmifed, that thefe hollows may be the natural confequences, and were all fretted into the Stones by the power of the Fire, let it be confidered, that they would then be without all regular form, none would be Circles, nor Ellipfes, there would be no perpendicular fides, nor thin partitions, nor plainly defigned communications, nor fmall and artfully-placed mouths, all which, it muft be confeffed, are the properties of thefe Monuments. Thefe are the difficulties, which, till they are anfwered and removed, muft prevent our thinking, that the Rock-Bafons were defigned for Altars of Sacrifice, or Holy Fires.

Thefe Veffels before us muft have been of more general ufe than either, for Libations of Blood, or, I may add, of Wine, Honey, or Oil; becaufe, for fuch ufes, they are too many, and too large.

Having now fhewn what ufes the feveral properties of thefe Bafons will not permit us to afcribe unto them, it will undoubtedly feem ftill more difficult to affign the real ufe, intent, and defign of them; the candid Reader will therefore, pardon the following conjectures, although he may not approve of them.

Among all the Pagan Superftitions there was hardly any one more anciently and more univerfally adopted, than that of Luftration and Purifications by water. The Ancients thought that the Soul itfelf was defiled by the impurity of the body [u], and therefore much care was taken of this outward purity : by frequent fprinklings and wafhings, they had perfuaded themfelves that all Sins were to be canceled, but without them no pardon was to be obtained; and befides the Rites neceffary for every private individual frailty, they never approached the Sacrifice, nor entered their place of Worfhip, nor lay down to their feftival entertainments, nor withdrew from battle, nor initiated their *Noviciates*, nor inaugurated their Princes, or Prieft, nor proceeded to their magick enquiries, nor, in fhort, engaged in any part of their endlefs Superftition, without either total or partial Wafhings.

SECT. IV. Purifications by Water, frequent and very ancient.

---

[t] As I obferved in a flat Stone at St. Michael's Mount.   [u] Porphyr. de Abftin. Lib. II.—Spencer, de L. Hebr. p. 1177.

R r r   There

There is no queſtion but theſe Rites of waſhing are as ancient as the inſtitution of the Moſaical Law ; but many of the learned carry their original much higher, and, conſidering how every Gentile nation, though divided into the extremities of the globe, had the ſame cuſtoms of purifying, think them as ancient as the Flood of Noah, and diſperſed with mankind from Babel[w]. This Rite, indeed, by its great ſimplicity, ſhews its early date; and though the purifications of Waſhing were, in many caſes, enjoined the Jews by God ; yet does it not follow, but that they might be much ancienter than the Law, and might probably be inſerted in the Levitical Ordinances, that the Jews (impatient always of reſtraint) might not think themſelves arbitrarily debarred of any innocent Rites, which the reſt of the world ſo univerſally embraced, and derived from ſo high a fountain as the reſtoration of mankind, after the Deluge.

Jewiſh Rites.

Not borrowed from the Gentiles. The Jews uſed not only Ablutions, but Libations alſo in the moſt early ages, after their Migration from Egypt. It is ſuppoſed by ſome[x], that as the Jews were not preſcribed the uſe of theſe Libations, and yet uſed them, they muſt have borrowed them from the Heathens, but the conſequence is not clear : and though Water-libation is no where ordained in the Levitical Law, yet this I take to be one proof of its Antiquity, and not of its being derived from the Gentiles ; for the Jews might practiſe it as one of thoſe Rites, which, being founded on the general ſenſe of mankind, needed not to be republiſhed, and it is recorded as a piece of worſhip performed under the eye, and therefore, it may be preſumed, not without the approbation, of that ſtrict Governour, Samuel; " The " Children of Iſrael gathered together unto Mizpeh[y], and drew " water, and poured it out before the Lord;" which, if not cuſtomary, it is not likely that Samuel would have ſuffered ; at a time too, when the people were to humble themſelves for too criminal a commerce already carried on with the Gentile Worſhip ; neither is it probable, that David (who was a man after God's own heart, more eſpecially on account of his avoiding every part of Idolatry and Superſtition) would have performed this ſame Rite of Water-libation[z], if it were no better authorized to him than from the practice of the Heathens. The Jews practiſing, therefore, this Rite without the Ordainment of God, is a ſtrong proof of its Antiquity, and its being derived (not from the Gentiles to the Jews, but) from the univerſal ſenſe of mankind.

---

[w] It was the general opinion of the Ancients, that the Earth was purified by the Waters of the Flood (Spenc. ib. 713.) " Primum inter Sacra " locum Ὑδροσπονδοις tribuit Porphyrius de Abſt." Lib. II. Sect. xx. Spencer (ib. 1099.) thinks theſe Rites as old as the Age immediately following the Flood.—" Hanc Ablutionem arbitror

" fuiſſe inter Inſtituta vetera orta poſt magnum " Diluvium in memoria aquâ purgati Mundi." Grot. ad Matt. iii. 6.

[x] Spencer, ibid. 1098.
[y] 1 Sam. vii. 6.
[z] 2 Sam. xiii. 16.

It

It muft however be acknowledged, that the Heathens are no The Gentile Rites. where found without Ablutions and Libations; the Egyptians, Ethiopians, Syrians, Perfians, Arabians, and the more Eaftern Idolaters, the Greeks and Romans in the Weft, Chriftians as well as Heathens, nations, however diftant, and in Genius, Climate, Religion and Manners, however different, all confpired to ufe thefe fame Rites; which is fufficient Teftimony, that they muft have been the Cuftoms of Mankind before the difperfion, and paffed Not borrowed from the Jews. into all Countries with the firft Planters of Nations; not borrowed from the fmall and little-noted people of the Jews, no more than from the Gentiles derived to the Jews; but having defcended to all from their firft common fathers, who practifed it when mankind was united in one common mafs, it could not but fpread itfelf with every fettlement, into every religious fect, though in fome more But as old as the Difperfion. ftrictly and fcrupuloufly performed, in others with lefs delicacy, devotion, and frequency.

Thefe Rites of Luftration, though at firft in all probability Differenty practifed. uniformly practifed, yet after the difperfion foon varied as to manner, fubftance, time, and ufe (as the cuftoms, dialects, laws, and religion took a different turn) fome preferring one time of the day, or month, fome another; fome enjoining frequent and feveral ftated daily Ablutions, others contenting themfelves with fewer; fome taught that the hands, others the head, others that the feet only needed to be wafhed, and they fhould be clean; whilft not a few infifted that nothing lefs than a total and frequent immerfion of the whole body was abfolutely neceffary. The juft, and every where prevailing notion, that facred things required fome preparatory, and more than ordinary purity, continued this Rite among all nations; but with fome it continued in its native fimplicity, whilft it grew by degrees, among the civilized and more cultivated nations, into a kind of Science. The water was confecrated with various ceremonies, nay in fome places worfhiped as a deity. The very temples were ritually befprinkled, not only when firft confecrated, but as often as the gates were opened, with this holy water; and the people, whenever they came to worfhip. The priefts were to wafh in one only kind of the pureft water, their veftments dewed, their victims, altar, and facrifical inftruments wafhed; they had their magical water to divine by, to foretell events, to try doubtful and criminal cafes; the pureft was poured out in libations to the Gods; their *noviciates* were initiated with no other than one particular fort of water; at ftated times; in certain appointed places; before particular perfons in proper habits; fo that it became one of the myfteries of the Pagan Religion, an emblematical fcience, of which the moft minute circumftance was not to be

omitted;

omitted; a science which no one but their Priests underftood, which, without the moft powerful folicitations, and timely probation, no one was admitted unto, nor fo much as to be prefent when another was admitted.

SECT. V.
Varieties of Holy-Water.

To obtain this external purity, various were the opinions concerning the Water, which fort was moft effectual and conducive. All nations agreed, that the pureft Water was to be ufed at thefe Solemnities; but which was the pureft Water, they did not agree. Some preferred the fountain, and river Water, and were particularly attached to fome noted fprings and rivers of their own Country.

Fountain and River Water.

The Romans thought it not lawful to ufe any other Water in their Sacrifices to Vefta, than what was taken from the fountain of Juturna where rifes the River Numicus: with this they fprinkled their Victims, and carried it in the *Futile* (a Veffel broad at the mouth, and fo narrow at the bottom, that it would not ftand on the ground), that it might not touch the common Earth, left it fhould be defiled: this Water was alfo brought to Rome for all Sacrifices[a].

The Athenians, for Sacrifices and Bridal Contracts, thought it unlawful to ufe any other than that of the Fountain Callirhoë[b]. The Syrians were fond of their own Rivers. " Are not Abana " and Pharpar, Rivers of Damafcus, better than all the Waters of " Ifrael[c]?" The Egyptian Priefts purified themfelves with no other Water than that which the Ibis had approved the purity of, by drinking of it.

Sea-Water.

At Heliopolis in Syria, not far from Lebanon, they never purified their Temple but with Water fetched from the fea, though at a great diftance[d]. In Sea-water the Greeks wafhed their hands before prayer[e].

The Jews had the fame cuftom[f]; but as lake and river Water is very impure, becaufe of the mud and filth which comes from Plants, Fifh, the Wind, and Animals; fo neither is the Sea without the like impurities, and, when not agitated by the winds or tides, has its unwholfome fmells, is foul, and corrupts the air with noxious fteams.

The pureft of all water is that which comes from the Heavens, in Snow, Rain, or Dew; and of this the Ancients were not ignorant[g], and therefore no Water feems to bid more juftly for the

---

[a] Servius Æn. 12.
[b] See Alex. ab Alexandro, Vol. I. p. 1096. The nicety of the Greeks, Perfians, Arabs, Egyptians, and Babylonians, in this particular.
[c] 2 Kings, v. 12.
[d] Spencer, ibid. ut fupra 775, 6, 790.
[e] ————————Τηλεμαχ⊙ δε,
Κειρας νιψαμεν⊙ πολιης αλ⊙·, ευχετ Αθη·η.
Strom. Lib. IV. Clem. Alex. p. 628.

[f] " Moris eft apud omnes Judæos manus aqua " marina lavare quoties Deum precibus vene- " rantur." Spencer, 789. ibid.
[g] Των ὑδατων κυφοταια τα ομβρια, και γλυκυταια, και λαμπροταια, και λεπλοταια. Hippocrat. Lib. de Aëre & aquis.

preference

preference in thofe facred Rites than this. For what is likely to be fo precious in the opinion of the Superftitious, fo fit to be offered unto the Gods, or to purify Man, as that Water which comes from the Heavens?

The people who performed Sacrifice to the infernal Deities were ⟨Dew.⟩ fprinkled with Dew[h]: " With pure Dew befprinkled, go ye to the " Temple," fays Euripides[i]; and from the frequent mention made of Dew, before they proceeded to the folemn Rites of Worfhip, we may infer it to have been the opinion of the ancients, that as the Dews of Heaven did wafh and purify the trees, herbs, and flowers, upon which they fell, fo did the fprinkling of any Sacred Water clean and purify the perfon who was to attend the Altar of the Gods; and indeed this *fprinkling* (of whatever kind the water might be) was borrowed (as it feems to me) firft from Nature; for the effect of Dews, and Rain, upon Plants, Leaves and Stones, was no fooner obferved in the days of primitive fimplicity, than thefe Celeftial Liquors (as if defigned originally to cleanfe all things they fell upon) became the fymbols of Purity, and probably the firft inftruments (becaufe the moft obvious) of ritual Purification. Among all the Ancients therefore, without exception, the cuftom of fprinkling ftill continued; although, with fome, Waters from Fountain, Well, Sea, or River, took place of the natural Dew, and Shower, from whence the phrafe, and the practice, were both at firft derived.

In the hot Eaftern Countries, it was no uncommon Rite to offer ⟨Rain.⟩ Libations, with thanks to the Gods for the former and the latter Rain: the Jews offered Water only[k], at the Feaft of Tabernacles; by this Rite, teftifying, that having gathered in their Fruits, they owed the Rain and plenty to God[l]. Some, fays Pliny[m], prefer the Rain-water preferved in Cifterns; and there is little queftion to be made, but that they ufed in Religious Rites that Water which they thought moft fweet, pure, and wholefome. Hofpinianus and Pontanus think that the Ancients ufed only that Water which was perfectly pure, without any mixture, to make their *Luftral*[n]. The Jews too had their Cifterns for preferving Rain-water, and every family feems to have been thus provided[o]. In thefe Cifterns they let the Rain depofit the *Fæces* which it could not but contract (collected as it was generally from the tops of houfes, or into pits), and then purified themfelves therewith[p].

---

[h] "Aqua abluebantur Sacrificantes Diis fuperis, " Rore afpergebantur Sacrificantes Inferis." Servius, Æn. ii. ver. 720.

[i] Euripides in Io.

[k] Spencer, ibid. 1101.

[l] " Pluviam & frugifera tempora Deo." ibid.

[m] Lib. XXXI. cap. iii.

[n] Danet, R. & G. Ant.

[o] It is one argument of Rabfhakeh to the befieged Jews, " That, if they would furrender to " his Mafter, every Man fhould drink the Wa- " ters of his Ciftern." 2 Kings xviii. 31.

[p] John ii, 6.

The

The Greeks too had their facred Rain; for Creon[q], coming upon the Stage, and feeing Oedipus (after he had deprived himfelf of his fight, upon his appearing to be the murderer of his Father, and the defiler of his Mother), begs the people prefent, if they had any reverence for the Sun, to whofe beams they owed all the plenty of the Earth, to take away Oedipus, whom neither the Earth could fupport without horrour, nor the facred Rain purify, nor the light of the Sun endure[r].

The Egyptians, probably[s], were the firft who improved the fimple ufe of purifying by Rain, Dew, and Snow, into an eftablifhed fyftem of fecret and ftrict ordinances, and indifpenfable prohibitions; for there being very little Fountain or Well-water in Egypt, and the Waters of the Nile generally foul, and of a muddy colour, and Rain falling alfo but feldom (and therefore the more precious); this laft became referved for, and dedicated to, facred ufes, as moft fuitable to the fervice of the Gods, and to all thofe myftical Purifications in which the Priefts of this Country were fo learned, and nice among themfelves, and fo unwilling to admit all others unto.

Snow-water.

Pliny[t] tells us, that as Rain was preferred to running ftreams, fo was Snow to Rain, and Ice (as reduced by the Chemiftry of nature to the utmoft lightnefs and purity) to Snow. The Egyptians, though idolizing at times the water of their Nile, were alfo, probably, the Authors (among their various Rites of Libation and Ablution) of dedicating Snow-water to facred ufes; for in all fuch fuperficial Purities they much exceeded others, were more ftrict and pompous, and being bound (from the moft ancient times) by a greater variety of Laws, they were to other nations, as it were, the Standard and Oracles of Purity, infomuch that the Romans went even as far as Egypt fometimes for Water, in order more ritually to befprinkle the Temple of Ifis at Rome.

> —— —— —— —— *Si candida jufferit Io,*
> *Ibit ad Ægypti finem, calidaque petitas*
> *A Meroë portabit aquas, ut fpargat in ædem*
> *Ifidis.* Juven. Sat. vi. ver. 525.

Polyphemus, in his addreffes to Galatea, reckons Snow-water as one of the moft inviting and precious treafures of his Cave[u].

---

[q] Sophocl. Oed. Tyr. Act v. Scen. iii.
[r] Ομβρ⊙· Ἱερ⊙·, well tranflated by Dacier, " La " Pluye Celefte, dont nous fommes arrofez aux " pieds des Autels."
[s] Herod. Lib. II. cap. xxxvii. " Λεβλαι δις της " ἡμερας ἑκαϛης, ψυχρῳ, και δις ἑκαϛης νυκ]⊙·; et ritum " illum recenfet inter alias puritatis externæ " ceremonias a primis ufque Superftitionis

" Ægyptiæ cunabulis ufitatas." Spencer, 1174. See Spencer, of the extraordinary nicety of the Egyptian Priefts, ib. p. 786.
[t] Ibid. ut fupra.
[u] Εϛι ψυχρον ὑδωρ, το μοι ἁ πολυδενδρε⊙· Αἰτνα Λευκας εκ χιον⊙·, ποῖον αμβροσιον, προῖη]ι.
Theocr. Idyll. xi. ver. 47.

That

That the Egyptians ufed Snow-water to purify themfelves before eating, is evident from Petronius [w].   Now the cuftom of fuch a nation as Egypt, fo celebrated in Theology, Magick, Science, and the deepeft Myfteries, could not but influence the cuftoms of the neighbouring nations; and in the ancient Poem of Job (who is generally fuppofed to have lived at no great diftance from Egypt) the fuperiour purity of rain and fnow-water is plainly taught.

In the 9th chap. ver. 30. Job acknowledges that all his endeavours after purity would prove ineffectual, and incapable of making him pure in the fight of God.   " If I wafh myfelf with " Snow-Water, and make myfelf never fo clean, and if I purify " my hands in a Ciftern" (viz. of Rain-water), " yet fhalt thou " plunge me in the Ditch, and mine own Cloaths fhall abhor me." Meaning, evidently, that the Waters of the Heavens (whether from Snow or Rain) did principally conduce to purification, but that, notwithftanding all his ablutions, in the pureft liquid that could be procured, he muft ftill appear, in the fight of God, full of Uncleannefs and Iniquity.

I muft here obferve that, in the latter part of this 30th verfe, our tranflation leaves out a whole cuftom of the Ancients, by deferting the original words, and (which is a manifeft defect) retaining only the general fcope of the author; but Spencer [x] tranflates thefe words as the Hebrew requires [y] : " *Si lavero me* " *in aquis nivis, & mundavero in cifterna volas meas.*"; and thence infers the probability of Job's exercifing himfelf in fuch Purifications. But more explicit ftill is *Caryll. ad loc.* p. 376.   " Others " conceive it (fays he), an allufion to that peculiar Rite in thofe " times when they took Snow-water to wafh with, rather than " Spring, or River-water, becaufe that came from the Heavens, not " from the Earth here below, and was therefore, in their opinion, " more excellent in its nature, becaufe it had a more excellent " original."   Thirdly, " Job (continues this Author), is thought " to fpecify Snow-water, becaufe, in thofe Countries, the Fountain " or River-water was not pure; and therefore they preferred Snow, " and took that Water to wafh and cleanfe with, as the cuftom ftill " is in thofe places where good Water is a rare commodity."

Now, it being manifeft that all nations who were in any degree intent upon cultivating proper diftinctions betwixt the facred and profane, expiating their faults, and reftoring themfelves to a purity becoming the facred myfteries, had fome or all of thefe Rites of Water-luftration, ablution, and libation,

SECT. VI.

That the Druids had thefe Rites of external Purificati-ons.

---

[w] " Tandem ergo difcubuimus, pueris Alex-
" andrinis aquam in manus Nivatam infundenti-
" bus." cap. xxxi.

[x] Ibid. ut fup. p. 779.
[y] See Buxtorf, in voce בור and Pagninus, ib.

It

It may with great probability be advanced, that so strict a sect as that of the Druids could not be ignorant of so universal a custom, nor knowingly forbear to adopt so ancient and specious a Rite for a part of their system: my opinion, therefore, is, that the Druids, as well as other Priesthoods, had the Rites of external purification by washings and sprinklings; for this, they had their Holy Water; that this Holy Water was Rain or Snow, or probably both; and that these Rock-Basons were vessels most ingeniously contrived to procure that Holy Water.

The great resemblance which the Druids bore to the Egyptians and Persians in other parts of their superstition will not let us believe that they could be so singular as to reject one of the principal and the most extended branches of their religion.

There is no reason to think but the Druids were as nice in this particular, and as strict, and valued themselves upon their superiour purity, and were as cautious of these imaginary defilements, as any sect in the world [z]; and it appears, by their gathering the Selago, that they had their Holy Water, and that, before the Priests could proceed to cut this sacred Herb, he was to be cloathed in white, his feet were to be naked, and washed in *pure Water* [a].

Here a Ritual Ablution of the Feet, in order to gather the Selago with greater devotion, is expressly mentioned of the Druids, and may with equal justice be inferred, to have preceded the forms of gathering the much more scarce and reverenced Misletoe: a Sect which prescribed rules so minute and circumstantial in their Ceremonial, named the hand, restrained the eyes (for they were not to look from the *Samolus* upon any consideration), prescribed the colour of the robe, ordained a preparation of fasting, and then commanded the gatherer, with naked and washed feet, to proceed to gather herbs, could scarce avoid being equally mystical and superstitious in their other Rites [b].

The Druids had their Waters of Jealousy as well as the Jews, and near the banks of the Rhine used the waters of that river to purge the suspected [c].

In the admonitions of St. Eloi, in the 8th century, we find him charging the Christians not to follow the several superstitions of the then Pagans and Gauls (who were doubtless of the Druid persuasion), " Qu'on ne fasse point de Lustrations [d];" whence it is

---

[z] " Les Druides etoient fecondes en Mysteres, " & rafinoient sur tout;" says Rel. de Gaul. p. 138. vol. I. very judiciously.'

[a] Plin. Lib. XXIV. cap. xi.

[b] The Celts used Lustrations, and even Baptismal Rites; and by Pope Gregory's Epistle, 122, to Boniface, it appears, that some Priests at that time sacrificed to Jupiter, and eat part of the Victim (which Rites must consequently have been Pagan), and then proceeded to baptise.

[c] " Le Rhin tenoit lieu aux Gaulois des eaux " de Jalousie. Ce fleuve, dit Julien l'Apostat, " vangeoit par son discernement l'injure qu'on " faisoit à la pureté du lit conjugal." La Rel. de Gaul. Vol. I. p. 56. 71.

[d] Rel. de Gaul. ibid. p. 71.

plain,

plain, that the Druids had the Rite of Luſtration; for that this is meant of the Druids is evident by what immediately follows, " Qu'on ne jette aucun charme ſur les herbes," that they ſay no incantations over herbs, i. e. over the Miſletoe, Samolus, and Selago as the Druids uſed to do.

Having reaſon therefore to conclude that the Druids had theſe Rites of waſhing and purification, let us next conſider whether theſe Rock-Baſons were Druid works.

That theſe Baſons are Druid works.

Although theſe Baſons could not be of any conceivable mechanick uſe[e], or ſerve the religious purpoſes of Druidiſm as to Libations, or ſerve as Altars, or as ſtages for their Holy Fires, yet there are great reaſons to believe that they are indeed Druid Monuments.

Theſe Monuments are generally on the tops of Hills, on the Crags, or Karns, in places which have the veſtiges of every kind of Druid Superſtition; which muſt not only ſuggeſt to us that they were Druid, but alſo Religious Monuments; and ſome way or other ſubſervient to the purpoſes of Paganiſm, as taught by the Druids. It may be objected, that the hiſtory of the Druids mentions very little of theſe external Purifications by Water; but it muſt be conſidered that whenever we find any cuſtom general among the moſt ſuperſtitious of the ancients, and diſcover Monuments in places frequented by the Druids, by their fitneſs correſponding with, and by their properties adapted to, and framed as it were for that general ſuperſtitious cuſtom, we have all the reaſon in the world to impute that cuſtom to the Druids, though it be not mentioned in the few ſcattered hiſtorical imperfect remains relating to that ſect.

We have no traces of ſuch works among the Roman or Chriſtian Antiquities; and they are too frequent and numerous to have been the works of ſuch ſojourners as the Danes, always engaged in wars, and either paſſing to, or repaſſing from, their own country; much leſs could they be the works of the Saxons, who were Chriſtians long before they conquered Cornwall: to whom then are thoſe Monuments to be referred but to the ancient Britiſh, and among them to whom ſo properly as to the Druids, who engroſſed all the Science, and whoſe Sect gave birth to all the Monuments (military excepted) of thoſe darkſome ages?

There being then great reaſon to conclude, that theſe Baſons are Druid works; let us take a review of the moſt remarkable properties of theſe Baſons, and from them (conſidered together with

SECT.VII. Of their Uſe in general.

[e] See before, p. 244.

T t t

the

the forementioned general Rites of Water-luftration) proceed to determine their ufe.

There are two forts of thefe Bafons; one fort has Lips, or paffages, through which, what they received run off. The other fort has none, but retain the Liquors which they receive. They are both on the higheft hills, in great numbers, on every Karn which has not been defaced. Both forts are alfo found on the tops of Logan, or Rocking-Stones; and both have their openings, or upper brim, widening towards the Sky.

What is more particularly obfervable in thofe which have Lips, is, that their floors, or bottoms, are horizontal, their Lips generally level with the bottom, fo as that the upper Bafon runs off what it contains into another below it, that into a third, and fo on, till the lowermoft Bafon has a mouth or lip to difcharge what it has received from the others either on the ground, or (which is moft likely) into a veffel or rock prepared underneath.

Examples.   I fhall only produce two Monuments to illuftrate what I have to fay, as to the ufe of thefe Veffels. The Tolmên at Conftantine has been already defcribed among the Rock-deities [f], but muft be alfo taken notice of here, as the moft aftonifhing piece of this kind of Fret-work, which perhaps the world affords. The whole furface A, is befpread entirely with Bafons (as may be feen in the little Plan, Pl. XX. Fig. IX. p. 219.) moft of which fupply and run into two very large ones, in comparifon of the reft, one at the South end *(b b)*, another at the North *(c c)*; but where the convexity of this vaft body of Stone fhelved off from the middle of its top towards the fides, there many little rills, or chanels (1, 2, 3, 4, 5. Pl. XIII. p. 174.) are cut in the brim of the Tolmên, to difcharge what the Bafons, next the edge, did contain; and underneath a great number of Bafons are cut into the natural Karns (ibidem, C, B, F) as if to preferve from wafte the precious Liquor as it fell.

To make this plainer ftill, I fhall here particularly defcribe the large flat Stone on Karn-brê (Pl. XX. Fig. VII. p. 219.) with the Bafons wrought into its furface.

The furface here is cut out into as many Bafons as the natural declivities of the Stone would permit. The parfimonious Artift has made the moft of his fubject: feven Bafons are contrived with fo much fkill as to fall from one level to another, from the higheft bunch of the Rock at *g*, down to *m* (pointing Wefterly), which on the very brim of the Stone has a chanel cut, *o*, by which all that was collected in thofe feven troughs (for they are large, three of them near fix feet long, and two feet deep) uniting, runs off, and is

---

[f] Lib. III. cap. iii. p. 174.

difcharged

difcharged eafily into any veffel placed under: to the left hand of thefe Bafons, the furface of the Rock falls quick, dipping away to the North, fo that here was room for Bafons, yet would not the level fuffer any communication with the Bafon *m*. Two Bafons therefore, *p* and *q*, were contrived, in order to make the moft of this remaining fpace; they are together an area of ten feet (i. e. four feet long by two feet and half wide at a medium); and becaufe the mouth at *o* was too high to ferve their purpofe, they have a chanel of their own at *r*, through which they yield what they were intended to receive.

Now if Fitnefs can decide the ufe (and where Hiftory is deficient, SECT. VIII. it is all reafon that it fhould), we fhall not be long at a lofs: for, Ufe of thofe why all this art and labour? why is all the area of thefe Stones Bafons which have employed, and no part left idle? why are all the openings fpread Lips. toward the Heavens, but to receive in greater plenty fomething which the Heavens were to beftow? and why fhould communications pafs from one to the other (from the higher to the lower), if it were not to convey fome Liquid? why fhould, what centered in the upper, run off from the place where it firft lodged, and the feveral Rills that proceeded from the feveral Bafons unite all at laft in the lower, if what was collected by them all, was not thought precious, and to be preferved with care? why is the fhelving fide of this laft Stone cut into two Bafons, *p* and *q*, although the level would not permit them to unite with the Bafon *m*; but with an evident defign to procure a greater quantity of the fame Liquid, than the other feven Bafons without them would afford?

The Lips do not all point one way; for what reafon? why they are directed to that part of the Stone whence the Liquor collected might be moft conveniently difcharged into, and be treafured up in fome veffel placed below.

They are moftly placed above the reach of Cattle, frequently above the infpection of Man; nay, the Stones which have thefe Bafons on them, do not touch the common ground, but ftand on other Stones. Wherefore? But that the Water might neither be really defiled by the former, nor incur the imaginary impurity, which touching the ground (according to the Druid opinion) gave to every thing that was Holy. Why they are placed above the infpection of Man will foon appear.

Thefe Bafons are found on the tops of hills; they could not more properly, according to the trueft Philofophy (as well as the laws of their Religion) be any where placed, for it is a known truth among Naturalifts, that the pureft Water is that of Rain, and Snow, collected in open Veffels upon the tops of Mountains g; and it is no

g Muffenbroek, p. 865.—Boerhaave's Chem. Engl. p. 312.

wonder

wonder that the Druids fhould be acquainted with this fuperiour
Purity of Rain and Snow-water, if we confider their celebrated
infight into the works of nature[h].

For catching the Rain and Snow, the little Walls, or Partitions
betwixt the Bafons, are as neceffary as the Mountains on the furface
of the Earth, and left purpofely, one would think, in order to catch
and diftill the Rain and Snow; for thefe (I mean the Rains and
Snow) fall not perpendicularly, but are driven in an inclined
direction, and are therefore very artfully intercepted by thefe fcreens,
which at once ftop the rain as it drives, and fhelter it from being
blown out of the Bafons when the Wind is tempeftuous.

Farther it muft be obferved, that fome of thefe Bafons have one
part of their hollow made more circular than the reft, forming a round
recefs, as if it were to receive the head, and the other part the body,
of fome human creature. What I mean is plainly vifible in the
Bofworlas Bafons, King Arthur's bed (Pl. XX. Fig. VII. p. 219.
D, and Fig. VI. *b)* as well as in feveral others which I could here
produce[i]. In the fmaller kind, I conjecture, they ufed to lay
Children, in the larger, Men, for particular diforders, that, by the
healing virtue attributed to the God who inhabited the Rock[k],
they might be cured of their ailment; or, by being proftrated on
fo holy a place, might be fitted for, and confecrated to, the fervice
of the Rock-deity, for which they were intended.

The number of thefe Bafons is very great in the Weft of
Cornwall; therefore the Druids muft have been very numerous here,
and the ufes they applied this their Holy Water unto muft have
been many, and frequent: we need only recollect the various ufes
to which the Ancients applied their Holy-Water (as recited Sect. 4.);
and then we fhall the lefs wonder that the Druids fhould be fo
ftudious to preferve, by fuch a number of Stone-veffels, fo great a
quantity of Rain and Snow-water.

SECT. IX.

Ufe of thofe
which have
no Lips

But there are fome Bafons which have no lip or chanel; and
therefore, as they could not contribute any of their water to the
common ftore, they muft have been appropriated to another ufe:
many large troughs of this kind have little Bafons round them,
which fupply the great one with what they gather; the maker
evidently proceeding upon this maxim, that the larger the concave
area was which was expofed to the Heavens, the greater would be
the collection of water.

---

[h] See cap. xi. Lib. II. p. 92.
[i] As the large Bafon at Hanterdavaz, in the parifh of Mabe, four feet two inches and a half wide, and feven feet nine inches and a half long, and the large Bafons on the top of the Tolmen in Conftantine, mentioned in the preceding page.
[k] See p. 169.

Now

Now thefe being found in the fame places with the others above-mentioned, which have outlets or mouths to them, muft have been fome way or other (as has been obferved before) fubfervient to the fame fyftem of fuperftition, though in a different method.

Thefe Bafons are fometimes found near 20 feet high from the common furface; and therefore, being fo far withdrawn from vulgar eyes, fo elevated from the ground (which was fuppofed, as I faid before, to defile all) they had likely a proportionably greater degree of reverence, and their waters accounted more holy, and more efficacious.

From thefe Bafons perhaps, on folemn occafions, the officiating Druid, ftanding on an eminence, fanctified the congregation with a more than ordinarily precious luftration, before he expounded to them, or prayed for them, or gave forth his decifions. This water he drank, or purified his hands in, before it touched any other veffel, and was confequently accounted more facred than the other Holy-water. To thefe more private Bafons, during the time of Libation, the Prieft might have recourfe, and be at liberty to judge by the quantity, colour, motion, and other appearances in the water, of future events, of dubious cafes, without danger of contra-diction from the people below[1]. This Water might ferve to mix their Mifletoe withall, as a general antidote ; for doubtlefs thofe who would not let it touch the ground, would not mix this their Divinity (the Mifletoe), with common water. Oak leaves (without which the Druid Rites did fcarce ever proceed) ritually gathered, and infufed, might make fome very medicinal or incantatorial potion. Laftly, Libations of water were never to be made to their Gods, but when they confifted of this pureft of all water, as what was immediately come from the Heavens, and partly therefore thither to be returned, before it touched any other water, or any other veffels whatfoever, placed on the ground.

As Logan Stones were fome of the *piæ fraudes* of the Druids[m], the Bafons found on them might be ufed to promote the juggle : by the motion of the Stone the Water might be fo agitated, as to delude the enquirer by a pretended Miracle ; might make the criminal confefs ; fatisfy the credulous ; bring forth the gold of the Rich ; and make the injured rich, as well as poor, acquiefce in what the Druid thought proper.

---

[1] The vulgar Cornifh have a great deal of this folly ftill remaining ; and there is fcarce a parifh-well, which is not frequented at fome particular times for information, whether they fhall be fortunate or unfortunate; whether, and how, they fhall recover loft goods, and the like ; and from feveral trials they make upon the well-water, they go away fully fatisfied for a while ; thofe who are too curious being always too credulous.

[m] See before, Book III. chap. iv. p. 179, &c.

There

There are some little single Basons cut into a few Stones in Bosworlas bottom, not higher from the ground than what the Cattle might reach to.

Were these the Stone-cisterns in which the Druids deposited their *Samolus*, for in some such Cisterns, Pliny [n] says, they used to bruise this herb, and make such an infusion as would keep off diseases from their cattle? or, were these small Basons to receive Libations of particular families, and, by the Sun soon exhaled, might be therefore thought to have been accepted, and well received by the Deity?

This then is the sum of what I have said, relating to these Rock-Basons:

That the Druids had the Rite of Water-Lustrations, is not without some traces in history, and very agreeable to the general tenour and cast of their superstition.

That they made these Basons, in consequence of such Rite, for the purpose of collecting Rain and Snow-Water (as an use most correspondent to the shape, direction, situation, and number of these Monuments), I have endeavoured to support in such a manner as I hope shall not injure truth, if it does not discover it; and it is so pleasant, to pursue truth, when we think we have first got it in sight, that, if I have been too diffusive and long in the pursuit, I hope the reader will excuse it: the consequences before drawn I take to be clear, that the Druids used Water-Purifications, because these Basons could serve no other use: but what parts, whether few or many, or all, of the Heathen ancient Libations, Ablutions, and Expiations the Druids adopted, or what distinction they made betwixt the two sorts of Basons above-mentioned, I do not yet find, so as positively to assert.

CHAP. XII.

Of the Gold Coins found at Karn-Brê in Cornwall, and what Nation they are to be ascribed unto.

IN the month of June 1749, in the middle of the ridge of Karn-brê-hill [o], were found such a number of Coins of pure Gold, as, being sold for weight, brought the finder about 16 pounds, sterling. Near the same quantity was found by another person, near the same spot, a few days after; all which were soon sold and dispersed:

[n] Lib. XXIV. cap. xi.
[o] Marked D. See Plate VII. Map of Karn-brê, p. 117.

some

Gold Coins found at Karn brè in Cornwall AD:1749.

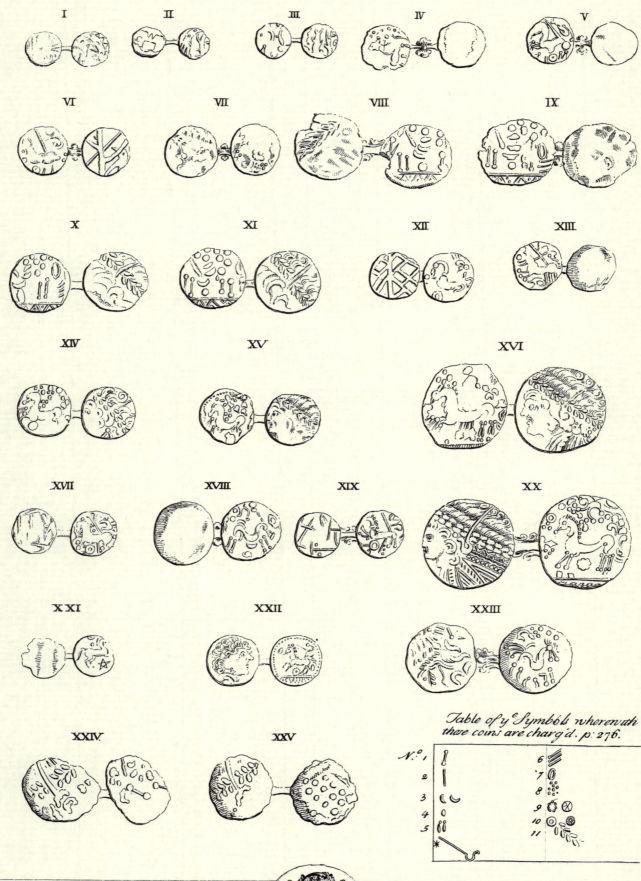

I II III IV V
VI VII VIII IX
X XI XII XIII
XIV XV XVI
XVII XVIII XIX XX
XXI XXII XXIII
XXIV XXV

Table of ye Symbols wherewith
these coins are charg'd. p. 276.

To Francis Basset of Walcot in Oxfordshire Esq

This plate engrav'd at his expence is with great respect inscrib'd by Wm. Borlase.

B

some were much worn and smoothed, not by age, or lying in the Earth, but by use, they having no allay to harden, and secure them from wearing.

Seventeen I here exhibit, in Plate XXIII, of different impressions, size, or weights; several others, found at the same time and place, I have seen, but being of the same sort as these Examples, I think it needless to lay them before the publick. I range the rudest, and those which have figures most unknown, first (as others engaged in treating of Medals have done), being, in all probability, the most ancient; the others follow according as their criterions seem to become more and more perfect, and modern. I mention their weight also, as a material circumstance (though omitted by other Authors) for classing them, and discovering what are, and what are not, the same sort of Coin. The size in the Plate is the real one by measurement of the Coins. The first has some figures upon it which I do not understand; its weight is 22 grains.

SECT. I.
Coins de-
scribed.

No II. has some figures on one side, which I do not so much as guess at; on the other side, it has the Limb, or trunk of a Tree, with little branches springing from it in one part; and what I take also for the body of a Tree, with two round holes, or marks, where the limbs have been lopt off, and roots at the bottom on the other part: it weighs only 23 grains.

No III. has a figure, which, in the Coin attributed to Cassibelan (by Speed, p. 30.), is more plain, and resembles two Dolphins turning their crooked backs to each other; on the other side it has a plain large stump of a Tree, with two branches breaking out on each side; it rises out of the ground, and stands between two smaller trees: it weighs 23 grains.

No IV. is quite defaced on one side, unless it be the outline of a human head; but on the other, it has some parts of a horse, and some little round studs, or button-like embossments, both which marks will be particularly dicoursed of when we come to explain the several uncommon figures which these Coins afford us: it weighs 26 grains.

No V. has one side effaced; the Reverse is a horse, betwixt the legs of which, there is a wheel, and from its back rises the stem of a spear, or javelin: weight 26 grains.

No VI. has the stem of a tree, with its collateral branches very distinct; in the middle, it is crossed slopewise by a bar like the shaft of a spear; the Reverse has the horse, the wheel, and spear, but somewhat differently placed on the gold. The weight is twenty five grains and a half, by which I conclude, that the side which is defaced in No V. was the same as in this Coin, for the Reverses are the same, and their weight corresponds to half a grain,

which

which may be allowed for the greater ufe that has been made of this than of the former.

N° VII. has on one fide fome appearances of a human head (which fide of the Coins we fhall henceforth call the *Head*, as Medallifts generally do, to avoid a multiplicity of words); on the Reverfe the remains are fo mutilated, that it can be only faid, that this Reverfe was much ornamented, but what the ornaments were, is not to be difcovered; it weighs 23 grains.

N° VIII. has the lines of a garland, or diadem on the *Head*. The Reverfe has the *Exergue* at bottom, fupported by jagged lines interfperfed with dots, above which are fome barbarous figures, which are to be explained, and their orderly difpofition here and in fome of the other Coins accounted for in their proper place; it weighs four penny-weights, three grains.

N° IX. has a head much defaced, but vifible, as is alfo the outline of the neck, and the ear; behind the forehead, and nofe, it has three femicircular protuberances; the Reverfe has the fame figure as the Reverfe of N° VIII. but has more little round ftubs on it (the Die, which gave the impreffion, being placed farther back in this than in the former), and difcovers therefore a circular figure, N° VII. with three pointed javelins, N° VI. underneath it, which the other impreffion has not; but, by the run of the Die, the former has one of the figures which is not in this. It weighs four penny-weights three grains, which weight, and the Reverfe charged with like figures (though differently placed) fhews that thefe two Coins were ftruck at one time, by the fame Die, and are of the fame value.

See the Table of the Symbols in Pl. XXIII.

N° X. has a laureated diadem, crofs which, at right angles, is a fillet, or rather clafp, and a faint appearance of a hook at the end of it, the reft defaced. The reverfe has a very diftinct *Exergue* at bottom; the fame figures partly as N° VIII, IX. but the Die was placed ftill farther back on the gold, therefore not altogether the fame, the javelins, or fpears (or whatever thofe pointed ftakes fignify), being in this Coin cut off by a defcending line, intimating that but part only of thofe inftruments were to be exhibited. It weighs four penny-weights two grains, by which it is probable, that it is the fame fort of Coin with the two foregoing, allowing one grain out of fifty for the wear.

N° XI. has the laureated diadem and clafp, above which the hair turns off in bold curls; the Reverfe has the fame charge as the three foregoing, but better placed, and it fhould be a Coin of the fame fort, but that it weighs four penny-weights and feven grains, fo that it muft have been much lefs ufed than the others, if of the fame time and value.

N° XII.

N° XII. has on the *Head* several parallel lines fashioned into squares, looking like the plan of a town of which the streets cross nearly at right angles, and the whole cut by one straight and wider street than the rest. On the Reverse are the remains of a horse with a collar or garland round his neck, and behind, something like a charioteer driving forward; underneath the horse is a wheel, and a few studs scattered near the extremities of the Coin; one penny-weight, three grains.

N° XIII. just shews the faint profile of a human face; the Reverse a horse, a spear hanging forwards towards the horse's neck, some appearance of a charioteer above the horse: it weighs only 23 grains.

N° XIV. has a laureated diadem round the temples, above which the hair turns back in large curls: the diadem has the clasp, or ribbon, which has a hook at the bottom of it, and on the shoulder is a *fibula* or button which tucked up the loose garment. The Reverse has a horse with a wheel below it, and many small and large studs above it; it weighed 25 grains.

N° XV. exhibits a distinct human face in profile; the head is laureated, clasped, and cirrated as the others, which plainly shews, that where there is only a simple laureated diadem now to be seen, as in N° X. XI. XIV. there the human face also was, though now worn out. The Reverse has a horse, with a wheel below it, and crescents, studs, and balls above it; weight 26 grains.

N° XVI. is the best preserved Coin, as well as largest and most distinct, which I have seen of the gold Coins found in Cornwall. The Profile is well proportioned, and neither destitute of spirit nor expression: and it is somewhat surprizing that an artist, who could design the human face so well, should draw the horse so very indifferently on the other side. This head has two rows of curls above the laureated diadem, and the folds of the garment rise up round the neck close to the ear. The reverse, a horse, a wheel, balls and crescents, as in the rest; it weighs four penny-weights, fourteen grains.

N° XVII. is the same weight as N° XIII. and the horse is nearly of the same turn, but here it has a crest of beads or pearl for a mane, as N° XIV. It has also some appearance of reins (as of a bridle) under the jaw; the horse is better turned than in any of them. Behind the wheel, it has something depending like a pole, which reaches the ground; whether a reclining spear, or what their scythes might be fastened to, or any other part of the chariot, is uncertain; but the charioteer is plain.

I perceive no letters on any of them; some are plain, or flat; some a little concave on one side and convex on the other, but not remarkably so.   X x x   Eight

Eight Coins are here fubjoined, from the cabinets of the curious, not yet publifhed, which may tend to illuftrate the foregoing; the five following are copied from the collection of the Rev. Mr. Gifford, of Queen-fquare, Ormond-ftreet, London, and were in his poffeffion before the Gold Coins above defcribed were found at Karn-brê, but in what part of Britain they were found is uncertain.

N° XVIII. on one fide a head emboffed; the Reverfe a very uncouth ancient horfe with its head to the right hand; the other ornaments as in the reft: the ufe we fhall make of this, fhall be to explain the marks of thofe which go before; where, though the fame, they are not fo diftinct, nor treated of by any author I have yet feen; it weighs four penny-weights, one grain; a little concave on the Reverfe.

N° XIX. Bars, ftakes, or fragments of fpears, or javelins croffing irregularly; Reverfe a horfe, with a fpear leaning forth over its neck, the fpear held (as it were) by an arm reaching forward; fplinters or pieces of fpears in other parts of the Coin; a garland round the horfe's neck, the mane made of a line of ftuds; a little convex on the Reverfe; weight 29 grains.

N° XX. a noble Coin; the head is ornamented in the fame manner as N° XVI. but has the clafp over the diadem much plainer; the hook at the bottom of the clafp alfo very plain, and fhews the fhape of this member, in N° X. XI. XIV. XV. where they are defective. It has more curls below the diadem, and the hair of the hinder part of the head feems traced in ribbons ftudded with pearl: it fhews alfo more of the habit than N° XVI. but it has either loft, or never had, the profile, in which particular it falls greatly fhort of the other. The Reverfe is a horfe in the fame ftyle, and furrounded with the fame ornaments, as N° XVI. the weight is four penny-weight, nineteen grains, which is five grains more than the above Coin; and if that difference may be imputed to the different ufe made of thefe Coins[P], they are of one age, were originally of one weight and value, and very likely of one and the fame prince.

N° XXI. the *Head* defaced. The Reverfe a horfe well fhaped, and of neat defign: underneath, is a ftar of five rays, formed very artificially by the interfection of three equal triangles[q]. Both the horfe and this geometrical figure fhew this Coin to be much more modern than any of our Karn-brê Coins; it is a little concave on the Reverfe, and weighs twenty grains and a half.

N° XXII. a well-preferved face, and of elegant workmanfhip. In the Reverfe the horfe is well proportioned, has a charioteer

[P] There are four grains difference betwixt N° IX. and XI. which however are certainly Coins of the fame fort.

[q] I find the fame figure in one of the Britifh Coins publifhed in Dr. Battely's Antiq. Rhutupianæ, p. 93.

behind

behind it, pointing forward the fpear, a wheel of dots under it
fupported by an *Exergue*, and the chariot wheel alfo clofe at the
horfe's heels : the mane of the horfe is a line of beads or pearls.
This Coin is ftill more modern than the reft, and is of the fame
fort in all appearance, as that publifhed in the laft edition of
Camden, Vol. I. Tab. II. N° xxx; though, for want of the weight
being fpecified, it cannot certainly be affirmed ; it weighs 29 grains
and a half.

N° XXIII. is a Coin from the cabinet of Smart Letheullier, Efq;
of Alderfbrook in Effex. In the *Head*, it has the laureated diadem
with fome curled hair above it, over which comes the clafp. Under
the diadem feems the collar-ornament of N° XX. but out of its
place ; underneath are two large crefcents, fo that this fide of the
Coin feems to be a collection of the ornaments of the *Head* inferted
together, and the face never intended. I find this Coin very near
the fame as Dr. Plot's Coin (p. 335. N° XXI. Oxfordfhire) who
takes it to contain two faces of Prafutagus and Boadicea, but I fee
nothing tending that way [r]. In the Reverfe is a horfe of the fame
ftyle as N°. XVII. but the wheel is larger, and the ears and tail of
the horfe more apparent, though of very clumfy defign ; the whole
favouring of great antiquity, and fhewing the low pitch of the art
of coining, at this time, in the nation to which this Coin belongs.
But the greateft curiofity of this Coin, and the reafon indeed for
which it is here introduced, is, that it is neither gold, nor wholly
electrum, or any imitation of gold, but feems to be copper
plated over with a mixed metal of the colour of gold.

N°. XXIV. and XXV. are filver Coins of the fame kind, from
the cabinet of the Rev. Mr. Wife, B. D. late Radcliff Librarian,
Oxford, and inferted here for confirming the defcriptions that go
before, as will be more particularly explained hereafter ; they were
found in the parifh of Swacliffe near Madmarfton Caftle, Oxfordfhire, A. D. 1746.

Having now defcribed the Karn-brê Coins, and produced fome
others which may in fome meafure explain them, let us confider to
what nation thefe Coins are to be afcribed.

As foon as the Gold Coins, above defcribed, were found at Karn- SECT. II.
brê, and got into the hands of the curious, it was by many imagined Not Pheni-
that they were foreign Coins, and fome thought that they were cian Coins.
Phenician. To this opinion the Reverfe, having generally a horfe

[r] The learned Mr. Walker (from whom Dr.
Plot had this Coin, which is alfo publifhed in
Camden, Tab. I. N° 29.) I find (fince my
writing the above) of the fame opinion, viz. that
it does not contain two faces ; " I fee no refem-
" blance (fays he, Camden, p. 116.) of one or
" more faces, I rather imagine it to be fome
" fortification;" which latter fuppofition, I
cannot but obferve, is as far wide of the truth as
Dr. Plot's ; as, by comparing this Coin with the
others here produced, will readily appear.

upon

upon them, gave at firſt ſome countenance, ſome of the Phenician Colonies having choſen that creature for their ſymbol; the place where they were found ſeemed to confirm this ſuſpicion, Cornwall having been (from the firſt appearance of Britain in hiſtory) celebrated for its Tin, which the Phenicians for many ages engroſſed to themſelves by their ſuperiour ſkill in Navigation. The only thing, then, that remains to be done, in order to determine them to be Phenician or not, is to confront the Coins found in Cornwall with thoſe confeſſedly of Phenician original, and conſider whether Coins of the ſame ſtyle have not been found in other parts of this our Iſle where the Phenicians never traded. Now the Phenician Legends will always be known by their letters, when they exceed the Roman Conqueſt of Syria (for after that Conqueſt they uſed either Greek or Roman Characters on their Coins); but there is not one Character to be found in theſe our Corniſh Coins. The ancient Symbol of the Syrophenicians was the Palm-tree, ſometimes the *Murex*; and of their Weſtern Colony, Hercules's Pillars; but there is no ſuch thing on our Coins. The Libyphenicians about Cyrene took, indeed, the horſe for their Symbol; but this horſe had either the whole Palm-tree, or its ſtalk ſtanding by it, alluding at once to their deſcent from the Syrians, and to the horſe for which their own country, Africa, was always ſo famous, and for the taming of which they were indebted to their principal God, Neptune.

But although this part of the Phenician people choſe the horſe for their Coins, yet could not our Coins come from thence, no trade having been carried on with this branch of the Phenicians ſettled ſo near Egypt; our Phenician trade was with thoſe of Cadiz, Carthagena or Carthage, herſelf. Now the Carthaginians had the head and neck of a horſe for their Symbol, alluding to the fable of their being commanded by Juno to build their city where a horſe's head was dug up [s]. Cadiz had her Hercules, his Temple, and his Pillars; but all theſe were modern and well executed, and of them nothing is to be ſeen in the Coins now before us, which are neither well executed, nor have any reference, or relation, to the Palm-tree, *Murex*, Buſt of the Horſe, Hercules, or his Pillars. But, one argument, which will ſtill weigh more than the above, is this, that coining Money came ſo ſurprizingly late into uſe among the Phenicians, that ſuch ſkillful Artiſts as they, and their Colonies were, could not coin ſuch artleſs Money as ours is. Of the Phenician Coins (certainly known to be ſuch) there are none extant more ancient than the time of Alexander the Great [t]; ſo modern are

---

[s] Æn. I. ver. 445.   [t] Wiſe, p. 217.

they,

they, that the Phenicians were many ages celebrated for their ingenuity and skill in other arts, before they ever coined money;
and, besides, having borrowed likely this art from the Grecians [u],
they cannot, with any probability be supposed to coin money of
so rude and mean design, as those of Karn-brê; arts among the
Greeks being arrived, as we all know, to their summit in the time
of Alexander the Great : history forbids us therefore to attribute
such Coins, as what are now under consideration, to so polite and
cultivated a nation as the Phenicians. Lastly, that they were not
brought hither by the trading Phenicians, seems to be plain, because they are found, not only in Cornwall, but in Wales, and
most parts [w] of Britain, where the Phenicians never came, their
trade being confined to Cornwall [x], and their business, Tin.

As these Coins cannot be ascribed to the Phenicians, so neither SECT. III.
to the Greeks nor Romans. That they are not of Roman work- Nor Greek
manship, the first sight of them plainly shews; much less can we nor Roman.
attribute them to the Greeks, whose Medals are still superiour to
the Roman in force and delicacy [y]. They must be either Gaulish,
therefore, or British; for people must be very fanciful indeed
(and extremely unwilling, or rather determined not to let their own
country Rights be impartially weighed) who will look out for a
foreign father of these Coins among the Spaniards, or Germans [z].

That they do in a few particulars resemble the Gaulish Coins,
must be allowed; and for this very good reasons can be given,
without admitting them to be Gaulish, as we shall soon see; in
the mean time, I must observe, that Cesar's seeming to assert, that
the Britans had no money in his time, having made several learned
men think that we had no coined money in Britain before the
Roman Invasion [a], and others being of a different opinion [b], I
will take all the care I can that the veneration which I have for
the latter may neither lead me blindly into their opinion, nor
the respect which I have for some of the others make me suppress
what I think to be right. The reasons must be weighed; the
passage of Cesar set in it's proper light; and the reader must determine.

[u] Ibid. p. 218.
[w] " Several gold Coins of the same kind, and
" also a rough Ruby were found not long ago
" in the Isle of Shepey." Letter from Smart
Letheullier, Esq;
[x] By Cornwall here, as oftentimes elsewhere,
I mean all that anciently went by that name,
viz. the South and Western parts of Devonshire, as well as what is West of the Tamar.
[y] Mr. Jobert, p. 3. translated by Gale.

[z] N. Salmon, Nova Angliæ Lustratio, Lond.
1728, p. 387, who thinks them coins belonging to the ancient Saxons.
[a] See Moreton's Northamptonshire, p. 500.
Walker in Camden, p. cxiv.—See Mr. Wise's
learned account of the Bodleian cabinet.
[b] Camden. Plot's Oxfordshire, Chap. X.
The learned Editor of Camden. Notes, ibid.
p. 774. The late Mr. Ed. Lhuyd. ibid.

Y y y   " Utuntur

Cefar ex-
amined.

" *Utuntur aut æreo, aut taleis ferreis ad certum pondus exami-*
" *natis pro Nummo* [c]." The Britans, fays he, ufe either Brafs
Money, or iron tallies inftead of Money.   This is the plain grammatical fenfe of Cefar's words, and in Plantin's Edit. p. 87. the
words run thus, " *Utuntur autem nummo æreo, aut annulis ferreis,*
" *&c. pro nummo* ;" by which it is plain that, according to
Cefar, the Britans had the knowledge of money, and that, in the
place he is there fpeaking of, they had Brafs Money ; from whence
it may be inferred, that the reafon why they had not Gold and
Silver Money there, as well as Brafs, was not becaufe they were
ignorant of the ufe of it (for the ufe of Gold and Silver Money
is much more obvious and convenient, for exchange or
purchafe, than that of Brafs, but becaufe doubtlefs they had
none of thefe Metals, and therefore could not coin Money of
them, but were obliged to be contented with coining the little Brafs
they had, and an endeavour to remedy the fcarcenefs of Brafs
Coin, by Iron Tallies, or Rings, of a certain weight.   Cefar is evidently here fpeaking of the maritime parts [d], in which they might
well ufe iron inftead of money ; for iron was found, fays he
(p. 92.), " *in maritimis*," on the fea coafts : in the fame place
they had brafs money, but their brafs was imported, " *ære utuntur*
" *importato* [e] ;" which argues, that the maritime coafts had no
brafs out of their own lands.   Neither had they gold or filver in
thefe parts, which is, doubtlefs, the reafon that they did not coin
any ; for of the four Kings, whom Cefar mentions in Kent, viz.
Cingetorix, Carnilius, Taximagulus, and Segonax, we find not one
Coin which has any part of their name upon it ; but this will by
no means infer, but that the other petty kingdoms of the ifland,
where thefe metals were, might have had gold and filver Coins
among them, although the other States, who had no fuch native
treafures, might be without them ; and that the other parts of this
kingdom really had gold and filver Coins, we fhall foon find fome
very ftrong arguments to believe.   It is plain, therefore, that
what Cefar fays, related only to that little part of Britain, in which
he paffed the fhort time he ftayed in this Ifland ; all his whole
account fhews, that he pretended not to give any defcription of
thofe inland parts which were at a diftance from the feat of
action ; let us add to this, that if the Kentifh men had any gold
Coin or Treafure, they certainly took all the care imaginable to

---

[c] Cef. Comm. Lib. V. Janf. Edit. p. 92.
[d] As appears by the whole paffage : " Britan-
" niæ pars interior ab iis incolitur quos natos in
" Infula ipfa memoria proditum dicunt ; Mariti-
" ma pars ab iis, &c." And then he goes on with

the account of the maritime parts, till he comes
down to *nummo* ; then he paffes on to the inland
parts : " Nafcitur ibi plumbum album in medi-
" terraneis regionibus, &c."
[e] Cef. Ibid.

conceal

conceal it from Cefar. But fuppofing that Cefar had pofitively faid that the Britans had no gold Coins, or Money, among them; if, by evidences unknown to him, and fince his time difcovered, it fhould appear extremely probable at leaft (if not as certain as things at this diftance can be made), that they really had fuch Coins; his authority muft give way, he muft be acknowledged to have been mif-informed; and the greater degree of probability muft determine our judgment.

There are feveral Coins preferved and publifhed in Camden, and Speed, which have been thought to bear the names of Britifh Princes; and I may add, that they have other evidences of their belonging to this Ifland. Let us examine them.

The firft Coin produced by Speed (p. 29), is that of COM. the Reverfe infcribed, REX; and is fuppofed by him, with great probability, to be the Coin of Comius, King of the Atrebatii in Britain, companion to Julius Cefar in his invafion. I will only make one remark upon the Reverfe, which is, that the horfe here is of much too great a defign to be among the firft Effays of the Britifh Coining, confequently the Britans muft have had Coins before this, or they could never have made this horfe and rider fo bold and fhapely.

The next Coin in Speed, is that of Caffibelan, which he read CAS; but Moreton in his Northamptonfhire (p. 500) reads it SCOV; the occafion of which difference is this: Moreton began with the S, goes on to the C, miftakes the Wheel (one of the Britifh Symbols) over the horfe's head for an O, and takes the A without its crofs-ftroke (as it was anciently written) for a V; fo that Moreton's objection to Speed's reading proceeds from his own miftakes, and he concludes too haftily, " That the Britans had not " the art of coining till they learned it of the Romans, and that " they did not mark their Coins with the names of Princes till the " time of Cunobelin." Speed's reading then remaining unimpeached, we have here a Coin of Caffibelan, who was General of the whole war againft Julius Cefar, and cannot be fuppofed to have learnt any art from the Romans, having been engaged continually in all the alarms of war from the time they landed to their departure. In the *Head* [f] (or the infcribed fide), the horfe is much better turned than in our Karnbrê Coins, and therefore later; for Arts and Sciences muft have time to ripen in fuch retired and uncultivated places as Britain; their beginnings will be rude, and the progrefs of every art towards perfection will be flow and gradual, efpecially where no Sifter Arts have been practifed, and therefore

---

[f] It muft be remembered, that one fide of a Medal is called the Head, whether it has a face on it, or not; and the other fide is called the Reverfe.

cannot

cannot lend their helping hand to forward and cheriſh that which is newly introduced.   The Reverſe of this Coin confirms the fore-going obſervation, the ornaments of it being a kind of ſcroll-work, intermixed with balls more uniformly diſpoſed, and the whole better digeſted, than our Coins, and therefore later.

Cunobelin's Coin is later ſtill than that of Caſſibelan, and more elegant ; the Horſe has ſhape and ſpirit ; and there is ſomething Roman in the turn of the head [g] ; but there is great difference in the countenance of this King's coins ; ſome are rude and of coarſe deſign, as Nº IV. V. VI. VII. XI. which may therefore be ſafely pronounced to be coined in his firſt years, either before his intimacy with the Romans, or before he could get the Artiſts into the ready and maſterly way of deſigning ; ſo that it may be inferred, from the coins of Cunobelin, that he did not learn, or firſt bring, the art of coining from the Romans, but that, having acquired ſome knowledge that way, he greatly improved this art.   Even this King's Coins have been diſputed, and by ſome inſinuated not to belong to the Britiſh King of this name, though his name be at full length upon four coins in Camd. Tab. I. and upon three of the ſame in Speed, ſo that theſe ſcruples are apparently without foundation.

The gold coin attributed to Caractacus by Camden and Speed, has the *Spica* well placed on the Reverſe ; and in the *Head* the horſe in full ſpeed is as well deſigned as poſſible, and therefore ſeems a cloſe imitation of the Roman manner.

That of Venutius has nothing Britiſh in it, but that the curls of the hair are formed of many contiguous circular rings ſtudded with balls, which is indeed in the Britiſh ſtyle [h].

Though the coins of Cunobelin were at laſt ſo greatly improved by approaching to the Roman manner ; yet theſe improvements ſeem to have been confined to his own dominions, for the coin of Boadicea, Queen of Verolamium (if it be of her), has nothing Roman in it, but the letters BODVA in the *Head* ; the Reverſe is of the ſame ſtyle as thoſe found at Karn-brê [i].

The ſilver coin aſcribed to Arviragus [k], has the Britiſh Wheel formed by eight detached ſtuds [l] ; but the Horſe is too good to be ancient.

The next coin attributed by Speed to Galgacus [m], but by Mr. Walker [n] to Cartiſmandua, has nothing of our coins, but the Wheel formed like a large Ring under the Horſe [o].

---

[g] See Nº 8, 9, 10. in Speed ; and 12, 13. p. 32.
[h] See the mane of the Horſe in Nº XVIII. XVI. XIX. XXI. Venutius in Camden, xiv. Tab. I. in Speed, xv. p. 34.
[i] Camd. Tab. I. Nº 8. Speed Nº 16. p. 34.
[k] Speed Nº 17.—Camd. ib. Nº 25.

[l] As in Nº XX. and XXII.
[m] Page 35. Nº 18.
[n] Camden, p. cxv.
[o] Other Britiſh Coins may be ſeen in Camden and Speed, but theſe may be ſufficient for our purpoſe.

As

As to the word TASCIA found on many of the coins abovementioned, whether it fignifies the Taxation, or Tribute-Money as Mr. Camden believed, or whether fuch coins of Tribute were ever ufed (coins being the enfigns of liberty and power, not of flavery), as other learned men doubt, I do not here enquire, there being no fuch word on our Cornifh coins[o]. Let it fuffice that here are feveral forts of coins produced; we muft next fee whether we have not fufficient grounds to think them Britifh, yet feveral of them not the oldeft of our Britifh coins, and fo trace up the art of coining among the Britans to its firft fimplicity, where we may poffibly find reafons to place many of the coins of Karn-brê.

All thefe Coins from Camden and Speed are found in Britain in feveral places, many in number, and the very fame in no other country[P]. Their Infcriptions, and feveral others which might here be mentioned, have either the firft or more fyllables of the names of Britifh princes, cities, or people, nay Cunobelin the whole name; why then fhould they not be Britifh[q]? If there be honey enough in our own hive, what need have we to fly abroad, and range into the names of neighbouring countries and kings, to find out refemblances in found, which are not near fo exact as what we find at home? Before we deprive our own country of the honour of coining the money found here, one would think it but reafonable that there fhould be produced from foreign countries, famples of the very Coins we find in Britain; and in greater number, as being doubtlefs more in plenty where they were ftruck, than any where elfe; but there is not one inftance of any number of Coins found abroad, which are of the fame kind as what we find here; although with regard to Roman Coins (which were not coined by little particular States, as the Britifh muft have been) there is nothing more common. It is very wonderful that all the Gaulifh Coins (for inftance), correfpondent to ours in metal and workmanfhip, fhould be deftroyed, and not one appear, or be dug up in Gaul; whereas in Britain they are numerous, which makes the learned Mr. Wife, though dubious at other times, conclude very juftly, that no country has a better title to the coining them than Britain[r]. But, I do not know how it comes to pafs, it is the unhappy fafhion of our age to derive every thing curious and valuable, whether the works of art or nature, from foreign countries; as if Providence had

SECT. V.
That thefe Coins are Britifh.

[o] Of the word TASCIA, fee the learned Mr. Pegge's Coins of Cunobelin, p. 21. publifhed in 1766.

[P] See Camden, p. 110.

[q] It is held by fome that there were no Gold Coins coined in England till Edward III. but this is probably a miftake, for " in the Saxon " and firft Norman times, vaft fums were paid " in Gold." The annual tribute to be paid by the Welfh and Cornifh to Athelftan, was 20l. of Gold, and 300l. in Silver, befides other

things. " And in Domefday, particularly, we " find Gold in Ingotts, contradiftinguifhed from " Gold Coin, viz. Libras auri ad penfum.— " Libras ad numerum.—Muft we fuppofe that " all this Coin was of Bizants, or other foreign " Coin?" Letter to the Author, 1753, from the Rev. Dr. Lyttelton, now Bifhop of Carlifle.

[r] " Maximo fanè numero in hac Infula eruun- " tur, adeò ut nulla regio poffeffionis jure magis " eos (viz. nummos) fibi vindicet." p. 228.

Z z z   denied

denied us both the genius and materials of art, and sent us every thing that was precious, comfortable, and convenient, at second hand only, and, as it were, by accident, from the charity of our neighbours.

That the Britans had both Gold and Silver in their own country, is plain from Strabo and Tacitus[s]; and it is observed[t], so lately as Camden's time, that Cornwall produced both these precious metals[u]; and this is confirmed by the reservation of both those metals to the Duke of Cornwall, in his grants to the Tinners. Gold discovered here I have seen[v] found among Tin grains in the Parish of Creed, near Granpont, in the year 1753; and both that, and native Silver, the produce of a Cornish Mine in the Parish of St. Just, I have now in my keeping; and it must be allowed, that people, who have materials ready at hand, will take the first hint of answering their necessities therewith. That the inhabitants of Kent, and the adjoining countries, had brass money, Cesar plainly asserts, as we have seen before; and when one part of the Island had experienced the use of brass money, and knew the art of coining it, the neighbouring States must have had very little communication one with the other, or been very void of understanding, if they did not perceive the equal and superiour convenience of Gold and Silver money, and for their own sakes procure it to be coined wherever they enjoyed the happiness of proper materials. Farther, that the Britans had and used money coined at their own mint is really plain, because the Roman Emperors published a severe edict to suppress all such Coins, and so forbid the use of any money in Britain, but what was stamped with the image of a Cesar[w].

If it be insinuated that the Gauls brought over this money to traffick withal; this is a circumstance which wants to be proved, nay wants probability, for it could not have escaped Cesar, and the Gold Coins must have been in greater plenty on the maritime coasts where he was, than in the inland parts, the merchants from Gaul coming to the sea-ports and coast of Britain, and having nothing to do with the other parts of the island[x]; but Cesar says, they used

[s] " Aurum et argentum fert Britannia." Strabo, Lib. IV.—" Fert Britannia aurum et argen- " tum et alia metalla, pretium Victoriæ." Tacit. vit. Agric. cap. 12.

[t] The Gold Mine of Cunobeline (being " lost) in Essex was discovered again, temp. " Hen. IV. as appears by the King's letters of " Mandamus, bearing date the 11th of May, " An. 2. Rot. 34. directed to Walter Fitz Walter " concerning it, and since that lost again." Plot's Oxf. from Sir John Pettus's Tradit. Regal, cap. ix. and xiii. Gold and Silver Mines also in Devon; see the Calendars of the Rolls in the Tower.—verbo MINERA et MINERATORRS.— And that the Romans did work in our Mines, see Brit. Baconica, p. 10. Pl. ibid. See more of

Gold found in Cornwall, Nat. Hist. of Corn. chap. xix. p. 213.

[u] " Nec stannum vero his solùm reperitur, sed " una etiam aurum & argentum." Camden, in Cornwalliâ.

[v] See Nat. Hist. of Cornwall, chap. xix. p. 213.

[w] " Cautum fuit Edicto Romanorum Impe- " ratorum severo ne quis in Britannia nummis " uteretur nisi signatis imaginibus Cæsarum." Leland, quoted by Sheringham, p. 391.

[x] " Neque enim temere præter mercatores illò " adit quisquam, neque iis, ipsis quidquam " præter oram maritimam atque eas regiones " quæ sunt contra Galliam notum est." Cæs. Lib. IV. p. 76.

æreo

æreo nummo, and takes no notice of any gold coin in thefe parts, which I think may make us reafonably infer, that the Gauls did not bring over any Gold Coins for merchandize; much lefs ftill can it be imagined that, if the Gauls did bring over fuch Coins, we fhould find them infcribed with names fo like at leaft to the names of our princes and cities. If any of the fame Impreffion and Legend with ours, found in many parts of Gaul, can be produced (which at prefent is far from the cafe), then let it be difputed whether the Gauls had thefe Coins from us, or we from them, both fides ftanding upon even ground; but till then, it is a piece of great partiality to foreigners, to deny the origin of thefe Coins to our own country; and I am furprized to find my countrymen fo fluctuating, and indifferent, not to fay carelefs, which way the beam may fall, in a point which concerns fo much the Hiftory of Medals in general, and affects the honour of their own country in particular.

But it will be faid, that there is a near refemblance between the ancient Gallick Coins and thofe found in Britain: it is true, there is a refemblance in a few particulars betwixt fome of the Gaulifh Coins and fome of the Britifh; and this is all that can be alledged, for it is not fo in all, nor in the greateft part. The reader will be convinced of this truth, by cafting his eye over the Gaulifh Coins of Plate LII. Tom. III. p. 88. of Montfaucon's Antiq. where he will find the refemblance they bear to ours of Karn-brê to be as follows:

SECT. VI.

Refem-blance they bear to Gaulifh coins ex-amined and accounted for.

There are in that table forty-feven different coins; upon the Reverfe of eighteen may be difcovered the horfe, a fymbol not peculiar to Gaul and Britain, but adopted by many other countries, as the moft fpirited and ufeful of all the brute creation. In the defigning part, there are thefe refemblances; fome of the horfes have wheels below, or above, or in both places; and beads, pearls, or balls, and rings, or rather pierced *Difcus's*, above and round them; but the horfes are all of another and better fhape than ours, and there are but two, which are N° 4. and N° 16. which are near the ftyle of the Cornifh Coins, and thefe have the manes of the horfes made of a ftring of beads, as in N° 16. and 19. before produced. This is the refemblance of the Reverfe; but when we come to the other fide, that is, to the *Head-part* (lately called by fome the *Obverfe*), they are entirely different, fome helmeted, fome infcribed, not one with a diadem about the hair, nor clafp, nor collar ornament; therefore, that there is fome refemblance in the charge of the Reverfe is true, but when the coins are brought to the teft, and the particulars in which they agree feparately examined, there are fo few that have any refemblance in the Reverfe, and even thefe few have their *Head* fo entirely different, that there is not the

least

leaſt grounds to ſuſpect from this ſmall reſemblance that our Coins were coined in Gaul. If the Gauls indeed had one peculiar manner or ſtyle in their Coins, which they invariably ſtuck to, as was the way of the Greeks and Romans, then the criterions would be deciſive and indiſputable, and we ſhould know Coins to be Gauliſh, whether inſcribed or not, as eaſily as we do the Greek and Roman; but this cannot be pretended; nothing is more vague than their ſtyle, if it deſerves that name; their Coins are as different from one another, as they are from thoſe of other nations, and here I cannot but obſerve, that many of the Coins found in Gaul may with much more reaſon be imputed to foreign nations: than ours found in Britain; for the Gauls being on the Continent, and continually almoſt at war with the Barbarians round them, and war not to be carried on without money, where the uſe of money was known; it is not at all unlikely that the Coins of the many German and Spaniſh nations lying round Gaul ſhould be more frequently brought in, dropt, and diſperſed there, than in an iſland, not ſubject to ſuch invaſions.

But ſuppoſing that there was a greater reſemblance betwixt the Coins found in Britain, and thoſe found in Gaul; it was not to be wondered at, nor would it prove the Coins found here to be Gauliſh. The Gauls and Britains were both uncultivated nations, and being of one Origin, one Language, one Religion, and Climate, divided only by a narrow branch of the ſea; there were frequent inter-courſes (eſpecially betwixt the inhabitants of the oppoſite ſea-coaſts); inſomuch, that their manners[y], cuſtoms, and buildings, were alike. Why then ſhould not their Coins have ſome reſemblance? but this reſemblance will not prove the Coins to belong to either nation ſeparately and excluſive of the other; for " the Coins of the " Anglo-ſaxons are not unlike thoſe of the firſt race of the Kings " of the Franks, who ſettled in Gaul near the time that the Saxons " invaded Britain[z]." The Saxons continued their ancient ſtyle; the Franks, doubtleſs, did the like, and the reſemblance continues. Are the Coins therefore the ſame? did not the Saxons as well as the Franks coin for themſelves?

Farther, it is not improbable, but the art of coining might be tranſmitted to the Britans through the hands of the Gauls, which might partly contribute to the reſemblance abovementioned; and we may go one ſtep farther yet, and with great probability con-jecture, that, though the Gauls were nearer to the ſeats of arts, and therefore had this art of coining before the Britans; yet, that they

---

[y] " Neque multum à Gallica differunt conſue-   " conſimilia." Ibid. p. 92.
" tudine" (viz. Cantii incolæ) Cæſ. Lib. V.   [z] Walker in Camd. p. cxiv.
p. 93. " creberrimaque ædificia fere Gallicis

could

could not have had coining among them long, before the mutual
resort of the Gauls into Britain, and the Britans into Gaul, on
account of traffick, aid, alliance, and religion, muft have communicated it to this Ifland, where there being Gold, Silver, and
Brafs, ready prepared, there was nothing wanting, but the hints to
improve and make ufe of what nature had fent. It is alfo to be
remembered, that fome Princes, as Divitiacus and Comius (and
others, probably, whofe names are not recorded) were Kings of part
of Britain, and part of Gaul, at the fame time.

All thefe circumftances confidered, can it be wondered at, that
the Britifh and Gaulifh Coins fhould be fomewhat alike, and
equally rude and barbarous in the beginning; but about the time of
Julius Cefar more improved, and the reprefentations of men,
animals, fruits, and the fymbols of War and Religion, more
naturally, or rather more artfully, performed?

The Coins of Countries then may refemble one another (as we
know the Greek and Roman do, and thofe of other neighbouring,
emulous nations) and yet be coined in different countries; and as
there can be very good reafons given why our Coins fhould refemble
thofe of Gaul, there is no reafon from this refemblance to conclude,
that our Coins (I mean thofe found here) were coined in Gaul, any
more than that the Roman were coined in Greece, or the Grecian
at Rome. In fhort, let it not furprize the Reader to find, that the
ancient Britans are here afferted to have had the art of coining; for
by N° XXII. it appears, that they had the art of counterfeiting
Coins too; and the very Coin which is here counterfeited by being
plated over, is found in Oxfordfhire in Gold, and publifhed by
Dr. Plot[a], which is another difcovery that may ferve to ftrengthen
what the learned Camden juftly fuppofes, viz. that the ancient
Britans had more arts among them than we feem willing to allow
them.

To fettle the age of our Karn-brê Coins is perhaps impoffible,
but that the Britans had, and ufed Coins of their own making, and
that the Romans forbad the ufe of Britifh money, has been obferved
before, p. 270. for which prohibition there could be no reafon, if
the Britans did not coin in a different manner from the Romans;
therefore, this different manner of ftamping their money, it is not
fo likely they fhould learn of the Romans, as that they had it before
the Romans came; for after the Conqueft, the Romans, we find,
infifted upon the head of Cefar's being upon all their Coins;
therefore, that thefe Karn-brê Coins are prior to the Roman

SECT.VII.
Of the Age
of thefe
GoldGoins.

---

[a] Plate XV. p. 335. Perhaps the Britans
ufed this Coin when there was a fcarcity of
Gold, or the State was diftreffed. Certain it is,
that fuch bafe Coins came into ufe among the
Romans, during the tempeftuous Triumvirate of
Auguftus, &c. Jobert's Medals, p. 14.

4 A   invafion

invafion is extreamly probable. Further, both the Gauls and Britans being invaded nearly at the fame time, and by the fame General, the firft conquered, the other frightened, both of them would either have had fome fymbol of their fubjection in their Coins, if they had been ftruck under the direction of their Conquerors, or would have borrowed at leaft fomewhat more of the Roman elegance than what we find in the Cornifh Coins. The infcribed Coins produced by Camden and Speed, about the Julian Age, confirm this conjecture, there being fomething of the Roman air and regularity in all of them, but in ours nothing at all of that kind.

There is one other ufe which I fhall now make of the infcribed Coins before-mentioned, and may contribute to fettle fome particulars relating to the age of thefe Cornifh Coins; which is, that thefe infcribed Coins could not be the firft Coins of the Britifh Mint; and confequently, that the rude uninfcribed money found in all parts of England are older than the infcribed, as favouring more of the beginning and infancy of the art.

The feries, in which money was firft introduced, and arrived by degrees to the Grecian and Roman perfection, feems to be this: firft they weighed pieces of metal, then found out the way of impreffing them differently, according to their weights, and the quantity and fort of cattle they would be taken for in exchange; fo as to fave them the trouble of weighing [b]; then they impreffed Symbols of the Religion, War, Arts, and Philofophy, peculiar to their country; then came in the heads of Demi-gods, and Princes; and then Infcriptions, more certainly to determine the Age, Works, and Perfons, fignified by the Coins.

As foon as the Gauls, or any other barbarous nations, faw the great ufe of money, as it was managed among the more polifhed parts of mankind; it is natural to imagine, that people of authority would endeavour to introduce the fame convenient way of exchange among their own people; but, being hafty and impetuous to have the thing done, were not over-nice in their choice of Artifts for the doing it. What firft and principally ftruck them, was the ufe of money; to have the money coined with beauty and expreffion, was what had no place in their firft conceptions, nor entered at all into their defign; hence came the firft Coins fo rude and inexpreffive; becaufe the art, though at full maturity among the Greeks and Romans, was forced to pafs through a fecond infancy among the Gauls, and like the Gold that was caft

---

[b] The firft Money ufed in Rome was of plain Copper, without any impreffion, till the time of Servius Tullius, who caufed them firft to be ftamped with an Image of an Ox, a Sheep, a Hog, whence it began to be called *pecunia a pecude*. Pliny.—Jobert's Medals, Engl. p. 35.

into

into the fire, could not come out a better molten calf than the hands, which were employed, were able to mold and fashion it. The money, therefore, coined at firft among the Gauls and Britans, could not but partake of the barbarity and ignorance of the times in which it firft came into ufe; and the figures muft have been much ruder, and more uncouth than thofe of the infcribed Coins. Of this firft kind of money are probably Laminæ ferreæ of which Cefar fpeaks, Comment. of the Gall. War, Lib. V. and of which Mr. Ed. Lhwyd, in his Travels through Cornwall, writes in the following manner, fending at the fame time the out lines of of the pieces he found to Tho. Tonkin, Efq; by letter dated at Falmouth, Nov. 29, 1700. " The fifth and fixth figures" (Pl. XXIV. Fig. 1. and 2. p. 287.) " are two iron plates of that form " and fize, whereof feveral horfe-loads were found about fix years " fince. Qu. Whether thefe may not be the Britifh money men- " tioned by Cefar in thefe words, *Nummo utuntur parvo et æreo,* " *aut ferreis laminis* c *pro nummo.*" On which Mr. Tonkin, MS. B. p. 193. remarks: " I am apt to believe that Mr. Lhwyd rightly " concludes, that this was the Britifh money mentioned by Cefar." And then adds, " This prefent year 1730, as they were pulling " down the great Tower and fome very old buildings at Boconnock, " the feat of the late Lord Mohun, in Cornwall, about a peck " of the fame fort, but of a larger fize" (Pl. XXIV. Fig. 3. and 4. p. 287.) " were found in part of an old wall there." Thofe Coins then, which are not infcribed, are moft probably elder than thofe of the fame nation which are infcribed; Infcriptions, or Legends, being a part of elegance and accuracy, which at firft were not at all attended to; but which after-ages conftantly practifed, confulting at once the conveniency of their commerce, and the glory of their country.

If this inference is right, our Coins at Karn-brê, and the like fort in Plot, and Camden's Englifh Edition, are elder than the infcribed ones produced by Camden and Speed, and confequently elder than the Roman Invafion.

There are many parts of our Britifh Coins, which, though SECT. VIII. faithfully enough copied by Engravers, are yet wrongly placed in Of their fe-the Plates; becaufe, indeed, they did not know what they had veral Mem-copied. This is the reafon that we find the Diadem fometimes Symbols. horizontal d, at other times perpendicular e; whereas we all know,

c In other editions called, " Taleis ferreis ad " certum pondus examinatis," and the late learned Mr. Moyle obferved that " Dr. Davis, " in his notes (viz. on the Commentaries), " with Lipfius, judges *Annulis ferreis* to " be the true Reading; and Dr. Clarke, " in his Edition of Cefar, has admitted it into

" the text, upon the authority of thefe manu- " fcripts, and the Greek Tranflation. I believe " it to be the true Reading." Moyle's Works, Vol. I. p. 171.
d Plot, Oxf. N° 21. p. 335.
e Wife, N° 1.

that

that this fhould rife floping from the ear to the forehead. In Mont-faucon's Plate, N° 16. the horfe is laid on his back with his legs uppermoft; and in N° 36. (ibid.) the horfe's body is perpendicu-lar, and fo is the line of the *Exergue*; which fame fault is com-mitted in placing the Reverfe of Plot's N° 21. p. 335. plain evi-dences, that the Engraver did not underftand the figure, though he drew the fize and fhape, not knowing what animal it was, or whether an animal or not: and whoever copied the fine Gold Coin in Camden's laft Edit. p. 833. N° 21. (of the fame age with fome of thofe at Karnbrê), moft certainly did not know what figure he had before him; and, therefore, it is no wonder that the learned Editor, depending on his Engraver, fhould place the Horfe upon his back.

There is one thing more neceffary to be obferved, in order to place thefe Coins with propriety, which is, that feveral of our Karn-brê Coins have not the horfe on the Reverfe (as N° VIII. IX. X. XI.), but inftead thereof, have certain members and fymbols adjufted together, in fuch a manner, as to imitate the fhape of a horfe, and become, when joined together, the emblem, rather than the figure of that creature, which the firft Engraver knew no better how to defign. Thefe feveral Symbols are not to be explained but by comparing the Coins, in which we find the fame parts inferted in the compofition of an intire figure, and others in which the fame parts are detached and unconnected.

The Legs of the Horfe.

The latter muft derive their light from the former. For exam-ple. In N° VIII. you find three of the figures marked in the Table of Symbols [f] N° 1. In N° IX. there are four of the fame Symbols; in N° X. two; N° XI. four. What fhould be the intent of placing fuch figures, in fuch numbers on thefe Reverfes? Why, in N° XVIII. and XIX. we find the legs of the horfe made in this unnatural fafhion; and it is obfervable, that where the horfe is not, there thefe legs (the moft ufeful parts of this creature) are placed. They are four in number in N° IX. and XI. and would have been alfo in the fame number and place in N° VIII. and X. (for, by the Weight and Symbols, thefe four muft have been Coins of the fame fort, time and value), but the mold in ftriking thefe latter was mifplaced [g].

They are placed two and two, with a ball or wheel between them, as in the Coins which have horfes intire. Between them the Half moon (of which by and by) dips his convex part, fome-thing in the manner of the horfe's barrel, above which another

[f] Plate XXIII.
[g] Thefe parts of the Horfe (viz. III.) are but very little better placed in Coins XVII. and XXII. where the Horfe is intire; thefe laft mentioned Coins therefore are next in antiquity to N° XI.

Crefcent-

Crefcent-like bunch forms the back; a round ball turns to fhape the buttock, and on the fore part, a thick handle of a javelin flopes upwards from the breaft, to form the neck and creft of the horfe. In Coin XI. we find thefe Symbols in full number (i. e. four) very diftinct, and as juftly placed as the Engraver's fkill directed. When thefe are placed double, as in Coin XVII, they feem intended to denote there being two horfes a-breaft, as was the ancient cuftom of drawing the fighting chariots. Two little figures of this fhape[h] are alfo placed in the later Coins, viz. N° XXIII. and XVIII. to form the upper and under jaw of the horfe's head. When therefore fuch figures occur in Britifh Coins, we need but refer to thefe of Karn-brê; and we find immediately, that they were intended for fome parts of a horfe.

Round the horfe's neck of N° XII. there is a Garland, or The Gar-land. Bracelet, which in N° XIX. is alfo plainly to be difcovered.

There is ufually a circular figure under the belly of the horfe, The Wheel, which in fome is a diftinct Wheel, as in Coins V. VI. XII. XIX. Tab. of Symbols, XX. XXII. XXIII. and therefore in the reft, where this figure is N° 7. 9. lefs diftinct, it muft be deemed an aim at, or rude imitation of, the fame thing.

The Wheel is to denote the Chariot to which the Horfe belonged. The learned Walker fays, "that the Wheel under the horfe, "amongft the Romans, intimated the making of an high way for "carts, fo many of which, being in the Roman times made in this "country, well deferved fuch a memorial[i]."

What the Wheel fignified among the Romans I fhall not difpute, but it could not be inferted in the Britifh Coins (as he feems to imply) for that purpofe; for there were no Roman ways made in Britain till after Claudius's conqueft, and we find the Wheel common in Cunobelin's Coins[k], and in Caffibelan's N° II. ibid. in N° XVI. XVII. XVIII. and in Plot's XXI; and alfo in the Cornifh Coins, which from all their characters appear to be older than the reft.

The Wheel is ufually placed under the belly of the Horfe, but is fometimes found in two places on the fame Coin (as in N°. 9. and 32. of Tab. II. in Camden) one above and one below the horfe, to denote (as I imagine) the two Wheels of the *Effeda*. One of thefe Wheels (viz. the upper one in N° 9. ibid.) Walker takes to be the Sun.

There are many balls, or globules, difperfed in all the Cornifh Of the Coins, which are of two fizes; thofe of the leaft kind are, or feem, Balls, or Globules.
Tab. of Symbols, N° 8.

[h] In the Table of Symbols, N° 5.   fame kind.
[i] Camd. p. cx. and in cxv. ibid. On   [k] See Speed, N° VIII. and XIII.
N° 2. and 3. he has an obfervation of the

4 B   meerly

meerly ornamental, being ftrung in rows like Beads or Pearls, and
ferve now and then in a regular figure to form the mane of a horfe
(as in Nº XV. XVI. XVII. XX. XXII); the circumference or outline of the Wheel (Nº XXII. and Mr. Wife's Bodleian Nº 2.), or a
kind of Bracelet, or Garland (two of which may be feen in one Reverfe of the Bodleian Nº. 11.) round the neck, or body of the Horfe.

Rings, or
Plates.
Tab. of
Symbols,
Nº 10.

There is another round figure in thefe Coins, which is of the
middle fize, and is a Ring, or *Difcus*, either pierced or emboffed.
They are larger in Nº IX. X. XI. than the Wheel itfelf, a difpro-
portion owing to the rudenefs of the art when firft practifed. When
thefe are emboffed, as I find them in a well-preferved Coin in the
Bodleian Cabinet, I imagine they are to reprefent either the fhield,
or rather the *Laminæ*, and may fhew that they had iron plates, as
well as rings, that ferved inftead of Money.

In Nº XX. fome of the Balls are plainly pierced; in Nº 12. of
the Bodleian they are plain, and placed where the roundnefs of the
Horfe's body, fhoulder, and buttock, made them fall in with the
fhape of the creature; there are others in the Bodleian collection,
and in the Reverfe of Speed's Caffibelan, but no where more plain
than in Dr. Plot's Nº 21. (p. 335. Oxfordfhire) where there are
five near the edge of the Coin, and more, though of a fmaller fize,
difperfed in the *Field* of the Coin, not only of the Reverfe, but of
the *Head*.

I am perfuaded that the little annular figures will make the learned
Reader eafily recollect the *annuli ferrei* of Cefar[k], and as eafily affent
to their being inferted on purpofe to reprefent the ancient money
which the Britans had before they coined after the Roman and
Grecian manner; and, perhaps, afterwards too, for a while, when
the Gold, Silver, and Brafs currency fell fhort of anfwering the
exigences of the State. Thefe Rings are taken notice of by Cefar,
as made of Iron, adjufted to a certain weight and ftandard, and
ufed inftead of money; and the figures of them on thefe Coins,
where this Symbol is pierced, may confirm the reading of that
paffage, to be as in Plantin's Edit. (Lib. V. p. 87.) " *annulis
ferreis*;" as the emboffed ones may in fome meafure affure us, that
they ufed alfo *Taleis*, or *Laminis*, as we read it in others. Where
there are many of thefe Symbols, they fhould fignify the plenty of
money in the little kingdoms where they were ftruck.

Crefcents.

In many of thefe Karn-brê Coins, viz. VIII. IX. X. XI. XVI.
and in Nº XXII. we find a Crefcent, or fome fuch figure (Nº 3.);
and in the *Head* of Dr. Plot's (Nº 21.) there are three; what
intended to fignify, is uncertain. We know the Crefcent was
among the moft honourable badges of the Druid Order; and from

[k] See before in this Chapter.

the

the Moon at fix days old, they regulated the beginning of their months, years, and ages, every thirtieth year; fo that the Moon was of conftant and efpecial note among the ancient Britans: but whether it be really a Crefcent, or not, I do not pretend to decide. It might poffibly be intended to reprefent the golden hook with which their Priefts with fo much folemnity cut their divine Mifletoe, or to record the hooks or fcythes faftened to the axis of their chariots of war, for fuch they had[1], and on thefe Coins we find feveral allufions to this manner of fighting. Which of thefe fuppofitions is moft likely, let the reader determine as he thinks beft.

There is a remarkable rectilineal figure, which leans obliquely in a line nearly parallel to the creft of the horfe, with which, or its emblem, it is always combined: it is feen in N° V. VI. more uncouth ftill in N° VIII. IX. XI. but very diftinct in XIII. This I take to reprefent the fpear, with which the Britans were fo dextrous in fighting from their chariots. In N° VI. it is placed crofs the tree, out of which the fhaft was made, and in gratitude perhaps to the tree, for affording the beft fhafts for thefe ufeful arms. *The Spear.*

In thefe coins then the principal figure is the horfe; the wheel (emblem of the chariot) conftantly attends the horfe; the fpear is vifible in ten of thefe Coins produced, and in N° XXII. the human figure is plain, pointing forward the fpear, or javelin, as if advancing to attack the enemy. In N°. XIII. there are fome traces of the fame kind, and more rude attempts to delineate the fame in N° VIII. IX. X. XI. for the fpear has the fame direction in all. *Why all thefe Symbols of, or belonging to, the Chariot.*

In N° XVII. the charioteer is very apparent—in fome winged like a victory—the bridle—and fomething like a trapping—a pendant or trailed fpear, or fcythe. To what other purpofe then are thefe warlike things collected and inferted in their Coins, but to fignify, that the chief glory of the Britans was their fkill in fighting from their chariots?

The Britans (fays Cefar, Lib. IV.) have the following manner of fighting from their chariots; "firft they advance through all parts of "their army, and throw their javelins, and having wound themfelves "in among the troops of horfe, they alight and fight on foot; the "charioteers retiring a little with their chariots, but pofting them- "felves in fuch a manner, that if they fee their mafters preffed, they "may be able to bring them off: by this means the Britans have "the agility of Horfe, and the firmnefs of Foot, and by daily exercife "have attained to fuch fkill and management, that in a declivity

---

[1] " Dimicant (fcil. Britanni) non equitatu " falcatis axibus utuntur." Pompon. Mela, " modò aut pedite, verum et Bigis et Curribus Lib. III. cap. viii. " Gallice armati. Covinos vocant, quorum

" they

" they can govern the horfes, though at full fpeed, check and turn
" them fhort about, run forward upon the pole, ftand firm upon the
" yoke, and then withdraw themfelves nimbly into their chariots."
The Britans being trained to, and excelling all others in this peculiar
manner of fighting (Cefar himfelf more than once acknowledging
the diforder into which thefe *Effedarii* had thrown the Roman
foldiers[m]) had nothing more glorious to record in their Coins than
fuch an artful and efficacious manner of combat; and no Coins, with
fuch fymbols, fo likely to be of any nation as of Britain. Thence
come the horfe, the wheel, the fpear or javelin, and the charioteer,
and perhaps the hook with which their chariot was armed. The
Britans were fo fenfible of their Glory acquired by Chariot-fighting,
that great Soldiers had an addition made to their names, for being
remarkable in this way of fighting, as the moft famous Romans had
from the feveral places they conquered, the Gauls from their habit,
and the Macedonians from their fpears. Hence we have thofe
Britifh names ending in *Rhôd* (which fignifies a fighting Chariot)
as Anau-rhôd, Cadrhôd, and Med-rhôd, as Mr. Rowland juftly
thinks.

In the firft fix Karn-brê Coins here exhibited, there is no
appearance of the human *Head*. In Nᵒ VII. and VIII. there are
fome faint traits of a diadem. In Nᵒ IX. the profile of the face, ear
and clafp, and outline of the neck is plain, but the diadem, which
was certainly there (as muft be inferred from Nᵒ X. and XI.) is
effaced, and the Coin has loft four grains more than Nᵒ XI. which
fhews that it has been fo much more ufed. In Nᵒ X. XI. XIV.
XV. XVI. the diadem is plain and ftrong. It is formed of leaves,
which have this peculiarity, that they point downwards; whereas,
in the ancient Roman and Grecian Coins, the leaves point upwards.
There is another difference between the diadem in the Karn-brê
Coins, and in the Greek and Roman; for, whereas, in the laft
mentioned, the fillet or ribband on which the diadem is grounded
(or by which it is bound together) makes a very elegant knot
behind the *Head*, the Britifh Coins have no fuch thing, but have a
ftraight bandage, or rather clafp which croffes the diadem at right
angles, and was doubtlefs defigned (like the fillet of the ancients)
to keep the diadem firm in its place, and clofe to the *Head*. This
is the meaning of that ftraight figure croffing the diadem in Nᵒ X.
XI. and XIV. and XVI. of the Karn-brê Coins; but is moft plainly
vifible in Nᵒ XX. XXIV. and XXV. with a hook or fcroll at the
end of it, and, but for thefe well-preferved Coins, would have ftill
remained uncertain, and unknown.

Marginal notes:

Of the *Head*.

Diadem. Tab. of Symbols, Nᵒ. 11.

Clafp. Tab. of Symbols, Fig. *.

---

m " Ordines plerumque perturbant." Lib.IV. p 83. " Perturbatis noftris novitate pugnæ." ibid. Lib. V. p. 93. " Equites Hoftium Effe- " dariique acriter prælio cum Equitatu noftro " in itinere conflixerunt."—" Novo genere " pugnæ perterritis Noftris." ibid.

Above

Above the diadem, the hair turns off in bold curls, fometimes in CurledHair.
one tire or row, as in N° X. XI. XIV. XV. but in the larger Coins
in two rows, as N° XVI. and XX[n].

Round the neck, in N° XIV. the habit of the prince juft appears; Habit.
in N° XVI. a kind of fcolloped lace or ornament of embroidery;
more of which is ftill to be feen in N° XX.

In N° I. II. III. VI. trees are placed in the *Head* part (as was Why diffe-
before obferved in the defcription) but there are few if any rings or rentCharges
balls: the reafon feems to be this; the riches of the country where in the*Fields*.
thefe were coined confifted in woods (not in money); and therefore
they took the tree for their fymbol, as the countries abounding
in corn took the *fpica,* and thofe which had plenty of pearls took
the globules refembling pearl, and thofe which had plenty of gold
and money, took the ringlets, or *Laminæ,* into their Coins[o].

The figure in the *Head* of N° XII. has been before obferved to
refemble the ichnography of a city, and was probably inferted in
the Coin by the founder, to record the erection of fome city: for
that the Britans had fuch cities, is very plain from the noble ruins
(containing in circuit about three or four miles), near Wrottefly, in
the county of Stafford, where (as Dr. Plot thinks, Staffordfh. p. 394.)
" the parallel partitions, within the outwall, whofe foundations are
" ftill vifible, and reprefent ftreets running different ways, put it
" out of doubt that it muft have been a city, and that of the
" Britans."

CHAP. XIII.

Of the Brafs Celts found at Karn-brê, and elfewhere.

IN the year 1744, in the fide of Karn-brê hill, were dug up
feveral hollow inftruments of brafs, of different fizes, called Celts,
whofe fhape is moft eafily apprehended from the drawings of two
of them, exhibited Plate XXIV. Fig. I. and II. with others from
different parts of the kingdom, placed together for the better
illuftration of one another.

With thefe inftruments were found feveral Roman Coins, fix of
which came into my hands; one of ANTONINVS AVG. N° 2.
uncertain. N° 3. DIVO CONSTANTIO PIO; Reverfe MEMORIA FELIX.
N° 4. defaced. N° 5. SEVERVS ALEXANDER. N° 6. defaced.

---

[n] The Gauls were called Comati, from their
long hair. The Britans had probably the fame
cuftom, for all uncultivated nations wore long
hair, except the Alani. (Lucian, Toxaris) it was
an inftance of their wildnefs.

[o] Camden thinks that tribute for woods was
paid in fuch coin, and that tribute-monies had
their impreffion from that deftination. The
reader will chufe which opinion he thinks moft
probable.

At

SECT. I.
Whether
and how far
they are to
be aſſigned
to the Ro-
mans.
At preſent let the Celts be the ſubjeƈt of our enquiry, what nation we ſhall aſcribe them to, and to what uſe that nation applied them.   As they are found here in Cornwall in company with Roman Coins, one would be apt to imagine that they were of Roman original.   Upon much leſs grounds are they aſſerted to be Roman by the learned Dr. PlotP, who, finding one of like kind, engraved in the Muſeum Moſcardi, immediately concludes all the Celts found at the ſeveral places there mentioned to be Roman (though no Coins of that nation were found with them), and deter-mines alſo the Barrows where they were found to have been ereƈted by that people.

Mr. Hearneq follows Dr. Plot, in attributing them to the Romans: others take them to be Britiſh.

Firſt, then, I do not take them to be purely Roman, foreign, or of Italian invention and workmanſhip.

They are made of Braſs, which the Romans of Italy would not have done after Julius Ceſar's time, when the ſuperiour hardneſs of iron was ſo well underſtood by that cultivated people, and ſo eaſily to be had from any of their conquered provinces.

They do not appear in the complete colleƈtion of arms on the Trajanr, or Antonine Pillar, which, if they had been Roman inſtru-ments, they certainly would have done.

There are but very few in the cabinets of the curious in Rome, Naples, and the other cities of Italy, as I am informed by a gentle-mans who has examined them with equal penetration and diligence (and has been ſo kind as to favour me with ſeveral informations relating to that ſubjeƈt), and " where they occur, they are looked " upon, by all the Italian Virtuoſi, as Tranſalpine Antiquities, and " not to have belonged to their predeceſſors."

In the great diſcoveries which have of late years been made among the ruins of Herculaneum, where weapons, tools, and utenſils for every occurrence in life, have been found, none of theſe inſtruments have been met with, as far as yet appears.

Spon in his Miſcellanea mentions none of them. " They occur " not in the Muſeum Romanum, publiſhed by Monſ. de la Chauſſe, " nor in the Muſeum Kercherianum publiſhed by Bonani.   In the " voluminous colleƈtion of Montfaucon, there are none engraved or " mentioned."   So far this learned Gentleman.

Now if theſe inſtruments had been of foreign original, and by the Romans introduced into Britain, they would have been frequently found in Italy, and very numerous in the colleƈtions of the curious,

P Staffordſhire, p. 403.   with P. S. Bartoli's notes.
q Leland, Vol. I. p. 127.   s Smart Lethieullier, Eſq; in his letter on the
r As publiſhed with Ciaconius's, or the Edit.   Celts.

and

and could never have efcaped the authors above-mentioned. I am therefore apt to believe that they are not to be afcribed in general to the Romans, nor ufed by the Roman legions in Italy and the Eaft; but that they were probably made and ufed by the provincial Romans of Britain, and by the Britans themfelves when they had improved the arts under their Roman mafters.

They are found here at Karn-brê, and have been found at Aldborough (the ancient Ifurium) in Yorkfhire, in company with many Roman Coins; the reafon of which feems to be this, when the Romans had thought fit to admit the natives of their conquered provinces into their armies (the very legions themfelves being, at laft, occafionally recruited out of fuch provinces), it is not to be doubted but the Britans were allowed to carry the weapons of war, which they had been trained up to, and were become eafy and habitual to them. And as we do not find thefe weapons of general ufe among the Eaftern Romans, we may conclude, that the Romans fuffered the Britifh difcipline, as to this particular, to prevail here in this province; and finding the Britans expert in the ufe of thefe arms, and the arms really of fervice againft the Picts, Scots, and rebellious Britans, not only indulged and encouraged the Britans in the ufe of them, but fell into the ufe of them themfelves. In fhort, moft of them feem to me too correct and fhapely for the Britans before the Julian conqueft; and yet the Romans do not appear to have ufed them beyond the Alps; I imagine, therefore, that they were originally of Britifh, Gaulifh, or Northern, invention and fabrick, and afterwards ufed by the provincial Romans, as well as Britans. Let us confider, in the next place, that they are frequently found in all parts of Britain.

Leland (Vol. III. p. 7.) tells us, that a few years before his being in Cornwall, there were found fpear-heads, battle-axes, and fwords made of copper, near the Mount[t], in the parifh of St. Hillary, where, by the fpear-heads, he certainly meant thofe which we (from Begerus, &c.) now call Celts[u]. Camden[w] fays, they were found not long before in Wales, and in Germany. Mr. Thorefby gives an account of fome found in Yorkfhire near Bramham-Moor, in 1709[x]. " Several of them have been found in a ftone quarry in " the fame county, many of which had Cafes exactly fitted to " them[y]. In May, 1735, were found above 100 on Eafterley-" Moor, twelve Miles N. W. of York, together with feveral lumps

SECT. II.
Places where found, and with what.

---

[t] According to Camden (Lat. edit. p. 79.) at the foot of the Mount, as they were digging for Tin; which gave occafion to Mr. Carew to think that they were ufually found in Tin-works (p. 8.), where he fays, " they were termed, " by fome, thunder-axes, making fmall fhew of

" any profitable ufe."
[u] A Cælo, to engrave; unde Cæltis, vel Celtis, quafi, An engraving tool.
[w] Ibid.
[x] Leland, Itinerary, Vol. I. p. 17.
[y] Mr. Lethieullier's Letter.

" of

" of metal, and a quantity of cinders, fo that no doubt remained
" of there having been a forge at that place for making them."
Mr. Rowland, p. 85. has publifhed fome (but all of one figure,
neareft to Fig. I. Plate XXIV.) found near the place where the
Romans made their attack upon the Britans, in the Ifle of Anglefea,
under Suetonius.

At Danbury in Effex, about twenty-two years fince, fome of the
fame kind were found, and at Fifield in the fame county, in the
year 1749, with a large quantity of metal for cafting thefe inftruments, feveral of which, with fifty pounds of the metal, were
fent, by the late Earl Tilney, to the learned gentleman before-
mentioned; part of the Celts, and Metal, he was fo kind as to
favour me with, at the fame time informing me, that he had fome
of the fame inftruments from Scotland, Wales, New-Foreft in
Hampfhire, and other places in Britain.

From all which circumftances it appears that they are fpread
every where in this ifland, that they were manufactured here, and
of general ufe among the natives. But though thofe found here
were Britifh, that is, made and ufed here, yet it muft not be imagined that they were peculiar to the Britans. Doubtlefs the Gauls
had the fame inftruments, their manner of living, fighting, worfhiping, their arts and learning, being the fame with thofe of the
Britans Neither is it any wonder that they fhould be found among
Germans, any more than that the Germans fhould have fwords,
fpears, the tools of arts, and inftruments of common life, as well
as the Britans; the fame neceffity of defending themfelves, offend-
ing their enemies, and preparing utenfils for their conveniency,
prompting them all to work up fuch metals as they could get, in
fuch manner as was proportioned to their fkill, and might beft
anfwer their neceffities.

SECT. III.
Various
Opinions of
their Ufe.
Various have been the opinions of the learned concerning the
ufe and defign of thefe inftruments; and, if they had not been advanced by men of learning, it would be fcarce excufable to mention fome of them, much lefs to refute them.

Some have taken them for the Heads of walking-ftaffs, fome
for Chizels to cut Stone withal, concluding, that fuch kind of inftruments [z] muft have been abfolutely neceffary in making the great
Roman ways in Britain; fome fancy them intended to engrave
Letters and Infcriptions; others as happily have imagined them to
be the *Falx* with which the Druids cut the facred Mifletoe. But
all thefe fuppofitions feem to me repugnant, either to their fhape,

z See Leland, Vol. I. p. 132.

or

or to the metal they are made of, to their fize or ftructure, or to all thefe equally.

They are found in too many places [a], and too many in number, to have been walking-ftaffs [b]; for, if we can fuppofe, that perfons of diftinction had fuch, the generality cannot be imagined to have run into fuch an expence.

The focket is not large enough [c], nor in a proper direction, for that of an Ax, nor the inftrument weighty enough, or properly fhaped, to do any execution on the victim [d].

The Socket is, it muft be owned, more like that of a Chizel [e]; but there are unfurmountable difficulties attending this hypothefis, which arife from the other properties. For firft and principally, it muft be objected, that the metal of which thefe inftruments are formed is very improper for an edge-tool (for cutting Stones efpecially, much too foft and brittle), being a compofition of Copper and Tin, or Lead. If they had been ufed in cutting Stone, they muft have been fcratched, and furrowed on every fide, by the hard and rough Stone; but the many I have feen have no marks of the leaft application to fuch an ufe; the edges of them are in fome parts jagged, in fome blunted, in others broke; but the fides, from the edge upwards, are ftill as fmooth as at firft from the mold, where the ruft has not corroded them. Round the brim of the Socket is fome imbofs'd work, more or lefs, which is much too delicate I imagine for Mafons Chizels. To moft of thefe inftruments there is a Loop, or Ring, which is to be found in no Chizels in the world. Some are fo thin in the blade, that they would bear no force, nor make any expedition in works of Stone; and they are all fo unequal to the laborious works of Mafonry, that, to fay no more of it, we may fafely conclude, that the Roman ways, from one end of Britain to the other, might well be executed without the affiftance of any fuch impotent tools as thefe.

To think they were intended to cut Letters [f], an art requiring the keeneft and moft lafting point, is ftill more abfurd.

Dr. Plot [g] takes one (the fame fort which I publifh here N° VIII. Pl. XXIV. from my own) to have been a Roman Reft, ufed to fupport the *Lituus*; but by its fhape, and having the fame marks of damage at the edge as others have, I fhould rather think it defigned for the fame ufe.

I fhall only obferve, that the hook for cutting the Mifletoe was of Gold among the Druids, not of Brafs, as the Celts are; and that

[a] See Sect. II.
[b] Thorefby.
[c] Being, in my largeft, but one inch and quarter; and in the leaft but five eighths of an inch diameter.
[d] Richardfon, ibid. Leland, Vol. I. p. 142.
[e] Mr. Hearne, ib. p. 135. &c.
[f] Begerus, ut fupra.
[g] Staffordfhire, p. 404.

4 D   the

the make of the Celts bears not any fimilitude to that of a hook, as the Druid inftrument is always formed; let me add in this place, that if we confider how curious and elegant the Ancients were, and the Moderns ftill are, about their arms; if it fhall appear that we have reafon to reckon thefe Celts among the weapons of war, it cannot be wondered at that they fhould be ornamented with mold- ings, and imboffed orderly-figured ridges.

SECT. IV. Ufe beft known from their Shape.
The true ufe of them is beft fuggefted by the things themfelves, that is, by the fhape, fize, and the metal they confift of. In the fhape we find three things remarkable; the Socket A, the Ring or Loop B, and the flat point or edge C. Round the Socket they have fome little moldings and lifts, D E; but as thefe are merely ornamental, and not conducive to, or expreffive of, the ufe of them, I pafs them by. Some have a Socket, but no Ring, as Fig. VIII. Some have a Ring, but no Socket, but, inftead there- of, a Groove on each fide, as Fig. VI. (of which Fig. VII. is the Section) and Fig. IV. and fome have neither Socket nor Ring, but the Grooves only, as Fig. III; and V has neither Socket, Groove, nor Ring, being quite flat, and its edge more circular; but, being found with the others before defcribed, is therefore to be affigned to the fame country and ufe, though of another model. They are different in fize, but of the fame metal. The ufe, which will beft agree with thefe properties, feems to me to be the *Head*, or arming of the Spear, the Javelin, or the Arrow.

Their Size.
They are of different fizes, and it is obfervable, that the Ancients had their *miffile* weapons of all fizes; for one Engine, fome were heavy, for another light; to throw at a great diftance, and to fight with near by; fome to affail the heavy armed, and others for the *Haftati*, *Velites*, and the light-armed; the larger and heavier feem to have been the *Heads* of Spears, the middle fort for Javelins, and the lighter and fmaller for the *Heads*, or arming of Arrows.

Socket.
See Section of the fame Fig. VII.
The Socket of Fig. I. II. and VIII. feems manifeftly defigned to receive a wooden haft. In Fig. VI. the Socket is divided in the middle by a partition A, to which a chink in the haft might eafily be adjufted, and the wood embracing this partition fecure the *Head*, better perhaps than where the Socket confifts only of one hole. Fig. III. and IV. feem alfo to have had their hafts, the timber of which was prepared properly to fill up the Grooves of each fide, and the tranfverfe welts (*b b*) to prevent the arming *Head* from finking too deep into the haft, by the refiftance it met with from the bodies it was thrown againft. Thofe which have no Sockets were faftened on to the haft in a different manner from the others; and, perhaps, by the driving a Ring round the handle, which did comprefs the timber, and keep it clofe to the *Head*. Fig. V. was more difficult to fix on to its haft, it having neither

Socket,

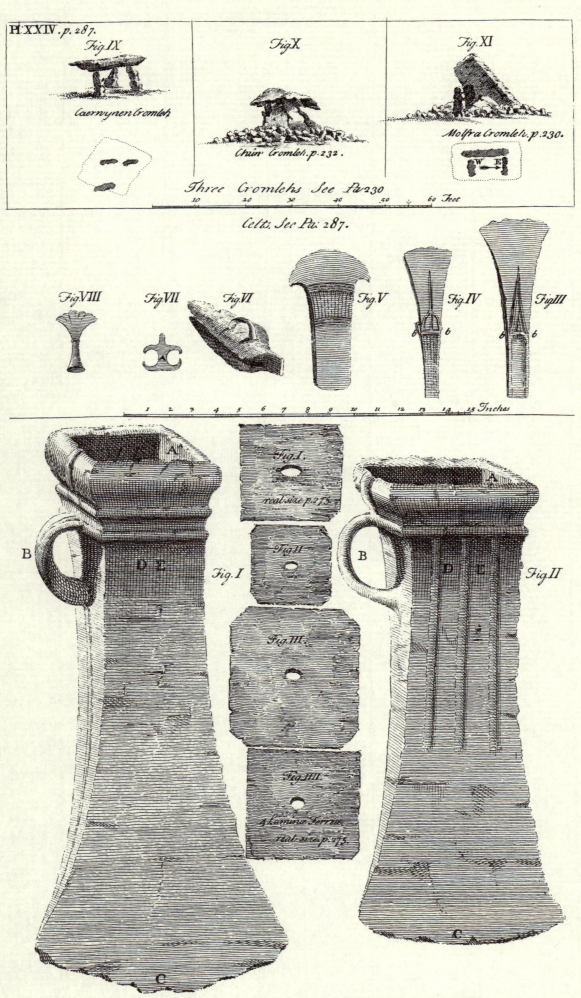

H.XXIV. p. 287.

Fig. IX

Caernynen Cromleh

Fig. X

Chun Cromleh. p. 232.

Fig. XI

Molfra Cromleh. p. 230.

W   E

Three Cromlehs See Pa. 230

10   20   30   40   50   60 Feet

Celts. See Pa: 287.

Fig. VIII   Fig. VII   Fig. VI   Fig. V   Fig. IV   Fig. III

1 2 3 4 5 6 7 8 9 10 11 12 13 14 15 Inches

Fig. I.

real size p. 275.

Fig. II

Fig. III.

Fig. IIII.

4 Lamina Ferrea.

real size p. 275.

A

B   D E   Fig. I

C

A

B   D E   Fig. II

C

Two Celts found at Karn Brè Cornwall of the Real Size.

see. p. 287.

W.B. Delin   J. Green Sculp

Socket, Loop, nor Groove; and therefore it might be doubtful, whether it fhould have a place among the offenfive weapons before-mentioned, but that we find the edge of the Spear-head made in this Crefcent-like form, in two Spears on the Trajan column[h]; fo that, however, they faftened this Celt to its haft, or the other Stone-axes (as they are called[i]) which are found in many parts of Britain, and much more difficult to fix than this, we may probably rank them among the weapons of war.

It muft be owned, that Spears and Javelins are for the moft part Edge. pointed for piercing; but it may be acknowledged as well, that they were fometimes edged flat for cutting, as appears from the two on Trajan's Pillar abovementioned, and from that publifhed by Dr. Plot[k] (of which fort he numbers four) which in the collection of Mofcardus, from which he publifhed it, is faid to be the arming of a weapon of war[l].

Of this latter kind is the Stone Celt exhibited in its natural fize, Plate XXVIII. Figures IX, X. p. 316. the only one I have yet heard of found in Cornwall. The ftone of which it confifts is white flint; it is ground to an edge, A, very fmooth and fharp; the face *c c c* is alfo fmooth and polifhed; it was alfo grinded thin at the fides B B, after which the fides were farther thinned by fplintering off part of the fide edge, and hollowing it into femicircular fhallow cavities *d d d d*, for the better faftening it, as I imagine, unto the handle or fhaft of the Spear[m]. To return now to the brafs Celts of Plate XXIV.

The greateft difficulty is, what this Ring, or Eye (Fig. I. II. IV. Ring or and VI.) fhould be defigned for. That it fhould be intended to Eye. faften on the arming to the haft, is an end that it would by no means anfwer, as is evident it being placed below the edge of the Socket in N° I. and II. whereas, in order to faften it to the handle, it fhould be placed above, and then (without another to anfwer it on the other fide), according to all the rules of Mechanicks, its *Power* could fecure but half the inftrument[n]: befides, if we obferve the Ring in N° II. it is too flight and weak to fix a bandage, or wire, for a *Head* of fuch weight and fize. Upon diligent con-fideration, therefore, the Ring could never be defigned for this ufe. Let us fee in the next place, whether even this part may not be reconciled to the arts of War.

[h] Montfaucon, Tom. IV. p. 65.
[i] Dugdale's Warwickfh.—Plot's Staff. p.404. Tab. 33. N° 3. 6.
[k] Staffordfhire, p. 404. N° V.
[l] Mofcard. Lib. III. cap. 174.
[m] This Inftrument of war was found in digging, Oct. 17, 1766, about three feet under the furface, in the new farm-yard (lately a field) at Clowance, the feat of Sir John St. Aubyn, Bart. who, with his ufual readinefs to oblige, was pleafed to communicate it, and to confent that, for the fatisfaction of the curious, it fhould be depofited with fome other Cornifh remains in the Mufeum at Oxford.
[n] Dr. Richardfon's conjecture therefore (Le-land, Vol. I. p. 142.) though ingenious, and his bandage neatly defigned, cannot be true.

It

Its Use con-
jectured.

It is not unlikely that this Ring, though it might poſſibly be of uſe to fix the *Labarum*, the Garlands of Victory, or the bunch of Ribbons (for all theſe we find placed at the Spear's *Head*[n], and therefore the Roman Spear muſt have been properly prepared to receive them) yet ſerved, more eſpecially among the leſs cultivated nations, to fix a line to, by means of which, the Soldier carried this Javelin more commodiouſly on his march by ſlinging it on his ſhoulder, and might throw it with more force in time of action, or by means of the faſtened line recover it to him again, after he had aſſailed his adverſary. For all theſe purpoſes this Ring is equally convenient.

Mr. Rowland ſeems to come the neareſt to the truth of any author I have read; where he ſays, p. 86, " that they might be uſed with " a ſtring to draw them back, and ſomething like a feather to guide " them in flying towards the enemy, and calls them Sling-hatchets;" but for ſuch weighty *Heads* there was certainly no occaſion for feathers; it was uſe and practice that brought the Soldiers to poiſe and throw their Javelins ſo dextrouſly; and as for ſlinging of hatchets againſt an enemy, I do not remember ever to have met with any inſtance, ancient or modern; and ſome of them are evidently too light to do any execution thrown from the hand.

The Greeks had darts projected by a ſtring, which they called Αγκυλη; that is, the *Anſa*, or handle, by which they took hold of, directed, and threw the dart: theſe Javelins were ſometimes called *Aclides:*

— — — *Teretes ſunt Aclides illis*
Tela, ſed hæc lento mos eſt aptare flagello[o].

VIRG. Æn. VII. ver. 750.

The ſtring was generally by the Romans called *amentum*, becauſe the ſoldiers brought it level to their chin, before they diſcharged the Javelin.

Theſe weapons were not confined to the Greeks and ancient Italians, but were alſo uſed by the Gauls, and by them ſometimes called *Cateiæ:*

Teutonico ritu ſoliti torquere Cateias.   Æn. VII. ver. 741.

on which Servius (ibid.) obſerves that the Gauls, having thrown theſe

---

[n] See deſcription of Antonine's Pillar, ibid. ut ſupr. Plate I. Fig. III.

[o] On which Servius — " Aclides ſunt tela " quædam antiqua: Legitur, quod ſint Clavæ " cubitoſemis factæ, eminentibus hinc & hinc " acuminibus, quæ ita in hoſtem jaciuntur " religatæ Loro vel Lino, ut peractis vulneribus " poſſint redire. Putatur tamen eſſe Teli genus " quod per flagellum in immenſum jaci poteſt."

Darts

FOUND AT KARN-BRE, CORNWALL.

Darts at their enemies, recovered them again by lines fastened to them.

The Gaulish weapons of this kind Cesar calls *Mataræ*; and, as Strabo says, they were like the *Pilum* of the Romans which the Gauls darted, and used generally in hunting and killing of birds; and this weapon was so common, and universally used by the Gauls, that it became a criterion of their nation, as the *Sarissa* (a very long spear) was of the Macedonians[o].

The Kerns, or Foot-soldiers, of the ancient Irish Militia bore Swords and Darts; to the last were fitted cords, by which they could recover them after they had been launched out [p].

But, if these instruments were designed for war, it may seem strange to some that they should be made of brass, when they would be so much more proper for all warlike uses if they had been made of iron. In answer to which I may observe, that in ancient times they had neither such plenty nor choice of metals as we have at present. The most ancient weapons were neither armed with Brass nor Iron.

SECT. V.
Celts, why made of Brass.

The Sarmatians[q], the Germans[r], and the Huns[s], for want of Metals, pointed the dart with bone. The Gauls had heads of ivory, and some of stone for their arrows; they had also what are called stone-hatchets, as appears by what have been found in their Sepulchres[t]; and the Britans, as is observed before, had flint heads for their spears and arrows, if they had not hatchets also of the same substance[u]. This was the most ancient way of making and arming their weapons, in the Western parts; but copper being found in many places, and very early among the Orientals, the way of tempering, hardening, and colouring it with Tin, Lead, or *Lapis Calaminaris*, soon followed, and was probably as ancient as the invention of Swords, which by learned men is supposed coeval with War; with this Metal it was soon found much easier to head their Spears and Arrows, than to grind a stone into the necessary offensive form; wherever, therefore, they had a sufficient quantity of brass, they threw aside the more operose preparation of stone-heads for these warlike weapons, and armed them with brass. But Iron was not found out till 188 years before the War of Troy, if we may believe the Arundelian Marbles; and this may be the reason that brass weapons are so

[o] Montfauc. Tom. IV. p. 37.
[p] See Camden and Chambers, in voce KERN.
[q] Pausanias, Atticis, Lib. I. p. 37.
[r] Tacitus de M. G.
[s] Amm. Marc. Lib. XXXI.
[t] Montf. Tom. V. p. 195.
[u] Plot, Staffordsh. p. 396. Sibbald, ibid. Dugdale's Warwickshire, p. 1081.

4 E

often

often mentioned in Homer, the ancients working in brafs much more early than in iron, according to Hefiod[w] :

Χαλκω δ᾽ εργαζονῖο, μελας δ᾽ εκ εσκε σιδηρος.

And Lucretius, Lib. V.

Sed prius Æris erat quàm Ferri cognitus ufus.

And when Iron became known, and its fuperiour hardnefs acknowledged, it was fcarce. The Sarmatians (a very extenfive nation) had no Iron in all their country[x]. The Germans had none in Tacitus's time ; and in Britain, Iron was very fcarce, as Cefar fays[y], and found only near the fea coaft, and that in fo fmall a quantity, and fo precious, that their money was fometimes made of that Metal. Thus it appears, that the ufe of Iron came late into the Weftern parts of Europe ; fo that it is no wonder that anciently their weapons were made of Brafs. Even among the Romans, their arms were of Brafs :

—— — *æratum quatiens Tarpeia fecurem.*   Æn. XI. ver. 656.
Æratæque micant peltæ, micat æreus enfis.   Æn. VII. ver. 743.

Their arrows alfo were tipped with Brafs, as appears by fo great a number of them found at one time, as loaded feveral boats[z].

The Spears of the Lufitanians, fays Strabo, were pointed with Brafs ; and to come nearer home, the Cimbrians and Gauls had Brafs for their weapons[a] ; the Danes made their fhort fwords, arrow-points, fpurs, and knives, of Brafs[b] ; and laftly, the Britans had the fame metal, and for the fame ufe, as appears by part of a fword found in Mên in Sennan, by the Brafs found in Trelowarren Barrow, by thofe publifhed by Dr. Plot, Staff. p. 396 ; and by the Spear-heads, Axes for war, and Swords of copper, wrapt up in linen before mentioned, found at St. Michael's Mount in this County, as well as by the feveral places in Britain beforementioned (p. 284.) which have yielded a fruitful harveft of fuch like weapons.

Befides the fcarcenefs of iron, there is another reafon which the Ancients had for making their weapons of Brafs, which is, that iron is not fo eafily worked up, caft, repaired (I mean recaft) and

<hr>

[w] Εργ και Ημερ, ver. 142.
[x] Paufan. ibid. ut fupra. See Montf. Tom. IV. p. 58.
[y] " In maritimis ferrum, et ejus exigua eft " copia," p. 92.
[z] Montfaucon, Tom. IV. p. 58.
[a] Camden.
[b] Worm. Mon. Dan. p. 48, 49.

polifhed ;

polished; nor indeed, after all, of so rich or lasting a colour as Brass. Montfaucon therefore rightly observes (though he assigns not the reason) that after the use of Iron was found out, the Ancients continued the use of Brass in making their weapons, and other things, for which at present we use only Iron. In short, all the fragments of Brass were serviceable, and easily to be re-melted, and cast a-new. And that the Britans put in practice this piece of good husbandry, is plain, from what was discovered at Fifield[c]; a great quantity of these instruments, some entire, some broke, with fragments of the same metal, but to what particular utensils they belonged, uncertain. These, with the quantity of unwrought metal found with them, are undoubted evidences of a furnace being here for casting such implements of war, and that here lived and worked an Artist, whose profession was that of a Founder or Caster of Brass; and I cannot but observe that spear-heads being found amongst the rest of these materials must make us conclude that the workman who made the Heads of Spears pointed, made the edged ones too called Celts, Javelins of all kinds, and Arrows, their use, intent, and substance being so much alike, that he who made the one, could not be ignorant of, or unpractised in making the other. This is therefore an equal proof of the Britans using Brass weapons, and of the instruments found there being weapons of war. There is another circumstance worth notice, in what has been mentioned before (p. 283.) which is, that some Celts, found in a stone-quary in Yorkshire, had Cases exactly fitted to them. Why inclosed in Cases? Why, doubtless, for the same reason as those found at St. Michael's Mount were wrapt up in linen, to preserve the keenness of the edge; and I must own it seems to me, that chizels for working Stone needed not to have been so cautiously sheathed; but rather, that the intention of the owner was, that by this means the edges of so tender a metal might be better kept for execution against the day of battle.

[c] As mentioned before, p. 284.

CHAP.

CHAP. XIV.

Of the Caves of the Ancient Cornish *Britans.*

OF these Caves I shall only describe three, nothing either of instruction, or pleasure, resulting from a multiplicity of measurements, where things are not materially distinct.

Description of Bolleit Fogou.

In the Tenement of Bolleit in the parish of St. Berian, in the Western part of Cornwall, at the end of a little inclosure, is a Cave called the Fogou; its entrance is about four feet high, and wide. The Cave goes straight forward, nearly of the same width as the entrance, seven feet high, and 36 from end to end. About five feet from the entrance, there is on the left hand a hole two feet wide, and one foot six inches high, within which there is a Cave four feet wide, and four feet six inches high; it goes nearly East about 13 feet, then to the South five feet more; the sides and end faced with Stone, and the roof covered with large flat stones. At the end fronting the entrance, there is another square hole, within which there was also a further vault now stopt up with stones, through which you see the light; and therefore I doubt not but here was a passage for light and air, if not a back way of conveying things into and out of these Cells; a property, which other Caves have as well as this. This Cave is not in the village of Bolleit, but about a furlong distant, and indeed, but for the entrance (the ground is so level above, and on each side of it), no one would suspect that there was a Cave below. There is a Cave of the same name in the parish of St. Eval near Padstow.

Bodinar Cave, called the Gyant's Holt.

In the tenement of Bodinar, in the parish of Sancred, somewhat higher than the present village, is a spot of ground amounting to no more than half an acre of land (formerly much larger), full of irregular heaps of stones overgrown with heath and brambles. It is of no regular shape, neither has it any vestiges of Fortification. In the Southern part of this plot, you may with some difficulty enter into a hole, faced on each side with a stone-wall, and covered with flat stones. Great part of the walls as well as covering are fallen into the Cave, which does not run in a straight line, but turns to the left hand at a small distance from the place where I entered, and seems to have branched itself out much farther

than

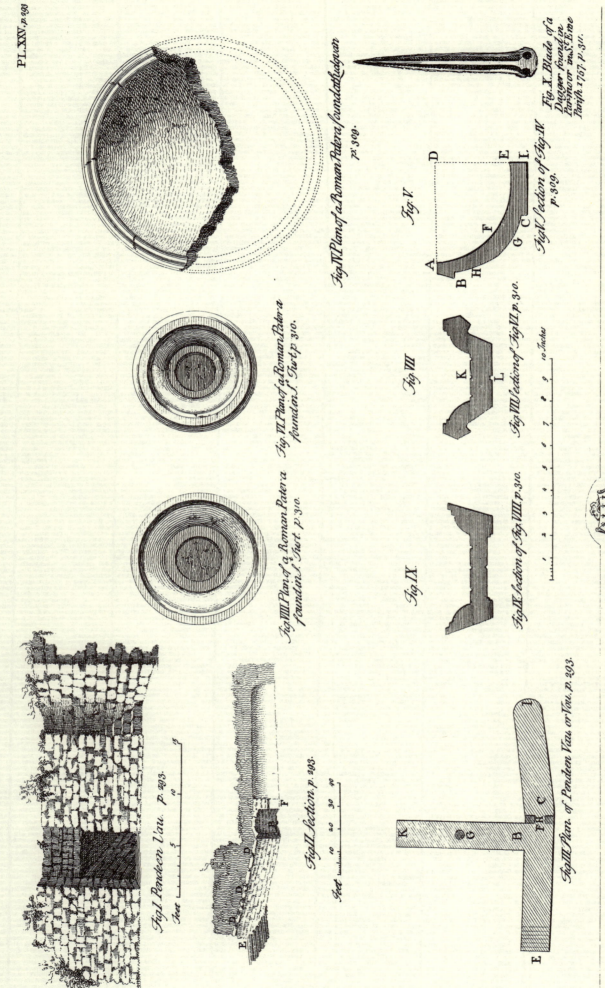

PL.XXV. p.293

Fig.1. Pendeen Vau. p. 293.

Feet

Fig.II. Section. p. 293.

Feet

Fig.IV. Plan of a Roman Patera found at Bufsalwan.
p. 309.

Fig.V.

Fig.VI. Plan of a Roman Patera found at Tweet p. 310.

Fig.VIII. Plan of a Roman Patera found at Tweet p. 310.

Fig.V. Section of Fig.IV.
p. 309.

Fig.VII.

Fig.VI. Section of Fig.VI. p. 310.

Fig.IX.

Fig.IX. Section of Fig.VIII. p.310.

Fig.VIII. Section of Fig.VIII. p.310.

Inches

Fig.X. Blade of a
Dagger found in
Park-moor in St.Erne
Parish. 1757. p. 311.

Fig.III. Plan. of Pendeen Vau. or Vau. p. 293.

To John Borlase of Pendeen in Cornwall Esqr.

This plate, engrav'd at his expence is with great duty

and respect inscrib'd by Wm. Borlase.

than I could then trace it, which did not exceed twenty feet. It is about five feet high, and as much in width, called the Giant's Holt, and has no other use at present than to frighten and appeafe froward children.   As the hedges round are very thick, and near one the other, and the inclofures within them extremely fmall, I imagine thefe ruins were formerly of much greater extent, and have been removed into the hedges; the ftones of which, appearing fizeable, and as if they had been ufed in Mafonry, feem to confirm the conjecture.   Poffibly here might be a large Britifh town (as I have been informed the late Mr. Tonkin thought), and this Cave might be a private way to get into or fally out of it; but the walls are every where crufhed and fallen, and nothing regular to be feen; I will only add, that this Cave, or under-ground paffage, was fo well concealed, that though I had been in it in the year 1738, yet, when I came again to examine it in the year 1752, I was a long while before I could find it.

Of all the artificial Caves I have feen in Cornwall, that called Pendeen Vau[d] (by the Welfh pronounced Fau) is the moft entire, and curious.   It confifts of three Caves or galleries; the entrance is four feet fix inches wide, and as many high; walled on each fide with large Stones, with a rude arch on the top[*].   From the entrance you defcend fix fteps, and advance to the N. N. E. the floor dipping all the way as in the fection[e].   The fides built of Stone draw nearer together, as they rife, the better to receive the flat Stones D D, which form the covering, and are full fix feet high from the ground; this firft cave is 28 feet long from E to F. Before you come to F[f], at right angles, turns off to the left hand the fecond Cave B, its fides the fame diftance, and roof formed in the fame manner as thofe of the firft Cave, but the roof only five feet fix inches high.   In the middle of this fecond Cave, obferving a low place, I caufed the floor to be dug, and found there a round pit, G, three feet diameter, and two feet deep, but nothing in it remarkable; in other parts, I afterwards tried the floor, and found the natural ground, as left when the work was finifhed: at the end K[†], it has a hole in the roof through which a man may climb up into the field.   This is all I found worth noteing in the fecond Cave.   At H, fronting the entrance, there is a fquare hole, two feet wide, and two feet fix inches high, through which you creep into a third Cave C, fix feet wide, and fix feet high, neither fides nor roof faced with ftone, but the whole dug out of the natural ground; the fides formed regularly and ftraight, and the arch of

Margin notes:
Cave in Pendeen Garden.

* Plate XXV. Fig. I.

† Plan ibid. Fig. III.

---

[d] Or Vou. Wallicè Fau. Dav. Dict.   [e] Plate XXV. Fig. II.   [f] Plan ibid. Fig. III.

4 F   the

the roof a semi-circle. The plan also ends in a semi-circle of the same dimensions at I, at the distance of twenty-six feet six inches. I caused the floor of this Cave to be dug in two places, but found neither Cell nor Grave, but the natural ground only, without any appearances of its having been moved. You see nothing of this Cave, either in the field or garden, 'till you come to the mouth of it, as much privacy as possible being consulted.

Norden, in his Survey of Cornwall, p. 40. tells us, " that the " tide flows into this Cave, at high water, very far under the earth," but the sea is in truth more than a quarter of a mile from any part of it.

The common people also thereabout tell many idle stories of like kind, not worth the reader's notice, neglecting the structure, which is really commodious, and well executed.

There are many other Caves still to be seen in these parts, and some have been rifled and destroyed by converting the Stones to other uses, but none have yet come to my notice, different enough from the foregoing to merit a particular description. I shall now proceed therefore to enquire into the use and design of those caves.

SECT. II. Their Use. In most countries the ancients thought themselves under a necessity of providing themselves with such private receptacles; and where their country did not afford them natural ones, they made to themselves, as here in Cornwall, artificial ones. They had more reasons than one, for betaking themselves to these retired places. In cold countries they retired into their Caves to avoid the severity of Winter, says Tacitus of the Germans [g]; and Xenophon, concerning the cold country of the Armenians, tells us that their houses were under ground, the mouth or entrance of them like that of a well, but underneath wide and spreading; there are ways for the cattle to enter, but the men go down by stairs [h]. This they did, doubtless, because, when the ground was frozen, or covered with snow, for any long time, their cattle as well as themselves, might go into the Caves where the ground was not affected not for Winter Retreats, by either, and the air less piercing. But the Winters are not so io severe in Cornwall, as that they can be reasonably supposed to have given occasion for the making those Caves.

nor Instruction, The Druids taught in Caves, and in Caves people were initiated into the mysteries of Mithras; but for both these purposes the Ancients made use generally of natural not artificial Caves.

[g] " Solent et subterraneos specus aperire, " gium hyemi, et receptaculum frugibus." De " eosque multo insuper fimo onerant, suffu- M. G. cap. xvi.
[h] De Exped. Cyri, Lib. IV.

It

It was a very ancient way of Sepulture (if not the firſt man- nor Bury-ing.
ner that obtained) to bury in Caves: thus Abraham buried Sarah
his wife in the field of Mackpelah (Gen. xxi. 19.), in which
chapter the ſacred hiſtorian gives us at length the treaty for pur-
chaſing this Cave, ſhewing how ſollicitous the Patriarch was to
have the property of it ſecured to him for a family burial-place:
this whole paſſage intimates, that it was then the cuſtom of
the greateſt princes to have ſepulchres (ſee ver. 6.) peculiar to their
families, either more ornamented, or more ſpacious, than the burying places of the vulgar, and that theſe ſepulchres were Caves:
but notwithſtanding the Cell which I found in Cave the ſecond (B)
of Pendeen Vau, I do not take that work to have been ſepulchral.
It may be ſuggeſted that there was an urn buried in this place
(for in ſuch Cells we often find them), and might be taken away
by perſons who had ſearched here before. This is poſſible; but
that a work of ſo much labour, and of three apartments, ſhould be
made for burying, and only one Pit, and one ſuppoſed urn, is not
at all probable. If this Cave had been deſigned for the dead,
many Cells would offer with their Urns, or many Graves. For Retreat in Time of War.
there is yet another reaſon why the ancients made theſe under-
ground ſtructures, a reaſon which prevails in all countries; and
that is, to hide and ſecure what they poſſeſſed and valued in
times of war and danger. Plutarch ſays [i], that the Characitanians
in any danger of war deſcended into their Caves, carrying in their
booty with them, free from all apprehenſions when they were
thus concealed: and of the Germans, Tacitus relates the ſame
cuſtom [k]. "In ſuch places as theſe Caves, ſays he, they endea-
"vour to ſoften the rigour of the ſeaſon, and if at any time an
"enemy approaches, he will lay waſte and carry off all that he
"can readily lay his hand on; but theſe ſecret ſubterraneous re-
"treats are either not known, or not thought of in the hurry, or
"eſcape notice for this reaſon, becauſe they muſt take up time
"in ſearching for." In ſeveral parts of Britain, Caves of this
nature muſt occur. "In the Iſland of Skie there are ſeveral
"little ſtone houſes built under ground, called Earth-houſes, which
"ſerve to hide a few people, and their goods in the time of
"war [l]." The ſame author tells us, "that in the iſle of Ila there
"is a large Cave called Vâh-Vearnag, or Man's Cave, which will
"hold 200 men." There is a remarkable one publiſhed and planned
in the Louthiana, (Lib. III. Pl. X. p. 16.) imagined by the author,
with good reaſon, to have been "intended originally for a ſort of

---

[i] In vita Sertorii.   [k] Ibid. ut ſupra.   [l] Martin of the Iſles, p. 154.

"granary

" granary to conceal corn, and, perhaps, other effects of value,
" from mountain-robbers. All this part of Ireland, continues he,
" abounds with such Caves, not only under Mounts, Forts, and
" Caftles ; but under plain fields, fome winding into little hills
" and rifings, like a volute, or ram's horn ; others running zig-
" zag, like a ferpent ; others, again right forward, connecting
" Cell with Cell : the common Irifh think they are fkulking-holes
" of the Danes, after they had loft their fuperiority in that
" ifland [m]." Upon which I cannot but obferve, that they would
have judged more rightly if they had attributed thefe hiding-places
to the natives than to foreigners, the latter having but little reafon
to flatter themfelves with any hopes of concealment from the
former ; but the former, born and bred upon the fpot, a great
deal of reafon to conclude, that many private places might be
retired to, which ftrangers and temporary invaders might never
difcover.

The true intent then of thefe Caves in Cornwall was, as I apprehend, to fecure their provifions, and moveable goods, in times
of danger [n] ; and the reafon that they are many in number, is becaufe Cornwall has been the feat of much war ; and, therefore,
few countries have had more occafion for fuch private ftore-houfes
than the Cornifh. That Cornwall has been the Theatre of much
war, appears by the multitude of entrenchments on the fhores,
particularly in the Weftern parts, where every promontory has its
fortification, every neck of land its ditch and *vallum* reaching
from fea to fea, and not a hill of any eminence without what we
call a caftle. Some ruined towns are alfo ftill to be feen, teftifying
the defolations of war. It was during thefe troublefome times
that I imagine the feveral Caves I have now mentioned, and others
of like kind, were made by the natives, to fecure their effects,
and, perhaps, the perfons of thofe of their family who were not
able to efcape, or keep the field, from the piratical invafions of
the Saxons and Danes. Expofed to the fea on every fide, as
Cornwall is, what is now looked upon as their greateft fecurity
by the inhabitants, proved at that time the perpetual inftrument
of their mifery. As foon as the Saxons came to underftand their
trade of piracy, they found it more for their advantage to attack
the Britifh nation in its extream parts, than at the heart and centre

---

[m] Ireland.

[n] Since the writing thefe papers, an ingenious modern author has given us an account
of the fame means ufed in time of diftrefs in
the Ifland of Minorca. " Their Caves, which
" they call Covas, have with incredible labour
" been fcooped out in the rock ; they are fo

" numerous and fpatious, as to contain all the
" inhabitants of the country in time of danger,
" and were ufed long after the erection of
" houfes, as places of fecurity for women,
" children, and moft valuable moveables upon
" any fudden alarm." Armftrong's Hiftory of
Minorca.

of

of the ifland; confequently Cornwall had its fhare of their vifits, in proportion to its remotenefs from the feat of protection and power, and the opportunities which its numerous creeks gave thefe fons of plunder to land and pillage. The Danes were ftill more troublefome and cruel, as they were more conftant vifitors, and continued many ages to wafte, burn, and deftroy, whatever fell in their way; fo that the poor Cornifh Britans becaufe of thefe rapacious enemies, as " the children of Ifrael becaufe of the " Midianites, made them the Dens which are in the Mountains, " and Caves, and ftrong Holds °.

° Judges vi. 2.

END OF THE THIRD BOOK.

Weftern View of Castle Treryn in the Parish of S.ᵗ Levin Cornwall   pa: 344   J Green Sculp

4 G   OF

O F

ROMAN REMAINS

IN

CORNWALL.

BOOK IV.

CHAP. I.

Of Roman Coins.

SECT. I.

Of Roman
Coins found
near Mines.

WE have already examined the reasons upon which authors have hitherto doubted whether the Romans were ever in Cornwall; and have shewn in general P, that Cornwall could not but be known to, and possessed by, that people: I have there also intimated, that great numbers of Roman Coins, and some Sepulchral Remains, have been found here, which confirm that supposition, and that upon enquiry it will be found probable, that there were Roman Forts, Camps, Towns, and Ways, in this County. I must now treat of these particulars separately, and first of the Roman Coins.

P Book I. Chap. **IX.**

About

About a century and a half fince, Mr. Carew mentions only one Roman Coin, found in this country; I fhall fpeak here of thofe few which I either have in my poffeffion, or have feen, or have been beyond all queftion informed of; and doubtlefs there are many more in the cabinets of the curious, which have not yet reached my knowledge, but may make their appearance hereafter.

There were two principal temptations which led the Romans into thefe Weftern parts; the plenty of Metals, and the excellency of our Harbours. That the Romans worked our ancient Mines, is extremely probable; for, having found out the way to the Caffiterides above 200 years before Julius Cefar, it is not to be fuppofed that they ever quitted that profitable trade, which was worth purfuing even from Italy, and muft needs therefore have induced the Romans to feize upon the Mines, the fources of thefe riches, when they came here, and were fo near the fountain's brink.

Some of the moft ancient Mines I have yet feen in Cornwall are as follows. There are fome in the higher parts of Wendron parifh, which being a wild of barren hills, that never appears to have been cultivated, it is not eafy to imagine what could draw the Romans here to live, and bury their dead, but the plenty of Tin. Yet here they were, for above thefe old heaps of workings there ftands a Stone-Barrow, called Golvadnek-Burrow, in which fome Roman Coins, and other things of the fame nation, were found in the year 1700, and will be particularly defcribed in the next chapter.

There were alfo ancient Mines near Karnbrê in the parifh of Illogan. On the South fide towards the foreft lies a Bal^q of ancient works called Karn-Kei. On the North-Weft, in the parifhes of Illogan and Camborn, many there are of like kind, and fome in the fides of Karn-brê Hill; and here many Roman Coins, at feveral times, in feveral parts, have been found. Some near the village, on the Eaftern end of this hill, I had given me by the Rev. Mr. Collins, Rector of Redruth, *viz.* an ANTONINVS, large fize, of the ancient lead (Coins of which Metal are very rare): Reverfe, a Triumphal Arch. Another much defaced, I think a FAVSTINA. 3. DIVO CONSTANTIO PIO. 4. Unknown. 5. SEVERVS ALEXANDER. 6. Unknown. At the foot of the fame hill, in a circle marked in the Map of Karn-brê W, one Mr. Bevan of Redruth difcovered, in July 1749, three feet under the furface, the quantity of one pint of copper Roman Coins, two only of which came to me; to wit, the fenior Tetricus, and the Roma, in Plate VII. Fig. IV. and V.

---

q A Bal is a clufter of Mines.

p. 117.

p. 117. A few years before, one Mr. Stephens of the same town found about a quart of old Coins of the same nation, in the same place.

That there were very ancient Mines in the parish of St. Just, in Penwith, cannot be doubted, considering that this coast is within sight of the Caffiterides, and resorted to as one of those islands[r] by the ancient traders for Tin[s].

There are also very ancient Mines in St. Agnes Bal, adjoining to which a Gold Valentinian was found that has reached my knowledge; and this is not the only evidence of this Bal being known to the Romans, as we shall see hereafter.

Harrison, in his Description of Britain, p. 65, speaking of the place where Arthur is supposed to have fought his last battle, on the banks of the River Camel, says, " Not long since, and in the " remembrance of man, a brass pot full of Romane coine was found " there, as I have often heard."

Mr. Carew tells us (p. 8, 1st edit.) that he had a Brass Coin of Domitian found in one of the Cornish Tin-works.

These Coins found near, and among, and even in our ancient Mines, far from Towns, Harbours, and Forts, must have been deposited either by the Roman Miners, or by officers appointed by that nation to superintend and guard the Mines which possibly the Romans might have worked more by the Natives than by themselves.

SECT. II. Roman Coins found near Harbours.

Several parcels of Roman Coins have also been found upon the hills, and banks, of our harbours.

" At Tredine (alias Treryn), the South-West point of Cornwall, " there was found (says Leland, Itin. Vol. III. p. 4.) in hominum " memoria, digging for the fox, a brass pot full of Roman Money." I have two silver Coins found near Penrose, which stands on a Lake called the Loe Pool, in the Eastern part of Mount's-Bay. One is of Trajan; Reverse, a female figure sitting: Exergue, PMO. The second is a face helmeted, the metal much eaten. Reverse, two horses, side by side as if drawing a chariot, full speed, no letters visible: both of the small size.

[r] I have not seen any Roman Coins found here; but I have been informed, by Mr. Borlase of Pendeen, that as some workmen were removing a bank in a Field belonging to the adjacent Tenement of Boscadzhil, they found near a hundred Copper Coins, which were all brought to him, and the greatest part of them by him disposed of as a present to William Harris of Hayne in Devonshire, Esq; the few which he retained in his own keeping are now lost, but ANTONINVS PIVS was very plainly to be read on some of them, as he well remembered. December 17, 1737.

[s] " In 1702, in the parish of Tawednack, be- " tween St. Ies and the Land's-end, were found, " under a prodigious rock of Moor-stone, called " the Giant's Rock, a large flat stone, supported " by four pillars of the same, an Urn full of ashes " with a round ball of earth by the side of it, " and in the said ball fourscore silver Coins, of " the latter Emperours, very fair and well pre- " served. I could not have the sight of more " than five of them, of which I got three, of " Valentinian I, Gratian, and Arcadius; the " rest were seized for the Lord of the Soil." Mr. Tonkin's letter to Bishop Gibson, Aug. 4, 1733. MS. B, p. 224.

On

On an arm of the Sea called Hêlford Haven, in the tenement of Condorah, in the spring of the year 1735, were found 24 gallons of the Roman Brass Money, several of which I have now by me, and many more I have seen, all which were of the age of Constantine and his family, and had either the *Heads* of those Emperours, or were of the cities of Rome, or Constantinople.

As these Coins were found in such a quantity, and so remarkably free from the Coins of preceding Emperours, there is no doubt but they were brought hither, and deposited, in the age immediately succeeding Constantine the Great. All I have seen were of the small size (*viz.* somewhat smaller than our common farthings) for which reason they must have been very incommodious for carrying on trade, or serving any other purpose than paying the common soldiers, whose daily portions were to be distributed in such small sums, as made the carriage of little money absolutely necessary, to every separate corps of troops: the place where they were found, by its ancient fortifications (to be treated of in their proper turn), will confirm the supposition that they belonged to soldiers.

On the other side of this Haven, upon one of the Creeks which run up into the parish of Constantine, were found forty Roman Coins. Four of the largest size, by the favour of the Rev. Mr. Collins of St. Erth, I have by me. The first of copper, IMP. CAES. DOMIT. AVG. GERM. COS. XIII. CENS. P. F. A bold impression, *Head* laureated; graceful. Reverse, FORTVNAE AVGVSTI. S. C. Plenty, with her *Cornucopia*.—The second of Trajan: bright brass, IMP. CAES. NERVAE TRAIANO AVG. GER. DA. Reverse, *figura galeata sedens*, s. c. the third defaced.—The fourth, FAVSTINA DIVA, the younger Faustina. Reverse, *figura vestita dextra serpentem, sinistra hastata.*

The other Coins which I have seen found here are of the lower Empire, and need not be particularized: the lowest was one of the Emperour Valens. DN. VAL. N. P. AVG. Reverse, SECV. REIPVBLICAE DAT. which brings this parcel about thirty years later than that which was found on the other side the Harbour. These Coins found on the banks of Helford Haven, belonging to the Soldiery, and deposited so near one time, will lead us to enquire whether there is any remarkable incident in history which may support the conjecture of the Roman soldiers being planted hereabouts in the age assigned to these Coins. I think there is.

The Saxon depredations were come to such a height in the time of Constantine the Great, that he thought it necessary to erect an office unheard of before, the sole business of which should be to

4 H   protect

protect the shores of Britain from those pirates [s] ; it may, therefore, be a probable conjecture, that the soldiers were placed at Condorah (where no Coins but those of him and his sons appear) in the time of Constantius and his brothers for this very purpose, as the others were deposited in the following reigns of Valens and Valentinian, by soldiers on the same errand ; and what seems to confirm this conjecture, is, that at the mouth of this Helford river there is a creek still called Porth Sauffen, or Saxon's Port, thereby shewing itself to have been formerly frequented by the Saxons.

But we are not to imagine that the Romans were not planted round our harbours till the time of Constantine, or that no other occasion drew them there, but to guard against the Saxon Piracies. Whenever they settled near the sea coasts, it was necessary for them to be masters of the adjacent harbour, and must have been one of the chief points that came under their consideration when they were upon determining their settlements, the conveniency of a harbour to a body of troops being of the last importance. To proceed therefore with Coins found on our harbours. In the month of October 1747, about two miles below the sea-port town of Truro, on a branch of Falmouth Harbour, in a ditch near Mopas Passage, in the parish of St. Michael Penkevil, were found twenty pounds weight of Roman Brass Coin. The Rev. Mr. Ley, Rector of Lamoran, who bought them all of the finder, writ me that he never met with more than one of Severus Alexander, and one of Valerian. I have examined about 3000 of this parcel, and find them all from Gallienus, who began his reign, A. D. 259, to Carinus, who with Carus and Numerian reigned about two years (viz. from 282 to 284[t].)

Mopas Coins.

These Coins having but one or two of the Emperours preceding Gallienus, and none below Carinus, appear therefore to have been deposited in the time of the last mentioned Emperour, and consequently before the Count of the Saxon shore was appointed, upon what particular occasion I do not presume to guess ; but that the Romans were very conversant about Truro, we shall have great reason to believe in the sequel of this chapter.

The next harbour, to the East, is that of Fawy[u], near which, in the neighbouring parish of Trewardreth, were many Roman Coins

Trewardreth Coins.

---

[s] The title of this officer was, Count of the Saxon shore; he had the honourable appellation of *Spectabilis* (Camd. Vol. I. p. 96.); he was one of the three commanders in the West under the Master of Foot (then chief over all the military affairs of Britain) by Ammian. Marc. styled *Comes Tractus Maritimi*; had under him seven companies of foot, two troops of horse, the second legion and a cohort.

[t] The several sorts which came into my possession were as follows : of Gallienus twenty-six, Salonina his wife two ; of Postumus nine ; of Victorinus ten ; Tetricus fourteen ; Tetricus jun. eight ; Marius two ; Claudius twenty-two; Quintillus four; Aurelian one ; Tacitus one; Probus two; Carinus one.

[u] In Linc, Taxation *Fawe*.

found,

found, and carefully preserved by the late worthy Philip Rashleigh of Menabilly, Esq; and now in the possession of his sister, Mrs. Hawkins of Pencoit [w].

I have only to observe, that Fawy lying about four miles below the Uxela (Ουεξελα) of Ptolemy, now called Lostwythyel, and at the mouth of the same navigable and (at Fawy) spacious river, this country and the coast was well known to the Romans, for they could not get at Lostwythyel by water without passing by Fawy; and indeed it is very likely that they had a station for their ships here, for on the other side of the river, about a mile below Fawy, there is an ancient village with a fair cove before it, still called Pol-rouan, signifying the Roman Pool, or, as I find it written sometimes, Port-rouan, that is, the Roman Port or Cove.

No Roman Coins found on the banks of the noble Harbour of Hammoze have yet come to my knowledge; but it being evident that the Romans were spread upon all the harbours to the West, we may safely conclude that their Coins have been, or will be found there; the excellency of this harbour being such, as could no more escape their possession, than their notice [x].

Let these parcels of Coins suffice to shew the Roman Settlements on our Harbours. Many scattered Coins found in different places I have received information of, and the late Mr. Tonkin died possessed of great numbers of his own collecting, and collected with a design to give light to the history of our county; but as his notes relating to them have not reached me, and as taking notice of all the Coins of this kind that have been found in particular places will more properly make a part of the Topography than of the present work [y], I shall detain the reader, on this head, no longer than to obviate a few doubts, by making some general observations on the Roman Coins found here.

These Coins are sometimes found single and dispersed, here and there one, or a few only together. In such case we may conclude them accidentally dropt, and lost; but whether by Britans, Traders, or Romans, will be uncertain, unless found near a Roman Way, Fort, or Habitation. *SECT. III. Single ones mostly uncertain.*

Sometimes they are found in heaps, as at Condorah twenty-four gallons, at Mopas twenty pounds weight; in which case, I apprehend, *Why found in large Parcels.*

[w] What have reached my notice of this parcel are the following sorts. Of Valerian one; Gallineus three; Victorinus twenty; Tetricus fifteen; Claudius nine; Aurelian one; Maximinus one; Constantin. Max. one; Constantin, jun. one; Urbs Roma one. Some other Roman Coins, found on the Eastern bank of Fawy harbour near Ethy, have lately come to the Author's knowledge, and will be taken notice of in their proper place.

[x] By the late Lady Carew of East-Anthony (seated on this harbour), I was favoured with the sight of several fair Roman Coins; but where they were found (though probably in that neighbourhood), I could not learn.

[y] The places where Roman Coins (as far as I have been yet informed) have been found, are marked in the Map of Cornwall, Plate I. with an Asterisk, by which it will appear that they have been dispersed in all the extremities of this county.

they

they muſt be conſidered, as part of the Roman Military Cheſt, it being equally abſurd to imagine that either Merchants or Miſers would lay up ſuch a heap of copper farthings (if I may call them ſo) or carry them from place to place to traffick withal, or that any but the Romans could have ſuch a quantity in their poſſeſſion for payment of ſoldiers. This money found in quantities, was purpoſely hidden in the earth, being always found covered (though ſome deeper buried than others); but for what reaſon it was ſo encloſed, learned men have been of different opinions.

Some have thought that the Romans buried their money in order to perpetuate their glory, and the memory of their conqueſts. That they incloſed Coins in the foundation of their Edifices, and in their Sepulchres, is true, and ſhews the zeal they had to continue the remembrance of their nation, and the age they lived in: but the glory of their nation required other proof than the precarious teſtimony which a few Coins buried in the earth might, and might never, give. We ſee the degeneracy as well as the perfection of their Arts in the Medals, and allow the uſe of them in adjuſting facts and dates; but the glory of their nation muſt be eſtimated by the ſpirit and the juſtice of their laws, their virtue, arts, and military exploits, and the ſcience as well as magnificence of their publick ſtructures.

Some think the great number of Roman Coins found in this Iſland were buried by the Romans when they were drawn off by Conſtantine and other Emperours, to fight their battles on the Continent, when the prize of victory was the Imperial Purple; but neither of theſe can have been the occaſion of hiding either of the two parcels found at Condorah or at Mopas, for the latter had no Coins but what what were 20 years before Conſtantine, and the former had thoſe of his ſons, and therefore could not be buried here at his time of leaving Britain, which was the beginning of his reign. Neither could they be hid here in the time of Maximus, for neither of them has any Coins of the three Emperours immediately preceding that Uſurper, which undoubtedly they muſt have had if depoſited in Maximus's reign.

Mr. Speed [y] ſeems to think that when the Romans took their laſt farewell they buried their money, and that this is the reaſon why we find ſo much coin of that nation. This may poſſibly be true of the money coined in the time of the laſt Emperours immediately preceding the Roman deſertion of Britain, but cannot be true of ſuch parcels which have none of the laſt Emperours intermixed; for as ſoon as ever Emperours aſſumed the Purple, one of their firſt

[y] See Chron. p. 187.

Acts

Acts of Empire was to coin Money in their own name, and to have their Effigies impreſſed ; and therefore no parcels can be later, as to their interment, than the laſt Emperour's time whoſe Coin is therein found. But I cannot ſee any reaſon why the Romans ſhould bury their Money when they left this Iſland ᶻ, for their deſertion was not forced, but voluntary ; they did not leave us in a hurry, but upon mature conſideration, that the ſafety of their own country required their aſſiſtance, preferably to that of any other. That the Romans, therefore, called off to fight their own battles, ſhould bury their Money, without which it is in vain for any people, however potent and glorious, to go to war, ſeems to me irreconcileable to common prudence. I ſhould rather think that every ſoldier, marching againſt an Enemy, or reſiding in Garriſon, either carried it about with him, by which means ſome ſcattered Coins, and even purſes of Money were loſt, by the death or careleſneſs of the owner ; or hid it in their tents, from which many a ſoldier goes upon an expedition, or to an engagement, and never returns again : when ſtrictly beſieged, or driven from their Caſtles and Towns, by enemy, or fire, upon ſudden aſſaults, it is likely they hid ſmall ſums as well as they could, or forgot, and neglected them ; but when we find ſeveral gallons together of this ſmall Coin, as at Mopas and Condorah, we cannot ſuppoſe them the property of ſingle perſons (every particular perſon being willing, for his own conveniency, to reduce Braſs into Silver, or Gold), but may juſtly conclude them part of the ſtores of the *Queſtor*, or Paymaſter of the Army, kept by him for the conveniency of the ſoldiers, and buried there where we find them, upon ſome unexpected alarm, when they could not be carried off. In ſhort, we owe the greateſt part of this kind of treaſure, to the confuſion and fatal events of War, the plundering Camps, burning Temples, Streets, and Cities.

Some may wonder, that we have ſo many Braſs Coins, and but few of Silver and Gold ; but when we conſider how much fewer and more portable theſe precious metals are than braſs, we may eaſily conceive that both Officers and Soldiers, on any ſurprize, were well able to carry off a ſum of great value in Silver and Gold, when without great incumbrance they could not diſpoſe of Braſs.

Why more Braſs than Silver or Gold Coins.

Laſtly, It may be obſerved of our Corniſh Roman Coins, that more of the lower Empire are found than of the higher. But we are not ſingular in this reſpect, for the ſame thing may be ſaid of the moſt Eaſtern, and indeed all parts of this kingdom. " Nor is " it ſtrange (ſays Sir Thomas Brown Hydriotaph. 8vo. p. 17.) to

Why moſt of the Lower Empire.

ᶻ As Kennett's Paroch. Antiqu. p. 11. " When at laſt they deſerted the Iſland they " buried their money in hopes of an opportunity " to return, and raiſe it up."

" find

" find Roman Coins of Copper and Silver among us (viz. in Nor-
" folk) of Vespasian, Trajan, Adrian, Antoninus, Commodus, Seve-
" rus, &c. but the greater number of Diocletian, Constantine, Con-
" stans, Valens, with many of Victorinus, Posthumus, Tetricus,
" and the thirty Tyrants in the reign of Gallienus." Whence we
see that not only in Cornwall, but in Norfolk, a country well and
early frequented by the Romans, the Coins from the thirty Tyrants
downwards are most common; one reason of which is, the more
frequent resort of the Roman Emperours and Soldiers to this Island
during the time of the lower Empire, than in the reign of the more
early Cesars; to which a second may be added, that in the latter times
of the Roman Power, the Soldiers were more distressed and hurried,
and more Britans in every part of the Island taken into the Roman
Soldiery, consequently the Roman money was more dispersed, and
common, in the latter, than in the former ages[a], and the greater
the plenty, the more there is to lose.

CHAP. II.

Of Roman Sepulchres, and other Remains found in Cornwall.

WHETHER the Urns found at Chikarn[b] (to the number of
fifty, many of them carefully placed, side by side, round the
principal Urn, which was carved, and lay in the center of the
Barrow) were Roman, and that Barrow a Family-sepulchre, I will
not take upon me to say, all the Urns being broke, or not to be
found; but certain it is, the Romans had such family burial-places[c],
and the same manner, if I do not mistake, of disposing their Urns.
Mr. Hals, in his Observations on Cornwall, mentions a Roman
Coin, found (as he says) in an Urn taken out of a *Tumulus* in this
county. The Coin must be as follows, by the letters he gives us,
IMP. CAES. M. ANT. GORDIANVS AVG.[d] the Reverse, PROVIDENTIA
AVG.

---

[a] Mr. Walker gives us another reason (Dedication of Coins and Medals, p. 7.) " Though
" very many Roman Coins be found here, yet
" not many of great rarity, they being generally
" of those who, setting up for themselves against
" the lawfully esteemed Emperors, were called
" Tyrants, especially such as reigned here, and
" in France; such were Carausius, Alectus,
" &c."

[b] See Book III. chap. x. p. 234.

[c] See Moreton's Northamptonshire, p. 528,
and 530.

[d] Mr. Hals says, it must be read, CESAR MANTIS
GORD. and the Reverse, PROVIDENTIA AVGVRIS;
not sufficiently informed that Gordianus assumed
the title of Marc. Antoninus, as many other
Emperours did, and that PROVIDENTIA AVGVSTI
is a common legend for the Reverses of most
Emperours.

Mr.

Mr. Carte tells us (Vol. I. p. 103. Hift. of England), that " a
" little while before he came into Cornwall" (which was in the year
1714.) " a fine Roman Urn was difcovered, with a cover to it, very
" large, on a hill oppofite to Karnbrê; it had afhes in it, and one
" Coin of the bignefs of a Crown-piece, with an infcription on it
" very legible, fhewing it to be a Medal of Auguftus Cefar."

" Within lefs than ten years before I was there, a quantity of
" Roman Coins (fome of which, by the brightnefs of their colour
" feemed to refemble gold) were dug up in one of the Barrows in
" the Parifh of Illogan. I have feen a great number of the Coins
" found here in fearching Barrows, but none later than Lucilla
" and Fauftina found in thofe Urns and Barrows, but in other
" places down along to Valentinian the third [e]."

By the neatnefs of the Lace-work round this Urn (Pl. XVIII. Sancred
Fig. VI. p. 208.), I fhould judge it to be Roman. Urn.

Near the Manfion-houfe at Kerris, in the Parifh of Paul, fome Kerris Urn.
workmen removing an old hedge in the year 1723, difcovered a
vault about eight feet long, and fix high, the floor paved with ftone,
and the roof arched over with the fame materials; within it was a
plain fair Urn, of the fineft red clay, full of earth (Pl. XVIII.
Fig. III.). By the largenefs and ftrength of this vault, the fmall-
nefs of the Urn, and the earth without any bones; this Urn muft
have contained the afhes of fome confiderable perfon [f]. But farther; by the delicate fhape of this Urn, and the fine clay it is
made of [g], compared with thofe we commonly find in Cornwall
(as Pl. XVIII. Fig. IV. V. VII. IX. ib.), and fome Coins found with
it (but not preferved, becaufe of Brafs); this may be juftly ranked
among the Roman Urns. For that the Romans had Sepulchres
of this vaulted kind, and Urns within them, in the Weftern parts
of Cornwall; the following relation, as I received it from the late
Thomas Tonkin, Efquire, a Gentleman well learned in the Antiquities of this county, in a letter dated March 1, 1727, will
place beyond all fufpicion, or doubt.

" In the year 1700 fome Tinners opening a Barrow of Stones, Golvadnek
" called Goldvadnek Barrow, in the parifh of Wendron, came at Barrow.
" laft to fome large ones difpofed in the nature of a vault, in which
" they found an Urn full of afhes, and a fine chequered brick pave-
" ment, which, together with the Urn, they ignorantly broke to
" pieces; they found alfo, in the fame place, feveral Roman Brafs
" Coins of the fecond fize, and a fmall inftrument of Brafs fet in

---

[e] Ibid. p. 104.
[f] See Chapter of Urn-burial, Book III.
Chap. X.
[g] Earthen Veffels and Fragments of this bright
red colour, being found at Cafter, with Roman

Coins, ruined walls, ridge-tiles, and bricks,
are evidences that the Romans made their Urns
of fuch clay. See Moreton's Northamptonfhire,
p. 510.

" Ivory,

" Ivory, which I fuppofe the Roman Ladies made ufe of about their
" hair.   The Coins were much defaced ; two of them, with the
" inftrument, were brought to me ; on the firft was very legible,
" DIVA FAVSTINA, the *Head* of the elder Fauftina, the Reverfe had
" only remaining s. c. ; the other, as well as I could guefs (for the
" Infcription was quite defaced, and the *Head* much fpoilt), was
" of LVCILLA, wife of the Emperour Verus, and daughter to Marc.
" Antoninus the Philofopher.   Since that, I had another given
" me, found, as well as I remember, at the fame time and place,
" of the Emperour MARC. ANTONINVS PIVS, hufband of the elder
" Fauftina, in which ANTONIN is plain ; Reverfe, a woman ftand-
" ing with the *Hafta* in her left-hand, the reft defaced, all but
" s. c."

In a letter, dated Auguft 4, 1733, of the fame Gentleman
(Mr. Tonkin) to the late Right Rev. Dr. Gibfon then Bifhop of
London, the laft paragraph runs thus : " Since that, I had three
" more (viz. Roman Coins) brought to me, which I believe came
" from the fame place : One of thefe was of Trajan, Æris magni,
" one of Nerva, and one of Marcus Aurelius Antoninus, both
" medii Æris, but all much defaced."   T. T. MS. B. p. 224.

Karn mene-
lezBarrows. About a furlong from Goldvadnek, on the hill called Karn-
menelez, ftand two Barrows of the fame kind ; thefe have alfo been
fearched, to what purpofe I cannot pofitively fay ; but the guide
who carried me to them informed me, that in one of them had
been found fome Coins of Julius Cefar; which relation, though I
do not credit (as to the name of the Emperour, Julius Cefar's
money being very fcarce in Britain), may, neverthelefs, have taken
its rife from Coins found here belonging to fome of the Cefars ;
thefe Barrows being fo near to Golvadnek (which was undoubtedly
Roman) make it the more probable, that thefe two were alfo of
the fame people ; and it is very remarkable that one of thefe is alfo
walled at the edge (five foot high when I faw it), which makes me
fancy that it muft have been erected in a Pyramidal or Conic
Figure ; an improvement upon the rude fhape of a Stone-barrow,
which is more likely to proceed from the Romans than from any
other people.   In this clafs, I think, may be reckoned the curious
Urn found about the year 1600, of which Mr. Carew (p. 157.
1ft Edit.), gives the following account : " Certain hedgers di-
" viding a clofe on the fea-fide hereabouts [h], chanced in their
" digging upon a great cheft of Stone, artificially joined, whofe
" cover they (over-greedy for booty) rudely broke, and therewithal
" a great earthen pot enclofed, which was gilded and graved with
" letters, defaced by this mifadventure, and full of black earth ;

[h] viz. Trewardreth-bay, where Mr. Rafhleigh's Roman Coins were found.

" the

"" the afhes, doubtlefs, as that the Urn, of fome famous perfon-
" age [i]."

At the foot of Karn-brê-hill, in a circle marked W in the Map, Roman Remains found at Karn-brê.
three feet under the furface, were found, together with one pint
of Roman Coins (mentioned before p. 300.), the head of an Animal in Brafs Pl. VII. p. 117. Fig. I.) the hinge of fome cover (Fig. III.), and a concave thin plate full of holes of the fame metal (Fig. II.). They are reprefented in their real fize. The head is hollow, and I take it for the head of a ram, and to have been the pummel of the handle of an ancient fword or dagger: one not very unlike this may be feen in Montf. (Tom. IV. Pl. XXIV. N° 6.). The hinge needs no explanation. Whether the other was the cover of the mouth of the *Simpulum*, or a veffel called the *Periranterium*, ufed to befprinkle the Sacrificers with Holy Water, or part of a mufical inftrument, or whether it might have been part of the lid of the Incenfe Pot, called *Thuribulum* (the perfume or incenfe to afcend through the holes), is uncertain, there being fcarce remains enough to decide what it really was; but there being fo many Roman Coins found with thefe things, and a few years before feveral other Coins of the Roman nation in the very fame place, makes me imagine that this brafs head, as well as the other things found with it, may have been of Roman original, though of the times in which arts began to decline in that Empire, forafmuch as the workmanfhip is not at all elegant in either, and the ROMA found among the Coins is evidently of the lower Empire, as fee Fig. V. ibid.

Fig. IV. Pl. XXV. p. 293. is the plan of a Bowl or *Patera*, and Roman Patera found at Ludgvan.
Fig. V. ibid. is the fection of the fame: it is ten inches in diameter, including the brim, which is half an inch thick, with a fmall drill or *fulcus* in the middle. The hollow is nine inches diameter nearly, See the Section. and the breadth from D to E is three inches, that is, one third of the diameter. The brim thickens as it defcends from A to B, and the line G H on the outfide is not parallel to the line A E F within, but contracts itfelf at H to give *relieve* to the lip B, and contracts itfelf again as judicioufly at G, to give the fame *relieve* to the bafe C, which bafe is five inches diameter, *i. e.* one half of the whole circumference. The depth of the brim from A to B is five eighths of an inch, and the thicknefs of the fhell at the bottom from E to I is exactly the fame; the projections alfo at C and B were without doubt the fame, but the edge at C is much worn by being applied to ufes for which it was never at firft defigned. The curious will eafily difcover that this harmony in the meafure-

---

[i] The Urn attributed by Guenebald to Chyndonax was inclofed in fuch a Stone-cheft, and probably Roman, the Greek Infcription having all the marks of a grofs impofition. See Guenebald, Reveil de Chyndonax.

4 K   ments

ments is what produces the proportion and beauty of this Vaſe; and that this agreement is ſo far from being accidental, that it can be no other than a reſult of the matureſt judgment, and, what is moſt likely, of Roman elegance.   I take it to be a ſacrifical *Patera*, to receive the blood of the Victim, and convey it as an offering to the Altar.   The Vaſe is of fine Granite, turned and poliſhed, and was found in an old hedge belonging to the Glebe of Ludgvan.   A fragment only remains, as repreſented Fig. IV. ibid.

Roman Pa-
teræ found
in St. Juſt.   Fig. VI. (ibid.) is a *Patera* alſo of Stone, turned and ornamented, within which are ſeveral hollow lifts or drills: Fig. VII. is its ſection, and ſhews, by the thickneſs of its ſides, that it was a work leſs elegant than the former.   It is entire, and was that kind of *Patera* from which they poured out the Libation of Wine, either upon the Altar, or between the horns of the Victim; and the center holes by which it was fixed in the turning-preſs, are ſtill viſible at K and L, Fig. VII.   It is made of a particular talky Moor-ſtone, or Granite, called commonly Ludgvan-ſtone, from the pariſh which it is moſt plentifully found in.

Fig. VIII. is another Stone Patera, of the ſame kind of Stone as Fig. VI.   It wants an eighth of two inches high, or thereabouts; the bottom cavity wants about an eighth of three inches diameter; the depth of that cavity wants a little of a quarter of an inch; the outer drill wants about an eighth of three inches and a quarter diameter; the baſe at bottom wants a little of three quarters of an inch; by which meaſurement of this, and the foregoing, it appears that theſe Vaſes were deſigned by a ſcale of inches, which inches were not ſo much as the Engliſh inch, which is a further confirmation of their being Roman; the Roman inch being but $\frac{967}{1000}$ of the Engliſh, of which it falls ſhort therefore one thirtieth part. Theſe *Pateræ* were both found in the Tenement of Leſwyn in St. Juſt, and 100 yards diſtance from them a large Urn; the *Pateræ* were given me in 1753, but the Urn was broke and loſt.

Varro (de Ling. Lat. Lib. IV. cap. xxvi.) ſays, that the *Patera* was a ſort of Cup to drink out of, and even to his age in Feſtival times they carried drink in the *Pateræ*, and uſed them alſo in ſacrifices to pour out Wine and Blood in honour of the God ſacrificed unto [k].

---

[k] " The flat Plates, or Diſcus's, with figures " emboſſed, are not Pateræ; but according to Be-" ger are the *Apophoreta* of Iſidorus, in which " they carried fruits and other viands to the ta-" ble; but, ſays Montfaucon's Supplement, Vol. " II. p. 67. they have figures in Relief, are al-" moſt always of copper, and many ſo ſmall, that " they do not appear to have been at all proper " for Plates. I ſhould rather think that they " fixed them as ornaments upon their Preſſes, " or Cup-boards; this laſt ſort is never found " either in Sacrifices, or on tables of repaſt among " the Ancients." Ibid.

" In

" In a Barrow on Lamburn Downs, in the parifh of Piran Sanz,
" was found an Earthen Pot, containing about two gallons, wherein
" was lodged much afhes, fome bones in fmall pieces, and
" charcoal; and by the fide of the faid pot were alfo found two
" fmall drinking cups of like clay, with feveral handles made of
" the fame matter." Hals's MS. What thefe handles were, I
cannot fay; but certainly, thefe drinking cups were Roman *Pateræ*,
placed (as before in Lefwyn) in the Funeral Monument of the
perfon interred; which I the rather believe, becaufe, in fome of the
Barrows of the fame Downs, which have been examined, have been
found pieces of iron, and brafs money, as the fame Author informs
us. Poffibly the handles here mentioned, might be the *Anfæ* of
the *Simpulum*, or of Lacrymatories, &c. and thefe Monuments,
in which fuch facred utenfils are found, were probably the
Sepulchres of Priefts.

In the year 1757, in a ftream-work in the parifh of St. Ewe,
Cornwall, in Par-moor, was found the blade of a Dagger; it was
of brafs, eight inches and quarter long, and one inch wide; its
handle was loft, otherwife it might have been determined with
more certainty, to what nation it belonged; but probably it was
Roman, for the workmanfhip is neatly executed. See Fig. X.
Pl. XXV. p. 293[1].

CHAP. III.

Of Roman Camps and Fortifications in Cornwall.

AS we have already tracked the Romans by their Coins and
Sepulchres, there can be no doubt of their having Camps and
Fortifications, neceffary for the fecurity of their forces in the field,
and in garrifon; it being one of the firft maxims among them, as
early as Agricola (as Tacitus fays) to fortify themfelves wherever
they advanced; whereas, before Agricola's time, the Romans
retiring to their Winter quarters (where only they had regular
ftations fortified) loft their ground in Winter, which they had
won in Summer. But fo many ages have paffed fince the Roman
times, and fuch great alterations by improvements and devaftations
(equal enemies to antiquity) have enfued, that entirely perfect Camps
and Forts can fcarce be hoped for. Let us therefore be content
with what remains, and fome rational conjectures relating to Roman

---

[1] Depofited in the Oxford Mufeum, in the year 1764.

Fortifi-

Fortifications, rather than always abfolutely pronounce them fo to be.

Little Di-
nas. The firft place which I think a Roman Fortification is that at Condurrah, in the parifh of St. Anthony (Meneâg) where the parcel of Coins of Conftantine and his Sons (p. 301.) were found. This hill is wafhed on each fide by the fea; and about a quarter of a mile from the ditch in which the Coins were lodged, there runs out a little tongue of land, called Dinas, and (to diftinguifh it from a much larger fortification, on the other fide the bay, called Pendinas[l]) this is called the little Dinas, in Cornifh, Dinas vean. This little Dinas has feveral modern fortifications on its Eaftern point (erected in the great Rebellion) but nearer to Condurrah it has an old Vallum ftretching from fea to fea, which is the remainder of a very ancient fortification, and in all likelihood Roman; for it is rightly obferved by Mr. Horfley[m], " the Romans were careful to have their ftations" (by which he means I fuppofe their Camps and Forts) " placed " near a river; and there is no fituation which they feem to be fo " fond of, as a *Lingula* (little tongue of land) near the confluence " of a larger, and fmaller river." Here I cannot but obferve, that this ftation at Condurrah has every one of thefe properties; on the right hand, as you front the Eaft, comes down the river Durrah, and with the fea makes a pretty pool, or cove, before St. Anthony's Church, in which fmall veffels may lye with great fafety; on the left hand comes down Hêl river, at this place near a mile wide, and what would be a very good harbour, but that it is within four miles of Falmouth, reckoned among the beft harbours in England. From the front of the hill runs out the *Lingula* of Little Dinas, about 500 yards long, and 200 wide at a *medium*.

Pendinas. As this place, therefore, has all the marks which its natural fhape, old *Vallum*, and Coins found, can give of its being a Roman Fort; fo, from the fituation of Pendinas, lying oppofite to it, of the fame name, and rather more advantageoufly fhaped for defence, and guard of a noble Harbour (called by Ptolemy, *Cenionis Oftium*); I fhould guefs it could never efcape the notice and ufe of the Romans : but as the hill is fortified in the modern manner, though not without fome veftiges of antiquity not far from the prefent works, and as no Coins, to my knowledge, have been found here, I leave this to be determined by future difcoveries.

Binnomay.

Walf-
borow. There are two fquare forts near Stratton, one at Binnomay[n], where fome old Brafs Coins were lately found; the other at Wallfborow. This latter is vulgarly, and, as I think, erroneoufly,

---

[l] i. e. The principal fortification, or, Fort on the Head-land.

[m] Brit. Rom. p. 393.

[n] In Camden's Map, laft Edit. Binaway.

called

called Whalesborow; but more properly, Wallsborow[n]; for on the higheft part of the Tenement, I perceived a very large Barrow, and as this place lies not far from the way called the Caufeway, leading from Stratton to Camelford, raifed above the common level high like a wall[o] (as is plain from the remains of it Weft of Stratton); I fufpect that this place was either called the Barrow on, or near the wall (i. e. Wall's Borow) or from the walled Fort there, now vifible above the houfe; *Gual* fignifying a Fort[p], and for one of thefe reafons, called by the Saxons Walls-borow. Both thefe fquare Forts lying fo near Stratton (and in all probability near a Roman way which paffed thefe parts) may not improbably have been little Roman Forts, fuch as they had by the fides of their ways in other parts of the kingdom[q].

Lancefton Caftle is a very ancient fortification, and in the plan of it there is a fquarenefs, and one round tower remaining on the angle (now called the Witches tower) which favour much of the Roman fhape. Some Roman Coins have been likewife found here, which will be taken notice of hereafter. Lancefton.

There is an angular Fort on the Barton of Wolvedon, alias Golden, in the parifh of Probus, which has a wide deep ditch, the outer edge (or counterfcarp) of which was faced upwards with Mafonry of thin ftones in cement, which had round Turrets, or Buttreffes (fuch as neither Saxons, Danes, or Britans, had as far as I can ever find) of the fame Mafonry, interfperfed with the ftraight lines of the ditch. This is very fingular in our country, where moft of our ancient fortifications are of a circular plan, without any projections, angular or circular, from the *Mafter-Line.* I can judge this, therefore, neither to be Britifh, Saxon, or Danifh, as being like no other works of thefe people; and from the artful fence of this ditch, as well as from the *Polygon,* which the whole forms, I guefs it to be a Roman Work. There is a large avenue, or a way from the North, rifing from an adjoining valley. Wolvedon.

There is a vaft intrenchment in the parifh of St. Agnes, which (from Porthchapel-Coom, to Breanik-Coom), extends near two miles in length. In the Weft, where the fides of Porthchapel-Coom are fteep and eafily defenfible, the ditch is fhallow, and the *Vallum* low; but as the Coom wears out into a plain, it grows proportionably larger, and about 200 yards above a cott called Gun-vrê, appears of its full fize, where the ditch I found to be 17 feet fix inches wide, and from the bottom of the ditch the perpendicular of the *Vallum* is at leaft 20 feet; from this place I traced, and St. Agnes Kledh.

[n] In Domefday, WALESBRAU.
[o] *Gual* fignifying any Ridge, or Vallum. See Plot's Oxfordfhire, p. 323.
[p] As Gual-hen, the old Fort. Camden, p. 164.

[q] At the Roman Wall in the North of England; thefe fquare Forts are from 100 t 150 paces for fide of the fquare. Horfley, p. 113.

dialled

dialled it more than a mile. The Work, throughout I judge to have been executed uniformly, according to the meafurement above expreffed, but in fome parts it is now much altered; the ditch has been widened in fome places, and levelled in others, to make gardens, and the *Vallum* has been carried off (where it was of clay) to make bricks, and levelled to make room for houfes in other places; it is alfo much defaced by Tin works, but is ftill a great work. From the Weftermoft point it runs in a ftraight line due Eaft, then makes another line fomewhat to the North of the Eaft to a village called Bolfter, for a quarter of a mile; about 500 yards beyond which, it comes into Pol-brêan Common, running Eaft by North, down to the Vicarage; about 100 yards below which it appears again, keeping very judicioufly the brow of the hill, and bearing N. E. by N. till it reaches the Coom, or bottom, below the Church-town called Breanik-Coom, which defcends to the fea. A work, furely, of equal fkill and labour, intended for the defence of St. Agnes Beacon, and its rich Bal, inclofing fome thoufands of acres by making a line of entrenchment from Portchapel-Coom, which lies to the Weft, and Breanick-Coom, which runs down to the fea on the Eaft of this Promontory. Within this entrenchment the late Mr. Tonkin (whofe paternal feat makes a part of the land inclofed) fays (in a letter to the late Learned Brown Willis, Efq;), that his father's fervant, in the year 1684, plowing, turned up a gold Coin of Valentinian[r], and thinks verily that this was a Roman work; but this fingle Coin is the only reafon which he gives, as far as I am at prefent informed; however, there are much better reafons to be drawn from the work itfelf; the grandeur of the undertaking, the judgement and conduct of the defign, the ftraightnefs of the lines, the uniformity of the work in all its parts, the *Vallum*, where not injured, being of one height, the ditch of one breadth, the judicious diminution of the labour, in proportion as the Cooms grow deep, and able of themfelves to form fome defence; all thefe are circum- ftances intimating too much art, and military fcience, for either Britans, Saxons, or Danes; add to this, that to the weft of the Beacon, on the top of the inclofed hill, is ftill to be feen, " the " remains of a fmall fquare fortification; adjacent to which are " three Sepulchral-Barrows;" which, if one may judge by the labour of erecting them on fuch an eminence, muft have been the monuments of fome great perfons. It is called the Kledh, which in Cornifh fignifies the Trench, or Fofs, and by the vulgar " faid " to be the work of a giant called Bolfter[s]."

[r] The Coin had this legened, DN. VALENTI- NIANVS. P. P. AVG. Reverfe, RESTITVTOR REI- PVBLICAE ANT. A. " It weighed feventeen " fhillings value in Gold." Letter to Bifhop Gibfon.

[s] T. T's letter to Brown Willis, Efq;

But

But the Romans did not always fortify in the square or rectilineal manner, but sometimes in the circular; for in encamping, the first point is to chuse proper ground, that is, proportionable to, and convenient for, the quantity of forces, and easiest to be made defensible; and the second great maxim, to suit the Lines to the natural site of the ground.

When they were to sit down on a plain and level ground, there is no doubt but they chose the square figure, as containing their troops in better order, easier to be inspected, and more ready for action, than any other figure; but when they were obliged to take up with a triangular or hexagonal hill, or rising, as it would be ridiculous to imagine them labouring contrary to the nature of the ground to throw the fences of their camp or garrison into a square, so I conclude, that whenever they met with the round top of a hill conveniently situated with regard to the enemy, and to their own forces, they fortified this round hill with circular Lines. Nay, the Romans made round hills probably, and fortified them with a Keep on the top; for the famous Mount of Marlborough, in the gardens of the late Duke of Somerset, was shaped out of the Keep of the castle, a Roman work, and in digging, brass Roman Coins were there found[t]; and an eminent *Tumulus*, on which the Keep, or Watch-tower of the Castle of Brinklo, in Warwickshire, did stand, is made no improbable argument for that to be a Roman structure[u]. The great fortification in Somersetshire, called Camalet *(alias* Arthur's Castle) must be a work of the Romans, as appears by the Roman Coins found there, and as is agreed by Camden, p. 77. and Dr. Gale's Comm. in Antonin. p. 93. and yet the work is round, four trenches and three earthen walls encompassing it. Maiden Castle near Dorchester is round, with a triple *vallum*, yet allowed Roman, being near so many other works of the same people, viz. their amphitheatre, ways, &c. So that, although the general shape of Roman intrenchments must be allowed to be square, yet this must not be understood (as Moreton well observes, Northamptonsh. p. 522. &c.) without its exceptions[w]; for the position of the enemy, and the shape of the ground, are two points which in the art of war will always carry a superiour weight, and controul the other subordinate rules, according as the safety of the whole body and the advancement of the service shall require.

[t] Camd. Annot. p. 129.
[u] Ibid. p. 612.
[w] Vegetius allows of Camps of different figure, sometimes quadrangular, and sometimes triangular, sometimes half round.

From

From thefe general obfervations on the Roman Camps, give me leave to obferve, that fome of our round intrenchments on the tops of round hills in Cornwall may be Roman works, if either ways pafs near or through them, or Coins be found in them.

But to pafs from conjectures to the ftrongeft evidence. In the year 1756, a Farmer at Boffens, in the Parifh of St. Erth, driving his oxen from the field, perceived the foot of one of them to fink a little deeper than ordinary into the Earth at A, Pl. XXVIII. Fig. VIII. Curiofity, and hopes of treafure, led him to fearch the place, where was foon difcovered a perpendicular pit, circular, of two feet and half diameter. Digging to the depth of 18 feet, there was found a Roman *Patera* (Fig. I. and II. ibid); about 6 feet deeper the Jug, Fig. III.; near by among the rubbifh the Stone, Fig. IV.; then a fmall mill-ftone about 18 inches diameter. Digging further ftill they found another *Patera* with two handles, in other particulars much of the fhape and fize as Fig. II. Intermixed were found fragments of horns, bones of feveral fizes, half-burnt fticks, and many pieces of leather, fhreds of worn-out fhoes. Having funk to the depth of 36 feet, they found the bottom of the pit concave, like that of a difh or bowl: there was a fenfible moifture and wet clay in all parts of the pit, in each fide there were holes at due diftances capable of admitting a human foot, fo that perfons might defcend and afcend: there is no doubt but this work muft have been intended for a well, but fo deep a pit of fuch narrow dimenfions could not have been funk through a ftony ground without great difficulty, and with tools very different from thofe now in ufe.

On the 22d of May, 1758, I went to view this place, together with Henry Davies, Efquire (Proprietor of the Land, who firft favoured me with notice of this difcovery); and on the higher parts of the Tenement, in a field called the Rounds, I perceived the remains of a Fort; the length from N. to S. is nearly (for it was covered with bufhes and briers) 152 feet; the breadth from E. to W. 136 feet. The fofs on the outfide is ftill difcoverable; the walls difmantled, in fuch a manner, that at firft fight it appears to be oval, but, on farther infpection, enough remains to fhew tha it was rectilinear with the angles rounded off, a manner of fortifying very common among the Romans, as may be feen by their ftations, *ad lineam valli.* Horfeley, p. 113.; and many other places.

At the north corner B, there was an additional building, which projected outwards beyond the Rampart; it was about 30 feet long, not quite fo wide. At the fouth angle alfo at D there was a building of the like kind; the Ancients called thofe buildings
Proceftria.

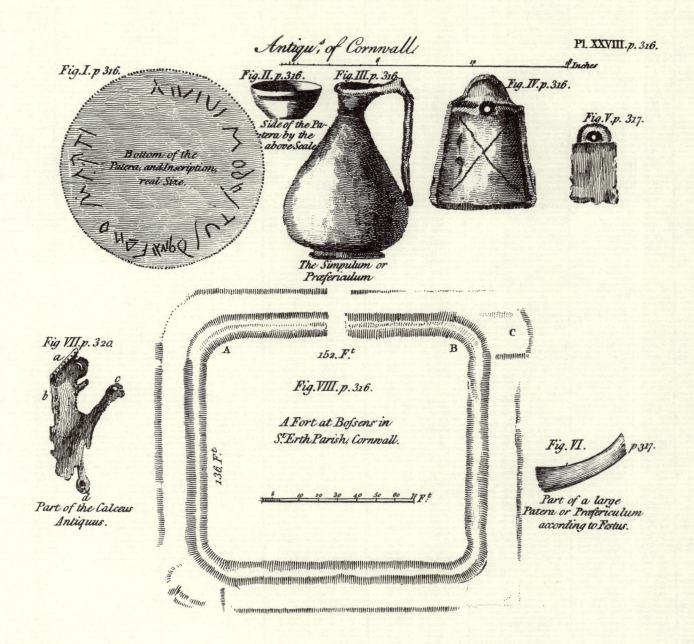

Antiqu.ʸ of Cornwall

Pl. XXVIII. p. 316.

Fig. I. p 316.

Fig. II. p. 316.

Fig. III. p. 316.

Fig. IV. p. 316.

Fig. V. p. 317.

Bottom of the Patera, and Inscription, real Size.

Side of the Patera by the above Scale.

The Simpulum or Præfericulum

Fig VII. p. 320

a
b
c
d

Part of the Calceus Antiquus.

A
B
C

152. Fᵗ

136. Fᵗ

Fig. VIII. p. 316.

A Fort at Bossens in Sᵗ Erth Parish, Cornwall.

5 10 20 30 40 50 60 70 Fᵗ

Fig. VI. p 317.

Part of a large Patera or Præfericulum according to Festus.

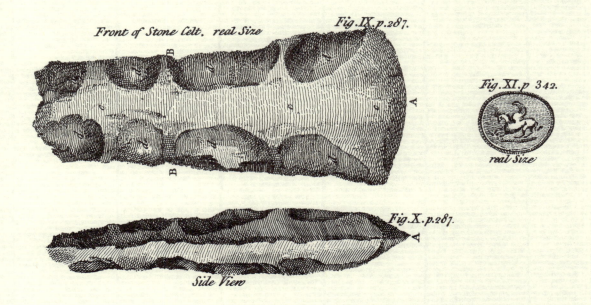

Front of Stone Celt. real Size.

Fig. IX. p. 287.

B
B
A

Fig. XI. p 342.

real Size

Fig. X. p. 287.

A

Side View

W. B. delin.

B. Green sc.

Proceſtria[x]. Examining the rubbiſh, beſides what is mentioned above, I found the ſtone Fig. V. and part of a large Vaſe of a curious ſort of grey granite (Fig. VI. ibid.) formed by turning, well poliſhed, but ſomewhat diſcoloured. I found alſo ſome fragments of leather, all deſcribed in the ſequel.

In Pl. XXVIII. p. 316. Fig. I. and II. are two views of the *Patera*, made of tin, of the 20th of an inch thick, four inches and half wide at the brim, but at the bottom, which was flat, two inches and half. The bottom of the inſide is repreſented, Fig. I. ib. of its real ſize. Fig. II. is the ſide of the ſame *Patera*, by the ſcale annexed. The Roman *Patera* was not always of the ſame dimenſions ; when it was of the larger ſize, its uſe is well known to have been for receiving the blood of the victim, or to be carried before the prieſts, containing other offerings ; but when of ſmaller dimenſions (as this is) either to offer Libations of water, oil, or wine (whence on medals the hand is ſo often ſtretched out holding the *Patera* over the Altar), or to participate the rites of Sacrifice by drinking. This *Patera* has no handle, but that which has been mentioned above, as found near it (and has ſince been unfortunately loſt) had, and thoſe found in England generally have. Mr. Addiſon, in his Travels [y], obſerves that it is not ſo common to find *Pateræ* with handles to them in foreign countries; but that a *Patera* without a handle would be as ſingular here in England, as one with it at Rome ; and Mr. Horſley, p. 191. ſays, that all *Pateræ*, which he had ſeen upon any altars in Britain had handles, though of different ſizes and ſhapes ; although the *Pateræ* found in Cornwall, which I have ſeen, never had any. It is more rare ſtill to find theſe ſeemingly trifling cups and diſhes inſcribed to a particular Deity ; but moſt uncommon to ſee them diſtinguiſhed by names of the Donor, and his Father, as well as the name of the Deity, to which it is dedicated. This *Patera* found at Boſſens is a ſingular inſtance of all theſe particularities, having the inſcription engraved on its bottom, as Fig. I. ; which, till better information, I read thus, LIVIVS MODESTVS DRIVLI (or DꝶIVLI) FILIVS DEO MARTI. The two firſt words are exceedingly plain, tho' a mixture of Greek and Roman characters. Livius is too well known to be Roman, to need any comment ; it is as well known, that the Virtues oftentimes gave name to perſons, and among the reſt Modeſty. Sometimes the perſon who had his cognomen from this virtue was called Verecundus, as DIIS MANIBVS VERECVNDI in a Roman Monument

---

[x] Οικηϱαία προ παρεμϐολης, Proceſtria dicitur. "Proceſtria ædificia dixit eſſe extra portam." ib. Horſley, p. 101. from an old Gloſſary. "Ælius [y] Addiſon's Works, p. 115.

at Skirway in Scotland [z]; here it is Modeſtus, of which we have alſo ſeveral inſtances [a].

Before I proceed farther, I would obſerve that the letters in general of this Inſcription are badly ſhaped, but in the third word particularly the letters are more perplexed than in the reſt. The firſt letter is the Grecian ſmall *Delta*; the ſecond I take to be the little *Ro* reverſed, *i. e.* with the long ſtroke on the right hand inſtead of its being, as uſual, on the left; the other letters are more truly delineated, though ſomewhat entangled, ſo that I take this word to be Driuli, a name which I do not recollect to have ſeen before; but if the ſecond letter, inſtead of being a *Ro*, ſhall appear to the learned to be more likely intended for the Greek dipthong ȣ, or *ou*, this word will then be *Douiuli* or *Duilii*, a name very honourable in the Roman genealogies. *F* ſtands for *Filius*, and the two laſt words are beyond doubt *Deo Marti*. Though the language here is Latin, yet the characters are for the moſt part proper to the Grecian alphabet, as the λ, δ, Δ, and η (which in both places where it occurs is uſed for the Latin *e*) and the ꟼ; the R in *Marti* is ſingular, approaching to the Latin P (which with the Greeks is the capital *Ro*); but inſtead of the ſemi-circular part joined to the upright, it has, through the incorrectneſs of the engraver, a demi-hexagon like a canopy ſpread over the upright line. The *o* is oval and angular, not round as with the Latins, and the A has no tranſverſe ſtroke; the other letters are common to the Romans as well as Greeks, but ſhould I think be aſcribed to the latter, becauſe the reſt are purely Grecian property.

That this Latin inſcription here in Britain ſhould have ſo many Greek characters in it is remarkable, and the reaſon not eaſily aſſigned. It is well known that the Druids uſed the Greek letters, though they writ not in the Greek language [b]. It is alſo certain, that among the Roman Legions there were many of the Greek nation. But whether the perſon, who conſecrated this *Patera* to Mars might have intruſted the engraving to one of the Druid Sect, or whether the Engraver was one of the auxiliary cohorts originally of Greece (as the Thracian and Dalmatian horſe were), it is in vain to enquire; but neither of theſe conjectures is improbable. There are, I think, but two inſcriptions in the Greek language as yet found in Great Britain [c]; but in the Latin language this is the

[z] Horſley's Brit. Rom. p. 199. and the ſame name is to be traced in another Monument, ib. Pl. 64 Nº X.

[a] Publius Ælius Modeſtus Præfectus, Pl. 16. ibid. Nº XLI. Caius Murrius Modeſtus Miles, ibid. Pl. 71. Nº II. And Sir George Wheler,

in his Travels, has a medal, Nº LXXXII. ſtruck at Trallis (anciently a conſiderable city on the River Alcander in Aſia) under the Conſulſhip of Modeſtus, p. 279.

[b] See before, Book II. Chap. X. p. 90.
[c] See Horſley's Collect. in Brit. Rom.

only

only one yet discovered in this island with so many Greek characters in it; and I believe there are but few instances of it in other countries [d]. I will only add, that as this inscription has neither ligature, nor point, nor the A any transverse stroke, which are so many evidences of its genuine antiquity, so its brevity and simplicity (including nothing but the names of the Donor, his Father, and the God to whom the *Patera* was dedicated) shew it to be truly Roman.

Fig. III. is a Jug or Jar (of Tin also) containing 4 quarts, 1 pint, and $\frac{1}{5}$ of a quartern, wine measure, its weight 7 pounds, 9 ounces and $\frac{1}{2}$. It is the Præfericulum of Antiquaries, *i. e.* a vessel used to carry the holy water, or other sacred liquor, to the Altar; it seems to have had that name from its being carried in procession before the Priests, standing in a kind of shallow bason, much after the same manner as the bason and ewer were used among our English Ancestors [e].

Fig. IV. and V. are of stone, the first and largest weighs 14 pounds 10 ounces averdupoise, and 11 penny weights. The second and smaller stone, Fig. V. weighs 4 pounds 1 ounce, and 7 penny weights. By the holes these stones have near the top, they were probably designed as weights whereby provisions were bought for, and afterwards shared out among, the Garrison. Whether these weights were originally of the Roman Standard (for they are not so now), and varied by time, or successive drought and moisture, or whether they might be the weights commonly used, in buying and selling, by the Natives of these parts, I shall not determine; but proceed to observe, that the Ancients in all countries oftentimes made their weights of stone, and of different shapes; some round,

[d] One instance was mentioned to me, as follows, in a letter from the late learned and worthy Robert Hoblyn, Esquire, of Nanswhydn in Cornwall, dated June 29, 1751. "I have some "recollection of an Inscription in memory of "one Gordianus a Gaul, and his whole family, "in the Roma Subterranea, in which, though "the Language is Latin, the Letters are a mixture of Greek and Runic; I believe Mabillon "takes some notice of it in his Iter Italicum. "Bishop Fleetwood says, in the Preface to "his Sylloge, speaking of the Orthograhy of "Inscriptions. — 'Utebantur enim N. Græco "sicut & aliis Græcorum literis promiscuè cum "Latinis, ut videre est, p. 328.'

"The Inscription is as follows:

Θ K

ΑΓΕ CΑΙορυεινος ετ

ΑΤΕΛΙΑC ετ ΠΑΔΙΟ

ΓενεC. ΚΟΜ ΠΑΡΑΟΥ

Η ΡΟVΛΤ CΙΒΙ ΕΤ CΟΥΕΙC

"I suspect this Inscription (which is at Rome) "is not fairly copied, it is very probable all the "Letters are Capitals, nor is the meaning of "some of the words to be decyphered. It is "quoted from Gruter (I believe), where possibly "others of the same kind are to be found." Dr. Jer. Milles, now Dean of Exeter, July 27, 1758, to the Author. These instances are from foreign countries, and more may occur, but in Britain none, as I believe, have yet appeared. See Gruter and Reinesius.

[e] Festus calls the Bason, or Charger, Præfericulum, and without any impropriety (as it seems to me); for as much as the broad Patera, or Bason, which was carried before the Priests in both hands of the attendant, might as often contain cakes, mola salsa, the Simpulum & Pateræ, as the Jar of wine, oil, and water; but in this point Festus is supposed by some to have been mistaken. Montf. de Pateris. Horsley, p. 191. 281.

as

as that mentioned in Kemp's Collection [f]; some rectangular, as Fig. V.; and some conical, as Fig. IV.; sometimes they were of marble, as those exhibited by Gruter, p. 221, 222 [g]; and the *Pondus antiquum marmoreum* of Kemp, ibid. These here described are both of the dove-coloured Cornish granite, discoloured somewhat by fire, or acrimonious moisture. But the ancients seem not to have made their weights of stone by choice, but for want of more proper materials; they could not be ignorant that lead, brass, or iron, was more compact, ponderous, and durable, and that stone was liable to become heavier, by assuming into its substance the moisture and weight of adjacent bodies, as also to be corroded, and become more porous, by any penetrating acid, or by heat, or drought, and thereby lose somewhat of its weight. These inconveniences of stone weights, the Ancients, I say, could not but foresee; they are alterations, which the materials could hardly escape; and, therefore, such materials they would never have made use of, but for want of better.

Fig. VI. I take to be part of that Vase called by Festus the *Præfericulum*; it was sometimes made of brass, or more precious metal, but is here of Stone [h], and by its gradually increasing thickness towards the bottom appears to have been of like design with that exhibited before, Pl. XXV. Fig. V. p. 293.

The small Mill-stone, by the smoothness of one side, shewed that it had been much used, and was such as without any material difference is still used in the Islands of Scilly, and elsewhere, for hand-mills to grind corn in times of siege and scarcity, and must be absolutely necessary in all garrisons.

The bones and horns belonged to animals either sacrificed or killed for the Fort; the ashes and half-burnt sticks are the remains of sacrifical or culinary fires: the fragments of leather are patched and coarsely sewn together for the most part; but some have no such evidences of inferiour use, and one piece which I found more entire may contribute perhaps to shew us the shape of the Roman Calceus of those times, and may be seen Fig. VII. by the same scale as the other figures. Some bits of leather were also pierced with circular holes; but whether parts of the cothurnus, calceus, or any border for the habit, armour, or vehicle of the officers, enough does not remain to decide.

This subject cannot be dismissed without observing, that every separate article here produced, is a fresh proof, establishing the

[f] Mon. Kempiana, p. 152.
[g] Kemp, ibid.
[h] " Præfericulum, inquit Festus, vas æneum " sine ansa appellatum, patens summum ut " pelvis quo ad sacrificia utebantur in Sacrario." Montf. Tom. II. p. 142.

opinion

opinion all along efpoufed in thefe Antiquities, I mean that the Romans came into Cornwall, conquered it even to the very extreme parts, and had all the appendages of victory, as Ways, Forts, Garrifons, and refided here as Governours, in the fame manner as they did in the other parts of Britain. For firft, this Fort is of that rectilinear figure, with the angles rounded off, which the Romans generally preferred to any others[k]. It is fmall in extent, as they generally made thofe forts, which they called Caftra Æftiva, which were of no certain determinate fize; but fuch only as might anfwer the neceffity of the fervice. It is fituated in a direct line[l], leading from Truro to Mount's bay, and the Land's end. It is alfo in the ftraighteft line from Falmouth Harbour (the Cenionis Oftium of Ptolemy), and there is at prefent a great ftraight road, which paffes within a bow-fhot South of this Fort, as the Roman ways generally did from their Caftra Æftiva[m]. But to obviate all contradiction here is found a Latin Infcription in undoubted Roman ftyle. The letters are Greek, and the Infcription is the firft and only one difcovered yet in Cornwall of fuch high antiquity, and will fatisfy the Learned, that the Romans had penetrated into the Wefternmoft parts of Cornwall, before the Empire became Chriftian; the Sacrifical veffels, the Pateræ, and Præfericulum, are of Tin, the natural product of Cornwall; the Vafe, the Weights, the Mill-ftone are alfo of Cornifh Granite; and by the Walls, the Religious Utenfils, Weights, quantity of Shoes, Bones, Horns, Vafes, and afhes; this Fort appears to have been that of a fixed Garrifon, not a temporary occafional Fortification[n].

CHAP. IV.

Of the Roman Geography of Cornwall, and the ancient and prefent Name and Limits.

THE Roman Geography of this County is fo imperfect, that little information can be drawn from thence, which can be depended upon.

Ptolemy mentions four towns; and all the light he feems capable of affording us, muft be drawn from their names, and the order in which he places them. His words are as follows:

[k] See Horfley's plan of the Roman forts " ad " lineam valli paffim."

[l] See the Map belonging to the Nat. Hift. of Cornwall.

[m] Such Forts were generally not contiguous to, but within call of, their great roads. Horfley,

p. 123. 151..154, &c.

[n] That the curious may the more eafily fatisfy their doubts, the Patera, one of the Weights, and the Pæfericulum, with the Vafe, are depofited in the Mufeum Afhmoleanum, at Oxford.

4 N

" Μεθ'

" Μεθ' ἐς Δ8ρολριγας, δυσμικωΊαΊοι Δ8μνονιοι, εν οἱς ϖολεις, Ουολιϐα,
" Ουξελα, Ταμαρη, Ισκα," *viz.* " After the Dourotriges (the people
" of Dorfetfhire), come the moft Weftern inhabitants of Britain,
" called Dunmonii [o], among whom we find thefe towns, Voliba,
" Uxela, Tamare, Ifka."   Voliba muft be a town in the moft
Weftern parts; for as Ptolemy ends with Ifca (undoubtedly Exeter,
as will be proved by and by) in the Eaftern parts of the Dunmonii,
he muft in all reafon be allowed to have begun in the Weft.   By
the name, Voliba fhould ftand fomewhere on the river Fal or Val;
and as the ancients for the greater fecurity from pirates and invafions,
chofe to build their cities (which they always placed, if poffible,
on navigable rivers) at a diftance from, rather than near the mouth
of the harbours, I think Granpont is moft likely to be the Voliba
of the ancients.   Ουξελα (or Vexela) comes next; farther to the
Eaft, certainly than the former, and by Camden thought to be
Leftwithel, but by Baxter peremptorily afferted to be Saltafh.
" *Pene quidem juraverim hanc* (viz. *Uxelam) fuiffe Salteffe, five uti*
" *hodie dicitur Saltafh* [P]."   I am, however, of opinion, that Uxela
is Loftwithel (Saltafh being much too near to Tamerton), though I
do not think with Camden, that ever this town ftood on the top of
a hill, or that the prefent name refembles much the ancient
one [q].

The third city is Tamare, in which the name of the river Tamar
is too ftrong to be queftioned; and Tamerton, on the eaftern
bank of this river, lies almoft oppofite to Saltafh, and muft have
been the place.

The fourth is *Ifca Dunmoniorum*, or Exeter, the winter and
wefternmoft ftation of the Romans, according to Antoninus's
Itinerary, capital of the Dunmonii, the common appellation of the
Devonfhire and Cornifh men.

Here, therefore, I muft beg leave to differ from the learned Mr.
Horfley, who (in his Britannia Romana, p. 462.) denies Exeter to
be the *Ifca Dunmoniorum*, making Ilchefter the wefternmoft ftation.
If Mr. Horfley " could never yet hear" (p. 462.) of any military
way leading to it, or from it, nor the leaft evidence of any fuch way
farther weft than what Dr. Stukely gives an account of in his Itin.
Curiofum, p. 153. (which is the only foundation of all his
arguments) I doubt not but he would be glad to be better informed;

---

[o] " It muft be written Dunmonii, from Dun a
" Hill, and Mwyn Metal;" fays Gale, Itin. p. 183.
fo therefore we fhall write it for the future,
however differently written by other authors.

[P] Gloffar. p. 257.

[q] Whatever gave name to Withyel at a few
miles diftance, gave alfo name to this, with the
addition of Loft (or Left rather), put before it;
but its being conveniently fituated near a river
(formerly of greater depth of water than now)
and at a middle diftance from Tamerton at the
Eaft, and Truro to the Weft, I fhould think the
Romans might have had their head quarters
here, and a ftation for fome fhips farther down
at Polruan, at the mouth of the river.

for

for by those who have examined the ground, I am well assured that there are two different Roman Ways, that plainly crofs one another near Honiton, about twelve miles to the Eaft of Exeter[r], and irrefragable evidences of Roman Ways to the Weft of that city, as we fhall foon fee. But Ways are not the only teftimonies of this truth; and fince this point has not yet been cleared up, I fhall beg the reader's patience whilft, from the name and fituation of it, according to hiftory, and alfo by its anfwering clearly to the diftances given by Antoninus, I prove Exeter to be the *Ifca Dunmoniorum.*

That the river Ex, on which Exeter ftands, is the Ifca of Antoninus, the very found of the word feems ftrongly to imply[s], whereas Il-chefter has the radical letter L in all its names[t]; and furely, becaufe it ftands on the river Ivel, it was named by the Saxons Ivel, or Il-chefter. Again, Ifca is placed by Ptolemy on the Southern fhore next above Tamar, whereas the Ifkalis runs into the northern fea, and by the fame author is rightly placed next to the Severn[u]. The Ifca is called *Ifca Dunmoniorum,* and therefore to be looked for in Devon; whereas Ilchefter is almoft in the middle of Somerfetfhire.

Now, if, befides thefe congruities of name and place, and appearance of Roman Ways, it fhall be found that the diftance alfo in the Itinerary of Antoninus does well agree to Exeter, I fhould think that this matter can be no more difputed; let us therefore examine the 12th Iter of Antoninus, and go no farther back than *Sorbiodunum* (Old Sarum), and fee whether the diftance from Old Sarum to Exeter is fuch as is there laid down from *Sorbiodunum* to *Ifca Dunmoniorum:*

From *Sorbiodunum* to *Vindocladia,* near Cranburn, XIII.
From *Vindocladia* to *Durnovaria,* now Dorchefter, XXXVI.[w]
From *Durnovaria* to *Muridunum,* likely Seaton
 (as by the name in Britifh) on the river Ax, } XXXVI.
From *Muridunum* to *Ifca Dunmoniorum*[x], - - XV.

} C.

---

[r] Feb. 21, 1754, as I came from Honiton towards Exeter, about four miles Weft of Honiton, I faw two plain fragments of what I take to have been the ancient Roman Road to the Ifca Dunmonii; one of thefe was the nobleft piece of Road that I remember to have ever feen.

[s] Nothing, indeed, is more natural to imagine, than that the Saxons, inftead of Ifk-cefter (where there are three Confonants after the I) for the eafier pronunciation turned the *fk* of the Britifh uifk into an *x,* writing it Excefter; as the river Axon, fays Baxter, p. 140. for Afkaun.

[t] Givelchefter in Florence of Worcefter; in the anonymous Ravennas (inverfedly, as Baxter fays p. 141.) Velox; in Ptolemy, Ifchalis.

[u] See Horfley, p. 357.

[w] The VIII. as in fome Copies, is a manifeft errour; for this would make it but fifteen miles Englifh, from Old Sarum to Dorchefter. Of this erroneous Number, fee Horfley of the 12th Iter. and ibid. p, 461. and Dr. Gale, Itin. Ed. 1709. p. 137. and the Map, ibid.

[x] Erroneoufly written in Anton. Scadumnunniorum; by the Anon. Rav. Scadumnamorum, & Scadomorum, *& in M.S. Regis Gall. Scadoniorum.*

Here

Here we have one hundred miles, according to the Roman meaſure; but the Roman miles are much ſhorter than the Engliſh, of which difference Mr. Horſley makes this, and I believe a juſt, calculation, after having maturely compared (as he ſays, p. 382.) and examined the miles uſed by both nations. " Sometimes the " *Ratio* (ſays he, p. 383.) may be as four to five, or leſs than this, " but three to four is the mean proportion;" ſo that theſe hundred miles from *Sorbiodunum* to *Iſca Dunmoniorum* make only 75 Engliſh miles, according to the *mean proportion*, and eighty, according to the *Ratio* of four to five, which comes ſo very near the real diſtance[y], that there can be no reaſonable diſpute but that Exeter not only anſwers to the name and place, but alſo to the diſtance given us in the Itinerary, and therefore muſt be the *Iſca Dunmoniorum*, the ſtation on the Roman Military Way mentioned in the 12th, and again in the 15th *Iter* of Antoninus.

Of the pre-ſentName of theCountry. What we now call Cornwall, is but a Portion of what in the Roman times was called *Dunmonium*. What the exact bounds of *Dunmonium*, were it is difficult to ſay. Mr. Horſley (p. 463, 464.) thinks that the South parts of Someſetſhire, where the inhabitants were not much unlike the *Dunmonii*, belonged formerly to *Dunmonium*; but, in truth, Borderers may contract a likeneſs in manners, language, cuſtoms, and religion, from a neighbouring country to which they do not belong, and therefore there is no ſettling the limits of a country without ſomething more deciſive than ſuch a reſemblance. Whether Alfred divided England into counties, and then fixed the limits of Devonſhire, where the ancient Eaſtern boundary was between the *Belgæ* and *Durotriges* on the Eaſt, and the *Dunmonii* on the Weſt, is uncertain, but not improbable; and, if true, will ſhew that ancient Cornwall included all the preſent Devonſhire, as well as what is Weſt of the River Tamar. When the Weſtern part of *Dunmonium* was firſt diſtinguiſhed by the name of Cornubia, I am not certain, no more than what were the bounds of the *Dunmonii*. What ſeems moſt probable (if it be not true, as I ſuppoſe it is) is, that though the Romans called this Weſtern part of Britain Danmonia, Dunmonium, or the Country of the Dunmonii; the native Britans (remarkable always for affixing ſuch names as Kernou. the natural properties of places ſuggeſted) called it Kernou[z], as

[y] The meaſurement (according to the poſt-road) is 89 miles from the preſent Saliſbury to Exeter; but meaſuring by the Wheel much exceeds the real diſtance (as meaſuring all the uneavenneſs of the ſurface), reaſonable allowances therefore on this account being made, this diſtance will appear as exact, as moſt of thoſe laid down in the Itinerary. The Roman Roads were alſo directed in much ſtraighter lines than the Engliſh, and therefore their meaſurement conſiſted of fewer miles than ours, in proportion to their length. It muſt be alſo

obſerved, that Ilcheſter is above thirty miles nearer to Saliſbury than the computed diſtance of Exeter.

[z] Pou Kernou, the country Kernou (ſays Mr. Lhuyd, Archæol. p. 222.) i. e. the county of Cornwal. This word is oftentimes writ Cornou (and the adjective derived Cornouak) and Cornow (alias Curnow) by the family of that ſurname, of which there are many remaining in Cornwall, but Kernou, as Mr. Lhuyd writes it, ſeems to be the true reading, Armoricè Qernou, Wallicè Cerniw, i. e. Horns.

they

they still call the Adjective Kernoueck (i. e. Cornish), and probably from the many sharp projections or promontories shooting on each side into the sea. After frequent communications with the Latin Language, first by means of the Roman governours, and afterwards an intercourse with the Church of Rome, this Kernou (or Kornou, for so it is also written) became Latinised into Cornubia [a]; thus it continued till the Saxons imposed the name of Wealas on the Britans driven by them West of the Rivers Severn and Dee (called by the Romans Ordovices, and Silures), calling their country in the Latin tongue Wallia. After which, finding the Britans had retreated not only into Wales, but into the more western extremities of the Island, which were called by the Natives Kernou, and in Latin Cornubia; the Latinists changed Cornubia into Cornuwallia; a name not only expressing the many natural promontories of the country; but also, that the inhabitants were Britans, of the same nation and descent as those of Wales [b], and from this Cornuwallia is derived the present name Cornwall [c].

This CORNWALL, as has been hinted before, reached anciently far beyond its present limits, if it did not include all the ancient *Dunmonium*; for the Britans gave way by degrees, and disputed the ground with the Saxons for several centuries: but the fortune of the Saxons prevailed; and the Cornish Britans being soon forced to leave the Eastern parts of *Dunmonium* in their possession, became bounded by the river Ex [d]. When England was divided into Counties, or Shires, it made no alteration in the habitancy of particular persons, nor any distinction betwixt Britan and Saxon. It is likely that Alfred, who probably made this division, separated *Dunmonium* into two portions, dividing them by the river Tamar, as a very natural and commodious division for the well governing of the two counties; but, notwithstanding this division, the Cornish Britans, lived at Exeter together with, and in equal authority to the Saxons [e], till the entire Conquest of their country by Athelstan in 936, when

Margin notes: Cornubia. Cornu-wallia. Cornwall. Limits.

[a] " Regnum, Latinizantibus Monachis Cor-"nubiam appellatum." Baxter, Gloss. p. 89.

[b] Camden seems to think that Wales and Cornwall, Wallia and Cornwallia were names first mentioned in the laws of King Ina. See Engl. Camden, p. 3. Vol. I.

[c] " Cornubia videlicet quæ Cornuwallia a "quibusdam dicitur. Demecia quæ Australis-"wallia appellatur, Venedocia quæ North-"wallia nuncupatur," says Mat. Par. reckoning the places to which the Britans were driven by the Saxons. Edit. Tran. of p. 104.

[d] Of this time we are to understand what Edward I. says (Sheringham, p. 129.) that Britain, Wales, and Cornwall, were the Portion of Belinus, elder son of Dunwallo, and that that part of the Island, afterwards called England,

was divided into three shares, viz. Britain, which reached from the Tweed, Westward, as far as the river Ex; Wales inclosed by the rivers Severn, and Dee; and Cornwall from the river Ex to the Land's-End.

[e] " Hanc urbem (scil Excestre) primus Rex "Ethelstanus in potestatem Anglorum (effugatis "Britonibus) redactam, turribus insignivit." Wm. Malmsb. p. 146. " Ab Excestra, quam "ad id temporis æquo cum Anglis jure inha-"bitârant cedere compulit, terminum Provinciæ "suæ citra Tambram fluvium statuens, sicut "Aquilonaribus Brit. amnem Wajam limitem "posuerat." ib. p. 28. And the fee farm of the city of Exeter is still the Duke of Corn-wall's; amounting to 21 l. 15 s.

they

they were confined within the Tamar. But even after this, the Cornish are said to have held as far East as Totness upon the river Dart; and this town was long after, even till the reign of Henry III. reckoned the Eastern part of Cornwall [f]. By these several removes were the Cornish Britans reduced to their present narrow limits, and as they retired Westward, the Eastern parts regained their ancient name of *Dunmonium*, or *Danmonium*; and, when the division of Shires took place, was called Davonshire *(quasi Danvon, or Danmonshire)*; and the name of Cornwall became appropriated to the Country West of the Tamar [g].

SECT. III.
Whether
any Roman
Towns in
Cornwall. Where the Roman stations were to the West of Exeter, is uncertain. Liskerd, alias Lescard, is certainly a very ancient town; and Tradition says, that a Roman Legion was stationed there, of which the present name of the Town is thought to bear some remains. But of the ancient Castle that was there, the remains are too small to draw any consequences from, especially, as I could see nothing in or round the Town to countenance any such great antiquity.

Some Authors [h] think that the word Caër, in the name of a Town, or Fort, is a proof of its being Roman, as Caër-leon, &c. and this may be a good argument, where history mentions the Roman exploits, and monuments frequently found, prove their residence. We have many places in Cornwall which begin with Caër [i], but as the Roman History of our country is but in its infancy, and more monuments will every day, I flatter myself, be making new discoveries, I shall lay no stress upon Etymology, where there are not the concurrent supports of Coins, Sepulchres, Forts, or Ways.

Stratton. One town, however, we have great reason to think of Roman original; for it has not only the name of many towns in England which are all Roman; but as far as I can learn, every other testimony; it is Stratton, at present not a considerable town, either for extent, trade, fortification, or beauty, yet formerly of such high account as to give name to the hundred in which it stands, which is more than any town in Cornwall was of figure enough to do, when the county was divided into hundreds, confessed to be done in

[f] See Note [d] p. 330. following.

[g] In the most ancient English Writers, and all the Records (I have seen) this name is written Cornwall, as it is also in Camden, and his Editor Bishop Gibson, in Carew, Norden, Speed, Selden, Baker, Ogilby, Bishop Kennett, Dr. Brown Willis, Ainsworth, &c. Others, however (as Lord Clarendon, in his Rebellion, Mr. Ed. Lhuyd, and Mr. Ray), of late have written this name Cornwal, with a single l, and perhaps with more propriety; but as this is a dispute, on the issue of which very little depends, I let the name stand as I find it in the Records, and the more ancient English Writers, many of them eminent for their knowledge in Languages and ancient history.

[h] See Moreton's Northamtonshire, p. 572. and Camden, passim.

[i] Caër in St. Germans — Caër-Dinham — Caër-gol — Caër-lean in Mawgon Kerrier — Caër-hays, and many others.

Alfred's

Alfred's time, about 900[k]. That the Romans placed their towns on their great roads, needs no proof; the Saxons called the Roman Roads Streets, as Watling-ſtreet, Icknild-ſtreet, and the like: the places where theſe ways paſſed rivers they called Street, or Stretfords, and the towns placed on thoſe Streets they called Street-towns, or Strettons, and the name properly muſt be ſo writ, although corruption in ſpeech has joſtled out E, and put the A in its place in this inſtance as well as many others[l]. Many Strettons there are in Warwickſhire, all which take their name, ſays Sir William Dugdale (ibid. p. 49.), from ſome great road, near unto which they are ſituate, as Stretton Baſkerville does from Watling-ſtreet (p. 50. ibid.). Stratton in Somerſetſhire, near the river Froom, lies on the Foſſe-way[m]. Near Cirenceſter there is a Stratton, on the Roman Way through Glouceſterſhire. In Shropſhire, Staffordſhire, and Oxfordſhire, the like[n]; and there is hardly any county where theſe great roads paſs, but that there is a town called Stretton near them; and their being placed ſo on the Roman roads is ſufficient authority to eſteem them of Roman original. This conſtant uſe of the Saxons in naming other places, muſt weigh with the impartial, and convince them that our Stratton had its name for like reaſon with the reſt, and conſequently is of Roman original as well as the others. Nor does this ſuppoſition entirely depend on ſound, as will be ſhewn in the following chapter.

C H A P. V.

Of the Roman Ways.

ROMAN Ways, as yet diſcovered, and already deſcribed, in Cornwall there are none, which can be ſpoken of with certainty; and no wonder, conſidering that it has been hitherto doubted whether the Romans were ever here or no. This latter point, however, can be no more diſputed; for that the Romans were here, and Maſters of our whole country, may, and, I think, has been proved beyond all doubt; and yet to pronounce abſolutely of their Ways may ſeem too preſuming. Even in counties, where

SECT. I.
Uncertainty of the Roman Roads, not only in Cornwall, but elſewhere.

[k] Hals ſays, that Leſnewth and Stratton hundreds are not mentioned in any record till 12 Edward III. both paſſing under the name of Trigmajorſhire: but this is a great miſtake, for in the Exeter Domeſday which was compiled in the year 1086, Stratton is reckoned one of the hundreds.

[l] Thus we ſay Aſton for Eaſton, Aſtley for Eaſtly (ſays Dugdale Warwickſh. p. 106.); and ſo we ſay Stratton for Stretton, and Stratford for Stretford.
[m] Camden, p. 87.
[n] Ibid. p. 658. Plot's Oxfordſh. p. 402.

the

the Romans have been known to refide, ever fince the time of Tacitus, we find the learned world not agreed, as to the rife and courfe of the four great confular ways. We find the *Iter* itfelf erroneous, or at leaft not underftood, and its laft learned Editor not always fuppofed to have hit upon the truth. In his Oxfordfhire, Dr. Plot, p. 321. hopes only to give a probable account, and (p. 323.) thinks he has reafon to depart from Hollenfhed, both as to the rife and courfe of the Icknild-ftreet; and (p. 326.) differs from Camden, and others, in their account of the Akeman-ftreet, which paffed (as he thinks) quite a different way from what they imagined; and the fame author tells us (in his Staffordfhire, p. 402.) that he could find no footfteps of the tenth *Iter* of Antoninus, as it is defcribed by Dr. Fulk. The anonymous Ravennas makes the way from London to *Veroconium* of the Cornavii go one way, the *Iter* of Antoninus another way°. In Antonine's ninth *Iter*, Dr. Gale fuppofes the firft ftation to have been at Taefborough in Norfolk; but Baxter very much alters the courfe of this *Iter*, and fuppofes the firft ftation to have been at Cambridge P. In fhort, we are not fure of the Roman roads, for any long way together; they flip us every now and then, and we are as uncertain where they end, as where they begin, fo that every one advances fuch a judgment of them as is moft reconcilable to his own obfervations. To fupport, and I am afraid, perpetuate this great uncertainty, the towns on the Ways are often mifpelt by copyifts, fo that learned men are not agreed, which, and where were the towns. The breaches made in the road for many miles together by cultivation and buildings, and oftentimes at fome turning, are another obftacle; fo that although it appears again afterwards, it fhall be dubious, whether it be the remains of the way we have left, or part of another. But what contributes moft of all to thefe uncertainties is the different ftructure of the ways themfelves, and the intended difcontinuance of them oftentimes by the Romans, in places where they thought them unneceffary.

SECT. II.
The ftructure of the Roman Ways.

Oftentimes the Roman ways are raifed into a Ridge, confifting of regular *ftrata* of Stone, Clay, and Gravel, ditched on each fide, running in a ftraight line, and the moft finifhed ones paved on the top, and the Stones oftentimes layed clofe in an arch correfponding to the general turn of the Ridge; where fuch a way occurs, it cannot be deemed any other than Roman.

But they are not all fo well conftructed. Icknild is not a raifed way q, nor Fofs r. Sometimes the Ways are raifed, and fometimes levels,

° See Baxter's Gloff. in DUROCOBRIVI, p. 114.
P Baxter's Gloff. ad TAVUM, p. 7.—Horfley on the ninth Iter.
q Plot's Oxfordfhire, p. 323.
r Horfley, p. 389.
s Plot's Oxfordfhire, p. 322.

and

and the raifed ones fometimes only of Earth, fometimes pitched, or
paved; fome have two Ridges, and a ditch in the middle, as that
near Dorchefter[t], that at Grimfdyke[u], and at Ellsfield[w]. Sometimes the Ridge turns to a ditch as Grimfdyke[x], and the Dyke turns
again to a Ridge, a little farther on, very high and lofty[y]. Two
ways are fometimes found, one near and by the fide of the other,
as Aves-ditch, and Portway[z], and in the Icknild-ftreet near Stoken-
church-Hills. In Staffordfhire the ways are only made of gravel,
dug all along by the fides of each Roman way, as appears by the
pits near Occamfley on the Watling-ftreet, and more plainly upon
the Icknild near Little Afton[a]: the fame is obferved by Dr.
Stukeley, concerning Ickling-dyke near Woodyates, where the
holes whence that road was raifed are ftill vifible[b], which I mention the more particularly, becaufe fomewhat of this kind appears
where there is great reafon, as we fhall fee by and by, to fuppofe a
Roman road in Cornwall. Add to this, that where new roads were
plainly unneceffary, either becaufe the March was to be over large,
dry, champain grounds (where the country-hills, or Sepulchral-
Barrows, might be a fufficient direction), or for that the foldiers
and the people were not diforderly enough to need fuch conftant
employment; the Romans difcontinued their ways as often as they
found them neither neceffary for the eafe nor the difcipline of
their people, and begun them again, when proper reafons or
difficult grounds made it requifite. Again, as fome of thefe ways
were Vicinal, and fmall in comparifon of the great roads, I muft
obferve, that the lefs thefe ways were (that is, the narrower and
lower) the fooner they were deftroyed and loft; and the more a
country has been cultivated fince the Roman Times, the more the
ways which they made have been ruined, which will ftill increafe
the difficulties, with regard to this county of Cornwall; for our
ways not being of the confular rank (if they had been, they muft
have had a place in the Iter of Antoninus) but Vicinal (that is,
from Town to Town) they were the fooner defaced; and the
cultivation of our barren grounds in Cornwall, being introduced
much later than in the more central parts of Britain, has deftroyed
the ways here much more than in other counties, which were cultivated during the refidence of the Romans, when all improvements
in hufbandry were obliged to conform themfelves to the military
ways of their Mafters, and leave them untouched.

[t] Ibid. p. 329.
[u] Ibid. p. 324.
[w] Ibid. p. 325.
[x] Ibid. p. 328. of the Akeman-ftreet.

[y] Ibid.
[z] Ibid.
[a] Plot's Staffordfhire, p. 399.
[b] Itin. Cur. p. 180.—Horfley, p. 460.

4 P   Amidft

Amidſt theſe difficulties, ſome common to the whole nation, and ſome peculiar to this county, I would not be underſtood to ſpeak poſitively of the Roman ways, which I think may be traced in Cornwall, but only lay before the reader what Tradition and authors ſay, and what has occurred to me in a few reſearches relating to this ſubject, in which I do not deſpair of evincing the probability of ſuch ways, or of giving a few hints, at leaſt, where they may be moſt ſucceſsfully ſought for.

SECT. III.
Romanways
Weſt of
Exeter.

As the Romans have been before proved to have had ſoldiers here in Cornwall, and in the very Weſtern parts to have poſſeſſed our mines and ſea-coaſt, it is not at all likely, that a nation ſo well ſkilled in making, and no leſs intent upon ſecuring their conqueſts, ſhould depart from one of their firſt principles of military policy, and leave themſelves deſtitute of publick roads. By all their hiſtory it appears, that they were very intent upon compleating the conqueſt of this Iſland ; and this could not well be done with ſuch few Legions as they had here, unleſs they conſidered above all things the convenience of theſe troops, and for their eaſe and connexion extended their roads as they enlarged their conqueſts. By the direction of the great roads now viſible in the more inland parts of Britain, we are ſure that the Romans laid out their ways with great ſkill, according to the length and breadth of the iſland. Of their four great ways, that called Icknild-ſtreet ſeems deſigned to have ſtretched away the whole length of the Province which we now call England (which is from Wintertonneſs in Norfolk, to the Land's End in Cornwall), in a line near W. S. W. for, as it has its name from the Iceni of Norfolk, and conſequently its riſe there, it is traced in many places bearing as ſtrait as may be towards the Weſtern parts of the iſland ; which made Dr. Plot imagine [c], that it goes " into Devonſhire and Cornwall to the " Land's End." Others think that it was not this Icknild-ſtreet (for there are ſuppoſed to be two of that name) which came into Cornwall, but another Roman way which has not been yet deſcribed [d].

In the Itinerary of Antoninus, it is true, there is no ſtation Weſt of Exeter ; but it is confeſſed, by all who have made this part of Geography their ſtudy, that there are Roman Ways in England,

[c] Plot's Oxfordſhire, p. 324.
[d] " I was always of opinion, that the Foſs " way, and not the Icknyld-ſtreet, was the great " Roman way which paſſes through Devon and " Cornwall : The Foſs, or Vorſe, as the So- " merſetſhire men call it, certainly enters De- " vonſhire, about the fair mile near Sir George " Yonge's, and gives name to Street-way-head, " a village juſt by. As to the Icknyld, Q. If

" the great Conſular-way, ſo named, be not " that which paſſes through Gloceſter, Wor- " ceſter, Warwick, Stafford, and Derbyſhire, " and ſo quite to Tinmouth in the North, ra- " ther than that from Norfolk. In the Pariſh " of Alvechurch, in Worceſterſhire, it was " called Ickle-Street." Right Rev. Dr. Lyttelton Biſhop of Carliſle.

on which no *Iter* has proceeded, nay, which have never been named, much lefs defcribed, by any author.

In Peutinger's Table there is a Roman Way far Weft of Exeter, and (if any thing could be gathered with certainty from this Table) muft be quite to the Land's End, where his *Riduno* is placed; and near this extremity of our County, we do indeed find Rin, and Treryn (not much unlike *Ridunum*), where the Brafs pot of Roman money, mentioned by Leland, was found [e]; but as this Table is unfortunately deficient, as well as confufed, in the Weftern parts, it is no fafe guide; and I am apt to think, from the numeral figure XV. near *Riduno*, that it is a miftake, as well as mifplacing for *Moriduno*.

Ptolemy's Geography is fo rude a fketch, and fo full of errours [f], that there is no following it. The anonymous Ravennas is ftill worfe, and the names of places fo dif-figured, that there is no knowing them. Places in Cornwall, or Devonfhire, we have none mentioned in the Notitia. We muft, therefore, depend upon the obfervation of the moderns; and, by what already appears, there is reafon to believe, that there are two Roman Ways leading into Cornwall, and therein to be traced; one by Exeter through Totnefs, paffing near Plymouth towards Lifkard; the other higher up, coming through Somerfetfhire, the North of Devonfhire, by Torington, to Stratton, Camelford, and Bodman, in the fame County.

That there paffed a road Weft of Exeter to Totnefs, Robert of Glofter (Temp. H. III.), tells us, fpeaking of the four great Roman Ways [g]. But we have better authority than that of this antiquated Poet for a Roman road to Totnefs. Whether it paffed to the Ferry below Exeter, as fome think (who take it for a branch of the Northern road through Worcefterfhire, Glofter, Somerfet, and Devonfhire), or through that city, and was only a continuation of the way through Dorchefter, Seaton, and Exeter, I fhall not now ftay to enquire; my bufinefs is to trace it Weft of the City, in which I fhall ufe the words of a late curious Gentleman. " The Roman road " is vifible at Kenford (about three miles below Exeter); there are " not bolder remains in the Kingdom of fuch ways than from the " paffage over the Ex, through Kenford and Newton Bufhel, to " Totnefs. It appears with a high Creft, and entire, moft part

---

[e] See before, p. 300.

[f] Horfley, p. 356, 361.

[g] " Fram the South into the North takith " Erminge-ftrete

" Fram the Eaft into the Weft goeth Ikeneld " ftrete

" Fram the South Eaft to North Weft that is " fum del grete

" Fram Dover into Cheftre goth Watlyng ftrete

" The ferth of thefe is moft of alle, that tilleth " from Totoneys

" Fram the one end of Cornwaile anone to " Cateneys."

Dugd. Warw. p. 8.

" of

" of the way, which is at least twenty miles: I travelled twice
" along it: at Totness I lost it; but about Brent, a small Market
" Town six miles farther, I imagine I struck into it again, whence
" it continues in as strait a line as that uneven rocky country ad-
" mits of, to Ridgeway, a small village near Plympton. In the
" neighbourhood of which place, in the grounds of Mr. Parker of
" Burrington, I observed a remarkable Camp, though of no great
" magnitude. Near this intrenchment, the said road, having passed
" the small river Plym, mounts a pretty steep ascent, crosses the
" main coach-road from Plymouth to Exeter, at a place called
" Nacker's-hole, and proceeds in a direct though narrow line to
" St. Buddox, where the ferry over the river Thamar brings us to
" Saltash, and thence into Cornwall. Near this Nacker's-hole is
" a small entrenchment (now a Bowling-green) which though of
" a circular form, I yet deem it Roman, and the *Castrum æstivum*
" of the Tamaris of Ravennas, at this day called Tamerton [h],
" about a mile below it on the side of the river Thamar." So far
the late learned Mr. Moulding, of Wichenford, Worcestershire, on
the Roman Ways [i] in the West, from his own observation; to
which he adds, " This way from Saltash, I have been told, pro-
" ceeds to an intrenchment near Lostwithel, where there is a cause-
" way leading directly to it. I am equally positive, there is another
" Roman direction into Cornwall." The causeway this Gentleman
mentions will be taken notice of in its proper place; I will only
observe, that this road being continued from Exeter to Totness, and
thence to the sides of Tamar, manifests that the design was to carry
it into the Southern coast of Cornwall; and that this design was
executed, there is more reason to believe, because in the ancient
MS. written by Richard of Westminster [k] (lately recovered from
obscurity), I find an *Iter* [l] laid down in the manner of Antoninus,
which, though imperfect, must needs lead us as far West as the
river Fal. The passage here follows: *A Londinio Ceniam usque
Sic. Venta Belgarum* XC. *Brige* XI. *Sorbioduno* VIII. *Venta
Geladia* [m] XII. *Durnovaria* IX. *Moriduno* XXXIII. *Isca Dumnonio-
rum* XV.—*Durio amne—Tamara—Voluba—Cenia.*

Here we may observe, that the distances below Exeter are not
expressed, but *Durio Amne*, seems to signify the river Dart (possibly
in the original *Dario*). The name of the town, which stood upon
it, is lost; then comes Tamarton; the intermediate town on the
river of Fawy (likely Vxela) lost; next the Voluba of Ptolemy,

[h] The Tamare of Ptolemy, now Tamerton Foliot.
[i] In a Letter to the Rev. Dr. Lyttelton, now Bp. of Carlisle, dated Aug. 22, 1743.
[k] Richardus Corinensis Monachus Westmo-nasteriensis, published by Charles Bertram in the year 1757.
[l] Iter XVI. p. 39. as published by Bertram.
[m] Pro Vindocladia Ant.

moft

moſt likely the preſent Granpont[n], whence the Fal deſcends to Tregeney, the Cenia probably of this author; the Cenio of Ptolemy, and the Giano of the anonymous Ravennas[o].

The reader will perceive that, according to this author, there was a Roman Way upon this Southern coaſt; and where I think are the remains of it, how it kept its courſe, and where it branched off, the following obſervations may in ſome meaſure inform us.

In the ſummer of the year 1752, I ſet out for Saltaſh, on purpoſe to ſearch after this road; and in my way from Loſtwythyel to Liſkerd, about a furlong to the Eaſtward of Loſtwythyel Bridge, ſaw an old Ridgeway on the right hand, but ſoon loſt it by keeping too much to the left, as I imagine; but, a quarter of a mile before I came to the ſecond Tap-houſe, ſaw on the left a high ridge, leading on near Eaſterly, large pits on the higher ſide of it, ſome ſquare, ſome ſhapeleſs, out of which the Ridge was raiſed. This way was ditched on both ſides, ten feet and half wide, in ſome places wider. It went ſtraight over the Downs (which was here level) from Loſtwythyel towards Liſkerd; on the ſide of it were many Barrows: hence it runs through ſome meadows (which lie round the Tap-houſe), beyond which I immediately joined it again, plain, high-creſted, ſlanting up the hill, ditched on both ſides, but wider than before; thence it is very plain as far as the third Tap-houſe, beyond which, in a ſtraight line, it continues for half a mile, then paſſes from the highway into a field, where it runs within the hedges for a quarter of a mile farther in a ſtraight line ſtill. I then loſt it; and thence to Liſkerd, and afterwards to Saltaſh, being through deep hollow ways and incloſures, I ſaw nothing more of it. That this is part of a Roman Way, I am inclined to think, from its keeping in a ſtraight line, from the places dug along its ſides to fill it [P], from its aſcending the hill in an eaſy ſlope, and from its being ditched on one ſide as much as on the other; whereas, if it had been a Camp, it would have turnings round the hills, and rounds or ſaliant angles on its turnings, and would have been ditched but on one ſide [q].

There is alſo a Ridgeway Weſt of Loſtwythyel, which runs down nearly parallel to the river towards Fawy; it runs by Caſtle-Doar

Remains of an ancient Road betwixt Loſtwythyel and Liſkerd.

Other Fragments of Ancient Ways on the South Coaſt.

---

[n] This Voluba cannot be Falmouth, for it is here placed to the Eaſtward of Cenia, whereas Falmouth lies to the Weſt of it.

[o] Cenia, lying ſomewhere on the Cenio river (or harbour of Ptolemy), muſt be either Tregeny or Truroe; but Tregeny bears faireſt to be this Cenia; for in the pariſh of Lamorran on this Creek, we find two Manſions called Tregennah; and in the adjoining pariſh of Verian, we find a tenement of like name, all taking their name from a River, or Creek, called anciently the Genna, or Cenio, as may be reaſonably ſuppoſed.

[P] See Occamſly pits, p. 329.

[q] Other inſtances of Roman ways in Cornwall, particularly the Giant's-hedge (as it is vulgarly called), running in a ſtraight line from Loo to Leryn-creek on the Fawy River, ſeven miles long, and in ſome places ſeven feet high, and twenty feet wide. See in the Natural Hiſtory of Cornwall, p. 325.

4 Q

(an

(an ancient encampment now almoſt demoliſhed), betwixt which, and Loſtwythyel, I ſaw many remains of a Riſbank about eight feet wide, ditched on each ſide; betwixt Caſtle-Doar alſo and Fawy, ſaw a high ridge-way ditched on each ſide, in a ſtraight line. What makes it probable that the Romans had a way here, running down from their great Weſtern road, the better to ſecure the mouth of Fawy harbour, is, that many Coins have been found hereabouts [r]; and a little below Fawy, croſs the River, is an ancient village, called ſometimes Polrouan [s], and ſometimes Portrouan, which by its name ſeems to have belonged to the Romans. I am informed that there is part of a Stone cauſeway leading from Bodman to Loſtwythyel: this Way Tradition attributes to the Romans: the remains of it are about midway betwixt theſe two Towns; they conſiſt of two fragments, the longeſt of them is about a hundred yards, and the other not ſo much; they incline a little with the road, are about ten feet wide, and are raiſed above the common level about a foot. It is not at all ſtrange that here ſhould be a Way, for the river Alan coming up from Padſtow-Haven, on the North Sea, and the river Fawy coming up from the South Sea, and Fawy to Loſtwythyel, do almoſt cut our narrow county in two, being within the reach of four miles one of the other [t], ſo that a way from river to river would in a manner connect the two Seas; and there could not be a more judicious piece of ground choſen either for a Way, or a Garriſon, than this, from whence the Troops could reach ſo eaſily from North to South Sea. To this let me add one obſervation more, that at Pencarrow there is a very conſiderable fortification overlooking the Alan, and on a hill near Bodman as conſiderable a Fort, leading directly from that of Pencarrow towards Loſtwythyel, called Caſtle-Kynek. By means of theſe two Garriſons, and one at or near Loſtwythyel, the paſſage between the two rivers was eaſily ſecured, and ſmall parties might traverſe with ſecurity.

Having tracked this way thus much about Loſtwythyel, I have ſeen no more of it; but there is reaſon to believe, that it kept on, through, or near St. Auſtle, to Granpont, the *Voluba* of the Ancients, and thence in a ſtraight line to Truro, ſix miles farther; but the grounds (altogether incloſed) will make it difficult to trace it here. However, about a mile Weſt of Granpont, there is a Tenement called Caerfôs, alias Carvoza [u], that is, the Caſtle, or Encampment, on the Dyke, or Foſs (by which name the ancient Ways are frequently called), adjoining to the High road to Truro;

r See, p. 303.
s Ibid.
t See Map—Plate I.

u I find by Mr. Tonkin's MS. that he alſo looked upon this Carvoza as a Roman Encampment. M.S. A. Creed pariſh.

and

and indeed the name of this laſt mentioned town (to ſay nothing of the Coins found near it taken notice of before [w]) makes me think that more than one way paſſed here [x]; ſo that Camden may be very little out in his derivation, when he ſays, that it is called in Corniſh Truru, *a tribus plateis*, from the three Streets. Probably the great Eaſtern road paſſed from Truro, near Penryn, there being a ſtraight lined fortification about midway between theſe two Towns (in the pariſh of Feock, as I remember), and ſo on towards Conſtantine, and Helford Haven, where ſo many Coins were found [y].

I have nothing farther to remark of this great Weſtern road, than that there is room to conjecture, from the *Iter*, juſt now produced from Richard of Weſtminſter, that a little beyond Granpont it ſent off a branch to the left hand down to Tregeny, on the river Val, which was formerly navigable far above this laſt mentioned Town; and what ſeems to confirm this conjecture, is, that midway betwixt Granpont, and Tregeny, is the encampment of Wulvedon, mentioned before, with an avenue pointing towards the Granpont road [z].

Beſides this Southern road, the Romans muſt have had another publick road into Cornwall, as Mr. Moulding, mentioned before, juſtly obſerves, for this one road could never ſend off ſuch convenient branches as to command the whole Country. For this purpoſe they muſt have had another Way coaſting along the North Sea, with Forts, or Towns, at proper intervals (as well as Croſs-roads ſtretching from the two principal ones) for to maintain a proper correſpondence between the forces on both. Of this Northern road I think there are plain remains ſtill to be ſeen at Stratton. *Fragments of Ancient Roads on the North;*

As this Town lies among hills, I was obliged to get up into the *at Stratton.* Church-tower to have the better view of the country round: from the battlements there, I ſoon ſaw a ſtraight road paſſing E. and W. and bearing directly for the Town, which in the main has the ſame direction, though ſome little by-ſtreets branch off on the ſides. The next morning, in my purſuit of this ſubject to the Eaſt, I eaſily found the ridgeway, which I had ſeen from the Tower the evening before, overgrown with briars, about ten feet wide, bearing in a ſtraight line up the hill;

---

[w] P. 302. At Mopas, which might be *Caſtrum Æſtivum* of the Garriſon of Truro, the *Caſtra Æſtiva* being ſometimes a mile or two at a diſtance from their Ways and Towns.

[x] I find this Britiſh Name wrtiten Tre-uro; in Domeſday it is written Treurgeu; in Henry the Second's time Treveru; Trivere in the 13th of Edward I. but in the 30th, Treveru, by which it appears that the firſt ſyllable of this name is *Tre*, a Town, and *vor*, or *vur*, is a Way, making in the Plural number, *vorou*; ſo that Trevurou, corruptly written in Domeſ-

day Treurgeu, will make Treurou (by dropping the V conſonant, which the Corniſh Language often does); conſequently this name will ſignify the Town of, or on, the Ways.

[y] See of Coins, p. 300, 301.

[z] " The Sea in former times brought boats " of reaſonable burthen far above Tregny to a " place called Hale-boat-rock, in which rock " are yet many ſtrong iron rings which ſerved to " tye boats unto." Norden's Survey of Cornwall, p. 6.

I rode

I rode by it till I came to Weft-leigh on the top of a hill, near two miles Eaft of Stratton, in the way to Torrington, about twenty miles Eaftward of this Town. There is a Way, parallel nearly to this, which runs midway betwixt the Lane leading to Lancell's Church and the forementioned Way, and this midway is called Small-ridge Lane. This may be a Collateral Way to the other, for fuch are found near the great roads, particularly in Oxfordfhire[a], and are fuppofed to be made either becaufe nearer or better Ways, or in order to keep feditious people and foldiers from worfe employments; but I do not take it to be the principal or moft ancient road, becaufe, I apprehend, there muft be a broad ridge-way near by, or that this could never with any propriety have been called the *Small-ridge*.

Having collected thefe hints to the Eaft, let us now pafs through the town of Stratton to the Weft, where, at the Town's-end, we find a raifed Way pitched with Stones called the Caufeway, flanting up the hill, and then running a mile and half as ftraight as the hilly furface will permit. About half a mile from the Town, and one furlong to the right of this Caufeway, there is a fquare entrenchment, containing about an acre of ground, where the houfe of the Blackminfters (once a great family in thefe parts) formerly ftood. It was moated round; but whether a little fort belonging to this Way (for the Romans were fond of the fquare figure), or layed out fo by the owners I do not pretend to fay; but in this place feveral Brafs Medals and fome Silver Coins have been lately found, as I was affured by (Mr. Marfhall) the prefent tenant of thefe lands, who found the former, and gave the four or five brafs old Farthings (as he called them) to his Children to play withall, as good for nothing. Before I go farther from this Town, I muft not forget to mention, that about two thirds of the Way from hence to Lancefton, there is a Barton called *Broad-ridge*, in which, as I am informed by Samuel Percival, Efq; Lord of the Soil, there is a large ridgeway ftraight for a mile together, in a line pointing North and South, that is, from one of thefe Towns to the other, which makes me imagine, that there was a Crofs road which ftruck off at right angles from Stratton to Lancefton, a place certainly of great antiquity, and a pafs of no lefs importance to thofe who would mafter Cornwall, as we fhall find when we come to give an account of the Caftle there. I return now to the Caufeway, which runs a mile and half Weft of Stratton, paffing away at the head of Bude Haven towards Camelford. I fhall not trouble the reader with my conjectures about the farther tendency of this Way at prefent.

[a] Dr. Plot's Map.

This

This is sufficient to shew that the Romans had a way in the North of Cornwall, though to be discovered now only in fragments; but the people hereabouts have done by this Way, as the vulgar and ignorant have dealt with the four great Ways in the other parts of the kingdom, they have attributed it to the most famous man that tradition records to have lived in these parts; they say the Causeway was first made by one of the name *de Albo Monasterio*, in English Blankminster, a knight Templar (whose effigies lies in their Church) who lived in the time of Edward the First, and gave lands to this Parish, as appears by a deed of confirmation granted by Queen Elizabeth. This Story may have so much truth in it as that it was repaired by some great man of this family, as it has been, at no small expence, within these thirty years; but the Romans, of all the Ancients, are eminently distinguished by their attention to publick roads; however, as we attribute all great works of the ruder kind to Giants, so the people of no knowledge in this part of history ascribe the great Ways to the greatest men they can think of. Thus Robert of Gloucester, from the fabulous British history, attributes the four great military Roads of Britain to King Belinus; and in like manner the Road through Westmoreland and Cumberland (though confessedly Roman) is called Michael Scot's Causeway [b], as is also that in the County of Durham about Binchester; whoever considers this custom, and at the same time the Road leading from the East, through the town of Stratton, must needs think that this Causeway to the West (though kept in better repair, because passing through more miry grounds) is only a continuation of the great Road which comes from the East.

Whether this great Road through Stratton comes from Exeter, or (as I am more apt to imagine) comes into the North of Devonshire from Somersetshire, crossing the river Ex above Bampton, thence to Romans-Leigh, and near Burrington, or Chimleigh (for *f*. Cheminleigh) passes on to Torrington, I leave to other Gentlemen, and future enquiry, as not concerning the design of these papers; but, I think, that the navigable Rivers, on which the two considerable trading Towns Barnstaple and Biddeford now stand, will abundantly justify the Romans for bringing their publick Road so far North, directly from Somersetshire, a way here in the North being altogether requisite for subduing this part of the Island, as well as opening a communication with Ireland; to this I must add, that Bude-Haven (as it is still called, though now only a sandy Creek for small vessels) appears to have been formerly much more commodious for shipping than it is now; for

[b] Horsley's Brit. p. 388.

4 R   the

the ground running up the valley from the Creek's-mouth (till it comes within half a mile, or thereabouts, of Stratton) is all a flat marfh, and moft certainly made fo by the Earth and Gravel wafhed down from the hills adjoining; the River here, being a plentiful ftream, always comes down charged with flime, when it is encreafed by the Land-floods, and has not the liberty to run it off into the fea, by reafon of the fands blown in by the Northern Winds; the fands increafing every age, as the prefent generation well remembers, muft have choaked this Haven long fince the Roman times. Nor is this a fingular cafe; deterrations have had elfewhere the fame effect on fome of the ancient Harbours[c], of which no one can doubt, who has read the judicious obfervations of Dr. Battely's *Antiquitates Rhutupianæ*.

Before this Marfh was formed, therefore, the Harbour of Bude muft have been a very pretty, and fecure one, being a mile and half long, and in many places more than half a mile over, the fea at Spring-tides even now reaching up more than a mile from the prefent mouth of the Haven, covering all this Marfh as it comes along. If Stratton then is an inconfiderable place at prefent, and, feemingly, not worthy of a Roman Way, it is becaufe its Harbour is choaked up, and it wants that refort which Trade naturally produces; but there is reafon to fuppofe, that it was formerly reckoned a Poft of fuch confequence, upon the account of its Haven, and oppofition to the Irifh Coaft, that it was conquered as early as the time of Agricola; into which point of hiftory, as not at all foreign to the Antiquities of our County, fince this place favours us with fo fair an opportunity, we will now enquire.

C H A P. VI.

Cornwall conquered by the Romans as early as the time of Agricola, in the Reign of Domitian.

MR. Edward Lhuyd, whofe authority in Britifh Hiftory will have great weight with the judicious, tells us (Archæol. p. 32. col. 3.) that " the Dunmonian and other Southern Britans, " being on account of their fituations earlier conquered, were " confequently more converfant with the Romans than the people " of Wales." Now the Welfh were conquered partly before Agricola's coming, and in his firft Summer; therefore, according

[c] Sandwich, Richborough, the Ifle of Thanet, &c.

to Mr. Lhuyd, the Dunmonians muſt have been conquered before Agricola. I will not, however, place it ſo early; but proceed to enter into particulars, and ſee what may be collected from the Ancients on this point.

In the firſt Summer of Agricola's command here in Britain, he vanquiſhed the *Ordovices* (i. e. the Britans of North Wales), and reduced Angleſea [d]. In his ſecond campaign, he made a great progreſs, conquering from Angleſea to Edinburgh [e], or, according to Horſley, Cumberland and Northumberland, in which, however, it muſt be implied, that the intermediate nations were before ſubdued, if not then, for Agricola would not leave an enemy at his back. In the third Summer, he advanced as far in Scotland as the river Tay, building ſeveral Forts. " The fourth Summer, " Tacitus ſays, was ſpent in erecting Forts upon the Iſthmus, " betwixt the Clyde, and the Frith of Edinburgh [f];" and, doubt-leſs, to pen up the Scots in the Northern part of Scotland, that he might be at liberty to turn his arms another way; for, in the fifth year, Agricola took ſhipping, and conquered nations before unknown to the Roman Eagles, and garriſoned that part of the country which lies over againſt Ireland [g].

The words of Tacitus run thus: " *Quinto Expeditionum anno* " *nave prima tranſgreſſus* (ſcil. Agricola) *ignotas ad id tempus* " *gentes crebris ſimul ac proſperis præliis domuit; eamque partem* " *Britanniæ quæ Hiberniam aſpicit copiis inſtruxit, in ſpem magis* " *quam ob formidinem.*" Tacit. vit. Agr. cap. xxiv. And, accord-ing to their Geography, nothing could be better ſituated for carrying on their purpoſes againſt Ireland than *Dunmonia:* " *Siquidem* " *Hibernia, medio inter Britanniam atque Hiſpaniam ſita, &* " *Gallico quoque Mari opportuna, valentiſſimam Imperii partem* " *magnis invicem uſibus miſcuerit.*" Ibid. The Romans thought Ireland to have lain midway betwixt Spain and Britain, and to have extended itſelf a great deal farther to the South than it really does; to promote the Conqueſt therefore of an Iſland, ſuppoſed to be placed ſo aptly for the connexion of Spain, Gaul, and Britain, nothing, he thought, could be more proper than conquering firſt *Dunmonia*, the moſt Southern and Weſtern part of Britain.

The queſtion is, who were theſe unknown nations ſubdued by Agricola in his ſhips this fifth year? The Brigantes, who extended as far North as the river Tine, were ſubdued by Petilius Cerealis [h]. The Welſh were already ſubdued (South Wales by

---

[d] From Tacitus.—Horſley, p. 42.
[e] Gordon's Itin. Sept. p. 15. ibid.
[f] Horſley, p. 43.
[g] This Expedition was in the 5th year of Agricola's Propretorſhip in Britain, which was

the firſt of Domitian. Domitian and Flavius Sabinus being Conſuls A. D. 83. according to the Savilian Faſti.
[h] Stillingfleet's Or. Brit. p. 243.—Tacit. Agric. cap. xvii. xviii.

Julius

Julius Frontinus, and the men of North Wales by Agricola in his first year); so that they could not be the Welsh; nor indeed their neighbours the Cangi, or those nations stretching from Chester to Bristol (as the late learned Dr. Musgrave imagines), for they, lying in the way to South and North Wales, could not be unknown to the Roman Generals, whose forces had made several campaigns (before the coming of Agricola) on those borders in Shropshire, Staffordshire, Hereford, and Monmouthshire, as they warred against the hardy Britans of Wales. Let it be considered, in the next place, that there was no reason for Agricola to go into his ships to conquer those inland Countries.

Mr. Horsley seems to me no happier in his conjecture than Dr. Musgrave, for he supposes these unknown nations were the people of Galloway, or the maritime parts of Cantyre and Argyleshire [i]: but is it likely that these nations should be unknown to Agricola, when they lay so near him in his marches the second, third, and fourth Summers? Is it likely that Agricola, so knowing in matters of war, would make his ships to sail so long and dangerous a voyage, on purpose to conquer, or attend the conquest of, what was so near at hand, and as it were contiguous to the Roman Garrisons, which he had placed on the *Isthmus* in his third and fourth Summers? It is certain, says Horsley (ibid.), that the Roman ships were in Clyde this (i. e. the 5th) Summer. I would ask how they should get there? They could not sail round Cathness without discovering the Orkneys, and the Orkneys were not discovered till the seventh year of Agricola [k]; so that plain it is, the Roman Fleet, which had its Winter Station at Portus Rhutupiensis near Dover, must have gone round the Land's-End, and up the Irish Ocean to the Frith of Clyde [l]. Is it probable, then, that the Fleet of one so curious, and equally intent upon Conquest and new Discoveries, should pass idly by the many promontories and harbours of the Western Coast, in a Climate much more tempting than the North, with the General and soldiers on board, without the least attempt on so great a scope of shores, till they arrived at the Frith of Clyde? No, surely.—In the West, therefore, were the *ignotæ gentes*. The Romans had possessed the middle and principal parts of England in the time of Claudius; his Lieutenants, and those of the subsequent Emperours, carried on the Conquests (as we find by their history) against all the Nations, from the *Belgæ*,

[i] Stillingfleet, p. 43.

[k] Horsley, p. 44.

[l] Bp. Stillingfleet treating of this Summer's Expedition (ibid. ut supr. 244.) omits the principal point; " nave prima transgressus;" and therefore takes the ignotæ gentes to lie beyond the Bodotrian Frith.

and

and the Britans in Wales, as far North as the river Tay in Scotland.

All the feveral nations of England, and the South of Scotland, were fo intermixed, that, upon any new infurrection, or frefh enterprize to employ the Soldiery, they muft at one time or other have fallen under the notice and power of the Romans. The *Belgæ* were probably fubdued by Vefpafian, of whom Suetonius faith (in Vefpaf. cap. iv.), " That he fought thirty battles, " conquered here two powerful nations, above twenty towns, and " the Ifle of Wight. By which we find his employment was " Weftward, and the *Belgæ* and *Dunmonii* were the two powerful " Nations that way [m]." But, with fubmiffion, the *Dunmonii* are not mentioned as conquered by Vefpafian; and as the Wars of that General reached from Wales, Southward, to the Ifle of Wight, the two powerful nations feem to have been the *Belgæ* and the *Durotriges*, which both lay contiguous to his other Conquefts, but the *Dunmonii* farther to the Weft. All this while we find no mention of the *Dunmonii*, they alone lying hid hitherto in a narrow angle of Britain, which was neither a thorugh-fare to other nations, nor had of itfelf provoked the Roman Power.

If we confider the Theatre of the Roman Wars to this time with a little attention, and how many battles were fought by Vefpafian, and how the Roman Armies were refident at different times in all the other parts of the Kingdom; we muft conclude, that the *Dunmonii* were the only Nations that could be unknown to the Roman people. This part of Tacitus's hiftory is, therefore, not intelligible, much lefs reconcilable to the confummate prudence of Agricola, unlefs we underftand him in the following manner, viz. That Agricola, having in his fourth year erected Forts on the Bodotrian Ifthmus, to fecure thofe Northern Limits, and being now at Liberty to make new difcoveries, and pufh his Conquefts another way, went into his fhips at Portus Rhutupienfis, and failing, down the Englifh Chanel, conquered the Weftern parts of the Ifland, till then unknown to the Roman Nation; thence paffing round the Land's-End, he placed Garrifons on the Shores oppofite to Ireland, not only that he might thereby better fecure the Conquefts he had made; but intending (like a man of extenfive views) one time or other to conquer that Ifland alfo; to which great defign, the different Harbours and Garrifons on the North of Cornwall and Devonfhire he thought might much contribute.

Before I clofe the account of the Romans refiding in Cornwall, and the Remains they left here, one article (though it might have

---

[m] Stillingfleet's Orig. Brit. p. 31.

been

been more regularly inferted in Chapter II. of this book if it had been more early communicated to the printer) requires fome notice.

There was an Intaglio found in this County fome time fince, which I think has undoubted marks of being a true Antique, and moft likely therefore to be Roman. It is the property of Philip Vyvyan, Efq; of Tremeal, was found in the parifh of Altarnun near Lancefton, and was then fixed, as a head to a gold bodkin, but is now fet in a ring as a feal (See Plate XXVIII. p. 316.).

The ftone in which the impreffion is cut, is green Jafper, re-markably ftreaked at the back, and zoned tranfverfedly with two flips of white, inclofing one that is brown in parallel lines, like what the Heralds would call a Bend Cotized: the texture of the ftone did not admit that high polifh, which the Drawing and erudition of the Defign deferved.

In the Area of the Seal, the chief figure is a Griffin, with its wings difplayed; three of the feet are fixed, the other is lifted up, as if to grafp fome fmall round things which lie before it, like pieces of money; the left wing is next to the eye, and very bold; the other is partly hid by the head and neck of the Griffin, but appears beyond the top of the head like a Creft of plumage: under-neath is an extended ferpent, which makes no improper bafe line for fupporting the principal figure.

In Aldrovandus's [n] Ornithologia, Tab. VIII. Fig. V. there is a Griffin, which will in fome meafure explain the fubject before us: it has the Serpent ftretched under its feet, and in one of his fore-paws uplifted he holds a dagger, fierce and attentive, guardian (as this bird was anciently fuppofed to be) of his collected treafures.

The Griffin, indeed, is an imaginary animal, as the Sphynx, Satyr, Gorgon, Syrens, Harpies, and Centaurs were of old, all creatures of the fancy, yet not unmeaning, nor to be looked upon as meer whims and monfters in any other fenfe than as they do not exift in Nature; they are mythological beings, confifting of feveral parts of different animals, adjufted and blended together, in order to convey fome moral, or heighten fome prevailing paffion above and beyond nature: this was one way among the Ancients of imprinting Caution and Wifdom; by a pardonable mixture of forms, they ridiculed and deformed Vice, fupplied Youth with inftructive and virtuous memorials, and contracted a leffon of im-portant and extenfive benefit within the portable compafs of a fhilling.

The Griffin (with which we are only at prefent concerned) has the Head, Breaft, and Wings of an Eagle, added to the body, and

[n] Aldr. Lib. X. cap. i. de fabulofis Avibus.

talons

talons of a Lion; the former to exprefs fwiftnefs, quicknefs of fight, and voracity, the latter to reprefent fiercenefs and ftrength. This compound figure was the Emblem of a Mifer, intent only upon gold (the fixed characteriftick of the Griffin), who by turns tenacioufly broods over his neft of treafure, or, with the fwiftnefs of an Eagle, and the rapacity of a Lion, preys upon, ftrips, and devours the orphan, the neceffitous, and improvident. In this Seal, the Griffin feems to be employed in pawing and fcraping together his pieces of money; and a Serpent, his ufual companion, lies underneath, either to denote the fubtilty of getting, or the watchful artifice of defending what is unjuftly gotten, or (which appears of equal utility), to warn the greedy Mifer, that though unjuft gain may give pleafure in the hoarding, yet at the laft it biteth like a Serpent, and ftingeth like an adder[m].

C H A P. VII.

Of Ancient Caftles in Cornwall; and firft of Hill-Caftles.

WE have feveral forts of ancient Fortifications in Cornwall; and becaufe it is difficult to affign them to their proper authours, but more difficult ftill to difcover the refpective age in which they were built, we will range them, by the reader's leave, according to the fimplicity of the works, beginning with thofe which have leaft of Art, and proceeding gradually to thofe which have more labour, and a greater variety of works in their compofition.

SECT. I. The Sorts of Caftles in Cornwall.

Our Caftles (for the Cornifh call them all fo, though, perhaps, improperly) may be divided into three Claffes. Firft, Walled Forts, or Lines, for Defence and Garrifon.

Secondly, Walled Caftles for Refidence, as well as Defence.

Thirdly, Artificial Hills, covered with a Building, fometimes called a Keep, fometimes a Dungeon; and a garretted Wall enclofing an Area below, called a Baffe-court. Of each fort I fhall defcribe one or two of the moft confiderable, and endeavour to affign them to that Nation which appears moft probably to have erected them, with fome obfervations on the occafion of their being built, and the choice of the ground they ftand upon.

[m] The Drawing is truly bold and good; the Eagle-part is magnified fo as to correfpond fitly to the fize of the Lion, and the whole is an elegant and expreffive compofition: indeed, the Griffin in general is fo fhapely a figure, that Architects in their capital works have enriched their Frizes with it, and Emperours in their Coins have fometimes preferred it to the Horfe for drawing their trumphal Carrs.

Of

Of the firſt Claſs we have two ſorts, ſome which incloſe a promontory, by a *Vallum* ſtretching croſs a neck of land from the edge of one cliff to that of another, which for diſtinction we may call Cliff-Caſtles; and ſome conſiſting of one *Vallum*, or more, of Earth, or a rampart of Stone on the tops of hills. Of the firſt ſort is Caſtle Treryn in the pariſh of St. Levin (Plate XXVI. p. 297). This Cape ſhoots forth into the Sea, bearing directly South; its farthermoſt Ridge conſiſts of three lofty groupes of Rock, to the North of which is a low and narrow neck of Land, croſs which there runs from the Eaſt to the Weſtern Cliff, a Stone Wall marked A; the ground then riſes pretty quick, and on the brow of the hill there is a *Vallum* of Earth B, and a ditch without it towards the land, but none within next the ſea. This *Vallum* runs alſo nearly Eaſt and Weſt, reaching from ſea to ſea; and without it towards the land there is another *Vallum* of Earth C, of like direction, but lower in point of ſituation, incloſing in like manner a greater portion of this promontory. To the Eaſt of this promontory there is a very commodious Creek called Penberth; and to the Weſt there are many landing places, which will give us ſome light hereafter into the occaſion of this and ſuch like Caſtles.

About a mile and half to the Weſtward of Caſtle Treryn, the cape called Tolpedn-penwith is divided from the main land by a Stone-wall, which coaſting along the brow of the hill extends from ſea to ſea. The Caſtles Karnijek and Boſcajell [n], in the pariſh of St. Juſt, are of the ſame kind, and many others on the ſea-coaſt. The remains of one are very remarkable, about half a mile N. W. of Tehidy, the Seat of Francis Baſſet, Eſq. They ſtand now on the very brim of the Cliff, and much more than what is now ſtanding is fallen with the Cliff into the ſea. This entrench-ment conſiſted of two Ditches, and conſequently two *Vallums* [o]: the inner and principal Ditch next the Cliff is now but ninety paces long, and twelve feet wide at the bottom, which, being very even, and full of graſs, is generally called the Bowling-green; it runs near E. and W. at each extremity ending in an inacceſſible Cliff, incloſing formerly a cape of land which ran into the North ſea, and at its Northern point, turning about to the Weſt, formed a Pool where veſſels might have had ſome ſhelter whilſt this cape remained entire, and Soldiers, under the fortifications above, might have had tolerable good landing: but the violence of the Northern ſea has eaten away all the neck of Land which joined this cape to the main, ſo that the Land and Sea alſo, which this forti-

[n] In Corniſh Karnnidzhek, and Boſcadzhel.
[o] By a Vallum, I mean what is thrown up out of the Trench into a Mound, or Ridge, in order to diſtinguiſh betwixt that and a Rampart, though Vallum in Latin really ſignifies both that Ridge, and a Rampart alſo.

fication

fication was intended to fecure, are both fo altered fince they were fortified, that, were it not for the remains of the fortification above, the place would efcape all notice ; and, on the other hand, unlefs we could trace this cape, and its alterations in the foft fhelfy Cliffs, and the remaining Rocks below, it would be impoffible to guefs for what reafon fuch a fortification fhould be here erected ; but the prefent appearance, well confidered, illuftrates the ufe and intent of this fortification to be the fame as of thofe which have been already defcribed.

Caftles of this fort, including Promontories and Rocks, with their trenches towards the Land, were made, as I imagine, by invaders, to fecure a place for landing men, when they made any defcent, and re-imbarking them upon their retreat. For this I have the following reafons ; the trench is always next the Land, implying, that the enemy expected was to come from the land, not the fea ; the inner *Vallum* next the fea at Tehidy, and at Treryn at C, is higher than that without it, and, doubtlefs, for this reafon, that they might make a double execution upon the enemy, by fhooting their arrows, darts, and ftones, both from above and below, at the fame time. It may be imagined, that thefe were retiring places for the Natives, when they were preffed by the enemy who were in poffeffion of their country, but this could not be ; the Natives would quickly have been ftarved into a furrender, amidft thefe Rocks and naked Capes ; there was no fhelter for their wives, children, or cattle, all which, therefore, they muft have abandoned to the mercy of their enemy, and upon every fuch in-judicious retreat find themfelves under an immediate neceffity of fubmitting, ftarving, or drowning ; befides, the Saxons and Danes, having fleets, were mafters of the fea, and, there being landing places near all fuch Caftles, the flight of the Natives hither would not by any means fecure them, for thofe who had fhips might eafily land, and fcale thefe Cliffs, without the leaft impediment from the fortifications towards the land ; fo that thefe Faftneffes could be of no fervice to the Natives ; but they were extremely proper for invaders ; for the line being fhort from Cliff to Cliff, and therefore eafily and quickly manned, and the invaders having eafy accefs to their fhips below for provifion, and every thing they wanted, could neither be forced nor ftarved ; as foon as they had feized a rocky Cape fit for their purpofe, they entrenched to prevent furprize, and, under the covert of thefe intrenchments, fome repelled the Natives, whilft others were bufy in dif-embarking their troops and neceffaries ; as foon as they were ready, they marched forwards into the land, leaving their fhips, and, doubtlefs, a Garrifon in thefe works, to fecure a retreat to their fhips. I

4 T   attribute

attribute thefe works, therefore, to the Saxon or Danifh invaders, for they fuit very well the purpofes of foreigners and pirates; but could by no means be of fervice to the Britans.

SECT. III.
Hill Caftles.
Bartinè.

The fecond fort of our military works is that which has one *Vallum*, or more, of Earth on the top of a hill. On the top of Bartinè-hill, in the parifh of St. Juft, may be feen a circular mound of Earth, with little or no ditch, never of any great ftrength; perhaps only traced out, begun, and never finifhed. Within this inclofure was funk a Well, now filled with Stones; and the only thing remarkable is, that near the centre of this Caftle lie three fmall circles, edged with Stones pitched on end, and contiguous to each other, the Northernmoft nine yards diameter, the others feven. It is uncertain whether thefe Circles were of military or religious erection; if of the firft, they were, as I imagine, the apartments or fepulchres of the Commanders; if of the fecond, places of worfhip, prior to the fortifying this hill. A view of this may be feen Plate XXIX. Fig. I.

Caerbrân.

That we may advance gradually, let the next Fortification be Caerbrân P in the parifh of Sancred, a circular fortification on the top of a high hill; confifting firft of a deep ditch fifteen feet wide edged with Stone, through which you pafs to the outer *Vallum*, which is of Earth, fifteen feet high, and was well perfected to the North Eaft; but not fo towards the Weft. Within this *Vallum*, paffing a large ditch, about fifteen yards wide, you come to a Stone-wall, which quite rounded the top of the hill, and feems to have been of confiderable ftrength; but lies now like a ridge of diforderly Stones: the diameter of the whole is ninety paces, and in the center of all a little circle. There are many others of this kind ftill to be feen q, and fome have been quite deftroyed r; and there are fome of thefe Hill-caftles which are more regularly built,

Caftleandinas.

and walled round, fuch as Caftleandinas in the parifh of Ludgvan, which confifted of two-ftone-walls built one within the other in a circular form, furrounding the area of the hill. The ruins are now fallen on each fide the Walls, and fhew the work to have been of great height and thicknefs; there was alfo a third and outmoft Wall built more than halfways round, but was left unfinifhed. Within the Walls are many little inclofures of a circular form about feven yards diameter with little Walls round them, of two and three feet high; they appeared to me to have been fo many huts, erected for the fhelter of the garrifon; the diameter of the whole Fort from Eaft to Weft is 400 feet, and the principal Graff

P " Dinas Brân, that is to fay, Brennus's " Court, or Palace." Hum. Lh. Brev. Engl. P. 53.

q As Caftle-Hornek, and Caftle Lefgûdzhek &c.

r As Rofcadzhel and others.

or

Bartine Castle in St Just

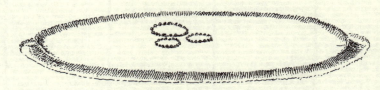

Caer brân Castle in S.^t ancred.

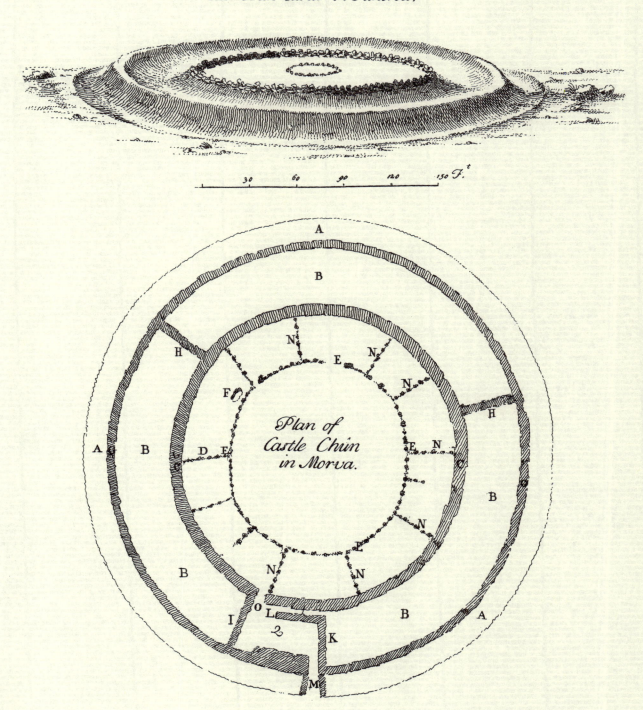

30   60   90   120   150 F.^t

Plan of
Castle Chûn
in Morva.

To William Lemon of Carclew in Cornwall Esq.

This Plate is with great   respect inscrib'd by Wm. Borlase.

or Ditch is fixty feet wide: towards the South the fides of this mountain are marked by two large green paths about ten feet wide, which were vifibly cleanfed by art of their natural roughnefs, for the more convenient approach to this garrifon: near the middle of the Area is a Well almoft choaked with its own ruins, and at a little diftance, a narrow pit, its fides walled round, probably dug for water alfo, but now filled with rubbifh: this is on the higheft hill in the hundred of Penwith; as to conftruction not materially differing from Caer-bran caftle; but the moft regular and curious of this kind is Caftle-Chûn in the little parifh of Morvah, a plan of which I have therefore here exhibited (Pl. XXIX. Fig. III.) and now fhall defcribe more particularly.

The entrance faces W. S. W. where having paffed the ditch A, you enter the outmoft Wall G, five feet thick at M, which is called the Iron Gateway, and leave on the left hand the wall twelve feet thick for ftrengthening the entrance; on the right, there is a wall, K, which traverfes the principal ditch, BB, thirty feet wide, till it reaches within three feet of the principal wall C eight feet thick at the prefent top, but in the foundation thicker; then turns away parallel to it, to L, leaving a narrow paffage of three feet wide, as a communication betwixt the entrance, Q, and the ditch K B H. The entrance Q, flanked on the right by the wall K, and on the left by an oppofite wall I, admits you by the paffage O, through the great wall C, into feveral lodgments which are formed by a circular line of ftone-work E E E, about three feet high, parallel to the wall C, and feveral partitions N N N, fpring as it were from the center of the whole work, and reaching from the line E to the principal wall C: thefe divifions are all thirty feet wide, but of unequal bignefs. The area within thefe works is 125 feet from Eaft to Weft, and 110 from North to South. The principal fofs B, has four traverfes; two, K, and I, which fecure the entrance; and two more HH, which divide the remaining part of the fofs nearly into three equal parts. At F, there is a Well, which has fteps to go down to the water. By the ruins of thefe walls, I judge that the outermoft could not be lefs than ten feet high, and the innermoft about fifteen, but rather more, and both well perfected; the apartments within were probably fhelters from the weather. Some rude ones of like ufe we have taken notice of in other examples; but thefe are much more regularly difpofed, and indeed the whole of this work, the neatnefs and regularity of the walls, providing fuch fecurity for their entrance, flanking and dividing their Fofs, fhews a military knowledge fuperiour to that of any other works of this kind, which I have feen in Cornwall. Many other walled Caftles we have upon our hills, as Torcrobm in

Lanant;

Caftle Chûn.

Lanant; Caergonin in Breague, and the like, but none materially different.

By whom built, and for what End. The age and authours of this fort of Fortification may beſt be determined by the form, number, and fituation of the works.

All of this kind, which I have feen, are either round or nearly fo; from which fome will pronounce them to be Daniſh; but this is too haſty a concluſion; for though the Danes fortified in this manner, as appears by entrenchments in feveral parts of England, inconteſtably of Daniſh ſtructure; yet by p. 315, it is plain that the Romans alſo erected their Forts fometimes in the circular form; and fo doubtlefs did the Saxons and the Britans; however, thefe Hill-Caſtles in Cornwall, I take to be Daniſh, for the following, and, as I think, more concluſive reaſons. In the narroweſt and Weſternmoſt part of Cornwall (viz. from St. Michael's Mount to the Land's-End), there are no lefs than feven of thefe Caſtles ſtill remaining[s]; fome are not one mile, none more than three miles diſtant from one another; fo that from the firſt you can fee the fecond, from the fecond the third, and fo on; from feveral of them you can fee both the North and South Chanell; but from all of them you can fee either one or other. This narrow fpot, in which the Caſtles ſtand fo thick, is no where above ſix miles from the North to the South fea, in fome places not four; and from the Weſternmoſt Caſtle of this kind, to the Eaſternmoſt, is not more than eight miles. In other parts of this county, we have Fortifications of the fame kind, but they are thinly planted. Now, why ſhould the natives crowd them together in a heap, and in ſuch a corner of the county, where they could be of no fervice to defend the moſt valuable and fpacious parts of it; and where there could not be room enough for the numerous inhabitants of a county fo well peopled as Cornwall was (before it was depopulated and in a manner ruined by the Danes) to retreat into?

Thefe Caſtles have no houfes within them (as moſt certainly they would have had, if erected by and for the natives), but only fome low huts for foldiers.

Moſt of them have fome part of either ditch or *vallum* unfiniſhed, which would not be left in that manner, if the natives had intended them for their fecurity; for the natives had intervals of quiet enough to have compleated thefe works. Again, all thefe Caſtles are difmantled, which the Danes could have no motive to do; neither can we imagine that the Britans would deſtroy their own forts; but now all thefe circumſtances argue, on the other

---

[s] All marked with a double circle in the ſmall Map.

hand,

hand, as much for their being Danish, as they do against their being British.

The Danes chose this Western part of Cornwall for disembarking their troops, and planting their garrisons, because small parties (as doubtless they were at first) were not so easily surrounded, forced, and cut off here, as they would have been in a more extended country[t].

They placed their Forts on hills in sight of one another, that the alarm might reach from one Castle to the other; that signals of distress, or assembling, and making ready, might be communicated in a minute.

They placed them near the Sea, to give notice to their fleet, receive notice from it, and discover the ships of the enemy; and all these are so many express testimonies that the Danes understood their business well.   The Castles indeed had only temporary shelters, because the Danes, accustomed to a much colder climate, wanted no more.   The outer parts of them were left unfinished, because the General, either satiated with plunder, or because of the advanced season, called off the garrison.   Lastly, they are all laid in ruins, probably by the Britans, who, as soon as the Danes were gone, had reason sufficient to wreak their spite, and demolish them, remembering how bitterly they had smarted by the garrisons they contained.

It may be asked, why should these Castles have British names, if of Danish erection? British names they have, it is true; but the single circumstance of a name cannot over-balance the reasons which go before.   What the Danes called them we cannot tell, though, for distinction sake, the garrisons had doubtless different names for the different hills; but the Danish names expired with the possession, and of the Danish language we find no traces which were owing to the intercourse of the Cornish and Danes of those times.   When the Danes left Cornwall, the natives named the Castle from some famous exploit, as the castle of the Bloody Field[u]; from its strong situation and works, as the Iron Castle[w]; from the name of the lands or manor on which it stood, as the castle of Chûn[x]; or from the remarkable height of the hill, as Castle-andinas[y]; but it can be no more concluded that the Britans erected these castles, because they have British names, than that the Saxons built Exeter or Salisbury because these cities have Saxon names.   And here I cannot but take notice of a common mistake,

t See map of the Hundred of Penwith, Plate I.   x Castle Chûn.
u Castle Lesgudzhek.   y Castle-andinas.
w Castle Hornek.

4 U   in

in calling and writing the name of the great caftle (of the fame kind we are now treating of) near St. Columb, and that in the parifh of Ludgvan, Caftle-an-Danis, as if it were called fo, becaufe it was a Danifh caftle. This cannot be the true name, as it would be no diftinction (which is the reafon of all names), for the inhabitants to call them Danis (i. e. Danifh), caftles, where there are fo many of one ftructure, and fo near one another, and all as much built by the Danes, one as another. It muft be written therefore Dinas (not Danis) for fo the Cornifh call the fortified hills, as Pendinas near Falmouth; Dinas, in Padftow; Little Dinas in St. Anthony. The reafons for the other Britifh names we have feen before; but this name they gave, by way of eminence, to the moft confpicuous and ftrongeft fort of any particular diftrict.

CHAP. VIII.

Of the Walled Caftles defigned for Refidence as well as Defence.

THESE are likewife of two forts, either with or without a Keep[z]. Thofe without a Keep were generally built Turret-wife, of which fort, we have but one now remaining, that I can fpeak of, in Cornwall[a], and that is Caftle Karnbrê, and even this has been fomewhat altered, to make it a Lodge for the old Park in which it ftands[b]. However, there is fomething fingular in the fituation, plan, and elevation of this caftle, for which reafon I have added Icons of it[c], and fhall defcribe it.

Caftle Karnbrê. Karnbrê Caftle ftands on a rocky knoll at the Eaftern end of Karnbrê-hill. The foundation of the building (Plate VII. Fig. A C. p. 117.) is laid on a very irregular ledge of vaft rocks, whofe furfaces are very uneven, fome high, fome low, and confequently the floors of the rooms on the ground-floor muft be fo too. The rocks were not contiguous, for which reafon the architect has contrived fo many arches from rock to rock, as would carry the wall above. The ledge of rocks was narrow, and the rooms purchafed with fo much labour, neither capacious nor handfome, as may be feen by the Plan, A D. The walls, as will beft appear in the elevation, have in one of the turrets, a, three ftories of

[z] A Keep is a building elevated above the reft by a Hillock (or *Tumulus*) for the moft part artificially raifed. See Trematon, Plate XXXI. and Lancefton, Plate XXXIII.

[a] The reft, as they were Britifh, being

deftroyed likely in the Danifh wars.

[b] Belonging to the family of Baffet, whofe anceftral feat, called Tehidy, is within two miles of it.

[c] Plate VII. p. 117.

windows,

windows, in *b* but one, and are pierced every where by small holes
to descry the enemy, and discharge their arrows, and some perhaps
added in the more modern times for muskets. There were some
Buildings (now all down) at the North West end which were the
out-works to this castle; but its greatest security was the difficult
approach to it, the hill being strewed with great rocks on every
side. This was certainly a British building, and erected in those
uncultivated ages, when such rocky, hideous situations were the
choice of warlike, rough, and stern minds.

The point on which this Castle stands is not the highest part of
the hill[d]; that is taken up by a circular fortification A M, about
300 yards to the West of the former[e]. Here we find the ruins of
a stone wall H, which ruins are twenty feet wide, and shew the
wall to have been of considerable height and thickness; it is called
the Old Castle: its Westernmost side was built on the foundation
of a sacred mound, which inclosed the greatest part of this hill, for
religion[f]; but its Eastern part deserted that mound at G L H, and
was determined by the height of the ground, as it ought to be.
That it was built by the ancient Britans, and as anciently as when
Druidism was the established religion in Cornwall, I have great
reason to think, because I find the large flat stones which have
most remarkable Rock-basons (instruments probably of Druid
superstition) at G and L, left entire, as if preserved out of devotion;
whereas, if this wall had been built by Saxons, Danes, or even
Christians, they would certainly have been clove up, as being of
the quoit or *discus* shape, and therefore commodious for the use of
building; in the next place I observe, that their wall does not cut
or mangle any of their sacred circles, which are numerous here;
whereas there is not that care taken of these places of devotion in
the Danish Fortifications. The Rock-basons of that vast crag
called Karnidsak were probably carried off to build Castle Chûn;
and at Castle Treryn (Plate XXVI.) I observe one of the Danish
vallums B, cutting one of the Druid holy circles, and passing quite
through it; and where the Danes have stone walls in their cliff
castles, we find few or none of the Rock-basons: all strong
evidences, that the Danes had no reverence for these works, and
therefore where we find them spared, we have reason to conclude
that they were spared by the Britans out of respect to their own
religion. There seems to have been part of a stone wall built on
the North side of this hill, running from the old Castle, nearly East,
towards the new; it was built on the foundation of the religious

[d] See the elevation of this hill at the end of Chap. xiii. Plate XXXVII. of this Book.
[e] See the Map, Plate VII. p. 117.
[f] See Book II. chap. xvii. p. 118.

mound

mound before mentioned ; but it does not reach within sixty yards of the new Caftle, and was never finifhed.

By the Military Remains on this hill, the Britifh Coins of Gold, the Roman Coins, Weapons of War, and other things (probably Roman) found here (not to infift upon the feveral Religious Monuments mentioned Book II. Chap. XVII.) this hill muft have been a place of ancient and great refort in times of war, as well as peace ; well known to the Romans, and frequented by the moft confiderable among the Britans [g].

Tindagel alias Tindogel Caftle.   Tindagel Caftle [h] (Plate XXX.) was built on a cape of land, the extremity of which was a *Peninfula*, a very lofty hill, E. Where this *Peninfula* joined the main land, there are the fortifications, partly on the *Peninfula*, and partly on the Main. Concerning this Caftle, a Poet has the following verfes, thus tranflated in the reign of Elizabeth, by the ingenious Mr. Carew, p. 121.

Eft locus Abrini finuofo littore ponti	" There is a place within the wind- " ing Shore of Severne Sea,
Rupe fitus media; refluus quem circuit æftus:	" On mids of rock, about whofe foote " The tides turn-keeping play ;
Fulminat hic late turrito vertice Caftrum	" A Tow'ry topped Caftle here " Wide blazeth over all,
Nomine Tindagium veteres dixere Corini.	" Which Corineus ancient broode " Tindagel Caftle call."

The Remains here are not at prefent confiderable. The Ruins on the *Peninfula* confift of a circular garreted wall D, inclofing fome buildings, among which there was a " pretty chapel of St. Uliane [i], " with a tomb on the left fide (ftanding in Leland's time, temp. " H. VIII.) and men then alive remembered a poftern door of iron." Leland (vol. II. p. 81.) calls this, improperly, the Dungeon (for it is indeed only the walling of the Bafecourt), and thinks the fituation muft have rendered it impregnable ; the cliffs, it muft be owned, are hideous, and not to be climbed without the utmoft danger ; but, with all deference to fo great a judge of antiquity, the ground here was badly chofen, the hill dipping fo very quick, that every thing within the wall was expofed to a hill over againft and fcarce an arrow-flight from it ; whereas the judgment was to have placed the Fortrefs higher, fo as it fhould have reached the top of the hill N. This would indeed have expofed the inhabitants more to the weather, but lefs to the enemy, which laft, in fuch

[g] Its elevation (as a hill that has afforded a great treafure of antiquities) may be feen at the end of Chap. xiii. of this book, Plate XXXVII.

[h] Rectius f. Tintughel ; viz. the high fortified hill.

[i] St. Juliane's Chapel in Tindagel Caftle. Lel. vol. III. fol. 95.

works

Pl. XXX. p. 362.

To M.rs Basset of Tehidy this View

of Tindagel Castle in Cornwall

is most gratefully

Dedicated by Wm: Borlase.

A

C

N

E

WB

J. Green sculp

works is moſt to be conſidered.   The walls on the Main incloſe
two narrow courts, and cover better than the other, and at the end
A, the higheſt part of this fortreſs, there are ſeveral Stone ſteps to
aſcend unto the Parapet for making diſcoveries.   The Walls were
garreted, and are pierced with many ſquare little holes as at
Karnbrê.   This part of the fortification was anciently joined to
that of the *Peninſula* by a Draw-bridge; but it was decayed before
Leland came there, and the want of it ſupplied by long Elm-trees
layed as a bridge[i]; but the gap c (purpoſely cut through the
Iſthmus at firſt for the ſecurity of the works D) is now much
widened, and the communication intercepted.   The whole was a
large work, and placed here for the ſake of ſhutting out the enemy
by means of the narrow *Iſthmus,* which errour in the firſt deſign
inevitably planted it ſo low, that little of what happened in the
country adjacent could be deſcried from it.   This Caſtle, ſo
noted for the birth of the famous King Arthur, about the end of
the 5th century, needs no proofs (though not without ſome
modern alterations) of its being originally a Britiſh Structure.
It was the ſeat of the Dukes of Cornwall at that time, how long
before we cannot ſay, but probably a product of the rudeſt times,
before the Corniſh Britans had learnt from the Romans any thing
of the art of war; for it cannot be conceived that any people who
had ſeen the Romans chuſe their ground, fortify, or attack, would
ever have placed a Fortreſs ſo injudiciouſly.   It continued to be
one of the Caſtles of the Earls of Cornwall to the time of Richard,
King of the Romans, who entertained here, his nephew David,
Prince of Wales.   After the death of Richard, and his ſon Edmund,
Earls of Cornwall, all the ancient Caſtles went to ruin; from
Palaces became Priſons and Gaols, and this among the reſt.
There was, however, a yearly ſtipend allowed for keeping this
Caſtle, till the Lord Treaſurer Burleigh, in Queen Elizabeth's
reign, aboliſhed it, as a ſuperfluous charge to the crown.

There is another Caſtle of this kind called Caerguidn (or White
Caſtle) in the pariſh of Sancred, which, becauſe it lies in the Side of
a hill, and has not in its ſituation the advantage of the ground, I
cannot think Daniſh, but Britiſh, and very ancient.

i Vol. VII. p. 106.

4 X   CHAP.

C H A P. IX.

Of Walled Castles for Residence and Defence, which have Keeps; and first of Trematon.

Trematon Castle. THE most entire Castle of this sort, but the least which we have in Cornwall, is that called generally Trematon[k], by Leland Tremertoun, in the parish of St. Stephen near Saltash. The Wall of the Bass-court, A (Plate XXXI. Fig. I.) is still standing, ditched without, and pierced in several places with certain loop-holes, some square (as those before in Karn-brê and Tindagel) some narrow, and high, as c, and some cross-wise, as D. There is no tower projecting from this Wall, but the gateway, which seems (together with the Walls near it) more modern than the rest of the building.

Bass-Court. The Bass-court was about three quarters of an acre, and once charged with several buildings which are now all gone. At one end of this Court is an artificial hill G, which, by the dipping of the valley at E, is there of a very considerable height, and has a large ditch round the bottom; but next the Bass-court is only about thirty feet perpendicular. On the top of this taper hill is **Keep.** erected the Keep F, of an oval figure[l], the outer Wall of which is still standing, ten feet thick, two feet of which is taken up with the garreted Parapet, the other eight make the breadth of the rampart. The entrance is towards the West, where the arch over the gateway is round, not pointed, and therefore the more ancient. The top of the Parapet is about thirty feet high from the area within, which is now converted into a garden of pot-herbs; but the man who shewed the Castle, and made the garden for his own use, remembers a chimney, and some part of walls standing, of which there are now no traces. The holes for the beams are plain, and in two rows, but both so near the top of the rampart, that, I imagine, there could be but one flight of rooms, and that the double beaming was contrived for the better supporting the roof, upon which in time of action the Soldiers did duty. There is no window in all this Keep, for which reason I conclude, they must have had a little Court (or Well, as the the builders term it), in the center of the Keep, to give light and air, in some such manner, as we shall find by and by in another Castle, and as is shewn in this by dotted lines in the plan annexed, at H. This little Court, it is

[k] In Domesday, TREMATONA.   [l] See the plan Pl. XXXI. Fig. II.

true,

Fig. III
Plan of the keep
of Launceston Castle
pa. 358.

Fig. IV Plan of the keep of Trematon Castle
pa. 354.

10 20 30 40 50 60 70 Ft

To Lady Caren Buller

Of Anthony in Cornwall

This View of TREMATON CASTLE is with great respect inscrib'd by Wm. Borlase:

true, would yield but little light, but it was to strengthen their rampart, that they denied themselves the pleasure of windows; and hence it was that these Keeps are often called the Dungeons of the Castles to which they belong.

Trematon Castle was the head of a Barony of the ancient Dukes of Cornwall. It appears by Domesday [m], that William Earl of Moreton [n] and Cornwall had here his castle and market, and resided here; but we are not to suppose that this William or his father Robert (half brother to the Conqueror) were the builders of all the castles which they had. For when the Conquerour came in, the last Earl of Cornwall of British blood (by some called Candorus; by Camden, Cadocus) descended from a long train of Ancestors, sometime called Kings, sometime Dukes, and Earls of Cornwall, was displaced, and his Lands as well as Honours given to Robert Earl of Moreton; and it is natural to think that, where the Residence of those ancient Earls of Cornwall was, there he occasionally fixed his Court, as at Lanceston, Tindagel, and Trematon. Mr. Carew, in his Survey (p. 112.) gives us this account of an ancient Monument found in the parish Church of St. Stephen, to which this Castle belongs. " I have received information (says he) from one averring " eye witness, that about fourscore years since, there was digged " up in the parish chancel, a leaden coffin, which, being opened, " shewed the proportion of a very big man. The partie farder " told me, how a writing, graved in the lead, expressed the same " to be the burial of a Duke, whose heir was married to the Prince, " but who it should be, I cannot devise; albeit, my best pleasing " conjecture lighteth upon Orgerius, because his daughter was " married to Edgar." Now this Orgerius was Duke of Cornwall, A. D. 959. and might probably have lived at Trematon Castle in this parish; but he was buried in the monastery of Tavistock (as W. of Malmsbury says, p. 146.), so that probably the Duke of Cornwall buried here was Cadoc, hereafter mentioned. Farther of this Castle, before the Conquest, I have not yet seen. Under Robert Earl of Moreton and Cornwall, it appears by the Exeter Domesday, that Reginald de Valletorta held the Castle [o]; but the inheritance came to William Earl of Cornwall, from whom it passed by attainder to the crown, with his other lands and dignities; then, as some think, Cadoc, son of the Condorus above-mentioned, was restored to the Earldom of Cornwall, lived and died at the Castle of Trematon, leaving one only daughter and heir Agnes, married to Reginald Fitz-Henry, natural son to Henry I.

[m] Camden, p. 21.
[n] Alias Mortagne, alias Moriton.
[o] " In ea Mansione habet Comes unum

" Castrum et Raginaldus (spoken of before as the Holder of the chief parts of the Manor) " tenet istud de Comite." fol. 67.

I con-

I conjecture, therefore, that this Cadoc muſt be that Duke (or rather Earl) of Cornwall, whoſe ſepulchre was diſcovered as above, his daughter being married to a Prince of the Royal Blood.   From Reginald Fitz-Henry, with one of his daughters and heirs this Lordſhip of Trematon came to Walter Dunſtavil, Baron of Caſtle-combe in Cornwall, whoſe iſſue (male) failing, it went with a daughter and heir to Reginald de Valletorta (temp. Ric. I.) who had fifty-nine Knights fees belonging to the honour of Trematon P. His ſon John de Valletorta had iſſue Roger (by others called Reginald), who, having only two daughters, Eglina married to Pomeroy of Bury Pomeroy in Devon, and of Tregeny in Corn-wall; and Jone married to Sir Alexander Oakeſton, Knight, ſettled this Lordſhip of Trematon on Sir Henry Pomeroy, Knight, his grandſon by his eldeſt daughter, Eglina; and this Sir Henry (or a ſon of the ſame name and title, as is more likely) did by his deed bearing date the 11th of Edward the third, releaſe to Edward the Black Prince (then created Duke of Cornwall) all his right and claim to the honour, caſtle, and manor of Trematon q.   It then became again, as it was moſt anciently, a part of the Dutchy of Cornwall, and ſo it ſtill continues.

Reſtormel Caſtle.

One of the principal houſes of the Earls of Cornwall was Reſtormel Caſtle, about a mile North of the town of Loſtwythyel. This Caſtle ſtands not on a factitious hill, for the architect finding a rocky Knoll, on the edge of a hill overlooking a deep valley, had no more to do than to plane the Rock into a level, and ſhape it round by a ditch, and the Keep would have elevation enough, without the trouble of raiſing an artificial hill (like that at Trematon) for it to ſtand on.   The Baſs-court was ſore defaced, as Leland ſays, in his time.   Some few ruins were to be ſeen in the lower part (in Mr. Carew's time), where the ditch is very wide and deep ſtill, and was formerly filled with water brought by pipes from an adjoining hill; on the higher ſide alſo leading to the principal gate there are traces of buildings to be found.   The Keep is a very magnificent one r; the outer Wall, or Rampart, is an exact circle, a hundred and ten feet diameter within, and ten feet wide at the top, including the thickneſs of the Parapet, which is two feet ſix.   From the preſent floor of the ground-rooms to the top of the Rampart is twenty-ſeven feet ſix, and the top of the Parapet is ſeven feet higher, garreted quite round.   There are three ſtair-caſes leading to the top of the Rampart, one on each ſide of the gateway

Baſs-Court.

Keep.

P Evidences from the Red Book in the Ex-chequer. Car. p. 45.

q In conſideration (as Mr. Hals ſays) of an annuity of 40l. per annum out of the Ex-chequer, which deed was extant when Mr.

Prince writ his Worthies of Devon, and in the poſſeſſion of Roger Pomeroy of Sandridge in Devon, Eſq;

r See the plan, Plate XXXII.

aſcending

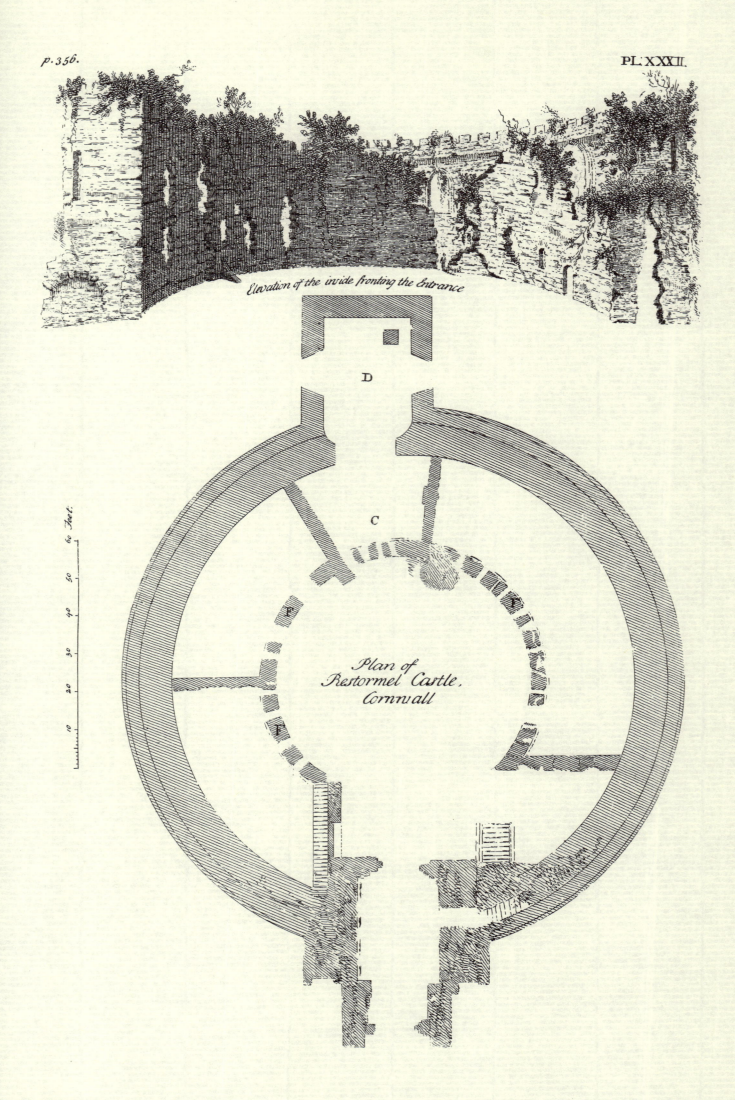

Elevation of the inside fronting the Entrance

D

C

60 Feet.

50

40

30

20

10

F

F

I

Plan of
Restormel Castle,
Cornwall

OF ANCIENT CASTLES IN CORNWALL.

afcending from the Court within, and one betwixt the inner and
outermoft gate.   The rooms are nineteen feet wide, the windows
moftly in the innermoft Wall F;   but there are fome very large
openings (in the outmoft Wall, or Rampart) now walled up,
fhaped like Gothick Church-windows, fharp-arched, which were
formerly very handfome and pleafant windows, and made to enjoy
the profpect, their recefles reaching to the planching of the rooms:
thefe large openings are all on the chamber-floor (where the rooms
of State feem to have been) and from the floor of thefe chambers
you pafs on a level to the chapel D.   This chapel is but twenty-
five feet fix, by feventeen feet fix;   but, that it might be the more
commodious, there feems to have been an anti-chapel c.   This
chapel, as Leland well obferves [r], is a newer work than the Caftle
itfelf;   and I may add, that the gateway, and the large windows
in the Rampart wall, are alfo more modern than the Keep, for
they were not made for war and fafety, but for pleafure and
grandeur;   and yet, as modern as thefe things compared with
the reft may appear, they muft be at leaft as ancient as Edmund
fon of Richard King of the Romans (temp. Edw. I.), for, fince his
death, I cannot find that any Earl of Cornwall refided here.
Richard King of the Romans kept his Court here, and in all probability made thefe additions (temp. Hen. III.).   The Offices
belonging to this Caftle, lay below it in the Bafs-court, where figns
of many ruins to the North and Eaft are ftill apparent, and, with
the ruins on either hand as you come towards the great gate from
the Weft, fhew that this Caftle was of great extent;   there was an
Oven (as Mr. Carew fays) of fourteen feet largenefs among the ruins
in the Bafs-court, and may ferve to give us fome idea of the hofpi-
tality of thofe times.   This noble Keep ftill holds up the fhell of
its turreted head, but within equals the ruinous ftate of the
Bafs-court below, over both which the following is Mr. Carew's
Lamentation, in his fomewhat antiquated but nervous ftyle:
" *Certes* (fays he, p. 138.) it may move compaffion, that a palace
" fo healthful for air, fo delightful for profpect, fo neceffary for
" commodities, fo fair in regard of thofe days for building, and fo
" ftrong for defence, fhould, in time of fecure peace, and under the
" protection of its natural Princes, be wronged with thofe fpoilings,
" than which it could endure no greater at the hands of any foreign
" and deadly enemy;   for the park is difparked, the timber rooted
" up, the conduit pipes taken away, the roof made fale of, the
" planchings rotten, the Walls fallen down, and the hewed ftones
" of the windows, dournes, and clavels, plucked out to ferve

[r] Vol. III. p. 24.

4 Y   " private

" private buildings ; only there remaineth an utter defacement to
" complain upon this unregarded diftrefs [s]."

The Caftle and Honour has never been alienated, as far I have
learned, from the inheritance of the Dukes and Earls of Cornwall.
There was a park round it, well wooded, and fuitable to the quality
of the ancient owners; but with feveral other parks in this county
(there having been formerly belonging to this Earldom nine Parks,
and one chace, or foreft [t]) difparked by Hen. VIII. at the inftance
of Sir Richard Pollard [u].

Bofcaftle.　　Bofcaftle, called fo from being the Caftle of the Lord Botreaux
(a family anciently of great poffeffions in this county), was a
Caftle of the fame kind as we are now treating of, and the round
artificial hill is ftill to be feen (called the Court); the hill was
fmall, and there are no other remains.

**Lancefton
Caftle.**　　Lancefton Caftle, Plate XXXIII. is the laft I fhall mention, and
was by far the ftrongeft of all our Cornifh Caftles. Leland, who
was a judicious traveller, and had feen the moft refpectable places
of England, fays, " the hill on which the Keep ftands, is large,
" and of a terrible height, and the Arx (viz. Keep) of it having
" three feveral wards is the ftrongeft, but not the biggeft, that ever
" I faw in any ancient work in England [w]."

Bafs-Court.　　The principal entrance is on the North Eaft, A, the gateway
a hundred and twenty feet long, whence turning to the right you
mount a terrace running parallel to the Rampart, till you come to
the angle, on which there is a round tower, now called the Witches
tower B. From hence the terrace turns away to the left at right
angles, and continues on a level, parallel to the Rampart, which is
nearly of the thicknefs of twelve feet till you come to C. Here
was a femicircular tower, and, as I fuppofe, a guard-room, and
gate : from this place the ground rifes very quick, and through a
paffage of feven feet wide you afcend the covered-way D, betwixt
two walls which are pierced with narrow windows for obfervation,
and yet cover the communication betwixt the Bafs-court, and the
Keep.　　Keep, or Dungeon, on the top of all, beginning at E. The whole Keep
is ninety-three feet diameter*. It confifted of three wards. The
*See the
Plan, Plate
XXXI. Fig
III p. 354.*
Wall of the firft Ward E was not quite three feet thick, and therefore, I think, could only be a parapet for foldiers to fight from,
and defend the brow of the hill. Six feet within E ftands the
fecond Wall F, which is twelve feet thick, and has a ftair-cafe three

---

[s] I think this Caftle muft have been built fince
the Norman Conqueft; for in the Exeter Domefday it is not named, nor in a Lift of the Earl of
Moreton's Lands and Caftles, communicated by
Francis Gregor, Efq; from a MS. in the Afh-
molean Library among the Dugdale MSS.
[t] Dodridge, p. 118.
[u] Car. p. 23.
[w] Vol. II. p. 79.

To S.ʳ John S.ᵗ Aubyn Bar.ᵗ Member of Parliament for Lanceston are most gratefully

These Ruins of Lanceston Castle in Cornwall engrav'd at his expence dedicated by Wm. Borlase.

feet wide, at the left hand of the entrance at G, running up to the top of the Rampart; the entrance of this ftair-cafe has a round arch of ftone over it. From G, paffing to H, you find the entrance I, into the innermoft ward; and on the left of that entrance, a winding ftair-cafe conducts you to the top of this innermoft Rampart, the Wall of which is ten feet thick, and thirty-two feet high from the floor K. The room K is eighteen feet fix diameter; it was divided by a planching into two rooms. The upper-room had to the Eaft and Weft two large openings, which were both windows, and (as I am inclined to think) doors alfo in time of action, to pafs from this Dungeon out upon the principal rampart F, from which the chief defence was to be made; for it muft be obferved, that the fecond Ward H was covered with a flat roof at the height of the rampart F, which made the area there very roomly, and convenient for numbers; thefe openings, therefore, upon occafion, ferved as paffages for the foldiers to go from one Rampart to the other. In the upper-room of K, there was alfo a chimney to the North; underneath, there was a dungeon which had no light. The lofty taper hill, on which this ftrong Keep is built, is partly natural, and partly artificial; it fpread farther into the town anciently than it does now, and by the *Radius* of it was three hundred and twenty feet diameter, and very high[x]. Norden gives us a Wall at the bottom of this hill; and, though there is no ftrefs to be layed on his drawings, yet it is not unlikely that it had a wall, or parapet, round the bottom of it, towards the town, for the principal Rampart of the Bafs-court breaks off very abruptly fronting the town, and feems patched, and maimed at M[y], and to have loft fome works at this place. The Bafs-court (half of which, or more, as I judge, is now covered with the houfes of the town) had formerly in it, the Affize-hall, a very fpacious building, a chapel, and other buildings, now all gone, but the county gaol N: at the Weftern end there is another gateway, O, into the town, but more modern than the reft.

The buildings which remain of this Caftle are of different ftyles, and fhew that the feveral parts of it were built at different times. For at the firft entrance through the great gateway, you have a flat but pointed arch over the firft gate; but within, at the fecond gate, you have a much rounder arch. There is a round tower B on the angle of the Rampart, which (if not built by the Romans) is undoubtedly of the Roman ftyle. There is a fquarenefs alfo in the Area of the Bafs-

[x] I took the height of it by a Quadrant, and made it from the Bafs court to the parapet of the Dungeon L, a hundred and four feet perpendicular; but, as it rained violently, I cannot depend on the obfervation; though, I believe, it is pretty near the truth.
[y] See the Elevation, Plate XXXIII.

court, which agrees with the manner of the Romans much more than any thing we have in our other Caſtles; but whether theſe parts are as old as the Roman times, I cannot ſay; however, that the Romans ſhould fortify here, is not at all improbable, conſidering that the ſituation of this Caſtle, near the ford of the river Tamar, makes it a paſs of great conſequence.   The river Tamar, running away to the South, is either dangerous or impaſſable below this place; and all learned men allow, that the Romans were not fond of the tedious work of building bridges, and it was therefore the more cuſtomary with them to take poſſeſſion of the Fords.   Now all below this place is ſecured by the Tamar, but near this Caſtle the river is fordable in ſeveral places.   Here, therefore, it was proper to have a garriſon, and, by placing another at Stratton on the North Sea (between which and Lanceſton there are the remains of an ancient way [z]), they formed a chain from the North at Stratton, to the South Sea at Plymouth.   This was therefore a ſtation of great importance, and not at all unworthy of the Roman attention, and that the Romans were here early, has been intimated before [a], and appears ſtill more likely from ſome Coins which have already reached my notice (viz. one of Veſpaſian, one of Domitian, found in the Walls of an old houſe, and a third found in digging a vault in the Church, with the letters IVLI plainly to be ſeen upon it); and will, it is to be hoped, be more confirmed, either by what are known to other perſons at preſent, or may hereafter be diſcovered in greater number.

I know it is generally held, that William Earl of Moreton and Cornwall built this Caſtle; but this is a vague expreſſion, and muſt not be underſtood, ſo as to ſuppoſe him the original, firſt builder, and founder of this Caſtle.   That he built ſomething here, is not unlikely; but, that he built all, can never be agreed to, when we conſider of what different parts it conſiſts, and recollect that it was a Caſtle long before the Normans came over.

The town was firſt built [b] by Eadulphus, brother to Alpſius, Duke of Devon and Cornwall, about the year 900; but the Caſtle muſt be much more ancient, for the town was evidently built for the ſake of the Caſtle, to be near the reſidence of the Prince, not the Caſtle to guard the town.   Of this there are ſeveral proofs; the high hill on which the Keep ſtands is a certain evidence that it was ſhaped in the manner we ſee it, before the town could be formed, for where there are houſes ſo thick, it would be madneſs to think of erecting a work of this kind.   The hill for the Keep muſt be certainly the firſt thing conſidered in all ſuch works, for to make

[z] See of the Roman Ways near Stratton, before, p. 336.

[a] Book IV. chap. vi.
[b] Hooker in Carew.

ſuch

fuch a hill after other fortifications, and after a town was built, would be tearing every thing to pieces. The garreted Walls, which went round the town, are manifeftly nothing more than a continuation of the Walls of the Caftle. In the Church of the town there is not the leaft mark of Antiquity, the Church being no older than Henry VII. as by the date 1511 on the Church-porch appears[b]. The only thing favouring of Antiquity in all the town is a door-cafe[c], carved according to the manner of the Saxons; and this was likely removed from the buildings of the Caftle, or from the collegiate Church of St. Stephen's, for where it ftands at prefent, it has no building near it to which it has any correfpondence, or can bear the leaft relation; fo that the town is modern in comparifon of the Caftle, and was built for it to enjoy the benefit of the Prince's Court, and to accommodate the perfons reforting to it. This Court was kept in the Caftle, which has large and Royal Jurifdiction ftill, entirely feparate and diftinct from the corporation of the town, having its own hereditary conftable, who had a houfe in the Bafs-court (temp. Eliz.[d]), and lived there. That there was a Caftle here before the Conqueft, is beyond all doubt, for Othomarus de Knivet[e] (faid to be of Danifh extraction) was hereditary conftable of the Caftle of Lancefton, and was difplaced at the Norman Invafion for being in arms againft the Conquerour; and Condorus Earl of Cornwall, at that time, being alfo divefted of his Earldom, the town and Caftle of Lancefton were given by the Conquerour, to Robert Earl of Moreton, with the Earldom of Cornwall, who with this honour had two hundred and eighty-eight Manors[f] in the county of Cornwall, befides five hundred and fifty-eight Manors in other counties[g]. William Earl of Moreton and Cornwall, fon and heir of Robert, kept his Court here, and likely made fome alterations and additions to the buildings. From him it fell to the Crown, with his other lands, and paffing with the Earldom of Cornwall, either into the Crown, or by grant from it, was at laft unalienably fixed to the Dukedom of Cornwall in the 11th of Edward III. and ftill continues part of the inheritance of the Dutchy.

It is called by Norden (p. 21.) " the Duke's moft ancient Caftle " in which dwelt divers Earls and Dukes of Cornwall before " William Earl of Moreton," (p. 92.). In the latter part of which

[b] " It was (viz. the Town-Church) from a " Chantry Chapel re-edified and enlarged in the " time of Hentry IV. and made fufficient to " contain the Inhabitants of the town." Not. Parl. p. 20. by Br. Willis, Efq;

[c] Now at the White-hart Inn.

[d] Carew, p. 117.

[e] Perhaps Dunhevet, having had this name from the Town called Dunheved; as the Dunhevets of Norfolk had (as Leland thinks, Vol. IX. xxxii.) though called afterwards Nevets; dropping the De or Du, as moft families now have done.

[f] Two hundred and forty-eight, fays Br. Willis, Efq. p. 16.

[g] Rapin, 8vo, Not. Vol. II. p. 253.

4 Z   affertion

affertion he is right; but whether this Caftle, though of larger jurifdiction, higher honours, and ftronger fortifications, may be more ancient than that of Tindagel, it is impoffible to determine.

Several Gentlemen in Cornwall hold their eftates of this Honour, by *Caftle-guard*, being bound to repair[g] and defend this Caftle.

" About fixty years fince, fays Mr. Carew, p. 117. were found " certain leather Coins in the Caftle wall, whofe fair ftamp and " ftrong fubftance till then refifted the affault of time." It is great pity but the Impreffion had been copied; however, a like difcovery, made at Carnarvon Caftle in Wales, may poffibly point out to us, if not the age, yet at leaft the occafion, of ftriking thefe leather Coins. " King Edward I. his leathern money bearing his name, " ftamp, and picture, which he ufed in the building thereof, to " fpare better bullion, were, fince I can remember, preferved and " kept in one of the towers of Carnarvon Caftle, and his Statue is " ftill upon the great gate of the town." Kennet's Paroch. Antiq. p. 697[h].

Of the Name of this Caftle. Lancefton.

Before I difmifs this fubject, give me leave to obferve, what feems to me a miftake, relating to the name of this Caftle and Town. The common opinion is, that Lancefton is derived from Lanftuphadon[i]; Launftaveton, as in Domefday; Loftephan[k], as in Leland[l], that is, the Church of Stephen; whereas they feem to me the names of two different places. The Church of St. Stephen is near a mile from the town of Lancefton, and had a College of Canons belonging to it before the Conqueft, with many dwelling houfes round it, which, as in other places of like kind, people always found it their intereft to build near the Monaftery, and might probably enough be called Lanftuphadon, i. e. the Town of St. Stephen's Church. Earl Harold poffeffed (as Lord of the Manor) this Lanftavedon, in the time of Edward the Confeffor, and here was held a market at that time; but the Earl of Moreton and Cornwall transferred it to his own Caftle, that is, to Lancefton. *Unum mercatum quod ibi jacebat ea die qua*[m] *R. E. F. V. & M. abftulit inde Comes de Moritonio & pofuit in* CASTRO SUO[n]. Now, if Lanftuphadon had been the fame as Lancefton, with what propriety could it be faid that the Earl of Cornwall took away the market from Lanftaveton, and fixed it in his own Caftle, that is, in the town, within the precincts and rights of his own proper Caftle? and therefore Lanftaveton and this

g Leland, Vol. VII. p. 114.
h Hift. of Alchefter written in 1622.
i Carew, p. 116.
k And in Wales, Kennett in his Parochial Antiq. p. 630, mentions the Lordfhip of Land-ftephan.
l Ibid. ut fupra.
m Rex Edvardus fuit vivus & mortuus.
n Exeter Domefday.

Lancefton

Lanceston (where the Earl of Cornwall's Caftle is) muft be two different places ; and it could never be called Lanftaveton Caftle, but by miftake, and the delufive affinity of names.   I am therefore of opinion, that Lancefton is the proper name of this Town, for the abovementioned reafons, as well as that neither our Towns nor our Caftles (in this county) take their moft ancient names from Saints ; but from fome notable property of fituation, fhape, the ufe they were defigned for, or river on which they are planted. Now Lancefton fignifies (in mixed Britifh) the Church of the Caftle, and in the Inquifition 20 Edward I. (A. D. 1293-4), I find it was rated by the name of *Capella de Caftro in Decanatu de Eaftwellfhire*.   Lancefton may alfo be a contraction of Lanceftreton ; for in the Bifhoprick of Durham we have Lanchefter, the Longovicus of the Romans, and Lancaftre (in Lancafhire) fhould have the fame derivation ; Langborough, that is, *Longum burgum*, a Long-town ; and it is not improbable, that the moft ancient name of this Caftle fhould have been Lanceftre, and the town thence called Lanceftreton, but by contraction Lancefton, in the fame manner as Chefhire, which is but a contraction of Cheftrefhire (its ancient name), and Chefton for Chefterton or Ceftreton, as in Kennett (Par. Antiq. p. 224.), for the eafier pronounciation[n].   This place has alfo another ancient name, Dunheved,   Dunheved. which is generally fuppofed Saxon, and to fignify the head of the hill[o] ; but the learned Baxter, in his Gloffary, thinks that Dunevet is the fame as the Nemetotacium (or, as it fhould be written *Nemetomagum* of the *anon. Ravennas*) ; and to his opinion I fub-fcribe, becaufe that Nemet is by the Cornifh pronounced and written Nevet, and Dun is *Magus* for *Pagus* (a Town or Village) and Dun-huedh fignifies, in the Cornifh language, the Swelling-hill, but Dun-hêdh the Long-hill.   I will only obferve farther, that if Baxter's Etymology is well grounded, it will prove this place as ancient as the Romans, and taken notice of in their Geography.

This manner of fortifying with a Bafs-court, an artificial-hill,   The Antiquity and and a Dungeon on the top of it, is very ancient ; was ufed, perhaps,   Ufe of this by the Romans, but certainly by the Saxons.   That the Romans   Manner of fortified fometimes in this manner, the old *Cunetium*, now Marl-   fortifying. borough in Wiltfhire, gives us reafon to believe.   " The Caftle " here[p] feems to have been a Roman work, by the Brafs Roman " Coins that were found in fhaping the Mount in the time of the " late Duke of Somerfet, which was contrived out of the Keep of

---

[n] As Glouceftre, not Glouchefter, Burcefter, Com. Ox. &c. Exceftre, &c.
[o] Kenn. Par. Ant. p. 633. Tien heved, or hefod, i. e. Caput de decem ; from heved comes the Englifh head.
[p] Camden's Annot. p. 129.

" the

" the Caftle." In Nottingham Caftle there are the remains of the Keep [q], and Dr. Gale places there the Gaufennæ of Antoninus. The Burgh at Leyden, which is a building of the fame kind, is thought to be Roman [r]. It muſt however be owned, that in the Military Architecture of the Romans in other parts, ſuch buildings do ſeldom appear. However that be, that the Saxons built in this manner, long before the Normans came in, one inſtance or two will be ſufficient to ſhew. Elfleda, daughter of Alfred the Great, and wife of Ethelred Earl of Mercia, in the end of Autumn, 915, built ſome fortifications againſt the Danes (which are ſtill called the Dungeon) upon an artificial hill at Warwick [s]. The ſame noble Lady built a work of the ſame kind at Tamworth, on the borders of the counties of Warwick and Stafford. She is ſaid to have built eight Caftles [t], all called Burrows, *alias* Burroughs, and very properly, becauſe they were fortifications raiſed on hills in the ſhape of Burrows, or *Tumuli* [u]. It is not likely that Elfleda was the inventor of this manner of Fortifying; her father Alfred ſoon diſcovered the neceſſity of ſtrong holds, preſſed as he was on every ſide by the Danes; and yet, as Aſſer obſerves, the Saxons were ſo indolent and ſtupid, that they could not be prevailed upon by the moſt preſſing inſtances of the King to erect any Caftles and Fortreſſes, till they were drove to it by the depredations of the Danes, and then Alfred cauſed ſeveral to be built. Here, therefore, we find fortification in its infancy among the Saxons, even when the country was over-run by the Danes; and whether they had then the leiſure to ſhape the natural hills, and where there were no natural hills to raiſe even mountains for the Keeps, or (as ſeems to me more likely) only built on theſe hills already raiſed, and ſhaped to their hand, we muſt leave undecided. One thing I would obſerve, that where the Saxons found any Roman fortification, they called it Ceafter, or Chefter; but what they erected themſelves in this manner they called Burghs, from the hills they ſtood on; and I am inclined to think, that the Saxons generally choſe to fortify in this manner (whether the hills were of their own raiſing or not) as ſuiting their purpoſe effectually againſt ſuch a roving enemy as the Danes were; whereas the Romans placed their forts any where, according as the circumſtances of the time and ground would permit, but generally in the manner of the encampment, ſquare, for the ſake of the health and order of their forces, and therefore called by the Saxons Ceafters, i. e. Caftles, or Encamp-

---

[q] Gale's Itin. p. 95.
[r] Breval, vol. I. p. 23. Travels.
[s] J. Roſſin Hiſt. Reg. Angli, p. 97. Dugd. Warwickſhire, p. 373.
[t] Named by Huntingt. p. 204.

[u] Whence, when theſe Caftles became numerous, and almoſt in every Town, ſuch Towns had the name of Burghs, or Burroughs, and Burrough came afterwards to ſignify a Town.

ments.

ments.   Whether the artificial hill, mentioned at Warwick, was at that time rais'd, or had only the Keep then built upon it, is not clearly exprefs'd; but the feafon of the year feems to intimate only the latter, autumn being a very improper time of the year, one would think, to engage in a work of fo much labour as the raifing an artificial hill, and a work alfo that required time to fettle, before it was capable of being built upon.   In fhort, it is not at all unlikely, that where the Saxons found thefe artificial hills erected by the Romans, they built new Keeps upon them, and added what works were neceffary to keep off the Danes.   Thefe artificial hills were works of time and labour, but as it was neceffary to build Caftles fometimes low, and among hills, to fecure a narrow pafs, or to command a creek, or a valley which had a navigable river [w]; it was almoft as neceffary to raife thefe artificial hills, and place Keeps upon them to overlook the country, difcover the enemy in feafon, and in times of extremity for the garrifon to retire to as their laft effort [x].

So far we have gone with the ancient Forts and Caftles of this county, which, if compar'd with the Fortifications of the prefent, and modern times, muft, doubtlefs, appear weak and trifling, confidering the improvements which Mathematicks, and the difcoveries of Gunnery and Engineering, have added to the latter; but thofe who compare only the modern fortification with the ancient, take not a proper way to form a true judgement of either.   Defence and fecurity is the proper end of fortifying, and the ancient manner might have anfwered that end as well as the modern, and therefore be of equal fervice in it's time.   The truth is, as fortifying has improved, fo has the Art of befieging and attacking.   The Arts of offence and defence have always grown together, providence nurfing them up, as it were, with equal care, to be a balance for, and a mutual check upon, one another; and the modern fortreffes, which look fo much better upon paper, more intricate, artful, and fubftantial, than the ancient, are no more impregnable than the others were; they may have all the advantages which the nature of the ground, improved by the greateft Artifts, can give them, but they muft yield to the fuperiour force of fhot, and bomb, and the equally improv'd method of approach, battery, and ftorm.   To fay no more of this, thefe ancient Forts, were, no doubt, equal and proportioned to the then method of at-

The Strength of fuch Fortifications.

---

[w] The Burgh at Leyden is plac'd fo as to command the River there. — Breval, ut fupra. — Trematon, on a Creek — Reftormel, to command the river and valley of Loftwythel — Lancefton, at the head of the fords of Tamar — Oakampton Caftle, in the narrow valley there.

[x] That fome of thefe artificial hills might be originally fepulchral *Tumuli*, is not improbable, efpecially in Ireland. (See Wright's Louthiana.) where thefe *Tumuli* are large and many, and Turrets, or little Caftles, built upon them; but, that they were all fo, is a miftake, thofe round hills in Cornwall being natural, as to the greateft part of them, and only fhaped by Art.

tack, and art of war; consequently, their use and security must be measured by the manner of besieging then in use.

There were but few of these Castles in England before the Normans came in [y], which much facilitated their Conquest, and William the First was so sensible of this errour in the Britans, Saxons, and Danes, and saw the use of these Castles so clearly, that he immediately promoted the building of them with all possible ardour; and his Nobles put in execution his commands with so much diligence, that in Henry II's time, there were reckoned no less than 1115 Castles in England.

When this Earldom of Cornwall was erected into a Dutchy (11 Edward III.) and fix'd either in the Crown, or the eldest son of the sovereign, all the Castles in Cornwall which had been the seats of their Earls or Princes from the Roman Times, if not before, were utterly deserted, and their dependant Towns, for want of that Princely resort, upon which they chiefly subsisted, went to ruin also; of which the Crown taking notice, an act passed in the 32d of Hen. VIII. for repairing those Towns, but this act came to nothing, and left that for trade and industry to do, which Law could not.

C H A P. X.

Of the State of Christianity in Cornwall before the Norman Conquest.

HAVING in the second Book given an account of DRUIDISM (the ancient Religion of the Britans in general), exemplified, and chiefly deduced from the Monuments remaining in Cornwall, I proceed now to consider the state of the Christian Religion, and at what time, and by what degrees, it succeeded the other, by what means it flourish'd at some times, and to what degree it was at other times depressed, together with the Christian Monuments which have reached my notice in Cornwall, before the Norman Conquest.

SECT. I.

Disadvantages of Christianity at first in Britain.

The Britans received the Faith of Christ very early, even, according to some authors, in the Apostolic Times [z], but there was no British King presumed to have been of the Christian Religion till Lucius, and the precise time when he was converted is not agreed upon, but is generally held to have been in the time of M. Aurelius, and Lucius Verus, and the beginning of Eleutherius's Popedom [a], who began his Rule, according to the *Savil Fasti*, A. D. 171, ten years before Commodus. It cannot however be imagined, that Pa-

y Dugdale's Warwickshire, pag. 426.
z Says Stillingfl. Ant. Brit. cap. i.
a Ibid. pag. 60. It must here be observed that,

besides some other doubts relating to this King Lucius, " his letter to Pope Eleutherius is an " evident forgery." L.

ganism

ganifm was every where abolifhed as foon as Chriftianity appeared; there were at that time, and from the very firft account we have in hiftory of the Britifh nation there had been, many petty principalities in Britain [b], for the moft part independent of one another, yet in times of diftrefs fubordinate, and obliged in matters of Council and War, to obey that Prince whom they elected to be the head of all. If it be allowed then, that Chriftianity was embraced by the King of Britain, as early as King Lucius, and that he was fupreme King of all the Britans [c], yet muft he have been under the direction of the Romans, and King only by their leave, and could have had no authority in Religious Matters over the other Princes of Britain; many of the little Kings therefore may be fuppofed to remain unconverted for a long time after.

I know that the learned Sir Henry Savil, in his *Fafti*, fays (in a note there, ad ann. 173.) that " about this time Lucius King of " the Britans (as he is call'd by Bede), at the inftance of Eleuthe- " rius the Pope, together with the whole nation of the Britans, re- " ceived the Chriftian Faith;" but this is altogether improbable, neither fuiting the limited authority of Lucius, nor allowing enough for the different tempers and circumftances of the other Princes.

Doubtlefs, the moft ftubborn, vicious, and bigotted, were lefs fufceptible of the divine precepts of the Gofpel, and continued many years after in their contented darknefs; and when the Princes became at laft converted, and baptized, the common people (every where fonder of fuperftition than truth) continued their attachment to the errours in which they were brought up.

From Commodus, to the time that the Roman Empire became Chriftian, Chriftianity, tho' adopted by the Britifh Kings, wanted really the fupport and countenance of the State, for the Romans (then Heathens) being lords of all, tho' the Britans had fome Churches, Bifhops, and a few Monafteries, the generality of the people (we may take it for granted) continued without controul in the Druid Superftition [d]. Again; the true Religion in it's infancy fuffered much under the perfecution of Dioclefian's reign, which lafted ten years, at which time it loft ground rather than advanced, tho', when thofe clouds were paffed, it fhone the brighter.

---

[b] Diod. Sic. lib. iv.—Strabo, lib. iv.—Mela, Lib. III. cap vi. Tacitus, vita Agric.

[c] Though fome think he was but a petty Prince. Stillingfl. ibid. pag. 63.

[d] And of this opinion I find Dr. Stillingfleet: " During all this time, the Church, fays he, muft " have labour'd under great difficulties; the Go- " vernours, and Provinces, before Conftantius, " and the generality of the people, being fet a- " gainft the Chriftians." Stillingfl. Orig. Brit. 74. And this feems to be what Gildas means when he afferts, " the continuation of a church here " from the firft plantation of the Gofpel (though " not maintain'd, fays he, with equal Zeal) to " the perfecution of Dioclefian." Stillingfl. Antiq. Brit. pag. 55.

In

In this perfecution, they not only deftroyed the Churches, but they prejudiced Church Hiftory beyond recovery, for as Velferus obferves [e], they burnt all the Monuments which concerned the Chriftian Church. 'Tis true, the perfecution in Britain did not laft fo long as it did in the Eaft, that is, did not rage with that violence, but the whole reign of this Emperor, is reckon'd by the above Author [f], one perpetual perfecution.

When Conftantine and the Empire became Chriftian, the Britifh Bifhops were fummon'd to the Council of Arles (314), and probably to that of Nice [g] (A.D. 325.), and of Ariminum in 359 [h]; at the laft of which, as well as at the firft [i], three Bifhops of Britain were prefent. Thefe Bifhops are ftyled by Hilarius (in his Epiftle to the Bifhops [k]) of the Provinces of Britain; and the reafon why only three were prefent, feems to be becaufe Britain was at that time divided into three Archbifhopricks. Under the Archbifhop of London was *Loegria*, and *Cornubia* (that is, from the river Humber to the Land's End); under the Archbifhop of York, all *Deira* and *Albania*, that is, all North of Humber to Cathnefs in Scotland; and under the Archbifhop of Caerleon, all Wales, called then Cambria.

SECT. II.

Difadvantages of Chriftianity in Cornwall in particular.

One great obftacle to Chriftianity's prevailing foon in Cornwall arofe from the retired fituation of the country, which, being at a great diftance from the heart of the kingdom, had fewer opportunities of being inftructed, than countries which lay nearer to the Imperial Court, which had already received the Gofpel.

Cornwall and Devon (then called Dunmonium) were at this time under the Archbifhop of London; they muft have fuffered greatly therefore in point of Religion, by means of their diftance from the Metropolitan See. The Gofpel might have been fupported in it's full purity under the Bifhop's eye; but, as the Bifhops kept moft of their Clergy about their perfons in thofe early days, and difpatched them occafionally only from their Cathedrals, to inftruct the more diftant parts, the Gofpel fhone more faintly in the remote corners of the Ifland. Druidifm had taken deep root, and it would not give way to weak efforts; hence it is, that after the Roman Empire, and much the greateft part of Britain had been Chriftian, we find many martyrs fuffering death in Cornwall for the Chriftian faith; and hence it is, that in the latter end of the fourth, during all the fifth, and moft part of the fixth centuries, we find fo many holy men employed to convert the Cornifh to the Chriftian Religion.

[e] M. Velfer. Rerum Vindel. Lib. VI.—Still. Ch. Ant. p. 42.

[f] Stillingfleet, pag. 70.

[g] As Stillingfl. ib. pag. 9. and Selden (ibid) in Eutych. pag. 115, 123. though by others this is doubted of, becaufe the Britans did not keep Eafter conformably to the directions of the Nicene Council. Spelman's Conc. Vol. I. pag. 141. from Bede. Lib. II. cap. xix.—See Prid. Connexion, 8vo, Vol. II. pag. 238, &c.

[h] Stillingfl. Or. Brit. pag. 176.

[i] See Stillingfl. pag. 74.

[k] Speed's Chron. pag. 79.

" The

" The state of Christianity among the Britans in Cornwall (at " this time) is accounted very uncertain[1]." Let us endeavour to discover what we can of it, by tracing the facts we have in history relating thereto.

About the middle of the fourth century, Solomon Duke of Cornwall seems to have been a Christian; for his son Kebius was ordained a Bishop by Hilarius Bishop of Poictiers in France, and afterwards returned into his own country to exercise that high function[m]. St. Corantine (now called Cury) was the first Cornish Apostle of note that we meet with; born in Brittany, he preached first in his own country, and Ireland, 'till, being driven away by violence, he again betook himself to the life of a Hermit, which he had quitted for the sake of travelling, to instruct the ignorant and the infidel: he settled at the foot of a mountain called Menehont[n], in the Diocese of Cornwall. Here the fame of his sanctity increasing, at the intreaty of Grallonus King of the Armoricans, he was consecrated Bishop of Cornwall by St. Martin, Bishop of Tours in France, and, being said to have converted all Cornwall, died in the year 401.

St. Piranus, born in Ireland in the year 352, must have come into Cornwall about this time, for he is said to have been buried here. But, notwithstanding the endeavours of these holy men, about the year 411, St. Melor (although son of Melianus Duke of Cornwall) suffered Martyrdom[o]. Capgrave, (p. 451.) says that this happened soon after the Britans had received the Christian Faith; by which Britans he must mean those of Cornwall, for the others had been converted above 200 years before. By persisting in their Druidism, the Britans of Cornwall drew the attention of St. Patrick that way, who about the year 432, with 20 companions, halted a little in his way to Ireland on the shores of Cornwall, where he is said to have built a monastery. Whether St German was in Cornwall at this time I cannot say; but, according to Usher, he was either in Cornwall or Wales; for St. Patrick is said, " *ad* " *Praeceptorem suum beatum Germanum divertisse, & apud Britan-* " *nos in partibus Cornubiae & Cambriae aliquandiu substitisse*[p]."

This was not the only visit of St. Patrick; for that holy Apostle having had great success afterwards in Ireland, in confuting the Druid Priests, and converting that nation to Christianity, undertook the same charitable task in Cornwall[q], and had an altar and church there dedicated to him, and much reverenced for the sake

---

[1] Inet's Orig. Ang. from Bede, Lib. V. cap. xix. Vol. I. pag. 123.

[m] Ush. pag. 1087. A. D. 369.

[n] I find it written thus, " Uberrimam Rec-" toriam de Manihont in Devonia." Parker's Eccl. Antiq. Drake, pag. 384. but some think it

Menhynnett in Cornwall.

[o] Capgrave, pag. 451.—Ush. Prim. p. 451.

[p] Ush. Prim. pag. 1100, and 842.

[q] The legend says, he was wafted over from Ireland into Cornwall upon this Altar, which was greatly frequented and reverenced for that reason.

of

---

of this excellent Paſtor. From the time of St. Patrick, Ireland began to be the ſeat of every kind of learning, which the chriſtian world was then acquainted with; and perſons of the higheſt rank not only deſerted Gentiliſm, but their crowns too, and became Preachers of the word of God; they neither ſhut themſelves up in Monaſteries, nor confined themſelves within the limits of their own Iſland, but travelled into Italy and France, frequently into the Iſles on the North of England and Scotland, and oftentimes into Cornwall, directing their courſe where they ſaw moſt need of their inſtruction.

St. Patrick who lived to a great age, ſome think 'till he was 120 years old (not dying till about the year 490), by his example equally and his inſtructions, animated his Diſciples to purſue his holy plan. Of his ſcholars, Fingarus, from Armorica (whither the like Druid ſuperſtition which had overſpread all the Weſt had probably called him), paſſing into Ireland, his native country, and finding it, by the labours of St. Patrick and his Prieſts, thoroughly converted to chriſtianity, gave up his right to a crown, by that time fallen to him (upon the deceaſe of his father Clito), and, with his ſiſter Piala, eleven Biſhops, and a numerous attendance, all baptized by St. Patrick, came into Cornwall, and landing at the mouth of the river Hayle, was there put to death, with all his company, in the year 460, by Theodorick King of Cornwall, for fear leſt they ſhould turn his ſubjects from their ancient Religion[r]. About the ſame time came over from Ireland St. Breaca (now called Breâg) attended with many Saints, among whom were Sinninus[s] the Abbot, who had been at Rome with St. Patrick, Germochus an Iriſh King (as Tradition ſays), and ſeveral others. She landed at Revyer on the Eaſtern bank of the river Hayle in the hundred of Penwith, where Theodorick (or Tudor) had his caſtle of reſidence, and ſlew great part of this holy aſſembly alſo.

In the middle of this fifth century the Saxons, being called in as friends, in a few years proved the moſt inveterate enemies to the Britiſh nation which the iſland to that time had ever felt; and the general diſorders which attend a weak government, and a potent enemy in the heart of the kingdom, engaged all hands in war, the Britans to defend their country, and the Saxons to ſeize it. Religion, in the general tempeſt, had her ſhare of the diſtreſs; an univerſal ignorance enſued, no one ſtudied Religion, becauſe every one was obliged to be in arms. Vortigern, hereditary King of Cornwall, and then advanc'd to the throne of Britain (from which

[r] Uſher. cap. xvii. pag. 869.——Dr. Cave, in his Hiſtor. Literar. among St. Anſelm's works, reckons Paſſio St. Guigneri ſive Fingari, Pialæ, & ſociorum, pag. 542.
[s] Aliàs Senanus.

he unhappily had invited the Saxons, as auxiliaries), neglected every thing sacred and civil, and was deposed in the year 454. His son Vortimer, being deservedly placed in the Throne, rebuilt the churches ruin'd by the Saxons, and did his best to restore the Christian Religion, then (as Speed says, pag. 266.) sorely decayed; but his reign being no longer than four years (as others say, seven), and most part of that spent in war, much could not be done, before, Vortimer dying, his father Vortigern was restored to his throne, and the Saxons, by his indolence and luxury, to a capacity of repeating with impunity their wonted desolations. About the year 470 [t], there was a Provincial Synod held in Britain, for reforming Religion, and repairing Churches. This Council, if held so soon, must have been in the last year of Vortimer; but, if ten years later, under the direction of Aurelius Ambrosius, who, having vanquished Vortigern, and succeeded him, and with great success repelled the Saxons, took that opportunity of convening the Princes and Bishops, in order to restore the true worship of God. Ambrosius died, King of Britain, in the latter end of the fifth century, or beginning of the sixth [u], and was succeeded by his brother Uther Pendagron, who by Igerna, wife of Gorlois Duke of Cornwall, had issue Arthur, who first succeeded Gorlos, in Cornwall, and, in the year 516, Pendagron, in the Imperial Crown of Britain. Arthur was a great lover of Christianity, as appears in all his history [w]; he came to the Crown, as some think, very young [x], and finding himself perpetually harassed with battles, by Cerdic the Saxon, is said, in his second year, to have allowed Cerdic, Hamshire, Surrey, Wiltshire and Somersetshire (to which were afterwards added Dorsetshire, and part of Devonshire and Cornwall); but, in this Treaty, King Arthur took care to provide for the Religion of his native country, and it was stipulated that Cerdic should allow the Cornish the free exercise of the Christian Religion, upon paying an annual tribute [y]. Here, it seems, there were some remains of Christianity, and some struggles of a few Britans, assisted by the Irish Saints, to preserve and cherish it; whereas in Somersetshire, Hamshire, Wiltshire, and places over-run by the Saxons, the Saxon Paganism had absolutely obtained.

But though Arthur made such provision for tolerating Christianity in Cornwall, the old superstition remained strong enough

---

[t] Speed, pag. 80.

[u] Biograph. A. D. 508.—Speed, pag. 268. A. D. 498.

[w] This may seem to be confirmed by the officious adulation of after-ages, which, in order to compleat the Hero, among other fables, assign him for a Coat of Arms, a cross with the Virgin-mother carrying Christ in her arms, although the custom of bearing Coats-armour was indeed never known in England till near five hundred years after his death.

[x] About fifteen or sixteen; but some understand this of his coming to the Crown of Dunmonium.

[y] Rudburn's Chron. Lib. II. cap. i.——Usher. cap. xiii. pag. 468.

Petroc.

to call forth the labours of the moſt learned and active of the Iriſh Divines.

St. Petroc therefore came into Cornwall, to preach the Goſpel: he was a native of Cumberland, and of royal blood; but forſaking his country, and right of ſucceſſion, went into Ireland (the great Weſtern Academy), in the year 498[z], and having ſpent twenty years there in the ſtudies of theology, under the moſt eminent maſters, came into Cornwall, A. D. 518. He ſettled in a monaſtery called, before his time, Loderic, and Laffenek[a], but from his name (as ſome think) Petrocſtow, now Padſtow. Here he had ſeveral Diſciples, illuſtrious for their learning and piety[b]; and, after paying a viſit to Rome[c], he returned into Cornwall, where, at that time, Tendurus, a man of a ſavage and cruel diſpoſition, and probably a Heathen, was King; and having reſided and taught there for thirty years, died about the year 564, was buried firſt at Padſtow, and afterwards tranſlated to Bodman Priory, dedicated to him.

SECT. IV.
Of the Monaſteries of the fifth Century.

Having mentioned the monaſtery erected by St. Patrick, and that which St. Petroc afterwards lived and taught in, it may not be amiſs, before we go any farther, to look a little into the nature and conſtitution of the Monaſteries of thoſe times, by which we ſhall be able to form a better judgment of the men that came from them, to whom the Corniſh were ſo much indebted for their inſtruction.

" The Monaſteries of the Weſtern Nations, before the time of " St. Benedict, ſuch as that of Bangor in England, and St. Martin " and St. Germans in Gaul, were chiefly intended as Nurſeries to " the Church[d]," to educate perſons in ſuch a manner as to make them able Miniſters of the word of God.

In the fifth century we read, of no diſtinct orders of Monks; they were not as yet called after any particular patron, as the Benedictines, Dominicans, Auguſtines, &c. in the following ages were; their deſign being to learn of ſome, in order to teach others, they were quite ſtrangers to the ambition, luxury, and idleneſs, which afterwards attended the monaſtick life: their zeal for Religion made them indefatigable in preparing themſelves for, and afterwards exerciſing their holy function. In the Monaſtery of Bangor (by ſome[e] accounted the firſt Chriſtian Monaſtery in the

---

[z] Uſh. Ind. Chron. in Pri. pag. 1112.

[a] Probably the ſame that St. Patrick had founded in the year 432; from which there is an eaſy paſſage to Wales, whither he afterwards went, before he paſſed into Ireland.

[b] Credanus, Medanus, Dachanus.

[c] In that age " the chief Univerſity of the " Empire." Stillingfleet, ibid. p. 210. which is the reaſon that people of the greateſt fame for

learning and ſanctity generally went to Rome to ſtudy ſome time, though born in the moſt diſtant parts of the Roman Empire; as St. German, St. Patrick, &c.

[d] Dupin's Eccl. Hiſt. Vol. II. pag. 291.—Stillingfleet, Orig. Brit. pag. 206.

[e] Bede, Lib. II. cap. ii.—Stillingfleet, Orig. Brit. p. 205.

world)

world) great numbers of Monks were bred up in a Collegiate manner, and daily, bodily labour was to fill up the intervals of their study and devotion. By their learning, they fitted themselves for teaching Religion; by their labour, they contributed in their turns to the support of the Religious numerous community of which they were members [f]. Many of these Monks were Bishops, of which seven at one time, with many other learned men from the same place, attended the Synod, called by St. Austin of Canterbury, about the year 600. St. German, St. Martin, and St. Patrick, all exercised the Episcopal Function, ordained, and appointed Bishops to their particular provinces. St. German Bishop of Auxierre, in France (but called over to assist the British Church), is thought to have established several Schools, or Seminaries, for young Divines here in England; and St. Patrick, who spent many years under the discipline of St. German, carried the same Collegiate or Monastick Education into Ireland [g], and, doubtless, brought the same into Cornwall when he came here. St. Patrick had also studied under his uncle St. Martin, Bishop of Tours, and from him received the habit of a monk, and with the habit, doubtless, the Institutes he was to observe; so that St. Patrick's Monasteries (for he founded many, as so many schools for learning) were of the same kind as those in France, in which he had his education [h]; and, by the history of those great Doctors, we see that their principal office was to preach the Gospel, to undertake the conversion of Infidels, now in one nation, and now in another, and to bring up other Monks under them, who might engage in the same holy task.

By this it appears that the Monastick Life, in those early ages of Christianity, was not what it generally is at present, viz. a life of inactivity and confinement, but a life of travel and preaching; and it was from such Monasteries, and such Monks, that we had our Irish Saints and Teachers [i], who, coming into Cornwall to preach the Gospel, were, after their death, generally reckoned among the Saints; and we have indeed great reason to think those holy men endued with as much piety and learning as any of the age they lived in, or any after them for many centuries.

[f] Hum. Lhuyd (in his Breviary) thinks some of these Monks were appropriated to labour, in order to maintain those whose genius carried them more eminently to study and learning; others think that labour was enjoined to all, at proper times, by their Institution.

[g] As Probus and Jocelin, the writers of his life, agree.

[h] At Armagh, it is said, he founded *Summum Studium Literale*, which, in the language of that time, is the same with an University (Stilling-

fleet. ib.); and in this School Gildas is thought to have been a Professor.

[i] " As the design of these Monasteries was " very different from that of the Monasteries in " after-ages, so was the faith of the ancient " church of Ireland, to which the Cornish had " so many obligations, very different from that of " modern Rome, as may be seen at large in " Archbishop Usher's Religion of the ancient " Irish." Letter from the Rev. Mr. Collins to the Author.

To name all these holy men and women, and particularly specify their coming into Cornwall, and departure elsewhere, might suit a Register, or Catalogue, but would be foreign to the intention of this Treatise, as well as tiresome to the reader. The design of them all was one and the same; they came to preach the Gospel, and by the strictness and severity of their lives to enforce their doctrine; and the consequence was suitable to their endeavours; by their means Christianity increased, Churches were built, and when, by a division of the Kingdom into parishes, each parish had it's Church, there was scarce a Saint from Ireland, or elsewhere, who had preached in Cornwall, but had his memory preserved by the grateful inhabitants, by having a Church, near the place he settled in, dedicated to and called after his name. Ireland continued to be a nursery full of holy and learned men even to the year 674 (as Marianus notes, Usher, Prim. pag. 1165.); and therefore we may reasonably suppose, that, till that time, she continued to send forth her Saints into the adjoining countries.

SECT. III.
Of the British Church in Cornwall under the Saxons.

To resume the thread of our narration. The Saxons prevailing after the death of Arthur (which happened in 542), did every thing in their power to extirpate Christianity, and Christianity (with the Britans) retreated before the Conquerours into the extremities of the Island; so that in the year 597 [k] Theonus, Archbishop of London, and Thadiocus, Archbishop of York, seeing all their Churches destroyed, their Clergy fled into Wales [l] and Armorica, and the Christians every where expelled from the country conquered by the Saxons, " retired with other Bishops into Corn-" wall and Wales, and by their labours so plentifully propagated " the Gospel there, that they made those parts, especially above " all other, glorious by the multitudes of their holy Saints and " learned Teachers [m]." In other parts the Saxons were in full possession, having, from their first coming, not only raged against religion, but against Learning too (as the Romans in Dioclesian's time, mentioned before pag. 334), and destroyed, wherever they came, all the books and monuments they could find, which is another great reason that our Ecclesiastical History of those times is, and must always remain, very much maimed and imperfect.

About the same time that the Bishops abovementioned retired into Wales and Cornwall, the Saxons, fatigued as it were with persecuting the Gospel, embraced (like a generous enemy) what

[k] Speed, pag. 80. from Bede.
[l] By Wales here we are to understand Wales properly so called, and West Wales too, as Cornwall was oftentimes called.
[m] In Wales and Cornwall they had preserved their Liberty and their Religion, tho' both attempted by the Saxons, and the Pelagian Hereticks. And Religion remaining in these two countries authorized and unsullied, was the reason that the British people, among all nations, were renowned for their constancy in their Faith. Historiola Winton. Ecclef. Ush. Prim. p. 576.

they

they could not deftroy. The kingdom of Kent firft became Chriftian, and the other Kingdoms of the Saxons quickly followed fo
good an example. But the condition of the Britifh Church did
not foon feel the benefit of this change; for Auftin and his fellow
Miffionaries not contented to convert the Saxons (in which it muft
be allowed they had great fuccefs) thought it incumbent upon them
to correct the errours of the Britans, who, being at a great diftance
from Rome, and perpetually at war, had not admitted the innovations
of that Church, but ftuck to the firft, plain Chriftianity, which they
had received (as fome think) four hundred years before. A Synod was
appointed about 601, and feven Britifh Bifhops, with many others
from the Monaftery of Bangor, appeared [n]; but matters between the
Saxons and Britans had been fo imbittered by continual wars, that
no agreement enfued: the Britans were as tenacious of their own
accuftomed time of holding Eafter (the great fubject of debate in
thofe days), and as refolute to maintain their independency on any
foreign hierarchy, as Auftin was eager to eftablifh his fuperiority,
and impofe the Romifh obfervation of that Feftival.

There feems to have been a third difpute betwixt Auftin and the
Britifh Chriftians; for the Saxons being now multiplied into feveral
and populous nations, all Heathens, and Auftin and his Monks few
in comparifon of the work they had to do; he feems to have propofed to the Britifh Clergy, that they fhould accept of a commiffion
from him, and, under his authority, preach to the Pagan Saxons,
and hold communion with thofe that were by him converted. This
propofal being refufed, St. Auftin told them, that fince they
refufed peace as brethren, they muft accept of war as enemies; and
as they would not preach the way of life to the Englifh, by the
Englifh they muft expect to fuffer death in return for fuch barbarity. Thefe words were probably menaces, defigned only to terrify
the Britans into a compliance; but afterwards, when the Saxon
King Edelbright had maffacred the Monks of Bangor, they were
looked upon as prophetical, and the effect of infpiration, by thofe
who were determined to admire and excufe every thing that this
Saxon Apoftle did, or faid.

The Cornifh Britans had either their own reprefentatives at this
Synod, or were reprefented by their brethren of Wales; and
Broch-well King of Powis, then General of the Britans, being foon
after defeated by the Saxons, and the Monks of Bangor (attending
the Britifh Army to pray for them) flain without mercy, to the
number of twelve hundred, Bellthrufius [o], then Duke of Cornwall,
fent aid to his fellow Britans of Wales, and by his affiftance in a

[n] Bede, Lib. II. cap. ii.   [o] Huntingt. p. 287.

great

great meafure it was, that the Welfh had the victory, and flew of the Saxons one thoufand and fixty-fix men. The difference about the time of Eafter lafted about a hundred years after this; and whereas the mutual right of Britans and Saxons to celebrate that high Feftival fhould have made them love one another as Chriftian brethren, a few days difference P in the time of obferving (which was a thing in itfelf of little importance) made them reproach and deteft one another, in a moft Unchriftian manner; infomuch, that Huntington (p. 187.) calls the Britans a perfidious nation, a deteftable army: Malmfbury (p. 28.) calls the Cornifh *contaminata gens*, a moft defiled people; and Bede himfelf does not fcruple to call the Britans a wicked and curfed nation, upon this very account.

The Saxon nation however (as it were to make amends for their former outrages) willingly, and more fpeedily than could be expected, fubmitted to the Chriftian Faith, and, as Chriftianity increafed, appointed Bifhops over particular provinces. Juftus had been made Bifhop of Rochefter, and Melitus of London, in 604; and in 635, Birinus was made bifhop of Dorchefter near Oxford, in the 24th year of Kingils, firft Chriftian King of Weft Saxony; and Cornwall (to which the Weft Saxon Kings, from the time of Arthur laid conftant claim, though never in poffeffion) was included in this bifhoprick. This was the firft Bifhop that ever the Weft Saxons had, and it was their only one, for it included all Weft Saxony: in the year 660, Winchefter was made an Epifcopal See, and then all Weft Saxony was under the Bifhop of Winton. As Chriftianity fpread to the Weft, a Bifhop was appointed at Sherburn in the year 705, and as Winchefter contained Hampfhire and Surry; Sherburn had Wiltfhire, Dorfetfhire, Berkfhire, Somerfetfhire, Devonfhire, and Cornwall. Aldhelm was the firft Bifhop of Sherburn, and his Epifcopacy lafted but five years; from him Geruntius King of the Cornifh Britans received a reprimand, becaufe the Britifh Monks of his country made ufe of a different *Tonfure* from that of the Roman Church. It feems the Cornifh fhaved only from ear to ear q; whereas the Romans fhaved all but the hinder part of the head. Aldhelm writ an epiftle to the King, and Priefts of Cornwall, on this fubject. But though the Saxon Bifhops

---

P The Afiatick Churches kept their Eafter upon the fame Day the Jews obferved their Paffover, viz. the 14th day of their month, chiefly anfwering our March; and this they did upon what day of the week foever it fell. The Britifh Church did the fame, and (as well as the Afiaticks) pleaded the practice of the Apoftles for doing fo. The Church of Rome, and moft of the Weftern Churches, kept Eafter upon the Lord's day next following the Jewifh Paffover; and it was ordained by the Oecumenical Council of Nice, that Eafter fhould be kept upon one and the fame day throughout the world, not according to the Cuftom of the Jews, but upon the Lord's day following their Paffover.

q " Rotundâ quidem tonfurâ, fed imperfecto " orbe ab aure ad aurem circumducto, &c." Ufh. p. 923.

pretended

pretended a right to direct and rule the Cornish in matters of Religion, yet in reality the Cornish were as averse to receive orders from the Saxon Bishops, as from the Saxon Princes, with whom being almost in constant war, they neither gave up their Civil nor Religious Rights; continuing Christians, but on the first plan; independent, though persecuted[r]; and, esteeming the Religion of the English as nothing, the Cornish would no more communicate with them than with Pagans[s], accounting that of the Welsh and themselves the only true Christianity[t]. At the same time they held constant communion with their fellow Christians of Wales, and some holy men passing from hence into Anglesea and other parts of Wales, gave names to the churches there[u]; and doubtless the Welsh did the same in Cornwall. All this while there had been no fixed Episcopal See in Cornwall that I can learn, and never was, till Edward the elder, in 905. But Cornwall was not singular in this particular, for the Kingdom of East Anglia had never a Bishop for above an hundred years, during the Danish Wars[w]. The ancient way in the Western Church was this; the Bishops usually lived in Monasteries, as appears from the seven Bishops at one time coming from Bangor to meet Austin. In London, York, and Caerleon, the Bishops had fixed residence from the beginning, but scarce any where else. To Cornwall, and most other places, bishops came either from France, Ireland, or Wales; and having taught, ordained, and stayed as long as they judged convenient, went to other places, with the same pious design, and returned, or not, as they were disposed.

Sherburn continued the Episcopal See of the Western parts of Britain, without any material accident or alteration, as far as I have read, till the year 897, when, Alfred being old, and the confusions of the Danish wars increasing[x] in these parts, there was no Bishop in all West Saxony, from that time till the year 905, which the Pope of Rome[y] being informed of, excommunicated Edward (then in the throne of his deceased father Alfred) and all his subjects. Edward, upon this, convenes a Synod (Pleimund Archbishop of

SECT. IV.

A Bishoprick erected in Cornwall.

---

[r] Winton. Hist. Monast. Anglican. Propylæum, from Bede, Lib. II. cap. xx.

[s] The Scots Christians used the Roman Bishops in the same harsh manner; and Laurentius, successor to Austin in the See of Canterbury, complains that Daganus Bishop of the Scots (Disciple of the Cornish St. Petrock) would never eat bread with the Roman Missionaries, nor in the same house with them. Malmsb. p.187. "His finibus (viz. Cornubiæ, "Demeciæ, and Venedociæ) quamvis eis invitis "contenti a fide tamen Christi nunquam re- "cesserunt sed in hoc tantum reprehensibiles "judicantur, quod semper gentem Anglorum

"etiam usque in hodiernum diem, quasi per "eos propriis finibus proscripti odio mortali "perstringunt nec illis libentius quam canibus "communicare volunt." Mat. Paris, Edit. Francofurti, p. 104.

[t] Usher, p. 1152. 576.—Geoff. Mon. Rog. Wendover.—Mat. Flor.

[u] Rowland's Mon. p. 154.

[w] Rapin, Vol. I. Lib. IV. fol.

[x] "Vi hostilitatis cogente," says Malmsb. p. 141.

[y] Malmsb. ibid. says it was Formosus, but he died in 896 (Dupin, Vol. IV. p. 335.); so that it must have been John IX.

Canter-

Canterbury being Prefident), in which it was determined to add three Bifhops to the two, which were before at Winchefter and Sherburn. The Pope approved of the propofal, and Pleimund ordained five Bifhops in one day[z]; Friedeftan for Winton, Adelftan for Cornwall, Werftan for Sherburn, Athelhelm for Wells, and Eidulph for Crediton in Devon. An ancient regifter in the Priory of Canterbury confirms this piece of hiftory, with this addition, that the council made a particular provifion for the Cornifh men, to recover them from their errours[a]. Rapin's remark upon this paffage has, I believe, a good deal of truth in it, " That, by " the errours of the Cornifh, we are to underftand their refufing " to acknowledge the papal authority[b]." The Cornifh See was fixed at Bodman, and the Cathedral Church was that of St. Petrock, at that time the chief Monaftery among the Cornifh Britans.

To this appointment, the Cornifh fubmitted, when it had refifted the Roman Hierarchy a great while after all the reft of Britain had fubmitted to it[c]. " The Britans in Cornwall (fays Mr. Rowland) " refifted the Romifh Ufurpations much longer than the reft of the " Britans, till about the year 905, when Edward the elder, with " the Pope's confent, fettled a Bifhop's See among them, which, " by the Pope's power, then greatly prevailing, in a fhort time " reduced them, much againft their will, to fubmit their ancient " faith to the conduct of papal difcipline, as moft of the Britans " were before forced to do[d]."

This new fettlement of the Church of Cornwall was followed by what fome hiftorians have ftyled the age of ignorance, fo that few materials of any confequence are to be met with for Ecclefiaftical Hiftory; the Monks and fecular Clergy difputed and contended with one another, but were both preyed upon without diftinction by the furious Dane.

The Bifhop's See continued at Bodman[e] till the year 981, when, that town and monaftery being burnt down by the Danes, the Bifhop removed his See to St. German's, where it continued till the year 1049, and in both places there fat twelve Bifhops in re-gular fucceffion[f]; — Athelftan, — Conan, — Ruydocke, — Aldred,

[z] Ibid. p. 26. Some fay feven, adding Kenulph Bifhop of Worcefter and Beornock of Selfey in Suffex. Rap. Engl. Fol. p. 113. Vol. I.
[a] Spelman's Councils, Vol. I. p. 387.
[b] Tranflat. Vol. I. p. 112.
[c] Rowl. p. 150.
[d] " This Bifhoprick was founded principally " for the reduction of the rebellious Cornifh to " the Roman Rites, who, as they ufed the lan- " guage, fo they imitated the lives and doctrine, " of the ancient Britans, neither hitherto, nor " long after, fubmitting themfelves to the See

" apoftolic." Fuller, Ch. Hift. Cent. X. B. II. p. 4.
[e] Mr. Rowland fays, the See was fixed at St. German's, and Edulph the firft Bifhop; but this is a miftake, and probably owing to this caufe, that Edulph or Wolf might be the firft Bifhop that fat at St. German's, but he was the feventh Bifhop from the firft erection of that Epifcopacy.
[f] See Heylin's Help to Englifh hiftory, where the year of inftallment of each Bifhop is men-tioned. — See Creffy, p. 832. where we find the names.

— Britwin,

Wm Dean

Kireen. Sculp Exon

To Sr John St Aubyn Bar^t This View of St Michael's Mount in Cornwall
engrav'd at his expence is most gratefully dedicated by Wm Borlase.

— Britwin, — Athelftan II. — Wolf, — Woron, — Wolocke, — Stidio, — Aldred II. — and Burwold g. After the death of Burwold, his nephew Livingus, Abbot of Taviftock, and Bifhop of Crediton, by his great intereft with King Canute, prevailed fo far as to unite the Bifhoprick of St. German's to that of Crediton, A. D. 1049; and Leofricus fucceffor to Livingus (becaufe of the ravages committed by pirates in the open towns of St. German's and Crediton) carried them both to Exeter in the reign of Edward the Confeffor, as to a place of greater fecurity, where the Epifcopal See for both counties of Devon and Cornwall ftill continues.

CHAP. XI.

Of Religious Houfes founded in Cornwall before the Norman Conqueft.

IT is not here intended to trace the Religious Houfes from the foundation, and, reckoning up their Benefactors and Donations, to run through all the changes they underwent. In one age they were plundered and ruined, in the next reftored; fometimes they were filled with Regulars, fometimes with Seculars, and then Regulars again; fometimes the Monks were of one Habit and Order, fometimes of another; fometimes the Houfes were independent, and at other times Cells to other and greater Houfes. Thefe particulars are too numerous for our prefent bounds. I fhall only give a fummary view of the moft ancient, and of fome particulars relating to them, leaft known, and moft remarkable.

The firft Religious Houfe which we read of, founded in Corn- SECT. I.
wall, was that erected by St. Patrick h, in the year 432. The place Of Padftow
where this houfe was fituate was called anciently Loderick, the Church and
houfe itfelf Laffenac; either from the Church's being built with Monaftery.
ftone i, whereas in thofe early times they were feldom built of fuch coftly materials k; or Laffenac, *quafi* Lan-manach, the Church of the Monks; as Bodvenah (now Bodman) from Bod-manach, the Houfe of the Monks; it ftood on the North Sea, at the mouth of a river, the place called then Heilemuth l; by Malmfbury, Lib. II. Hegelmith: the river was what we now call Alan, formerly called by the name

---

g Called alfo Birthwald, and Brithwald.
h " Ubi (in Cornubia fcil.) & Meneviæ " Cœnobium conftruxiffe ferunt."—Ufher, p. 1100.
i Quafi Lan-menek, the M (according to the Cornifh idiom) paffing into an U.
k Their walls being ufually wattled, and of

clay or wood.
Alfred the Great, almoft five hundred years after this, introduced building with ftone. Rap. Vol. I. p. 96.—Spelman's Councils of Britain, p. 15.
l Rog. Wendover, Ufher, p. 1014. Heiel muth, i. e. the Mouth of the River.

of Hayle, or Heyle, a common name for any River. In this church Laffenack, there was an Altar dedicated to St. Patrick, much reverenced in thofe times, as fuppofed to be the fame on which (according to his Legend) that Saint fwam from Ireland into Cornwall, to avoid the pomp and ceremony with which the Irifh continued to teize him[m]. This church was called afterwards by the name of St. Patrick[n]; and I fhould think that the town was afterwards, in commemoration of this Saint, called by the Saxons Padftow, or Patrick-ftow[o]: others think it called Padftow from St. Petrock, a Difciple of St. Patrick, who fettled in the fame Houfe, and built here; and, after thirty years labour in the word of God, died and was buried here, A. D. 564.

SECT. II.   The Monaftery of Padftow being near the fea fhore, and expofed
of Bodman. to the piracies of the Saxons[p], and after them of the Danes, the Monks removed to Bodman, and, bringing the body of Petrock with them, the church there was dedicated to that faint (who paffed fome part of his retirement formerly in this place[q]); and the town was called by the Saxons Petrocftow, but by the Britans Bodmanna, that is, the habitation of the Monks. As this was the moft ancient fociety, and moft flourifhing in Cornwall, and placed conveniently for that purpofe; Edward the elder fettled here the epifcopal See, A. D. 905. Athelftan, fucceeding his father Edward, abfolutely conquered the Cornifh Britans about the year 936; and, being a Prince as generous in his donations to the Clergy, as he was valiant and fortunate in war, among the reft of his liberalities, gave the Religious here fuch privileges and lands, that he was ever after regarded as their Founder. " He found the Monks following the " rule of Benedict," fays Bifhop Tanner (p. 66.); and it is not improbable but they might have admitted this rule of the Romifh Church when they had their new Bifhop. Here the Bifhops of Cornwall refided till the year 981, when the town, church, and monaftery, being burnt down by the Danes, the Bifhops removed their feat farther Eaft, to St. German's on the river Lyner. The Monaftery feems to have continued in ruins for fome time, and went into the poffeffion of the Earl of Moreton and Cornwall, at the Conqueft; but was foon after [r] re-edified, and reftored to its former ufe, by a nobleman called Algar, with the licence of the King, and affiftance of William Warlewaft, Bifhop of Exeter.

[m] Ufher, p. 877.
[n] " Ibidem ftatuitur Ecclefia, St. Patricii " nomine." From the Glaftonb. Records.— Ufher, p. 879.
[o] The Irifh calling him Padraick. Ufher, ib. p. 895.

[p] Whence it feems to have had the name of Loderick, that is, the Creek of Robbers.
[q] Leland, Itin. Vol. II. p. 84.
[r] Viz. in 1110, or 1120, according to Tanner.

Leland

Leland fays (Vol. II. p. 84.) there were in this houfe, firft Monks, then Nuns, then fecular Priefts, then Monks again, then Canons; and it was Algar that placed the black Canons regular here, between the years 1110 and 1120. About fixty years after this, there happened a remarkable conteft about the body of their Saint and Patron, Petrock, for " Martin, Canon Regular of this " houfe, ftole the body of St. Petrock from the Church of Bod- " man, and carried it into Britany in France, and lodged it in " the Abby of St. Mein there. The theft being difcovered, Ro- " ger, then Prior of the Church of Bodman, with the honefter part " of this Chapter, went to Henry the Second, then King of England, " with their complaint, who, without delay, ordered the French " Abbot and his Convent to reftore the body to the Prior of " Bodman; and, in cafe of refufal, Rolland de Dinant, chief Ju- " ftice of Britany, had orders to take it away by force, and reftore " it. The Abbot, fearing the King's difpleafure, reftored the bo- " dy, at the fame time fwearing upon the Evangelifts, and the " Relicks of the Saints, that it was in no wife altered or diminifh- " ed fince it came into his cuftody [s]." Such a treafure the Monks of that age efteemed the bones of their patron. And here I cannot help mentioning, how precious every part of this Saint was reckoned in ancient times. King Athelftan was remarkable for every act of piety which was in fafhion in his time; he was particularly curious in collecting Relicks; they were prefented to him as the moft acceptable gift [t], and he beftowed them with great devotion, as he faw moft proper; among other prefents, he is faid to have given part of the bones, the hair, and the garments of St. Petrock to the Monaftery of St. Peter's at Exeter [u]. The fhrine of St. Petrock, and his tomb, were both ftanding, in the Eaftern part of the great Church, in Leland's time [w]. The black Canons, placed here by Algar, continued till the diffolution, when Thomas Wandfworth (laft Prior) with his Monks delivered it up into the King's Hands, in 1539. It was ftiled " the Priory of St. Mary, and St. Petrock, and valu- " ed at 270 l. 11 d. by Dugdale, 289 l. 11 s. 11 d. by Speed [x].

King Athelftan is reckoned to have founded this priory, and to have dedicated it to the honour of St. German, Bifhop of Auxierre, in France, but a ftrenuous preacher here in Britain, being delegated by the French Bifhops (A. D. 429 [y]), together with Lupus Bifhop of Troy, to come hither, and oppofe the Pelagian He-

SECT. III.
St. German's Priory.

[s] Hoveden's Ann. pag. 324.—Ufher, pag. 1014.
[t] See Malmfb. pag. 28.
[u] Monaft. Angl. pag. 226.
[w] Temp. Hen. VIII. Itin. Vol. II. pag. 84.
[x] Tanner, pag. 66.
[y] Ibid. pag. 77.

5 E

refy.

refy.   Here were fecular Canons at firft, and King Athelftan is
faid to have appointed one Conan Bifhop here (A. D. 936).   King
Edred, brother to Athelftan, who began his reign in 946, and died
955 [z], is alfo faid to have ordained St. German's to be a Bifhop's
See ; but as all hiftories agree, that the Bifhop of Cornwall did
not remove from Bodman till the year 981, it is very unlikely
that there fhould be a Bifhop here before that time (as Bifhop
Tanner rightly obferves) ; neither does it feem neceffary, that there
fhould be two Bifhops in fo narrow a flip of land as Cornwall,
and but one at Crediton, for all Devon, a country of fo much
larger extent.   The following particulars may ferve, in fome meafure, to difcover the truth : I find Edred a benefactor to the See
of Bodman ; for Henry the third confirmed to the Monks there
the Manor of Newton in the fame manner as King Edred had
granted it.   Very likely this was given in order to augment the
revenues of the Bifhoprick there ; and, for the fame reafon, he
might have appointed the Bifhop of Bodman to be Bifhop of St.
German's too.   Again, Conan is faid to be the name of the firft
Bifhop, placed here by King Athelftan.   I find alfo that Conan
was fecond Bifhop, in the See of Bodman, in the time of King
Athelftan ; it is poffible therefore that Athelftan might annex his
new Priory of St. German to the See of Bodman, for the better
maintenance of the Epifcopal Dignity, and ordered alfo that St.
German's fhould partake of the Epifcopal Title, by which difpofition, I imagine, that Conan, at that time Bifhop of Bodman,
became Bifhop of Bodman and St. German's too, in the fame manner as we have now the Bifhop of Bath and Wells, and the Bifhop
of Litchfield and Coventry ; and this might give occafion to the
miftake of St. German's being one Bifhoprick, and Bodman another ; but thefe things I offer only as conjectures : one thing, I
think, we may reft affured of, that there were not two Bifhops in
Cornwall at one time.   In 981, the Cornifh Bifhop fettled here,
and, by the date, it muft be one of the middle Bifhops in the lift ;
for, in all, they were but twelve ; and to the year 981, the Bifhoprick had lafted, at Bodman, feventy fix years, and from the
year 981, to the tranflation of the See to Crediton (in 1049), is
fixty eight years, fo that the perfon who removed muft, likely, be
the feventh Bifhop from the foundation ; and the name of the
feventh Bifhop was Wolf, who firft placed the See at St. German's ;
and this gave rife to another miftake, which is, that the Bifhoprick was firft placed at St. German's, and that Edulph, or
Wolf, was the firft Bifhop ; whereas, indeed, he was (at leaft as it
feems to me) only the firft Bifhop that fat and lived at St. German's.

[z] Speed, Chron. pag. 346.

Leofri-

Leofricus, succeffor to Livingus in the See of Crediton (then the only See for the counties of Cornwall and Devon), is thought to have changed the fecular into regular Canons, and was therefore looked upon as their Founder, and it was called a Priory of the foundation and patronage of the Bifhop of Exeter [a]. Whether the regular Canons of Leofric, firft Bifhop of Exeter, were difplaced, and the feculars reftored, I cannot fay; but it is faid by Leland, that Bartholomew, Bifhop of Exeter (temp. Hen. II.) introduced Regulars here. Robert Swimmer, the laft Prior here, with eight black Canons, yielded it up into the King's hand (March 2), in the 30th of Henry VIII. The Monaftick Church is as ancient a building as any at this time extant in Cornwall, and was formerly inclofed by the Priory. " Befide the high Altar " on the right hand is a tomb in the Wall with an image of a " Bifhop, and over the tomb eleven Bifhops painted, with their " names, and verfes, as token of fo many Bifhops buried there, " or that there had been fo many Bifhops of Cornwall that had " their feat there [b]." On this paffage, let me obferve, that there were twelve Bifhops in all, from the firft eftablifhment, by Edward the Elder, to the laft Bifhop; the firft, called Athelftan, fat at Bodman before the Conqueft of Cornwall; Conan was the fecond, and, from him included, to the laft Bifhop, there were eleven in number, as painted here in this Church, which may ferve to confirm the above conjecture, that Conan was made Bifhop of St. German's, as well as of Bodman, by Athelftan, and confirmed by Edred, and that, though there were twelve Bifhops in all in Cornwall, St. German's could only reckon eleven, and therefore has only that number painted on the wall. Their Names, with the order of fucceffion, are mentioned before, pag. 378.

King Athelftan, having fet his heart upon the Conqueft of SECT. IV. Cornwall, thought it could not be compleat, unlefs he reduced the Of St. Berian. Scilly Iflands, which he had a view of from the Weftern Promontories. He vows, therefore, a Religious houfe, in cafe he returned with victory, and being returned according to his wifh, he acted according to his Vow; he built a Collegiate Church in fight of thofe Iflands, and dedicated it to St. Berian a holy Woman of Ireland (who had at that time an Oratory, and was buried here), placing a Dean and three Prebends in the College.

This King had now done with conquering, and his Princely mind had nothing farther to exert itfelf in, but making free and amplifying thofe immunities, which, by his conqueft, he had ta-

[a] Prideaux's Excerpta—Tanner, pag. 67.   [b] Leland's Itin. Vol. VII. pag. 113.

ken

ken away; the firft he did for his glory, the fecond was the ufual dictate of his generous nature.

This Religious Houfe was exempted from all Epifcopal, and every other authority, but that of the Pope of Rome [c]. He alfo made it a fanctuary [d], and, perhaps, extended his bounty to this Church in the fame manner, if not in the fame words, which he made ufe of in endowing the Church of Beverley,

" *Alls free make I thee—As Heart may think, or Eye may fee* [e]."

To build Religious Houfes was, in thofe days, the way which the moft religious Princes took to fhew their gratitude to Providence for delivering them from the accidents of War; and the donations were generally in proportion to their danger, or victory. At the Norman Conqueft, there were fecular Canons here; and in the 20th of Edward the Firft, a Dean and three Prebends. " The Dean-" ry" (confifting of three Churches, and as many Parifhes, viz. St. Berian, St. Levin, and Sinnin, alias Senan) " was feized into " the King's hands, in the reign of Edward III. (becaufe John " de Maunte, then Dean, was a Frenchman); and, as Alien, was " given in the 24th of Hen. VI. to King's College, Cambridge, " and in the 7th of Edward IV. to Windfor College; yet neither " of thefe Societies long enjoyed it, or had any benefit from it, " for it was all along, and ftill continues, an independent Deanry, " either in the gift of the Crown, or the Duke of Cornwall [f]." It was valued in the 26th of Henry VIII. at 48 l. 12 s. 1 d. per ann. The remains of the College were wantonly demolifhed by one Shrubfall, Governor of Pendinas Caftle, during the ufurpation of Cromwell.

The following Deans, before the fuppreffion, occurred to the learned Bifhop Tanner [g]—Walter de Gray, 1213.—William de Hamilton was fucceeded, in the year 1296, by Ralph de Manton. —Matthew de Baylew elected 1303.—John de Maunte (alias de Meunte), elected 1318.—Tho. de Crofs elected 1338.—John de Hale, Robert de Stratton, and Richard de Wolvifton, all three elected 1350.—John Saucey was fucceeded by David Maignard, 1354.—Alan de Stokes elected 1386; but he was Dean of Berian A. D. 1372, as appears by the copy of an inftrument he was witnefs to that year, figned Alan de Stokes Doien de Sanct Berien [h].—John Boor elected 1394. Nicholas Slake elected 1395.— William Lochard 1410; he was Dean of Berian, and by his Mo-

[c] Leland, Vol. III. pag. 113.
[d] Ibid. p. 6.
[e] Holland, Infert. pag. 4.
[f] Tanner, pag. 67.
[g] See his Principals of Religious Houfes, ad fin. Notitiæ.
[h] M.S. Survey of the Dutchy of Cornwall, temp. Edward III. nuper penes R. Elliot Arm. def.

nument

nument in Hereford Church[h], died Oct. 24, 1438, Adam Moleyns 1439.—Peter Stukler occurs 1444.—Robert Knollys elected 1460, occurs 1486; to which we may add, John Rese " of late " time[i], Dean of St. Berian's."

King Athelstan is also said to have founded a priory of Black *Bonury.* Canons to the honour of St. Petrorsi, at Bonury in this county; but where that Religious House was, I cannot say, probably it was soon after annexed, and the Monks translated to some larger house, by which means it lost all notice[k].

The Church of St. Stephen near Lanceston was Collegiate, and *SECT. V.* in the College secular Canons before the Conquest. It was given *Of St. Ste-* to the Bishop and Church of Exeter by Hen. I. and suppressed *phen's near* *Lanceston.* about 1126, by William Warlewast Bishop of Exeter, who removed the Canons from the hill into a more retired situation under the Castle, about half a mile nearer to the Town, where he founded a Priory for Canons of the order of St. Austin, and dedicated it to St. Stephen as the College had been before[l]. This Priory was the richest in Cornwall, and in the 26th of Henry VIII. was valued at 354 l. 0 s. 11 d. says Dugdale; 392 l. 11 s. 2 d. says Speed. The Prior and eleven Canons subscribed to the supremacy, A. D. 1534. It had the privilege of a Sanctuary, as appears by 32 Hen. VIII. cap. xii. sect. 3.

When the Monks first settled here, is uncertain: Edward the *SECT. VI.* Confessor found Monks here serving God, and gave them by charter *St. Mi-* the property of the Mount and other lands; first obliging them to *chael's* *Mount.* conform to the Rule of St. Benedict. But, long before this, this place seems renowned for its sanctity, and therefore must (according to the custom of the first ages of Christianity) have been dedicated to Religion; for St. Kayne, or Keyna, a holy Virgin of the blood royal, daughter of Braganus, Prince of Brecknockshire, is said to have gone a Pilgrimage to St. Michael's Mount in Cornwall[m]. Now this Saint lived in the end of the fifth Century, and as she probably dwelt in the Eastern part of this county (where her Church and Well are still to be seen, and her festival is celebrated on the 30th of September[n]), it is not at all improbable that she should come this pilgrimage to St. Michael's Mount; a fact farther confirmed by the Legend of St. Cadoc (though disfigured by Fable),

[h] Willis, Cathed. p. 539.
[i] Leland, Vol. III. p. 46.
[k] Bishop Tanner, Not. f, p. 66. thinks it the same with Bodman.
[l] " It was founded and endowed (says Hals) " by the Earls of Cornwall, and Bishops of " Bodman, long before William the Con- " queror." Reginald Fitz Henry, Earl of

Cornwall, was a great benefactor to it, and endeavoured to bring back the Bishoprick of Cornwall to it, but in vain.
[m] Carew, p. 130.—Capgrave, p. 204.— Willis, Not. p. 103.
[n] " By the Romish Calendar, her feast was " held October 8." Letter from Dr. Milles, now Dean of Exeter, Dec. 11. 1755,

5 F   who,

who, according to Capgrave (fol. liv. and ccv.), made a pilgrimage to St. Michael's Mount, there saw, and conversed with St. Kayne, and on his return, parched with thirst, miraculously produced a most plentiful and healing fountain in a dry place, and had a church dedicated to him in Cornwall, where this miracle was performed; from which it appears that this place was dedicated to Religion, at least as anciently as the latter end of the fifth century, above five hundred years before the grant and settlement of it by Edward the Confessor.

When the Normans came in, this Monastery (with many other lands and honours) came into the power of Robert Earl of Moreton and Cornwall, who built here, and, out of regard to his Mother-country, annexed it as a Cell to the Abby of St. Michael *de Periculo Maris* in Normandy; the Monks were of the reformed Order of the Benedictines called Cistercians, and of the Gilbertine kind, a rule introduced into the Cistercian Order by Gilbert of Sempringham in Lincolnshire, A. D. 1148. By this rule, Monks and Nuns were placed in one house; and the Nunnery was lately standing on the Eastern end of this Monastery, with a Chapel dedicated to the Virgin Mary, as in all Cistercian Monasteries these Chapels were. The Nunnery was detached a little from the Cells of the Monks, and a great deal of carved work both in stone and timber (to be seen a few years since) shewed that it was the most elegantly finished of any part of this House. In Richard the first's time, one Pomeroy, a gentleman of great possessions in Devonshire and Cornwall, having committed murder, took refuge here, having a Sister in this Nunnery, and being (as Leland says, Itin. Vol. VI. p. 54.) " at that tyme Lord of the Castelle of the " Mount of St. Michael," where, finding the hill on which the Monastery stands steep and rocky, he fortified it, though to little purpose; however, from this time, it was looked upon as a place fit for defence, and made use of as such upon several occasions, and the Commander of the Garrison had a lodging in the Monastery[n].

This Priory continued a Cell to St. Michaels's in Normandy till that connexion was destroyed, with all those of like kind throughout the kingdom, in the time of Edward the third.

When Henry VI. endowed his New College in Cambridge, he gave this Religious House to it (Pat. 20 Hen. VI. p. 4. m. 3.); but Edward IV. annexed it as a Cell to Sion Abby in Middlesex, and so it continued till the general dissolution. At the first seizure of it by Edward III. the farm of it was rated but at ten pounds

---

[n] In Patent 5. of Hen. IV. p. 1. m. 21, for repairing this Priory, it is called Fortalitium, i. e. " a place of defence and security in time of " war, to all the country round." Rym. Fœd. Vol. VIII. p. 102, 340, 341.

per Annum ; but in the time of Hen. VIII. the lands belonging to this Houſe (as parcel of Sion) were valued at one hundred and ten pounds, twelve ſhillings, and one halfpenny[o].

Of this Mount and Priory, as the moſt entire Religious Houſe now ſtanding in Cornwall, I prefix the proſpect to this chapter[P].

At Crantock there were Secular Canons in the time of Edward SECT.VII. the Confeſſor, and a Collegiate Church dedicated to St. Carantocus Carantoc. (ſaid to be a diſciple of Patrick), in the patronage of the Biſhop of Exeter. " In the Lincoln taxation[q], there were reckoned here " eight Prebendaries without a Dean, but Le Neve's MS. reckons " a Dean and ten Prebendaries." Tanner, a Dean, nine Prebendaries, and four Vicars choral[r]. The founder of this Religious Houſe is not yet known. The Secular Canons continued here till the general ſuppreſſion, when their Revenues were valued at 89l. 15s. 8d.

Here was a Monaſtery in the time of Edward the Confeſſor, SECT. VIII. founded in honour of St. Neot, brother, " or (as others think) a St. Neot's. " near relation" to King Alfred the Great. St. Neot is ſtyled by Fox, Abbot in Cornwall ; he died, A.D. 890, and was buried here, and from him the place was called Neotſtow, having had the name of St. Guerir till that time. His body was afterwards removed into Huntingtonſhire[s]; where alſo he gave name to the town, before called Arnulphſbury (alias Aimſbury), but, ever ſince, St. Neot's, from this Saint. In 1213 the poor body ſuffered another removal ; for Henry, Abbot of Croyland, thinking his Abby a fitter ſhrine for ſo great a Saint, took up his bones from St. Neot's in Huntingtonſhire, and beſtowed them in Croyland Minſter[t]. From this Church of St. Neot's in Cornwall, the Earl (as Exeter Domeſday calls him), that is, William Earl of Moreton and Cornwall, took away all the lands, excepting one acre, which he left to the Prieſts ; and the ſame Earl ſeems to have annexed it to Montacute Priory in Somerſetſhire, of which he was the founder, for to this Houſe it did belong[u]. The founder of this Monaſtery is not known, but likely it was Alfred, or ſome of his family ; for Aſſer, in his Life of Alfred, tells us, that King Alfred, being ill, proſtrated himſelf in the Church of St. Guerir, and there performing his devotions with great zeal was ſurprizingly recovered ; and St. Neot dying here, with great reputation for his ſanctity, and being here interred, it is not unlikely that Alfred (by whom

[o] Perhaps, inſtead of Lands, it ſhould be Revenues, which might be advanced by means of the Fiſhery ; formerly of little value, but of late ages much increaſed ; at preſent, the moſt conſiderable part of the Revenue of this Site and Manor, and ſtill likely to increaſe.

[P] Plate XXXIV. p. 379.

[q] Tanner, p. 68.

[r] Spelman's MS. of the Lincoln Taxation, in the Bodleian Library, names ten Prebends.

[s] To the palace of Earl Alric (alias Alfric) in Huntingdonſhire. Spelman's Life of Alfred, (p. 139.), then converted into a Monaſtery.

[t] Spelm. Life of Alfred, p. 139.

[u] Tanner, p. 69.

he

he was highly honoured after his death[w]), or his son Edward, might found a Religious House of Clerks (as Spelman calls them) in this place, in grateful remembrance of the abovementioned recovery, as well as to do honour to the name of so near and worthy a relation.

SECT. IX.
St. Piran, alias Piran-Sanz.

" In the days of Edward the Confessor, here was a Dean[x] and
" Canons endowed with lands, and the priviledge of a sanctuary.
" The Church was given by King Henry I. to the Bishop and
" Church of Exeter. Afterwards, here was a Cell of Cistercian
" Monks subordinate to Beaulieu Abby in Hampshire[y]."

John of Tinmuth, in his Life of Kiaranus, says, that in Cornwall, where he was buried, he was called Piranus; the same author adds, " that his father was called Domuel, and his mother " Wingella," and this might be true of St. Piran, but other parents are ascribed to Kiaranus in a MS. which Archbishop Usher says[z] he had then in his possession, for his (viz. Kiaranus's) father was said to be Lugneus, " *de nobilioribus gentis Osraigi*," and his mother, called Liadain, " *de gente quæ dicitur Corculaigde*," and that he was born and brought up " *in Clera Insula in regione Corculaigde*," whereas Piranus was *ex Ossoriensi Hiberniæ provincia*, son of Domuel and Wingella. However, from John of Tinmuth, as I suppose, Leland[a] calls the parish church " of St. Keveryn, alias of " Piranus;" but whatever name St. Piran had before he came into Cornwall, St. Keveryn, and St. Piran were certainly different persons; for Domesday[b] says, " the Canons of St. Pieran held " Lan Piran;" that is, some lands which (from their belonging to a Church of that Saint) had the name of Lan Piran; and at Piran-Sanz[c] the Bishops of Bodman had a Manor called Lan Piran, now almost entirely overrun by the sands; and so great esteem had the Cornish for the name of this Saint, that we have at present three parochial Churches dedicated to him, and two of them are at present in the patronage of the Church of Exeter.

St. Kiaran, alias St. Keveryn, f. St. Achebran.

But St. Keveryn does not appear to have had any connexion with the Bishop of Exeter, any otherwise than as its Diocesan. The patronage is in Lay hands[d]; and here seems to me to have been a distinct Religious House, with lands called Lanachebran, which we find mentioned as one of our Religious Houses in Cornwall, but have not known hitherto where to fix it. " There was a Society " of Secular Canons in a place of this name, at or about the " Conquest[e], dedicated to St. Achebran;" and it appears from the

[w] Spelm. ibid. p. 139.
[x] Domesday, Exon. p. 435.
[y] Tanner, p. 69.
[z] Prim. p. 784, and 1091.
[e] Tanner, p. 69.
[a] Itin. Vol. VII. p. 110.
[b] Tanner, p. 69, Not. c.
[c] Piran-Sanz, i.e. St. Piran.
[d] ——Bulteel, Esq; of Devon.

Domesday

Domefday in Exeter Cathedral library[d], that thefe Canons held Lanachebran in the time of Edward the Confeffor. Now this St. Achebran is not to be found in Cornwall; but St. Chebran there is commonly called Kevran, the fame doubtlefs as Kiaranus[e], now called St. Keveryn, in the hundred of Kerrier[f]. Several confiderable Ruins are ftill to be feen, about a quarter of a mile from the Church of St. Kevern, at a place called Tregonin, where there is a Tradition among the neighbours, that formerly there ftood a Priory; and a part of thefe Ruins is ftill called the Chapel. This likely was the Houfe, and St. Kevern the Collegiate Church, of thefe Canons Secular.

There was a little Priory on the ifland of Trefcaw (alias Inifcaw) SECT. X.
in Scilly, at leaft as early as the reign of Canute, though by whom Sulley, alias Scylley, et placed there is uncertain; but probably by Athelftan, who (as in Scilly. this lift of Religious Houfes we have all along obferved) was very intent upon converting, and furthering in the ways of Religion, thofe whom he had fubdued in war. It was dedicated to St. Nicholas (from whom the whole ifland is fometimes called St. Nicholas's Ifle), and belonged to Taviftock Abby before the Conqueft[g]. Whether that be true or not, Henry I. by his charter[h], " grants all the Churches of Sylley (or Sully), with their appur- " tenances, and the land, as the Monks or Hermits held it in the " time of Edward the Confeffor, and Burgald (alias Burwald, or " Birthwald) Bifhop of Cornwall, to Ofbert Abbot of Taviftock, " A. D. 1120." By which charter (as it grants rather than confirms), though its connection with Taviftock earlier than this date may be rendered doubtful, yet the Monaftery's being as old as Canute at leaft (in whofe reign Burgald died at St. German's) becomes unqueftionable. The remains of the Priory Church are ftill to be feen, called the Abby; but the Monaftery is wholly deftroyed. The Monks were of the Benedictine Order[i].

There was a Collegiate Church of Secular Canons here, dedicated SECT. XI.
to St. Probus, before the Conqueft[k]. The Manor, which the Probus. Canons had here, is called Lanbrabois in Domefday[l], erroneoufly, for Lan Probus, and was held by Edward the Confeffor himfelf, fo that it muft have been granted to the Canons by Edward the Confeffor, or after him. " The Church was given to the Bifhop " and Church of Exeter, by King Henry I." (fays Tanner); but I find, by Henry I's Charter[m], that he only reftored it to St. Mary, and St. Peter's Church in Exeter, " for the abfolution of his fins,

[d] Page 433.
[e] In the Lincoln Taxation (20 Ed. I.) called Ecclefia S[ti] Kiorani, by Mr. Carew writ Keyran.
[f] The letter A before Chebran (whereby they make a Saint Achebran) is no more than a prepofition in the Cornifh language, fignifying of, prefixed to the name of the Saint Chebran, or Kevran.

[g] Tanner, p. 69.
[h] Monaft. Ang. p. 516 and 1002.
[i] Tanner, p. 69.
[k] Domefday, in Not. (h) ibid.—Tanner, p. 69.
[l] Exon. p. 434.
[m] Pen. T. Hawkins, Arm. Dom. de Manerio de Probus.

5 G   " and

" and the good of his foul, together with the other Churches of
" St. Petrock, St. Stephen, Peran, and Tohou, as free in every
" refpect, and quiet, as the famous Kings, his predeceffors, apppear
" by their charters to have granted them." There were five
Prebends here[n]. Henry de Bolifh was made Dean by the Bifhop
of Exeter, in 1258[o]; and I find by an extract (ex Regift. Exon.)
that Henricus de Bollegha (doubtlefs the fame man), by his inftrument of Donation[p], bearing date the 14th of Feb. 1268, grants
the perpetual Patronage of the Prebends of Probus to the Bifhop of
Exeter, and his fucceffors for ever. After this Henry, I have found
no mention of a Dean; but " William, Bifhop of Exeter[q], foon
" after gives the Church of Probus, with all its rights of prefenting
" and nominating the Prebends, and Vicar, the impropriation of the
" Tithes (a particular portion being referved to the Prebends), and
" every appurtenance (faving the rights and dues of the Vicar), to
" the Treafurer for the time being of the Church of Exeter, moved
" thereto, by the great expence which the faid Treafurer was put
" to in maintaining perpetual Lamps in the Church of Exeter."
For the better fupport of which, efpecially on the Feaft of the
Dedication of the faid Church, the Feaft of the Nativity, Feafts of
St. Paul, and our Saviour's Circumcifion, this was granted by the
Bifhop, with the confent of the Chapter. A few years after this,
viz. in 1312, Walter Stapledon, Bifhop of Exeter, eftablifhed a
Partition of the Tithe Corn, between the Treafurer of his Church,
and the Prebends here. In which inftrument (called *Divifio
Garbarum)* the five Prebends are named. There were alfo five
Prebends at the general furrender; their names were Matthew
Hull; Thomas Parker; George Chudleigh;——Perot; Richard
White; they had a Salary each[r], which in the whole amounted but
to 16l. 9s. 4d. " The endowment of the Treafurerfhip in the
" 26th of Henry VIII. was valued at 22l. 10s. per ann." And to
the Treafurer of the Church of Exeter the Patronage of this Church
ftill belongs.

Conftan-
tine.

     There feems to have been a Religious Houfe at Conftantine; for
in Domefday[s], " *Sanctus Conftantinus habet dim. hidæ terræ,
" quæ tempore Regis Edwardi (fcil. Confefforis) fuit immunis ab omni
" Servitio, poftquam Comes* (viz. de Moreton) *accepit terram, femper
" reddidit Gildum.*"

---

[n] In the Linc. Taxat. but four Prebends, fays
Tanner, ibid. but I find five in Sir Henry
Spelman's excellent copy of that Taxation in
the Bodleian Library; five in 1312, twenty years
after the Linc. Taxat. and five alfo at the
fuppreffion.

[o] Regift. of Bronfc. Bifhop of Exeter.
[p] Pen. Thomas Hawkins, Armig.
[q] Suppofed Bifhop Brewer.
[r] Tanner fays but four had penfions, but this
feems to be a miftake.
[s] Exon. p. 435.

Thefe

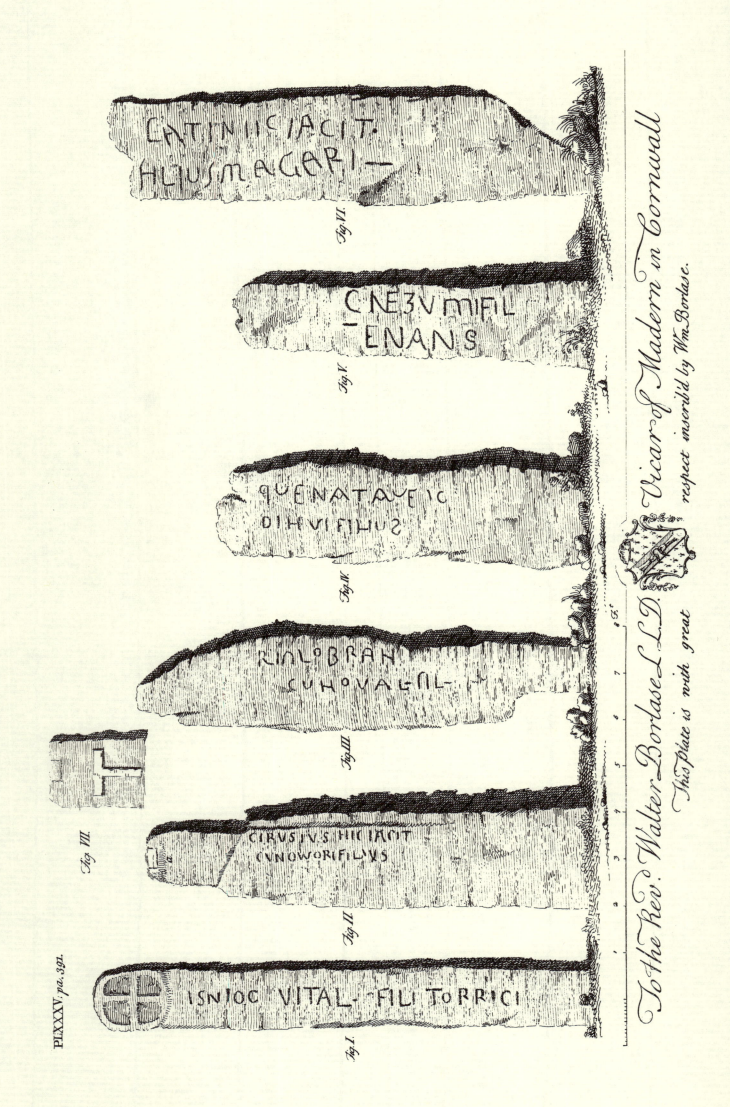

Fig. VII.

CATINIISIACIT.
HLIUSMAGARI—

Fig. VI.

CNE3VMIFIL
ENANS

Fig. V.

QVENATAVEIC
DIHVIFILIVS

Fig. IV.

RIALOBRAN
CVNOVALIIL·

Fig. III.

CIRVSIVS·HIC·IACIT
CVNOWORIFILIVS

Fig. II.

ISNIOC· VITALI· FILI· TORRICI

Fig. I.

To the Rev.ᵈ Walter Borlase L.D. Vicar of Madern in Cornwall
This plate is with great respect inscrib'd by Wm. Borlase.

Thefe are all the Religious Houfes which were founded in Cornwall before the Norman Conqueft, that I have met with ; the reft of more modern date, may be feen in the Monaft. Angl. and Bifhop Tanner [s], and may one time or other (as well as thefe which have gone before) come to be more particularly confidered, if God permit.

CHAP. VII.

Infcribed Monuments before the Conqueft.

THIS Stone ferves, at prefent, to hang a gate to, on the Vi-carage ground of St. Clement's near Truro. By the purity of the character, I judge it to be one of the moft ancient Chriftian fepulchral Monuments in this county. It's infcription is in one line, and, if at full length, the words would be thefe following : *Ifniocus Vitalis filius Torrici*; there is not the leaft deviation from the Roman Capitals, but only that the under dexter ftroke of the R in *Torrici* is too fhort, and too horizontal.

SECT. I.
Plate
XXXV.
Fig. I.
ISNIOC.

There is another very good argument for the great antiquity of this Infcriprion, which is, that here are two names of the perfon interred, a thing fo common among the Romans, and fo feldom met with, during their Empire, in the Monuments of other nations, that where the character concurs, it may be looked upon as a decifive criterion of a Roman Infcription, or at leaft nearly bordering upon their reign here in Britain; but this is ftill more confirmed by a remark, which will readily occur to the curious, which is, that *Vitalis* is actually a Roman Name; fo that *Ifnioc* the *Prænomen* is Britifh, and the *Cognomen Vitalis* is Roman [t]. This Stone has at prefent a large Crofs on it in bafs relieve, which is fingular; and as the other Stones infcribed, which cannot be fo ancient as this, have no Croffes, I queftion whether the Crofs may not be of later date than the infcription, and cut on the ftone in thofe times, when it was none of the meaneft parts of Religion to erect Croffes in every Church-yard, and at the meeting of highways [u]; but of this I am doubtful, it being a very early cuftom among the Chriftians to blefs and dignify their memorials with the fign of the crofs [w].

---

[s] Pag. 70.
[t] See Dr. Mufgrave, of Julius Vitalis.
[u] The Copy of this Infcription was firft fent me by Francis Gregor, Efq; taken at his inftance by the Rev. Mr. Walker, and Mr. War-

wick of Truro; and, after I had drawn it on the fpot, I muft do them the juftice to fay, their copy was very faithful.
[w] Moyle, in Pofthum. Works, Vol. I. p. 187. thinks, " that there are feveral inftances to be

" A mile

" A mile off (viz. from Caftledôr) is a broken Crofs," fays Leland [x], " thus infcribed : *Cunomor & filius cum Domina Clufilla.*"
But Mr. Lhuyd, who was better acquainted with the old character,
reads the infcription (as publifhed in Camden, from his papers,
pag. 18.) *Cirufius hic jacet—Cunowori filius.* The fame learned
perfon juftly thinks the W to be an M reverfed, the W being but
lately [y] introduced into the Britifh Alphabet. This Stone is in-
corrrectly publifhed in Camden [z], and alfo in Mr. Moyle's Poft-
humous Works [a]. In the top of it, *a*, there is a little trough, or
pit funk, marked with dotted lines, fix inches long, three deep,
and four wide. On the fide, oppofite to that infcribed, there is a
Crofs emboffed, of the fhape and fize as Plate XXXV. Fig. VII. p.
391. This Monument is called the Long-ftone. It was removed, about twelve years fince, from the four Crofs-ways, a mile
and half North of Fawy, and lies now in a ditch, about two bow-
fhots farther to the North, in the way from Fawy to Caftledôr.

Mr. Edward Lhuyd abovementioned, in a letter to Thomas
Tonkin Efq; dated at Falmouth, Nov. 29, 1700, fays, that this
infcription is probably of the fifth or fixth century. Mr. Moyle,
in his letter on this infcription, fays [b], " The letters refemble the
" common infcriptions of the fourth and fifth century."

Who this Cirufius was, I do not pretend to fay; perhaps, the
fame who gave name to a little Creek, not far from this place,
called Polkerys [c], as Mr. Lhuyd conjectures; but we have the
name of Cerys in other parts of Cornwall alfo, by which it may
be concluded, that Cirufius was a name of note among the Cornifh
Britans.

As to the name of *Cunomorus,* I find in Rowland [d], that Kin-
warwy, fon to Awy, a Lord of Cornwall, gave name to a Church
in Anglefea, which was built A. D. 630 [e]. This feems to be the
fame name as Cunomorus (which, as Mr. Lhuyd rightly obferves,
in Welfh, and fo in Cornifh, was writ Kynvor [f]), and the termination Wy was affumed, as denoting the father Awy, from whom
he was defcended [g]. If the Kynvor, mentioned by Rowland,
was the fame as here interred, this Monument muft be of the middle of the feventh century, unlefs the reputation of his fanctity

---

" found in Aringhi's Roma Subterranea of
" Chriftian Monuments, with croffes engraven
" on them in the fame (viz. the fourth) centu-
" ry, and earlier."
   [x] Itin. Vol. III. p. 26.
   [y] About the year 1200, ufed firft by the Britans. See Lhuyd, Archæol. Brit. p. 229.
   [z] Camd. ut fupra, p. 18.
   [a] Vol. I p. 189.
   [b] Lhuyd, Archæol. Brit. p. 229.
   [c] The Cornifh common people pronounnce
it Pol-kerus. Moyle, ibid. p. 182.

[d] Mon. Illuftr. p. 154.
[e] Ibid. p. 189.
[f] Mr. Moyle thinks it only a flip of Mr.
Lhuyd's pen, when he fays it fhould be written
in Welfh ap Kynuor, and that it fhould be
Kynmor; but this is a miftake, the m, in Welfh
and Cornifh compofition, changing ufually into
a V. Conmor was a Royal name among the
ancient Scots; he was King of Inis huna.
" Ceafe, Love of Conmor, ceafe." Fingal.
   [g] According to the cuftom of the Britans, as
Ap Rice, ap Howel, now Price, and Powel.

may

may be fuppofed to have occafioned the nomination of that Church, after his deceafe, which might poffibly be the cafe.

In a croft about half a mile to the North Weft of Lanyon, in the parifh of Madern, lies a Stone, called by the Cornifh, Mên Skryfa, i. e. the infcribed Stone. The dimenfions are nine feet, ten inches long, one foot eight wide, and one foot feven deep, or thick.

SECT. III.
Plate
XXXV.
Fig. III.
RIALO-
BRAN.

This Stone ftood upright, and the infcription begins at the top (as moft of our ancient Cornifh Infcriptions do), and is to be read downwards, quite contrary to the method of the Runick Infcriptions, which generally begin at bottom, and are to be read upwards [h]. The Infcription is,

Rialobran — Cunoval — Fil.

At length, the words would be, *Rialobranus Cunovali filius.*

It is a fepulchral Monument fignifying that *Rialobran,* the fon of *Cunoval,* was buried here.

The firft name is likely compounded of *Rialo* (a name taken from Rhial, a Britifh word, fignifying noble), and Bran, or Bren, in the fame language, fignifying a Prince, as Brennus, Brendanus, and the like; both names are found in the Britifh Hiftory [i]. After the Saxon invafion, the Britans, hard befet, difperfed into Cornwall and Wales; others, under the conduct of *Rioval,* took poffeffion of of *Armorica,* in the year 454 [k].

Harold, fon of Earl Godwin, had alfo a brother called Rivallo (alias Rywalhon), whom, with his brother Blegent, he appointed to fucceed Griffin King of Wales, whom he had conquered [l].

As to the other name; Cun, or Kyn, is a Head, *metaph.* a Prince; and Mawl (which, in compofition, the Cornifh turn into Vawl) fignifies to praife or glorify [m].

As to it's age, nothing certain can be faid; but probably it is one of the oldeft Monuments we have in Cornwall. The lines are well kept in the writing, and the mark for contractions at the end of each word proper. It was written before the alphabet was corrupted, that is, before the letters were joined together by unnatural links, and the down-ftrokes of one made to ferve for two; which corruptions crept into the Roman alphabet (ufed by

[h] Worm. Mon. Danica.
[i] Brennin (Wallicè), a King. Bren (Cornubicè), fupreme.
[k] Ufher, Prim. p. 1110.
[l] Malmfbury, p. 53.——Rualhonus the fixteenth prince of Armorica, from Conan Meri-

doc.——Carad. Lang. by Powell, p. 2.——Rywalhon, King or Prince of Wales, time of Edward the Confeffor.
[m] Malglocun feems to have the fame original, the radixes being inverted.

5 H

the

the Cornifh Britans) gradually, after the Romans went off, and increafed more and more, until the Saxon letters came into ufe, about Athelftan's conqueft. The moft obfervable deviation from the Roman orthography in this Monument is this, that the crofs ftroke of the Roman N is not diagonal as it fhould be, nor yet quite horizontal (as it is obferved by the learned to be under the fixth century [n]); wherefore I fhould think it highly probable that this infcription was made before the middle of the fixth century [o]. The learned E. Lhuyd, in his letter to Mr. Tonkin [p], fays, " the " reading in Britifh [i. e. Welfh] is Rhwalhvran map Kynwal, " names not uncommon in our old Welfh pedigrees ; I take it to " be a thoufand years ftanding."

Mr. Moyle [q] thinks it moft likely that Rialobran was a Heathen, though for what reafon it is not faid. I rather imagine it a Chriftian Monument ; for, to make ufe of that gentleman's own argument [r], if D. M. (i. e. Diis Manibus) being wanting in Dr. Mufgrave's Infcription of Julius Vitalis fhews it plainly to be the Monument of a Chriftian, why muft not the omiffion of it in Rialobran be admitted as equal evidence for his religion ? If he was a Heathen, he muft have been of the Druid perfuafion ; and we know how averfe the ancient Druids were, to commit any thing to writing. It is true, there is no crofs at the beginning of this Infcription, as we find upon fome of our ancient infcribed ftones ; but there being no fymbol of the Heathen Religion here, and the Infcription written in the fame concife ftyle and the fame character with others, which (as the following pages will fhew) have croffes on them, will sufficiently prove that this is a Chriftian Monument, and erected, poffibly, before it became ufual to place the crofs before the name.

SECT. IV.
Plate XXXV.
-Fig. IV.
QUENA-TAU.

In Barlowena bottom, as you pafs from the Church of Gulval to that of Maderne, in the hundred of Penwith, there is a ftone, one foot eight inches wide, thick one foot, long feven feet nine inches, lying crofs the brook, as a foot bridge. It is thus infcribed,

Quenatau ≡ *Ic-* ⎫ ⎧ In words at length, it would run,
dinui filius. ⎭ ⎩ *Quenatavus Icdinui filius.*

This Infcription cannot be fo old as either of the former, for here are two forts of the letter N, the firft true Roman, the other as ufed in the fixth century ; that is, as the Roman H. There

[n] See Bernard's Alphabet of the Latin language, and Moyle, p. 198.
[o] See Fig. IV. The N in Icdinui, and Infcriptions in Camden.
[p] MS. penes Rev. Ed. Collins, p. 38.
[q] Pofthum. Works, p. 199.
[r] Moyle's Works, Vol. I. p. 173.

are

are three daſhes at the end of the name, ᴈ, inſtead of one; the ſecond I in *filius* is linked to the L, and the S is inverted. The
croſs ſtroke in the A is not ſtraight, but indented. Theſe are arguments, that the Alphabet then in uſe was farther departing
from the Roman exactneſs, and conſequently more diſtant from the
Roman times. Mr. Lhuyd, abovementioned, in his letter to
Mr. Painter of Boſkenna[s], thinks the perſon here interred would
have been called in Wales Kynadhav ap Ichdinow, and places the
age of this Monument near the end of the ſixth century.

In the highway leading to Helſton, near the pariſh church of
Mawgon, ſtands, what is generally called, Mawgon Croſs. The
Inſcription is,

SECT. V.
Plate
XXXV.
Fig. V.
CNEGUMI.

Cnegumi fil-Enans.

It is very erroneouſly publiſhed both in Camden's laſt Edit. p. 16.
and in Mr. Moyle's Poſthumous Works. The icon annexed is
the exact ſize and ſhape of the ſtone, and letters as they are
placed, by the ſame ſcale as all the inſcribed ſtones here publiſhed.
Mr. Moyle, in a letter to the late Sir Richard Vyvyan (May 12,
1715), ſays, that " by the characters this muſt be above 1200
" years ſtanding;" but by the firſt E being joined to the firſt N,
and by the ſhape of the G in *Gumi*, I ſhould take it to be two,
if not three centuries later; the G being the ſame as we have in
a Monument [t] evidently of the ninth century.

Enans is ſaid by Mr. Lhuyd to be " ſtill a common name in
" Wales, where this Inſcription would run thus, Knegwm ap En-
" nian;" to which we may add, that Ennian is a Royal Name, the
ſon of Malgo, fourth King of Britany, being ſo called[u].

This inſcribed Stone, nine feet nine inches long, and two feet
three inches wide, was formerly a foot bridge near the late Lord
Falmouth's ſeat of Worthyvale, about a mile and half from Camelford. It was called Slaughter Bridge, and, as Tradition ſays,
from a bloody battle fought on this ground, fatal to the great
King Arthur. A few years ſince, the late Lady Dowager Falmouth, ſhaping a rough kind of hill, about 100 yards off, into
ſpiral walks, removed this Stone from the place where it ſerved as
a bridge, and, building a low piece of Maſonry for it's ſupport,
placed it at the foot of her improvements, where it ſtill lies in one
of the natural grots of the hill.

SECT. VI.
Plate
XXXV.
Fig. VI.
CATIN.

[s] Moyle's Works, Vol. I. p. 173.
[t] Doniert.
[u] Geff. M. p. 97.—It is alſo written Emman,
Anian, and Eneon; ſee the liſt of Kings of Britain, chapter following. Eneon, ſon of Cadi-
vor, Lord of Dyuvet, was a Welſh nobleman,
aſſiſtant to Fitz-hamon, Granville, and other
Knights, in the conqueſt of Glamorgan, temp.
Wm. II. A. D. 1094. Evan probably is no
other than Enan, the N being liquidated as yet
by the Corniſh (as ſee Lhuyd, Corniſh Grammar) into an U, or a V, as Tyner, Tyuver, tender, and Bevan (a Surname well known). Qu. an
non ap Evan, as Price from Ap Rice.

This

This Stone is taken notice of by Mr. Carew [w], in the following words: " For teſtimony of the laſt battle in which Arthur was " killed, the old folkes thereabouts (viz. round Camelford) ſhew " you a Stone bearing Arthur's name, though now depraved to " Atry."

This Inſcription has been lately publiſhed [x]; but ſo incorrectly, that it may be ſtill reckoned among the non-deſcripts. It is ſaid there, that " this Stone lay at the very place where King Arthur " received his mortal wound."

All this about King Arthur takes it's riſe from the five laſt letters of this Inſcription, which are by ſome thought to be Maguri *(quaſi magni Arthuri)*, and from thence others will have it, that a ſon of Arthur was buried here; but though hiſtory, as well as tradition, affirms that Arthur fought his laſt battle, in which he was mortally wounded, near this place, yet that this Inſcription retains any thing of his name, is all a miſtake. The letters are Roman [y], and as follows:

Catin hic jacit——filius magari——

By the I in *hic* being joined to the H; by the H [z] wanting it's croſs link, the bad line of the writing, the diſtorted leaning of the letters; I conclude, that this Monument cannot be ſo ancient as the time of Arthur, nor indeed as the foregoing [a].

SECT. VII. In the pariſh of St. Clare, about 200 paces to the Eaſtward of
Plate Redgate, are two Monumental Stones, which ſeem to me parts of
XXXVI. two different Croſſes, for they have no ſuch relation to each other
Fig. I. & II. as to make one conclude that they ever contributed to form one
DONIERT. Monument of that kind.

Fig. I. is like the Spill of a Croſs, ſeven feet ſix inches high above ground, two feet ſix inches wide in the under part D, but in the above A, two feet, and one foot thick. The ſide of the ſhaft B is adorned with ſome diaper work, conſiſting of little aſteriſks of two inches diameter, diſpoſed in the *quincunx* manner; the lower or pedeſtal part D is ſomewhat thicker, but has no ornament. In the top of this Stone at C, there is part of a mortice, which, doubtleſs, had ſome tenon fitted to, and fixed in it, in ſuch ſhape as to form a croſs; but the making this mortice ſeems to have ſhattered the Stone, for part of the ſhaft, which reſted on D, is cloven off, and not to be found, from which defect, this is called,

---

w Pag. 123.
x Gent. Mag. June, 1745.
y The M in the Gent. Magazine is ſaid to be Saxon; but this is a miſtake, it is a Roman little m, placed, as frequently we find it, for a

great M.
z See the Figure in the Plate.
a St. Machar is mentioned in Spotſw. p. 102. We have a Church in Cornwall dedicated to a Saint of this Name.

the

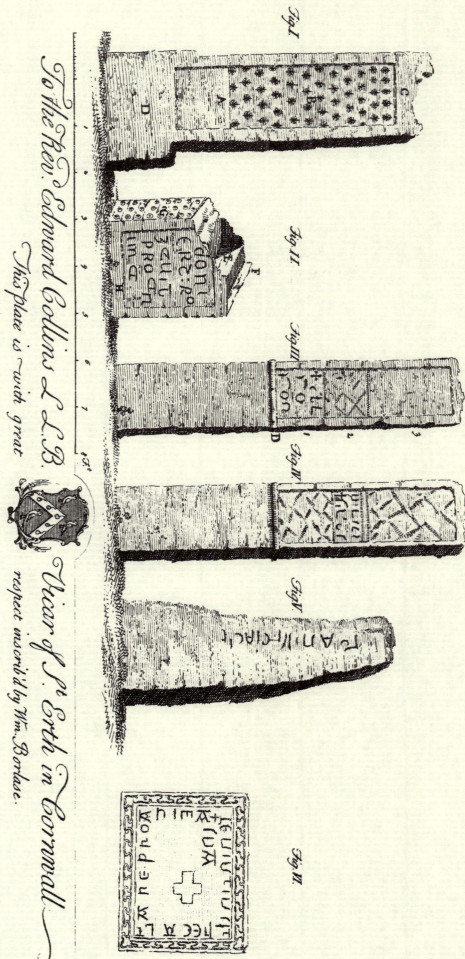

Fig.I.

Fig.II.

Fig.III.

Fig.IV.

Fig.V.

Fig.VI.

To the Rev.ᵈ Edward Collins L.L.B. Vicar of S.ᵗ Erth in Cornwall.

This plate is with great respect inscrib'd by W.ᵐ Borlase.

the *other-half-stone:* the ground about this Stone has been much tumbled and searched by digging; and in one of the hollows is the Stone H, Fig. II. On the top of it was a square socket E, very regularly sunk, the sides and top well smoothed, above which the brim rises into a thin edge F, that ranged round the whole surface. One side G is diapered, as in the former Stone, and in another side (surrounded with a rectangular *sulcus)* is the following Inscription, *Doniert rogavit pro anima.* The Masonry of Fig. II. is greatly superior to that of the other; and I apprehend it might be the Pedestal or Plint of a Cross, and that the other Fig. I. was either placed at the other end of the Grave, or was erected for some other person about the same age.

That by Doniert is meant Dungerth King of Cornwall, about the beginning [a] (or rather middle) of the ninth century, drowned in the year 872 [b], or 873 [c], cannot be disputed (the G, before an E, being sometimes pronounced in British as an J consonant, as *Geon,* a giant), and also because the letters are exactly the same with those on a Monument in Denbighshire put up by Konken, King of Powis, in the very same age [d].

The name is a name of Dignity [e]; and this Donjert was not only a Prince, but a man of great piety, as this solicitude for his soul testifies.

Of the person here named there can be no reasonable dispute, but the meaning of the Inscription is doubtful. Some think, it may signify that Doniert gave those lands to some Religious Purpose [f]. Cressy [g] had the same information, and calls this " a Monument " very ancient," with this imperfect Inscription, " Doniert gave " for the benefit of his soul, namely, certain lands:" " this solici- " tude," says the same author, " he had in the time of his health, " for at his death he could not shew it being unfortunately " drowned [h]; but Cressy was misinformed, for he says this Monument is at Neotstow, or St. Neot's, whereas it is three miles and a half distant, in the parish of St. Clare. Secondly, the registering such gifts upon Stone is unusual, and, I believe, in that age among the Britans without precedent: besides; the make of this Stone evidently shews, that it was part of a Cross, and why should the grant of lands be inscribed on a Cross?

Others have thought that this was a place of devotion, and that Doniert usually prayed here for the good of his soul, and erected

---

[a] Lhuyd's letter to Mr. Painter, Nov. 30, 1700.
[b] Carew, p. 78.
[c] Cressy, p. 746.
[d] Lhuyd, ibid.

[e] One Dungardus died King of Scotland A. D. 457. H. Boëthius. Usher, p. 671.
[f] Camden, last Edit. p. 20.
[g] Cressy, ut supra.
[h] Ibid. ut supra.

this

this Crofs himfelf, being willing that his name and piety fhould defcend together, in order, by fuch an illuftrious example, to raife
the emulation of pofterity.   But it was very uncommon, not to
fay vain, and unbecoming a fincerely Religious Man, to record his
own acts of piety in fuch a manner; befides, the word *Rogo* cannot
properly fignify to pray to God.

I rather think that Doniert defired in his life time, that a Crofs
might be erected in the place where he fhould be interred, in order
to put people in mind to pray for his foul.   So that this is, in my
opinion, a fepulchral monument; and, if we take it in this fenfe,
the word *rogavit* is proper, and the whole Infcription intelligible,
and according to the ufage of ancient times.

Chriftians generally placed a Crofs (about this time) at the beginning of Infcriptions; and, I think, part of one (the corner of
the Stone being here broken off) may be feen in this, before the
D.   When praying for the dead came into ufe, it was a general
cuftom (as in the Catholick countries it is at prefent), to intreat all
comers to pray for the foul of perfons buried there; and that they
might after death have (as they thought) the benefit of frequent
prayers, fometimes a Church or Oratory was erected [i], at other
times it was only an Altar; fometimes it was a Tomb-ftone, that
defired the prayers of the reader; and fometimes a real Crofs of
Stone; and all thefe memorials were faid to be erected *pro animâ*,
for the good of their fouls, becaufe their intent was to excite the
devotion of perfons that paffed by, in favour of the dead.

When thefe Memorials were erected by perfons in their life-time,
there was generally infcribed *Pofuit*, or *Poni curavit*; but moft
commonly they were erected either by the command, or at the
defire, of the perfon departed.   When by the command or order
of the deceafed, the word *Juffit* was made ufe of; when at the defire, *Rogavit*.

That the Ancients erected Croffes in the middle ages of Chriftianity, we have an inftance in the Infcription near Neath in Glamorganfhire, in the Church-yard of Lan Iltud vawr, where there
are two Stones as here, one infcribed, and one not.   That not infcribed, is about the height of our *Other-half-Stone*; the other
Stone was part of a Crofs, very likely the Pedeftal [k], and on one
of its fides has this Infcription, *Samfon pofuit hanc crucem pro animâ*

---

i As there was at this place, if what Mr. Hals
fays, in his account of Cornwall, be true.   " At
" the Pedeftal of the Stone Monument of Do-
" niert, called the Half-ftone, is yet extant a
" vaulted and arched Chapel under ground,
" wherein were lately feen certain feats in Stone,
" or Coffins, within which pots, or urns, dead

" men's bones and afhes were ufually put by the
" Britans and Romans."   Tonkin's Extracts
from Will. Hals's Dictionary.
  k " Once the Shaft or Pedeftal of a Crofs."
Camd. p. 736. Very different things; but the
Stones are not well defcribed, nor the Infcription
well placed.

ejus.

ejus. Now the meaning of this Inscription is (as is obferved in Camden, ibid) that one Samfon erected this Crofs for his foul, that is, that prayers might be faid at this Crofs for the good of his foul.

Of Monuments fet up by the command of perfons for their fouls, we fhall give an inftance prefently.

That people defired the erection of fuch Monuments for their fouls, and that *Rogavit* was the word ufed upon fuch occafions; we find an inftance in Godwyn's Catalogue of the Bifhops of Lan-daff [l], where, fpeaking of Theodoric King of Glamorganfhire's laft battle againft the Saxons, in which he was mortally wounded, he has thefe words, " Having received a wound in the head which " he knew to be mortal, he haftened back into his own country, " that he might expire among his friends and relations, firft de-" firing his fon *(Rogato priùs filio)* to build a Church on that fpot " where he fhould breathe his laft (in cafe he fhould die on the " road), and bury him alfo there." Here we fee the dying The-odoric only *defired* the Monumental Church, and therefore it was not *Juffo*, but *Rogato filio*; and, in the cafe before us, I conjecture, that Doniert requefted, and did not command, that this Crofs fhould be erected, and prayers faid there for the good of his foul, and therefore it is *Rogavit*, and not *Juffit*. Whether the Long-ftone was placed at one end of the grave, and the infcribed Pedeftal with the pillar of the Crofs at the other end, or whether there was an Oratory here (as there was erected for Theodoric abovementioned [m]), and the Long-ftone erected for fome other perfon who defired to be interred near Doniert, is all uncertain.

That " *hanc crucem*" fhould be omitted in this Monument, will not feem at all ftrange to thofe who are acquainted with an-cient Monuments, which (contrary to the modern ones), were to have as few words as poffible on them. I have only further to ob-ferve, that this Doniert was probably reckoned among the Saints, and was the fame under the name of Donanwerdh mentioned by Leland, whofe reliques were held in great efteem at Beckley [n], formerly the Capital Seat of the Honor of St. Walery, Oxfordfhire, and place of Refidence of Richard King of the Romans and Earl of Cornwall, and his fon Edmund fucceffor to him in the Earldom of Cornwall.

In the parifh of St. Blafey ftands a high and flender ftone, the form beft known by it's icon, feven feet fix inches high, one foot

SECT. VIII.
Plate XXXVI.
Fig. III. & IV.
ALRORON.

[l] Ufher's Prim. p. 562.
[m] Ibid. p. 564.
[n] This Town of Beckley (Kenn. Par. Ant. p. 295.) had a reputation for the Reliques of St. Donanwerdh (I fuppofe) a Britifh Saint, as I find entered among the collections of Leland, " St. Donanwerd apud Beckleiam." Collectan. MS. Tom. II. p. 369.

fix

fix inches wide, eight inches thick (Plate XXXVI. Fig. III. and
IV.); it is publifhed in Camden very erroneoufly, in Moyle's Works
better, but incorrectly, and in both without fcale, and rather by
guefs than meafurement.

It is a very fingular Monument, infcribed on both fides, the Infcription not to be read from the top downwards, but horizontally,
as Doniert, and therefore lefs ancient than thofe that go before.
There is fuch a mixture of the Saxon writing in the letters, A, R,
S, but efpecially the firft, that I think it muft be more modern than
the year 900. It is the only one of thefe ancient Monuments that
has the Saxon A, fo that it can fcarce be lefs than 50 years below Doniert.

It has been judged by fome to be the ftone fet up by the Saxons, to fhew how far Weft they penetrated. What has given rife
to this opinion is, that the Infcription was never underftood. The
late learned Mr. Ed. Lhuyd in a letter to Thomas Tonkin, Efq;
dated November 29, 1700 [n], writes, that he did not at all underftand this Infcription [o]. " By a Gentleman, F. R. S. the firft
" Infcription (Fig. III.) was interpreted to John Hicks, Efq; of
" Trevithick, CIL, or CIVL SOSON [p], *hucufque Saxones*, fo far came
" the Saxons; but he could make nothing of that on the other
" fide." Now on the other fide (viz. Fig. IV.) the laft Word is
plainly *filius*, which will decide this Monument to be no Trophy,
nor to have any relation to the Saxon Invafion of Cornwall; but
that it's Defign and Stile is one and the fame with thofe defcribed
before in the XXXVth Plate, reprefenting, firft the name of the
perfon interred, and then that of his father.

The Monument is fepulchral. The Infcription on the South
fide in the compartment (N°. 1.) contains the name of the perfon
interred, ALRORON [q], in three lines, with a crofs before the firft letter.
Above the Infcription there is a little compartment of net-work,
confifting of diagonal tranfverfe fulcus's (2), and over that, a plain
rectangle (3), fhaped out by a fulcus (parallel to the edges of the
ftone) which defcends fo far as to become footed on the aftragal
D, projecting from the body of the ftone about one inch, and
going round the whole. On the North fide (Fig. IV.) upon a level,
and of the fame fize with the compartment (1), is the net-work;
above which there is a compartment anfwerable to (2) on the other
fide, which has the name of the father of Alroron in one line,
which is either VILICI, or ULLICI (for the fecond letter is fomewhat

[n] T. T. MS. B. p. 193.
[o] D°, in a letter to Fran. Paynter, Efq; dated November 30, 1700, recited in Moyle's
Pofthum. Works, Vol. I. p. 237.
[p] T. T. MS. G. p. 74.

[q] Or it may poffibly be Alfofon, or Cilfofon;
but I chufe the former reading, becaufe the fhape
of the letter, which I read R, is very different
from the Saxon S, in " filius."

defaced),

defaced), I judge it to be the former. The next line has a Crofs, and, moſt certainly, *filius*. The characters are much worn, and muſt have been at firſt very barbarouſly written. Above this Inſcription, the rectangle, which is plain in the South front, is here ornamented with the tranſverſe chanels; ſo that the ornaments of this ſtone were purpoſely counterchanged.

I find Euroron among the names of the Welch nobility [r]. But there is reaſon to conjecture that Alroron was the ſame name as Aldroen (or Auldran [s]), of which name I find a King of Armorica, of Britiſh deſcent, the fourth from Conan-Merodac; and poſſibly this Monument might be erected to the memory of ſome one called Aldroen, but in a rough and ignorant age pronounced Alrorn, and as ignorantly written Alroron.

In a little meadow adjoining to the place where this ſtone now ſtands, many human bones have been found; and I ſuſpect that this Crofs may have been removed from thence.

In this Stone (which I accidentally met with about four miles Eaſt of Michel) the letters are much worn, eſpecially the ſecond; but the R is the ſame as in the foregoing Monument, and the line worſe kept. I judge it of the ſame age as that above, and read it, *Ruani hic jacit.* SECT. IX. Plate XXXVI. Fig. V. RUANI.

In Cornwall we have three pariſhes called Ruan, doubtleſs from a ſaint of this name. This name alſo occurs among the Princes. One Prince of this name was ſon of Maglocunus, who reigned in the latter end of the ſixth century. I find three Princes more of the name of Rûn from the year 808, to 1020 [t]; and Rouan, and Rouanes, is, among the Britans, a name of Dignity, and ſignifies Royal, not improbably derived from the name by which the Britans diſtinguiſhed the Roman people.

This is a flat ſtone three feet five inches long, by two feet nine inches wide. It lies at preſent a little without the church yard of Camborn, but I do not at all doubt that it was either in the Church, or ſome Oratory or Chauntry near it, and ſerved as a covering to an Altar there, at which it had prayers ſaid for the good of the ſoul of the man whoſe name it bears. The Inſcription, ſurrounded with a fillet of wreath work, is as follows: SECT. X. Plate XXXVI. Fig. VI. LEUIUT.

Leuiut juſit hec Altare pro anima ſua.

By the character ſo mixed with the Saxon, I judge it to be near the ſame age with Alroron, the writing being equally bad, the letter R exactly the ſame, and the Latin very barbarous.

Leuiut is a Corniſh name, and ſignifies pilot, or ſailor; as may be ſeen in the Vocabulary.

[r] Car. Langarv. p. 183.
[s] Ibid. Edit. Powel, p. 2.
[t] See Caradoc of Langarvon, Edit. Powel.

CHAP,

C H A P. XIII.

Of the Princes and civil Government of Cornwall, from the earliest Account of it to the Norman Conquest.

IT would be in vain to attempt a regular succession of the Princes of this County since it has been taken notice of in history. All before the times of Cesar is very uncertain. We have however several Princes said to be Kings, and at other times Dukes and Earls of Cornwall, before Julius Cesar invaded Britain [u]; but there are great chasms in the list; by which we may suppose that Cornwall was sometimes governed by it's own distinct Princes, and at other times governed as a Province, or part of the whole, by the same Prince that ruled over the other parts of Britain; that some of the Princes did nothing worthy of note, and that what was recorded of the most worthy in the songs of the Bards has been in a great measure lost. These several causes having concurred to make our history defective, scattered memorandums are all we can now expect; and even the truth of these, far from being unquestionable, rests in a great measure upon the fidelity of Geoffry of Monmouth, who is said by some to have forged them, though by many learned and candid men to have only copied them from Annals, and translated the Records which he had the good fortune to meet with, but (like other Records of such distant times) labouring under the misfortune of fable, and a disturbed chronology. Another unhappy cause of the defects of British history was the Druid tenet of writing as little as possible, for whatever may be said in favour of teaching things *memoriter*, and transmitting them to posterity by oral tradition, it cannot be denied that it was very unfortunate for the history of those times and places in which this unsociable maxim prevailed: I call it unsociable, because History unites us to the company of our ancestours; it is the scale, or Ladder, by which we ascend into the regions of Antiquity, and by which the actors of the ages past descend to us; and, in proportion as History is defective, all communications are interrupted, and what has passed before is, to posterity, as if it had never happened.

After the Saxon invasion, the Britans sometimes chose their King from among the Princes of Wales, sometimes from those of

---

[u] " Certum est (vel hac quam habemus histo-
" ria testante) Loegriam, Albaniam, Cornubi-
" am, &c. suos ferè semper habuisse Regulos."
Dr. Powel's Epist. to Fleetwood.—" Cornwall,
" a distinct province of great antiquity among

" the Britans, long before the Romans subdued
" it, nay some hundreds of years before Christ,
" if we may believe the British MSS." Rowl.
p. 171.

Dunmo-

Dunmonium (or Cornwall), and in after-times from thofe of Armorica, as being originally all of one nation, and of the blood royal of the Britans. The prince fo elected was thenceforth called King of the Britans, and King of Britain, though he had little more power than commanding their armies in time of action; and the Saxons, foon after they came in here, became entire mafters of the greateft part of Britain, the ancient Britans having only Wales and Cornwall, to which fometimes, upon preffing exigencies, Armorica united [w]. The King refided fometimes in Wales and fometimes in Cornwall, according as the neceffity of the publick weal required. But, if we may believe the Britifh Hiftorians, Cornwall afforded many Kings and Princes to all Britain, long before the Saxon and even Roman conqueft; fo that indeed it cannot well be apprehended at what time we had diftinct Princes here in Cornwall, and when we had none, without inferting the fucceffion of the Britifh Kings. I fhall therefore in this chapter lay before the reader the feries of Kings, according to the Britifh Hiftorians [x], with the age of the world. Where the Britifh Kings ceafe (as they did with Cadwalader about 690), I take in the Kings of Weft Saxony, and after them the Kings of England, until the Norman Conqueft, marking down in each reign, what has occurred to me relating to the Princes and affairs of Cornwall.

For the amufement of the curious, I begin with the reign of Brute; not entering into the difpute whether the account we have of him be hiftory or fable, but laying hold of it as the only account we have of thofe ancient times, and in which, it is likely, we have fome truth, though all be not fo [y]; neither fhall I pretend to reconcile the differences between our Britifh Chronicle-writers. It muft fuffice, that by comparing, and bringing things into the fame view, and difpofing them (as well as I can) in their proper periods of time, fome light may be gained; but dim, I own, it muft needs be, and unfatisfactory to the critical eye.

[w] There were alfo fome of the ancient Britans in Cumberland, who contributed to the common Caufe, what their diftant fituation would permit.

[x] According to Harding's Chronicle, and Dr.

Powell in his edit. of Gir. Camhrenfis.

[y] Vid. Dr. Powel's Epift. to Serjeant Fleetwoode ad fin. Gir. Cambr. p. 282.——See alfo Book I. Chap. VII. p. 25.

A CATALOGUE

A CATALOGUE of the KINGS of BRITAIN,

With the PRINCES of CORNWALL,

And the moſt important INCIDENTS relating to that COUNTY

Interſperſed according to their Order of Time.

Abbreviations in this Catalogue.——G. M. Geoffry of Monmouth.—Gir. Camb. Giraldus Cambrenſis.—P. V. Ponticus Virunnius. H. Harding.—P. Powel.—A. M. Anno Mundi.—Not. Notes.—A. D. Anno Domini.—r. reigned.

A. M.

2859 BRUTUS began to reign, and reigned according to Harding 60, to Powel 15 years.

CORINEUS came into Britain with Brute, and choſe Cornwall for his ſhare of the kingdom. (Unde Corineia, & populus Corineienſis, ut vult G. M. ix. b. & Gir. Camb. p. 241.)

2874 LOCRINUS reigned according to Harding 10, to Powel 20.

2894 GUENDOLEN reigned according to Harding and Powel 15 years. She was the daughter of Corineus, married to Locrinus, by whom being divorced after the death of Corineus, ſhe retired into Cornwall, (temp. Sam. Prophetæ, Pont. Vir. p. 6.) rais'd an army, routed and killed Locrinus, got the kingdom, and when her ſon Madan was fit to rule, reſigned, and retired into Cornwall, which, as her paternal inheritance, ſhe had reſerved for herſelf. P. Vir. ibi.

2909 MADAN reigned according to Harding and Powel 40 years.

2949 MEMPRICIUS (omitted by Harding) reigned according to Powel 20 years, when Saul was King in Judea. G. M. f. xii.

2969 EBRAUC reigned according to Harding 60, to Powel 40 years.

3009 BRUTUS II. (alias Greneſhylde) reigned 12 years.

3012 LEYLE (alias Leir) reigned 25 years. He built Carliſle, alias Caer Leil.

3046 RUDHEDEBRAS (alias Hudibras) reigned according to Harding 39, to Powel 29.

3085 BLADUD, who built the City of Bath, reigned 20 years.

LEIR II. (omitted by Harding) reigned according to Powel 40 years, partly by himſelf, and partly with Maglan and Heninus.

Heninus Duke of Cornwall, married Raguna daughter of King Leir the ſecond, with whom he had only one half of the Iſland, but was afterwards diſpoſſeſſed, and what was given with Raguna, taken from him by King Leir, and given to his other daughter, Cordeilla.

3141 CORDELL (alias Cordeilla) reigned five years.

3170 CUNEDAGIUS (alias Condage) reigned with his kinſman Morgan, and alone, 33 years.

Cunedagius ſucceeded his father Heninus in the Dutchy of Cornwall and Cambre. He took Cordeilla priſoner, and ſhe killing herſelf in priſon, he and his couſin-german Morgan divided Britain betwixt them. Morgan had all north of the Humber, Cunedagius the reſt; but a quarrel enſuing, and Morgan being ſlain, Cunedagius became ſole Monarch of Britain. This happened at the time of the building of Rome. G. M. xvi.

3203 RIVEALL (alias Rivallus) reigned according to Harding 22, to Powel 46 years.

A. M.

GURGUSTIUS (pacificus, ebrietati addictus, 3249 not. in Pow.) reigned according to Harding 15, to Powel 37 years.

SCICILIUS (alias Siſillius) reigned according 3287 to Harding 14, to Powel 49.

JAGO (alias Jacobus) reigned according to 3336 Harding 10, to Powel 28.

KYMAR (alias Kynmarcus, alias Kinimacus) 3364 r. according to Harding 28, to Powel 54 years.

GORBONIAN (alias Gorbodug) reigned ac- 3418 cording to Harding 11, to Powel 63 years.

CLOTANE (alias Cloteius) then Duke of Cornwall was next heir.

At this time the Kingdom was divided into five parts, betwixt Rudac King of Wales—Clotenus King of Cornwall—Pinnor King of Loegria—Staterus King of Albany—Ywen or Owen King of Bernicia;—but Clotane dying after a reign (reckoned by Harding) of ten years, Mulmutius his ſon overcame the reſt, and became ſole King of Britain. Not. in Powel.

DUNWALLO MODUNCIUS (alias Mul- 3529 mutius, alias Molmutius, fil. Cloteii) reigned 40 years.

BELINUS and BRENNUS, ſons of Dun- 3574 wallo Molmutius, reigned according to Harding 41, to Powel 26 years.

To theſe two princes it was propoſed, that Belinus, the eldeſt, ſhould have Loegria, Cambria, and Cornwall, and Brennus, the ſecond ſon, all from the river Humber to Cathneſs in Scotland. The brothers agreed, afterwards fell out, and Brennus is forced out of all. Belinus, at peace, makes a great Way, the whole length of the iſland, and eſtabliſhes laws, which Gildas the hiſtorian and poet turned into Latin, King Alfred into Engliſh. Pont. Vir. pag. 10.——Harding, pag. 26. G. M. 18.

Theſe were the two brothers, who after their quarrel (agreeing at the intreaty of their mother Cornuenna) went afterwards, ſubdued great part of Gaul, and ſacked Rome. P. Vir. p. 11. Now betwixt this Britiſh chronology, as to the ſacking of Rome, and that of the Roman Faſti, there is only about twenty years difference.

GURGWIN ſon of Belinus (alias Gurgwin- 3596 tus Barbtrucus) reigned according to Harding 30, according to Powel 19 years.

GUYTELIN BATRUS reigned according 3614 to Harding 10, to Powel 27 years; (*qu. an non pro* 37.)

SCICILIUS the ſecond reigned according 3650 to Harding 24, to Powel 7 years, in whoſe time the Picts landing in Britain took poſſeſſion of that part of the Iſland now called the Marches of England and Scotland. Not. in Powel.

KYMAR

3657 KYMAR the second reigned according to Harding 21, to Powel three years.

3661 DANIUS (alias Elanius) reigned according to Harding 10, to Powel eight years.

3669 MORVYLE (alias Morindus) reigned according to Harding 17, to Powel eight years.

3676 GORBONIAN, his eldest son, reigned 10 years.

3686 ARTHEGAL his second brother (alias Argallo) reigned one year, and was deposed, Harding, pag. 31.

3687 ELEDOUR the third brother, (alias Elidurus, alias Heliodorus Pius) reigned according to Harding five, to Powel three years.

3690 ARTHEGAL the second time being advanced to the throne, reigned 10 years.

3700 ELEDOUR (alias Elidurus Pius) coming again to the throne, reigned according to Harding 13 years, to Powel one.

3701 JUGEN (alias Vigenius, alias Ingenius, alias Oenus) and Peredour (alias Peredurus) reigned jointly, according to Harding seven, to Powel eight years.

Then PEREDOUR reigned alone four years, according to Harding.

Then ELEDOUR abovementioned came a third time to the Crown, and reigned according to Harding 10, to Powel four years.

From this place Dr. Powel reckons only the names of the Kings, but not the years they reigned; imagining, as I guess, that the computation of the following chronicle was more suspicious, and more irreconcilable than the former; but says, that they were 33 Kings, and reigned, all together, 185 years. Belinus Magnus was the 35th King; and in the following Catalogue Harding makes the years 186, the Kings 33, as Powel; but in the number from Porrex to Capoirus there are 24 Kings; 15 of them only reigned but one year each; and the whole 24 reigned 57 years. —This is somewhat unlikely.

GORBONIAN 3us (alias Refus Gorboniani fil.) reigned ten.

MORGAN (fil. Archigallonis) fourteen.

EMMAN (alias Emerianus, alias Anianus alias Eneon) Morgani frater, seven.

IVAL, alias Idvallo, alias Edoallus, fil. Oeni, 20.

RIMO, alias Runo, fil. Pereduri, 16.

GERENNES, alias Geruntius, Eliduri fil. 20. CATELLUS, fil Geruntii, 10.

COYLE, alias Coyllus, alias Coelus, 20.—PORREX, 5.

CHERYN, alias Cherimus, one.—FULGEN, fil. Cherini, one.

ELDRED, alias Eldadus, fil. Cherini, one.—ANDRAGIUS 3us fil. Cherini, one.

URYAN, fil. Androgei, 3. — ELIUDE, alias Elvidius, 5.

DEDANICUS, alias Dedacus, alias Cledaucus, reigned 5.

DETENUS, alias Clotenus, 2.

GURGUNTIUS, alias Gurgineus, 2.

MERIANUS, alias Meiriaunus, 2. BLEDUD, 2.

CAPPE, alias Caphus, 2.—OWEN, 2.—SCISILLIUS 3us, 2.

BLEDUD 2dus, alias Blegabridus, alias Blegoredus, 10.

ARCHYVAL, alias Archemaillus, 2. ELDOL, alias Aido, 2.

REDON, alias Redion, 2.—REDRIKE, alias Rothericus, 2.

SAMUEL, alias Penisel.—PIRRE, alias Pir, and Pyrrhus, 2.

PENEYSEL, 2.—CAPRE, alias Capoirus, 2.

ELYNGUELLUS, alias Gligueilus, alias Gilguellus, fil. Gapoiri, 7.

HELY, alias Bely, reigned according to Harding 60, to Geoffry of Monmouth 40 years. The Britans call him Beli Mawr, that is, Beli, or Belinus the Great; and the Welsh Bards, in tracing all Genealogies, have nothing more to do, than to rise as high as this Belinus the Great, because thence (as Dr. Powel says, Not. on Girald. Camb. pag. 246.) quite up to Eneas, the pedigree of the Britans is sufficiently known and allowed. Henry VII. sent into Wales purposely to enquire into the pedigree of Owen Tudor his Grandfather, and it was traced up to this Belin the Great, and no higher; a copy of which pedigree Powel was then possessed of. (ibid.)

3895 LUDUS, son of Belin the Great, reigned according to Harding 40, to Powel 11 years.

3908 CASSIBELAN (alias Cassivellaunus, Ludi frater) reigned according to Harding 33, to Powel 15 years.

In this reign Jul. Cesar, invading Britain, made it tributary to the Roman Empire. Here let us pause a little, and weigh the imperfections of this British Chronology, and, perhaps, we may find it come nearer to the Computations of the modern Chronologers (who, learned as they are, all differ from each other) than is generally imagined.

The destruction of Troy, according to Marshall's tables, was before Christ, 1184; out of which take 69 years, at which time Brutus, great Grandson to Eneas, came into Britain, 1115 years before Christ; Eli had been judge of Israel then 18 years; for Eli was born A. M. (according to Archbishop Usher's Annals, pag. 45.) 2790, and judged Israel 40 years, dying at the age of 98; consequently he was 58 years old when his Magistracy began, and the 18th year thereof must have been the 76th year of his age, which added to 2790 (the year of his birth) makes 2866. Now according to Abp. Usher (Annals, p. 1.) the vulgar Christian Era is A. M. 4004, out of which deduct 2866, and Brute will have come into Britain 1138 years before the birth of Christ.

Let us see now how the Chronicles of these British Kings agree with this computation. From Brutus's first year of reigning in Britain to the 33d year of Cassibelan, Harding's Chronicle makes in all 1003. —— —— 1003

To this add 20 years for the reign of Mempricius omitted by Harding, but by G. M. said to be torn in pieces by Wolves in the 20th year of his reign. —— 0020

To this add what Leir the 2d, Maglan, Heninus and Arthegal reigned, not mentioned by Harding, but by Dr. Powel reckoned 37 years. —— 0037

Julius Cesar came into Britain 50 years before the birth of Christ.—Suppose this to be in the latter end of the reign of Cassibelan, for he had made his two sons one King

5 L   of

of Cornwall, the other King of Kent, before Cefar's coming, and muft therefore have been advanced in years; place this therefore in the 25th year of Caffibelan, for about feven years after he died, fays Pont. Vir. (pag. 26.) from which time there being 50 years to the birth of our Saviour, and eight of them reckoned above in the 33 years, there remains according to Harding 42 years. —— —— 0042

According to H. Chron. from Brute's coming into Britain to the birth of Chrift. } 1102

According to the vulgar computation from the 18th year of Eli's Rule, in which Brute came in, to the birth of Chrift. } 1138

Difference 36 years according to Harding.
Difference 38 —— according to Powel.
" Caffibelan had two fons; to the firft, called
" Androgeus, he gave Kent, and the Province of
" the Trinobantes; to the fecond, called Theo-
" mantius, he gave the Dukedom of Cornwall,
" referving the imperial Diadem to himfelf."

3921 TENANTIUS, alias Theomantius, fon of Lud, reigned according to Harding 17; to Powel 22 years.

THEOMANTIUS was Duke of Cornwall when Cefar came, (Pont. Vir. 17.) " but Dr. " Powel fays, (ibid.) that he was fon of Lud;" and Cefar fays, one Imanuentius King of the Trinobantes was killed by Caffibelan; and his fon Mandubratius came over to Cefar's party, and was by him made King of the Trinobantes in oppofition to Caffibelan. De Bell. Gall. lib. v.

3944 CYMBELINE, alias Cunobelin, reigned according to Harding and Geoffry of Mounmouth 10, to Powel 29 years.

In the 22d year of this King, Jefus Chrift was born in Judea. (Powel, ibid.)

His name fignifies King Belin, which adds fome proof to Belinus being King of Britain before, A. M. 3574; and again 3890. He is faid

A.D. to be fon of Theomantius. Pont. Vir. 26.

7 GUIDERIUS, eldeft fon of Cunobelin, made great refiftance againft the invafion of Claudius Cefar, but was treacheroufly flain by Hammo, Pont. V. p. 26. He reigned according to Harding 24, to Powel 28.

45 AGRESTES (the Arviragus of Geoffry of Monmouth, and Powel, fuppofed the Prafutagus of Tacitus, alias Caractacus, the Cateracus, alias Caradocus, of Hum. Lhuyd) reigned according to H. 64, to P. 28 years.

" This Arviragus, fecond fon of Cunobelin,
" after much bloodfhed, makes peace with Clau-
" dius, who by his affiftance fubdues the Orca-
" des, and the Iflands adjoining to the Roman
" province in Britain." [fcil. Loegria] Pont. Vir. pag. 28.

But in fact the Orcades were never difcovered by the Romans till the 6th year of Agricola's command, many years after this. See of the Rom. Conqueft, before, p. 340; and Stillingfleet allows no fuch King as Arviragus till Domitian. ibid. 34.

In this reign, viz. A. D. 17. Jofeph of Arimathea is faid to have come into Britain, and to have had Glaftonbury, then called Mewtryn, given to him and his 14 companions, Hard. f. 40, Nennius 42, and Mewynus 44; a forgery of the

Monks of Glaftonbury, fays Stillingfleet in his Antiq. Brit. chap. i.

In his time, according to Powel, ruled the Roman Legati in the following order;—Aulus Plantius.—P. Oftorius Scapula.—A. Didius Gallus. —Paulinus Suetonius.—Petronius Turpilianus. —Trebellius Maximus.—Vectius Volanus.— Julius Frontinus.

It muft here be noted that thefe Princes, called Kings of Britain, Kings of Cornwall, &c. were, indeed, fubjects to the Roman Legates, and yet fuffered to enjoy the title of King.

MARIUS, alias Maurius, alias Mavus, Manius & Mayricus, reigned according to Hard. 73 63, to Powel 52.

In this reign, Julius Agricola was Roman Legate of Britain, and in his 5th year failing round the Land's End probably conquered Cornwall. See Book IV. ch. vi.

This King Marius is faid by Harding, pag. 42. to have been fomewhat informed of the Faith of Chrift.

COYLUS (Coillus, alias Coëlus) the fon of 125 the foregoing King, fucceeded and reigned according to Hard. 13, to Powel 40 years.

He was inftructed fomewhat in the Chriftian Faith, but not fully, fays Hard. pag. 43.

LUCIUS, fon of Coëlus, reigned according 165 to Hard. 54, to Powel, 43.

He, firft of all the Kings of Britain, embraced the Chriftian Relgion, according to Powel, A. D. 177; but, according to the Savilian Fafti, betwixt the years 173 and 176.

He was baptized A. D. 190, 1° Eleuth. Papæ; founded Archbifhopricks and Bifhopricks, in the room of three Archiflamens, and 28 Flamens. H. 43, Pont. Vir. 31.

The Archbifhop of York in his Province had all North of Humber. Archbifhop of London had Loegria and Cornubia; Archbifhop of Caerleon, Wales. Ibid.

This ftory is much difputed, and juftly as to the Flamens. Lucius died without Children. Pont. Vir. 32. fays, he died in 158, and was buried at Glocefter. That there was fuch a perfon, with Royal authority in fome parts of Britain, a Chriftian, and promoter of Chriftianity, is proved from the concurrence of authors, and from two Coins mentioned by Archbifhop Ufher, one filver, and the other gold, the image of a King on them, and Crofs, the Letters LVC. as far as they could be difcerned. Stillingfl. ibid. pag. 39. conjectures him to be King only in Surry and Suffex; but thefe bounds are rather too narrow: though to think that he had fo much influence as to change the whole ftate of religion throughout the Ifland, is on the other hand allowing him more power than hiftory will warrant.

In his time, the Roman Legates were Cn. Trebellius.—Julius Capitolinus.—Pertinax.—Clod. Albinus.

SEVERUS, Roman Emperor, (defcended 207 from Androgeus, eldeft fon of Lud, fays Hard. p. 44.) was in Britain four years, and died in the 5th, viz. A. D. 212.

BASSIANUS CARACALLA, called alfo 211 Antoninus, reigned according to H. 7, to P. 6 years.

CARENCE, alias Caraufius, reigned according to H. 4, to P. 7 years. 218

ALEC-

225 ALECTOR, alias Alectus, reigned according to Hard. 3, to Powel 7 years.

About this time one Lyr was a great Lord, or Duke in Cornwall; and the Britans, enraged at the death of Carausius, slain by Alectus, made Asclepiodotus Duke of Cornwall, (perhaps the son of Lyr) their King; (Pont. Vir. pag. 34.) and he reigned according to H. 10, to P. 30 years, and was killed by Coëlus Duke of Colchester, who succeeded him in the throne A. D. 262, and r. according to H. 11, to P. 27 years.

N. B. Carausius was not killed by Alectus till the year 293-4. (see Speed, 151, &c.) and Asclepiodotus served under Constantius Chlorus, who came into Britain on that occasion, so that Asclepiodotus could not begin his reign over the Britans till 293, and he is therefore placed much too early by the British Historians.

289 CONSTANTIUS CHLORUS CESAR, r. according to Harding 15, to Powel 17 years; he was sent into Britain to reduce the rebels there; upon Coëlus's submission, takes hostages, names the tributes to be paid by the Britans, and married Helena daughter of Coelus, by whom he had Constantine the Great; who being but 16 years old when his father died in Britain, succeeded him, and reigned here, till, being solicited to set up for Roman Emperour, he assumed the Purple, conquered the Tyrant Maxentius, and fixed himself in the imperial throne.

330 When Constantine left Britain, Octavius King of North Wales (called Duke of Cornwall in Heylin's Help to History, pag. 15, and by Rowland reckoned so, A. D. 330.) rebelled against the Roman Proconsuls appointed by Constantine, and, having slain them, made himself King of Britain; is dispossessed by Trahern brother of Coëlus abovementioned, sent for that purpose into Britain; but Trahern being treacherously murdered, Octavius regained the throne.

350 SOLOMON * (perhaps the son of Asclepiodotus abovementioned) was Duke of Cornwall about the year 350. He was father of St. Kebius, who died in Anglesea, A. D. 369. Usher's Prim. pag. 786. and ibid. 1086, 1087.

360 About this time Caradocus, son of Lewellyn, who was Uncle to Helena the mother of the Emperor Constantine, and by him advanced in the rank of a Roman Senator, was King of Cornwall; and Octavius King of Britain, having only one daughter, Helen, Caradocus advised the Nation to send to Rome, and invite one of the most noble Romans to come and marry her, and succeed her father. Conan Meriadoc, then King of South Wales, nephew of Octavius, thinking to succeed his Uncle, opposes this motion; but Caradoc sending his son Mauritius to Rome to propose it to Maximus, alias Maximian, son of Trahern, (Hard. pag. 51.) he accepts the terms. Pont. Vir. 36, and Powel's Note, ibid.

383 MAXIMIAN, alias Maximus Tyrannus, r. according to H. 34, to Powel 5 years.

Maximus, being reconciled to Conan Meriadoc, conquers great part of Gaul, plants 30000 British Soldiers in Armorica and makes Conan King of them; from whom Armorica (as Pont. Vir. chimerically, pag. 39.) received the name of Little Britain. This Maximus is said to have

* " Coriniæ Regulus."—Lel. de Scr. Britan. p. 65.

depopulated Britain, and left it exposed to the incursions of the Picts (ibid. 41.) All groundless! The Britans had not Armorica till a long while after this. See before, pag. 39. and Stillingfl. Antiq. Brit. pag. 291.

DIONOTUS succeeded his brother Caradoc, and was Duke of Cornwall, A. D. 383. (Matt. Westm.—Carew, p. 77.) He is said fabulously to have sent 11000 Noble Virgins (at the instance of Conan Meriadoc) and 60000 of inferiour rank, to people Maximus's new Colony of Britans in Armorica, but all dispersed, drowned, or taken prisoners by the Barbarians. Pont. Vir. 40, 41. Hard. 153.

390 GRACIAN, surnamed Funarius, alias Gratianus Municeps, was General in Britain, according to Powel, four years. He was father to Valentinian the Emperor. Camd. p. xcvii. There happened then an *Interregnum*, during which I find Melianus Duke of Cornwall, father to St. Melor, who suffered Martyrdom, A. D. 411. Jan. 3.—Ush. Prim. p. 451. Capgrave places this Martyrdom on the Kalends of October, that year.

433 CONSTANTINE, son of Solomon, King of Armorica, according to Rowland, and brother of Aldroen, afterwards King of the same country, reigned 10 years.

443 CONSTANS, eldest son of Constantine, r. according to Hard, one, to Powel three years.

446 VORTIGERN, of Royal Parentage, was Earl of Cornwall. [Speed, p. 264, &c.] and thence elected King of Britain, betwixt the years 430 and 452. He called in the Saxons, reigned according to H. 18, to P. 8 years, and was then deposed.

464 VORTIMER, son of Vortigern, succeeding, reigned according to Powel 7 years, and, as some say, was deposed, as others, killed.

THEODORIC, King of Cornwall, about the year 460, put to death St. Guigner, and his company from Ireland. Usher's Prim. 869, p. 1113. He was a Heathen, and by his being appointed King (after Vortigern was elected to the throne of Britain) it appears that whoever appointed him (whether Vortigern or the Nobles of Cornwall) could not have the interest of Christianity much at heart. His subjects also were Heathens; for he put to death the Irish Saints, lest they might turn away his subjects from their old religion. Ush. ib.

471 VORTIMER being dead, Vortigern again ascends the throne, and r. according to P. 9 years.

481 AURELIUS AMBROSIUS, second son of Constantine abovementioned, [as Hard. 58.] r. according to Harding, 13, to Powel 19 years.

He is fabled to have erected Stonehenge (called the Stone Hengles, by Harding) at the advice of Merlyn, as a sepulchral monument for the British Lords, there treacherously slain by Hengist, and to have been buried there himself. Hard. 59.

About this time Gorlois was Duke of Cornwall, and lived at Tindagel Castle.

500 UTER PENDRAGON, third son of Constantine, reigned according to Hard. 13, to P. 16 years. He was famous for his strength and valour, died A. D. 516. and was buried (as Harding says, p. 79.) at Stonehenge.

516 ARTHUR reigned 26 years. This Prince having succeeded his nominal father, Gorlois, in
the

the Kingdom of Dunmonium (by the British Historians always, though prematurely, called Cornwall), as Duke of Cornwall, is said to have assisted greatly Aur. Ambrosius against the Saxons. [Rapin, pag. 34.] He succeeded Uter Pendragon (as some think his real father) in the year 516. He is said to have been born at Tindagel Castle in Cornwall ; and in the Country near that place, every thing that is grand, uncommon, or inexplicable, is attributed to this Arthur. Here we have his Hall, his Bed, his Way to Church, and the like ; which things may strengthen the Tradition, and serve to assure us, that there was such a person ; and the Tombstone found in Glastonbury Church, even though suppositions, will confirm the tradition that there was such a famous Prince, or the monks would never have attempted such a forgery in favour of the Dignity and Antiquity of their Monastery. The Inscription may appear to some to be more modern than the Interrment of King Arthur ; be it so, it may not however impeach the matter of fact of Arthur's being buried here ; for, from the constant Traditions, and perhaps Registers of the house, it appearing that K. Arthur was buried in such a place, it is not unlikely but, in some after-time, when disputes ran high about Relicks, and the fame of Arthur was more and more celebrated, it was thought no part of deceit, to ascertain the Tradition, and appropriate the honour of such Remains to the Abby of Glastonbury, by recording that distinguished name in the stone found there. The Inscription may be seen in Camden's last Edit. Vol. I. pag. 80. See Stillingfleet's Antiq. Ecclef. Brit. cap. 1. In short, there was certainly such a person ; but the year when born, whether the son of Gorlois or of Uter, or the same person as Uter, is not agreed. Another thing of him may be asserted without doubt, that he was a valiant Warriour, and true Christian ; but his real actions, great as they were, cannot now be separated from his false and suppositions ones, so intimately are they mixed with fable. Merlin, in his Prophesies, calls him the Cornish Boar *(aper Cornubiæ)* because born *in maritimo castro Tintagel.* Ush. Prim. p. 518.

Arthur being advanced to the Crown of Britain, his half brother [as Harding says, p. 77, 79.] CADOR, who must therefore have been son of Gorlois by Igerna before Arthur (as Hard. thinks p. 63.) was made Duke, and (after many great actions in war, under the command of Arthur) stiled King of Cornwall ; he is by some thought the son of Aur. Ambrosius. The British History in Rowland says, that Uter Pendragon made Cador Duke of Cornwall ; if so, Arthur, as Duke of Cornwall, could not have been so early upon the stage as Rapin says above.

About this time Indualis, surnamed the White [Candidus], was *Domnonensis Patriæ magna ex parte dux nobilissimus.* Usher, Prim. pag. 558. In Arthur's time, Gereint ap Erbyn, Admiral of the British Fleet, Nobleman of Cornwall, was killed at Longborth.

542 CONSTANTINE, son of Cador, reigned 4 years ; he was made King of Cornwall by King Arthur, and by Geoffry of Monmouth is reckoned King of Britain, but was only King of Cornwall as Usher thinks, ib. p. 537. He is said by Cressy, p. 258, to have resigned his Kingdom, and turned Monk, A. D. 583 ; but his conversion in the Ulton. Annals is placed in the year 588. Ush. ibid. pag, 1148 ; and he is said to have died in 590. Usher, ibid. Perhaps he might be elected King of the Britans in 542, at the death of Arthur ; and in those tumultuous times deposed after four years, and then retired into his hereditary country of Cornwall, where Gildas's Epistle found him in the year 583, and made such an impression on him that he turned Monk. This will reconcile the two accounts of this Prince.

He is supposed to have suffered Martyrdom, and is therefore reckoned a Saint. We have a Church dedicated to him, in the gift of the Church of Exeter ; and the Parish-feast is on the nearest Sunday to the 11th of March, according to the Martyrology cited by Usher. [Prim. 541.] " He was called by the Britans Cystennin Go- " ronawg" [i. e. the Cornish Constantine, as Rowland says, because he was the last King of Britain of the Cornish Family] ; " and his issue " is said to have continued Dukes of Cornwall " a long time." Rowland, pag. 170. He is said to have been buried at Stonehenge. Hard. 79. Ush. ibid. 541.

AURELIUS CONANUS (nepos Constantini) reigned according to Hard. 3, to Powel 2 years. He is supposed to have been King of Powis, or some other Province in Wales (Ush. ib. 537.) ; by some King of Cornwall after Constantine's being killed by him. {568 H. {546 P.

VORTEPER [& Vortiporius King of Demetia. Ush. 537.] reigned according to Hard. 7, to Powel 4 years. {571 H. {548 P.

TENDURUS was King of Cornwall when St. Petrock came last to visit the Cornish Britans, about the middle of the 6th century, A. D. 557. Ush. ib. 1141.

MALGO, alias Maglocunus, King of Venedotia. Ush. ib. 537. reigned according to Hard. 22, to Powel 5 years. {578 H. {580 P.

GERENNIUS was King of Cornwall about the year, according to Powel, 585, to Usher, [pag. 1150.] 589, who [pag. 559.] thinks him successor to Constantine, to whom he was grandson ; he lived at Dingerein [i. e. the fort of Gerennius], which, most likely, was somewhere near the Church called from this Prince (as 'tis supposed) Gerrans, and gave name to the harbour, thence called Dingerein port. Ush. 560. When the yellow plague raged, even to the depopulating South Wales, and among the rest had carried off King Maglocun, Theliaus, then Bishop of Landaff, with some suffragan bishops, and several attendants, came into Cornwall, and was there kindly entertained by Gerennius. From thence St. Theliaus went into Armorica, and after staying there seven years and seven months, being upon his return to his own country, visited Gerennius again, found him dying, and gave him the Sacrament, and then proceeded to Landaff. [Ush. 560.] This Gerennius is thought to be the person mentioned before, and celebrated in a particular Ode called Cowydd Gereint ap Erbyn, by Lowarch Hen, a British Prince and Poet, who flourished about that time. [Rowland Mon. 187.] Mr. Lhuyd, in his Arch. Brit. pag. 260. gives us the following account of this Ode:

" In

" In Epicædio Geruntii docet [fcil. Lhywarx " Hen.] cujus filius fuerit, et ut fupra," (viz. pag. 240, col. 1.) " innuimus, locum ubi oc- " ciderit defignat, pugna fortaffis navali, nam in " portu Lhongborth dicto peremptum refert. " Deinde Arthuro tam egregium militem Long- " portæ fublatum dolet." But it muft be noted that this Gerennius King of Cornwall fell not in battle, but died in his bed, as above; and fecondly, that time will not permit them to be one and the fame perfon; for the Gerennius who is the Hero of this Poem was killed at Longborth, in the time of King Arthur; the Poet laments that King Arthur had loft fo ex- cellent a foldier as Gerennius the fon of Erbyn, who muft therefore have been elder than Geren- nius King of Cornwall by many years.

H. 600 ⎱
P. 586 ⎰ CARICIS, alias Careticus, reigned according to H. 3, to P. 2 years, over all Britain, and in Wales and Cornwall 25 more.

At this time the Britans were, by the Saxons, and Gormund, a King of Ireland (who came into Britain, A. D. 596, according to Ufh. ib. p. 1151.), driven into Wales and Cornwall, with their King Careticus (Not. in Powel's Cata- logue), who in Wales and Cornwall, after this retreat in his fecond year, feems to have reigned 25 years; for, according to Powel, he was not fucceeded till 613.

To Gerennius fucceeded a King of Cornwall, who gave the land of Glaftonbury to the Monks there, at the inftance of Worgrez, then Abbot, A. D. 601. The name of this King, Ufher fays, they could not find out, becaufe the paper and writing was decayed. Ufh. p. 1054. But Ge- rennius dying feven years and a half after Malgo, who died, according to Powel, in 586, muft fix the death of Gerennius to 593, or [as Ufher has placed it in p. 1150.] in 596, or a little after, according to H. At this time I find Bel- thrufius, Bletius, or Bledericus, called Duke, Prince, and King of Cornwall. [G. M. xciiii. —Caradoc of Lhancarvan, by Wynne, p. 17, 21, 23.] He was fent to for aid againft the Saxons, who had maffacred the Monks of Ban- gor. Now this maffacre happened, according to Ufher [from the Ultonian Annals, p. 1157.], A. D. 613. He was Generaliffimo in a confi- derable battle on the River Dee, in the year 617, againft Ethelbrith King of Northumberland, where he won the battle, but loft his life. [G. M. ibid.] This Prince is alfo mentioned on account of the above battle by Nic. Trivet. [Wilk. Conc. p. 28. and in Spelm. Con. vol. i. p. 28.] By his living fo near the date of the grant of Glaftonbury to the Monks, and no one named betwixt Gerennius and him, I conclude him the perfon who granted thofe lands. Nor is it unlikely, that the Kings of Cornwall fhould have power to grant thefe Lands, for as much as it appears to have been part of their heredi- tary dominions, which was the reafon, that though Arthur was wounded mortally in a battle in Cornwall, yet was he neverthelefs carried [" a nobili matronâ quâdam ejufdem cognatâ et " Morgani vocatâ (corpus fcil. Arthuri) eft de- " latum, quod poftea defunctum, in dicto Cœ- " meterio facro eadem procurante fepultum." Ufh. Prim. 523.] to the Abby of Glaftonbury to be buried, as a place of the greateft fanctity,

within the bounds of his own inheritance. [Bp. Stillingfleet, however, queftions whether there was ever fuch an Abbot as Worgrez *; but I cannot underftand for what reafon.

CADVAN reigned according to Hard. 13, to Pow. 22 years. He reigned over the Britans, and the Weft part of all Wales and Cornwall. Hard. 85. He was great Grandfon to Malgo, alias Maglocunus; for Malgo begat Ennian, who begat Belin, who begat Jago, who begat Cad- van. [G. M. xcvii.]   ⎱ 603 H. ⎰ 613 P.

CADWAL, alias Cadvallonus, fon of Cad- van, reigned according to Harding 61, to Powel 48.   ⎱ 616 H. ⎰ 635 P.

By the fate of War, Cadwallo was forced to take fhelter in Armorica. Brian, his Nephew, convoked an affembly of his Britifh Subjects; they met at Exeter, and ordered all the Nobles (univerfis Britonum proceribus) to put their towns in a proper pofture of defence, and prepare for the reception of their King, Cadwallo, who would foon return with aid from Britany [G. M. pag. xcviii.], which he accordingly did, and became afterwards Mafter of all Britain (excepting what the Saxons held), ibid. xcix. He died according to Harding, pag. 113. A. D. 676.

CADWALADER, fon of Cadwallo, reigned according to Hard. 12, to Powel 3 years.   ⎱ 676 H. ⎰ 683 P.

CADWALADER, laft King of the Britans, died and was buried at Rome A. D. 690. Hard. p. 96.

Here fell that moft ancient Kingdom of the Britans, which, continuing from the time of Heli the High-Prieft to this time, during the fpace of 1825 years, may be juftly reckoned to have ex- ceeded in duration all other Kingdoms of the World. Vid. Rob. Cœnal. Lib. ii. and Not. in Powel's Catalogue.

From the Death of Belthrufius, A. D. 617, the Dukedom of Cornwall feems annexed to the crown of Britain, for Cadvan reigned over Cornewayle [Hard. 85.], and fo did Cadwallo his fucceffor [G. M. xcviii.], as appears by the Affembly of Britans held at Exeter by his Nephew, during his exile in Britany, and fo pro- bably did Cadwalader; but, upon Cadwalader's death, though the Britans afterwards had never one King in common to Wales and Cornwall, yet the firft had feveral petty Princes, or Reguli, and the latter its own Ruler, fometimes called King, and fometimes Duke, as will appear in the following remarks.

GERUNTIUS was King of Cornwall in the year 690. Archbifhop Ufher, Prim. pag. 1167. places the Epiftle he received from Al- delm (mentioned before, pag. 343.) in this year.   690

The addrefs of this famous Epiftle, relating to the Sacerdotal Tonfure, and keeping of Eaf- ter, is fomewhat remarkable. It runs thus, Creffy, pag. 481.

" To my glorious Lord Geruntius, King of " the Weftern Kingdom, whom I, as God " the fearcher of hearts is my witnefs, do " embrace with brotherly Charity, and like- " wife to all God's Priefts inhabiting Damno- " nia," &c.

* Antiq. Brit. pag. 27.

5 M   GERUN-

GERUNTIUS, King of the Britans in Cornwall, was vanquifhed by King Ina [Hunt. 193. Creffy, p. 522.—Sax. Chron. ad ann. 710.]; and Ina got great glory by his wars with the Cornifh. [Rapin, 8vo. Engl. p. 209.]

730 RODERICK MOLWYNOC, Grandfon to Cadwalader, perceiving that Ethelhard, King of the Weft Saxons, had deftroyed Devonfhire with fire and fword, drew the Cornifh together, and, upon that King's entrance into Cornwall, gave him battle, defeated him, and forced him to retire with all fpeed to his own dominions: this victory the Britans call Gwaeth Heilyn from the place where this battle was fought. [Caradoc of Lhangarvon, pag. 15, 16.] Roderick was afterwards forced to forfake thefe Weftern parts, and died in North Wales, A. D. 755. [ibid. Wynne's Hift. of Wales, pag. 18.]

BLEDERIC is faid to have been Prince of Cornwall at this time, and to have joined Roderic. [Car. lib. ii. pag. 97.—Carad. Langarv. Edit. Powel, pag. 16.]

743 This year Cuthred obtained a confiderable
753 victory over the Cornifh. [Hunt. 196.] In this year he obtained another victory here. [Hunt. ibid.]

755 At this time the Britans in Devonfhire and Cornwall were forced out of every thing worth notice [Wynne, p. 18.]; but Ivor fucceeding his father Alan the fecond in the Kingdom of Britany, in this year came over into Cornwall to affift the Britans, by which affiftance the Cornifh recovered their country from the Saxons. Leland [It. Vol. VIII.] mentions three battles, one at Heyl in Cornwall, the fecond at Gardmailanc, the third at Pentun; in all which the Britans, under the command of Ivor, overcame the Saxons.—Lhuyd's Pref. to his Cornifh Grammar, and Third Letter in Rowl. Mona.

This Ivor is called the fon of Cadwalader, by Lel. It. Vol. VIII. The particulars of this Hiftory of Ivor will admit of fome doubt. [See Powel's Edit. of the Hiftory of the Princes of Wales.]

About the year 766, Kynewulf had wars with the Cornifh, for his fuccefs in which he gave certain lands to the Church of Wells. [Cam. pag. 84.]

780 In the time of Conan, fon of Ivor (who both feem to have had the chief power in Cornwall), the Britans were again difpoffeffed. [Wynne, ibid.] Kynewulf is faid to have been very victorious in his wars with the Britans. [Hoveden, pag. 235.]

787 In the third year of Brithricus, the Danes came into Cornwall. [See before, pag. 42.]

806 In this year the Danes came into Cornwall, and brought a fleet there at the invitation of the Cornifh. They joined forces, and, continuing the war fome time, were met at laft by Egbert in the year 813 [as the Sax. Chron. or 809, as Rapin, pag. 214.], vanquifhed, and all Cornwall over-run.

824 In the 24th of Egbert, the Cornifh and Danes engage the Devonfhire men at Gavulford, [Sax. Chron. ann. 284.] but were worfted; which being the firft battle recorded betwixt the De-

vonians and Cornifh, inclines me to think, that the Devonian Britans were for the moft part driven out of that county, and that what remained there had at this time fided with the Saxons, and that by the Devonians here we are to underftand principally the Saxons who were fettled in Devonfhire. Hunt. pag. 198. fays, that many thoufands fell on both fides. So fays Hoveden.

The Cornifh, with their auxiliary Danes, 835 marched Eaftward to fight the Saxons, and in the firft battle put Egbert to the worft [Wm. of Malm. pag. 20.], and the coming on of the night was the only thing that prevented the difgrace of a total defeat; but in the next battle at Hengefdune, the Cornifh and Danes were entirely overthrown.

In this year Caradocus, fecond of that name, 851 feems to have been King of Cornwall [G. M. lib. v. cap. xv.]; and at this time the Cornifh were overcome in battle at Wenbury Wicgambeorg by Cheorl Earl of Devonfhire. Hoveden, pag. 258. Cheorl is a Saxon name, and confequently the Saxons ruled at that time in Devonfhire.

ETHELBALD, King of England.   857
ETHELBERT, King of England.   862
ETHELRED, King of England.   867
ALFRED was in Cornwall in this year. 871 [Creffy, p. 742.]

DUNGARTH, or Doniert, King of Corn- 872 wall (likely the fon of Caradocus), was drowned in this year, and a Crofs at his defire (or an Oratory) erected where he was buried. [See in Plate XXXVI. Fig. I. and II.]

ALFRED was in Cornwall again in this year. 892 [Sax. Chron.]

EDRED, Duke of Damnonia, [Davene in Hunt.] intimate companion of Alfred in his wars, died A. D. 901. one month only before Alfred. [Hunt. p. 202.]

In Alfred's time, the Saxons appointing an Earl of Devon, feem to have given him alfo the title of Earl of Cornwall, though Cornwall was not as yet fubdued.

ALPSIUS Duke of Devon and Cornwall. 901 [I find, by a note of Mr. Hals, that this Duke gave the manor of Cargol to the Bifhop of Bodman.]

The Cornifh were beaten by Edward [Malm. pag. 25.]; and a Bifhoprick was erected at Bodman.

ETHELSTAN conquered the Cornifh en- 936 tirely; and, as they before claimed a right to Devonfhire as far as Exeter, ordered, that thenceforth the river Tamar fhould be the Eaftern boundary of their country.

EADMUND, King of England.   940
EADRED, King of England.   946
ORGERIUS (alias Ordargus, Comes Dom- 959 nonienfis, Pater Elfridæ Regis Eadgari ux.) Duke of Devon and Cornwall, was a great benefactor to the abby of Taviftock, where he is regarded as a founder, and lies buried. [Malmfb. pag. 146.]

EADULPHUS, fon of Ordgarus, famous for 959 his great ftature and ftrength of body. [Malmfb. pag. 146.] buried at Taviftock.

When

When Eadgar was taking his pleasure on the river Dee in the year 973, and, sitting in the stern of his boat, was rowed along by eight Kings who were subjects to him, Cressy [pag. 878.] says (upon what authority he does not mention) that Duffnal, one of those Kings, was King of West Wales.—Very likely this might be Eadulphus.

975 EDWARD the Martyr, King of England.

980 AYLMAR, alias Athelmar, was Earl of Cornwall. [Monaft. Angl. Tom. I. pag. 258.] —See Cressy [pag. 783.] who places him as early as the reign of Eadgar; but Eadulphus was living in Edward's time [as Malmsb. says, pag. 146.], and therefore outlived Eadgar. This Aylmar (by his name should be Saxon) and therefore the Royal Blood of the Britans was either by this time displaced, or had adopted Saxon names. [See Cressy, pag. 896.]

981 The Danes, now enemies to the Cornish, burnt and destroyed Bodman, and forced the Bishop to St. German's.

997 The Danish Fleet, sailing round West Saxony, entered the mouth of the Severn, and sometimes landed and plundered North Britain [Sudwales, says Hunt.] now and then Cornwall, and sometimes Devonshire, at Weced port (now Bydeford); and, having burnt many villages, and killed a great number of people, sailed back again round the Land's-End, landed at the mouth of the river Tamar, and wasting both sides of the river (Cornwall, as well as Devon) without opposition, till they reached Lideford, burnt that Town, and then proceeded to Tavistock, where the Abby, being first plundered, underwent the same fate. [Hoveden, pag. 246.]

EDMUND Ironside, King of England. 1016
CNUTE, the Dane, King of England. 1017
HAROLD, King of England. 1036
HARDECNUT, King of England. 1040
ALGAR Earl of Cornwall, A. D. 1046. 1046 [Mon. Ang. ibid. pag. 1022.] founded the Abby of Bruton in Somersetshire. [Leland, It. Vol. V. pag. 49, & 79.] " Odda constitutus fuit Comes super Defenashire, Somerset, Dorset, and Ofer Wealas." [Sax. Chr. ad pag. 1048.]

CONDORUS, alias Cadocus, last Earl of 1066 Cornwall of the royal British blood (says Camden, pag. 123.) was displaced by William the Norman, to make room for his half brother Robert Earl of Moriton. He had issue another Condor, whose daughter and heir Agnes was married to Reginald, base son to Henry the First. [Carew, pag. 79.]

Others say, this Reginald married the daughter of William Fitz-Richard, a potent man in Cornwall. Tonkin's notes on Carew, MS. B. pag. 150.

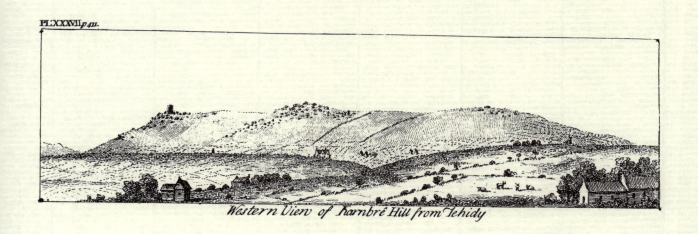

Western View of Karnbré Hill from Tehidy

PL XXXVII p 411

NATAL?

N A T A L I S O L O S.

MR. Lhuyd obferves, in his Preface to his Cornifh Grammar, " That to preferve any old " Language in Print is, without all Doubt, a moft pleafant and obliging Thing to Scho- " lars and Gentlemen, and altogether neceffary in the Studies of Antiquity."

It was in Hopes of throwing fome Lights upon the Hiftory of my native Country, that I under- took the Tafk of infpecting the few Things that remain in the Cornifh Language, and forming out of them, as far as my Time and Reading could reach, the little Vocabulary that follows.

I am fenfible that it is not fo compleat as I could wifh, the Reafon of which may be partly owing to the Authour, and partly to the Subject, and partly to the Materials. If the Authour had no other Points of Antiquity to divide and fhare his Attention, he would be more inexcufable that it is not more correct. Had not the Subject been difufed among People of Literature for fo many Ages, it would have been eafier compaffed ; and if the Materials had been in greater Plenty, there would have been more Choice, and the Work might have been better executed. But the Materials were not only few, but they were much difperfed ; and fo many as fell into my Hands might not probably have come to the Share of another, and the Helps for fuch a Work were ftill growing fewer by Time and Accident ; it being with Languages as with Buildings, when they are in a State of Decay, the Ruins become every Day lefs diftinct, and the fooner the Remains are traced and copied out, the more vifible both the Plan and the Superftructure will appear.

The fooner therefore fuch a Work was undertaken, the greater Likelihood there was that more of the Language might be preferved, than if the Attempt was deferred ; and as fome who had a Regard for their Country lamented, that it fhould utterly lofe its ancient Language, and thofe who were curious had a mind to underftand fomething of it, I found the Work was much defired ; and I was willing to do fomething towards reftoring the Cornifh Language, though I might not be able to do all that fewer Avocations would have permitted.

As incompleat as the following Vocabulary is, I am perfuaded, that it will be of fome Ufe. In the prefent Language of my Countrymen, there are many Words which are neither Englifh, nor derived from the learned Languages, and therefore thought Improprieties by Strangers, and ridiculed as if they had no Meaning ; but they are indeed the Remnants of their antient Language, efteemed equal in Purity and Age to any Language in Europe.

The technical Names belonging to the Arts of Mining, Hufbandry, Fifhing, and Building, are all in Cornifh, and much oftener ufed than the Englifh Terms for the fame Things. The Names of Houfes and Manors, Promontories, Lakes, Rivers, Mountains, Towns, and Caftles in Cornwall (efpecially in the Weftern Parts), are all in ancient Cornifh. Many Families retain ftill their Cor- nifh Names. To thofe, therefore, who are earneft to know the Meaning of what they hear and fee every Day, I cannot but think that the prefent Vocabulary, imperfect as it is (and as all Vo- cabularies, perhaps, are at firft), will be of fome Satisfaction.

The Helps I have received, I muft acknowledge chiefly owing to the Archæologia of the late Mr. Edward Lhuyd, above mentioned, Keeper of the Mufeum at Oxford, who has publifhed a Grammar of the Cornifh Tongue[a], and therein preferved the Elements of this Language, which had otherwife wholly perifhed with him, and his Friend Mr. John Keigwyn, who was, indeed, Mr. Lhuyd's Tutour in this Point of Learning, and died a few Years after him. In the Comparative Vocabulary, and in other Parts of the Archæologia, there is a great Number of Cornifh Words ; moft of which, if not all, I be- lieve, the Reader will find in the following Vocabulary. I have alfo called in the Affiftance of the Armo- rick Vocabulary (publifhed in the fame Work) ; and where I met with no Radix of like Sound in the Cornifh, I have there inferted the Armorick Word, putting after it *Ar.* to note that it has only oc- curred to me as yet in the Armorick, tho it may in the reading of others either be found in the Cornifh MSS. or be of Service to explain Words which are omitted by me at prefent. Some *Radix's* alfo are taken from the Welfh and Irifh, as what may at one time or other explain Parts of the Sif- ter-Dialect, the Cornifh. Befides what Mr. Lhuyd has printed, he left feveral MSS. behind him, and among the reft a Cornifh-Englifh Vocabulary, which [in his Arch. pag. 253.] he tells us, he had then by him, " written about fix Years before," that is, in the Year he was in Cornwall, [viz. 1700.] " and that he had lately improved it with what Additions he could." I had the favour of perufing all the MSS. relating to Etymology, which could be found in the Library of Sir Thomas Seabright, Bart. where the Literary Remains of Mr. Lhuyd were thought to have been depofited. Among them I met with an imperfect Englifh-Cornifh Vocabulary ; and in the other fcattered Memorandums, I found feveral Cornifh Words I had not feen before, which in the following Work are inferted ; but

---

[a] Arch. pag. 225, &c)

the

the Cornish-English Vocabulary was not among thofe Papers, and therefore is fuppofed to be loft, and always to be regretted by the Curious.

Befides Mr. Lhuyd's Works, I have been favoured [b] with the Perufal of a curious MS. written by the late Mr. Scawen of Molinek in Cornwall; in which, firft, there was Part of a Cornifh MS. called Mount Calvary, with a verbal Englifh Tranflation (no fmall Help to a Beginner); and in the latter End, the Excellency of the Cornifh Language, and the feveral Reafons of its Decay, are well fet forth, together with fome Proverbs, Sentences, and other Affiftances, for the better underftanding, and for the encouraging fome one to endeavour to reftore it. Mr. Scawen's MS called the Cornubrita-nick Antiquities was alfo communicated [c]. I had alfo the Favour [d] of the MS. of the late Tho. Tonkin, Efq; in which there is a Tranfcript of the MSS. now in the Bodleian Library, in Cornifh and Englifh, which were copied under the Direction of the late Mr. Lhuyd, at the inftance of Mr. Tonkin, who intended to print them, with fome Dialogues, and other Cornifh Compofitions, contained in the faid Manufcript.

I had the Favour [e] of perufing what the late William Gwavas, Efq; (after Mr. Keigwyn, and, Mr. Lhuyd, the moft knowing of his Age in the Cornifh Tongue) left behind him; and a few MSS. [f] of the late Mr. Bofon, Part of Mr. Hals's Cornifh Vocabulary, and fome Tranflations of feveral Parts of the Holy Scripture. Laftly, I have inferted the Cornifh Vocabulary [g], which is in the Cotton Library, London; a MS. as Mr. Lhuyd thought [h], about feven hundred Years old; fo that, I hope, though what follows is not compleat, it may lay a Foundation, and provoke fome one of more Leifure to add to it an Englifh-Cornifh Vocabulary, and a more exact Lift of the Words which are to be found in the two laft Cornifh Manufcripts of the Bodleian Library, which, with the Grammatical and Philological Collections I have made in order thereto (and fhall readily communicate to any Perfon of Learning who will undertake the Tafk), will recover, and may continue, as much of this dead Language as may be ufeful to my Countrymen, and fatisfactory to all who will not be too Scrupulous and Critical.

I fhould here have inferted a Contraction of Mr. Edward Lhuyd's Cornifh Grammar, as I at firft intended; but as the Number of Sheets, which this Work was to confift of, will be more than com-pleat without it, and as the whole Grammar is already printed by Mr. Lhuyd, to print it here would needlefsly fwell the prefent Work; and it is hoped that the Addition of feveral Chapters, and feveral Copper Plates, more than were at firft engaged for, will fufficiently compenfate for this Omiffion.

[b] By the Rev. Dr. Lyttelton, then Dean of Exeter, now Bifhop of Carlifle, whofe kind Affiftance, in every thing relating to this Work, I can never forget.

[c] By Francis Gregor, of Trewarthenik, Efq;

[d] From the Rev. Mr. Collins, Vicar of St. Erth.

[e] From William Veale of Trevailor, Efq;

[f] From the Rev. Mr. Uftick of St. Juft.

[g] For an entire Tranfcript of which I am obliged to the Rev. Dr. Jer. Milles, then Precentor, now Dean, of the Church of Exeter.

[h] Letter to Th. Tonkin, Efq; in 1702-3, pen. W. B.

[i] As Mr. Edward Lhuyd's Cornifh Grammar, publifhed in his Archæologia, Tit. VI. pag. 222. is fcarce, and little Hopes of feeing Etymology fo much countenanced as that it fhall be foon re-publifhed: It might not, perhaps, be unacceptable to the Studi-ous in Britifh Hiftory to have that Cornifh Grammar re-printed from pag. 222, to pag. 232. viz. down to (aberh an tfhei omma), at the bottom of the firft Co-lumn. From thence there is in Mr. Lhuyd a long Digreffion not immediately relating to the Cornifh Tongue till you come to pag. 240. Col. 2. where the third Chapter begins—from hence to the End, pag. 251. may be publifhed together with the St. Levan man of Tfhei an Hor, in modern Cornifh, with the Englifh Tranflation of it from Mr. Tonkin's MS. pag. 177.

ABBREVIATIONS in the following VOCABULARY.

A. Adjective.
Ad. Adverb.
Ar. Armorick.
B. Bochart.
Baxt. Baxter's Gloffary.
Bof. Bofon MS.
C. Cornifh.
Car. Carew's Survey.
Comp. Compound.
Cott. Cotton Vocab.
Dav. Davies's Dict.
f. forfitan.

G. Gallicè.
Gr. Greek.
Gw. Gwavas MS.
Heb. Hebrew.
id. idem.
Ir. Irifh.
J. T. Tregere MS.
L. Latin.
Lh. Lhuyd, Arch.
LMS. Lhuyd's MS.
Pa. Participle.
Pl. Plural.

Pr. Pronoun.
Pre. Prepofition.
Pri. Primitive.
Qu. Quære.
R. Rowland's Welfh.
S. Subftantive.
Sc. Scawen MS.
Sing. Singulariter.
T. T. Tonkin MS.
V. Verb.
Uf. Uftick MS.
W. Lhuyd's Welfh.

A CORNISH

A.

A, *Of; from; and;* a Prep. or Conjunction, *it is either, separate, or annexed.*

A, prefixed to the infinitive mood of Verbs, supplies the want of the Participle of the Present Tense; as, a debbry, *eating;* a cusga, *sleeping.*

A, *as;* A mi a môz, *as I was going.*

A, is the sign of the Preter and Future Tenses; it is also used sometimes, in the Present Tense, thus, A leversys, *thou sayest;* A nethas, *thou spinnest.*

A, *I will go;* as, My a, *I will go;* Ty a, *thou shalt go;* Moz being understood.—See more of the use of this Particle before the Verb, Lhuyd's Cornish Gram. Arch. pag. 25, 26.

A, *my;* as, a Vester, a Vestrez, *my Master, my Mistress.*

A, is united to the pronoun personal when sign of the Preter, or future Tense, as, Am, *hath me;* Ath, *have thee,* &c.

A, the Article, answers to the English *a,* or *an.*

A, is sometimes put before the Substantive, when mi is used; as, dho a bredyr vi, *to my Brother.*

A, *out of;* a kez glaz, *out of green Cheese.*

A, *by,* or *with;* as, a Eleth splan, *with Angels bright.*

A, Oh; an Interjection; A Dâs, *O Father!* A Venen, *Ah Woman.*

A, *which,* or *that;* a Pron. Relative, as Avo, *that is,* or *which is.*

A, *if;* A'm cothvaz, *if thou knewest me;* A mennas, *if thou wilt.*

A, *his,* or *her's;* as, a dhillaz, *his,* or *her cloaths*

A B

Abaff, *dizziness; rashness.* Ar.

Aban, *above; forasmuch as; when; since that;* it is written Aba, before an N.

Abardtat, *an Uncle;* a *Father's Brother.*

Abarhmam, *an Uncle;* a *Mother's Brother.*

Abarstick, *insatiable.*

Abat, *an Abbot.* Cott. Abod. W. id.

Abec, *a Cause.* Ar.

Abell (apell, id.), *far off.*

Abem, *a Kiss.* Gw.

Aber, *a Ford;* a *fall of Water;* a *mouth of a River;* a *meeting*

of two Rivers. W. id.

Aberveth, Aberth, and Oberth, *upon; within.*

Abestely (abozdol, id.), *Apostles.*

Able, *whence.*

Abosdol, *an Apostle.*

Abrans, *the Eyelid.* Cott. W. Amrant.

Abys, *to beseech;* ny a bys, *we do beseech;* wy a bys, *you shall beseech.*

A C

Accoyes, *to assuage; abate.*

Ach, *Issue; Offspring; root of a Tree.*

Acheson (Achesow), *Guilt;* ab Achesa, *to impeach; accuse.*

Achlefs, *Defence; Protection.*

Acr, *vile; base.* Ar.

Achta (it. Ehtas, id.) *a Possession; Inheritances.*

A D

Ad (ath, id.) *of; on; concerning; thy.* Cott.

Ad, *aliquando otiosa particula;* as Ny ad wra, *we will make.* Cott.

Ada, *to feed;* (C. haza.) Ar.

Adail, *a Building.*

Addel, *loose Rubbish; Filth.* W. addail. id.

Addeuli, *to worship.* Ar.

Aden, *the Leaf of a Book.* Cott.

Adhurt (adheuorth, adhiuort, id.) *from.*

Adhellar, *after; behind.*

Adletha, *a Soldier.* Cott.

Adoth, *Haste; Readiness; Vow.*

Adre, *homewards.*

Adro, *about; on; upon.*

Adwra, *thou shalt endure.*

Adzhan, *to know; perceive.*

Adzhyi, *within;* agy, id. LMS.

A E

Ael, *a brow;* Aeltavon, *the brow of a River.* Moreton.

Aer, *a Snake; Air.*

Aeran, *Plumbs.*

Aerva, *a Defeat.* See Lh. 155.

A F

Aff, *I; me;* war aff, *on me;* 'tis suffixed to Verbs, as, allaff, *I can;* dampnyaff, *I condemn.*— 'Tis suffixed also to Prep. as, ragaff, *for; by me.*

Aff, *a Kiss.* Ar.

Aflavar, *an Infant;* one that cannot speak. Ar.

Affo, *swift; quick.* Ar.

Aga, *them; theirs.*

A G

Agan, *ours.*

Agan honan, *our selves.*

Agan bys, *let us pray.*

Agan, f. *the stomach of an Animal;* so the Cornish call the stomach of a Pig.

Agans, *with;* (a præfix).

Agary, *contrary, Enemy to.*

Agathyas, *seized upon;* (a præfix.)

Agaz, *your;* agaz Pedn, *your Head.*

Agerou (et Agheri), *to open; stretch.*

Agis, *you; your.*

Agolan, *a Whetstone.*

Agoz, agyz & guz, *your.* This Pronoun possessive loses often the three first Letters, and has the last annexed to the end of another Word, as, Evos kowl, *sup up your Broth;* for evough agoz kowl.

Agos, *near;* Ogaz, id.

Agowsys, *said;* (a præfix) a Kouz, *to say.*

Agris (or agreis), as, Me agreis, *I do believe;* pres. t. of Cresy, *hear,* or *believe.*

Agroasen, *a Shrubb.* Ar.

A H

Aha! *So ho!*

Ahanav, *from me.*

Ahanaz, *from; out of thee.*

Ahanen, *from us.*

Ahuel, *a Key.*

Aho, *Offspring; Pedigree.* Lh.

A I

Ai (pro A), *have;* as, mi ai didhinuys, *I have promised.* Lh.

Aidlen, *a Fir Tree.* Cott.

Aidhlen, id.

Ail, *an Angel.* Cott. Archail *Arch-angel.*

Ailga, *Slaughter.*

Ailla, *most beautiful;* pl. aluin. LMS.

Ailne, *Beauty.*

Aincamheach, *blemished.* Ir. ib.

Ainisle, *mean; low.* ib.

Annaisle, id. ib.

Ainmhidh (pl. ainmhidhe), *a Beast;* vulg. Cornish, Bestaz. ib.

Airos, *the stern of a Ship.*

Aise, *gentle.*

Aithbhear, *to blame.*

Aiuma, *to kiss,* ib.

Aizia, *to ease;* to lessen; to disburthen.

A L

Alan, *Breath.*

Albalastr, *a Cross-Bow.*

Alenc,

A L

Alau, *white Water Lillies.*
Alemma (alebma, id.), *from hence.*
Alene, *from thence.*
Ales, *abroad*; (unles, id.) *spread, broad.*
All, *another.*
Allaff, *I can*, ny allaff, *I can't.*
Allas, *couldst*; ny allas, *thou could'st not.*
Allec, *Herring*; *Pilchards.*
Alli, *Advice, Counsel.* Ar.
Allos, *ought*; Dallos, id.
Alloys, *Grief*; *flowing.*
Alra, *a Maid-Servant.*
Als, *a Cliff*; *ascent, or descent*; *a Shore.* Cott. Alz, id. Lh.
Alsest, *mightest*; ti'a alsest, *thou mightest.*
Alt, *a Grove.* Ar.
Alta, *wild*; Beathuige alta, *wild Beasts.*
Altrou, *a Father-in-law.*
Altruan, *a Step-Mother.*
Aluedh, *a Key.* Lh.
Alwed, *an Inclosure.* Cott.
Alyek, *a Key.*

A M

Am, *my*; *me.*
Am, *round about.*
Am, *hath me*; neb am gurek, *who hath made me.*
Amal, *Plenty, or Store.*
Amane, *a Kiss.*
Amann, *above*; aban, id. uar, id.
Amar, *a Knot, or Tye.* Ar.
Amas, *did kiss.*
Ambodlaun, *unwilling*; anbodlaun, id.
Ambreth, *shaking.* Hals.
Amenen, *Butter.* Cott. Emenin, id.
Amman, id. Ar.
Amesek, *a Neighbour.* Ar.
Amnuid, *a Beck, or Nod.* LMS.
Amneidio, *to becken*; gogwyddo pen, id. viz. *to bow the Head.*
Amontye, *to reckon.*
Amplek, *pleaseth*; Mar thym amplek, *it much pleaseth me.* LMS.
Amser, *Time*; Anser, Cott. id.
Amwyn, *to defend*; *assist.*

A N

An, *him, or it*; Mi an guelaz, *I saw him, or it*; Ev an gevyth, *he shall find it.*
A'n, *of the*; *from the*; *the*; This Article is not only placed before Nouns, as, an Dên, *the Man*, but before Pronouns; as, an rena, *those*; and also inserted between a Noun and Pronoun, as, pa an dra, *what thing?* where it is otiosa par-

ticula, or redundant, as, pa an cheyson, *what Accusation?*
An, a Particle privative, as, anlavar, *mute*; *without Speech*; an coth, *not known.*
Anadlu, *to breath*; anadl, *breath.* Lms. anal, id.
Anallod, *before*; *before that*; *of old.*
Anat, *plain*; *manifest.* Ar.
Anau, *an Evet.* Cott.
Anav, *a spot, or blemish.* Cott.
Anavel, *a storm*; ab an, & avel, *a calm.*
Anbodlaun, *unwilling.*
Ancar, *a Hermit*; it. *an Anchor.* Cott. ancar, id. Lh.
Anchel, *an Arm.*
Ancouth, *a stranger*; *one not known.*
Androw, *Andrew.*
Anedhi, *of her.*
Anered vur mor, *a Pirate.* Cott. alias, angredar, id.
Anethe, *of them*; annedhe, annydha, *from or concerning them.*
Aneval, *a beast*; *any quadruped.* Ar.
Anfur, *imprudent.* Cott. *without wisdom.*
Anghel pur, *unlike*; *unequal.*
Anghygred, *hardness of belief.*
Anglod, *to blemish*; *spot*; *spoil.*
Angor, *an anchor.*
Angov, *fogetfulness.*
Angredar mer, *a Pirate.*
Angus, *anguish*; *pain.*
Aniâk, *weak*; *infirm.*
Anken, *Grief.*
Ankevys, *forgotten.* See Kovys.
Ankow, *Death*; ancou, & ancouyns, id.
Anlavar, *mute*; avlavyr, id. Lh.
Anludd, *bucksome.*
Annerh, *Honour.*
Annez, *Cold.*
Annodho, *thereof.*
Anow, *a Name*; pro hanou, id. also *a Mouth*; pro ganow.
Anser, *Time.*
Ansueth, *a Curse*; kymmys ansueth, *such a Curse!*
Antarlick, *a Play*; *a Comedy.*
Antel, *Danger.*
Antromet, *Sexus.* Cott.
Anvab, *barren*; anvabat, *barrenness.* Cott.
Anuan, *an Anvil.*
Anvein, *weak.* Cott.
Anwyd, *cold.* Cott.
Anz (ut, & onz, & oinz), *they*; a Pronoun personal suffixed to denote the third Person plural, as, Guelanz, *they see.*
Anzaoue, *Prosperity*; *Opportunity.*

A O

Ao, *ripe.* Ar.
Aor, *Earth*; Oar, id.

A P

Ap-haul, *filius Solis*; scil. Apollo, R.
Apert, *publickly*; *openly.* G.
Aperth, *a Victim.*
Apparn, *an Apron.*

A R

Ar, *a still Lake.* Hals. Qu.
Ar, *the*; an article before Nouns.
Ar, *Land*; qua. pro aor, *Slaughter*; har, id. Lh. Aras, Ir. id.
Arwerthel—Arwinic. Qu. Ar-devora—Arvôs. Harlyn.
Ar (for war), *on, or upon*; ardour, *upon the Water.*
Ara, *to cause*; *make*; *do*; id. ac wra, or awra, *we shall cause.*
Ara, *flow.*
Araderuur, *a Plowman.* Cott.
Arall, *another*; pl. erel, *others.*
Arat, *a Plow*; it. arad, id. Dho araz, *to plow.*
Arbednek, *used*; *customary.*
Ardar, *a Plow*; Ardur, *a Plowman.*
Arghans, or argan, *Silver.* Lh. arhans, id. Lh.
Argila, *to recoil.*
Argraphyz, *printed*; Levar argraphyz. Lh.
Arha, *to command.*
Arhadou, *Commands.*
Arho, *a Goad*, Lh. stimulus, L.
Arleth, *a Lord*; *a Chief, or Master.*
Arludes, *a Lady.* Cott.
Arluit, *a Lord.* Cott. Arluth, id. pl. arlydhi. W. Arglwydhi.
Armas, *cried out*; a arme, *they cried out.*
Armor, *a Wave*; *a Surge*; Lh.
Armoriou, *Arms in Heraldry.* Ar.
Aroaz, *Tansie.* Ar.
Aroc, *before.* Ar.
Arouez, *a sign, or token.* Ar.
Arrez, *a way*; *path*; *course*; *pace.*
Arrîa (vulg. for ria), *O strange!*
Arse, *commanded*; from arrha.
Arte (& arta), *again.*
Arth, *a Bear*; orth, id. Gr. αρκτος.
Arv, *a weapon*; *arm thou*; pl. Arvou.
Arvez, *ripe.*
Arvis, *early in the Morning.*
Aruit, *Air.* Cott.
Arvor, *the Sea shore*; Ar. quasi war môr.
Arvordir, W. *a place by the Sea side.*
Arweddiad, *behaviour, manners.* LMS.

Arwydd,

AR

Arwydd, *a brand*, or *mark*; ib.
Arwyl, *a burial*, or *funeral*; ib.
Arwyddocan, *to betoken*, or *fore-shew*.

AS

As, *them*; (*us*, id.) *they*.
As, a Termination of the imperf. Tenfe, as, y foras, *they did grieve*; y reforas, *they did much grieve*.
Afcable, *cavilled*, or *fquabbled*.
Afcient, *one out of his Senfes*; *a poffeffed*; (guan, id.)
Afcle, *the Bofom*; afcra, id. Lh.
Afderbynas, *compelled*. V.
Afen, *an Afs*; it. *a Rib*; pl. afon.
Afenza, *an Afs-colt*.
Afenguil, *a wild Afs*. Cott.
Afew, *it be*; (V. a præf.)
Afgarn (afgorn, id.), *a Bone*.
Afgornek, *bony*.
Afgura, *will make them*; (as præf.)
Afkal, *a Wing*; pl. afkelli.
Afkal, *a fhell Fifh*; *a Naker*; it. *the fin of a Fifh*. Lh.
Afkellen, *a Thiftle*. Cott. Afkallan, id.
Affaz, *thou art*.
Affon, *we are*.
Aftell, *a Board*, or *Plank*. LMS.
Aftyllen, id. *a Shelf*; *a Shingle*. Lh.
Aften, *to enlarge*.
Aftor, *Offspring*; dry aftor, *to bring forth Iffue*.
Afwonas (afwothas, id.), *do know*.

AT

Ate, *fpite*; mar ate, *fo much fpite*.
Ath, *hath thee*; *have thee*; *will thee*; meathkelma, *I will bind thee*.
Ath, *thy*; mez ath, *out of thy*.
Ather, *a Paunch*; *a Belly*; lean eu athor, *fill my Belly*. Gw.
Atis, *a perfuafion*; *Advice*. Ar.
Attal, *a Bolt*, or *Bar*.
Attamye, *to redeem*.
Attret, *fweepings*. Ar.

AU AV

Au, *the Liver*. Ar.
Avain, *an Image*. Cott.
Aval (Avell, id.), *an Apple*; *all forts of fruit*.
Avallen, *Apple Trees*. Cott.
Auan, *a River*. Lh.
Avan (aban, id.), *above*; ita & man, pro aman, id.
Avani, *to imagine*.
Auartha, *above*.
Auc, pl. auen, *Vallis fontibus ri-*

gata Ab ahis, vel ahvis *aqua, flumen*. Keyfler.
Aveas, *by*; *through*; aus, *out of*.
Avez, *without*; foràs.
Auel, *Aura*; *weather*. Cott. Ar. *Wind*.
Auel teag, *fair Weather*; auel vas, *a calm*; hagar auel, *bad Weather*.
Auelek, *windy*.
Avell, *like to*; (haval, id.) *likenefs*.
Aueth, *alfo*; *equally* (aweth & auedh, id.); fcribitur aweyth, awyth, awyethe, id.
Aueil, *the Gofpel*. Ar. Aviel.
Avin, *will*; *wilt*; ni au'n moz, *we will go*. Lh.
Aules, *a Cliff*; aules ewhal, *a high Cliff*; whêl aules, *work in the Cliff*.
Aultra, *a Godfather*.
Aultruan, *a Godmother*.
Avon (auan, id.), *a River*.
Avor, *towards*; avor thys, *towards thee*.
Avorou, *to-morrow*. Cott.
Auoz, *fo that, notwithftanding*; *above*; avoz travyth, *above any thing*; *for the fake of*; as, auos den vyth, *for the fake of any Man*. LMS.
Aure, *he that*; (fuel, id.); q. fee awre.
Aufa, *to adorn*; *prepare*. Ar.
Aufillen, *an Ozier*. Ib.
Aut, *the Sea-fhore*; *bank of a River*.
Autrou, *a Mafter*, or *Lord*. Ar.
Avi, *the Liver*, or *Breaft*. Cott. *Spite*; *Envy*; *Difcord*; avey, & avy, id.

AW

Awatta, *to behold*. LMS.
Awen, *the Jaws*, or *Chops*. Ar.
Awothe (awothy, id.) *he felt, or knew*.
Awre, *he made*.
Awy, the old Word for *River*. R.
Awyr, *Air*.

AY

Ay, *that*; *his*; ay oys, *that Age*.
Aydn, *one*; peb aydn, *every one*.
Ayûh, *over*; *above*; ayuhav, *above me*; ayûh y pen, *over his Head*.

AZ

Azan, *a Rib*; it. *a Pipe-ftave*; (afen, id.) pl. afou.
Azgran, *a Wing*; kanifer hethen

gen afgran, *every Fowl with Wings*. Bof.
Aznat, *evident*; *plain*. Ar.
Azrek, *Sorrow*. Ib.
Azrouant, *a Devil*. Ib.
Azroue, *a Sign*; *Token*. Ar. See arouez.

B.

"Hum. Lhuyd affirmeth bold-"ly, that there is not any Bri-"tifh Word whofe firft Radical "Letter is B." Speed. Chron. p. 7. But H. L. p. 8. adds, what Speed does not, " abideth "any change into P, or Ph."
Many Words beginning primarily with a B, begin alfo in the fame Authours, fometimes properly (viz. by Grammatical Permutation), fometimes improperly (contrary to Rule) with a V, or F. B is changed into F, and M, as, Bara, *Bread*; o fara, *out of Bread*; fymara, *my Bread*.

BA, *who*.
Baal (bal), *a Shovel*.
Baar, *a Bolt*, or *Bar*.
Bach (bagl, id.), *a Stick*.
Badeza, *to baptize*. Ar.
Badna, *a Drop*; banne, id.
Badus, *a Lunatic*.
Baedh, *a Boar*; bahed id, bora, id.
Bagat, *a Troop*, or *Crew*; *an Affembly*, or *Council*.
Bagaz, *a Bufh*; bagaz eithin, *a bufh of Furfe*; bhaid, *about*.
Bahau, *Hooks*, *Hinges*; bahau an darras, *Hinge of the Door*.
Baiou, *kiffes*; a baye, *to kifs*.
Bai, *blame*; difai, *blamelefs*.
Baicwl, *a blamer*; *a fault-finder*.
Bail, *a Bery*.
Baiol, *Enula, the Herb Elicampan*.
Bairfighe, *brawling*
Bakken, *Bacon*. Gw.
Bal, *a Plague*; *a Place*; *a Place of digging*.
Balas, *to dig*; Palas, id.
Balaven, *a Butterfly*. Ar.
Bali, *a high grown Wood*.
Balliar, *a Barrel*; it. *a Tub*.
Ban, *up*; *high*. W. *a Place*. [Lugban, alias ludvan, *a high Tower*.]
Ban a fevy, *up he ftood*.
Banal, *Broom*; bauathel, id. Cott. Ai balan. Lh.
Baneu, *a Sow*.
Baniel, *a Banner*.
Bankan, *a Dam*, or *Bank*.
Banna *could*; V. (vynna, id.) as, n'y wely banna, *he faw not a glimpfe*, i. e. *could not fee*.

Banneth,

B A

Banneth, *a Blessing.*

Bar, *the top,* or *summit.*

Bara, *Bread*; bara heb gwèl, *unleavened Bread.*

Barbur, *a Barber*; W. *Cneifiwr,* id.

Bardh, *a Mimic*; *Scoffer*; barz, Ar. writ also, barth.

Barev, *a Beard*; id. Lh.

Barf, & Baref, *a Beard.*

Barfufy, *Codfishes*; pl. from Barvàs, *a Cod.*

Barges, & bargos, *a Kite.*

Bargidnyas, *did bargain*; dho bargidnias, *to confent*; *agree.* Lh.

Barh, & bara, *with*; barh an dzhei, *with them.*

Baris, *readily*; paris, id.

Barliz, *Barley*; W. id. Lh.

Barlen, *the Lap,* or *Bofom.*

Barn, *to judge.*

Barner, *a Judge.*

Bart, *a Side*; *a Scoffer*; warbarth, *altogether.*

Barri, *to divide*; debarra, *to feparate.*

Barth-hirgron, *a Trumpeter.*

Basdhour, *a Ford,* or *Pass over the Water.*

Basghed, W. & C. *a Basket*; Basket-dorn, C. *a Hand-basket.* Lh.

Bastord, *a Bastard*; pl. besterd. Sic W. & A. & Ir.

Bat, *Money.*

Bâth, *Coin*; *Money.* Lh.

Bather, *a Coiner*; *a Banker*; gwas bathor, *ailigent, a monied man.*

Bathon, & bathyn, *a Bafon.*

Battiz, *Staves.*

Baye, *to kifs.*

Baz, *a Pole,* or *Staff.*

B E

Be, *he hath been.*

Bealtine, *Fires lighted to Belus.* Ir. N. B. The Cornish for Fire is Tan; but to tine, or light a a Fire, is still used in Cornwall, unde Bartine, *the fiery top,* i. e. *the hill of Fires.*

Beazen, beaze, beazenz, *we, ye, they had been.* V.

Beazez, *thou hadst been*; beaze, *he had been.*

Beb, *every one*; pub, id.

Bech, *a Voyage.* Ar.

Bechye, *to thrust.* V.

Bederow, *Prayers.*

Bedh, & Bez, *be thou.*

Bedh, *a Grave*; pl. bedhîow, bethow, id.

Bedhav, *I will be*; bedhi, byd, *thou, he will be.*

Bedhez, boez, bìz, *let it be.*

Bedhon, bedhoh, bedhanz, *we,*

B E

ye, they will be; *let us be,* or *be ye.*

Bedhon, bezen, *we should be.*

Bedhe, beze, *he should be.*

Bedhiz, beiz, *thou should'st be.*

Bedhynz, bezenz, benz, *they should be.*

Bedewen, *the Poplar Tree.*

Bedhigla, *to bellow like an Ox.*

Bedho, & bedewen, *a Birch Tree*; pl. behu.

Bedidio, *to baptize.*

Bednath, & benath, *a Blessing.*

Bednuaaz, *Madam*; pro benenvâz.

Bedzhinidia, *a Christening*; *baptifm.*

Bedzidvaen, *a Font,* i. e. *a stone for baptizing.*

Befer, *a Beaver*; *Animal.*

Beghan, bean, bîan, *little*; vighan, id.

Beghas, *a Sin*; peghas, id.

Bêgel, *the Navel*; it. *a Bofs.*

Begol, *a Shepherd*; bizel, id.

Bein, *I should be.*

Beifder, *a Window.*

Bel, *long*; *far*; vel, & velha, id. o bel, *afar off.*

Belee, *a Priest*; pl. belein. Ar.

Belender, *a Miller.*

Beler, *Creffes,* i. e. *the Herb Carifta.*

Belgar, *the calf of the Leg.*

Belyny (velyny, id.), *railing*; *malice.*

Belin, *a Mill*; velin, id.

Ben, *bended*; *a Head,* for pen.

Bena, *to cut.* Ar.

Benary, *hourly*; *continually.*

Benans, *Penance.*

Beneas, *banned*; viz. in the Church; quafi benidnias, *confented*; *agreed.*

Benegys, *blessed.*

Benen, *a Woman*; pl. benenas, & ez.

Benen-vat, *a Matron.*

Benen-rid, *Female.*

Benen- nowydh, *a Bride.*

Beneuas, *an Awl*; beneuez, id. Lh.

Benidnia, *to confent.*

Benk, *a Bench*; fkân, Ar. id.

Bennak, *foever,* piua bennak, *whofoever*; pandra bennak, *whatfoever.*

Benthygio, *to borrow.*

Beol, *a Trough,* or *Manger.* Ar.

Bêr, *a Spit.*

Ber, & berr, *short*; beranal, *a Shortness of Breath.*

Bera (en bera), *within.*

Bera, *to drop*; *slide*; *flow.* Ar.

Berges, *a Citizen.*

Bern, *a Heap*; *a Rick,* viz. of *Hay,* or *Corn.*

Berna, *to buy*; perna, id.

B E

Bernigan, *a Limpet*; Lh. pl. breunik, id.

Berri, *Fatness.*

Berthog, *rich.*

Bers, *Defence.* Ar.

Berthuan, *a Jay*; *a Magpye.*

Bes, *but*; *yet.*

Bes, f. for bofs, as res for ros.

Befadow, *Prayers.*

Befga (for bifgueth), *never*; *ever.*

Befgan, *a Thimble.*

Befl, *Mufcles*; it. Gall, *bitterness.* Lh.

Best, *Mofs*; ne vedn nevra kuntl best, *will never gather Mofs.*

Befte, *thou hadst been.*

Beftyll, Gall; *Bitterness.*

Befy, *to intreat*; V. (pify, id.) *needful.*

Betan urma, *hitherto.*

Betegyns, & betygons, *neverthelefs.*

Bethens, *be*; *let him be.*

Beu, *alive*; (biu, & bewe, id.) beua, *to live*; na illy beu, *could not live.*

Beunans (veunas, bounaz, id.) *Life.*

Beva te, & bethys, *be thou.*

Beven, *the hem of a Garment.* Ar.

Beuk, *Cow*; beugh, or biuh, pl.

Beuzet, *drowned.* Ar. See bidhyz.

Beuzi, Ar. *to dip,* or *drown.*

Beyn, *Pain*; plr beynis.

Bez, *a Finger,* or *Toe*; it. *but. yet.* pl. byzias.

Bezau, *a Ring.*

Bezo, *a little Hoop, Circle,* or *Wheel.*

Beze, beuch, bedhec, bezech, *ye should be.*

Bezl, *the Gall.* Lh. it. *a Mufcle Shell.* Lh. alias, mefklen.

B I

Bideven, *a Hawk*; Bydhin, id. Lh. Kryffal, faucan, id.

Bidhen, *a Meadow.* Lh.

Bidhyz, *drowned.*

Bidn, *against*; *towards.*

Bidnepein, *a Hawk*; *a Crane.*

Bidzheon, *a Dunghill.*

Bigel, *the Navel*; begel, id.

Bylien, *a Pebble.*

Bilwg, *a hedging Bill*; W. gwddi, id.

Bindorn, *a Hall,* or *Refectory.*

Bis, *a Finger*; bez, id. pl. befs.

Bifgueh, *perpetual*; *conftant.*

Bifou, *a Ring*; pro bezau.

Biftel, *the Gall.*

Biftruit, *a Toe*; i. e. *Finger of the Foot.*

Bithen, *a Meadow*; bedhein, id.

Biu

B I

Biu en lagat, *the Pupil of the Eye.*

Biz, *there will be*; biz reiz dhodho, *he will be obliged*; viz. *there will be a necessity for him.*

Bix, *the Box Plant.* Mod. C.

B L

Blaidh, *a Wolf.* W.

Blaguro, *to branch out.*

Blaz, *Taste.* Ar.

Bledhan, *the Year*; pl. blethaniou, blidhen, id.

Bledhîan, *a Flower*; pl. blegyow (bledzhan, id.)

Blegadou, *things agreeing.*

Bleit, a *Wolf*; bleiddie, blaidh, id.

Blek, *pleasant.* Ar. blific, id.

Blem, *pale*; *wan.* Ar.

Bleû, *Hair*; bleuak, *hairy*, gols, id.

Bleu, *a Parish*; mui vel ol an bleu, *more than all the Parish*, bleu, id.

Bleuak, *rough*; *prickly*; *unpleasant.* Lh.

Bleûenlagat, *the Eyelid*, viz. *Hair on the Eye.*

Bleuynpen, *the Hair of the Head.*

Bleut, *Meal.* Ar.

Blêz, *Meal*; blez fin, *fine flour*; it. *Powder*; *Sawdust.* Lh.

Blipen, or bliwen, *the Year.*

Blith, *Milk*; W. *that hath Milk.*

Bloaz, *the Year.*

Blodeno, *to blossom*; bloden, *a Flower.*

Bloeddio, *to bawl,* or *cry.*

Bloesy, *a Stammerer.*

Blonek, *Fatness*; *Grease*; *tallow*; Ar. Bloanek.

Blonet, id. it. *Fat*; *Tallow.*

Blot, *Meal*; *soft*; *tender.* Ar.

Blou, blew; Glaf. id.

Blythen, *Blows*; bluthen, *to beat.*

Blyzen, id. yn blyzen, *with blows.*

B O

Bo, *thee*; a pr. *is,* V. *he may be.*

Boayok, *a Parasite*; bohauok, id. bowhoc, & bauhoc, id. Cott.

Boas, *Custom*; *Fashion.* Ar.

Bod, *a Den,* or *Dwelling.*

Bodn, *the Teat,* or *Nipple*; bron id. tidi, id.

Bodo (G. bodun, profundum), *deep.*

Body-guerni, *a Buzzard.*

Bogan, *the corner of a Sack,* or *Bag.*

Boghan, *little.* See bychan, & vîan.

Bôh (bock, bok), *a Cheek.* pl. Byhou; bôch, W. & Ar. id.

B O

Bohatna, *the smaller*; from bohan, compar. benna, & bohatna, & bohadna.

Bohosak, *poor,* pl. bohosogyon.

Bolder, Qu. 'tis boldering weather, i. e. lowring, inclinable to Thunder.

Bolenegeth, *the Will.*

Bolee, *a Calve's House*; qua. bodleau.

Bolla, *a drinking Cup*; *Intrenchment.* T. T. *A Bowl*; Skala, id. Lh.

Bonas, *that there was*; *may be.* V.

Boncyff, *a Block*; *a Stem of a Tree.*

Bondhat, *a Circle*; Spira.

Bom, *a Bank,* or *Causeway.* Ar.

Bonez (Poz, id.), *to be.*

Bora, *a Boar*; baedh, id.

Bor, *fat.*

Bord, *a Border.*

Bore (y bore), *betimes*; y fore, id.

Boregeth, *on a Morning.*

Boren frwyd, *a Breakfast.*

Bareles, *the Herb Cumfry.*

Boreys, *that it was*; a comp.

Borsach, *to boast*; Frostis, W id.

Bos (boz, id.), *but*; *he*; ha bos, *and that he*; *is,* f.

Boseias-triez, *Toes of the Foot*; bozias, *Fingers.*

Bos, *a House.*

Bosse, *to lean*; bosse y bên, *to lean his Head.*

Bothan, *a bump*; or *bunch.*

Bothell, *a Blister.*

Bothak, *a Bream Fish.*

Bothas, *bore*; V. borthas, id.

Bothur, *deaf*; it. bothack, id. Gw.

Bottaler, *a Tankard-bearer.* Lh.

Bottas, *a Boat.*

Bounder, *common Pasture*; as, park an vounder, *the Field of Pasture*; bounder tre, *a Village,* or *Town,* Lh.

Bouch, *a he Goat*; byk, id.

Boucq, *soft*; Ir. *a Bog.*

Boudzhi, *a Cow-house*; (a comp.) *a Fold*; Lh. boudzhe de vas, *a Sheep-fold.* Lh.

Bouesua, *Rest*; ny a bouez, *he will rest.* V.

Bouët, *Meat*; Ar. Ir. biath, id.

Bouin, *Beef.*

Bounaz, *Life.* Lh.

Bouperic, *the Hoop Bird.*

Bowesas, *rested*; my re bowesas, *I rested.*

Bows (Pows, id.), *a Coat.*

Boynedh, *daily.*

Boys, *Meat*; buz, buyd, & bos, id.

Bozzorrez, *to sing after others.*

Boz, *to be*; boz talvez, *to be able.* Lh.

B R

Brae, W. *Colliculus*; bre, or brêh, id. pl. breon. *Mons*; *Collis.*

Brâg, *Malt.*

Brakat (bregaud, id.), *Metheglin.*

Bram, *Ventris crepitus.* Ar. Brabm.

Brân, *a Crow*; bran vrâz, or marvrân, *a Raven.*

Brandre, *a Rook*; (a comp.) viz. *a Town-crow*; Frau, id.

Brandzha, *a Neck*; y vedn trehe gyv brandzha, *he'll break your Neck.*

Brandzhian, *the Gullet,* or *Throat*; brangain, id.

Braôzder, *Greatness*; mourder, id.

Brâs, & braôn, *gross*; *great*; brâz, id. *cruel*; *outrageous*; brafa, *greatest*; braôz-oberyz, *magnificent*; *noble.*

Broza, *greater.*

Brath, *a Mastiff*; brath kei, *a Mastiff Dog.*

Brawd, *a Brother.*

Brawdoliath, *Brotherhood*; a brawder, *Broth.*

Brawan, *Brawn*; bahed kyg, id. viz. *Boar Flesh.*

Brechol, *a Sleeve*; brohal, id.

Bredar, *while*; *broad*; *a Brother*; pl. brederi.

Brederys, *bethought himself*; prederys, id.

Bredion, *a boiling*; coctio.

Bref, *a Serpent*; hagar bref, *a foul Serpent*; prev, id.

Breferud (brefu, id.), *to bleat like a Sheep.*

Brefusy, *Prophets.*

Brêg, *a Breach*; *Seizure.*

Bregaud, *Hydromel*; *Mead.*

Bregeth, *preached.* V.

Bregowthys (cum a præf.), *thou preachest.*

Brê, *a Hill*; pl. breon. Dav.

Brêh, *an Arm*; pl. breas, or brehs.

Brein, brenn, brennyn, *supreme, Royal.* R. Ar. *Futidus.*

Breinaff, *I rot, stink.* Ar.

Breily, *a Rose*; breilu, id. and *Primrose.*

Brelyr, *a Baron.* Qu. breyr, id. Lh. ac pot. Qua. brê wyr, *a Man that lives high.*

Breman, *now*; *already*; *at length.*

Brennik, *a Limpet.*

Brennyat, *a Fortress*; *a Pilot.*

Brenmat, *a Boatswain.*

Brenol, Lh. *brittle*; Qu. an non, id. ac brettol.

Brerthil, *a Mullet.*

Bres, *Judgment.*

Bresel, *War.* Ar.

Breson, *a Prison.*

Bresq,

BR

Brefq, *brittle.* Ar.

Breffel, *Argument ; Dispute.*

Breft, *Brass.* Lh.

Brefys, *questioned.*

Brefych, *a Cabbage.*

Brethal, *a Mackerel ; a bryth, streaked;* brethil, id. Lh.

Brettol, *brittle.*

Breva, *to waste.* V. Ar.

Breuha, *Food.*

Beur, *Brother ;* Ir. brathair. W. Braud.

Breuyonen, *a Crumb of any thing;* Ar. brienen, id.

Breyr, *a Baron.* See brelyr.

Brêz, *the Mind.* Lh.

Brezeler, *warlike.*

Brezonnek, *Armorique,* viz. *Bretonique.*

Brianfen, *the Throats.*

Bridzhan, *to boil, seeth ;* brudziar, id.

Brienen, *a Crumb.* Ar.

Brihi, *Malt-liquor ;* gara brihi, *to brew.*

Bris, *a Berry.* Ar.

Brith, & bruit, *various;* i. e. *of different Colours ;* Cott. bryth, id. pl. brithion.

Britty, vel abritty, *a Mackerel;* from brit, *speckled,* or *spotted.* Lh.

Brôch, *a Badger ;* Ar. *a Vessel of Clay,* or *Wood ; Bank of a River ;* Gale. it. *a Yew-tree.* Mod.

Broche, *a Buckle, Clasp,* or *Bracelet.*

Brochi, *cruel; unruly.*

Broden, *the Lungs.*

Brodit, *President of a Country ; Lord lieutenant.* Lh.

Broen, *a Rush ;* broenek, *rushy.* Ar.

Brohal, *a Sleeve ;* brechol, id.

Brohalek, *having Sleeves.*

Bron (brun & brodn, id.), *Breast,* or *Pap ; a Mill-stone.*

Bronkis, *brought ; led ;* hombronkyas, *they led.*

Bronter (praunter, id), *a Priest.*

Bros, *a Sting,* or *Prickle ;* inde f brufs, *Furse-dust.*

Brou, *a Coast ; an Edge ;* brou an môr, *the Sea Coast ;* it. *a Mill.* Ar. bro, *a Country.*

Brouion (broufian, id.), pl. breyonen, *Crumbs.*

Brouda, *to sting ; nettle.*

Broufta, *to bud.*

Broza, *greater ;* broz for brâz.

Brudnyan, *Gerts.* Gw.

Brudzhiaz, *boiled ;* fod. Lh.

Bruha, *Victuals ; Provision.* Lh.

Brunnen, *a Bull-rush.* Lh.

Brufs, *Furse-dust.*

Brychan, *a Bull-rush.*

Brydnan (brydn, id.), *a Rush.*

BR

Bry, *Clay ; Earth.*

Brych, *a Blot,* or *Blur.*

Bryn, *a Hillock ;* brine, id. W. *a Hill,* or *Cliff;* brynkyn, W. id.

Brys, *Account ;* den a brys, *a Man of Account, of Council.*

Bryth, *spotted ; speckled.* Lh.

BU

Bu (Ar. Byuh, Ir. bo), *an Ox,* or *Cow.*

Buanegez, *Madness ;* Ir. banegas, *Anger.*

Bubbuen, *a Botch,* or *Boil.* Ar.

Bucellat, *to low; bellow.* Ar.

Buddiol yw, *it behoveth.*

Budgeth andour, *the face of the deep.*

Budh, *Conquest.*

Budicaul (bydhygol, id), *victorious.*

Buel, *he that.*

Bugale, *a little Boy.* Ar.

Bugel, *a Shepherd.*

Buhan, *quick ; swift ;* byhan, *soon.*

Bûl, *an Axe.*

Bulch (W.), *a Passage ;* as, bulch Guortigern, *Vortigern's Passage.*

Bulhorn, *a Shell-snail.*

Bulligan, *an Angle-touch,* or *Angle-worm.*

Bunta, *to push,* or *jolt against.* Ar.

Burman, *Yest,* or *Barm.* W. Swyf.

Burzut, *a Wonder.* Ar.

Buttein, *a Bawd;* ind. puttendy, *a Bawdy-house.*

Buth, *a Cottage.*

Bûyd, *Food;* buit, id. bûz, id.

Buyth, *a House ; a Cottage ;* veth, id.

Bûz, *eating ; a Bait for Fish or Birds ; but ;* bes, id.

Buzuguen, *a Ground-worm ; a Grub ;* pl. buzug.

BY

Byan (ni vian, id.), *we have been.*

Byck, *a Buck Goat.* W. Ewyg, id. boch, id.

Byddin, *a Band,* viz. *a Company.*

Bydh, *he will be.*

Byhan, *soon.*

Bydredhy, W. *to defile ; pollute,* or *corrupt.*

Byghel nôs, Ar. *a Hobgoblin, a Bugbear.* Lh.

Bym, *I have been.*

Byn an lugat, *the Ball of the Eye.*

Bynk, *a Stroke ; a Blow ; a Blast,* or *Puff.* Lh. Bank, id.

Bynkiar, *a Cooper.*

BY

Bynollan, *a Beefom ; Broom.*

Byoh (huei a vyôh, id.), *ye have been.*

Byonz, *they have been.*

Bypur, *hourly ; continually;* qua. peb ur.

Byr, *brief ; short ;* cuttu, id.

Byr-luan, *the Morning Star.*

Byrdruethwd (W. f.), *a Breviary ; a Mass-book.*

Byrla, *to embrace.*

Bys, *even ;* bis, id.

Bys pan, *then ; until.*

Byfma (Bys, id), *this World ;* beis, & beaz, id.

Bys (abys, id.), *to beseech ;* ny abys, *we do beseech.*

Byte (vyte, id.), *Pity.*

Byth queth, *never ; ever ;* na byth, or vyth, *never; nothing.*

Bythak, *deaf;* id. ac bothak.

Bytheirio, *to belch.*

Byuh, *a Cow,* or *Ox.*

Byu an lagat, *the Ball,* or *Apple of the Eye.*

Byz, *but.* Lh.

Byzias, *the Fingers.*

C.

Note, that many Words placed under C, by some Authors are begun by K, or G, by others, & vice versa ; " for K we use C." Hum. Lhuyd Brev. C, for good sound, is turned into G, Ch, and into N G H. Hum. Lh. p. 3.

CABAN, *a little House.* Ir. Ar. Cabell, *a Hood.* Ar.

Cabin Lygeazhah, *Squint eyed.* Lh.

Cabin thavas, *a Rainbow.*

Cablas (Cublas, id.), *cavilled; quarrelled ;* fcable, id.

Cabledd, *Blasphemy;* Serthed. id.

Caboun, *a Capon.* Ar.

Cabydul, *a Chapter.*

Câd, *an Army.* R. *a Battle.*

Cad, *any Liquor.*

Cadair, *a Chair.* Ar. Cador, id.

Cadarnle, *a Bullwark ;* Cadernid.

Cadr, *strong.*

Caduit. Cott. Qu. f. Cadwyr, *a Soldier.*

Cadzhel, vulgo Cagel, *a Castle,* as Roscadzhel, Boscadzhel — Kaftelh. id.

Caer, *a City; a walled Town.* Ar. Ceer, & C. Geer.

Caethiwed; *Bondage ; Slavery ;* Caeth, *fold.* Gurkaeth, *a Bond-slave,* Lh.

Cafor, *Brucus.* Cott. Qu.

Cafos, *found;* Cafons, *we find ;* gafe, *I find.*

Cafudhd,

CA

Cafudhd, *a Stile; a Stone Stile.*
W.

Cagal, *Rubbiſh; Rubble; Dirt; Sheep-Dung.*

Cahout, *Wealth; Riches.* Ar.

Caid, *a Servant;* Caid-pinid, *a Slave.*

Caihir, Ir. Caer, Ar. *Fair; Pretty.*

Caillar, *Dirt; Mire.* Ar.

Caines, *a Nun.*

Caithes, *a Maid Servant.*

Câith, *a Servant; a Slave.*

Cal, *cunning; lean.*

Cala, *Straw; Stubble.* Ar. Colo, id. Calav. id.

Cale. Ar. *A Wood.* Ir. Coill; C. Kelli, id.

Caleh, *Chalk.*

Callo (Calle, id.), *might; could.*

Callys (Calys, Calliſh & Cals, id.), *hard; ſmart.*

Cals, *many; much* Ar.

Calter, *a Kettle;* Kalhtor, id.

Cam, *crooked; evil;* Pl. camou. Iriſh, Caum.

Camen, *ſo.*

Camgyhuddo, *to belye one.*

Camhinſic, *injurious; croſs; unjuſt.*

Camhilik, id. Cott.

Camniuet, *a Bow.*

Cams, *a Surplice.*

Canaſow, *Meſſengers; Apoſtles.* Ar. Cannat, *a Meſſenger.*

Cane, *to crow; or ſing;* Can. Ar. *a Song.*

Canego, *Bogs.*

Canel, *a Pipe of Wood to draw off Liquor;* Tap an canel, *the Pipe and it's Peg;* quaſ. à canalis, *a Chanel or Conduit,* ut & Gannel.

Caniad, *a Ballad.*

Cann, *the full Moon.*

Cannu, *to whiten, or blanch.*

Canores, *a ſinging Woman.*

Cans, *a Hundred.*

Canſgur, *a Wife; any Female.*

Canſrueg (Canſfreg, id.), *a Huſband.*

Cantrev, *a hundred; becauſe it contained formerly 100 villages.*

Cantulbren, *a Candleſtick.*

Cantuil, *a Candle.* P. Cyntulu.

Caouen, *an Owl.* Ar.

Caougant, *abundant; very much.*

Car, *a Friend.*

Câr, *a Chariot;* R. ind. Caradoc.

Capt, *of Chariots; a Charioteer;* Kyncâr, id.

Cara, *as; ſicut; it. to Love.*

Caradow, *beloved.*

Carayos, *a Kinſman.*

Carchur (Carchurdy, id.), *a Bridewell.*

CA

Carchar. Ar. *a Priſon.*

Carder, *beautiful; comely.*

Cardotta, *to beg;* Cardottin, *a Beggar.*

Cariad, *Benevolence.*

Carn, *a Heap of Rocks; a high Rock.* Pl. Carnow.

Carnſow, *Cliffs.*

Carogos, *a Kinſman.*

Carou (Lh. Karo), *a Deer;* Caruu, id. Cott.

Carru, *a Plow.* Car.

Carreg, *a Rock;* Pl. Cerigi; as, Cerigi Drudion; *Columnulæ Druidum.*

Carthu, *to clear; purge.*

Cath, *a Cat.*

Caſaus, *odious.* Ar.

Caſadou, *Countenance; ill-favoured; withered.*

Caſat, *any Veſſel.*

Caſmai, *an Ornament.*

Cau, *to ſhut; or incloſe.* R.

Cauen, *an Owl.*

Caul, *Gruel; Pottage; Cole.*

Caur-march, *a Camel.*

Caus, *Cheeſe.*

Cawg, *a Baſon.*

Cawr (Gaur, id.), *a Gyant.*

Cazau (Caſſec, id.), *a Mare.*

CE

Ceany, *to ſup.*

Ceard, *or* Keard, *an Artificer.*

Ceg, *a Mouth; or Throat.*

Ceibal, *a Barge.*

Cel, *or* Cil. Ir. *a Church, or Cell.*

Ceirſio, *to wind, turn, or twiſt.*

Cendel, *fine Linen.*

Cerig, *Stones, or Circles;* Crig, Crug, id.

Ceriſs, *loweſt;* Pul-keriſs, *loweſt Stream.* R.

Cern, *a Turn; Circle.* Ar.

Ceulan, *Bank of a River;* ind. Glan. f.

Cevn, *a Ridge, or Bank.*

Centowen (Contuen, id.), *a Gnat.*

CH

Chabenrit, *a Torrent.*

Chaden, *a Chain.*

Chain, *a Carrion.* Ar.

Charnel, *a Place where dead Bodies are laid.* Ar.

Chaſty, *to Chaſtiſe.*

Chaſy, *to chaſe;* Chaeyes, *chaced.*

Cheber, *Vulva.*

Chechys, *taken.*

Chee *thou;* ge *(erron. for* chee*),* id.

Cheſals, *a Limb; artus.*

Cheſindoc, *omnipotent.* Cott.

CH

Chein, *the back;* Kein, id.

Chelioc guit (or Ghod), *a Gander.*

Chelioc, *a Cock.*

Chemel, *to tarry.* Ar.

Chen, *a Cauſe.*

Cheniat, *a Singer.*

Chereor, *a Cobler; a Shoemaker.*

Cherhit, *a Heron;* Keridh, id.

Cheritè, *Dearneſs, Charity.* Ger. id.

Cherniat, *a Player on the Horn.*

Cheſpar, *Conjux.*

Chetua, *a Meeting; Convention.*

Chever, *to; unto;* chever tyller, *unto the Place.*

Chic (Kyg, id.), *Fleſh.*

Chil, *the Neck.*

Choantek, A. *greedy; covetous;* Lh. W. Chuannog, id.

Choar, *Siſter.*

Choareil (Ir. Corgas), *Lent.* Ar.

Choarion, *ſports;* ab Huare.

Choch-dibi, *a Cymbal.*

Chom, *to inhabit.* Ar.

Chuervan, *a Whirling.* Lh. 172.
y Chugfyons, *they bethought.*

Chuillioc, *an Augur.*

Chuillioges, *a Witch,* or *She-diviner.*

Chuivian, *to fly away;* Lh. 215.

Churiſigen, *a Bladder; a Bliſter;* Guzigan, id.

Chuyth, *Wind;* Lh. 122.

Chyffar, *a Bargain;* yn chaffar, *in the Bargain.*

CI

Cib, *a Shell; a Cabinet.*

Cin. Ar. *a Swan.*

Cinkla, *to caſt.* Ar.

Ciſt, *a Cheſt.*

CL

Claatgueli, *Bolſters; fulcra.* L.

Clabitter, *a Bittern.*

Claff, *ſick;* Clevys; Clevas; Clef, Claf, id. Pl. Clevion. Klav. id.

Clafhorer, *a Leper.*

Clafn, *the Blade of a Sword.*

Claiar, *warm.*

Clamderys, *fainted.* V. *Was in Want.*

Clao, *an Inſtrument, or Iron Tool.*

Clapier, *to ſpeak;* clapier Kernuak, *to ſpeak Corniſh.*

Claſq, *to gather; look for; beg.* Ar.

Clathoree, *fallen; lapſus.*

Clauſt (Cloiſt, id.), *a Bar; Incloſure.*

Clawd (Kled, id.), *a Dyke; a Foſs;* Clawd Offa, *Offa's Dyke.*

Clecha, *a Eell-place;* Lucar. id.
Clechic,

C L.

Clechic, *a little Bell; a Clock, or a Bell.*

Cleddif, *a Belt.*

Cledr, *a Rafter.*

Clehe, *Ice.*

Cleis, *A Chalk.* Lh.

Clemmow, *Clement; a Man's Name.*

Clenniaw, *a Hip, or Thigh.*

Clefkher, *the Skin of the Leg.*

Clethe, *a Sword, a Knife, a Dagger.* Kledheid.

Cleuth, *a Ditch.*

Clenzen, *a Tree.* Ar.

Clewet, *a Distemper, or Sickness.*

Clewo (Glewo, id.), *to hear;* Clewys, *heard.*

Clicket, *Clapper of a Bell; Latch of a Door.*

Clithio, *to bait, or entice.*

Clo (Cleg, Clog, Cluid, id.), *a fort of hard Stone, between a Moor stone and a Marble.*

Clocen, *a Shell;* Clocen ui, *an Egg Shell.* Ar.

Cloch, *a Bell;* Kloh, id.

Cloch-muer (or Maur), *a great Bell.*

Clode, *Praise; Fame* (Klos. Ir. Cloth); Klod, id. Klodvaur. W. *a famous Man.*

Clôf, *Lame; maimed.*

Clo-gris, *the grey Clo;* Clo-du, *the black Clo.* Hals.

Cloireg, *a Clergyman.*

Clone (Cluain. id.), *a Cave, or Den.* Ir. (ind. f. Treglone, in Cornwall; *the Town of Caves; or near the Cave*), it. *a Park.* Lh.

Clor, *neatness;* yn clor, *neatly.*

Clorian, *a Pair of Scales;* Mantôl. id.

Clot-boffan, *a Trype.* Gw.

Clouar, *warm.* Ar.

Cluddias, *a Bar, or Hinderance.*

Cluddu, *to bury.*

Clugea, *to perch; or sit.* Ar. inde *to cluck as a Hen going to sit.*

Cluit, *Breast.*

Clymmu, *to buckle.*

Clynk, *to swallow.* Qu.

C N

Cnil (Cnill Clil, id.), *a passing Bell.*

Cnithio, *to strike.*

Cnoi, *to bite, or gnaw.*

C O

Coant. Ar. *fair; handsome.*

Coar, *wax.* Ir. Ceir.

Cob, dho Cob, *to break, or bruise.*

Cobber, *a Bruiser of Tin.*

Coch, *Purple;* Coccus, *Red* (Ar. Merda.);

C O

Codgroen, *a Budget.*

Codnabreh, *the Arm-wrist.*

Codnatale, *the Forehead.*

Coed, W. *a Wood;* Cos & Kûz, id.

Coegdale, *purblind.*

Cof, cov. See kov, kovys.

Coff, *a Belly.* Ar.

Cofgurhehel, *Utensils.*

Coggas, *a Priest.*

Coifinel, *Running Betony; wild Thyme.*

Coillinhat, *the herb Angelica.*

Coir, *Wax.*

Coit. See Koit (& Kûz, id.); *a Wood.*

Col (Colin, Conyn, id.) *Sting of a Bee.*

Colewuys, *heard;* glavis, T. T. id.

Côlbran, *fierce; Lightning.*

Colhen, *a Hazel.*

Colhlwyn, *a Grove of Hazel.*

Coll, *Loss;* Coll restoua, *Loss beset him.*

Collet, *a forlorn; a lost Person; perditus;* à Kellye, *to lose;* it. *Loss.*

Collon (Colan, id.), *a Heart.*

Colmas, *bound.*

Colmen (Pl. Colmenou). *a Knot.*

Colmur, *a Binder.* Pl. Colmurian.

Colmye, *to bind.*

Coloin, *a Whelp.*

Coltel, *a Penknife; an engraving Tool.*

Colter, *the Plow-knife.*

Colwiden, *a Hazel Tree.*

Colyd, *a Beard of Corn.*

Colyek, *a Cock;* Keilliog, id.

Comer, *Pride;* Lh. 215.

Comiska, *Stirring;* Gw.

Commaër, *a Godmother.*

Commol, *a Cloud; Darkness.* Ar.

Compez, *right; even;* tha geil compez, *to do right;* N'un compez, *the plain, even Downs.*

Compofter, *Form,* heb compofter, *without Form.*

Conerioc, *mad; raving; foolish.*

Conna, *the Neck;* codna, vulg. id.

Connar, *Rage; Fury.* Ar. it. C.

Contreva, *to dwell; commoror.*

Contrevac, *a Neighbour; one of the same Town.*

Contowen, *a Gnatt.*

Conze, *Matrix.* Gw.

Coom (cwmm, id.), *a Valley.*

Coone, *Sugar.* Gw.

Coot (kooth, id.), *a Beating; to give one his Coot; i. e. his Beating.*

Coppa, *the Top, or Summit.*

Côr (cor, id.), *Ale; Manner;*

C O

war nep cor, *in any Manner.*

Cor, *a Dwarf;* Ar. cornandon, & corrig, id.

Corden, *a Pipe.*

Corf, *a Body; a dead Body;* pl. corfou.

Corfil, *a little Body.*

Corgwenyn, *Bees-wax.*

Corn, *a Horn.*

Cornbrican, *a Pipe; Fistula;* tolcorn, id.

Cornwyd, *a Bile, or Sore;* gweli, id.

Corol, Ar. *a Dance;* corolli, *to dance.*

Cors, *a Place full of small Wood; a Den; a Bog;* figlen, id.

Corfen, *a Reed; a Pipe.* Ar.

Corsfruynen, *a Bull-rush.*

Coruf, *Beer;* coref, id.

Côs, *a Wood.*

Coske, *Sleep; sleeping.*

Coste, *the Herb called Zedoary.*

Coth, *old;* den coth, *an old Man.*

Cothas, *to find.*

Cothas (pro wothas), *knowest; sufferest; feelest; findest.*

Cothewell, *he felt.*

Cothys, *fallen;* gothys, id.

Couat, *a Shower; a Cloud.*

Coueno, *Swelling; Inflammation.* Ar.

Covi, *extreme Heat of the Sun.* Ar.

Coulm, *a Pidgeon.*

Couls, *Time.* Ar.

Coûn, *Memory.* Ar.

Couniel, *a Rabbit.*

Couz, *speak thou.*

Coweidliuer, *Glove.*

Cowethas, *to lie down.*

Cowethe, *a Companion.*

Cowethys, *acquainted.*

Cowlas, *a Bay of Building.*

Cowlez, *four;* leath cowlez, *four milk.*

Coyntis, *wrought.* V.

Coz, *old;* cozni, *old Age;* id. ac Coth.

C R

Craf, *covetous;* kraff, id.

Crakye (crakya, id), *to break.*

Craouen, *Nuts.*

Crapat, *to anchor.* Ar.

Crafa, *to dry.* Ar.

Creader, *a Creator.* Ar. Crouer, id.

Crech, *high;* crechen, *a little Hill.* Ar.

Crêd, *Belief;* credzhi, id. Lh.

Cref, *strong; abundant;* crif, id. Cott.

Creft, *Art;* creftor, *Artifex,* Ib.

Creft, & creftor, id. Qu.

Creg, *Stammerer.*

Cregaud, *Hydromel.* Qu.

Cregys,

CR

Cregys, *hanged*; gregy, *to hang.*
Cregyans, *Faith.*
Crehyllys, *crushed.*
Creiz, *Mud*; *Dirt.* Ar.
Cren (kern, id.), *round*; Ir. cruin, id. Ib.
Crene, *trembling*; crenna, *to tremble.*
Cres, *a Garment*; Ar. pl. cresiou.
Creven, *a Crust.*
Creulon, *barbarous.*
Crez, *the middle*; Ar. creis, id.
Crib, *a Comb*; criban, id. (Ir. Cir.)
Criedzy, *to believe.*
Crin, *dry.*
Criz, *cruel*; crizder, *Cruelty.* Ar.
Crob, Qu. tre, an crob, Qu.
Crobman, *a Hook*; crobman ithen, *a Furze-hook.* Gw.
Crocadur, *Creatures, created things.*
Crochen, *a Skin*; Ar. C. Croin.
Crochan, *a Pot*, or *Kettle*; crochadn, id.
Crockan, *a Springle.* Gw.
Croider, *a Sieve*; Ar. crouezer, id.
Croin, *the Hide*, or *Skin.* Cott.
Croinoc, *a Land Toad* that frequents the Bushes; Cott. *Rubeta*; cronek, id.
Crois, *a Cross.* Cott.
Cronnys (curnys, curunys, id.), *crowned.*
Cronou, *Thongs.*
Crqueg, *a Gibbet.*
Croum, *crooked*; krum, id. crobm, id.
Crousel, *the Top of a Hill.*
Crou, *a Fold*; crou an devet, *a Sheep Fold*; Crou an gueffer, *a Goat Fold.*
Crow, *utmost*; yn crow, *to the utmost*; it. *Gore*; *Blood.*
Crowethe, *in Bed.*
Crows, *a Cross.*
Cruguel, *a Hillock.* Ar.
Crunckia, *to beat.*
Crunnys (crummys, id.), *stagnated*; *curdled.*
Cruffu, *to broil.*
Crwst, *an Eating between Meals.*
Cryk. See Kryk.

CU

Cudiri, *Hair.*
Cudon, *a Dove.*
Cuen, *a Wedge.* Ar.
Cueny, *Moss*; *Mouldiness*; *Hoariness.* Germ. vinnigh.
Cueth, *Weariness.* See Gweth. it. *short*; as, cuedth anadl, *short Breath.*
Cugol, *a Hood.*
Cugdd, *a Butcher.*
Cuhupudioc, *an Accuser*; cuhu-

CU

thudioc, id.
Cuic, *bleer-eyed*; *one-eyed.*
Cuit, *a Wood.*
Cul, *Lean.*
Culm, *Chaff*; *Straw*; ufion, id.
Cumah, *now.*
Cummyas, *Leave*; ty ary cummyas, *thou shalt give Leave*; kibmiaz, id.
Cûn, *sweet*; *affable.* Ar.
Cunhinfik, *a just man.*
Cuntellet, *an Assembly.*
Cuntullys, *gathered*; cûntle, id.
Cur, *a Cure*; grwa cûr, *do a Cure.*
Curo, *to beat*; *punish*; *bounce*, or *knock.*
Curun ray, *a Diadem.*
Cufcadur, *a Lethargy.*
Cufki, *a Dormitory.*
Cuffin (guffin, id.), *a Kiss.*
Cufual, *soft*; kuzal, id. kyzoleth, *Peace.*
Cufyll, *Advice*; *Counsel*; cuful, id.
Cufulioder, *a Counsellor.*
Cuthens (cuthys, id.), *covered*; Par.
Cwkw, *a Boat*; bhaid, vel baid, id.
Cuyttyn, *short*; *little.* W.
Cûz, *to loiter.*
Cuziat, *a hiding Hole.*
Cwas, *a Shower*, or *Skud of Rain.*

CY

Cyff, *a Block*; *a Stem of a Tree*; boncyff.
Cyffin, *a Boundary.*
Cyfoeth, *Honours*; *Wealth.*
Cyhoeddwr, *a Crier of a Court.*
Cymmun, *a Legacy.*
Cymmuno, *to leave by Will.*
Cynddeiriog, *a Bedlam.*
Cyulym, *swift*; *rapid.*
Cyweithas, *kind*; *courteous.*
Cywelu, *a Bedfellow.*

D.

D is changed into Dh, and N, as, Duw, God, (W.) O Dhuw, out of God; Fynuw, my God. Hum. Lhuyd, pag. 4. Note, that D is not so often radical as T.

D A (dha, & dah, id.), *good.* Da, *thy*; tha, id.
Da, *a Doe.* Cott.
Daal, *a Stock*, or *Family.* Ir.
Daffar, *Conveniencies*; *Furniture.*
Dagel, Qu. unde Tindagel; an a dagh, vel dah, *good*; & hêl, *a Moor.*
Dagrou, *Tears*; δαχϱυ, Gr.
Daiarou, *to bury*; *to interr.*
Dain, *sent*; mi rig dain dythi,

DA

I have sent unto him.
Dal, *worth*; travyth ne dal, *nothing is worth*; it. dark. Lh. E dal, *it should or ought*; Lh. oportet; Lh. rez, id.
Daladur, *a Plane.* Ar.
Dall, *blind*; (tiwal, id.) dallu, *to make blind.*
Dallath, *to begin*; it. *a Beginning.* Lh.
Dalpen, *Top of a Hill.* Ar.
Dalvith, *to requite.*
Dalv, *Palm of the Hand.*
Dama (damma, id.), *a Mother.*
Dama-widen, *a Grandmother.*
Damenys (Danvonys, & tevenes, id.), *sent.*
Dampnys, *to condemn*; thamnys, id.
Dan, & dadn, id. *below*, *inferiour*; (unde ut B.) Danmonii, the Corn. & Dev-men.
Dan, *a Tooth* (danz, pl. denz, id. deins, id.), pl. dannet.
Dans, *an Elephant*; *Ivory.*
Daneuel, *to tell.* Ar.
Danin, *to send.*
Danta, *to bite.*
Daol, *a Cause*; *Suit*, or *Process*; Ar. kein van, id. haul, id.
Daôz, *to come*, or *go.* Lh.
Daphar, *to prepare*, or *provide*; it. *Furniture.*
Dar, *an Oak*; glaftan, & glaftanen, id.
Daradur, *a Doorkeeper.*
Daralla, *a Tale*; *Narration.*
Darat, *a Door*; daras, id.
Dareden, *Lightning*, Ar.
Darken, *inflicted*; warkerd, id.
Darllawydd, *a Brewer.*
Darlow, *to brew.*
Darn, *Pieces*; mil darn, *a thousand Pieces.*
Darniegeal, *to wag*, or *waver.* Ar.
Darrar delkar, *the back Door*, or *postern Gate.* Lh.
Darras, *a Door* (darat, id.), Pl. Darasou; darras rag, *the fore Doors.* Lh.
Daryvas, *Discovery*; *Meaning*;
Daftor, *to yield*; *yielding*; das, *a Father*; a das, *O Father.*
Datguddio, *to bewray a Secret.*
Datheluur, *a Speaker*; *an Orator.*
Dâtho, *to him.*
Dau, *he will come.*
Davaz, *a Sheep*; pl. devez; (davat, & devet, id.)
Davydh, *David.*
Dawns, *a Dance*; guare dauns, *a Ball where many dance.* Lh.
Dayl (dalt, & dolle, id.), *oughtest*; ny dayll, *thou oughtest not.*
Daz, *answers to the Latin* re, as, dazveua, *to revive.*

Daze,

DA

Daze, *a glittering Stone from the Mine.*
Dazprena, *to redeem.*

DE

De, *Day; Yefterday; this Day; it. Thy; as,* de hanno, *thy Name.*
De Jeu, *Thurfday.*
Deas, *fwore;* ef a deas, *he fwore.*
Deag, *Tythe;* Deaug. Ar. id.
Deau, *two.*
Deauon, *Gods;* Deuiou, *id.*
Debar, *down.* See dybour.
Debarn, *a Scab; an Itch.* Ar. debron.
Debarris, *divided; feparated.*
Debm, *to me;* dho debbry, *to eat;* Lh. deori, *id.*
Deder, *Goodnefs.*
Dedh-goil, *Holy-days;* degl, & degol, *id.*
Dedwh, *a Law.*
Dedwyddwęh, *Blifs; Happinefs.*
Deez, *come thou;* à dyvoz, *V. to come.*
Deck, *a Neck-jewel; Monile;* deck, Lh. id.
Defendis, *put out; forbidden.*
Deffry, *foon.*
Dêg, *Ten;* dêg, uar nigans, *Thirty.* Lh.
Deghenzete, *the Day before Yefterday.*
Deglftul, *Epiphany; Twelfth-day.*
De-guenar, *Friday.*
Degylmy, *to untie.*
Degys, *taken; carried;* dregy, id.
Dehen, *Cream.* Gw.
Deheubarth, *the Right Hand Side;* i. e. *the Southern Part, fays Camden.* — *Name of South Wales.* Hum. Lh.
Dehilians, *Forgivenefs.*
Dehou, *South;* i. e. *on the right;* as Gleth, *the left Hand, fignifies North.*
Dehoules, Cott. *Southern Wood.*
De Jeu, *Thurfday.*
Deifkin, *to defcend.* Lh.
Dele, *the Yard of a Ship.*
Delen, *a Leaf.* Pl. deil.
Delin, *Monday.*
Delk, *a Leaf.* Lh.
Dell, *fo; as; by.*
Della, *like;* an della, *likewife; thus;* Lh. an dellana, id.
Dellit, *Merit; defert.* Ar.
Delly, *to hole;* telly, *id.* und. toll, *a Hole.*
Delt, *moift.* Ar.
Delw, *an Image.* R.
Delyou, *Leaf; Leaves.* Ar. &c. Delk.
Demarhar, *Wednefday.*
Demer, *Tuefday.*
Demigou (yn demigou, id.) *particularly.*

DE

Demytho, *to marry.*
Dèn, *a Man;* Pl. dynion, dyn, o deân, id. Cott. Pl. Tiz-Lh.
Den an cloc, *the Bellman; Sexton;* deân deu, *a pious Man.* Lh.
Denater, *unnatural.*
Dentofkor, *a Client.*
Dendle, *to get;* dendle peth, *to get Riches.*
Dendzall, *to bite;* danheddu, & deintio, id.
Denethys, *born; begotten.*
Denevoit, *a Bullock;* denevoid, *a Yearling.*
Denhuêl, *a Servant; a Workman.*
Denjack, *a Hake Fish.*
Dennas, *Drew.* V. dene, id.
Dên nowydh, *a Bridegroom.*
Denfdhellor, *Jaw-teeth.*
Denfhoc dour, *a Pike, or Jack-fish.* Cott.
Denfrag, *the Foreteeth.*
Denfys, *hunger; hungry.*
Denunchut, *a Stranger.*
Denys, *fucked;* tenys, id.
Denythyans, *a Generation.*
Denz klav, *the Tooth-ach.* Lh.
Deoriad, *a Brood of Chickens.*
Deow, *Two.*
Depbro, *eat it;* dibbry, & tibbry, *to eat.*
Dera, *or* tera, *was; did;* dera vî labiria, *I do labour.*
Deragla, *to chide; fcold.*
Dereat, *handfome; decent.* Ar.
Derevas, *lifted up;* deraffas, id.
Dereval, *to build; to hoard up; to ftir up;* as, dho dercual aman, id.
Deriaeth, *a Nourifher, or Bringer-up of any one.* Cott.
Derrez, *by; or through your.*
Derry, *to break.*
Derven, *an Oak;* Ar. dair. Pl. Deru, Ar. id.
Defethys, *ftirred up.*
Defgibl, *a Scholar; Difciple.*
Defimpit, *a Lethargic.*
Defkans, *Skill; Knowledge.* Lh.
Defkîans, *an Ignoramus; a Fool.* Lh.
Defky, *to learn;* dho defge, id. Lh.
Deflam, *an Excufe.*
Defo, *to thee.*
Defpyth, *Vexation; Spite.*
Deftrias, *over;* Deftrias enefou, *over Souls.*
Defty, *to tafte.*
Det (deth, id.), *a Day;* Pl. dethiou; dydh, id. Pl. dydniou.
Dethewys, *chofen.*
Deu, *God;* a Dûe; W. Dyu, id.
Deuas, & dewes, Lh. *Drink.*
Deve, *ought.*

DE

Deveeder, *a choak Sheep.*
Develo, *weak; impotent;* guadn, id. Lh.
Deveras, *dropped.* V. thiveras, id.
Deûergy (Quaf. dour kei), *an Otter.*
Deuefys, *chofen.*
Devethes, *we come; came;* devedhez dre, *brought back again.* Lh.
Devez, *Sheep.* Pl.
Deugh, *come.* V.
Devidhyz, *quenched; choaked;* tegez, Lh. id.
Devra, *a Bofom;* (afcra, id.) a Lap; it. *a Haven.* Lh. 151. Tîr devrak, *a Fen, or Marfh.*
Devys, *grew up.*
Dew (Deo, id.), *God;* Pl. Deuion. See Dû, & Dewou.
Dewerryan, *Drop.*
Dewcth, *an End;* yn deweth, *at laft;* diuedh. Lh. id.
Deuiggans (dowgans, id), *Forty.*
Dewle, *Hands;* thewle, id.
Dewolgow, *Darknefs.*
Dewr, *valiant.* R.
Dewfcol (Dowfcol, id.), *all abroad.*
Dewy, *David;* Landewi, *David's Church.*
Deyow, *Thurfday;* Duyow, id.
Deyfif, *a Petition.* δεησις.
Dez, *to thee;* thys, id.
Dezadarn, *Saturday.*
Dezan (tezan, id.), *a Cake.*
Dezil, *Sunday.*
Dezkryffa, *to diftruft.*

DH

Dh'an, *to the; as far as; to thee.*
Dhanleiah, *at leaft.*
Dhanna, *with;* an golou dhanna, *with the Light.*
Dhedhe (dhedhynz, id.), *to them.*
Dheffa, *to come;* neb a dheffo, *he that fhall come.*
Dhellar, *back;* doz uar dhellar, *to come back;* uar delhar, *behind.*
Dhelledzhaz, *delayed; protracted.*
Dhem, *and* dhebm, dhym, dhymmo, *to me.*
Dheth, *came;* V. it. *unto thy;* as, dheth corf, *unto thy Body.*
Dhiguydha, *to fall;* kuedha, Ar. id.
Dhiu (dhyuch, dhuich, id.), *to you.*
Dhive, *thou comeft.*
Dhiz, *to thee;* dheyz, & dhehî, id.
Dho, *to;* Sign of the Infinitive Mood before Verbs; as, dho dibbry, *to eat.*

Dhodhans,

DH

Dhodha, *unto thy.*

Dho-douria, *to moisten, soak, or water.* Lh.

Dhodhans, *of them; to them.*

Dhodhe (dhydhe, id.), *to, or unto him.*

Dhofergi. See Dourgi.

Dhora, *bring;* mi a dhora, *I will bring.*

Dhoroaz, *brought;* (dhroz, & dhroys, id.)

Dhort, *from;* dhortam, *from me.*

Dhov, *to come;* mî dhove, *I will come.*

Dhy, *thy;* (the, tha, da, thy, id.)

Dhybba, *hither.*

Dhyg, *did;* mî a dhyg tôn, *I carried.*

Dhygav don, *I did carry;* me a dhygav dôn, *I will carry.*

Dhyn (dhynni, id.), *to us; to the;* as dhyn vôz, *to the Maid.*

Dhyso, *for thee; to thee.*

Dhyz, *to your.*

DI

Di (deiz, id.), *a Day; thou.*

Di, *without;* id. ac a priv. Gr. as dibitti, *merciless,* i. e. *without Mercy.*

Diagon, *a Deacon.*

Dialthyet, *a Key;* f. *without a Key.*

Dianaff, *spotless; chaste;* inde Diana. R.

Diaul, *a Fury, Fiend, or Hag.* Lh.

Dibbry, *to eat.*

Dibêh, *guiltless; without Sin.*

Dibenna, *to behead, kill, or butcher.* Lh.

Dibre, *a Saddle;* W. kyvruy, id.

Diberh, *divided.* V.

Dich, *potent; powerful.*

Dichon, *to be powerful.*

Dicreft, *a Sluggard; Blockhead.*

Dicreft, *a Rogue.*

Didhiuys, *promised.* Pa.

Didirio, *to banish.*

Didra, *poor,* i. e. *without any thing.*

Diegus, *idle.* Ar.

Dien, *Cream.* Ar.

Diesgiz, *unshod.*

Dieu, *both;* an dieu, *one and the other.*

Diffenner, *an Excuser; Defender.*

Diffig, *Want; Defect.* R.

Diffry, *Duty.*

Difroedd, *Banishment.*

Difroi, *to banish.*

Difyddio, *to deprive.*

Dignas, *opposing;* o dygnas, *were opposing.*

DI

Digthtyas, *restored; used; led forth; did provide.* V.

Digwyddo, *to befall, or happen.*

Dikref, *silly; weak;* i. e. *without Strength.*

Dilecha, *to depart; to go away.* Lh.

Diliis, *manifest;* δειλ☉. Gr.

Dilla (dolla, id.), *to cheat; deceive;* delhas, id.

Dilladzhi, *to cloath;* Dilladzhas, *cloathing.*

Dillat-gueli, *Bedcloaths.*

Dillun, *Monday.*

Dimedha, *Marriage;* it. *to marry.* Lh.

Din, *worthy.* Ar. it. C.

Din (tin, id.), *a fortified Hill,* " sometimes used as the pro-" per Name of round steep " Hills." Lh.

Dinevour, *a Fort on the Sea;* (à din & mor), inde Moridunum. Lat.

Dinam, *clean.*

Dinar, *a Hold; a fenced Place;* R. dinas, id. *a Penny;* Lh. dinair, id. Lh.

Dinas Beli, *Belinus's Palace, or Court.* Hum. Lh.

Dinaz, *a Fortress, or Bulwark.* Lh.

Dinerz, *weak;* à nerz, *Strength.*

Dinful dezil, id. (devfull, id.), *Sunday;* it. *a sunny Hill, or Hill dedicated to the Sun.*

Diogel, *secure; certainly;* endiogel, *doubtless.*

Dîog, *slow; lazy.*

Diolacht (dileuchta, id.), *Fatherless.*

Diot, *Drink;* diautvrac, *Malt-drink;* it. *a Sot.* Ar.

Dioul, *the Devil.*

Diowenes, *Loss; Damage.*

Diwog, *the Great-Grandfather.* Proavus. Cott.

Dippa, *a Pit.* (Tinners Term.)

Dir, *Steel.* Ar.

Direttha, *latter; posteriour.*

Direvall (dereval, id.), *to build.*

Diriair, *Money.*

Dirra, *to last, or hold out long.*

Discar, *to break down; to ruin.* Ar.

Discebel, *a Disciple.*

Discorvanait, *Madness.*

Dise, *a Rick, or Mow;* parc an dise, *the Rick-Field.*

Diskient, *simple, ignorant;* diskìans, *Madness; Folly.*

Diskuedha, *to discover; shew; accuse.* Lh.

Diskys, *taught; learned.*

Dislarg, *behind;* dislôr, id.

Disliu, *deformed; discoloured.*

Dislonka, *to swallow.*

Dislough, *immediately.*

DI

Dismigo, *to suspect.*

Distrippas, *stripped; spoiled.*

Díu, *black* (Ir. div, id.); diuat, and duat, *Blackness.*

Diua (díuath, id.), *a Bound.* Terminus. L.

Diua (teua, id.), *at last.*

Diuadha, *to finish;* diuadh, *End;* war an diuadh, *finally.* Lh.

Divetha, *the worst.*

Diuethaz, *late; serus.* L.

Diuglun, *the Reins.*

Diuorte, *from him.*

Diures, *an Exile.*

Dizhanih, *a Breakfast;* dizanhih, id.

Dizil, *to undo;* dizurythyl, id.

DL

Dle, *a Debt.* Ar.

Dluzen, *a Trout.* Pl. Dluz.

DO

Dô, *tame;* maggo do, *as tame as.*

Doal. See Dôl.

Doan (dôn, id.), *to bear; carry.*

Dobby, *Robert.*

Dochye, *to touch.*

Dodnan, *Earth; Soil.*

Dof, *a Son-in-law; Gener.* L.

Dogan, Ar. *a Cuckow.*

Dohadzheth, *Afternoon;* dyhodzhydh, id.

Dok, *gave;* (thuek, & thoke, id.)

Dôl, *a Share.* Ir. daal, id. doal, id.

Dol, *a Valley;* (Ir. Dal, id.) W. *a Meadow.*

Dole, *a Plain; Plainness.* B.

Dolla, *do.* V. na ylly dolla, *could not do;* it. *to deceive.*

Dony, *damp.*

Dôr, *Earth;* doar, doer, & dayer, id.

Dor, *from* (dorte, id.); dor y vam, *from his Mother.*

Doreganas, *to charge.* V.

Dorre, *broke;* torhas, id. *to break.*

Dôrgis, *an Earthquake.*

Dormont, *to torment.*

Dorn, *a Hand; a Handle;* Lh. pl. dula.

Dorne, *back;* it. *Hands.*

Dorngliken, *on the the left Hand;* the Cornish call a left-handed Man Glik, or Klik-handed.

Dorossen, *a Mole-hill.* Ar.

Dos, *come;* dose, *he comes;* daôz, id.

Dotha, *on him;* dothans, *to them;* for dho.

Dothye, *he came;* dothyans, *they came.*

Dova, *to tame, subdue.*

Dovi, *a House.* R.

Doul, *a Purpose; a Design.*

Doun,

DO

Doun, *deep*; town, id.
Dounder, *Deep*; viz. *Sea*; *Depth*; *a Gulf*.
Doun, *we will come*; douh, donz, ye, *they will come*.
Dour, *Water*; Gr. ὕδωρ. Durra, or deura, id.
Dourgi, *an Otter*, devergi, id.
Dous, *they*.
Douthek, *Twelve*; *taken off*.
Dowlyn, *the Knees*; Dewlyn, id.
Dowyll, *shady*; R. und. f. thule, *a dark Place*; it. *a Tool*.
Doy, *Yesterday*.
Doyn, *to thee*; *to bring*. V.
Doys, *swore*.
Dôz, *to come*. Lh.

DR

Dra (tra, id), *a Thing*; it. *is*. V.
Draff, *Grains*; i. e. Remains of the Malt after Brewing. Qu.
Dragun, *a Dragon*. Ar. id.
Dre, *by* (der, id.); *a Town*, for Tre.
Drê, *Home*; moaz drè, *to go Home*; for Tre.
Dreath, *sandy Shore*, or *Beach*; it. *gravel*; dreath lenky, *a Quicksand*. Lh.
Dreau, *lusty*; *lively*. Ar.
Dred ha, *through thy*.
Dred hev, *by me*.
Drefen, *although*; *because*.
Dregas (tregid), *tarried*; *dragged*; *forced along*.
Drehevy, *raised*; drehevell, *to rise*; it. *bred*; *bore*; *brought up*.
Drei (dho drei), *to afford*; *præbeo*; Lh. dho rei, id. Lh.
Dreizan, *a Bramble*; *a Thorn*; pl. dreis; drachen, and drize, id.
Dremas, *just*.
Dren, *a Bramble*; parc-andren, *the Bramble Field*; drein, and drain, id. Cott.
Dres, *Being*; S. *Nature*; *Profession*; ladron dres, *Thieves by Profession*; it. *above*; as moaz dres, *to be above*; for dris. f.
Dret, *a Share*. Ar.
Drethe, *through*.
Drethough, *between*.
Dreval, *to lift up*; *to take away*.
Drevas, *Tillage*; *cultivated Land*.
Drevethys, *proceeded*; *came forth*.
Drew (Deew, id.), *is*; *being*. Pr.
Drey, *a City*; ut dre pro tre.
Dreyson, *Treason*.
Dreyn, *Prickles*; f. pl. of dren.
Drez, *over*; *beyond*. Lh.
Drilgy, *Noise*; *Hurry*. f.
Drindaz (drendzer, and drindzis, id.), *the Trinity*.

DR

Driskyn, *drowned*. Pa.
Dris, *according to*; *above*; drís pubtra, *above every Thing*.
Dro, *about*; *on every Side*; pou adro, *the Country round about*; it. *thereabout*. Lh.
Drô, *bring thou*. V.
Droaga, *to hurt*.
Drocger, *Infamy*; *Scandal*.
Drocgerut, *an infamous Man*; drog-ober, *a wicked Work*; drokgeryt, id.
Drogbrêz, *Spite*; *Grudge*; *ill Will*.
Drohas, *cut*. V.
Drok, *Hurt*; *Wrong*; *Grief*; drwg, it. *Heart*; *wicked*; *malicious*. Lh.
Drok-davazek, *ill-tongued*.
Drossen, *brought*; dhrôz, id.
Droys, *bought*; it. *Feet*.
Druesy, *mournful*. Lh.
Druic, *a Dragon*.
Druilla, *to pare*; *slice*. Ar.
Drusher, *a Thresher*. Lh.
Druw, *a Druid*, as tre'r druw, *the Druidstown*; maen ydruw, *Druid Stones*.
Druz, *a Foot*; Lh. *Greazy*, Ar.
Dry, *what*.
Dry, *to bring*.
Drychinog, *boisterous*; *stormy*.
Drydhi, *through her*.
Dryff, *Purpose*; adryff, *on Purpose*.
Drygaer, *to blemish*; anglod, id.
Dryk, *to tarry*; ef a dryk, *he shall tarry*.
Dryllio, *to break small*; i. e. *into Pieces*.
Drylyas, *wrapped*.
Dryppan, *a Drop*.
Dryst, *an Oak*; *Grove*. δρυς Gr.
Drythyll, *bucksome*, *gamesome*, an ludd, id.
Dryz, *come thou*.

DU

Du, *God* (Ir. Dia, Ar. Dove, id.); pl. Duou, Duy, and Duvo, Cott, id. Deu. Lh.
Du, duw (Cott. id.), *black*; du ha glas, *black and blue*.
Du (pro De) Pasch, *Easterday*.
Du (pro De), -yow, *Thursday*.
Duat, *Blackness*.
Dues, *a Goddess*; Diuies. W. id.
Dûg, *a General*.
Duganz, *Forty*.
Dule, *Comfort*.
Dulw, *a Base*, or *Pedestal of a Pillar*.
Dûn, *a Hill*; din, id.
Dunuves, *a Steer*, or *Bullock*; f. pl. à Denevait.
Durdalatha, *I thank*. V.
Durra & deura, f. *Water*; as

DU

ardeura, côndurra, &c. *all on the Water*; and the River at Gillan Creek, coming down from Manachan, is called the Durra; and Condurra and Tindura lie upon it.
Durt, *from*, pro dort.
Durva, *watery*.
Dûs, tûs, *a Man*.
Dustuny, *a Witness*; pl. dustunnou.
Du-taith (teutates), *the Traveller's Deity*.
Duyfron, *the Breast*. Lh.
Duyfronneg, *a Breast-plate*.

DY

Dy, *of thee*; *there*; Ad. it. Privat. as dygomfortis, *without Comfort*; dy, W. *Ink*.
Dyal, *Revenge*.
Dyantell, *hazardous*.
Dybarth, *a Separation*.
Dybour, *lowly*.
Dyenar, *Pence*.
Dyerbine, *to revive*.
Dyfen, *a Prohibition*.
Dyfn, *Depth*. R.
Dyfout, *Fault*. See Diffout, *Crime*.
Dyg, *to bring*; ef ai dyg hym, *he brought it unto me*.
Dygnahas, *to deny*.
Dygow, *right*; barth dygow, *Right-side*.
Dyhodzheth, *in the Afternoon*. See dih, &c.
Dyhou, *right*. Lh. See dehou.
Dyhuanz, *quickly*.
Dyliez, *revenged*. V. Mevedn boz dyliez, *I will be revenged*.
Dyllas, *Cloaths*. See dill.
Dylla gudzh, *Phlebotomy*; *drawing Blood*.
Dyller (tyller and tellar, id), *a Place*.
Dylly, *ceasing*; Heb-dylly, *without ceasing*.
Dylofni, *a Bunch*, or *Bundle*.
Dylyr (& dilvar, id.), *to deliver*.
Dymme, *Value*, S. na ro dymme, *value it not*; *deem it as nothing*.
Dymmo, *valued*. Pa.
Dymmyn, *Pieces*; ol the dymmyn, *all to Pieces*.
Dyn, *sharp*, it. *a Man*; tyn, id.
Dynerchy (dynerhi, id.), *to salute*; *to greet*.
Dyns, *Teeth*.
Dyrag, *before*; coram. Lat.
Dyrgwys, *raised*.
Dyskas, *a Guide*.
Dyskyans, *Learning*.
Dyskyna, *to descend*.
Dyskyblion, *Disciples*. See Disk.
Dyson, *a Blessing*.
Dyspresias, *despised*. V.

Dyssantye,

DY

Dyssantye, *to deceive.*
Dysuleuuit, *the Top of the Head.*
Dyswe, *tell.* V.
Dyswithy, *to shew, inform;* dysquethas, & thyswethas, id.
Deswrys, *undone; destroyed.* Pa.
Dyth, *a Day;* Pl. dydiou.
Dythygtys, *was framed; prepared.*
Dyvere, *to drop;* guraf dyvere, *I should drop.*
Dyueth, *scornful.*
Dyuetha, *last; utmost.* Lh.
Dyvethaz lak, *long a coming.* Lh.
Dyun, *let us come.*
Dyvot (dyvoz, id.), *to come.*
Dyweddio, *to betroth.*
Dywolou, *the Devils;* à Dioul.
Dywort, *from.*
Dyz (dez, id.), *equivalent to the English Dis, or un,* as
Dyzkydha, *to discover.*

D Z

Dzarn, *an Orchard; a Garden.*
Dzeziou, *Jesus, the Saviour.*
Dzhei, *they; them.*
Dzherken, *a Jerkin.*
Dzhiaul, *the Devil.* Lh.
Dzhiunia, *to join together; to couple;* kydio, W. id.
Dzhyi, *a House; they.*
Dzhyrna, *a Day.*

E.

E, *He; him; it; of him; of it; his.*
E, V. *is;* this E, before Verbs of the Present Tense, is joined to the Verb, as Dew ewyr (for dew e wyr), *God knows.*
Eage, *Spar-thatched.*
Eal, *an Angel;* pro El.
Eanes, *Lambs;* Parc an Eanes, *the Lamb's Field.*
East, *August.*
Eaustic, *a Nightingale.* Ar.
East, *just* (f. pro yst), *Justus,* [a proper Name], as Pronter Est, *the Priest of St. Just.*

E B

Ebal, *a Colt.*
Ebat, *a Play.* Ar.
Ebilhocra, *a Nail, or Spike.*
Ebilio, *to bore a Hole;* tyllou, id.
Ebral, *April.*
Ebron, *the Sky.*
Ebscob, *High-Priest; Bishop.*

E C

Echuydh, *the Evening.*
Echrys, *a Blasting, or Strokeing with a Plant.*

E D

Ed, *into; in;* as, ed eskaz vî, *into (or in) my Shoe.*
Eddrak (edrek, id.), *Sorrow; Repentance.*
Edhen, *a Bird.*
Edhenor, *a Fowler.*
Edn, *narrow; slender.*
Ednak, *only; to wit;* enednak, id.
Edris, *learned;* caer edris, *a learned City.*
Eduyn (Ir. eadhan, id.), *scilicet; to wit.*
Edyack, *a Simpleton.*

E F

Ef, *he;* (E, id.)
Efin, *June;* Ephan, & Ephou, id.
Efyddu, *to braze;* pressu, id.

E G

Egery, *to open;* Egoru, id.
Egliz, *a Church;* W. egluys; Ar. ilys, id. eglos, id.
Egr, *a Daisy;* egr deu, id. neonin, id.
Egruath, *to roll; voluto.*

E H

Ehal, & eal, Lh. *a labouring Beast; an Angel;* Lh. el, id. Pl. E.
Ehan (eghen, id.), *a Kind; a Sort;* as, neb ehan, *every Kind;* Ar.
Ehaz, *Health; Safety; Greeting.* Lh.
Ehog, *a Salmon;* ehoc, & ehauc, id.
Ehual, *high;* as, bal-ehual, *the high Bal.*

E I

Ei, *wilt;* tî ei môz, *thou wilt go.*
Eiddo, *proper; one's own.* Gr. ἴδιον.
Eigion, *the Bottom, or Ground of any thing.*
Eiloh, *can;* huî eiloh, *ye can.*
Eineach, *a Face.*
Eiriasdan, *a Bonefire;* tanllwyth, id.
Eirinen, *a Plumb;* Ar. *a Sloe.*
Eifin, *Bran;* ysgarthion, id.
Eithick, *huge, very;* eitnick da, *hugely (or very) good.*
Eithin, *Furze.*
Eithav, *inward.* Lh.

E L

El (ehal, & eal, Ail. Cott. Ir. aiglile, id.), *an Angel;* Pl. elez.
Elar (elor, W. id.), *a Bier.*

E L

Elau, *an Elm Tree.*
Elec, *Alexander.*
Elerch, *a Swan;* Elerhe. Cott. & Elerchy, id.
Elesker, *the Shin; Shank.*
Elestr, *Matt; Tapestry; Carpet.*
Elestren, *Sedge; Waterflag; Sheer-grass.*
Elgeht, *the Chin.*
Elhylbon, y mor, W. *Nereides, the Fairies of the Sea.* Lh.
Elin, *a Cubit; an Angle, or Corner.* Gr. ωλενη. id.
Ella, *the Night-mare;* unde f. *Elves, or Fairies;* W. elkylh nôs. Lh.
Ellaz, *Alas.*
Elhil, *an Idol, or Hobgoblin.* R.
Ello, *may, or can;* neb na ello, *who cannot.*
Els, *a Son-in-law; a Stepson.*
Elfes, *a Son-in-law by a former Wife, or Husband.* Cott.
Elvenuaf, *to sparkle.* Ar.
Elven, *an Element; a Spark of Fire.*
Elydr (elydn), *Brass.*

E M

Emdhal, *to strive;* ombdhal, id.
Emeas, *without.*
Emenin, *Butter.*
Emlodh, *Fighting; a Fight.*
Emmet, *an Ant;* Qu.
Emperr, *an Empress.*
Emperur, *an Emperour.*
Emskemmunys, *accursed.*

E N

En, *an Intensive Particle,* as, enkledhyz, *buried;* for kledhyz, it. *the;* for an.
En (for enys, in Compos.), *an Island,* as, enmaûr, *the great Island.*
Ena, & enaff, *the Soul;* it. *there; then.*
Enap, *a Face;* it. *against;* bidn, id.
Enbera, *into.*
Enbît, *the World;* (Quas. an bys.)
Enc, *narrow;* encat, *to make narrow.*
Enchinethel, *a Gyant;* enquelezar, id. Ar.
Ene (ena, id.), *there; then.*
Eneb (enep, id.), *the Page of a Book.*
Enederen, *the Bowels.*
Enef (enaff, & ena, id.), *the Soul;* Pl. enevou.
Eneval, *a Beast;* enevales, *a She-beast.*
Enez, *Shrove tide;* it. *an Island,* (pro Enys), Pl. Enezou.
Enezek,

EN

Enezek, *an Iſlander.*

Enfys bwagwlaw, W. *a Rain-bow.*

Engil, *Fire.* R.

Englennaf, *to ſtick,* or *adhere to.* Ar.

Engurbor, *a Diſh.*

Enys, *an Iſland* ; W. ynys ; Ar. Enezen, enyzyz, id.

Enkledhyas, *buried.*

Encois, *Frankincenſe* ; *Incenſe.*

Enlidan, *the Herb Plantain.*

Ennill, *Gain.* R.

Enniou, *Joints* ; *Seams.*

Enogoz, *near.*

Enradn, *partly.*

Ens, *are.* V.

Entredes, *Warmth.*

Enuedh, *alſo.*

Envenough, *often* ; liaztorn, li-aſtre, id.

Enuoch, *againſt* ; *a Face.*

Enwedhan, *an Aſh-tree.*

Enwyth, id.

Enys, *an Iſland.* Lh.

E P

Epat, *laſting* ; *during.* Ar.

Ephan, *Summer* ; miz ephan, *Summer Month* ; viz. *June.*

Eppilio (qu. an euillio), *to breed,* or *be with young.*

E R

Er, *an Hour* (urna, id.), it. *upon.*

Er, *an Intenſive Particle,* like ιει, Gr. valde ; it. *new* ; *freſh* ; it. *Snow* ; Lh. as, eri.

Er, *au Eagle.*

Er (pro erw), *a Field* ; as, ertêg, *a Foir-field.*

Era, *which* ; *how* ; as, pelea era, *how far.*

Era (pro dera), *do* ; as, mi dera lavirias, *I do labour.*

Erberou, *Gardens.*

Erchyll, *dreadful* ; *Hercules* ;

Erchys, *commanded.*

Eren, *to tye* ; ere, *a Band,* or *Tye.*

Ergh (yrgh, id.), *to call earneſt-ly.*

Ergiz (for egiz), *a Shoe.*

Ergyd twrwf, *a Thunderbolt.*

Erhmit, *a Hermit.*

Erieu, *the Temples* ; viz. *of the Head.*

Erigea, *to ariſe.*

Ernoyth, *undreſſed* ; *unclad* ; *naked.*

Ero (erov, erven, id.), *a Ridge,* or *high Furrow.* Ar.

Err, *Snow* ; 'ma kil err, *it ſnows* ; it. *new* ; *freſh.*

Erra, *was* ; *had been.*

E R

Erres, *a flat, even Plot* ; *Floor of a Houſe.* Ar.

Erthebyn (ortheby, erybyn, er-byn, erdhabyn, id.), *againſt.*

Ervinen, *a Turnip.*

Ervyes, *he is circumſpect* ; ab

Ervyr, *to perceive.*

Ervyz, *armed* ; ab arv, *arm thou.*

Erw, *a Field* ; ager. L.

E S

Es, *is* ; eſen, id. eſa, *were* ; ens, & ez, *are.*

Es, *that* ; *which* ; es guaya, *which moveth.*

Eſcob, *a Biſhop* ; eſcoben, & eſ-cobon, Pl.

Eſcuit, *nimble* ; *ſwift.* Ar.

Eſe (eve, & ve, id.), *was.* V.

Eſgara, *to leave,* or *forſake.* Lh.

Eſgiz, *a Shoe* ; eſkaz, id.

Eſkidieu, *Slippers.*

Eſkynna, *to aſcend.* T. T.

Eſel, *a Limb,* or *Member.*

Eſou (eſoz, id.), *already.*

Eſquet, *a Felon.*

Eſt, Yïſt, Iſt, *Juſt* [a proper Name] ; Re Yïſt, *by St. Juſt* ; W. Jeſtin for Juſtin.

Eſtren, *an Oyſter* ; Pl. eſtreu.

E T

Et (pro etaf), *it* ; *in* ; as, et a phokkat, *in my Pocket.*

Et, *Corn.* Ar.

Eta, *itſelf* ; *it.*

Etau, *a Firebrand.* Ar.

Eth, *he went* ; ethons, *they went.*

Ethas, *the eighth.* Lh.

Ethiaz, *is* ; *there is.*

Edhnou brodzan, *Starlings.*

Etho, *am* ; Etho ve, *I am* ; tho, id.

Ethon, *bear Children.*

Ethowon, *Jews* ; Edzhewon, Pl.

Ethym, *did* ; me a ethem moaz, *I did go.*

Etre, *between* ; emeſk, id. Lh.

Ettanz, *in them* ; *therein.*

Etto, *yet* ; *ſtill* ; Gr. eti.

E U

Eu, *he* ; (ef, Ev, id.)

Eva, *to drink.*

Evef, *Eve.*

Even, *patient* ; pur even, *very patient.*

Evêz, *out* ; *without.*

Eugh, *go* ; *get out* ; eugh yn mes, *get you out.*

Euhal, *high* ; ehual, eukella, id. W. uchel, id. *haughty.* Lh.

Euhelder, *Height.*

Euhelet, *Altivola* ; *a Lark,* or *Bird that flies high.* Lh.

Evî, *of me.*

E U

Ewidit, *a Lark.*

Euig (euhig, id.), *a Hind* ; *a fattened Deer* ; loch, & leauh euig, *a Fawn* ; euhig luyd, *a fallow Deer.*

Euincarn, *a Hoof.*

Euit, *an Uncle* ; *a Father's* or *Mother's Brother.*

Euithr, id.

Euleiok, *at leaſt.*

Eun (even, id), *ſtreight* ; *right.*

Euna, *to rectify.*

Eunhilik, *a juſt Man* ; camhilik, *an unjuſt.*

Evodh, *Leave* ; dregyz evodh, *by your Leave.*

Evos (for evough aguz), *drink your.*

Evough, *Drink ye* ; from eva.

Eure, *a Goldſmith.*

Eur, *Happineſs* ; eurmat, id. Ar.

Eus, *Horror* ; *Abomination.* Ib.

Eus, *a Nightingale.*

Euth, *alſo* ; ruth, id.

Euin, *a Nail* ; Ind. Euincarn, *the Hoof of a Horſe.* Lh.

E Y

Eye, *they* ; Y, id.

Eyll, *the one* ; yld, id.

Eyn, *Cold* ; garm eyn, *cold Cry.*

Eynog (kining eyinok), *Gar-lick.*

Eyriſder, *Happineſs.*

Eyſye, *to extol, praiſe.*

Eyſyll, *Hyſop.*

E Z

Ez, *is* ; V. it. *your,* as, der ez kibmiaz, *by your Leave.*

Ezall, *low.* Gw.

Ezen, *I was* ; it. *a Bird,* for ed-hen.

Ezhov (ydzhov, id.), *I come.*

Ezom, *Poverty.* Ar.

Ezzez, *thou wert.*

F.

N. B. The Letter F, Primary Initial, never alters in the Welſh, Corniſh, or Armoric. Lh.

"We uſe F always for V, "when it is a Conſonant, as, "Lhan fair, is in reading called "Lhan uair." Hum. Lh. So Fou, or Fau, *a Cave* in Welſh, is Vou, or Vau, in Corniſh.

Inſtead of the Latin F, the Welſh always uſe Ph, or Ff.

F Adic, *(profugus),* *a Run-away.*

Faellu, *to err* ; *make to err.* φαλλω. Gr.

Faidus (fardus, Cott), *beautiful.*

Fàl,

FA

Fâl, *a Shovel*, hez ou âl, *Length of my Shovel.*
Fall, *Doubt*; heb fall, *without Doubt.*
Falladou, *Fraud*; *Failing.*
Fallia, *to cleave*; *split.*
Falfney, *Falshood.*
Falfury, *falfely.*
Fan, *Dominus*; *Deus*; Celtic. Keyf.
Faneq (Ar.), *Mud*; *Mire.*
Farvel, *a Buffoon*; Ar. *a Jester.*
Fas, & yn fas, *clearly*; *Strength*; *Face to Face.*
Faftfens, *Faftnefs*; it. *prefently*; it. *faft*; an Ad.
Fatel, *how*; fatla, & fatl, id.
Favan, *a Bean*; Pl. fav; ponar, id.
Faucun, *a Hawk.*
Fauns, *a Fall*; *a Caft*; *a Throw*; a wreftling Term.
Faut (fout, id.), *Want*; *Lack*; *a Crime*; ma faut, *I want.*
Ffau, ffay, Lh. *Fovea*; *a Den*; Dav; C. vau, & vou.

FE

Fe, *was*; *fhould be*; ve, id,
Fehas, *Sin*; (pro peghas, id.)
Fein, *neat*, *handfome*; fêg, id. *witty.*
Fekyl, *fhewed* (fecle, id.); *made*; *feigned.*
Feldzha, *to cleave*; id. ac fallia.
Felen, *Wormwood*; fuelein, id.
Fell, & feld. See Gueal.
Fella, *further*; na fella, *no further*; fel, id. as, vorfel, *the further Way.*
Fellores, *a Player on the Pipe*, or *Violin*; *a Woman Piper.* Cott.
Felpen, *a Piece.* Ar.
Fen, *End*; yn fen, *in fhort*; *finally.*
Fenochel, *the Herb Fennel.*
Fentan, *a Spring*; *a Source*; fyntan, id.
Ffenwith, *End*; heb ffenwith, *without End.*
Fer, *the Leg* (Crus). Cott.
Ferclin, *Meat*; *Dainties.*
Ferhiat, *a Thief*; lader, id.
Fernoyth, *bare*; *naked*; *poorly clad.*
Ferue, *to die*; merwc, id.
Feryl, *Danger.*
Ffefont, *a Pheafant.*
Feft, *quickly*; *Meafure*; feft cref, *abundant Meafure.*
Feftinna, *to make Hafte.* Lh.
Feth, *Face*; it. *fhall be*; fyt, id.
Fethys, *taken*; fedh, id.
Fettow, *faid he.*
Feunt, *would*; y feunt, *he would.*

FE

Feur, *a Fair*; *Market*; fêr, id.
Feyn, *Smart*; *Pain*; beyn, peyn, id.

FI

Fia, *had*, or *did*; vîa, id.
Fìal, *a Buckle.*
Fiala, *a She-piper.*
Fickya, *copulari.*
Figbren, *a Fig-tree.*
Figges, *Figs*; figges ledan, *broad Figs*; figgez an houl, *Raifins of the Sun.* Gw.
Filgeth, *Soot.*
Filh, *a Hook-bill*, *a Hook*; *a Sickle.*
Fin, *againft*; fyn, id. it. *fubtil*; *wary*; *provident*; it. *white*, pro gwyn.
Finval, *to ftir*; *remove*; *part from.* Ar.
Fiol, *a Cup.*
Fìr, *wife*; *cautious*; fir, id. Lh.
Fiflak, qu. (go you little fiflak), fiffelek, f. *a Knave*; Lat. *lepidum Capitulum*; *Puerulus.*
Fiffel, *Ventris Crepitulus*; *Peditum.*

FL

Flair, *a Smell.*
Flacraf mâd, *to fmell well*, or *ftrong.* Cott.
Flam, *a Flame.* Lh. Ar. & W. id.
Flaw, *a Cut*; φλαω. Gr.
Fledgiow, *Children.*
Fleheffig, *a little Child*; flehefou, Pl. & flechet, id.
Flem, *a Sting.* Ar.
Floh, *a Child*; Pl. flehys.
Flo, *very fmall.*
Flookan, qu. (an à Flaw), *a Cut*; it being a Parcel of Ground which cutteth off one Part of a Load from another? a Tinner's Term: fleukan, *a foft Vein.* T. T.
Flown an, *a proud Maid.* Gw.
Fflur, *Brightnefs.*
Flurr (flurrag, id.), *Prow of a Ship.*
Flyran, *a Lock of a Door.*

FO

Ffo, *Flight.*
Foath, *the Town of Fawy* (Carew), quafi Fau-weath; in Leland, Fawathe, Cornifh for Fawy; Faw-uedh, i. e. *the Bed*, or *Grave of the* Fau, *from it's Depth near the Town*; f. Fau-warth, *on* (i. e. *the Banks of*) *the* Faw.
Fod (fed, id.), *a Place.* R.

FO

Fodic, *happy.*
Foen, *Hay.*
Foge, *a Blowing-houfe for melting of Tin.*
Fogou, *a Cave*; quaf. foghou, id. ac fou, vel fod-gou, à fod & govea, *to lie hid*; viz. *a hiding Place*; ogo, quaf. vogo, id.
Fol, *a Fool*; par (or pur) fol, *a very Fool.*
Ffollach, *a Bufkin.*
Follat, *a Handkerchief.*
Folneth, *Folly*; Foloreth, id.
Foltgufke, *frantick*; foltregufke, id.
Foltre, *frantick.* Lh.
Fon, *let it be.* V.
Fonn, Ar. *Plenty*; fonna, *to abound.*
Fons, *may be*; fens, *we were.*
Font, *the Bottom.* Ar.
Ford, *a Way*; (forth, & vor, id.) P. furru.
Forh, *a Pitchfork*; *a Prong.*
Formyys, *formed.*
Forn, *an Oven*; Ar. *a Prong.*
Forrior, *a Thief*; φωρ. Sam.
Forth, *a Way*; it. *why?*
Fôs, *a Wall*; marhas an fôs, *the Market on Wall*; fôs. Lh. id.
Fofaneu, *a Shoe*, or *Slipper.*
Fou (vou, id.), *a Den*, or *Cave*; Pendîn vou, *Pendin Cave*; Pl. fouiz, *Dens.*
Foulz, *falfe*; *perfidious*; *treacherous.* Lh.
Foys, *a Table.*

FR

Fra, *why*; rag fra, *wherefore?* Lh.
Fraga, *why*; praga, id. rag praga, id.
Frank, A. *free.*
Franki, *Francis.* Gw.
Frao, *the little horned Owl.*
Ffras, *born*; inffras, *to be born.*
Frat, Qu. *for all your Frat*; *Noife*; *Objection.*
Frâu, *a Rook*, or *Town Crow*; Lh.
Frêg, *a Wife*; gurêg, id.
Frehez, *vexed.* Gw.
Frenna, *to buy*; perna, id.
Frez, *diftinctly*; *eafily.* Ar.
Fria, *to fry*; Lh. W. frio, id.
Fries, *a Husband.*
Frigau, *a Nose*; trein, id. Ar. fri.
Fron, *the Nose.*
Frôs, *the Tide of the Sea.*
Frot, *a narrow Sea.* Cott. *Alveus.*
Frôth, *a Crumb*; *a small Piece.*
Frou, id. ac frôs.
Frouden, *Fancy*; *Humour*; *Frolick.* Ar.
Frouyn, *to part*, or *feparate.* Lh.

5 R

Frûc,

FR

Frûc, *the Nose* ; Cott. Ar. fri.
Fruyn, *a Bridle.*
Ffrwyth, *Effect* ; *Fruit* ; Ar. frouez, id.
Frya, *to Fry.*
Fryns, *Prince.*
Fryth, *a Hawthorn* ; kellifryth, *a Grove of Hawthorns.*

FU

Fual, *a Buckle* ; fial, id.
Fuelein, *Wormwood.*
Fulen (fulien, id.) *a Spark of Fire.* Ar.
Funil, *Fennel.*
Funten. See Fenten.
Fur, *wise* ; W. fwyr, anfur, *imprudent.*
Furaat, *to be wise.*
Furf, *a Form*, or *Shape.*
Furgan, Qu. *to give a Boy his Furgan*, i. e. *to correct*, or *chastise him.*
Furnez, *Wisdom.*

FY

Fyal. See Fual.
Fyas, *fled.*
Fye, *to exile* ; *drive away* ; fys, *scattered.*
Fykyl, *lying* ; fykyl lavarou, *lying Words.*
Fyllel, *fail* ; heb fyllel, *without fail.*
Ffylly, *ought* ; dous fylly, *they ought.*
Fyn, *an End* ; *a Boundary* ; tyr-fyneau, *Lands.*
Fynnas, *would* ; vynnas, id. V.
Fynny, *to prosper.*
Fyr, *wise* ; *cautious.* See Fur.
Fysadou, *Prayers.*
Fysel. Qu. See Fiffel.
Fysta, *to thresh.*
Fysteene, *haste.*
Fyth, *Faith.*
Fyvar, *an Edge.*

G.

" G, in the first Place vanish-
" eth away." H. L. Brev. E. 3.
So in Gûn, *Downs*, the G shall vanish, as in Boscawen ûn, Lan y ûn.
N. B. Where the same or like Word begins with a K or C, and also with a G ; that with a K, or C, is to be reckoned the Theme, and the K, or C, changed into a G, Euphoniæ gratia.

GAchyns, *seized* ; gathyas, & agathyas, id.
Gad, Ar. *a Hare* ; gat, id. ib.

GA

Gael (for gavel), *to find.*
Gafe (cafe, & cafos, id.), *to find* ; *to contrive.*
Gahen, *the Herb Symphoniaca.*
Gajah, *a Daisy* ; Gajah broaz, *the Great*, or *Horse-Daisy.*
Gaiav (guav, id.), *the Winter.*
Gain (cain, & gainor, id.), *Fair.*
Gainz (pro guenz), *Wind.*
Galarou, *to lament* ; it. bitter *Pangs*, or *Wailings.*
Galarouedges, *suffered.*
Galdrum, *Inchantments* ; *a Delirium*, or *Absence of Reason* ; vulg. Gualdrums ; Galek, *French.*
Galla, *to may*, or *can.*
Gallydhog, *mighty* ; galluidoc. Cott. id.
Galles, *didst lose* ; *art lost* ; à kelly, *to lose.*
Galli (hali, id.) *Holy.*
Galliard, *a Jigg* ; *a Dance.*
Gallons, *obtained* ; *persuaded.*
Gallous, *to go.* V.
Galloys, *Eagerness.*
Galluster (galluzack, id.), *mighty* ; galludek, A. *able.*
Galse (galso, & Gulse, id.), *gone* ; *lost.*
Galu (galua, id.), *to call.*
Gamma (omgamme, id.), *bowed down* ; à kam, or kabm, *bowed.*
Gan, *in* (id. ac gen), *by* ; *with.*
Gan (for gwen, or can), *white* ; as, godolgan. . . . dourgan, *white Water* ; it signifies also, *a Hollow* ; *an Opening*, or *Mouth of a River*, or *Valley* ; as, Treworgan, *Habitation on the Opening of the Valley* ; from ganau, genee, C. Ar. genee, id. W. genee, Lh. 110.
Ganau, *a Mouth* ; gene, id. Lh.
Gangys, *changed.* Pa.
Gannel, *Chanel*, or *Arm of the Sea* ; f. gan-hel, *white River*, or *River's Mouth.*
Ganou, *a Mouth* (genau, id) ; genuous, *their Faces.*
Gans, *with.*
Gans-henna (or hema), *hereupon.*
Ganfa, *with you.*
Ganzo (gonzha, id.), *with him.*
Gan-zingy, *to draw in any thing.*
Gara, *beloved* ; gare, *Love* ; *loved* ; pro cara.
Garan, *a Crane* ; γεραν⊙.
Garera, *to leave* ; gara, id.
Gargabm, *bandy*, or *crooked legg'd.*
Gargat, *a Garter* ; gargettou. Pl.
Garlont, *a Garland* ; an arlant, *the Garland.*
Garm (Ir. gairm, id.), *happy.*
Garme, *bewailing* ; yn un garme, id.

GA

Garou, *rough* ; *cruel* ; garo, id. hagar, id.
Garr, *the Leg* ; Pl. garrou, *Legs*, *Feet*, or *Knee.*
Garras, *to go* ; *come* ; *pass* ; *proceed.*
Garres, *left* ; gwell gerres, *better left.*
Garthou, *a Goad* ; guân, id.
Garz, *a Hedge* ; Ar. Pl. guir-zier.
Gasa (gase, id.), *to leave* ; gaz, *leave thou.*
Gath, *went* ; *came.*
Gathya, *to seize upon.*
Gav, *forgive thou.*
Gavael, *a Tenure* ; *Lands-bounded.* R.
Gaval, *to get.*
Gavar, *a Goat* [Ar. gaor, id.) ; Pl. Goûr ; gever, *a She-Goat* ; Cott. bock, *a He-Goat.* ib.
Gavar môr, *a long Oyster* ; *from its Horns called a Sea-Goat by the Cornish.* Lh.
Gaunak, Ar. *barren.*
Gawr, *valiant* ; *mighty* ; ind. cawr, *a Giant.*
Gaws, *to get* ; *gotten* ; *got.*

GE

Ge, *their* ; as, dho ge Deauon gow, *to their false Gods.* See Ghee, and Ghee.
Geauel, *the Gospel* ; Geawel, id. Cott.
Gedn, *a Wedge* ; ind. gad, *an Iron Wedge.*
Geêy, *to bring forth* ; *to fole* ; *the Mare was ready to geey*, i. e. *to cast her Fole* ; f. for kiy.
Geffi [tî a geffi, or gevyth, *thou shalt have*] ; *to haste* ; *hold.*
Geffo, *found* ; *have* ; *had.*
Gefys, *left* ; [gefys, id.]
Geien, *a Sinew* ; *Nerve.*
Geien, *a Back.*
Geir, *by.* Lh.
Gêl, *a Horse-leech* ; Gelauch, f. id. Lh.
Gelchi, *to wash thoroughly.*
Gele, *to swear* ; V. *another* ; gelle, id.
Gelen, *an Elbow*, or *Cubit.*
Gelli, *Hazels* ; Tregelli, *Town of Hazels.* Hum. Lh.
Gellon, *a Cubit* ; gelin ; Pl. gelinou, id.
Gelvyn, *a Bill*, or *Beak* ; gilbin, id.
Gen, *with* ; it. *on* ; *for* ; *near to.*
Genas, *with thee* ; genes, & genez, id.
Genau, *the Mouth.*
Genaued, *a Morsel* ; A. & C.
Gene, *a Chin.*
Genedigveth, *Birth* ; *Nativity.*
Gennen,

G E

Gennen, *with us*; gennam, *by us*.
Genouh, *with you*.
Genre, *with them*.
Gens, *are*; gennas, *id*.
Genfy, *with her, or with him*.
Genvar, *January*.
Genys, *born*; *begotten*.
Genzynz, *with them*.
Gêr, *a Word*; gervas, *a good Word*; ger da, *id*.
Gerches, *to fetch*.
Gerdin, *the Bloody-flux*.
Gerenfe (grenfye, *id.*), *Sake*; *Love*; pro Carensa.
Gerhas, *did go*; gerys, *gone*.
Gero, *let*; gero ni guil, *let us make*.
Gerut-da, *a famous Man*.
Ges, *jeering*; yn ges, *in Sport*; *is*; V. nyn ges, *is not*.
Gêft, *a Bitch*; Pl. gefti, *Dogs, or Bitches*.
Gethe, *a Day*; Pr. deth.
Geve, *had*; *took*; *ought*; gevo, *he had*; na geve, *there was not*.
Geuelhorn, *a Hand-wiper, or Towel*.
Gever, *Duty*; et i gever, *in her Duty*; it. Pl. of gavar.
Gevern, *a Hundred*; *a District*.
Gevyn, W. *Fetters*; *Gives*; *Shackles*.
Gevyons, *forgiven*; Geve, *to pardon*.
Gew, *a Spear*; gyw, *id*.
Gewar, *Rage*.
Geyleifio, *to tickle*; γιϚγιλιζειν. Gr. id.
Geyll, *Scoff*.

G H

Ghe, *them*; ne el e ge debre, *he can't eat them*.
Ghenev (for gen y vi), *with me*.
Ghel, *a Horfe-leech*; gêl, *id*.
Gheluyz (& ghiluyz, *id.*), *called*.
Ghenouch (ghenok, *id.*) *with you*.
Ghennyz, *with your*.
Gheon, *a Giant*; treva gheon, *Gyants Town*.
Ghera, *do*; ghera vî, *I do*.

G I

Gi (ge, *id.*), *they*; *them*; ha gorafgi, *and he put them*.
Giâr, *a Hen*; 'mab giar, *a young Hen*.
Gigal, *a Diftaff*; Kogol, W. *id*.
Gîl, *to make*; guil, *id*. gero ni gil, *let us make*. It is often redundant.
Gilbin, *a Beak, or Bill*.
Gilliz, *gone*; *loft*.
Ginnow, *a Pair of Bellows*.
Gir (for ger), Pl. giriou.

G I

Girak, *the Gar-fifh*; *the Needle-fifh*; *a Needle*. Lh.
Girr, *a Loofenefs*; an girr, *the Loofenefs*.
Dho githa, *to hide*. Lh.
Givians, *Pardon*. See Geve.

G H

Glaine (Ir. gloine, *id.*), *Glafs*; W. Gleini nadroeth, *the Glafs Adders*, viz. the Anguinum of the Druids; in Scotland called Adder-ftones.
Glân, *the Bank of a River*.
Glane, *clean*; glannith, Lh. *id*.
Glannuthder, *Cleanlinefs*.
Glaouen, *a Coal*; Ir. gualan, *id*.
Glâs, *Green*; *Grey*; *Afh-coloured*; it. *the Stomach*; Cott. glayis, & lays, *id*. glaz, id.
Glafenye, *Green water*. Norden, p. 49.
Glafennith, *Viridis Nidus*. Leland.
Glafgarn, *a Kingdom*.
Glaftan (& glaftanen, *id.*), *an Oak*.
Glafuidd, *blueifh*. R.
Glau, *a Shower*; *Skud of Rain*; gleau, *id*.
Glavethas, *a Midwife*; à clav, f. bennen glyvedh, *id.* & vethys, viz. *looking to fick Women*.
Gleab, & gleb, *moift* (pro glib), it. *Weft*; W. gulyb, *id*.
Gledh, *Left*; as, *Left-hand*; it. *North*; it. *Chickweed*; Gogleth, *the North*.
Gleny, *to flick*; *cleave to*; *take hold of*; glenys, Pa.
Glefin, *the Herb Sandyx*.
Glevyon, *the fick*; Pl. of clef.
Glewas, *to hear*; clowas, *id*. gleu, *heard*. Pa.
Glez, *a Swarm of Bees*.
Gliber, *Moifture* (ind. glib), *flippery*; *moift*; *fmooth*; glybor, *id*.
Glihi, *Ice*; iâ, *id*.
Glikin, *left*; dom glikin, *Left-hand*. Lh.
Glin, *a Knee*; Ir. glun.
Glit, *Water-fnow*; *Hoar-froft*; *Froft*.
Glos, *Grey*; Ar. glâz, *id*.
Glow, *a Coal*; glou, *id*. Lh.
Gloyndiu, *a Butterfly*.
Gloys, *Pulfe*; gloys cref, *ftrong Pulfe*.
Gloz, & glauz, *Cow-dung*.
Gluan, *Wool*; gulân, *id*. Ar. gloan.
Glud, *Birdlime*.
Glut, *Glew*; *Pafte*; *Solder*. Lh.
Gluth, *a Bed, or 'Bed-chanber*; it. *Dew*; Ar. geiz.
Gluys, *pleafant*; *White*.

G L

Glyd, *a Lord*; it. *vehement*; Lh.
Glyn, *a Valley*; Ir. glin, glean, glan, *id*.

G O

Go, *was*; nyn go, *was not*.
Goac, *foft*; *tender*. Ar.
Goaguen (goagren, *id.*), *a Wave*. Ib.
Goall, *evil*; *wicked*. Ib.
Goap, *Mockery*.
Goar, *a Hufband*. See Gûr.
Goas (Ar. pro guaz), *a Man*.
Goath (Ar. pro gôth), *old*.
Goaz, *a Goofe*.
Goazen, *an Arm of the Sea*. Ar.
Gobennudd, *a Bolfter*.
Goch, *a proud Woman*. Hugh goch, i. e. Hugh the Red-head; W. from Godhz, *Blood*.
Gochus, *a proud Man*.
Gockorion, *foolifh People*; Pl. Goky.
Gôd, *a Mole*; godh, *id*. gudh-doar, *id*.
Goden-truit, *Sole of the Foot*.
Godhaz, *Lees of Drink*; godho, id.
Dho Godhaz, *to know*. Lh.
Godho, *Geefe*, Pl. à goaz.
Godoryn, *a Broil*; *Tumult*.
Godrabben (gudrabm, *id.*), *a Pain, or Swelling in the Hand*; *a Cramp*.
Gofail, *a Workman*; à gov. f.
Gofe (goffe, goyff, & gov), *a Smith*.
Gofys, *bloody*.
Gôg, *a Cuckow* (Goky, *a Fool*); ind. f. Gogwell, *the Cuckow's Town, or Work*.
Gogleth, *the North*.
Gogwyddo, *to bend, or fhake*; ind. gogwyddo pen, *to beckon*.
Goil, *a Sail*.
Goitkenin, *Dog's Bane*.
Goky, *a Fool*; affos goky, *you are a Fool*; *a gog*, *a Churl*.
Gôl, *Holy*; it. *a Veil*; ind. Ca-ergol, *Holy Town, or Fortrefs*; goil, *id*. Lh.
Y Gol, *the Holy*; a Cornifh Oath.
Golas, *lower* (pro wolas).
Golaz, *a Bottom*; lêr, *id*. golaz truz, *Sole of the Foot*.
Golch, *a Bath*; golchfa, *a hot Bath*.
Goleou, *Marks*, Pl. goleou pals, *frefh Marks*. See Golu.
Goleuder, *Splendor*.
Golhan, *a Knife*; holhan, *id*. kolhel, *id*.
Goleur, alias golor, *Plenty*; *Abundance of any Thing*.
Golhya, *to wafh*,
Golhys, *wafhed*.

Goll,

GO

Goll, *to lose*; gollas, *loft*; it. *hidden*; gyld, id.

Golli, *to deſtroy*.

Gollon (collon & hollon, id.), *a Heart*; it. *a Hart*, or *Deer*.

Gollow, *a Light*; goleuad, W. id. golouas, *Lightning*.

Golmas, *bound*; *fettered*.

Golo, *a Coverture*; golo ar guele, *a Coverlid*.

Goloff, *to cover*. Ar.

Golom, *a Pidgeon*; *Columba*.

Golovas, *Childbed*; *Travail*; bennen yn golovas, *a Woman in Childbed*.

Golou-leſtre, *a Lamp*; *a Candle-ſtick*; incoiſe left, *an Incenſe Pot*.

Gols, *the Hair*.

Golſowas, *to kearken*.

Golu, *a Mark*.

Goluan, *rejoicing*; *Midſummer*; i. e. *the Time of Lights*, or *Bone-fires*.

Golvan, *a Sparrow*; gylvan, id.

Golvinak, *a Curliew*.

Golwiden, *a Hazle-tree*. Lh.

Golwyth, *Burnt-offerings*.

Golyough, *watch ye*; goolyas, *to watch*; golzyas, id.

Gomfortye, *to comfort*. V.

Gon, *ours*.

Gonalen, *a Shoulder*.

Gonidog, *a Servant*; *Attendant*.

Gonnyon, *white*; carrig gonnyon, *White Stones*.

Gonon, *none*.

Gons (Mod. Corniſh), *Vulva*.

Gonyaz, *a Moth-worm*.

Gonys, *with them*.

Goon, *a Down*; *a Plain*; goon glaz, *the Sea*, or *green Plain*; gûn, & ûnn, id.

Goober (gober, id. guber, id.), *a Reward*; *Wages*; gubar, Lh. id.

Googoo, *a Cave*, or *Den*; W. ogoh.

Gophen, *to aſk*.

Gor, *put*; *cauſe*; *do*; à gorra.

Gor, *an Intenſive Particle, ſometimes only an Expletive*.

Dho gora, *to put*, or *ſet in Order*; *to frame*, or *make*, Lh.

Gorchymmia, *to bid*, or *command*.

Gorephan, *July*; Miz Gorephan, *the Month of July*; Miz gorphennav, W. id. i. e. *the Month in the Height of Summer*.

Gorfenne, *to make an End*; gura fen, id.

Gorguith, *be careful*.

Gorgwethens, *they covered*; à gueth, *a Cloth*.

Gorha, *Hay*.

Gorhmenna, *to command*. Lh.

GO

Gorhemmenau, *Commands*.

Gorlan, *a Church-yard*; it. *a Sheep Cote*.

Gormenna, *to command*.

Gormola, *Praiſe*.

Dho gorou, *to open*.

Gorra, or gora, Lh. *to put*; *lay down*. See Gurys, or gorris.

Gorre, *that which is above*. Ar.

Gorſedd, *a Seat of Judgement*; gorſeddaddleu, *a Bar in a Court of Juſtice*.

Gorthewyth, *Bed-ſickneſs*.

Gorthyans, *Worſhiping*.

Gorthyn, *muſt, or ought*.

Gortha, *to tarry*; gortos, *to ſtop*.

Gortys, *eſteemed*.

Goruedh, *to lie-down*.

Goruer, *a Cloud*.

Gorweythy, *ought*. V.

Gorweddar, *to brood*, or *ſit on Brood*.

Gorwfel, *a Snake*.

Goſkaz, *to ſleep*; me ry goſkaz, *I have ſlept*.

Goſkordhy, *a Houſhold*; *a Family*.

Gôſteggion, *Banns of Matrimony*.

Goſteyth, *obedient*.

Goſtotter, *Shelter*.

Goſys, *bloody*.

Goth (for koth), *old*; *formerly*; it. *Pride*.

Goth, *ſee*; V. *back*; *ought*; *becomes*.

Gothas, *they fell*; pro cothas, *to fall*.

Gothaff (pro wothaff), *I know*; ind. gothewys, *known*.

Gothihuar, *the Evening*.

Gothoan, *Fools*.

Gothvethough, *know ye*.

Gov, *a Smith*; gov-diu, *a Blackſmith*.

Goval, W. *Care*; *Induſtry*; *Diligence*.

Govail, *a Smith's Shop*; *a Workman*.

Govaytis, *Covetouſneſs*.

Gouas, *to have*; *to hold*; gevas, id. dho gouas (dho gaval), *to hold*, *poſſeſs*, or *obtain*.

Goucen, *a Nerve*.

Gouea, *to lie hid*; A. kudha, kudhet, id.

Gouegneth, *Fraud*; *Falſhood*.

Goulaff, *to weep*; *I weep*.

Govenek, *Remembrance*.

Gouer (gouea, id.), *a Brook*, or *Bog*; Ar. W. gover, gouern, id.

Gover, *a Rivulet*; as, polgover, *a Rivulet Pool*, or *Head of the Rivulet*.

Govidzion, *Sorrows*.

Gouiles, *the Herb Avadonia*. Cott. Qu.

Goular, *Coral*. Ar.

GO

Gouleveriat, *a Lier*.

Goullenwel, *to fill*; *fulfill*.

Goulo, *void*. Ar.

Gouris, *a Girdle*.

Gouwan, *a Moth*; Lh. gouyan.

Govy, *ſad*.

Govynnas, *aſked*; govyn, id.

Gow, *a Lie*.

Gowak, *a Lier*; Pl. gouîgnion, gûak, id.

Gowethas, *Company*.

Gows (pro cowz), *Speech*.

Gowſyn, *I ſpake*.

Goyf, *Winter*; guaf, id.

Goyne, *Supper*; kone, id.

Goyn, *a Sheath*.

Goyntys, *Courteſy*; *Covetouſneſs*.

Goys, *Blood*; gudzh, & woys, id.

Gôz, *your*; for agoz, id.

Gozer, *ſtrived*; Gw.

Gozan, *a hard Vein*, or *Lode croſſing another*. T. T.

Gorowas, *hearken*. Gw.

GR

Grachel, *a Heap*; *Tumulus*; L. berk, id.

Grachya, *to break*; *crack*.

Grambla, *to climb*. Lh.

Grân, *Command*; an deag gran Deu, *the ten Commandments of God*. f. Contraction from gormen, or gormenna.

Gras ('ras, & grage, id.), Pl. araſou (grath, id.), *Grace*; *Thanks*.

Graſſys, *thankful*.

Grat, *a Step*; L. *Gradus*.

Gravar, *a Barrow*; gravar dowla, or dula, *a Hand-barrow*; gravar rôe, *a Wheel-barrow*; *a Vehicle*. Lh.

Gravior, *a Sculptor*; gravia, *to engrave*. Lh.

Grawn, *a Berry*.

Grayth, *Trouble*.

Gregar, *to cackle as a Hen*.

Gregy, *to hang*.

Grehan, *Leather*; ſkelligrehan, *Leather wings*, viz. *a Bat*.

Greiah rag, *to require*; *to enquire for*.

Grelin, *a Lake*; W. id. & lhuch, Ar. laguen; Ir. lôch.

Grên, as, Polgrên, Tregrên, i. e. *the Green Pool*; *the Green Town*, or *Dwelling on the Green*. Scribitur & Gryn, as, Grynſey in Scilly, quaſi *Green Sea*.

Gres, *do*; dell rethe gres, *ſo they ſhould do*.

Greſt, *Chriſt*; Griſt, id.

Greunen, *a Grain*; Ar. C. gronen.

Greut,

GR

Greut, *Earth* ; *Powder* ; *dusty Grains* ; *Grit*.

Grevye, *painful* ; *heavy* ; grevys, *grieved*.

Grew, *caused* ; à gura, *to make*.

Grez, *Faith* ; gris, id.

Grigear, *a Partridge* ; quas. grygiar ; grugyer, id. *a Heath-poult*.

Grigiz, *a Girdle* ; *a Band*. Lh.

Grill, *a Crab*.

Gris (agris, id.), *I believe*, grys, id.

Grisill, *thin* ; *small*.

Grisla, *to grin* ; mân kei y grisla, *the Dog grins*.

Gro, *Ballast* ; pro grou, f.

Groes, *Heat*. Ar.

Gromercy (or gwra mercy), *Thanks to thee*.

Gronen, *the Skin* ; *a Grain*.

Gronkye, *to beat*.

Grontys, *a Grant* ; *granted*.

Grou, *Gravel* ; *Sand*, &c.

Grouan, id. grouder, id.

Grouanen, *a Pebble*.

Groudel, *a Fidler*.

Growedh, *to lie down* ; ke groweth, *go*, *lie down*.

Grownzebas, *let him do*.

Groyne, *a Seal* ; *Vitulus Marinus*. Leland.

Gruah, *an old Woman*.

Grûan, A. *Gravel*.

Grud, *a Cheek*, or *Jaw* ; grydh, id.

Grueirten, *a Root*.

Grug, W. *a Mount* ; pro Cryg, id.

Grushens, *the Dregs*, or *Lee*.

Grussons, *they took* ; grussons cusyl, *they took Counsel*.

Gry, *Noise*.

Grydh, *a Cheek* ; *Jaw* ; or *Chin*.

Gryg, *Heath*. W.

Gryglans, *Sticky Heath*.

Grygys, *a Belt*, or *Girdle* ; gouris, id. grug. Cott. id.

Grym, *bony* ; *strong*. R.

Grys, *to believe* ; me a grys, *I believe*.

GU

Guadhel, *Houshold Stuff*.

Guadan, *a Foundation* ; *the Base of a Pillar*.

Guadn, *weak* ; pro guan.

Guadngyrti, *to strangle*.

Guaeldgu, *a Sorry Fellow* ; boudhyn, id. Gw. Lh. 65.

Guaf, *chaste*.

Guag, *Hunger* ; *Penury* ; en guâg, *in vain* ; *empty*.

Guahalgeh, *an Officer of State* ; *a President*, or *Governor of a Country*.

Guailen rayvanadh, *a Scepter* ; guailen, *a Scepter*. Cott.

GU

Guain (nain, id.), *a Meadow* ; it. *a Sheath*.

Guainten, *the Spring Season*.

Guaith, *a Work* ; guithorion, *Workmen*.

Guâl, *a Wall* ; *a Fort* ; guâl hen, *an old Fort* ; as, Wallenford, Camd. & gwal, *Murus*, Dav. ut Gwal Sever, *Severus's Wall*.

Guallofwr, *a Butler*.

Guan ascient, Cott. *one besides himself*.

Guân, *a Sting* ; ind. Guana, *to pierce*.

Guan, *weak* ; *sickly*.

Guana, *to pierce, boar*, or *enter*.

Guanan, *a Bee* ; Pl. guenen ; kaual guanan, *a Bee-hive*.

Guanath, *Wheat* ; bara guanath, *Wheaten Bread*, i. e. *White Bread* ; quas. à Guen, *white*.

Gwander, *Weakness* ; guandre, *Wandering*. Lh.

Guar, *the Neck* ; *Collum*. L.

Guarac, *a Charter*, or *Patent*.

Guardy, *Theatre*. Lh.

Guare (huare, id.), *to play*, or *sport*.

Guarhaz, *the Top*, or *Summit* ; guarhaz ganou, *the Roof of the mouth*. Lh.

Guarimou, *Theatres*.

Guarnys, *warned*.

Guarth, *a Garrison* ; *a Place of Safety*. Gale, *a high Place*.

Guarra, *to sell* ; guertha, id.

Guarrak, *a Bow* ; *Arcus*. L. *An Arch*, or *Vault*. Lh.

Guarrhog, *all Manner of Cattle* ; eal, id. Lh.

Guarthav, *the Top*, or *Summit*.

Guasga, *to press* ; guasge dorn, *to lay Hands on* ; *to ravish*, or *deflower*. Lh.

Guashevyn, *a Magistrate* ; *Primas*. Lh.

Guaskettek, *shady* ; guastad, W. *steddy* ; *constant*.

Guastia, *to destroy* ; dho toula dyveas, id.

Guâv, *Winter*. Ar. *a Spear*.

Guaya, *to move* ; es guaya, *that moveth* ; *that creepeth along* ; ind. guayans, *moving*.

Guaglen, *a Rod*, or *Twig*.

Guayn, *Advantage*.

Guaynia, *to gain, win*, or *profit*. Lh.

Guaz, *a Man* ; *Fellow* ; *Servant* ; Pl. guession ; guaz hegin, *a Skullion*.

Gubar, *pay, reward* ; aguz, gubar, *your Pay*.

Gubman, *Sea Weed* ; *the Alga*.

Gûdh, *a Goose*.

Gudhân, A. *to harden*.

Gudh, *a Mole* ; gudhor, id. &

GU

gudhthaur, id. Lh. gudh dhaôr.

Gudra, *to milk*, or *milch*.

Gudrak, or guedrak, *the first Milk before the Cow has Calf*.

Gudreva, *the third Day hence*.

Gudzh, guydh, id. (goys id.), *Blood* ; *Parentage* ; *Descent*. Lh.

Gudzhigan, *a Black Pudding*.

Gueadar, *a Weaver*.

Guêal, *a Field* ; *Farm* ; *Manor*.

Gueder, *Glass* ; gwydr.

Guedeu, *a Widow* ; guldeu, Cott.

Guêdh, W. *Custom* ; *Fashion*. Lh.

Guedhan, *a Tree* ; guydhen, id. Lh.

Guedhan knyfan, *a Hazle Tree*.

Guedhar, W. *a Weather Sheep*. Lh.

Guedho, *deprived*. Pa.

Guedhra, *to be dry* ; *to dry up* ; dho scha, id.

Guedn hogian, *a Wart*.

Guedran, *a Glass* ; guedran avin, *a Glass of Wine*.

Guedrek, *glassy* ; *green*.

Guedrys, *weak* ; *flagging*. Lh.

Gueid, *Work*.

Gueid uur-argans, *a Silversmith*.

Gueiadar, *a Weaver*. Lh.

Gueiduur-cober, *a Brazier* ; *a Tinker*.

Guein, *a Sheath* ; it. for gûn, *Campus* ; pou izal, id. Lh.

Gueith, *Trees* ; Pl. à guedhan.

Guelan, *a Yard* ; guelan gol, or goil, *the Sail Yard*.

Guelaz, *to see* ; it. *Sight* ; Lh. guellys, *seen* ; welsons, *they see* ; miraz, id. Lh.

Gueldzha, *a Pair of Sheers*.

Guele, *a Bed* ; penguele, *a Bolster*.

Guelen, *a Rod* ; Welen, id. Pl. gueel.

Guella, *to yield* ; *amend* ; *correct* ; it. *best* ; dho ouna, id.

Guelz, *Grass* ; *Straw* ; *all kind of Herbs*. Lh.

Guelu, *a Lip* ; guelv, id.

Guelvan, *to weep* ; ind. vulg. *to belve*, or *weep aloud*.

Guelyst, *thou hast seen*.

Guelz, *Woody* ; *wild* ; as, Idhin guelz, *wild Fowl*.

Guelzen, *I had seen*.

Guen, *Campus* ; *a Plain*. Cott. pro Gun.

Guenan, *a Pimple* ; *a Blister* ; *a Speckle*.

Guenar, *Love* ; *Beauty* ; ind. f. Venus ; W. Didh Guener, *Friday* ; inde Guenwar.

Guenez, *stung* ; guenez gen nadar, *stung with an Adder*. Gw.

Guennol,

GU   GU   GU

Guennol, *a Swallow.*

Guenoiurciat, *a Witch* ; Cott. guenoiureat, & gunethiat dren, id.

Guent, *Monmouthshire.*

Gûenuit, *sagacious* ; *subtil* ; *cunning.* R.

Guenuyn, *Poison* ; *Witchcraft.*

Guenyz, *pierced* ; guinys, id. qua. à guan.

Guenz, *Wind* ; *Breath* ; *Spirit* ; guinz, id.

Gueol, *a Mouth.* Ar.

Guer, *a Village* ; Ar. *a Word.*

Guêr, *Green* ; guirdh, L. *Viridis.*

Gueras (weras, id.), *Help.*

Gueret, *the Ground* ; *moist Earth.*

Guereugh, *shew ye.*

Guerha, *to brag.*

Gueriff, *to lay Eggs.*

Guern, *the Mast of a Ship.*

Guernen, *an Alder Tree.*

Guersyn, *a Spindle.*

Guerthe (werthe, id.), *to sell.*

Guerthyd, W. *an Axle-tree.*

Gueruelz, *Feeding Ground* ; *Pasture* ; *Green Field* ; bounder, id. Lh.

Gues, *wild.* Lh. 59.

Guesga, *to wear Cloaths* ; *to rub* ;

Gueskys, *clad* ; *cloathed.*

Gueskeuyn, *a Primate* ; *a Magistrate.* Lh.

Guesk, *a Husk.*

Gueskall, *to contend.*

Guespeden vrâz, A. *a Hornet.*

Guest, *a Garment* ; ind. *a Vest*, Engl.

Gueth, *Glothing* ; *a Cloth* ; guethens, Ar. *to cover.*

Guetho, *deprived.*

Guethy, *weaved.*

Gueuan, *a Heel.*

Gueus, *the Lips.* Cott.

Guew, *a plain Field.*

Guezga, *to rub, thresh, or crum.* Lh.

Gugl, *a Veil.*

Gugy, *is.*

Guher, *a River* ; id. f. ac gover, *a Brook.*

Guhidh, *a Daughter-in-law* ; guhit, id.

Guhien, *a Wasp* ; & guhyen, id.

Guhuthas, *to accuse.*

Guîa, *to weave* ; *knit, or compose.* Lh.

Guiat, *a Webb.*

Guiban, *a Fly.*

Guibedn, *little stinging Flies.*

Guicgur, *a Merchant.*

Guid, *a Vein.*

Guiden, *a Tree* ; Guetha, id.

Guidhi, *thou shalt know.*

Guidhili, *Irishmen.*

Guidthiad, *a Keeper* ; *a Guardian.*

Guihan, *a Periwrinkle Shell* ; a

Wrinkle.

Guik, Ar. *a Village* ; Guêr, Ar. id.

Guikyr, *a Merchant* ; *a Farmer.*

Guil, *the Sail of a Ship.*

Guilan, *a King's-Fisher.*

Guili, *a Bed* ; Pl. gueliau.

Guilleia, *a Beggar.*

Guillua, *a Watch* ; *watching.*

Guilskin (guilkin, id.), *a Frog.*

Guilter, *a Mastiff.*

Guin, *Wine* ; win, id.

Guin-bren, *the Vine-tree.*

Guindod, *Excellency.* R.

Guinenddhy, *brown.*

Guins, *the Wind.* Lh.

Guins a dro, *a Storm.* Lh.

Guinzal, *a Fan.*

Guîrion, *a Man of Veracity.*

Guirioneth, *Truth.* Lh.

Guîrleveriat, id.

Guirt, & gwird, *green* ; *viridis.* L.

Guis, *an old Sow.*

Guisc, *a Cloathing* ; *a Garment* ; guisk, id.

Guest, id.

Guisetti, *a Basket.*

Guisgdy, *a Wardrobe.*

Guistel, *a Hostage.*

Guit (& gwydd, id.), *a Goose.*

Guîth, *Noise*, Lh. 52. it. *Anger,* 73. it. *a Vein,* ib. 170.

Guitha, *to preserve.*

Guith, *to keep* ; guitha dhort, *to withhold, or keep back.* Lh.

Guitsil, *a wild Beast.*

Guithorion, *Workmen.*

Gul (guil, id.), *to do* ; gull peghes, *do Sin.*

Gulad, *a Country* ; wlas, W. id. gulot. Cott. id.

Gulan, *Wool.*

Gulbredengu, *the Pin-bones.*

Guledh, *a Feast.*

Guledh-iz, *the Corn.*

Guledhiz, *the Corn-feast.*

Guleit, *Roast-meat.*

Gulen, *to require.*

Gûlhel, *Houshold Goods.*

Gulhys, *washed* ; *washing.*

Gulî, *a Wound* ; Pl. Gollyou.

Gullan, *a Gull* ; Pl. gullez.

Gullas (for wollas), *lower* ; as, gueal gullas, *the lower Field.*

Gulloar, *Abundance* ; *Plenty.* Qu.

Gumsellet, *Vinegar.*

Gumpas; *a Plain* ; n'ûn gumpas, *the plain Downs.*

Gun, *our* ; *our Health* ; gun ehaz.

Gûn, *a Scabbard* ; *a Heath* ; *a Down* ; it. *a Gown* ; Pl. gunniau. Lh.

Gunbrê, *a Hill on a Down.*

Guneual, *to dine* ; dho guneual gondzha, *to dine with him.*

Gûner, *a River, or Brook.* Lh.

Gunio, *to sow* ; as, gunnes haz, *to sow Seed.*

Gunithiat ereu, *a Husbandman.*

Gunthas (guathas, rectiùs, id.), *kept.*

Guon, *I know* ; mi a uon, *I know.*

Guorhemmyn, *a Command.*

Guorhyans, *Glory* ; *Renown.*

Guothso ev, *he may know* ; mai guoth ev, *that he may know.*

Guoze (guodzhi), *after.*

Guozemma, *hereafter* ; udzhemma, id.

Guozena (udzhena, id.), *afterwards.*

Gûr, *a Man.*

Gur-a-vau, *an Hermaphrodite* ; *Vulvatus Homo.*

Gura, *to cause* (wra, id.), gurys, *done.*

Guradn, *a Wren.*

Gurâh, *an old Woman* ; bennen goath, id.

Gural, Ar. *Amber.*

Guraminadou, *Commandments* ; à guorhemmyn ; gurhemynadow, id.

Gurâz, *he has done.*

Gurbor, *a broad Dish.*

Gurbulloc, *mad.*

Guredhan, *a Root.*

Gureg (grueg, & freg, id.), *a Woman* ; *a Wife.*

Gureg uedhu, *a Widow.* Lh.

Dho gurei, *to make* ; *to create* ; gil, id.

Gureithon, *we have done.*

Gurek, *Wreck.*

Gureoneth, *Truth.*

Gures, *Heat* ; grês, id. n'un grez, *the Hot Down.*

Guressauk, *hot.*

Gurgettan, *Garters.*

Gurhal, *a Ship* ; goroll, id. Pl. Garhaliou.

Gurhemin, *a Command* ; *an Ordinance* ; Lh. *a Charge* ; *Commission* ; gurhmenniz, id.

Gurhog, *a Great-Great-Grandfather.*

Gurhthit, *a Spindle.*

Guridnias, *pressed* ; *squeezed* ; *crushed.*

Guriz, *a Girdle.*

Guria, Ar. *to surround* ; *encompass.*

Gurjovene, *a young Man.*

Gurkaeth, *a Prisoner* ; *a Man taken in Battle.*

Gurpriot, *a Bridegroom.*

Gurra, *to impose* ; *deceive* ; *beguile.* Lh.

Gurria, *to worship.*

Gurruid, *a Male* ; *a Man* ; *the Male of any Creature.*

Gurythys, *rooted.*

Gurthvi¹,

GU

Gurthvil, *a Beaſt; a wild or other Beaſt.* Lh.

Gurthuper, *in the Evening.*

Gurthyd, *a Spindle;* kerdhit, & guerzit, id.

Gurvedhu, *to lie;* ha gurvedhu en guili kala na, *and lie in that Straw Bed.*

Gurychin, *a Briſtle.*

Gurys, *put; carried;* uras the mernans, *to put to Death.*

Guryſſen, *done;* mî a vryſſen, *I had done.*

Guryſſys, *thou haſt done.*

Gus (for aguz), *yours; you.*

Guſel, *did;* guſell dre envi, *did it out of Envy.*

Guſendzhi, *to lay;* mi vedn guſendzhi, *I will lay.*

Guſke, *frantick.* Lh.

Guthemin-ruif, *a Royal Law.*

Guthot, *Meal.* See Guloth, & Gloth, id.

Guthyl, *All-heal.* So the Ancients called the Miſletoe. Keyſl. 307.

Guthyl, *doſt; canſt; to make.*

Guver, *a Brook;* gûner. Lh.

Guy, *Water;* uy, id. Baxt.

Guyader. See Gweadr. Ir. Fiadoir.

Guyd, *a Fault; or Errour;* kûl bai, id.

Guydh, *conſpicuous; high.* See Gwydh.

Guydh-grug, *a High Mount.*

Guydnach, *a Whiting; a Fiſh.*

Guydhbedyn, W. *a Knat, or little Fly.*

Guydhvaen, *a high Stone;* ind. f. Penwyth, or Penguydh, *the High Promontory; the Weſtern Hundred of England.* Qu.

Guydhelek, *Iriſh.*

Guydhuydh, *the Woodbind, or Honeyſuckle.* Lh.

Guyles, *the Herb Libeſtica.*

Guylfym, *I ſhall ſee;* mar guylfym, *if I ſhall ſee.*

Guyr (& fyr gwyr), *Truth,* it. *a Man;* guyr an chy, *Man of the Houſe.*

Guyraf, *Hay.*

Guyrthiadereu, *a Huſbandman.*

Gûys, *an old Sow.*

Guyſketh, *ſtricken;* gweſka, & gwaſka, id.

Guyſtel, *a Hoſtage,* or *Pledge in War.* Lh.

Guyth, *Times; Seaſon;* komero wyth, *take Care; Opportunity.*

Gwyth, *Name of the Iſle of Wight.*

Guythyad, *a Guardian.*

Guzen, *a Rope; with.*

Guzigan, *a Bladder.*

GW

Gwaeddi, *to bawl; cry out.*

Gwaedling, *bleeding at the Noſe.*

Gwaedu, *to bleed.*

Gwaeth, *a Field;* Gwaeth Heilyn, *the Field of Heilyn; Field of Battle; a Battle.*

Gwailbeth, *a Bawble.*

Gwâl, *empty;* R. gwael, *vile.* Ib.

Gwâl, *Murus;* L. Dav. *a Wall.*

Gwarha, *Lover.* Gw.

Gwarthav, *the Top,* or *Summit of any thing;* gwarthe, id.

Gwarth, *Shame.* R.

Gwawdio, *to befool one.*

Gwef (gwelh, id.), *ſad.*

Gwêl, *Leaven; Barm;* bara gwêl, *Leavened Bread.*

Gwell, *better;* guella, *beſt;* guella guaz, *beſt Man.*

Gwells, *wild.* See Guelz.

Gwelltfa, *a Bean Stalk.*

Gwelyfod, *a Bedchamber.*

Gwen, *white;* gwin, & wyn, id.

Gwep, *to bill as a Pidgon.*

Gwer, *green.*

Gwerches, *a Virgin.*

Gwern, *a Place of Alder Trees.*

Gwethy, *to weave; weaved.*

Gweyth, *the contrary;* gweth, *worſe;* it. pro vyth, as, tergweyth, *three Times.*

Gwg, *Fierceneſs; Anger.* Ar.

Gwiſe-pren, *Bark of a Tree.*

Gwlás, *the Kingdom;* wlas, & gulaſker, id.

Gwothemys, *ſee; know;* wothaff, gothaff, *I know.*

Gwregus, *a Belt;* cleddiff, id.

Gwrelle, *to make.*

Gwydd, *a Gooſe.*

Gwydh, *perſpicuous; eaſy to be ſeen;* as, gwydhgruc, *a conſpicuous Heap;* gwydhfa, *a conſpicuous Place;* the higheſt Mountain in Britain, in Caernarvonſhire. H. Lhuyd's Brev. fol. 17.

Gwydr, *Glaſs.* R.

Gwylvyth, *have ſeen.*

Gwyn, *glorious; a Court;* as, brein-gwyn, *a ſupreme Court.* R.

Gwyn, alias gwydn, *white.*

Gwyne, *Wine.*

Gwyns, *Wind;* guenz, id.

Gwyrthiadereu, *a Huſbandman.*

Gwyrif, *a Batchelor; an unmarried Man.*

Gwyro, *to bend.*

Gwythe, *to preſerve; hinder; hold;* gwethe, & wythe, id.

Gwythres, *Quarter; Part;* yn pub gwythres, *in every Quarter.*

GY

Gy (dzhei, id), *they; them.*

Gybeddern, *a little Hammer.*

Gydhaz, *Judgment;* it. *Opinion; Advice.* Lh.

Gydhivaz, *to brim as a Sow,* i. e. marem appetere.

Gydhihuar, *the Evening.* Lh.

Gydiuhar, *the Evening Star; Even-tide.* Lh.

Gyff (gyff, id. a cafos quas), wy a gyff, *ye ſhall find.*

Gyhydha, *to accuſe;* kyhydha, id.

Gyk (pro kych, or kyg, id.), *Fleſh.*

Gylchynu, *to beſet.*

Gyliangê, *a Hedge Sparrow.*

Gyllin, *can;* ni a yllin, *we can.*

Gylvan, *a Sparrow;* golvan, id.

Gylvan ge, *a Hedge Sparrow.* Lh.

Gylwyr, *Maker.*

Gylwys, *called.*

Gylyua, *to ſhine.*

Gymyn (gemyn, id. cummyn, id.), *to commend; reſign; give Leave to.*

Ghyn (ghen, id.), *our.*

Gyndan, *a Debt.*

Gynez, *to ſow.*

Gynnodar, *a Sower.* Lh.

Ghynſi, *with her.*

Gynſy, *Uſe;* the wull gynſy, *for it had Uſe.*

Gyrgcrik, *a Partridge.* Lh.

Gyrheffias, *offered; proffered,* or *given.* Lh.

Gyrr, *the Gripes; Flux; Dyſentery.*

Gyryn, *a Crown;* t'an ghyryn, *to the Crown.*

Ghyſenzhi, *to lay.*

Gytheffys, *offered.*

Gyu (gew, id.), *able; is; but; only; due; ought;* nyn gyw, *'tis but; 'tis not.*

Gyw, *a Spear.*

Ghynzhanz (genzynz, id.), *with them.*

Gyz (goz, id.), *your;* gyz honan, *your own.*

Gyzigan, *a Bladder.* Lh.

Gyzyuaz, *liſtened* or *did liſten; to hearken;* gwel yw guzuwaz, *it is better to hearken.*

H.

Ha, *and;* oh! hag, *before Vowel.*

Habadın, *Bondage, Slavery.*

Haddal, *a Ladle.*

Hafaid, *ſummerly; æſtivus;* Hâf, *Summer.*

Hagar, *foul; ugly; cruel; wicked;* hagra, & hacera, *more ugly.*

Hagar-

HA

Hagar-auel, *bad Weather, Time,* or *Season.*
Hagen, *but* ; *yet.*
Hagenzol, *also* ; *likewise.* Lh.
Haheyz, *wholly* ; *altogether.*
Hai, *and her* ; *she* ; *her* ; *of her* ; *hay,* id. hodda, id.
Hain, *and our.*
Haiarn, *Strength* ; R. 'trehairn, gwethairne, ib.
Hail, *liberal* ; *huge* ; *very great* ; ind. Hailmên Tor, *the great Stone Tor.* See Heyle.
Hâl, *a Hill,* or *Hillock* ; Pl. halou ; halou-nei, *our Hills* ; it. *a Moor* ; ker th'an hâl, *to go to Moor,* i. e. *to work for Tin* ; halgaver, *the Goat's Moor.*
Halan, *Calends, first Day of the Month.*
Hale theez, *Pull to thee.* Gw.
Halein, & haloin, *Salt* ; halen, id.
Hali (Teuton), *Holy.*
Halle, *he might.*
Hallough (yllough, id.), *ye,* or *you may,* or *can be.*
Hallus, *Sweat* ; re hallus, *with the Sweat.*
Hallyah, *pulling.*
Halogu, *to bribe,* or *corrupt.*
Haloiner, *a Salter.*
H'am, *and my* ; *and I am* ; ab ha & om.
Hamblys, *prepared* ; *Preparation* ; hablys, id.
Hambrokkya, *to wash.* Lh.
H'an, *and the* ; *for* ha-an.
Hanadzhans, *a Sigh.*
Hanaf, *Hanapus.* Cott. Qu.
Hanath, *a Cup,* or *Bowl* ; hanaf, id. bolla, id. fîol, id.
Hanchi, *a Linx* ; *a spotted Beast.*
Hanes, *those.*
Haneth, *he* ; *this* ; *this Night.*
Haneu, *a Swine* ; *a Sow.*
Hanou, *a Name.*
Hanter, *betwixt* ; *middle* ; hanternos, *Midnight.*
Hao, Ar. *ripe.*
Hàr, *Slaughter* ; *Murther* ; Ar. quod pro aor, *Land Earth* ; *plowed Land.* W.
Harau, *a Harrow* ; W. oged. Ar. oget.
Hard, *earnestly* ; hard, W. *seemly* ; *comely.*
Harfel, *a She-piper* ; *a Viol* ; *a Harp* ; it. *a Drink-pot* ; Lh. *in Phiale.*
Harfellor, *a Player on the Pipe.*
Harlot, *a vile Fellow.*
Harow, *bitter* ; yn harrow, *bitterly.*
Harthy (hartha, or harrah), *to bark as a Dog.*

HA

Haru, *rough* ; *beggarly.*
Harz, *a Bound* ; *Limit* ; *Hinderance* ; Ar. as, mên-hars, *a bound Stone.*
Hat, *a Hat* ; het. W. id.
H'ath, *and thy.*
Hâv, *Summer* ; Cott. hâf, id.
Haval, *Likeness.* See Aval, Avel, id.
Havas, *found* ; cafos, id.
Haun, *a Haven* ; as, Porthkarnhaun, in Endellyan, Par.
Hauns, *thee.*
Haunsel, *a Breakfast* ; dishunish, id. Lh.
Havodty, *a Cottage.* Lh. 167.
Havrek, Ar. *a fallow Ground.*
Hauz, *a Duck* ; haz, id. Pl. heidzhe, hoet, id.
Hawlsons, *they cried out* ; ab helwys.
Haz, *Seed* ; *Nature* ; it. *a Duck* ; kuliagaz, *a Drake* ; *a Mollard* ; Plur. heidzhe.

HE

He, *the Skin.*
Hêan, *a Haven* ; goran hean, *put into the Haven.*
Heb, *without.*
Hebford, *impassable.*
Hebrenciat phui (oferiat, id.), *a Priest of the Parish* ; it. hebryngkiad, *an Elder* ; *a Presbyter.*
Hebrenciat, luir, *a General.*
Hecka, *Richard.* Gw.
Hedda (hed, id.), *that.*
Heddre, *whilst.*
Hedh, *easy* ; *feasible.*
Hedha, *to stretch out* ; *to reach at.* Lh.
Hedra, *October.*
Heene, *drowsy.* Gw.
Heeneth, *Generation.* Gw.
Hegar, *a Captive.*
Hegar, *lovely* ; ab hedh, & gare, *easy to be loved.*
Hegarat, A. *Mild* ; *gentle.*
Hegaratyz, *Health.* Lh. Pref.
Hehen, *one* ; pub hehen, *every one.*
Heid, *Barley.*
Heidzhe, *Ducks.*
Hel, *a Hall* ; Cott. hêll, id. it. *a River,* or *Moor.*
Helak (helik, heligen, or helagan, id.), *a Willow Tree.*
Helek, *Moory* ; *Marshy* ; *full of Brooks* ; ab hêl, *a River* ; *a Moor.*
Helfia, *to hunt.*
Helhwar, *a Hunter* ; *a Huntsman.*
Heltheys, *hunted.*
Helu, *Brine* ; gulyber, id.
Helviat, *one that pursues,* or *hunts* ;

HE

helyad, & helyûr, id.
Helwys, *to cry out.*
Hemdrez, *Dream.*
Hemlodh, *to fight* ; hemladh, id.
Hen, *that.*
Hênath, *Generation* ; *Age.*
Henbidhiat, *sparing* ; *frugal.*
Hendat, *a Grandfather.*
Hengog, *the Great Grandfather's Father* ; *a Great Grandfather.* Cott.
Henn, *old* ; Ir. sean, id.
Henna, *this* ; *he* ; *then.*
Hent, Ar. *a Way.*
Henuir vi, *I shall be called.*
Henvill, *Vigil.* See Heuyl.
Henwys, *called* ; *stiled* ; henuelez, id.
Henz, *before* ; *first* ; *for* kenz.
Heor, Ar. *an Anchor.*
Hepmar, *doubtless.*
Hepparou, *incomparable* ; *matchless.*
Hepeu, *To-day* ; *this Day.*
Hepuil, *watchful* ; hichh puil, *very watchful.*
Herdya, *thrust forth* ; *prominent* ; ind. f. lyzherd, *a chief Place thrust forth,* or *Head-land jutting forth.*
Hernan, *a Pilchard* ; hearne.
Hernan guidn, *a Herring,* i. e. *a white Pilchard.*
Herniah, *to shoe* ; herniah an verh, *to shoe the Horse.*
Heruedh, *in Respect of* ; heruedh nep, *without Respect of whom.*
Herwith, *Attendance.*
Heschen, *a Reed,* or *Sedge* ; *a File* ; Pl. hesk. pendiuen ; id.
Heskyz, *dry* ; beuh heskyz, *a dry Cow.*
Hesp, *a Lock.*
Hethe, *to reach* ; *stretch* ; hethys, pa.
Hethen, *a Bird* ; Cott. adglaer, id. f. *an Eagle.*
Hethow, *this Day.*
Heved (Sax. *a Head*), Qu.
Heuel, *visible* ; *easy to be seen* ; ab hedh, or he, *and* guêl.
Hevelep, *like* ; ab havel.
Hevez, *a Shirt,* or *Shift* ; heuis, Cott. id.
Heeuhal, *lofty* ; mar heuhal, *so high.*
Heuul, *the Sun.* Cott.
Heuyl, *watchfull.*
Heyle, *a River* ; hêl, id. hail, id. heil, id.
Heys, *the Length of any thing by Measure.*
Hez, *a Swarm.*
Hezuek, *Ease.* ἡσυχια. Gr.

HI

Hi, *she* ; *of her.*
Hibblyth, *pliant* ; *supple.*

Hidhu,

HI

Hidhu, *To-day.*
Hieauvén, *Ivy.*
Hîg, *a Crook; a Hook.*
Higa, *to play with.*
Higolen, *a Whetstone.*
Hihsommet, *a Bat.*
Hillah, *the Night Mare.*
Hilliv, *I may, or can; as, mai hilliv, that I may, or be able.*
Hingerlin, *a Bastard's Bastard.*
Hinon, Ar. *the clear Firmament.*
Hîr, *long;* Tremenhîr, *the Town of Long-stones;* Hêr, *id.*
Hîrath, *a longing after; a coveting.*
Hirgherniad, *a Trumpeter.*
Hirgorn, *a Trumpet; a long Tube, or Horn.*
Hirrahat, *to procrastinate.* Ar.
Hisommet, *a Bat.* Lh.
Hitadver, *Harvest.*
Hiubren, *a Cloud.*
Hiuhelder, *Height.*
Hiuhvoeliet, *a Helvetian; a Highlander.*
Hiuin, *the Yew-tree;* hivin, *id.*

HO

Ho (He, id.), *easily; when prefixed to an Adjective; as, ho-gil, feasible; as bilis affixed in Lat.*
Hoalea, *to weep.*
Hoar, *a Sister;* hôr, huyr, *id.*
Hôarn, *Iron;* hoarnek, *of or belonging to Iron.*
Hoary, Ar. *a Sport;* C. huare, & guare, *id.*
Hôch, *a Sow; Pig;* hôh, *id.*
Hochuayu, *a Hunting Pole.* Lh.
Hochuaiu, *id.*
Hodda, *she; that; there;* honna, *id.*
Hodna, *a Neck;* ter (for der), y hodna, *about her Neck;* godna, *id.*
Hoedel, *Life; Age.*
Hoet, *a Duck;* hos, id. Cott.
Hogan, *a Hawthorn Berry.* Ar.
Hogen, *vile.*
Hogil, *easy.*
Hoirnier, *an Ironmonger.*
Hoizias, *Hoarseness;* hôz, *hoarse.*
Hokye, *Delay.*
Holan, *the Heart;* for golan, *id.*
Holan, *a Knife.*
Holan (& holoine), *Salt;* Lh. pro halen.
Hollyas, *followed;* holliou, *follow ye.*
Holm, *the Holy Tree.*
Holi, *Watch;* ketwell holy, *keeping Watch.*
Hombronkyas, *led;* V. it. *to wash.*
Hon, *this Female;* homma, *this Woman here.*
Honon, *himself; one's self.*

HO

Honou, *Honour.*
Dho honua, *to name, or call;* dho kriha.
Hôr, *a Ram;* Pl. Hyrroz, it. *a Sister.*
Hora, *a Whore; a Miss.* Lh.
Hordh, *a Ram.*
Horfe, *Body,* for corfe.
Hos, *a Boot; a Harness for the Leg.* Lh.
Hostleri, *a Tavern; Alehouse.*
Hot, *Caputium.* L.
Houl, *the Sun;* sul, id. heul, id. Lh.
Houl-dreval, *the East, or Sun-rising.*
Houl-zethza, *the West, or Sun-setting;* houlzedhas, id. Lh.
Hounsal, *Breakfast;* Gw. See Haunsel, & Halsel.
Hôz, *hoarse.* Lh.

HU

Huanen (huadnan, id.), *a Fly; a Flea;* for guanan.
Hual, *on high; above; upon;* uhal, id. ehual, id.
Huarfo (as, pan huarfo, *when I shall do);* à gwra, *to do, or cause.*
Huath, *yet; it. anew; afresh;* W. eto, id.
Huchot, *above.*
Hudol, *a Magician.*
Hudur, Ar. *foul; nasty.*
Huedh, S. *a Swelling.* Lh.
Huedhi, *to swell;* huedhyz, *swoln.*
Huedzha, *to vomit.*
Hueffas, *the sixth.*
Hueg, *sweet; dear; delicious;* wek, id.
Hueger, *a Mother-in-law.*
Huehag, *sixteen.*
Huei, *ye; you; of you.*
Huekter, *Sweetness.*
Huel, *a Work; a Mine;* huel stean, *a Tin Mine;* Pl. huelio.
Huelder, *Bounty.*
Huelen, *a Hill.* Ar.
Huellam, *I may see;* Huellaz, *seen.*
Hueret, *the Ground.* Cott.
Huerhen, *Laughter.*
Huerthyn, *to laugh, or play;* hwerwin, id.
Huero, *rough;* Ar. *bitter.*
Huerval, *February;* corruptly for Huevral, id. Lh.
Huethia, *to blow.*
Huethvians an dour, *a Bubble of Water.*
Huetlo, *a Tale-teller;* W. chuedlæ; Lh. χuedel, W. *a Rumour.*
Huettag, *sixteen.*
Huez, *Sweat;* hueza, *to sweat.*
Huhuthas, *to accuse;* guhuthas, id.

HU

Huî (dheu, huyhui, id.), *unto you.*
Huibanat, *to whistle.*
Huido-wenyu, *a Swarm of Bees;* faith-beach, id.
Hujeth, *huge;* hujeth tra, *a huge thing.*
Huigan, *Meal, or Flour; Medulla Panis.*
Huigeren, *a Father-in-law.*
Huîh, *six* (huè, id.), hueffas, *the sixth.*
Huil, *to do; make.* V.
Huila, *to seek* (huillaz, id.), *to ask, seek, or demand.* Lh.
Huilan, *a Beetle; a Spider.*
Huirnerez, *a Hornet; a Wasp.*
Huis, *an Age,* & huys, id. Lh.
Huist, *Silence.*
Huitel, *a Story;* Pl. huitelou.
Hule, *an Owl.*
Humthan, *conceived; breeding;* ma hy a humthan, *she here is breeding.*
Hun, Ar. *Sleep.*
Hunnyn, *of us.*
Huvel, *humble;* hyvel, W. id. Lh.
Huveldot, *Humility.*
Huwelwur (& huweluair), *a Nobleman; a Viscount; a Sheriff;* quas. Uchel wyr.
Huweltag, *a Patriarch.*
Huyl-bren, *a Beacon.*
Huyn-dhe-sympit, *the Lethargy.*

HY

Hy, *he, or she.*
Hycheul, *very watchful.*
Hychol, *above.* Lh.
Hydheyl, *Soot.* Ar.
Hydhr, *bold.* Ib.
Hydol, *an Impostor; Sorcerer.*
Hydruk, *brittle.*
Hyeis, *an Age;* huis, & huys, id.
Hyfder, *Boldness.*
Hygoeled, *Credulity; Superstition.*
Hyll, *fierce;* it. *the hinder Part of the Neck.*
Hyller, *to follow.*
Hylly, *might;* hyllyf, *I may, or can.*
Hylwys, *to cry out.*
Dho hynadzha, *to groan, or sigh.* Lh.
Hynadzhan, *a Sigh, Groan, or Howling.*
Hyrch, *to command;* αρχη. Gr.
Hyrliau, *Hurling; a Cornish Custom of playing with a Ball:* Hyrliau, yu ghen guare nyi, *Hurling is our Sport.*
Hysty, *haste; haste.*
Hyuelar, *noble.*
Hyveldot, *Obedience.* Lh.

Hyuelvair,

H Y

Hyuelvaiŕ, *a Sheriff; a Viscount.* Lh.

Hyvla, *to obey.* Lh.

I.

I, *They* (for y), *his; her; war* i progath, *upon his Sermon.*

Ja, *but; rather; it. Ice.*

Jach, *sound; safe; healthy; it. low.*

Jakeh, *John.*

Jammeh, *James.*

Jâr (rectiùs yâr), *a Hen.*

Jar, *a Stalk.*

I C

Icot, *below; Deorsum.* Cott.

I D

Idhen, *a Bird;* ethen, *id.*

Idhio, *the Ivy Tree;* eideu, *id.* W. *id.*

Idnak, *the eleventh.*

Idne, *narrow; it. a Fowler.* Cott.

Idzhek, *hooting; sounding;* Qu. as, Karn-idzhek, *the hooting Karn, so called probably from the significant, prophetic noises which consecrated Rocks were supposed by the Ancients sometimes to emit.*

Idzhin, *we;* ni idzhin aguelaz, *we see.*

N. B. Two Pronouns personal for one. Lh. 245, Col. 1.

I E

Jedhewon, *Jews;* Edzhewon, *id.*

Jef, *Ice.*

Jein, *cold; chill; frigid.*

Jên, *Cold; it. a Yoke.*

Jeu, *the Ridge of a Hill.*

Jevam, *a young Man; Prince; Jupiter.* R.

I F

Ifarn, *Hell;* Als-yfarn, *the Hellish Cliff; viz. as deep as Hell.*

I G

Ig, *a Hook.*

Iganz, *twenty.*

I K

Ik (yk, ick, id.), *a common Termination of Creeks in Cornwall, as, Pordinik, Pradnik, Portyssik, f. A'uik, or Gûik.*

I L

Il, *can, or may;* tî a îl, *thou can'st;* ni illi, *he cannot.*

Ilin, *an Elbow.*

I M

Impinion, *the Brain.*

Im, *into my.*

Impoc, *a Kiss;* impog, *id.* pok-kail, *id.*

I N

In, *they.*

Inguinor, *a Workman; Inventor; Contriver.* Lh.

Inhans, *down;* inhans in hâl, *down in the Moor.* Qu.

Inniadou, *Repulses; Denials.*

Inkois, *Frankincense.*

Inkois-lestr, *a Censer.*

Innanz, *now.*

I O

Jor, *Lord;* bâd-ior, *the Governor's House.* R.

Jorkhes, *a Roe; a She-goat.*

Jot, *Hasty-pudding; Pulse.* Cott.

Joul, *the Devil;* Dzhiaul, *id.* Joulou, *Devils.*

Jowan, *John;* Dzhuan, *id.*

Jorwerth, W. *Edward.*

I R

Ira, *to anoint.*

Irat, *sweet Ointment.*

Irch, *Snow;* Cott. S. irk. Lh. *id.*

I S

Is, *any thing low; inferiour.* Gale.

Isav, *the Bottom.*

Iscaun, *slight;* treviscaun, *a slight Dwelling.*

Isel (isall, id.), *humble; low.*

Iselhat, Ar. *Humility.*

Iseldor, *lowest, or deepest Part; even with the Ground.*

Isge, *Water;* Ar. visge, *id.*

Ision, *Chaff; Palea;* L. kulin, *id.* Lh.

Iskel, *Broth;* isgal. Lh. *id.*

Iskinat, *to provoke; to challenge.*

Isod (isot, id.), *below; downward.*

I T

Ithen, *Furze;* eithen, *id.*

Ithik, *immense; cruel; fat; valiant;* ithik tra, *very much; most of all.*

Itta, *in;* itta 'o guili, *in the (or my) Bed.*

I U

Ives, Ar. *also.*

Jugye, *to judge.*

Juh, *upon, super.* L.

Juin, *a Nail;* Pl. juinaz, *Unguis.* L.

Juntis, *Joints; viz. of the Limbs.*

Ivre, *Darnel.*

Jurna, *a Day;* dzhurna, *id.*

I Y

Iyn, *young.*

Iyngh (Iynkar, id.), *a Youth.*

I Z

Iz, *Corn;* iz saval, *id.* Lh.

Iz-diu, *a Hurtle-berry.*

Izal. See Isel.

K.

Mem. No K, in the British Language, says Moyle, Lett. Vol. I. pag. 182. Posthum. Works, till the Year 1200, when the W was also introduced.

N. B. The K is very rare in the Cott. MS. But Mr. Lhuyd often uses it; and by other Moderns the C, K, and Ch, are indifferently used.

Kabin garick, *bandy-legged.* Kabin lugadshok, *squint-eyed.* Lh.

Kabin sghudak, *crook-backed.* Lh.

Kac, *a Field.*

Kad, W. *War; Battle.*

Kadar, *Honour; Reverence.*

Kadven, W. *a Chain.*

Kaeth; *sold;* gurkaeth, *a Bond-slave.* Lh.

Kael, *to find;* gael, & gavel, *id.* Lh.

Kaff (kaou, id.), *a Cavern.* Gale.

Kaffel, *to have;* Verbs that want the Present Tense Indicative, have it supplied by ma d'hymmo, *I have,* i. e. *there is to me;* kavaz, *id.*

Kah, *caco;* kaha en guili, *cacavit in Lecto;* Gw. *it. the Crop, or first Stomach of a Fowl.*

Kahen-ryd, *a Torrent.*

Kaîk, *Lime.*

Kairder, *an outward Form; Shape; Pretence, or Picture.*

Kaithes, *a Maid Servant;* kaith, *a Man Servant.* Lh.

Kakan (Pl. kakez), *a Cake.*

Kal, *a Phallus; Membrum Virile.* L.

Kala, *a Straw.* Lh.

Kalagueli, *a Bed of Straw.*

Kalan (halan, id.), *the Calends, or first Day of the Month.* Lh.

Kalanedh, *Murther.*

Kalatza,

KA

Kalatza, *hardeft.*
Kalch, *Lime.*
Kaletter, *Hardnefs.*
Kalifh, *hard;* kalifho, *difficult.*
Kall, *crafty.*
Kallaminghi, *Tranquillity;* Calm.
Kalonnek, *valiant.*
Kaltor, *a Kettle;* pêr, id.
Kamdhavas, *a Rainbow.*
Kamhinfek, *partial.* Lh.
Kams, *a Surplice.* Lh.
Kân, *white;* bara-kan, *white Bread;* it. *a Song; a Poem.*
Kana, *to fing;* kans, *finging.*
Kankar, *a Crab-fifh;* Ruft; Blaft *of Corn;* Pl. kenkraz.
Kanna, *a Flagon.*
Kan-pur (f. kanwur), *Athleta; a Wreftler.*
Kans, kana, *a Song, or Tune.*
Kanftel, *a Bafket.*
Kantl, kantuil, Pl. kyntulti, *a Candle.*
Kanvas, *to flout, rattle, make a Noife.*
Kanz, *a hundred.*
Kaol, *Cabbage.* Lh.
Kâr, *a Friend;* Lh. *a Kinfman.*
Kara, *to love;* Lh. it. *as if; as it were.* Ib.
Kâràk, *a Rock;* kraig, id.
Kardouion, *Friends.*
Karedig, W. *Wind.*
Karenza, *Love.*
Karéfk, *Exeter City.*
Karetys, *a Parfnip, or a Carrot.*
Karhar, *a Jail, or Prifon.*
Karlath, *a Ray-fifh, or Thornback.*
Karn, *a Heap of Stones.*
Karnedh, *a Heap of Stones;* W. & Ir. karnân, id. it. *a rocky Heap of Witnefs.*
Karnkolhan, *the Handle of a Weapon.*
Karo (karu, id.), *a Stag, or Deer.*
Karogos, *a Kinfman;* Lh. qua. kar-agos.
Karol, *a Choir; a Confort of Mufick; a Song.* Cott.
Karr, Ar. *a Cart, or Waggon.*
Karrak, *a Rock;* W. Kraig. Lh.
Karrog, W. *a Brook, or River.* Lh.
Karrog, *a River.* [Qu.]
Karwedha, *to lie;* ma'n ladar y karwedha, *the Thief lies;* i. e. *down.*
Karven, W. *a Cart, or Waggon.*
Kaftelh, alias kaftal, Lh. *a Caftle.*
Kâth, *a Cat.*
Kavaethiaz, *Covetoufnefs.*
Kaval, *a Hive; a Bafket;* W. *a Hamper.*
Kaval guanan, *a Bee-hive.*
Kavankis, *to efcape.*
Kavarn, *a Grot, or Den.* Lh.
Kavat, *any Kind of Veffel.*
Kavatfh, *a Cabbage;* kaol, id.
Kauaz, *to have;* it. *to find.* Lh.

KA

Kaudarn, *a Caldron;* pêr, kaltor, id.
Kauh, *Dung.*
Kaul, *Herbs; Pottage.* Lh.
Kaurvarch, *a Camel.*
Kauz, *to talk.*
Kâz, *Reafon; Caufe.*
Kazal, *the Arm-pit.*
Kazek koit, or koat, *a Woodpecker.* A. & C. Lh.
Kazer, *a Sieve.*

KE

Ke (kei, id. W. kae, id.), Pl. keaw, *a Hedge.*
Ke, *fall thou; go thou.*
Keann, Ir. *a Head.*
Dho keaz, *to fhut up; to fhut faft.* Lh.
Keber, *the Rafter of a Houfe; a Beam of Timber;* it. pro cheber.
Kebifter, *a Halter.*
Kedha, *a Fall.*
Kedva, *an Affembly; a Synod.*
Keer, *Love; Affection;* carer, kerd, ker, id.
Keffrys, *between.*
Keg, *a Cook;* kog, id. Cott.
Kegaz, *Hemlock.*
Keghin, *a She-cook; a Kitchen.* W. id.
Kehedzhe, *a reaching, or ftretching of the Body.*
Kei, *a Dog* (kì, id.), Pl. kên, gi, id. in Compof.
Kein, *the Back.*
Keinak, *a Shad-fifh.*
Keirch, *Oats;* bara keirch, *Oaten Bread.* Cott.
Kekyffrys, *alike; likewife.*
Kelednak, *kind.* Gw.
Kelegel, *a Cup;* Calix, L. Cott.
Kelin, *the Weed of ftanding Pools.*
Kelinen, *the Holly Tree.*
Kelinnek, *a Place where Holly Trees grow.*
Kelionen, *a Fly;* kilionen, id.
Keliok reden, *the Ferncock; Grafhopper.*
Kelli, *a Grove.* Cott. Lh.
Kellys, *fallen; loft;* killys, id. à kelly, *to lofe.*
Kelma, *to bind.* See Colmye.
Kelmy, *to bind; to thruft in;* takkia, id.
Keluedhek, A. *a Grove, or Tops of Hazel Trees;* kelhi. W. id.
Kembra, *a Britan;* Chî an Kembra, *the Houfe of a Britan.* Pl. Kembrion.
Kemer, *to take.*
Dho kemera kerr, *to take away* (kymeras, *to take,;* Lh.
Kemerys (hemerys, kemerag, & gemerag, id.), *taken.* Pa.
Kemifkys, *mixed; a Mixture.*

KE

Kên, *although; before; otherwife; as if; before that.*
Ken, *Pity;* hebken, *without Pity.*
Kendereu, A. *a Coufin-german.*
Keneual, *to dine.*
Kenin eynoc, *Garlick.*
Keniat, *a Singer.*
Kenkraz, *Crabs.*
Kennkia, *to contend; quarrel; guefkal;* id.
Kens, *rather; before that;* kyns, id. & *before-hand.*
Kenfa, *firft; Chief;* kenza, id.
Kenfemmyn, *e'er now.*
Kenfenna, *e'er that.*
Kent, *before.* Lh.
Kentro, *Nails* (Claves, L.), *Spurs;* kentar, *a Nail;* pidn, id.
Kenyver, *every;* (kanifer, id.), *any.*
Kenzhoha, *the Morning;* en kewzboha, *in the Morning.*
Kepar, *as, even as; furely.*
Kêr, *a Dwarf;* kerr, *far away;* procul; L. it. *dear; coftly; beloved;* hueg, huegol, id.
Kerd, *Affection.*
Kerden, *the Mountain Afh.*
Kerdinen, *a Branch, or Bough.*
Kerdy, *Cords;* kereor, *a Shoemaker.* Lh.
Kerh, *Oats;* ker-iz, *Oat Corn.*
Kerheis, *a Heron.* Lh.
Kerhez, *to fetch;* kerhys, *removed; gone.*
Kerhidh, *a Heron.* Lh.
Kerghys, *made ready.*
Kern, *a Horn;* kernias, kerniat, *a Piper;* it. *round.*
Kerna, *to tremble; trembled;* ev rigkerna, *he did tremble;* krenna, id.
Kernat, *a Pipe; a Blower of a Clarion.*
Kernou, *Cornwall;* fo Cymru, W. *Wales.* R.
Kernuâk, *Cornifh; of or belonging to Cornwall.*
Keroin, *a Cup.*
Kerrys, *loved.*
Kerydhy, W. *to condemn.* Lh.
Kefer, *Hail;* kezzar, id.
Kefkar, *Poverty.*
Kefker, *to wander.*
Kefkewetha, *familiar.*
Kefkyans, *Confcience.*
Ket, Adv. implying an Equality; as, kettoth, *as foon as.*
Ketchys, *taken.*
Ketella, *fo; in fuch Manner.*
Ketelma, *this Manner.*
Ketep, *every.*
Keth, *People; the fame; fuch; Acquaintance.*
Kethel, *a little Knife; a Knif.*
Kerthes, *to walk;* gerthes, id.
Ketorva, *the Groin;* Inguen. L.

Kettoth,

K E

Kettoth, *as.*

Ketwell, *to keep.*

Keu, *hollow.* Lh.

Keuar, *a Storm*; *a Tempeſt*; hagarauel, id,

Keuar-diu-mis, *December.*

Kevelep, *alike.*

Kevnen, *a Hill,* or *Hillock.*

Keweras, *help.*

Kewſel, *to ſpeak*; kewſens, *they ſpake.*

Keyſon, *Charge, Accuſation.*

Kez, *a Cheeſe*; kezn, id.

Kezan, *a Clod,* or *Turf*; Pl. kezau.

Kezzar, *Hail.* Lh.

K I

Ki, *go thou.*

Kibbal, *a Bucket*; *a little Tub*; Ar. quibell, id.

Kibmiaz, *leave*; kummyaz, id.

Dho kidha (dho dereval, id.), *To hoard*; *hide*; it. *to build.*

Kidniadh, *Autumn*; kidniaz, *Harveſt*; kyniau, id.

Kidnio, *a Dinner.*

Kig, *Fleſh.*

Kigel, *a Diſtaff.*

Kiger, *a Butcher.* Ar. id.

Kigiiu, *Fleſh-colour.*

Kigty, *the Shambles.* W. id.

Kiguer, *a Fork*; *Furca*; L. vorh, id.

Kil, *a Neck*; chil, id. polkil, *top of the Neck*; it. *a Retirement.*

Killîn, *to lie along*; killynia, *to lie ſhelving.*

Kilymmiar, *a Pigeon House*; klymmiar, id.

Kimêr (for keimawr), *a great Dog.*

Kinak, *a Worm*; Pl. kinakas.

Kinbyk, *a Wether-goat.*

Kinethel, *a Generation*; en kinedhel, *a Giant.*

Kinidern, Ar. *a ſhe Couſin-german.*

Kinin, *a Leek*; *a Slip of Land.*

Kinguer (ſee Kiguer), Cott. Qu.

Kinnis, *Fewel*; *hot*; kynnes, id.

Kîo, *a Snipe.*

Kiſtan, *a ſmall Cheſt.* Lh.

Kitha, *to hide*; keeth, id. keether, *hidden*; leath kither, *ſcalded* (viz. *hidden,* or *covered) Milk.*

Kiulat, *a Coverlet.* Lh.

K L

Klabitter, *a Bittour,* or *Bittern.*

Klâv, *ſick.* Lh.

Klechic, *a little Bill.* Lh.

Kledh, *a Trench* (Pl. kledhiou), *a Dyke*; kleudh, id. Scots

K L

Cluith, *as,* Alcluith. W.

Clawd, *as,* Clawd Offa, *Offa's Dyke.*

Kledha. See Clethe.

Kledha bian, *a Dagger.*

Kledhe, *a Sword*; *Knife*; it. *the Left-hand*; kledhek, *Left-handed.* Lh.

Klevas, *a Diſeaſe.*

Klevas y mân tedh, *the Stone in the Kidneys*; klevaz an my tern, *the King's Evil.*

Klevet, *the Hearing.*

Klihi, *Ice.*

Klittro, *to ſhine*; o es klittra, *that is ſhining.*

Klo. See Clo.

Klôdai, W. *Credit*; *Honour.* Lh.

Klodzha, *to harrow.* Lh.

Klodzhaz, *a Harrow*; *to harrow*; ma e a klodzhaz, *he harrows.*

Klôh, *a Bell*; kloch, id.

Kloppek, *lame*; *a Cripple.* See Clof, & Klof, id.

Klouaz, *to hear*; dho glouaz, id.

Klunk, *to ſwallow.* f. Qu.

Klut, *a Rag*; *a Clout.*

Klut-leſtre, *a Diſh-clout.*

Kluyd, *a Hurdle of Rods*; W. id. Ar. kluet, id. *the Breaſt*; duyvron, id. Lh.

Klymiar, & klomiar, *a Pigeon-houſe.*

K N

Kneff, *ſorry.*

Kneu-glan, *a Fleece of Wool.*

Kniſkan, *a Flagon.*

Knyfan, *a Hazzle*; guedan knyfan, *a Hazzle Tree.*

K O

Kô, *Remembrance*; ema ko dho vi, *I remember*; kof, & cof, id.

Koat (for coit), *a Wood*; kûz, id.

Kober, *Copper*; *Braſs.*

Kodha (dho kodha), *to fall.* Lh.

Kodna, *a Neck*; kodna brêh, *the Arm Wriſt*; kona, id.

Kodna-guidn, *a white Neck*; i. e. *a Weazel.*

Kodna-huilen, *a Lap-wing.*

Koeten, *Quoit*; as, koeten Arthur, *Arthur's Quoit.*

Kof, & cof, *Remembrance.*

Koir, *Wax.*

Koiſen, *the Calamus,* or *ſweet Cane.*

Koit, *a Wood*; as, penkoit, W. coed.

Koith-gath, *a wild Cat,* i. e. *a Wood Cat.*

K O

Kok, *a Boat*; ſkath, id.

Kolan, *a Cole*; it. *the Heart.* Lh.

Kolannak, *courageous*; à Colon, *a Heart.*

Kolh (kolhed, id.), W. *Hurt*; *Damage.* Lh.

Koliaz, *ſailing.*

Koll, Ir. *a Head.*

Kollel, *a Knife*; kolhel gravio, *a Graving Inſtrument.* See Coltel.

Kollet, *Loſs*; *Damage.*

Koloin, *a Whelp.*

Komolek, *dark.*

Kompas, Ir. *a Circle*; it. C. as, n'un gompas, in St. Juſt, *the Down by or of the Circle.*

Kona, *a Neck.*

Kone, *Supper*; Pl. konnes.

Koneriok, *mad.*

Kong, *a Look.*

Kontlez, *gathered.*

Kopher, or Kophor, *a Box*; kopher-brâz, *a Cheſt.*

Kôr, *Beer*; *Ale*; *Wax*; *a Male Dwarf*; koruv, id. i. e. *Ale*; korguella, *beſt Beer.*

Kor, W. *a Sheep*; Ir. kaor, id.

Korf, *a Body.*

Korhlan, *a Burying-place*; *a Sheepfold.* W.

Korn (C. W. Ar.), *a Horn*; kern, id.

Kornat, *an Angle.* Lh.

Kornat, *a Corner*; *Angulus.* L.

Korolli, *to dance.*

Koron, *a Crown*; *a Coronet.*

Korph maro, *a Corpſe*; *a dead Body.*

Korres, *a Female Dwarf.*

Korſen, *a Reed, Stalk*; *a Quill.*

Kortez, *to ſtay.*

Koruedha, *to lie down*; *to lie.*

Kofgar, *Lads*; *Boys*; it. *a Guard*; Satellitium. Lh.

Kofgaza, *ſhade,* or *defend thou*; kofgezyz, *ſhaded.*

Kofkor, *depending*; Dên kofkor, *a Tenant.*

Kofkough, *ſleep ye*; à Kuſge, *to ſleep.*

Kofoua, *to lift up.*

Koſtan, *a Buckler,* or *Target*; *a Defence.*

Koſtrel, *a Pot, Bottle,* or *Flagon.* W.

Kota, *a Peticoat, Coat,* or *Jerkin.* Lh.

Kôth, *old*; *of old Time.* Lh.

Kov (kyv, id.), anſwers to the Latin *con* in confirmo, &c. as, kovlenuel, & collenuel, *to fulfill.*

Kouaith-liver, *a Manual.*

Kouat, *a Storm of Rain.* Lh.

Kouaz, *to get*; *to enjoy*; potior. L.

Kovlenuel, *to fulfill*; koullenweugh, *fulfill ye.*

Koulrty,

KO

Koultyr, *the Coulter of a Plough.*
Kovys, *mindful ; remembring.*
Kouz (koums, id.), *Discourse ; Talk ;* dho kouz, *to chat ; to tell.* Lh.
Kowl, *Broth ;* evos kowl, *sup up your Broth.*
Kozal, *slow ; soft.* See Kuzal.

KR

Krâf, *covetous.* Lh.
Krâg, *Provision ; Meat.*
Kra-ma, *if not.*
Kramia, *to creep.*
Krampez, *a Pie ;* as, gil krampez l'avalou, *to make an Apple-pie.*
Krampothan, *a Fritter ; a Pancake ;* Pl. krampedh.
Krana, *a Crane.* Lh.
Kranag, *a Frog ;* kranag diu, *a Toad.*
Kredzhans, *Faith ; Honesty ;* Lh.
Kreft, *Art ; Science ; Skill.* Lh.
Kreis, *a Smock ; a Shirt ;* hevez, id.
Kreiz, *called ; invited.* Lh.
Krên, *a Spring ; a Source ;* pedn an kren, *the Head of the Spring.* Gr. κρηνη.
Kren, & kern, *round.* Lh.
Krena, *to shake.* Lh.
Kreshaz, *increased ;* an devaz yn kreshaz, *the Sheep are increased.*
Kreshia, *to increase.*
Kreshudnian, *Christians ;* Krishonion, id.
Krev, *stout ; strong ;* cref, id.
Krevan, *a Crust.*
Krevdar, *the chief Point of Business ; Firmamen.* L.
Krêz, *the Middle ;* bêr-krez, *the Middle-finger.* Lh.
Krîb, *a Ridge ;* krib an chi, *Ridge of the House.*
Kriba-mêl, *a Honey-comb.*
Kriba, or kribaz, Lh. *to card ; to comb ;* dho kriba an pedn, *to comb the head ;* sybbona, id. Lh.
Kriban, *a Comb ; the Crest of a Lapwing, or other Bird ; a Tuft ; a Plume.*
Kridzhi, *to think ; conjecture.*
Kriha, *to call ; name ; to cry.*
Krio, *to weep.*
Kriv, *crude ; raw ; bold.*
Krobman, *a Hook.*
Krodar, *a Sieve, or Sierce.*
Krogan, or krogen, *a Shell ;* Pl. kregin.
Kroglath, W. *a Snare, or Trap.*
Krohan, *the Skin ; Hide ;* kroin, id. Lh.
Krois, *a Cross ;* krouz, id.
Kronek, *a Toad ;* kronek melyn, *a Frog.*
Krongkia, *to beat, lash, overcome, or strike ;* terhi, id.

KO

Krou, *a Hut ;* krou môh, *a Hog's-stie.*
Kroude, *a Fiddle.*
Krum, *crooked ;* cromb, id. cam, id.
Krun, W. *round.*
Krûst, *an Afternoon's Luncheon.*
Kryhiaz, *to neigh as a Horse.*
Kryk, *a Hillock ;* for kryg, id. Ir. kruach, id.
Krylliaz, *curled ;* bleu krylliaz, *curled Hair.*
Krys, *a Shirt, or Smock ;* hevez, id.
Kryssat, *a Hawk.*
Kryvedhe, *a Bed.*

KU

Kuarre, *a Quarry ; Fodina.* L.
Kuartan, *the fourth Part of any Thing.*
Kuaz, *a Shower of Rain ;* kuas, id.
Kubma, *to fall, perish, or be slain.*
Kudnik, *crafty, cunning.*
Kueia, *if ; si.* L.
Kuer, *Hemp ;* it. pro keuar, *a Storm.*
Khuero, *cruel ; fierce.* See Huero, *rough,* id.
Kueth (or gweth), *Cloathing.*
Kuethiou, *Cloaths ;* kuethiou kod-penna, *Neck-cloths.*
Kuf, *Wife.*
Kugol, *a Monk's Cowl ; a Hood.*
Kuhuthe, *to betray ;* kyhydha, id.
Kuik, *a Blinkard ; One-eyed.*
Kuilioc, *an Augur ;* kuilioges, *a Witch.*
Kuilken, *a Frog ;* kranag melyn, id. Lh.
Kuilkiores, *a Wasp ; a Hornet.*
Kuillan, *a Quill, or Reed.*
Kuit, *a Wood* (koit, kuz, id) ; penkuit, *Head of the Wood.*
Kuitha, *to keep, preserve, or guard.* Lh.
Kuithizi, *Keepers ; Guardians.*
Kul, *lean ; macer.* L.
Kulhu, *a Beard of Corn.*
Kulin, *Chaff.*
Kulliag, *a Cock ;* Kelioc, id.
Kulliag-gini, *a Turky-cock ;* & jar-gini, *a Turky-hen.*
Kulliaghaz, *a Drake, or Cockduck.*
Kulste, *could'st ;* mar kulste, *if thou could'st.*
Kuluwi, *to lighten ;* idzhi kuluwi ha tredna, *it lightens and thunders.*
Kundura, *a Post, or Stake.*
Kunivias, *Sheers ;* V. ef a kunivias e dhevaz, *he sheers his Sheep.*

KU

Kûr, *the Coast, or Border of the Country.*
Kurel, W. *Coral ;* A. Gular, id.
Kurkath, *a Ram-cat.*
Kurtaz, *lingering.* See Kortes.
Kusga, *to sleep ; to be slow, or dull.* Lh.
Kuth (Ir. *a Head*), *a Cod, or Husk.*
Kuthu, *Chaff ;* kuthn pez, *Pease Cods.*
Kuthyl, *Harm.*
Kûz, *a Wood* (W. koed) ; Pl. kozou ; kuit, id. Lh.
Kuzal, *clear ; serene ; soft ; pleasant.*

KY

Ky, *a Dog ;* kel, id. ky-hir, *a Greyhound.*
Kydas, *fallen ;* cothas, id.
Kydhman, *a Companion ; a Friend.*
Kydhon ; *a Ring-dove ;* a *Pigeon ;* a *Dove.*
Kydiad, W. *Coitus, Copulatio ;* it. *a Joint, or Closure.*
Kydiorch (kytiorch, Cott. id.), *a Male Kid ; a Roe-buck ;* an quaf. koed jurk? Lh.
Kydnik, *Crafty.*
Kydynnou, *Hair of the Head.*
Kyffes, W. *Confession ; Acknowledgement ;* Kofes, A. id.
Kyffris, *in Respect of.*
Kyffys, & kefys, *found.*
Kyg, *Flesh.*
Kyl, *lean.* Lh.
Kylednak, *sincere ; kind.*
Kylhan, *a Knife ;* kolhen, id.
Kylighi, *Cockle shells.*
Kyll, *can ;* mar a kyll, *if he can.*
Kylmys (kelmys), *bound ; thrust in.*
Kylobman, *a Pigeon.*
Kylyrion, *the Bowels ; Entrails.*
Dho kymeras, *to take ;* dho sezia, id.
Kymmis, *so much ; every ; always ;* kynnis, & kemmys, id.
Kymmisk-bleid (or ki, *a Lynx*), *a spotted Beast ;* hanchi, id.
Kympez, *a ways ; as much as ;* id. f. as kymmis.
Kyn, *Head ; Prince ;* as, Kynvelyn, sc. Cunobelin, i. e. *yellow Head.* R.
Kynak, *a Louse ; Tinea Capitis.* L.
Kynava, *a Rogue.*
Kyndan, *a Debt ;* dha bos en kyndan, *to owe ; to be obliged.*
Kynihias, *neighing.* L.
Kynin, *a Rabbit.*
Kynivias, *to clip, or sheer, or reap.* Lh.
Kynnen, *Strife ;* ind. f. Trekynnen, *a Town of Strife.*
Kyn·l, *to gather ; collect.*

5 U

Kynyphan,

KY

Kynyphan, *a Nut*; kynyphan Franc, *a Wallnut*. Lh.

Kyr, *dearly beloved*; *chosen*. Lh.

Kyran, W. *a Buskin*; folhach, id.

Kyriak, *a Pimple*.

Kyrtaz, *to stay behind*; remaneo, L.

Kysga, *to sleep* (kufga, id.)

Kyssel, *Counsel*; Pl. kyssylgou. W. id.

Kystris, *between*.

Kyvadhas, *profitable*; *fit*; *agreeable*; it. *a Companion*.

Kyuedh, *a Fellow*; *a Collegue*. (& kyuedhiad), *a Copartner*.

Kyvedhach, W. *a Banquet*; guledh, id.

Kyveether, *Omnipotent*. Cott.

Kyvelak, *a Woodcock*.

Kyueras, *Help*; *Succour*.

Kyvetha, *drunk*.

Kyvethidog, *able*; *potent*.

Kyuiat, *a Coverlit*; *Tapestry*; *Hangings*. Lh.

Kyw, *a Chick*. W.

Kywely, *a Bedfellow*. W.

Kyzalath, *Peace*; kusual, id.

Kyzalatha, *to reconcile*; *make Friends*; *make Peace*.

Kyzauleth (Cott. id.), *Peace*.

L.

L is sometimes premised for found sake, as, guedhan lavəlu, (for avalu), *an Apple-tree*.

Laboucc, *a Bird*. Ar.

Labscou, *coarse Diet*; *poor Meat*.

Lader, & ladar, *a Thief*; purra lader, *the veryest Thief* (ladron, id.); Pl. ladrou. W. lheidir, id.

Dho lâdh, *to kill*.

Ladn, *a Bank*. In Carew, pa. 144, 'tis written Ladu, but that is printed wrong; Mr. Carew meant Ladn, for he is giving the Etymology of Lan in Lanherne.

Laduit, *Nothing*.

Laë, *high*.

Laferrya, *to work*; lavyrrys, *wrought*; *laboured*.

Lagadzhek, *quick-sighted*.

Lagam, *a Pool*, or *Lake*; laguen. Ar.

Lagas, *the Eye*; lagat, id. legadzho, id. lagas-auel, *the Weather's Eye*; *the Weather Dog*.

Lagat, id. Pl. legeit. Cott.

Laha, *a Law*; Pl. lays.

Laian, *loyal*; *good*; leal, id. dislaian, *unfaithful*; *seditious*.

LA

Laig, & leig, *a Layman*.

Laines, *a Nun*. See Leanes.

Lait (lath, leath, id.), *Milk*. W. blith, Ar. leth, id.

Laka, *worse*; lacka, id.

Lakka, *a Well*; *a Pit*.

Lam, *space*.

Lam to rez, *beaten soundly*.

Lan, *a Church*; *a Rest*; *an Inclosure*; yn lan, *in Rest*.

Lan, Ar. *Furze*, or *Gorst*.

Lanek, *of or belonging to the Church*; as, Insula Lenach (a little Island near the shores of Anglesea), i. e. Insula Ecclesiastica propter Sanctos ibi sepultos.

Lanherch, *a Forest*; *an inclosed Wood*; it. *a Leap*, or *Skip*. Lh.

Laôl, *to speak*. See Laul.

Laouer, *a Trough*.

Lappior, *a Dancer*. Cott.

Lappiores, *a She-dancer*.

Lasche, *strongly*.

Lask, *a Cradle*; lesk, id.

Latha, *to kill* (ladh, id.); hanter e ladha, *to half kill him*.

Lau, *a Hand*; lof, id. layff, & leyff, id. la, Ar. id. it. *Furz*. Lh.

Lavalou, *Apples*; for Avalou.

Lavar, *a Saying*; *Proverb*; *Book*; Pl. Leffrou; Ar. lenfr, id.

Lauenez, *Joy*; lauenik, *glad*. Lh.

Laversough, *ye have spoken*.

Lavethas, *a Midwife*; Germo Mahtern, Breag Lavethas, i. e. Germo *was a King*; Breag *a Midwife*.

Laul, *to say*; ema radn a laul, *there are some who say*.

Launter, *a Lantern*.

Lavrak, *Breeches*; lavarrak, & laudr. id.

Lavrok-pan, *an Apron*.

Lausq, *slack*; *loose*.

Lavur, *sweet*.

Lawennek, *merry*.

Lays, *green* (for glaz, id.); glays, id.

Lâz, lâs, *Land*; vôn laz, *the furthest Land*; i. *the Land's End*.

LE

Le, *a Place*; it. *less*; it. *a Condition*. Lh.

Leadan, *huge*.

Leal, *faithful*; *loyal*; *innocent*. Lh.

Lean, *Slate*; lehan, id.

Llean, *a Pilchard*.

Leana, *to fill*, *fulfill*; lenal, *fill ye*.

Leanes, Ar. *a sacred Virgin*.

Lear, Ir. *the Sea*.

LE

Leas, *many*.

Leath, *Milk*; *Half*; Ir. & W. as, lhediaith, *half Language*, or *Barbarism*.

Leau-ewig, *a Fawn*; Cott. loch ew hic, id.

Leauh, *a Calf*; loch, id. Ar. levè, id. it. *the Ague*; Pl. lee; parcan lee, *the Calves Field*.

Leb, *which*; lebba, *whom*; *who*.

Lebben, *now*; merough lebben, *see now*; *look now*.

Lebma, *to whet*, or *sharpen*; ind. lemmys, *sharpened*.

Lebmal, *to skip*, or *dance*. Lh.

Lêch, *a flat Rock*; W. id. Ar. id. Ir. leac, lêh, id. ind. crumlêh, *a crooked flat Stone*.

Ledan, *large*; *broad*; Ar. leadan, id.

Ledan-en (ledan-lês), *Plantain*.

Ledhaz, *slain*; *killed*. Lh.

Lediaith, *a Barbarism*.

Ledîor, *a Reader*; lediores, *a Female Reader*. Cott.

Lednow, *Whittles*; *Swaddling-cloaths*.

Ledradeth, *Secrecy*; *privately*.

Ledres, *stolen*.

Ledryn, *ignoble*.

Ledzhek, *a Heifer*.

Leeshann, *a Sur-name*; i. e. *Name from a Place*.

Leesmam, *a Step-mother*. Ar.

Leff, *a Voice*; it. *a Hand*.

Legast, *a Lobster*; legesti, it. *a Polypus Fish*.

Legriaz, *a Change*; legryz, *changed*.

Lêh, *a flat Stone*; W. llech, id. Pl. lêhau; lehan, id. Lh. it. *a Tyle*.

Leiah, *least*; dhan leiadh, *at least*; en leiah, id. Lh.

Leid, *an Offspring*; lwyth, id.

Lein, *a Dinner*; *a Feast*.

Leith, *a Tribe*, or *Ward*. See Leid.

Lemal, *to leap*; lebmal, & lemmell, id.

Lemmyn, *now*; *but*; luman, id. Lh.

Lemmys, *sharp*; *sharpened*; leym, id.

Lempia, *lame*.

Lên, *full*; leun; luen; lwn, id. it. *honest*.

Len, Ar. *a Pond of standing Water*; it. *a Kind of Blanket*; Sagum. L. *a Short Cloak*.

Lenez, *a Ling Fish*; Pl. lenezou.

Lenol, *the Tide*; lenol môr, *Tide of the Sea*.

Lêr, *a Floor*; *a Bottom*; *the Foundation*; *the Earth*; it. warler, *after*; wariler, *after him*.

Lês,

LE

Lês, *Breadth*; Ar. *a Court-Hall*; lez, W. lhys, id.

Lês, *Profit*; it. *any Herb.*

Les-derth, *Feverfew*; lefderthen.

Les-dufhoc, *Betony.*

Les-engoc, *the Sun-flower*; *the Marygold.*

Lefk, *a Cradle.* Lh.

Lefkyz, *burning*; karn lefkyz, *the Rocks of burning*; lefkez, id.

Lefkyad, *a burning Coal*; W. llofgiad, id.

Les-lûit, *Mugwort*; *white Whorehound.*

Les-ferchoc, *the Burr*; *Burrdock.*

Lefter, *a Ship*; Pl. liftri.

Leftezius, *lowzy.*

Leftre, *a Dish*; *any thing that holds or receives another thing*; as, cantuil-leftre, *a Candleftick.*

Leth, *Side.* Sc.

Letfhar, *a Frying-pan.*

Lethys, *killed.* See Latha.

Lêu-guthal, *the Rudder of a Ship*; ind. leuiut, *a Pilot.*

Llevain, *to lament.* R.

Levar, *the Bark of a Tree*; *a Book.*

Leven, *bald*; *smooth*; por-leven, *the smooth Port.*

Leuenik (louan, & louenak, id), *pleasant.*

Leuend-lac, *sweet Milk*; Cott. leuerith, id.

Leverell, *speak*; leverys, *said.*

Leuiar, *a Dyer.*

Leuilloit, *the Milt*; *Spleen.*

Leuirgo, *the Seale-fish.*

Leuiût, *a Pilot*; *Master of a Ship*; leuyidh, id. Lh.

Leur, *a Piece of flat, even Ground.* Ar.

Lew, *a Lion*; lheû, id. Lh.

Lewte, *indeed.*

Lezow, *Bretagne*; *Armorica.*

Lezr, *a Skin*; Ar. *Leather.*

Lezron, *the Thighs.* Ar.

LI

Lî, *a Breakfast.*

Liam, *a Knot*, or *Tie.*

Lian, *Linen*; lien. Ar.

Liana, *to bury.* Ib.

Lian-buz, *a Table-cloth*

Lian duylou, *à Hand-cloth*; *a Napkin.*

Lian-gueli, *a Bed-sheet*; it. *Codex.* L.

Liafder, *Plenty*; *Wealth*; peth, id.

Liaz, *thick*; *close*; *frequent*; *much*; *a Band*, or *Company.*

Liaz-tre, *often*; lias termen, *oftentimes.*

Lic, Ar. *wanton.*

LI

Liden, qu. This is your Liden, i. e. *this is your Way of talking.*

Lidden, *a By-word.* Car.

Lidzhiu, *Ashes.*

Ligan, qu. penny-ligan, i. e. *last Stake*; *last Penny*; *Pennyless.*

Lili, *a Lilly.* Lh.

Lligruer, *a Barbarism in Speech*; llediaith, id.

Lill, *lascivious*; Trelill, *a Town of Wantonness.*

Lin, *a Lake*; it. *Flax*; Ar. *a Pond.*

Linaz (linhaden, id.), *a Nettle.*

Linva, *to flow*; linvat, *an Inundation.* Ar.

Linyn, *Thread*; *Yarn.*

Lis, . . . Ir. *a Fort*; unde Lifcarol & Lisfinuy, ibid. & Lifkerd, in Cornwall.

Lit, *a Feast*; *a Merriment*; lit an ilis, *the Wakes of a Parish.*

Litherau, *an Epistle*; *Learning*; *Scholarship.*

Litheren, *Letters*; Cott. it. *a Letter in a Book*; Pl. litherou. Lh.

Litiauc, *angry.*

Lituen, *a Pipe.* Cott.

Liu, *Colour*; ind. liuiar, *a Dyer*; liuor, *a Painter*; ynliu, *of one Colour.* Lh.

Livan, *the Leaf of a Book.*

Liver, *a Bark of a Tree*; *a Book*; Pl. livrou. Lh.

Lîvern, *the Ancle-bone*; lifern, id.

Liumelet (minium, L.), *Redlead*; *Paint.*

Livris, *fresh*; lez livris, *fresh Milk.* Ar.

Liy, *an Egg.*

Liz, *a Gulf of Water between two Lands.* Hals.

Lizer, *an Epistle.* Ar.

Lizherd (the Southermost Promontory of England, quaf. liazherd, *much thrust out*), *a projecting Headland.* See Herdya, *to thrust out.*

LO

Lo, *a Spoon*; loc. Cott. id. Pl. leu; lo, *Water*; Lh. *in Aqua.*

Loak, qu. do loak, i. e. *do I pray.*

Loar, *enough*; laur, lûr, id. it. *the Moon.*

Lobmaz, *a kind of Bream Fish.*

Loch, *a Calf.* Cott.

Lodes, *the Herb Artemisia.*

Lodn, *a Bullock*; Pl. lodnou; Lodn-guarack, id. viz. *a Bullock.* Gw.

LO

Lodn, *a Sluggard*; lodn an parnu, *such a Sluggard!*

Lodn-davas, *a Wether Sheep.*

Lodr (Pl. lydrau), *Stockings*; *Breeches*; lydrou, id.

Lodzhon (see Lodn), *any Bullock.*

Loe, qu. Cott. *Regula.*

Lof, *a Hand.*

Logan, f. *shaking*; qu. à Logan Stone, viz. *a rocking, moving, Stone*; qu. an a leâgan, Ir. *a Rock*, or *great stone.* Lh.

Logel, *a Pocket*; Cott. loghel, id.

Loggas, *Mice*; Treloggas, *Micetown.*

Logoden, *a Mouse*; lygodzhen, id.

Logoden fer, *Calf of the Leg.*

Lodofa (hlodofa, id.), *wild Saffron*; *Dog's-bane.*

Lollas, *America*; *the West Indies*; Dour tubm Lollas, *Rum*; i. e. *West India Spirit*; Dour tubm Franc, *French Spirit*, or *Brandy.*

Lommen, *a Mess*; lommen coul, *a Mess of Pottage.* Gw.

Lonath, *a Kidney*; *the Reins*; diuglun, id. Lh.

Lôr, *a Staff* (lorch, id. Cott.), it. *a Floor*; *the Earth*; *the Moon.*

Lor-vraôz, *a Club.*

Lofgi, *to burn.* Lh.

Lofk, *Corn Smut: Ustilago.* L.

Lofq, *a Burning.* Ar. id.

Loft, *a Tail*; *a Rump*; Pl. lofio.

Lofteg, *a Fox* (loftek, id.), qua. *large Tail.*

Loftlydan, *a Beaver.*

Lov, *a Hand.*

Lovan, *a Rope*; loch-lovan, *a Rope of the watry Place.*

Louan, *pretty*; *cheerful*; louen, Cott. *Merriment.*

Louas, *Lightning*; goleuas, id. Lh.

Loven, *a Bed.*

Lovennan, *a Weazel.*

Lougurchel, *Utensil*; *any thing for Use.*

Loui, *to wax mouldy*; louedy, Ar. id.

Loum, *a Drop of Water.*

Lour, *down*; *downward*; ind. f. *a lowring Look.*

Loufaouen, *Grass*; *Herbage.* L.

Louzall, *to unloose*; laxo. L.

Llow, *Chief*; W. lloworch, *a Chief*; *a Governor.*

Lowarth, *a Garden*; luar, id.

Lowene, *Joy*; lowan, *gladly.*

Lower, *many*; lower le, *many Places.*

Lowyz, *Gray*; W. lhuyd, id. ludzh. id.

Loyen,

LO

Lòyen, *a Louse.*
Lôys (aloys, id.), *flowing.*
Lozou, *Ashes.*

L U

Lû, *the Vulgar ; the Mob.*
Llû, *an Army* ; Cott. ly, id.
Luan, *a House* ; Pl. Lou.
Luar. See Lowarth.
Luarn (luern, id.) *a Fox* ; los-teig, id. Lh.
Lucar, *a Bell-place* ; clecha, id.
Lhuch, W. *a Lake* ; Ir. loch.
Luder, *a Peer of the Realm* ; *a Ruler.*
Ludin, *a Meadow.*
Ludnou, *Cattle* ; reban ludnu, *by the Cattle.*
Ludzh, *Gray-haired.* W. Lhuyd, A. Gwen, id.
Luck, *enough.* Qu.
Luedik, *stinking.*
Luerid, *sweet Milk.* Ar.
Lluesu, *to be calm.*
Lug, *a Tower* ; Ar. *a Crow.*
Lugu, Pl. *Crows ; Ravens.*
Lugarn, *a Candle* ; *a Lamp.*
Luh, *a Lake* ; W. lhuch, id. inde luh, *River* ; luh, *Pool* ; Ir. lough, Scot. loch.
Luhas, *Lightning.*
Luid, *Battle-array.*
Luid, *a Precinct.* See Leid.
Luir, *the Moon* ; lûr, id.
Llun, *a Lake* ; Gale. See Lin.
Lur, *enough* ; it. *the Moon.*
Lurgy, qu. feaver lurgy, i. e. *the Fever of Laziness* ; *a pretended Fever* ; i. e. *no Fever at all.* Qu.
Lushan, *a Herb* ; lyzuan, id.
Luu-listri, *a Fleet* ; *a Ship-army.*
Luwet, *Lightning.*
Luworch-guit, *a Shrub* ; lyuorch guydh, id. So Kuz, *a Wood* ; W. Koed.
Lûz, *grey* ; W. llwyd, id.
Llwyn, *a Grove* ; Pl. lhwynau, R. See Lhyn.

L Y

Ly, & lhy, *an Army.* Lh.
Lyle-stri, A. *a Fleet.* W. id.
Lyble, *the Inscription* ; *Character.*
Llydaw, W. *of or belonging to Shore.*
Lyder, *a President of a Country* ; *an Officer of State.* See Luder. Cott.
Lydrou, *Stockings.* Lh.
Lyfr, *a Book* ; Pl. lyffrou.
Lyg-vraoz, *a Rat.* Lh.
Lygarn, *a Candle.* Lh.
Lygodzhan, *a Mouse* ; Pl. logaz.
Llygud, *the Eye.* See Lagad ;

LY

ydn lygadzhak, *One-eyed.* Lh.
Lyhuetha, *to lock* ; lyhuetha darras, *to lock the Door.*
Lyk [& Iaur], *enough* ; it. luek, & laver, id.
Llymman, W. *an Ensign* ; *Flag.*
Lyn, *Humour* ; *Water* ; it. *although.*
Lhyn, *a Grove* ; as, pellyn, or pellhyn, *the Head of the Grove.* W. id.
Lynneth, *Offspring* ; *Lineage.*
Lyrgh, *after* ; war ylyrgh, *after that.*
Llys, *a Manor House* ; lees, Ar. *a Royal House*, or *Court* ; lis, Ir. *a Fort.*
Lytherau, *Letters.*
Lyv, *a Deluge* ; *a great Flood.* Lh.
Lyuorch-guydh, *Suckers of Trees* ; *young Sprouts.*
Lyw, *a Countenance* ; *Complexion.*
Lywar, *Liquor.*
Lyzûan (it. lysuan), *a Herb*, or *Plant.*

M.

MA, *this* ; dên ma, *this Man* ; it. pro ymma, *is* ; a V. it. *my.*
Ma faut dhọ, *I want*, or *lack.* Lh.
Mab, & map, *a Son* ; Pl. meib, Ar. map ; Ir. mak ; W. mâb. Lh.
Mab an lavar, *an Infant.*
Mabmeithrin, *a Foster Child.*
Mach, *a Bail* ; Pl. meichian.
Machenno, *to be Bail for any one.*
Machno, *defensible Places.*
Madam (for me vadam), *I will.*
Madere, *the Herb Sinitia.* Cott. Qu.
Madhekneth, *Physic* (Ir. f.)
Madra, *to study.*
Mael, *Steel* (metaph.), *Hardness* ; *Armour* ; tegvael, *fairly armed.*
Mael-gyn, *Vulcan.* R.
Maen, *a Stone* ; *a Rock.*
Maen-flent, *a Flint-stone.*
Maengluadh, Ar. *a Quarry* ; in Cornish, *a Trench of Stone* ; maengledh, id.
Maer (mair, Cott. id.), *a Lord* ; mester, id. " Celtis, *Præpo-* " *situs*, à quo *Major* Angl. " *non* à Latino Fonte." Keysl.
Maerbuit, *a Stewad* ; i. e. a *Dispenser*, or *Orderer of Food.* Cott.
Maes, *a Field* ; R. Gale. Ar.
Maeth, *Nourishment.* Ar.
Maethu, *to bast*, or *beat one.*
Mâg, *to breed* ; megyz, & mighyz, *bred.*

M A

Maga, *to feed* ; *nourish* ; it, *Corn.*
Maga, *as* ; maga tek, *as fair* ; so ; mar, id. Lh.
Magata, *also.*
Magdulans, *the Pot-herb* ; *Colewort.*
Magl, *a Blur*, or *Blot.*
Maglen, *a Halter* ; *a Snare* ; f. à magal, W. *ensnaring.*
Magon, *a Field* ; *a House* ; magwyr, *a Habitation* ; *a walled Dwelling.* W. R. und. C. machno. Pl.
Mahtheid, *a Virgin.* Lh.
Maidh curd, W. kaus maidh, *Cheese* ; *Runnet.*
Maidor, *an Innkeeper* ; *Caupo.* Cott. *a Victualer* ; *a Suttler.*
Maillart, *a Drake* ; Ar. Engl. *a Mallard.*
Mair, *an Overseer.* Lh.
Maister-meibion, *a School-master.* Cott.
Maithez, *a Maid Servant.* Gw.
Mako dho vi, *I remember* (perkoh. See ko, kovys), *there is Remembrance to me.*
Ma, *a Joint* ; Pl. malou, Ar. *a kind of Sack* ; it. *that.*
Malagma, *Ointment* ; *Soap.* Lh.
Malan, Ar. *a Sheaf of Corn.*
Malc, *a Path-way.*
Mall, *deserved.*
Malou, *the Herb Mallows.* Cott.
Mam, *good* ; nyn yw mam, *it was not good* ; it. *a Mother.*
Mam guenyn, *a Stock of Bees.* Gw.
Mamard (mammath, id.), *a Nurse.* Cott.
Mamen, *a Spring* ; *Source*, or *Head.*
Mamteilu, *Mistress of a Family.*
Manach, *a Monk* ; Cott. ind. Bodman, *a House of Monks* ; Pl. mench. Lh. A. id.
Manaes, *a Nun.*
Manak, *a Glove* (manek, id.), Pl. menik, it. manegou.
Manal, *a Handful* ; *a Sheaf of Corn.*
Manan, *useless.*
Maner, *Manner* ; maner o, *it was the Manner* ; Ar. *a Gentleman's House.*
Manno, *many Times* ; liaz termyn, id Lh.
Mans, *maimed.*
Mantel, *a Mantle* ; *a Towel*, or *Napkin.* Lh.
Manyn, *Butter* ; amenen, id.
Mao, Ar. *merry.* Dho mâoz, *to walk.* Lh.
Mar, *if* (maro, id.), *very* ; *as* ; so ; as, marwhek, *so sweet.*
Mar-bel, *so long* ; *so far.*
Marburàn, *a Crow.* Cott.

Mare,

MA

Mare, *Time*; Ar. da bap mare, *at all Times.*

Marg, *Ruſt*; Ir. meirg, id.

Marh, *a Horſe*; Pl. merh; Ar. & W. March.

Marhar, *a Horſeman* (W. Marchwr, id.); it. *Mercury.*

Marhaz, *a Market*; ind. marhazion, or marhaz-dzuhon, *Market of the Jews*, or marhaz-zian, *a Market on the Sea Shore*; tſhymarhazno, *a Market-houſe*, or *Place.*

Marhtheid, *a Virgin*; mattheid, or mahtheid, id.

Marnans, *Death.*

Marow, or maro, *dead*; maruo, *to die.*

Marth, *Wonder* (marthan beas, *the Wonder of the World*), Pl. merthas.

Marra, *to break Earth*, or *dig*; marradek, *dug up.* Ar.

Marreg, *a Soldier*; marhag, *a Man of Arms*, i. e. *a Horſeman.*

Martezen, *ſee well*; f. marth ezen, *It is a Wonder.*

Maru, *Marrow.*

Marudgyon, *Wonders.*

Maruo, *to die*; maru, id.

Marya, *Mary.*

Mas, *but.*

Mâs (for mat), *juſt.*

Mat, *good*; vat, id. Ir. maith, id.

Matern, *a King*; megtern, id.

Mat-oberar, *an honeſt Act*, or *Actor.*

Math armeſſur, *a Buſhel*, or *Strike.*

Maur, *great*; bras, & braoz, id.

Maurugo, *the Thighs.*

Maw, or mau, *a Lad*; an mawna, *that Lad*; maw teg, *a comely Youth.*

Mawl, *to praiſe*, or *glorify.*

Mawr-wyſk, *powerful*; R. und. *Maurice.*

Maxy, *Mundic*; *a Corruption of* Marchaſite.

May, *that*; *there.*

Mayn, *Means*; mayn ave guris, *Means were found out.*

Maythys, qu. maithez, id. See maethu, *a Maid Servant.*

Maz, *good*; dâ, id.

ME

Me, *I*; mi, id.

Mè, *May-month.*

Mean, *a Stone*; mên, id. Pl. myſtin, & mein; mean bîan, *a Pebble.*

Mèare, *much*; mêr, id. mear-lè, *much leſs*; rag mêr a dounder,

ME

over much of the Deep.

Mêas, *out of*; *from*; *ſince*; *for*; *according to*; Lh. e mêas, id.

Meath, *a Plain.*

Meaul, *with a Miſchief.* Ad.

Mechain, *a defenſible Place*; Pl. f. machno.

Mechiek, *ſtinking.*

Medal, *ſoft*; *gentle*; medaldher, *Softneſs*; meddal, Lh. id. aiſe, id.

Medd, *Metheglin*; medu, id. & medhu.

Meddonz, *they will.*

Meddou, *a Meadow.* Lh.

Medge, *to reap.*

Medh, *ſaid*; Methens, *they ſaid.*

Medhas, *Drunkenneſs.* Lh.

Medhec, *a Phyſician*; *a Surgeon.*

Medhecniad, *Phyſic*; à Medhec, *a Phyſician.* Cott.

Medho, *to drink*; *drunk*; *drunkenneſs*; ind. vedho, *a drunken Woman*; meſuiff, Ar. *drunk.*

Medi, *to mow*; mediur, *a Mower.*

Mediner, *a Hinge.*

Mediud, *Mowing.*

Medra, *to behold*; mira, id.

Meen, *an Edge*; min, id.

Meervell, *to die.*

Megganu, *the Mob*; *the Vulgar.*

Meginou, *a Pair of Bellows.*

Megis, *ſtifled*; quaſ. à megy.

Megouzian, *Reapers.*

Mêhin, *Lard*; *Fat of Bacon.* Cott.

Mehil, *a Barbel*; *a Mullet*; mehal, id. meill, id. Ar. Pl. meilli.

Meidhio, W. *to dare*; *to preſume*; Lh.

Mein, *a Face*, or *Countenance.* Lh.

Meini-gwyr, *Men-pillars*; R. *Stone-men*; *erected Stones like Men.*

Meinek, *ſtony*; meinig, *ſtony*; *made of Stone*; Ar. C. menek, or meneg; und. meneague, vulg.

Meîth, *Whey.*

Mèl, *Honey*; ind. melys, *ſweet.* W. id.

Melhuez (melhuek, id.), *a Lark*; Celtic, & Corn. Lh.

Melhyonen, *a Violet.*

Meliaz, *to grind*; dho melias yz, *to grind Corn.*

Melin, *a Mill* (velin, id.)

Mellyn, *a bright Yellow*; Cott. milin, id.

Melwiogel, *a Houſe-ſnail.* Ib.

Melyen, *a Snail*; *a Dew-ſnail*, or *Slug.*

Melyn-ôi, *the Yolk*, or *Yellow of an Egg.*

Menas, *meer* (menas belyny, id.),

ME

meer Reproach.

Mener (menar, id.), *a Hill*, or *Mountain*; as, drez menar Brownuello, *over Brownwilli-Hill.*

Meneth, *a Mount*; monedh, id. menydh, id. Pl. menedhiou, Cott. menit, id.

Men-glâs *a Slatt*; Ar. mengleudhier, A. *a Stone-cutter*; men-gluedh, *a Quarry of Stones.*

Menjam, *I will*; me amenja, id.

Meniſtror, *a Butler*; *a Servant.* Cott.

Menn, *a Place*; mann, id.

Mennaz, *he would*; mennen, *I would.*

Mennen, *we*; mennen, *ye*; mennenz, *they would.*

Mennyz, *thou wouldſt.*

Menouc, *often.*

Menough, *many*; *frequent*; it. *ye will.*

Mên-pall, *a Quoit.* Ar.

Men-pobaz, *a Baking-ſtone.*

Ment, *Size*; *Greatneſs.* Ar.

Menta, *thou wilt.*

Mente, *the Herb Mint*; it. mentula. Lh.

Menwionen, *an Ant.*

Menwynnen—in Ludgvan, & Illugan, *the Windy Place.*

Menz, *wherein*; *in which*; *that which.*

Menzhon, *I would*; *I had been willing*; menzhez, *thou*; menzhe, *he would*, &c.

Meppig, *a little Boy.*

Mêr (mar, môr, id.), *Water*; *either Lake or Sea Water.* Bax.

Meraſtadu, *it mack, thank God.*

Merâſtawhy, *I thank you.*

Mêre, *a Lake.* Celtic.

Merel, *Ruſt*; Ar. merela, *to grow ruſty.* Ib.

Meren, Ar. *a rere Supper*; merenna, *to take a Repaſt after Supper.*

Merh, *a Daughter*; it. *March-Month.*

Merlê, *much leſs.*

Meroin, *a Girl.*

Mernans, *Death* (marnens, id.), *Let him die.* V.

Merrow, *ſee*; à meras, V. *to ſee.*

Merth, *Deſire.*

Merthyn, *a ſtanding Pool.* Lh.

Merthuſy, *wondrous.*

Merwy, *to die.*

Mes, *but*; *out*; mer amês, *abundantly.*

Meſclen, *a Muſcle-fiſh.* Cott.

Meſen, *an Acorn*; A. id.

Meſk, *among.*

Meſkat, *mad*; *furious*; *fierce*; meſkatter, *Madneſs*; diſkians, id.

5 X   Meſkymera,

ME

Mefkymera, *to miftake*; mefky-meraz, gyz vordh, *miftaken your Way.*

Meflan, *a Maftiff*; guilter, id.

Mefternges, *a Kingdom.*

Meftre, *Mafter.*

Meftry, *Power*; *Victory.*

Meth, *Shame*; *Sorrow.*

Methia, *to nurfe*; *nurfing.*

Metin, *the Morning.* Lh.

Metol, *Steel*; f. *any Metal.*

Metui, *in the Morning.* Cott. Qu. an non pro mettyn, vel mettin, Ar. *the Morning?*

Mevionen, *an Ant.*

Mevys, *moved.*

Meyny, *within.*

Mêz, *a Field*; *without*; it. *Modefty.*

MI

Mî, *I.*

Midil, *a Mower.* Cott.

Midzhar, *a Reaper*; *a Mower.*

Midzhi, *to reap.*

Mien, *a Face.*

Mighterne, *a King*; materne, id. ind. mighteruas, *a Kingdom.*

Miginau, *a Pair of Bellows.* Lh.

Mihâl, *Michael.*

Mikan, *a Morfel*; *a fmall Piece.*

Mîl, *an Animal* (it. *a thoufand*); ourthvil, id. Lh.

Milin, *yellow.* Cott.

Mill, *a Poppy.*

Milprêv, *a thoufand Worms*; it. *the Anguinum* (Ovum Druidum), called fo from the Spawn of the Adder inclofed in the Lump; it was called alfo Gleinneidr, or *Glafs Serpent*, which was the artificial Imitation of the natural Anguinum, made of Glafs, fuppofed a powerful Amulet. See Gleininadroeth.

Mil-wyr, *a Knight*; R. quaf. *Captain of* 1000 *Men.*

Min, *the Brink*, or *Borders of a Country*; *an Edge*; miniog, id. Lh.

Min, *a Kid*; Lh. parc an min, *the Kid's Field.* See Mynnan.

Minarvau, *Temperer of Tools.*

Minfel (milfel, f.), *the Herb Millefolium.*

Minne (*Pocula Diis facrata.* Keyfler. *Pateræ*), *Cups of Sacrifice.*

Minne, *I alfo.*

Minnis, *little*; tacklouminnis, *fmall Things.*

Mins, *a Table.*

Mintin, *in the Morning.*

Mira, *look you*; mirough, *fee ye.*

Miraz, *the Look*; *Mien*; *Af-*

MI

pect.

Mîs, *a Month* (Ar. *Expence*); Pl. mifou, miz, id.

Mis Genuer, *January.*

Mifcheurer, *February.*

Mis Meurz (alias Merh), *March.*

Mifeprell, *April.* Ar. id.

Mis Mê, *May.*

Mis Mefuen (f. Mifuen), *June.*

Mis Gouare, *July*; i. e. *Play-Month.*

Mif-Eaft (or Eaufti), *Auguft.*

Mis Guengolo, *September.*

Mis-Hezre, *October*; miz hedra, id. Lh.

Mis-Diu, *November*; i. e. *Black-month.*

Mifguerdiu, *December*; i. e. *Month of black Storms.*

Mifcoggan, *Fools.*

Mifke, *among.*

Mifkymeraz, *to err*; *miftake*; myfkymerrians, *Error.*

Mius, *a Table*, or *Board*; Lh. bord, id.

MO

Moal, W. moall. Ar. See Moel.

Moaren, *a Blackberry*; moras, id.

Moccio, *to mock*; μοκιζω. Gr. Sc.

Moch, *a Pig.*

Modereb, Cott. *an Aunt*; modryb, id. abarhmam, id. modrap, id. Lh.

Modereuy, *a Bracelet*; *a Ring*, or *Rings.*

Moel, *a Bald-top*, or *Tops of Hills.* Pl. moelion; ind. W. moelcen, *Baldnefs.*

Moelh, *a Black-bird*; mola-diu, id.

Môg, *Smoke*; W. mûg, id.

Mogyon, *the Vulgar.*

Môh, *a Hog*; krou moh, *a Hog-ftie.*

Moid, *a Woman.*

Moign, *maimed.* Lh.

Mol-huydzhon, *a Snail*; i. e. *a naked*, or *Dew Snail.*

Mola-dhiu, *a Black-bird.* Lh.

Mola-laz, *a Fieldfare.* Lh.

Molaud, W. (A. meulendi), *Praife*; *Renown.*

Moli, *to praife.*

Molletha, *to curfe.* Lh.

Mollethians, *a Curfe.*

Mollough, *that they may be*; for may yllough.

Molth, *a Curfe* (molath, id.); molothek, *curfed.*

Molythia, *to curfe*; molletha, id.

Mon. See Mûn.

Monadh, *a Mountain.* Lh.

Monez, *to go*; V. mynez, id.

MO

Monnah, *Money*; fo's, id. Lh.

Mor, *if*; mor menta, *if thou wilt*; for mar.

Môr, *the Sea*; Ir. mair, môr, mur, id. mordrai, W. *the Ebb of the Sea.* Lh.

Mor-nader, *the Lamprey*; mornerdyr, id.

Mor-nader, *a Lamprey.* Lh.

Moran, *a Berry*; moran diu, *a Black-berry.*

Moran-kala, & fivi, *a Strawberry.*

Morboit, *the Hip*, or *Thigh.*

Mor-difeid, *the Sea*; *the Ocean*; Cott. mor diveid, id.

Moreth, *Sorrow*; morethek, *Melancholly.*

Morhoch, & morhuch, & moruch, *a Porpoife*; i. e. *a Sea-Swine.*

Moroin, *a Girl.*

Morraz, *a Hip*; *a Thigh*; klyn, W. id.

Mortholl, *a Hammer*; morzol, id.

Mortot, *the Ocean.* Cott. Lh. An môr brâs, id.

Morvah, *a Place by the Sea*; W. id.

Mor-vîl, *a Whale.*

Moruerches, *a Mermaid.*

Môs (môz, id. & mouas), *to go*, or *come.*

Moth, *Shame.*

Mouar, *a Mulberry.*

Mourder (from maûr), *Greatnefs.*

Moureriak, *high-flown.*

Mourobrur, *magnificent.*

Mowlz (molz, id.), *a Wether Sheep.*

Mowys, *Mouths.*

Mouzak, *ftinking.* Cott.

Moy, *more*; muy, id.

Moygha, *moft.*

Moyrbren, *a Mulberry-tree.*

Môz, *a Maid* (moaz, & mauz, id.), Pl. muzi, & mozi, it. *to go*, or *come.*

MU

Much, *a Daughter*; Cott. merh, id.

Muin, *fmall*; *thin.* Ar. moan.

Muis, *a Table.* Qu.

Mul, *bafhful.*

Mulder, *Bafhfulnefs.*

Mun (mooun, or moowyn id. W.), *any fufible Metal*; ind. dunmwyn, *a Hill of Metals*; unde Dunmonii, *the Cornifh Britans*; fecund. Gale.

Mungys, W. *ftuttering*; *ftammering.*

Munugl, W. *the Neck*; Ir. muin.

Mûr, *much*; *fo*; *many*; it. *a Wall.* R.

Murrian,

M U

Murrian, *an Ant*, or *Pifmire*; murianean, id. meuionén, id. Lh.

Muy, *more*; moy, id.

Muydion, *Marrow*. Lh.

Muyglen, *a Bawd*; ind. f. *to fmuggle*.

Mûyn, *Metal*.

Muys, *a Bafket*; bafcaeid, id.

Muzel, Ar. *a Lip*; unde f. *to muzzle*.

M Y

My, me; *I*; *whence*.

Mydzhovan, *the Ridge of a Hill*; L. *Jugum*.

Myfyrion, *a Place of Study*.

Mygfaen, *Brimftone*.

Mygilder, *Warmth*.

Myhtern, *a King*.

Myll, *Thoufands*.

Mylyge, *curfed*.

Myngar, *a Cord*; *a Collar for Horfes*.

Mynan, *a Kid*; myn, & min, id. Ar. menn, id.

Mynneu, *the Alps*. See Lh.

Myns, *as many*; *how much*; warth an myns, *upon the whole*.

Mynyd (W.), *a Hill*.

Mynyth (menyth, vynnyth, id.), *wilt thou*; *would'ft thou*.

Myrough (myrugh, id.), *fee ye*.

Myftite, *a Miftake*.

Myyn (for mêan, or mein), *a Stone*.

N.

NA, *not*; *no*; *neither*; nag, *before a Vowel*, id.

Na neite, *neither of the two*.

Na, *that*; often annexed; as, an mawna, *that Lad*; an marhna, *that Horfe*.

Naddyr, *a Snake*; *an Adder* (nadar, id.), ind. glein-naddyr, *a Snake of Glafs*. fcil. *Anguainum*.

Nâdelik, *the Nativity*; viz. *Chriftmas*.

Nadzhedh, *a Needle*.

Nag, *not*. See Na.

Nagas (naughas, id.), *denied*.

Nago, *it was not*; nagoff, *I am not*.

Nagonnon, nagonen, Lh. *none at all*; *none were*.

Nam, *that*; as, nam vyo, *that it might be*.

Nam-na, *almoft*.

Nan, *now*; as, nanfyw, *now is*; it. *us*; as, warnan, *on us*; it. *not*; as, nan Ethewon, *not the Jews*.

Nans, *a Valley*; it. *now*; as, yn nans, *even now*.

N A

Nant, *a Fountain*; cornant, id.

Naou, *nine*; nau, id.

Nauhuas, *the ninth*.

Naun, *Hunger* (naoun, Ar. id.); naounek, *hungry*.

Nauy, *more than ordinary*.

Nawanyo, *not yet*; *it was not*.

N E

Ne, *not*; prefixed, as, nel e, *he cannot*; for ne el e. Neg, before a Vowel, id.

Neag, *Mofs*; *moffy*; mean neag, *a moffy Stone*; keneggy, i. e. f. ke-neag-gwy, *the moffy Hedge by the Water*.

Neb, *whom*; *why*; *he who* (nebmêr, *much ado*); nef, id.

Nebaz, *a little*; *fomewhat*.

Nebyn, *any*; *fome one*.

Nedelek. See Nadelik.

Nedhan, *a Nit (Lens. L.)*, Pl. Nêdh.

Nêdhez, *twifted*; *wreathed*.

Neff, *Heaven*; *above*; *joyful*; R. neb, & nev, id.

Neffre, *never*; *neither*; *for ever*; *ever*.

Negis, *Errand*; *Bufinefs*.

Nehuer, *laft Night*.

Neith, *a Neft*; Pl. neithio. Nid, id. Lh.

Nel, *Power*; Dre ou nel, *by my Power*, or *Strength*.

Nenbren, *the Roof of a Houfe*.

Nenna, *from thence*; *then*; *moreover*; nena. Lh.

Nenpynion, *the Brain*; quaf. an enpynion.

Nentydd, *a narrow Paffage for Waters*. R.

Neonin, *a Daify*.

Nep, *any*; prefixed, as, yn neppow, *in any Country*.

Neppeth, *fomething*; *fometimes*; Nepyth, & nebas, id.

Nerg (nerh, & nerth, id.), *Strength*; it. *a Nerve*.

Nês, *nigh*; neffa, *nearer*; *the fecond*, or *next*.

Nefheuin, *a Neighbour*.

Nethyn, *Birds*; quaf. an edhen, und. 'n ethen.

Never, *Number*; heb never, *without Number*.

Neûn, Ar. *to fwim*.

Neung, *it was not*.

Newawdd, *a Hall*; *Habitation*. R.

Newidio, *to barter*, or *exchange*.

Newothou, *News*; neuydho, id.

Neyl, *one*; anneyl, *on one Side*.

N I

Ni neb tra, *Nothing*; ni traveth, id. laduit, id.

Nied, *a Neft*. Cott.

N I

Niedga (ga pron. as, ja) *to fly*; *fwim*.

Nigans, *twenty*.

Nintell, *Yarrow*; *Millefolium*. L.

Nivera, *to reckon*, or *number*.

Niull, *a Cloud*, or *Mift*; L. *Nebula*.

Nith, *a Niece*. Cott.

N O

Noaudho, *News*. See Newothou. id.

Noath, *bald*; *bare*; leven, id. Lh.

Noaz, *naked*. Ar.

Nod, *a Mark*; noz, id.

Noden, *a Thread*; *Yarn*.

Noffddyfn, *over the Deep*; R. ind. *Neptune*.

Noi, *a Grandchild*; it. *a Prodigal*; Lh. L. *Nepos*.

Noith, *a Niece*; noit, id.

Nonce, Qu. *Purpofe*; provided for the nonce, i. e. *Purpofe*.

Nôr, *Earth*; Gw. quaf. an oar, id.

Nos, *Night*.

Notho, *him*.

Notuydh, *a Needle*.

Notye, *to remark*; *obferve*, or *note*.

Nough, *ye*; warnough, *on ye*; genough, *with ye*; and fuffixed to Verbs, as, vynnough, *will ye*.

Noundzhak, *nineteen*.

Now, *Noife*; qua. an ow.

Nowydh (noweth, id.), *new*; Pl. newothow.

Noydh, *naked*; noath, Lh. id.

N U

Nuddic, *the hinder Part of the Head*.

Nudol, *a Magician*. Cott. See Hudol.

Nuel, *only*; *alone*.

Nuefs (*Iflandic*.), *a Nofe*, or *a projecting Piece of Land*; und. f. nefs, id.

Nugan, nogen, vel hogan, *a Loaf of Bread*; *Pie-cruft*; velin nogen, vel hogen—*the Loaf Mill in Gulval Parifh*; i. e. *the Mill where Loaves, or Pies are fold*.

N Y

Ny, *not*; *we*; *us*; Gr. nic, id. nyn, before a Vowel.

Nyddu, *to fpin*. Gr.

Nyethy, *Nuts*.

Nyidzha, *to fwim*; *fly*, or *leap*.

Nym, *not to me*.

O, *was*;

O.

O, *was*; V. *he was.*
O, *Oales, a Hearth.*
Oan, *we are* (on, id.), it. Ar. *a Lamb.*
Oanic, *a little Lamb.*
Oar, *Earth*; aor, id.
Oare, *can*; for Or.
Oat, Ar. *Age.*

O B

Obel, *far off*; *eminus.* L.
Ober, *Work*; *Wages*; rag an ober, *for the Work.*
Oberur, *a Workman*; *any Artist.*

O C

Och, *Oh! Woes me.*
Ochre, *an Edge.* Camden.

O D

Odgha nena, *afterward.*
Odians, *a Court*; *a Town-hall.*
Odhiuorto, *from him.*
Odzhi, *ye*; as, huî odzhi a guelez, *ye see.*
Odzhon, *an Ox,* or *Cow*; ohan, id.

O E

Oerni (oerfel, oerder, id.), *bleak*; *cold.*
Oezenz, *they were.*
Oezy, *ye were.*
Oezyn, *we were.*

O F

Of (av, id.), *I am.* V.
Ofergugol, *a Hood.* Cott.
Offeren (L. *Missa,* id.), *Mass.*
Offeiriad, *a Priest.* Lh.

O G

Ogall, *a Pulpit.*
Ogas, *near*; ogas o, *it was near.*
Oguet, Ar. *a Harrow.*

O H

Oh, *ye are.*
Ohan, *Oxen.*

O I

Oi, *an Egg.*
Oich, *Cold.* Cott.
Oilet, f. *a Frying-pan,* or *Gridiron.*
Oin (oan, id.), *a Lamb.*
Oinz, *they*; suffixed to Verbs, to shew the third Person Plural.

O I

Oiz, *thou*; ti oiz aguelez, *thou seest.*

O L

Ol, *all*; Pl. ollow.
Olaz, *a Hearth*; ollaz, id.
Ole, *weep*; olough, *weep ye.*
Olegaddow, *Agreement.*
Olen, *Salt*; Ir. Ar.
Olifans, *an Elephant.* Cott.
Oleu, *an Olive.*
Oleubren, *an Olive Tree.*
Ollna, *Lamentation*; olva, id.

O M

Om, *him*; *himself*; prefixed to Verbs and Substantives.
Oma, *I am.*
Ombdenas, *out*; *fled.*
Omdhal, *to contend*; *cross*; *thwart*; *chide*; *rebuke.*
Omgamme, *wryed,* or *turned him awry*; from cam, *crooked*; gamma, *to crook*; and, with om prefixed, omgamma, *to bend*; *turn crooked,* &c.
Omgregy, *to hang himself.*
Omlanas, *lame.*
Omma, *here*; *this*; ymma, & uppa, id.
Omma, is contracted and placed after Substantives, as, anbyzma, *this World,* and velenma, *this Woman*; so that ma, at the Termination of Nouns, seems but an Abbreviation of Omma.
Omsettyas, *set himself.*
Omstumunys, *astonished him.*
Omwethe, *preserve, keep him.*
Omwrello, *seeks him.*

O N

Onest, *honest.* Lh.
Ongel, *a Cabbage.*
Oni, *we are.*
Onn, or ynn, *a Spear.* Celtic.
Onnen (on, id.), *an Ash-tree.* Cott.
Onowr, *Honour.*

O R

Or, *a Bound*; *Terminus.* L. Ir. Ore, id.
Or, *can,* or *know*; mîor, *I can,* or *know*; oare, id. ni ôr den veth, *no Man knows.*
Orch (oruch, id.), *eminent*; *supreme*; W. as, llow-orch, *chief Government.* R.
Orchinat, *a Shoe,* or *Sock.*
Ord, *of*; *on*; *upon*; orth, id.
Ordan, *by*; *juxta.* L. orta eff, *by him.*

O R

Ordnys, *ordained.*
Ors, *a He-Bear.* Cott.
Orta. See Ordan.
Orte, *thereupon.*
Orthin, *to us*; *for,* and *unto us.*
Orthiv, *to me.*
Orthyz, *unto thee.*
Orz, *a Hammer.*

O S

Os, *thou art.*
Ose, *art thou*; it. *behold*; otese, id.
Ossav, *I am*; ossam, id.
Ost, *a Host,* or *Landlord.*
Ostia, *Lodging.*

O T

Ota (& ote, id.), *behold.*
Otham, *Necessity*; yn otham, *necessary.*
Otho, *him*; warnotho, *on him.*
Otte, *he is.*

O V

Ov, *are*; as, ov ry, *are giving*; it. *I am.*
Ouch, *ye are.*
Overgugol, *a Cottage*; *Cabin*; *Tent.*
Ouna, *to amend*; *rectify*; *to fear*; *Fear*; S. oun, Lh. ounek, *fearful.*
Ounter, *Uncle.*
Our, *an Hour*; ouer, id. Lh.
Ourlen, *Silk.*
Oure (anowre, id.), *farewel.*

O W

Ow, *of me*; *mine.*
Ow (now, id.), *Noise*; heb ow, *without Noise.*
Owel, *a Cliff* (voel, id.), aul, or aules, id.
Owleou, *Marks*; goleou, id.
Own, *Fear.*
Ownek, *a Coward.*
Owr, *Gold*; *Aurum.* L.

O Y

Oyech, *an Outcry*; oyez.
Oyha hemma, *know this*; oyha hedda, *know that.* Gw.
Oyrech, *fiery*; *red-hot.*
Oys, *Age*; ay oys, *that Age*; oze, id.
Oyv, *I*; as, oyv a guelez, *I see.*

O Z

Oz, *thou art.*
Ozhoz, id. as, Ozhoz tôz, *thou comest,* or *art coming.*

Every

P.

Every British Word whose first Radical is P, T, or C, hath in writing three Variations; so that Radical P is sometimes turned into B, into Ph, and into Mh. H. Lhuyd, p. 3.

PA, *which ; when ; see-ing that ; o pa an ruiva-nedh, of what Country is he?* Lh.

Paal, *a Spade,* or *Shovel.*

Pad, *a Cloth* ; padn, id.

Padal, *a Pan.*

Padar, *(the Lord's Prayer)* ; *a Father.*

Padarn, W. *of or belonging to a Father.*

Padelh, *a Frying-pan.*

Padelhoern Cott. id), *an Iron Frying-pan.*

Padn, *Cloth* ; L. Pannum.

Padzhar, *Four* ; padzhar iganz ha dêg, *ninety,* or *four-score and ten.* Lh.

Padzhuera, *the fourth.*

Pairchemin, *Skin* ; parshmennen, id. *Parchment.* Lh.

Pais, Lh. *a Coat* ; peis. Cott. id.

Pâl, *a Shovel* ; W. A. id. unde, by inserting *d,* to padle, i. e. *to stir, and shake the Water to and fro.*

Paladr, W. *Straw* ; *Stem* ; *Reed* ; kala, id.

Palf, *the Palm of the Hand.* Cott.

Palfat, *a Companion* ; Ar. palfat mat, *a good Companion,* ib.

Palmes, *Branches.*

Palmoryon, *Pilgrims.*

Palores, *a Cornish Chough,* or *Daw.*

Pals, *fresh* ; *recent* ; goleou pals, *fresh Marks,* or *Stripes.*

Paltowat, *Fertility.* Cott.

Pan, *when* ; *that* ; *what* ; *until.*

Pandra, *which Thing.*

Panan (Pl. panez), *a Parsnip.* Lh.

Panvotter, *Sorrow.*

Panyn, *whether of them* ; *which of them.*

Papar, *Paper* ; Lh. W. pappyr. id.

Parad, *a Separation.* R.

Paravii, *Pleasure* ; *Preparation* ; qu. Paravij gwaynten, *Pleasure of the Spring.*

Parc, *a Field* ; Ir. pairc.

Parch, *to esteem,* or *bless.* R.

Pardec, *mildly* ; Quaf. pur dêk, *very good.*

Paret *(coctus,* L.), *baked,* or *boiled.*

Parkemmin, *Parchment.*

Parkmennik, *like Parchment.*

Parkenniat, *hurtful.*

PA

Paris, parez, Lh. *ready* ; *pre-pared* ; *readily.*

Parleth, *a Parlour,* parledh, id.

Parou, Ar. *the Country.*

Parthy, *to honour* ; party ma-teyrn, *honour the King.* See parch. W.

Pasch, *the Passover* ; *Easter.*

Passiez, *past.* Lh.

Patshan, *a Buttock* ; *a Haunch* ; peuklyn, id.

Pattek, *a Simpleton* ; *a Fool.*

Pattel, *how* ; fattel, & patla, id.

Paugen (Cott. *Pedula*), *a Wrap-per for the Feet.*

Paun, *a Peacock.* Cott.

Paut, *enough* ; *Abundance.* Ar.

Pautr, *a Boy.* } Ar.
Pautres, *a Girl.* }

Payltye, *beat* ; *to beat* ; ind. f. *pelted.*

Pâz, *a Cough.*

Pazuardhak, *fourteen.*

PE

Pe, *what* ; *although* ; *where* ; *or.*

Pea, *to pay* ; *to rue* ; Pemet, *Pay-ment.*

Peal, *a Spire* ; und. karn an peal, *the Spire Rock.* Hals.

Peb, *every.*

Peba, *to bake* ; pebas, *baked* ; pe-bar, *a Baker.*

Pebouch, *tune ye.*

Pechadyr, *a Sinner.*

Pechadyres, *a Woman Sinner.*

Pedar, *four* ; peswar, id.

Pedhigla, to *bellow* ; *(rugio,* L.), *to roar like a Lion.*

Pedn-diu, *a Blackhead* ; *a Frog-spawn.*

Pedniz, *the Earl of Cornwall.* Lh.

Pednglin, *a Knee.*

Pednpral, *a Skull* ; W. penglog.

Pedrain, *a Buttock,* or *Haunch.*

Pedresiv (pedrevor, id.), *a Li-zard.* Cott.

Pedrevan, id. pedrevan au dour, *a Water Evet,* or *Lizard.*

Pedyr, *Peter.*

Pesyr, *bark as a Dog.*

Peg, *Pitch.*

Pega, Ar. *to bite,* or *sting.*

Peghe, *Sin* ; beghas, id. pek, id.

Pehadorion, *Sinners.*

Pehadur, *a Man Sinner* ; peha-duras, *a Woman Sinner.*

Peidgy, *to pray.*

Peidwurty (Peidwura, id.), *an Architect.* Cott.

Peis, *a Coat.*

Pekar, *as* ; kepar, id.

Pêl, *a Ball* ; pelen, id. it. *a Bowl,* or *any round Thing* ; *a Spire.*

Pelgyp, *a Battledore.*

PE

Peliha, *which* ; *which of the two.*

Pell, *far off* ; *long Time* ; pella, *further.*

Pellen, *a Bowl* ; *a Globe* ; *a hard Pudding* ; *a Bottom of Yarn* ; Pl. peliou.

Pellist-ker (pellistgur, id.), *a Fur Coat* ; *a Leather Pilch.* Lh.

Pema, *where.*

Pemdhak, *fifteen.*

Pemp, *five* ; pempas, *fifth.*

Pen, *Head* ; *a Promontory* ; pedn, id. Pl. pennou.

Pen braoz, *a Jolt-head* ; pen-maur, id.

Penakyl, *a Pinnacle.*

Pencanguer, *a Centurion.*

Pencion, *a Gift* ; *a Pension.*

Penclâs, *Head of a College,* R.

Penclun, *the Buttock* ; Cott. pen-klyn, id.

Pendevig, *a Prince* ; *a Princess* ; Pl. pendzhivigion.

Pendiuen, *a Reed* ; *Arundo.* L.

Pendruppia, *to nod, shake,* or *drop the Head* ; *to beckon.*

Pendzhivig, *a Gentleman* ; Pl. Pendzhivigion.

Pengaled, W. *stubborn* ; *per-verse.*

Pengarn, *a Gurnet* ; qu. *hard,* or *Rock-head* ; Pengurn, *a Gurnard,* id.

Pensgruet, *Bed-cloaths.*

Pengughrek, *a Fur-coat* ; pellist ker, id. pengughgret, Cott. *a Quilt,* or *Rug.*

Penhalurick, quaf. pen-halou-rick, *Head of the rich Moors.*

Penkast, *Whitsuntide* ; Pencas, id. Lh.

Penklyn. See Penclun.

Pennaeth, *chief* ; *uppermost.*

Pennou-tiês, *the head Men of the House.*

Pens, *Pound* ; dek pens, *ten Pounds.*

Penteileu, *Master of the Family.* Cott. penteyly, id.

Penuar, W. *a Halter,* or *Col-lar.* Lh.

Penwith, *the Left-hand Promon-tory* ; *says* Camden. — But I find the South called by the Ancients the Right, and the North the Left. — Now Pen-with is one of the two Sou-thernmost Hundreds of all Britain.—Penguith, or guydh, *the most conspicuous high Land,* or pen-niêt, *the Head of the Island.* See Baxt. in Mictis ; and Humph. Lhuyd's Brev. on the Isle of Wight, pag. 17.

Penyle, *which of the two* ; penyle an dûs, *which of the two Men?*

Penys, *Pains* ; *Punishment* ; pe-nas, id.

Penzivik,

P E

Penzivik, *noble.* See Penzhivig.

Pepynnag ol, *whatsoever.*

Pêr, *a Pear*; Peran, id. perbren, *a Peartree*; it. *a Cauldron*; it. *sweet*; as, aval pêr, *a sweet Apple.* Ar.

Perag, *before*; *coram*, L. *wherefore.*

Pergho (for perko), *remember.* See Ko.

Pergrin, *a Foreigner*; pirgirin. Cott. id.

Perhen, *Owner, or Possessor of any Thing.*

Perna, *to buy*; *redeem*; pernas, *bought.*

Perpoz, *the Plaice Fish*; Pl. perpezou.

Pers, *partial.*

Perseit, *a small Cask*; *Amphora.* L. Cott.

Pertal, *the Porch.*

Pertha, *to honour.* See Parthy.

Perthyans, *Patience.*

Peruez, Ar. *learned*; *expert.*

Pês, *payed.* See Pea.

Pesa, *to pray.*

Pêsk, *Fish*, pusgar, id.

Peskzal, *Salt-fish.*

Pesough, *pray ye to.* V.

Pestriores, *a Witch.*

Pesy, *pray, praying*; pidzhi, id. besy, id.

Pêth, *Plenty*; Pez, id. *Goods*; *Riches*; it. *a Lump, or Mass*; *a Part, or Portion*; as, peyth.

Peth-tshyi, *Houshold Stuff, Furniture*, &c. Lh.

Peualtra, *how many.* Qn.

Peuare, *a Farthing.*

Peul, *a Stake.*

Peulia, *to round with Stakes.* Ar.

Peuri, *to graze*; Ar. und. peurvan, *Pasture Ground*; Ar. *Commons.*

Pew, *whom.* See Piu.

Pewi, *to own*; as, me a pew, *I do own.*

Pewo, *was*; pew, *is*; V. ve, id.

Peyny, *to punish.*

Peynye, *a Token*; *a Sign.*

Peyth, *Part*; *Share*; as, nep peyth, *some Share.*

Pez, *Pease*; Ar. *a Piece*; it. *a Finger, or Toe*; as,

Pez-braz, *the Thumb, or great Toe.*

Pezealla, *how many*; *so many as.*

P I

Piban, *a Pipe* (pib, id.), *Fistula*, L. *of any Kind.*

Pibidh, *a Maker of Pipes*; *a Piper.*

Pibououl. See Piban.

Picol, Ar. *great.*

P I

Pidde, *a Coat*; f. pro peid, id. ac peis.

Pidn, *a Pin*; *a Nail*; *a little Stake.*

Pidnian, *the Brain.*

Pidzhi, *to pray*; piedgy, pidgy, & pidzha, id.

Pig, *Cuspis.* L.

Pig, *a Pig*; pig binau, *a little Pig.* Lh.

Piga, *to prick* (*pungo*, L.), pigaz, *pricked*; ev rig pigaz, *he pricked.*

Pigol, *a Mattock, or Pick.*

Pilecur, *a Parasite.*

Pilez, *bald*; pen-pilez, *a bald Head.*

Pilgudhar, *a Molehill*; *a Hillock.* Lh.

Pill, *Castrum*, L. *a Bullwark.*

Pillen, *the Skirt, or Hem of a Garment.*

Pilliz, *pilled Corn*; *a Kind of Oats* called by Ray Avena nuda.

Pilm, *Dust*; *Chaff*; *Stroil.*

Pîl-tyil, *a Dunghill.*

Pimuschoch, *Bleer-eyed*; Qu. an wimuschoc.

Pinbren, *the Pine-tree.*

Pindy, *musty*; the Flour is pindy, i. e. *musty.*

Pinuidic, Ar. *rich.*

Pip, *a Song*; *Musa.* L. Cott.

Piphit, *a Songster*; *a Player on the Pipe*; & pibit, id. ibid.

Pisgirin, *a Stranger*; *Peregrinus.* L,

Pisch, *a Fish*; Cott.

Pisclin, *a Fish-pond*; i. e. pisclyn.

Pisky, qu. f. *a Fairy.*

Pitshar-pîza, *an Urinal.*

Piu, *who? which?* pu, piua, id. Den o piua, *of what Country is the Man?* Lh.

Piuns, Ar. *a Spring, or Well*; Ir. fians, id.

Pîz, *a Part*; *a Piece*; Ar. *Sparing*; *Niggard.*

Pizaz, *Urine.*

P L

Plankan, *a Table*; *a Plank*; Pl. plenkos, & plynkennou.

Plås, *a Palace.*

Plans, *Sole of the Foot*; it. *a Plant.*

Ple, *where*; prefixed generally, as, plemonz, *where they are*; peleh, pelech, and plech, id.

Plegvyz, *pleasing*; por blegvyz, *very pleasing*; *obliging.*

Plegya, *to wrap, or fold in*; *implico*, L. it. *to bow down to.*

Plema, *where.*

Plen, *united.* Ar.

P L

Plena, *to unite.* ib.

Plenkos, *Boards*; Pl. plynkennou.

Plenys, *that*; *quòd.* L.

Plêu, *a Parish.*

Pleyntye, *accusing.*

Plezia, *to please.*

Pliskin, *an Egg-shell.*

Plobm, *Lead*; plobm rydh, *Red-lead.*

Plos, *Dust*; it. *a Sow.*

Plousen, *a Straw*; *Chaff.* Ar.

Pludn, *a Pool*; na reaw môz war an pludn na, *do not go on that Pool.*

Plumbren, *a Plumb-tree.* Cott.

Pluuen, *a Pen*; plyven, id. Pl. plîv.

Plymon, *a Plumb*; pluman, id.

Plynche, *to bow.* V.

Plysg, *Shell of a Nut.*

Plyvog, *a Cushion*; plufoc, Cott. id.

P O

Po, *or*; *either*; *when*; *where is*; po marh leddres, *when a Horse is stolen.*

Poan, *Grief*; *Pain.*

Pobaz, *to grind, bake*; mên (mân, Lh.), pobaz, *a baking Stone*; ba, id.

Pobel-tiogou, *the Vulgar*; pobyl, id.

Pob-faen, *a Brick*; pob-vaen, *a baked Stone.*

Pob-tî, *a Bake-house.*

Poceuil, *a Kiss*; *Basium*, L. Cott. Ar.

Pocq, id. pokkail, pokkuil, f. id.

Podar, *rotten*; *corrupt*; it. *mundic*; *ugly.*

Podrak, *a Witch*; pydrak brâz, *a great Witch.*

Podzher, *a little Dish.*

Poenis. See Peynye.

Poès, *Weight*; Ar. id. poesa, *to weigh.*

Poesygys, *very hot*; *torrid.*

Pokar, *as if*; *such*; *like*; *equally*; *as*; kâr, id.

Poken, *but if*; *else*; *otherwise.*

Pokkail, *a little Mouth*; *a Kiss.*

Pokkia, *to thrust, or push.*

Pokkys-frenc, *Lues Gallica.* L.

Pokkys miniz, *the Small Pox, or Measles.*

Pol, *a Pool*; Cott. *Puteus*, L. pull, Ar. id. (T. T. *a Top, or Summit*; Qu.), *a Pit*; it. *Dirt*; poldoun, *a deep Pit*; Pol is often put before the Pits dug for Tin, as, Polbreon, Polgooth, Poldys, because their ancient Workings were attended with much Water before they found out the

Way

PO

Way of making Adits, and draining with Engines; it. *Dirt*; *Mire*; Lh.

Pollan, id.

Poldoun, *a deep Pit.*

Poldys, i. e. *St. Dye's Pit,* or *Work.*

Polgover, *the Pool of the Brook.*

Polgooth, *the old Pool.*

Pol-Hendra, *Hendra-Pool.*

Poli, *a Province.*

Pol kil (*Occipitium*), *the hinder Part of the Head.* Lh.

Polkil, *Top of the Neck*; T. T. f. *Pit in a Slip,* or *Neck of Land.*

Pollan-troillia, *a Furrow*; *a Mote.*

Pol-pry, *Mud,* viz. *Pool-clay.*

Polot, Ar. *a Ball*; choari polot, *to play at Balls.*

Pol-roz, *the Pit under a Mill-wheel.*

Pols, *while*; un pols, *u while.*

Polstên, *a Tin-pool,* or *Pit.*

Poltrigas, *Buskins, Spatterdashes.*

Polvellan, *the Mill-pool.*

Polhûel, *the Pool-work.*

Ponar, *a Bean.*

Poni, *unless*; pyni, & ponag, id.

Pons, *a Bridge*; ponz, id. pont, id.

Ponteodi, *a Draw-bridge.*

Ponyas, *ran*; ef ponyas, *he ran.*

Pooc, or puuk, *a Heap*; as, a Pooc of Turves, Pooc of Hay, i. e. *a Heap of Turves*; *a Hay-cock.*

Poran, *streight*; poran war, *streight over.*

Porchel, *a little Pig*; L. *Porcellus*; Pl. pocelli, Porhal, id.

Porh, *a Haven,* or *Creek*; por, id. porth, id.

Porogga, *to gather*; *to steal*; ind. f. *progging.*

Porris, *it must be*; *needs*; *fain would*; *of Necessity.*

Portal, *a Porch, a Threshold*; *an Entry.*

Porth, *a Gate*; Pl. Porthou, *a Door*; *folding Doors.*

Portheres, *a Woman Porter.*

Porthwys, *a Ferryman.*

Poruit, *the Wall of a House.* Cott. *a Wall.*

Pos, or poz, *a Post of Wood,* or *Stone*; *a Prop*; *a Pillar.* Cott. post, id. Lh.

Posigr, *empty.*

Potguidn, *a Bag-pudding.*

Pottro, *rots*; pottro ol dha gîg, *all thy Flesh rots.*

Pour, *Rule*; *Dominion*; gwrens govas pour, *let Dominion be given.*

Pouruei, *to prepare.* Ar.

PO

Pouis, *a Burthen*; W. Ar. poes, C. poîs, & poiys, id.

Pow, *a Country*; *a Province*; pow izal, *a plain Country*; pou an zouzn, *England,* or *the Country of the Saxons.*

Powes, *a Coat.*

Powesough, *rest ye.* V.

Poys, *heavy*; *grievous.* See Puz.

PR

Prag, *why*; praga, id.

Praidh, W. *a Prey*; *Flock*; *Herd*; C. praed, f.

Prania, *crows*; V. ân kuliak a prania, *the Cock crows.*

Praonter, *a Priest*; prounder, id.

Prontir, Pl. prauntirion, id.

Predery, *to consider*; predirio, id. *to meditate*; *to study*; prediri, id. Lh.

Pregoth, *breathing.*

Pregeth, *a Preaching*; as, pregeth awre, *made a Preaching*; ind. progath, *a Sermon*; progathar, *a Preacher.*

Pren, or predn, *a Stick*; *a Tree*; *a Lot* (f. because by Sticks the Druids divined); Pl. prenyer.

Prenest, *a Window*; L. *Fenestra.*

Prenoyth, *seize*; *take.*

Prenol, *a Box. Arca.* L.

Preson, *a Prison*; presonys, *a Prisoner.*

Prest; *but*; *soon*; *readily.*

Prev, *a Worm*; *a Viper*; mil prev, 1000 *Worms*; Prev-nor, *an Earth-worm.*

Prêva, *to prove*; mal dho prêv, *that he might prove,* or *try*; prevys, *proved.*

Prevan, *a Moth-worm*; *a Cheese-worm,* or *other Worm.* Lh.

Prêv'nor, *an Earth-worm.*

Prev pren, *Eruca,* L. *a Caterpillar.*

Prez, *Time*; *Opportunity.* Lh.

Prez-buz, *a Feast*; *a Banquet*, scil. *a Time of eating.*

Prî, *Clay*; peulprî, *a Clay Pit.*

Prideras, *careful*; *cautious*; *sad*; *Studious*; pryderys, Lh. id.

Pridit, *a Poet,* Cott. prydydh, W. id.

Pries, *a Husband*; ou fries, *my Husband.*

Prinnis, *Princes.*

Priot, *a Bride*; bennen priot, *a Bride-Woman.*

Prit, *an Hour.*

Privia, *to bleat*; dhavas a privia, *the Sheep bleats.*

Priz, *Price*; Lh.

Profuit, *a Prophet.* Cott.

PR

Progath, *an Oration,* or *Speech*; progathar, *a Preacher.* Lh.

Pront, *swift.* Ar.

Provycha, *to incense*; *provoke,*

Prunnys, *pardoned.*

Prumpl, *a Boss,* or *Stud of a Bridle.*

Pryderys, *pensive*; *sorrowful.*

Prydydh, *a Poet.* Lh.

Prydzhan, *boiling.*

Pryi, *Clay*; it pry, id.

Prys, *Time*; pres, & prez, id.

Pryvia, *to procure.*

PU

Pu, *who.*

Pub, *every*; pub-er, *whatsoever*, pypenag, id.

Puberoll, *every where.*

Puill, Ar. *abundant.*

Puir, *a Sister.* Cott.

Pul, *a Stream.*

Pulcolan, *the Breast* (f. *the Heart beating,* or *Palpitation*). Cott.

Puludoc, *rich*; ib. *wealthy.*

Punder, *a Priest*; ib. Qu. if not Prunder.

Pundesimpit, *a Lethargy.* ib.

Punnio, *to run away*; *escape,* or *flee*; Lh. redek, W. A. id.

Punt, *Weight*; L. *pondo.* Ar.

Pupprys, *always*; pupûr, *continually*; *every Hour.*

Pur, *being*; pa, pur ylwys, *being called.*

Pur, *snivel*; it. *very* (par, per, id.), pura, *veryest.*

Purcheniat, *a Sorcerer*; Cott. *wicked*; *mischievous.* Lh. it.

Purvan, *a Rush*; *a Pith of a Rush.*

Put, Ar. *four*; as, avalou put, *four Apples.*

Puttendy, *a Bawdy-house.*

Puz (powz, id.), *heavy.*

Puza, *to press*; *lean*; maw, napuza, *Boy, do not lean.*

PY

Py, *whether?* Lh.

Pydzhadou, *a Prayer.* Lh.

Pyg, *the Beak of a Bird*; gylsin, id.

Pygimmis, *how much*; quas. pythkemys.

Pykar, *like*; *as it were.* See Pokar.

Pylta, *much*; pylta guêl, *much better.*

Pyltye, *to beat*; pylt, f. *a Stroke,* or *Blow.*

Pymthek, *fifteen*; à pemp-dek.

Pyni, *except*; *unless.*

Pyni, alias poni, *unless.* Lh.

Pynyon, *the Brain*; pidnian, id.

Pynz, *a Pound*; pymthag pynz, *fifteen Pounds.*

Pyrdzha,

PY

Pyrdzha, *to purge.*

Pyrkat, *a Pulpit; Chair; Roftrum.* L.

Pys, *to pray.* V.

Pyfder, *Heaviness*; à pûz.

Pyfga, *a Fish* (pefk [pyfgaz, Pl. *Fishes*], & pyzgh, id.)

Pyfgadar, *a Fisherman.*

Pyfgadyr, yn mytêrn, *the Halcyon,* or *King's-fisher*; Lh. pifk lîn, *a Fish-pond.* Lh.

Pyfgetta, *a Fishing*; Lh. it. *to fish.*

Pyftege, *Wounds*; T. T. pyftege, id. Sc. Qu.

Pyftryor, *a Sorcerer*; peftriores, *a Witch.*

Pyteth, *Pity*; pyte, id.

Pyth, *what; it. shall be*; as, mar pyth, *if he shall be.*

Pyuha, *who.*

Pyuha, bennak, *whosoever.*

Q.

This Letter is rarely used by the Cornish, often by the Armoricans; and as in some Cornish MSS. Words may occur written after the Armorican Manner, the following Armoric Words are inserted from Lhuyd, marked Ar.

QUAE, Ar. *a Hedge*; ind. f. *a Quay,* or *Hedge, Mole,* or *Pier built into the Sea.*

Queiquel, *a Diftaff*; Ir. cuigeal, id. C. kigel.

Quelen, Ar. *Holly*; it. *to teach,* ib.

Quelguen, Ar. *a Fly.*

Quellida, Ar. *to bud; spring forth.*

Quelvezen, *a Hazel.* Ar.

Quemefq, *to mix.* Ar.

Quenet, Ar. *Beauty.*

Quenver, Ar. *an Acre.*

Querchen, Ar. *the Lap,* or *Bosom.*

Quetren, Ar. *a Particle.*

Queuneut, *Fewel*; queuneuden, *a Log,* or *Billet.*

Quevvret, Ar. *the East*; Auel quevvret, *the East Wind.*

Quignen, Ar. *Garlick.*

Quill, *the Nape of the Neck.* Ar.

Quilquin, *a Frog.*

Quoit, *a broad thin Stone,* or *Rock*; koeten, id.

R.

RAbman, *Rubble*; that Mixture of Clay and Stone which has not been moved fince the Flood, and generally lies over the Karn.

Racca, Qu. Cott. *Comedia.*

RA

Raden, *a Fern*; reden, & Ir. rathin, id.

Radna, *to divide* (radn for ran, *a Share*), dho barri, id. Lh.

Raf, *I shall do*; wra af, id.

Rafarîa, *a Miracle,* or *Wonder.* Lh.

Rag, *for; from; before*; suffixed and prefixed. Rak, id. Lh.

Ragdazu, *Forefathers*; or rhagdazu.

Ragos, *for thee.*

Ragou, *before you*; rago huei, *for you.*

Ragta (ragthe, id.), *for him,* or *it.*

Ragteken, *a little while.*

Rahaya, *to sneeze.*

Rakkan, *a Rake; a Harrow*; Lh. W. kribyn, Ar. Raftel.

Rambrea, Ar. *to doat.*

Rampa, Ar. *to slip,* or *slide.*

Rân, *shall do*; dzhyi a'rân, *they shall do.*

Ran, *a Part; a Share* (rans, id.), pedar rans, *four Shares*; rhanniad, id.

Randigal, Qu. what a Randigal (viz. *Rout, Noise,* or *Tumult*) is here?

Rane, *broke; rent; shared; divided.*

Raneie, Sc. (rauny, T. T. id.), *vexing.*

Raoula, *to grow hoarse.* Ar.

'Râs, *Grace; Virtue*; der'râs, *by Virtue of; good Will*; for grâs.

Rath, Ir. *a circular Fortification*; à radt, f. in Celtic, *a Wheel.*

Raz, Ar. *Lime; a Rat.* ib.

RE

Re, *that; who; some; whilst*; it. Sign of the Future Tense; as me a re gelfes, *I will heal.*

Re, *too much; also; quickly*; a Particle encreasing the Force of Verbs and Nouns and Adverbs; as rebehas, *I have too much sinned*; reforras, *is very angry*; redegua, *a Course*; f. *violent one.*

Re, often used for rig; as, me re gufges, *I have slept.*

Rêa (rîa, rêa reve, id.), *O strange!*

Reâu, *Frost*; rêu, id. rhewi, & reui, Ar. *to be very cold.*

Reb, *of; by; nigh; near.*

Rebe, *were*; rebee, *was*; revye, *it was before.*

Rebea, *to begin*; a nombris rebea, *began to number; to begin.*

Rebet, Ar. *a Fiddle*; rebetter, *a Fidler.*

Rebeuten, Ar. *a very Whore.*

RE

See Puttenty.

Redan, *a Fern.*

Redanan, *a Brake of Ferns.*

Redegua, *a Course*; Cott. Curfus; L. retaden, Ar. id.

Rhedec, *Swiftness*; W. & Ar. Gr. ῥέω.

Redha, *well; very well.*

Redic, *a Radish*; rhedhîc, id.

Redy, *surely*; yredy, *readily.*

Redyn, *to read*; Engl. und. redior, *a Reader.*

Reeg, *did*; y a reeg gore, *they did put*; for ryg.

Regeth, *is settled.* V.

Reighten, *a Coal,* or *Ember.* Cott. *Pruina.* L.

Rego, *against*; as, aga rego, *against them.*

Reguezen, Ar. *a burning Coal.*

Dho rei, *to give; to grant,* or *offer.*

Reig, *Ice*; po an reig dho derhi, *or the Ice to break.*

Relewte, *indeed*; relawta, & rulewte, id.

Rello, *to make; be.* V.

Remenat, *the Remnant*; Pl. remenadow.

Rên, *the Mane of a Horse.*

Ren, *to bring; lead*; pa. reet. Ar.

Ren, *him; the same; the ren, to him*; reth, Pl. rena, id.

Renêag, *to deny,* or *refuse*; *Renegado,* Span. quasi à Lat. renego-are.

Renki, or renkia, Lh. *to snore*; Gr. ῥέγχειν. id.

Rhengkias, *snoring.*

Renniat, *a Sharer*; *a Carver.* Cott. *Discifer*; *a Waiter at Table.*

Rera, *Father.* Sc.

Rês (for ros), *a Valley*; as, Reftormel, refcadzhill, &c. *Places in Vallies*; as, bes for bos.

Refas, *gushed; flowed*; Gr. ῥέω. *fluo.* See Rezek.

Reffa, *done*; ev a reffa, *he had done.*

Refteffo, *that he might be.*

Reftoua, qu. f. *to befet; to rest upon.*

Reth, *they; them*; it. V. *be caused.*

Retheruid, *a Fisherman.*

Rêv, *an Oar*; *a Shovel*; as, rêvtan, *a Fire-shovel.*

Reu, *Cœlum,* L. Cott. See Nêf.

Revadar, *a Rower.*

Revarîa, *by our Lady,* scil. by the *Virgin Mary*; a common Expreffion of Aftonishment and Surprize.

Revewfe, *to abide*; revefe, id.

Reugh,

RE

Reugh, *go* ; eugh, id. it. *do* ; as, na reugh, *do ye not.*

Reun, *the Hair of Beafts.* Ar. W. rhaum, id.

Reux, Ar. *Misfortune.*

Rew, *Hafte* ; yn rew, *in Hafte* ; it. *Froft* ; as, reau.

Rewrenfys, *thou haft done.*

Rey, *to give* ; re, id.

Reys (rez, & rys, id.), *needs* ; as, reys yw, *needs be* ; L. *oportet.*

Rezek, *running.*

RH

This afpirate is always in W. fometimes in Ar.

Rhaith, Ar. *a Law.*

Rhei an guella, *to permit,* or *confent.*

Rhied, *Nobilium Statio.* L. R.

Rhies, *a Princefs* ; *a Lady.* R.

Rhifglaff, Ar. *to flide.*

Rhittia, *to rub, chafe,* or *fret.* Lh.

Rhôs, *Heath.* R.

Rhyvedhod, Ar. *rare.*

RI

Rib, *of* ; *by* ; *through.*

Ribla, *to rake* ; *fwagger.* Ar.

Ridar, *a Kind of Sieve,* or *Riddle.*

Ridar, *a Kafher* ; *a Sierce* ; krodar, id.

Rig, *did,* or *have* ; Sign of the Preter Tenfe ; never joined to the Verb.

Rigol, *Rigour* ; Ar. it. *a Slip, Gap,* or *Cleft.* Lh.

Rilan, *flowing into.*

Rimadel, Ar. *a Romance* ; *a Fable.*

Rine, *a Quail.*

Riou, *Cold* ; *Froft* ; riua, *to be cold.* Ar. See Reau.

Rifk, *the Rind of a Tree* ; e rîfk, *it's Bark* ; *a Shell,* or *Pill.*

Rift, *fad* ; trift, id.

Ritan, *the Wind-pipe.*

RO

Ro, *a Gift* ; Pl. robou ; à rofe, *gave* ; tero, *you give* ; un ro, *one Gift.*

Roath, *Form.*

Robbia, *to fpoil* ; rob ; *plunder.* Lh.

Roch, Ar. *a Rock* ; G. id.

Rochet, *a Shirt* ; Ar. rochueden, *a little Shirt.*

Rocca, *a Roach-fifh* ; talhoc, id.

Rhod, *a fighting Chariot* ; R. whence Britifh Names ; as, Anau-Rhôd, Cadrhôd, Medrhôd.

RO

Rodella, *to turn,* or *wind about.* Ar.

Rhodl, *a Branch.*

Rodothye, *gave Gifts to thee.*

Rogeth, *fettled.*

Rolle, *to give* ; rolla, *might,* or *did give.*

Ronkye, *fnoring* ; renky, id.

Rooge, *to rooge to and fro,* i. e. *to remove* ; *to transfer from one Place to another by meer Strength* ; Lat. *ægrè portare.*

Roulers, *Rulers* ; *Governors.*

Rofen, *a Rofe* ; ros, Ar. Ir. *Rofa,* L. id.

Rhos, *habitable Land* ; rhofydh, *Heathy Ground.* R.

Rôs, *a Mountain* ; *Meadow,* or *Mofs* ; *Heath* ; *a Wheel.* Lh.

Rôfh, *a Valley,* or *Dale* ; nans, id.

Roftia, *to roaft.*

Rouan, *Roman* ; as, Pol-rouan, *the Roman Pool.*

Rouden, Ar. *a Foot-ftep.*

Roue, Ar. *a King* ; rouanes (fee ruyfanes), *a Queen* ; & rouentelez, *a Kingdom* ; G. roy, &c. C. ruy, Cott. rhy, riog, id. Ar.

Rouenner, *a Mite* ; *a Weevel.* Ar.

Roueft, *Confufion* ; roueftla, *to confound.* Ar.

Rouez, *thin* ; *flender,* Ar.

Rouffen, *Wrinkles* ; *Plaits* ; *Folds.* Ar.

Rougn, *a Scab* ; rougnus, *fcabby.*

Rouhen, *a Span.* Ar.

Roulia, *to guide,* or *rule.*

Rounzan, rouzan, & rofin, id. *an Afs.*

Row, Qu. as, the Row-tin, i. e. *the large grained, rough Tin* ; rowtor, i. e. *the rough Hill* ; quaf. ab huero, *rough.*

Rowas, *obtained.* V.

Rôz, *a Wheel* ; gravar-rôz, *a Wheel-barrow* (Ar. rot, id.).

Rozellen, *a Whirl for a Spindle* ; i. e. *little Wheel.*

RU

Rual, Ar. *to rufh* ; *batter* ; *throw.*

Rud, *red-coloured.* See Rydh.

Rûeik, *a Prince* ; prins, id. Lh.

Rug, *made* ; ryg, arug, id. as, arug cry, *made a Cry.*

Rugfi, *fhe bore.*

Ruibht, *Brimftone* ; mygfaen, id.

Ruilla, *to roll.*

Ruif, Cott. *an Oar* ; ruifadur, *a Rower* ; *a Waterman* ; ruiv, ruivadar, id.

Rum, *hath* ; *haft me* ; ty rum gruk, *thou haft made me.* Ar. *fomebody.*

RU

Runa, *Myfterium* ; *Vates* ; Celtic, as, Runa Goths, *Dei Confilium.* Keyfl.

Runen, *a Hillock.* kryg, id.

Rufk, *the Bark of a Tree.* Cott.

Rut, *a Path* ; A. Lh. it. ib.

Rute, *the Herb Rue* ; ryte, id.

Ruthveyn, *a Multitude.*

Rhuttia, *to rub* ; as, rhytti marhna, *rub that Horfe.*

Ruy, *a Prince* ; Cott. *a King* ; brenin, W. id.

Ruyd, *a Net* ; Ar. red, id.

Rhuydh, W. *eafy.*

Rhuyfanes, *a Queen.* Cott.

Rhuygo, *to tear,* or *rend.* W. R.

Ruyvanaid, *a Kingdom.* Cott.

Rûz, *a Net.*

RY

Ry, *to give* ; *give* ; reyth, *giveft* ; rys, *gave.*

Ry, *to caufe* ; rys, *Caufe* ; ryfyw, *there is Caufe* ; *did.*

Ryb, *of* ; *by.*

Rybbon (rebbon, id.), *by,* or *near us.*

Ryd, *a Ford* ; ryd-helik, *the Willow Ford.*

Rydh, *red* ; rydhik, *reddifh* ; ryudh, Ar. ridh velin, *a deep yellow.*

Pedn-rydh, *red haired.* Lh.

Ryel, *royal.*

Rygthe, *to charge* ; *command.*

Rymys, *divided.*

Rhyn (W. *a Promontory*) ; C. *a Chanel.* Gr. ῥιν.

Ryn, *a Bill* ; *a Nofe* ; W. rinn, id.

Rynen, *a Hillock.* Cott.

Rys, *was.*

Ryfeve, *received.*

Ryfy, *to extoll.* T. T.

Ryte, *Rue.* Lh.

Rhyth, *Appearance.* R.

Rhyttia, *to rub.*

Rhyven, W. *Rome* ; C. Ruan.

Rywïer, Ar. *a River* ; und. f. Ryvier in Phillak, on Hayle River.

S.

SAUT, *Meat* ; *Dainties* ; Cott. Sach-diaul, *a Demoniac* ; *a poffeffed.* ib.

Saëfnek, *Englifh* ; *Saxon.*

Safar, Ar. *Noife* ; fafari, *to make a Noife.*

Sagen, *a ftanding Pool.*

Saim, *Fat* ; *Oyl.*

Sairpren, *a Carpenter.* Cott.

Saithor, *a Shag* ; *Bird* ; Cott. *Mergus.* L.

Sâl, *vile.* R.

Salver, *a Saviour.* Ar. id. Lh.

Sam,

S A

Sam, *a Burthen* ; *a Charge.*
San, Ar. *a Conduit.*
Sanaill, *a Mow-hay.* Ar.
Sanqua, *to prick* ; *pierce.*
Sans, *holy* ; Speris Sans, *the Holy Spirit* ; Sanz, *a Saint.* Lh.
Sant, Lh. *Food* ; *Meat.*
Sarn, *a Caufey*, or *Pavement.* W.
Sarra, *Sir* ; farra wheag, *fweet Sir.*
Satheluur, *an Orator* ; *a Speaker.* Cott.
Satnas, *Satan.*
Sâu, *fafe* ; *but* ; *except* ; *fave that.*
Sav, *rife up* ; *ftand up* ; à fevys.
Savarn, *Smell* ; *Savour* ; drog favarn, *ill Smell.*
Savas, *a Chanel* ; penfavas, *Head of a Chanel.* Gibf. Camden, pag. 13. Qu.
Saudl, Ar. *a Heel.*
Savig, *the Branch of a River.*
Saunt, *Noife* ; *Difpute.* What a Saunt is here ? Qu.
Sautra, *to foul* ; *bewray.*
Sawe, *a Seam* ; *a Horfe-load* ; war an fawe, *by the Seam.*
Saweh. Cott. Qu.

S C

Scacel, *a Prop.* Ar.
Scaff, *nimbly* ; marfcaff, *fo nimbly.*
Scala, *a Difh* ; *Patera,* L. *a Goblet,*
Scân, *a little Table.* Ar.
Scao, *an Elder-tree* ; fcauan, id. Ar. id.
Scarz, *fhort.* Ar.
Scavel, *a Bench* ; fkaval, id. Lh.
Scedgwith, *Privet.*
Scherewneth, *Pride.*
Scherewys, *the Scribes.*
Scevens, *the Lungs* ; Cott. Ar. fqueveat, Ir. fcaven, id.
Scinin, *an Ear-ring* ; ib. fkinen, id.
Scloqua, *to chirp like a young Bird,* or *Hen.*
Scobman, *a Chip of Timber*— Scobman vîan, *a little Chip.*
Scoch, *common* ; fcoch-fôr, *the common Way.*
Scod, *the Shade* ; *Umbra,* L. Cott. fkez, id. Ar. fqueut, id.
Scol, *a School* ; fcolheic, *fcholaftic* ; yfkol, W. id.
Scolchye (fcolcheth, id.), *a Fugitive* ; ind. f. *fkulking,* or *lying hid.*
Scolys, *fpilt.* Pa.
Scon, *immediately* ; mar-fcon, *as foon as.*
Sconyth, *fhunneft* ; fconyas, *refufed.*

S C

Scorgyas, *to fcourge,* or *lafh.*
Scorren, *a Branch,* or *Bough* ; fcourr, Ar. id. it. *a fmall Vein of Tin,* or *other Ore.*
Scôs, *a Change* ; *to exchange.*
Scoth, *a Shoulder* ; fcooth, id. See Scuid.
Scovern, *the Ear.*
Scoul, *a Kite* ; Cott. bargus, id.
Screfys, or fkrephys, *written* ; mean-fcrefys, *the infcribed Stone.*
Skrepha, *to write.* Lh.
Skrift, *a Writing* ; fkrividh, id. Lh.
Scren, *a Bone,*
Scriven-danven, *an Epiftle.* Cott.
Scriviniat, *a Writer.* ib.
Scrivit, *Writings.*
Scryrya, *forfaken.*
Scubellen, *a Broom* ; fcubilen, Cott. id.
Scudell, *a Difh* ; *a Quoit* ; *a broad Difh* ; fkydel, id. Pl. fcudellou ; fgudh, & fkaydh, id.
Scuid, Cott. *Scapula,* L. *Shoulder* ; fcuidlien, *a Cloak to put over the Shoulder.* Cott.
Scuilla, *to fhed,* or *fpill.* Ar.
Scuiz, *weary* ; *tired.*
Scuiza, *to be weary.* Ar.
Scût, *a fmall Piece of Money.*
Scyle, *a Proof* ; fcyle vâs, *good Proof* ; it. *plainly* ; ken fcyle, *other,* or *more ado.*

S E

Se, *them* ; ganfe, *with them.*
Seadha, *to fit* ; *fit down* ; fethas, feithva, fittis, *did fit.*
Seafys, *dried* ; *drying.* See Seha.
Seban, *Soap* ; Gr. σκπων. Sa.
Seera, *a Father.*
Segernath, *lazy* ; *dull.*
Segeris (fegyr, & figer, id.), *empty* ; *void.*
Seha, *to wipe* ; *to be dry* ; *to fcour.* Lh.
Seis, *Silk* ; feizen, *a Ribbon.* Ar.
Seitag, *feventeen.*
Seith, *a Pot* ; Cott. it. *feven.* Lh.
Seithas, & feythvez, *the feventh.*
Seithyn, *a Week.* ib.
Sekerden, *Security.*
Sel, *a Foundation* ; Cott. W. fail, id.
Selda, *a Cellar.*
Sell, *a Look* ; *Sight* ; fellet, *to look.* Ar.
Selliz, *falted.*
Sely, *Arms.*
Sempla, Ar. *to flacken.*
Senedh, *an Affembly* ; *Synod.* Cott.

S E

enfys (from fendzha, alias fenze, *to hold*), *held.*
Serra, *to clofe* ; *fhut up.*
Seruic, *a Shrub.* Cott.
Seth, *an Arrow* ; fethy, *to fhoot.*
Sethek, *fet down* ; fethas, *did fit* ; fettyas, *placed.*
Setfans, *preffed* ; *earneftly intreated.*
Seuadh, *a Taylor* ; feufad, *a Patcher* ; *Mender.*
Sevi (fyvi, id.), *Strawberries.*
Seuades, *a Woman Taylor.*
Sevys, *flood* ; fefsons, *they flood.*
Seuzl, *the Heel.* Ar.
Sew, *ye be* ; fens, *they be.*
Seweth, *fadly.*
Sewillaf, *to loofe* ; L. *folvere.*
Sewyas, *followed.*
Seygh, *dry* ; pren feigh, *a dry Stick* ; fekh, id.
Seygh, or feugh, f. id. i. e. as, the Cow is gone to feugh, i. e. is gone dry ; *without Milk.*

S G

Sgân, *an Elder Tree* ; fkauan, id. C. & A.
Sgâu, *light* ; fgav, id. i. e. *not heavy* ; fgavder, *Lightnefs.*
Sgenip, *inceftuous* ; Cott. fguenip, id.
Sgein, Ir. *a Flight.*
Sguattia, *to tear in Pieces.* Lh.
Sgûth, *a Shoulder-blade.* Lh.
Sguthlien, *a Cloak,* or *Hood.* Lh.
Shagga (farthor, id.), *a Cormorant* ; *a Shag.*
Shanol, *a Chanel* ; *a Pipe* ; *a Gutter* ; A. kanal, & ganhel, Lh. id. as, Ganhel in Carantok Parifh, & Canal in St. Iffy ; as, Canal-Idgy, or Idzhy, i. e. St. Iffy Creek.
Shimbla, *a Hearth,* or *Fire-place.*
Shode. Qu. *fmoothed Tin-Ore.*

S I

Sibuit, *a Fir-tree.*
Sicer, *Peafe.* Cott.
Sichen, *a Chair* ; *a Seat.*
Sichor, *Drought* ; *Thirft.* Cott.
Sidan, Ar. *a Linnet.*
Siell, *a Seah.* Ar.
Sîger, *hollow* ; *full of Holes* ; tollek, id.
Siglen, *a Bog.*
Silien, *an Eel* ; Pl. filiou.
Sim, *an Ape.*
Sindzhy, *to hold* ; dho finlzha, *to feize.* Lh.
Sinfiat, *tenacious.* Cott.
Sioas, *alas!*
Sionge, *honourable.*
Sioul, *filent.*
Sira, *a Father.*

Sira,

S I

Sira-gwydn, *a Grand-father.*
Sirig, *Silk* ; Gr. σηρικον. Sa.
Sizl, *a Strainer* ; fizla, *to ſtrain.*

S K

Skarkeas, *a Shark-Fiſh.*
Skat, *or* ſkuat, *a Buffet,* or *Blow of the Fiſt.* Lh.
Skath (ſkaph, id.), *a Boat* ; ſkath ruz, *a Boat with Nets* ; ſkath hir, *a Long-boat.*
Skauan, *an Elder-tree* ; ſcauori-an, id. ſkaun. Lh.
Skavarnak, *a Hare.* See Sco-vern.
Skeans, *pretty* ; *lepidus.* L.
Skelli, *Wings.*
Skelligrehan, *a Bat* ; *Leathern Wings.*
Skent, *ſcanty* ; *ſhort.*
Skentyll, *learned* ; ſkyntyll, id.
Skenys, *Sinews.*
Skephans, *the Lungs.* Lh.
Skeſy, *eſcape* ; ny wra ſkeſy, *ſhall not eſcape.*
Skêth, *weary.*
Skez, *a Shadow* ; ſcod, Cott. id. und. f. ſkeſy.
Skibia, *to bruſh,* ſconr, *or ſweep.* Lh.
Skibor, *a Barn.*
Skidal, *a little Diſh.*
Skientoc, *wiſe* ; Cott. ſkientik. Lh.
Skinan, *a Pin.*
Skiran, *a Bough* ; Pl. ſkirau ; ſcorren, *a Branch,* or *Bough.* Lh. Grefen, *a Sprig.* Ar.
Skîth, *weary* ; *jaded* ; *ſpent.*
Skival, *a Porringer* ; ſcudel, id.
Skogan, *a Fool.*
Skreft (ſkrividh, id.), *Scripture.*
Skriga, *to ſcreech* ; na ſkrig, *do thou not ſcreech.*
Skrivinas, *to ſcratch, claw,* or *rub.*
Skuattia, *to ſtrike* ; *to break.*
Skud, *a Shoulder.*
Skudel, ſkydel, *a Diſh,* or *Plate.* Lh.
Skuerryon, *Eſquires.*
Skul, Qu. towle the Skul, *to take in vain,* ſcil. *the Name of God.*
Skul, *a Shoal* ; *a Quantity of Fiſh* ; *a Skul of Pilchards.*
Skyhans, *Wiſdom.*
Skylia, *ſcatter thou.*
Skylur, *a Scholar* ; Pl. ſkylurion.

S L

Slavan, *dirty* ; loh-ſlavan, *dirty Pool.* Hals.
Sleane, *a Conger-fiſh.*
Sleppia, *to ſlip,* or *ſtumble* ; rag dout why dho ſleppio, *for fear you do ſlip.*
Slev, *cunning* ; *ſkillful* ; und. ſley-neth, *Skill.*
Slottere, i. e. *dirty, ſlovenly.* Qu.
Slumyas, *to reproach.*

S N

Snell, *to him.*
Snod, Cott. *a Fillet* ; *a Hatband* ; *a Garland.* Lh.

S O

Soa, *Tallow* ; *Suet.* Ar.
Sobman, *a Chip* ; ſobman vîan, *a little Chip.*
Soch, *the Plough-ſhare.* Cott.
Sofl-jar, W. *a Quail.* Lh.
Sog, f. *a Doze* ; *Numbneſs* ; *Drouzineſs.*
Sogal, *Rye* ; bara ſogal, *Rye-bread.* Gw. Lat. *Secale.*
Sogete, *a Diſcovery.*
Sol, *a Shilling* (Ar. *a little Gird-er*), hanter ſol, *a Six-pence.*
Soler, *a Throne* ; *a high Seat,* or *Bench* ; it. *a Sun-dial.* Lh.
Sols, *Money.*
Sonas, *bleſſed.*
Sonta (ſouta, id.), *to ſolder.* Ar.
Sorca, *to charm* ; *bewitch.* ib.
Sorchenni, *to rave.* ib.
Sordys, *raiſed.* Pa.
Sorras, *angry* ; *jealous* ; reſorras, *very angry* ; ſor, id.
Sort, *a Hedge-hog.*
Sos, *thou beeſt* ; ſota, *thou art* ; ſoge, *be thou.*
Sôs, *a Friend,* or *Companion.*
Softer, *a Siſter.* Mod. Corn.
Soth, *riſe.* S.
Souba, *to hop,* or *ſkip.* Ar.
Soubla, *to ſweeten.* Ar.
Souez, *Admiration* ; ſouzea, *to admire.* Ar.
Soul, *Straw* (W. ſool, id.), ti ſoul, *a thatched Houſe.* ib.
Soweth, *curſed* ; yn ſoweth, *ac-curſedly* ; it. *Alas !*
Sowmens, *Salmons.*

S P

Spâl, *a Sconce* ; *Amercement* ; *For-feiture.*
Sparf, *a holy Water* ; *a Sprinkling.* Ar.
Sparl, *a ſhort Cudgel* ; ſparla, *to bolt.* ib.
Sparria, *to ſpare.*
Spas, *untill* ; *as long as* ; *whilſt that.*
Spauen môr, *Æquor.* L. Cott.
Spaz, *a Gelding* ; ſpaza, *to geld.* Ar.
Speal, *an Acquaintance.* T. T.
Specyal, id. *intimate* ; ſpecyal brâz, *very intimate.*
Spedye, *to ſucceed* ; *haſten* ; ta ſpedye, *to ſpeed well.*
Speitia, *to ſpite* ; *vex.*
Spekkiar, *ſpeckled.*
Spendys (ſpengas, id.), *ſpent* ; *waſted.*
Spens, *a Buttery* ; L. *Promptua-rium.*
Speris, *Spirit* ; ſpyr, id. ſprîte, id.
Spern, *Thorns* ; Pl.
Spernabyll, *ſtedfaſt* ; ſpernaſyll, T. T. id.
Spernan, *a Thorn* ; ſpernan diu, *a black Thorn.* Lh.
Speur, *an Incloſure.* Ar.
Spezaden, *a Gooſeberry.* ib.
Spillen, *a Pin.*
Spiziz, *a Ghoſt* ; *Hobgoblin* ; *Hag.*
Splan, *clear* ; *bright* ; *excellent* ; ſplanna, *to ſhine* ; ſplen, id. ſpladn, *illuſtris.* L.
Splander, *Brightneſs.*
Spluſen, *a Pippin* ; Ar. ſpluſek, *a Nurſery of Pippins.* ib.
Spong, *a Spunge.*
Spont, *dread* ; ſpontus, *dreadful.* Ar.
Spoue, *Cork.*
Spoum, *ſcum* ; ſpouma, *to ſcum,* ib.
Spykes, *Spikes* ; *large Nails.*

S Q

Squardya, *to tear* ; ſquardias, *he tore.*
Squarinek, *long-legged.* Ar.
Squattia, *to pluck,* or *tear in Pieces.* Qu.
Squei, *to knock* ; Pa. ſcoet. Ar.
Squeigea, *to cut off* ; *pare,* ib.
Squenip, *Inceſt* ; *Uncleanneſs.* Lh.
Squeull, Ar. *a Ladder.*
Squilfou, *Claws.* Pl. Ar.
Squyth, *weary.*
Squytzder, *Wearineſs.* l. T.

S T

Stagen, *a ſtanding Pool.*
Staquel, *the String of the Tongue* ; und. f. ſtaqual, *to clatter,* or *gnaſh.* Ar.
Stal, *a Shop.* ib.
Stanconni, *to prop* ; ſtanconnou, *Stays.* Ar. id.
Stanc, *a Pool* ; *a Pond of ſtanding Water.* Ar. id.
Stanquen, *a Valley* ; *a low Place.* Ar.
Staoun, *the Roof of the Mouth.* ib. See Stefenic.
Starda, *to quench.* ib.
Start, *firm* ; *faſt.*
Stèan, *Tin.*

Stefenic,

ST

Stefenic, *the Palate of the Mouth.*
Stella, *every Day ; always.*
Stemmyn, Qu. *to work out his Stemmyn,* i. e. *to do his Share of Work.*
Stempel, *a flant Beam ufed in Tin Mines.*
Stên, *a Milking Pail ; alfo a Water Veffel.*
Stener, ftenor, Lh. *a Tinner ;* it. *a Water-Wag-tail.*
Stequi, *to choak ;* Ar. See Taga.
Steren, *a Star ;* Cott. fterran, & fteyr, id. fterran lefki, *a Comet ;* fterran guandre, *a Planet.* Lh.
Stervys, *to catch Cold.* See Stevys, id. T. T.
Steva, *to find ; found ;* ni fteva whans, *found no Defire.*
Stevel, *a Chamber ; a Dining-room ;* Cott. *Triclinium.* L.
Stevys, *to be very cold.*
Stich (hule, id.), *an Owl.* Cott.
Stifak, *a Cuttle-fish.*
Stigna, *to reach ; extend ; difplay.* Ar.
Stikedn, *a Stake ;* Pl. ftukednaw.
Stil, *a Beam of a Houfe.*
Stkaf, *a Stammerer.*
Stlapa, *to caft,* or *fling ;* Ar. id. ind.
Stlap, *a Stroke,* or *Blow.*
Stlegea, *to draw,* or *drag.*
Stoath, *ftifled.*
Stoc, Cott. *the Trunk of a Tree.*
Stol, *a loofe Garment.* Cott.
Stollof, *a Glove ; a Handful.*
Stollowfet, *a Towel,* or *Napkin.*
Stopan, *bend thou ;* ftopan we-then, *bend the Tree ;* ind. f. *a Stope.*
Storc, Cott. *a Stork.*
Stouet, *to kneel.* Ar.
Strail, *Tapeftry ; Mats ;* ftrail-leftre, *a Mat.*
Strath (Scotifh), *a Dale,* or *Valley,* or *Plain ;* W. *a Vein,* or *Soil of Land ;* as, Strad Alyn, Strad Towyn, i. e. *a Vein on the River Alyn,* or *Towyn.* H. Lh.
Strecha, *to tarry ;* ni ftrechaff, *I will not tarry.*
Streil, *a Curry-comb ; a Flefh-brufh.* Cott.
Streing, *a Buckle.* ib.
Strêk, *a Stream ;* ftrek brâz, *a great Stream ;* ind. f. Strakes, *to go to* Strakes.
Stret, *Spring-water.* Cott.
Strevy, *ftrived.*
Strifor, *contentious.* Cott.
Strihue, *fneezing ;* ftrihui, *to fneez.*
Strìk, *fwift ; active ; lufty ; courageous.*

ST

Strill, *a Drop :* ftrillic, *a little Drop.* Ar.
Stringua, *to caft,* or *hurl.* ib.
Striz, *narrow ; ftreight ;* ftriza, *to bind faft.*
Strokofou, *Stripes.*
Strollat, *a File ; a Rank.* Ar.
Strop, *a Thread,* or *String.* Ar. id.
Strouez, *Prickles ; Thorns.* Ar.
Stûan, Qu. *He gave him a Stûan,* i. e. *a Blow.*
Stut, *a Knat,* or *little Fly ;* Cott. Ar. *a Rudder.*
Stynnar, *a Peuterer.*

SU

Sûas, *O ftrange !* fioas, Ar. *alas !*
Suben, *a Kind of Pudding ; a Morfel.* Lh.
Sudronen, Cott. *a Drone.*
Suel, *he that.*
Suellak, *a Field-fare ; a Bird.*
Suidnan, *a Draught ; Hauftus.* L.
Suif, *Tallow.* Cott.
Sul, *the Sun ;* fol, id. Ar. id.
Suler, *a Floor.* Ar. id.
Sumbul, *a Goad.*
Sutal, *to whiftle ;* Ar. futellez, *whiftling.*

SY

Sybottia, *to think ;* fyppofia, f. id.
Sygal, *Rye ; the Grain Secale.* L.
Sygan, *Sap ; Soaking ; Juice ; Moifture.*
Syl, *although.*
Syllyas, *the Conger-fish.* See Silien.
Sylwans, *Salvation ;* fylwys, *faved.*
Syns, *he be ;* it. *I hold.*
Synfy, *retained ; held.*
Synt, *a Saint ;* re Synt Gylmyn, *by Saint Golman.*
Sythyn, *a Week ;* feithyn, id.
Syueth, *alas ! ah !* fywêth, id.

T.

" T is changed into D, into
" Th, and into Nh." Hum.
Lh. p. 3.
N. B. T and D are often ufed indifferently.

TA, *Good ;* yn ta, *after Good ; goodly ;* it. *thou.*
Tabarlanc, *a Cloth of State ; a Canopy.* Ar.
Tabm, *a Piece ; a Morfel.* Lh.
Tach, *a little Nail ; a Nail ;* tacha, Ar. *to nail,* or *tack together.*
Tachen, *a fpacious Plain,* or *Piece of Ground ;* tachen glaz, *a*

TA

green Place. Ar.
Tadder, *Goodnefs.*
Tadvath, *a Nurfer ; Bringer up ;* talvat, Cott. id.
Taga, *to choak ; devour ;* tagou, id.
Taghir, *the Skuttle Bone,* or *Bone of the Cuttle-fish.*
Tahua, *a Sea-calf.*
Taig, *a Club.* Ar.
Takkia, *to fix ; to drive,* or *thruft in.* Lh.
Taill, *a Tax ;* tailla, *to impofe.* Ar.
Tair, *three ;* fem. g. tre, m. Lh.
Tairnant, *Ointment ;* Cott. *Soap.*
Takkys, *faftened to ;* ind. f. *to have the Tack ;* i. e. *not to be able to move.*
Taklolaz, *a Creature ;* taklolaz gwayans, *a moving Creature.* B.
Taklou, *Creature ; Thing ;* as, taklou minniz, *fmall Things ;* ind. f. *Tackle ;* as, *good Tackle ;* i. e. *good Things ; fit Inftruments for the Bufinefs ;* & è contra, *bad Tackle ;* viz. *unfit,* &c.
Tal, *high : tall ; a Forehead ;* W. *a Region ;* R. & W. *a Beginning ;* und. talar, *a Headland ;* it. *a Seal ;* as, tal-gellth, *Sigillum ; Cellarium.* Lh.
Talch, *Bran.*
Taleden (talguen, id.), Ar. *a Fillet.*
Talhiar, *a broad Plate,* or *Difh ; Lanx.* L.
Talien, *a Brow ; a Forehead-cloth ;* f. koruadh, id.
Tallafqua, *to be idle ;* Ar. See Talfoch.
Talfokh, *ftupid ;* talfoch, Lh.
Tallok, *a Roach-fish.*
Talm, *a Clap of Thunder ;* Ar. tarzcurun, id.
Talfoch, Cott. *a Dunce ; Blockhead.*
Talvat, *a Nourifher.*
Talvega, *to reward.* I. K.
Talvez, *able ;* bôz talvez, *to be able.*
Tam, *piece* (tabm, id.), *at.*
Tamal, *to rebuke.* Ar.
Taman, *upright ; that.*
Tam, or Tamny, *Names of Rivers,* as the Greek Ποταμ☉, und. f. Tam-mawr, or Tamar, fcil. *the great River ; the largeft in Cornwall.*
Tamouez, *a Sieve.* A.
Tan (odditan, & tanodd, id.), *beneath ;* tanou, *under me.*
Tan, *Fire.*
Tan-llwyth, *a Bon-fire ;* Ar. tantez, tan, id.

Tantât,

TA

Tanau, *thin; slender; small; lean.*

Tanauder, *Thinness.*

Tantat St. Jan, *Midsummer Bonfires; sc. St. John's Fires;* tantat, *good, or holy Fires.*

Tanter, *a Wooer;* tymarrhar, id.

Taran, *Thunder;* tredna, id.

Tardar, *an Augur; a Gimblet;* und.

Tardha, *to bore, prick, sting, or nettle;* Lh.

Tardhak, *thirteen;* trethak. id.

Tarfin, *a Boundary.*

Tarian, *a Buckler.*

Tarneidzha, Lh. tarneudzha, *to swim over.*

Tarneuhon, *the Loin; Hanch, or Flank.*

Tarnutuan, *a Phantasm;* Cott. *a Whim; a Chimera.* Lh.

Tarthas, *gushed forth.*

Tarw, *a Bull;* Lh. taro.

Tarza, *to prick; stir.* Ar.

Tarzas, *to burst.* V. Neut.

Tarzell, *a Nook, or Corner.* Ar.

Taserghys, *the Resurrection.*

Tatinus, *contentious.* Ar.

Tâu, *hold your Tongue; be silent.*

Tavantec, *poor;* tavanteguez, *Poverty.* Ar.

Tavarchen, *a Turf.* Ar.

Tavargn, holsteri, id. *a Tavern; an Alehouse.*

Tavaz, *a Tongue;* tavazek, *talkative;* it. *a Token;* Pl. tavazou.

Taul, *a Blow;* taulen, *a Table.* Ar.

Tavolen, *a Dock;* Cott. Dilla. L.

Tavot, Cott. *the Tongue.*

Taw (Cott. *Cereus,* L.), *Waxen.*

Taz (tad, id.), *Father;* tazguidn, *a Grandfather.*

TE

Te, *thou.*

Teak (teg, pro ték, id.), *fair; good;* und. tekter, *Beauty.*

Teaut, *Tongue.* Ar.

Tear, *rude.* ib.

Tebel, *wicked.*

Tebri, *to itch;* ma dorn a tebre, *my Hand itches.*

Techet, *to fly.* Ar.

Tedha, *to melt; thaw; dissolve.*

Tedna, *to lead; convey; draw; strain; wring, or bind.* Lh.

Teed, *a Tide;* trig, id.

Teen, *a Man;* dien, id. for deen, quas. pro dên, id.

Teffa, *should;* teffe, *might come.*

Teffen (en teffen), *awake.*

Tefighia, *to tire;* tevigia, id.

Têg, *pleasant;* Lh. *honest; fair.*

TE

Tegauel, *a Calm; fair Weather.*

Teghez, *choaked.*

Tehen, *a Firebrand;* it. *to light; kindle,* or *set Fire to;* tewyn, id.

Tei, *to thatch,* or *cover with Straw;* Ar. C. tey, id.

Teil, *Dung; Ordure.*

Teill, *a Raspberry.* Ar.

Teirgueth, *thrice.* Lh.

Teithioc, *a Bond Servant, Male or Female.*

Teken, *a little while;* rag teken, *for a while.*

Tekter, *Beauty; Comeliness.*

Telein, *a Harp.*

Teleinior, *a Harper.*

Telhar, *a Palace; Palatium;* L telhar marhaz, *a Market-place.* Lh.

Tellou, *Land-taxes.* Ar.

Tellys, *holed.*

Temigou, *Bits; Fragments;* Pl. of temig, *a Bit;* qua. from tam; demigou, id. Lh.

Temptys, *tempted.*

Tena, *to suck.* Lh.

Tene, *sucking;* denys, *sucked.*

Tenewen, *a Side of the Body;* tyrnenuan, id.

Tenn, *rude; rustic.* Ar.

Tensa, *to chide; scold.* ib.

Têr, *a Field; a Manor;* quas. *Terra;* L.

Tera, *was;* dera, & thera, id.

Terebah, *until; as far as.*

Termen, *a Time;* thermina, id. Pl. termin; un termen ma, *hac Vice;* Lh. pubtermin, *all Times;* enmên, *after that.* Lh.

Tern, *an Oven; a Furnace.*

Ternewan, *the Side;* terneuan an auan, *the Bank of a River.*

Ternewen. See Tenewyn.

Ternôs, *the Day following.*

Terri-andzheth, *Dawn,* or *Break of Day.*

Terry, *to break, cut, saw,* or *rend;* torras, & dorras, *broke;* trehez, *cut.*

Tês, *Heat;* Cott. R. id.

Tescaoua, *to glean.* Ar.

Tesky, *to teach.*

Tempell, *a Temple;* Pl. templys.

Tethan, *an Udder;* also *a little Teat.*

Tetholl, *Day; all Day;* pubtetholl, *every Day.*

Têu, *fat; thick;* Ar. teo, id. brâz, id.

Teua, *Home;* môz teua, *to go Home;* it. *at last;* quas. à deweth.

Teva, *to grow; increase.*

Teual, *dark; brown;* Pl. tulgu.

Tevas, *merciful.*

TE

Teuder, *Thickness;* Ar. tevahat, id.

Teuel, *to be silent.*

Tevenes, *sent;* damenys, id.

Teuth, *a Nation;* Ir. tuath, id.

Teuzi, *to melt.* Ar.

Tewlas, *cast; decreed; designed;* dewlys, id.

Tewlel (tyulel, id.), *to cast.*

Teyrn, *a Prince.* R.

Teys, *Thatch;* chy teyz, *a thatched House;* Ar. Toen, und. toer, *a Thatcher.*

Tez (tiz, id. Pl. f. à den), *Men.*

Tezan, *a Cake.*

TH

Tha, *thy;* da, id. thy, the, dhy, id.

Thadder, *Goodness.*

Thagan, *to us;* thagan sawga, *to save us.*

Thâl (for tal, *a Forehead*); rum thal, *by my Forehead.*

Tharnou, *Pieces;* ol the tharnou, *all to Pieces.*

Thâs (tâz, tâd, id.), *a Father.*

Thât, *I shall,* or *do go;* à theth.

Thavaz, *a Token;* cabm thavaz, *a Rainbow;* i. e. *a crooked Token.*

The, *to; from;* thethe, *to them.*

The (athe, id.), *comes;* V. thês, *do you come;* deez, ind. f. *come thou.*

Thecsyngh, *ye carried;* à thegis.

Thefregh, *Arms.*

Thegis, *to bear,* or *carry;* thek, id.

Thegough, *bear ye.*

Thehes, *at length.* Ad.

Thelle, *was; might,* or *could be;* delle, id.

Thelhar (thellurgh, id.), *back;* warthellurgh, *backward.*

Then, *this.*

Thens, *they were.*

Theravas. See Derevas.

Therevel, *to raise; repair; rebuild.*

Thermaz, *dearly; beloved.*

Thefe, *were;* thefe fethek, *were set down.*

Theskerny, *to grin.*

Thesky (disky, tisky, id.) See Tesky.

Thesympys, *immediately.*

Theth, *went;* theves, *they went;* thethons, id. *came;* à toz, vel doz, *to come,* or *go.*

Thethoras, *to rise;* ef a thethoras, *he rose.*

Thethoryans, *the Resurrection.*

Theveth, *a Curse.*

Theugh, *you; to you;* thewna, *they; themselves.*

6 A

Thevyth,

T H

Thevyth, *take Care* ; qua. à theveth, *a Curse.*

Thew, *a Side* ; Pl. thewen ; it. *is* ; y thew, *it is.*

Thew, *Dew* ; *two* ; dho thew, *to threaten.*

Theweth, *End* ; *Death* ; Deweth, id.

Thewhans (tewans, id.), *fast* ; per thewhans, *very fast* ; i. e. *secure.*

Thewleff, *Hands* ; viz. *two Hands.*

Thewlyn, *Knees* ; dowlyn, id.

Thewsys, *Pains* ; it. *Choice.*

Thillas, *Cloaths* ; dillas, id.

Thîs, *a Servant* ; ou thîs, *my Servant* ; qua. tez, or tiz, it. *at all.*

Thiftiplys, *Disciples.*

Thistrewy, *to destroy.*

Tho, *him* ; it. (pro dho), *to* ; as, thotho, *to him* ; war tho, *on him.*

Tho, *am* ; V. as, tho ve, *I am.*

Thoke, *carried* ; *taken* ; à thegis, or thek.

Tholle, *deceived* ; *to deceive.*

Thom, *I am* ; thom kimerez, *I am taken.*

Thons, *they* ; often suffixed in the End of Verbs, to shew the third Person Plural ; it. *they come.*

Thorians, *the East* ; viz. *Sun's Rise* ; thuyran, id.

Thort, *from.*

Thoutyth, *carest* ; ny thowtyth Du, *Carest thou not for God ?*

Thragta (thrayta, T. T. id.), *to betray.*

Thraytor (traytoar, id.), *a Traitor* ; thraytorou.

Thrig, *the Tide of the Sea.*

Throppys, *dropped.*

Thugsyons, *they thought.*

Thum, *my* ; *to my* ; thum lavarou, *my Words.*

Thuthy, *to her*, or *him.*

Thy, *to his* ; thys, *to thee* ; *to her.*

Thyasseth, *stedfast* ; *settled.*

Thyatye, *to dispose.*

Thyfar, *a Bargain.*

Thyghou, *right* ; leffe thyghou, *the Right-hand.*

Thyguethys, *shaved* ; trysyvethas, id.

Thym, *to us*, thymmo, *to* or *for me.*

Thynny, *we* ; *us.*

Thytsyas, *provided.* Pa.

Thyvas, *should.*

Thyveth, *dismal.*

T I

Ti, *a House* ; Pl. ties, Ar. id. Ir. eagh, id.

Tiwarnal, *a House upon the Moor* ; scil. ti war an hâ'. N. B. Four Words put together, to make a Name expressive of the Situation.

Tiah, *to swear* ; ind. toan, or tyan, *an Oath* ; Ar. touet, *to swear.*

Tiak, *a Farmer* ; *a Housholder* ; *Master of a Family* ; Ar. tiek, id.

Tidi, *a Dug* ; *a Breast* ; *a Nipple* ; Lh. W. diden, têth.

Tigan, *a large Sack* ; *a Wallet.*

Tign, *Scurf.* Ar.

Tikkideu, *a Butterfly* ; gloindiu, id.

Tîm, *Thyme.*

Timat, *swift.* Ar.

Tin (dyn, id. & tyn), *sharp* ; *terrible* ; *severe.* Διωθ'. Gr.

Tinel, *a Tent.* Ar.

Tîr (tyr, id.), *Land* ; Pl. tiriou, & terros.

Tir-devrak, *a Moor*, or *Marsh.*

Tisky, *teaching* ; *Learning* ; disky, & thesky, id.

Tist, *a Witness.* Cott.

Tithe, *thou also.*

Tithia, *to hiss.*

Tivia, *to grow.* See Teva.

Tiwulgou, Cott. *Darkness.*

Tîz, *Men* ; tuz, duz, tez, id. *a People* ; *a Tribe*, or *Family* ; tyd, A. id.

Tizout, *to reach* ; *attain to.* Ar.

Tiz-rum, *Romans* ; *Men of Rome.*

T O

To, *than* ; T. T. Qu. it. *a Roof.* Cott.

Toan, *an Oath.*

Toas, *Paste* ; Ar. toasez, *a kneading Trough* ; ind. f. to tôas, i. e. *shake the wet Tin to and fro, to cleanse it of the Earth.*

Toc, *a Hat* ; *a Cap* ; *a Bonnet.* Ar.

Todn, *Lay-ground* ; *Land on a Downs.*

Toim, *hot* ; tom, id.

Tokko, *he may bring* ; mai tokko, *that he may bring* ; f. à degy.

Tollgarrik, *the holed Rock.*

Toll, *a Hole* ; tell, id. tolvên, *a holed Stone* ; toll y gwint, *a Vent-hole.*

Toll-karn, *the holed Heaps of Rocks.*

Tollek, *hollow.*

Tollkorn, *a Trumpet* ; clarion, *a Crozier.* Lh.

Tollur, *a Man that inspects and superintends Tin-bounds* ; so called f. because Bounds are terminated by Holes cut in the Earth, which must be renewed and visited once in a Year, or because he receives the Tolls, or Dues, of the Lord of the Soil.

Tolva, *a Custom House.*

Tombder, *Heat* ; Pl. tummasou, tom, id.

Tomals, *Quantity* ; *great Heaps of any Thing.* Lh.

Tôn (tûn, id.), *to bear* ; porto, L. it. *a Billow* ; *a great Wave.*

Tonek, *a Flock*, or *Herd.*

Tonen, *the Rind*, or *Paring of Fruit*, or *Plant.* Ar.

Tonnel, *a Tub* ; *any great Vessel* ; Cott. tonwel, *a Barrel.*

Tons, *they come.*

Tor, *a Tower*, or *high Place* ; as, Helmantor, Rou-tor ; Torcrobm ; it. *the Belly* (Ar. tur, id.), Pl. torr.

Torandorn, *the Palm of the Hand.*

Torch, *a Hog* ; towrch, Ar. Ir. torc, *a Boar* ; f. *a wild Boar* ; à tor.

Torchat, *a Bundle* ; Ar. torcha bleo, *a Lock of Hair.*

Torgocc, Ar. *a Dwarf.*

Torh, *a Loaf* ; torth, id. torz, Ar.

Torkhan, *a Fire* ; *Hatred* ; *Envy.* Lh.

Torlan, *Bank of a River.*

Tornad, *a Breach.*

Torneuan, *the Sea Shore* ; *the Bank of a River.*

Tôs, *to come* ; me tôz, *I come* ; dôz, id.

Tosoanna, *to provoke*, or *vex.*

Tost, *near.* Ar.

Touçec, Ar. *a Toad.*

Toula, *to cast* ; *to pour* ; toula emeas, *pour out.*

Toun, *an Oath.* Lh.

Tourni, *Noise.* Ar.

Touse, *a Noise* ; *Disturbance* ; as, What's the Touse there ? Qu.

Touzier, *a Table-cloth.* Ar.

Towan, *an Otter.*

Towl, *some* ; *away* ; Qu. *a Fall.*

Towne, *deep* ; maga towne, *very deep.*

Towyll (dowyll, id.), *a Tool* ; *a working Instrument.*

Towyn (tuyn, id.), *a Turfy Down* ; ind. portowyn, & towyns, *Hillocks of Turf* ; W. in Dav. *Gleba* ; *Cespes* ; L. Belg. Duyn est Tumulus arenarius, five Collis sabulosus objectus Oceano—and so are the Towyns in Cornwall. See Lye's Junius in Voce DOWNES.

Traeth

TR

Traeth (Tractus, viz. Marititimus), *a Sea-shore*; trai, Ir. id.

Trafferth, *a Bustle*; *a Noise*.

Trahaue, *proud*.

Trahezi-mean, *Stone-cutters*.

Trailia, *to turn*; traillia an ber, *to turn the Spit*; treyl, id.

Trangiak, *a Dream*; *Exstasy*; *Delirium*; *a Difficulty*.

Traoue, *a Valley*; Ar. traoun, *low*, id.

Travethak, & trauedhak, *lamentable*; *sad*.

Traûst, *a Beam*.

Trauythes, *thin*; *rare*; *excellent*. Lh.

Tre (id. sonat ac L. Trans), as, tremenez, *to traverse*; *transgress*.

Tre, *that*; *as*, trevedna dama, r'hei, *that my Mother will give*.

Tre, *a Town*; trev, id. a *Walled Town*, or *City*. Lh.

Treage, *the Muscle-fish*.

Trêas, *Gravel*; *Pebble*; *coarse Sand*. Lh.

Trebath, *a Trivet*, or *Brand-iron*. Lh.

Trebe, *until*.

Trebez, *a Trivet*. Ar.

Trech, Cott. *Fruit*; *a Trunk*, or *Stem of a Tree*; *a Blockhead*. Lh.

Trechi, *to surpass*. Ar.

Tredhek, *thirteen*.

Tredna, *Thunder*; trenna, id.

Tredzha, *the third*.

Tref, *Lands annexed to a House*. R.

Treffia, *to spit on*; und. trifiaz, *spitting*.

Trefraint, *a Borough*, or *Corporation*, qua. trefranc, *a free Borough*.

Trege, *to dwell*; tregis, & dregas, pa. dho trega, id.

Tregva, *a Dwelling*; alias trega, as, tregavara, *the Bread Town*; tregaminion, treganebris.

Trehar, *a Taylor*; *a Cutter out*.

Trehe (try, trybo, id.), *as far as*; *until*.

Trehi, *to cut*; *chop*; ind. troher, *a Coulter*; trehys, *cut*; tresheys, *to cut*.

Trei, *three*.

Trein, *the Nose*. Cott.

Treiz, Ar. *a Passage*; *a Strait in the Sea* (und. treiza, *to pass*); it. *a Town of Corn*.

Trekh, *the Trunk of a Tree*; treugen, id. Ar.

Trem (or threm, W.), *the Sight*.

Tremen, *a Passage*; tremenvan, id. Ar.

Tremengue, *a Ladder*. Ar.

TR

Tremôr, *foreign*; *beyond Sea*.

Trene, *sharp-tasted*.

Trenk, *a Sower*.

Trendzha, *the Day after Tomorrow*.

Trens, *among them*; *beyond them*.

Trenydzha, *to fly to and again*; *to fly over*, or *across*.

Tres, *moreover*; yn tres, *in the midst*.

Três, *Trouble*.

Treffe, *three*.

Trethe, *among them*.

Trethon, *betwixt us*; trethynz, *betwixt them*.

Tretury, *Treachery*.

Trev, *a Village*; *a House*; Pl. trevou; Lh. treven, W. *a Tribe*; R. treu, id. as in Domesday, Coven treu, for Coven trê, ind. Treuro, f.

Trevedic, *a Countryman*; Cott. *a Cottager*; *a Clown*.

Trevedig-doer, *a Sojourner*.

Treus, *Cross*; treusou, *a Threshold*. Ar.

Treust, *Powder*; *Dust*.

Treut, *lean*; Ar. Qu. See Teu.

Trevith, *Nothing*.

Treuth, *the Entry*. Lh.

Treuzhen, *a Blockhead*. Lh.

Trew. See Trev, Tre, id.

Trewe, *spitted on*. See Treffia, Treefa's, & Drewys, id.

Trewesy, *feeble*; *sorrowfully*; it. *Fit*; dreuesy, id.

Treys, Pl. of Troys, *the Foot*; troat, id.

Trez, Ar. *Sand*; trezou, *Linen Cloths*; it. *betwixt yours*.

Trìa, *to tempt*; *to prove*; *to assault*.

Tribedh, *a Brand-iron*, or *Trivet*; Τρίπος. Gr. it. *a Gallows*.

Tridal, *to start*. Ar.

Trifiaz, *Spittle*.

Trig, *a Flowing*; f. Trig, & Trigshire, Cornwall, it. *an Inhabitant*; *Recessus Maris*. Lh.

Trighia, *to inhabit*; kontreva, id.

Trîkkin, *a Tucker*, or *Fuller*; trykkiar, id.

Trincha, *to flatter*. Ar.

Trist, *sad*; Cott. tristys, & tristans, *Sorrow*.

Triuadhek, *meek*; *gentle*.

Triuath, *Pity*. See Truez.

Tro, *a Turn*; Pl. troiou, trova, id.

Troheaul, *a Turn-Sol*, or *Sun-turn*, such as the Druids made, and the Inhabitants of the Western Isles still make, in Salutations and Worship.

Tro, *that*; *as*; *how*; *then*; *than* (try, id.)

Troaz. See Trôs; it. *Urine*;

TR

und. troaza, *to make Water*.

Trocha (troha, & trogha, & traha, id.), *towards*.

Trodzhan, *a Starling*.

Troed, *a Fool*; troedlydan, *broad-fooled*; Lh. W. See Truz.

Troet, *a Turtle*.

Troher, *the Plough's Coulter*.

Troidella, *to compass*. Ar.

Troill, *a turning Reel*; Ar. *a Term in Hunting*.

Tron, *a Hose*. Lh. an tron. Qu.

Tronsal, *to truss*; *tuck up*. Ar.

Trôs, A. trus, W. trust, id. *Noise*; *a Bounce*; *a Din*.

Troster, *a Beam*. Cott.

Trossol, *a Bar*, or *Bolt*.

Trot, *miserable*; Cott. troth, id. *Poor*.

Trouviaz, *found*; V. G. Trouver.

Trui, *through*.

Tru, tru, *sad!* *sad!* ogh tru, tru, O *sad!* *sad!*

Trud, *a Trout*.

Truez, *Compassion*; truath, id.

Trugarez, *Mercy*; qua. *Pity* and *Love*; und. trucaraue, *merciful*.

Truillou, *Rags*; truillek, *ragged*. Ar.

Truit, *the Foot*. Cott.

Trulerch, *a Path*; *a Foot-path*.

Trull, *a Buttery*.

Truz, & druz, *a Foot*; truzu an daraz, *a Threshold*; it. *a Louse*; Pl. treiz; trûyd, id. Lh.

Truz-blat, *Splay-footed*.

Truz-ebal, *the Colt's Foot*; *Tussilago*. L.

Trwydon, *Swimming*; und. R. triton.

Try, *whilst*; spas, id. Lh.

Tryan, *Clay*, or *Clob*; as, chytryan, *a House of Clob*, or *Clay Walls*.

Trychans, *three hundred*.

Tryygans, *sixty*; tryngens, id. trei-igans. Lh.

Trylya. See Traillia.

Tryn, *to feed*, or *look after*. R.

Trysa, *the third*.

Tryssor, *a Bank*, or *Public Stock*.

TS

Tshappal, *a Chapel*.

Tshappen, *a Capon*.

Tshattal, *all Manner of Cattle*.

Tshauka, *a Jack-daw*, or *Chough*; W. koguran; palores, id.

Tshei, *a House*; tshei hora, *a Brothel*; chi, id. Pl. treven. T. T.

Tshikuk, *a Swallow*.

Tshimbla, *a Chimney*.

Tshomber,

T S

Tſhomber, *a Bed-room*; *a Chamber.*

Tſhoun-ler, *a Candleſtick.*

Tſhofar, *a Chafindiſh.*

Tſhyrkog, *a Tavern*, or *Victualling-Houſe.*

Tſkekk'er-eithin, *a Titmouſe.*

T U

Tu, *Side*; pub tu, *on every Side*; Ar. *a Coaſt.*

Tuban, *a Bank*; Lh. *Dam*; *Dike*; ind. tubans, f. i. e. *great Clods of Earth.*

Tubby, *Thomas.*

Tubm, *warm*; *lukewarm*; from tubmy, Lh. tubma, *to heat.*

Tui (tyi, id.), *ſworn*; e rig tyi dho vi, *he ſware unto me.*

Tull (toll, id.), *a Hole.*

Tulgu (tuyldar, tewolgou, id.), *Darkneſs.* See Teual.

Tulla, *to bore through*, or *hole*; und. f.

Tulle, *Deceit*; and tullor, *deceitful.*

Tummaſou, *Heats.*

Tunder, *Heat.* Cott.

Tuogu, *common*; pob'el tuogu, *the Rabble*; *the common People.*

Tûr, Cott. *a Tower*; tûrmas, id. Lh. kaſtal, id.

Turen (Cott.), *a Turtle*; turan, id. Ar. turzunell.

Turques, *a Pair of Pincers.*

Twrgwelied, *a Beacon*; huyl bren, W. id.

Turiat, Ar. *to dig the Earth, as Moles.*

Turnupan, *a Turnip*; Pl. tyrnyppyz.

Turumel, *a Molehill.*

Tûs, *Men*; dûs, id.

Tutton, *a Chair*, or *Seat*; und. f. Tutts, or *Haſſocks.*

Twyllo, *to beguile*, or *deceive.* See Tulla.

Tuyn, *a Hillock.*

Tuyſog, W. *a Captain.*

T Y

Tŷ, *Thou*; te, id. it. *Side*; as, anty man, *on this Side.* Lh.

Tybakko, *Tobacco.*

Tybyans, *Thought*; *Imagination.*

Tyd (tydhyn, W.), *Land*; C. id. from tydhyn to tydhyn, i. e. *from Pariſh to Pariſh.*

Tyffonz, *they come*; may tyffonz, *that they come.*

Tyha, *towards*; as, tyhan temple, *towards the Church*; war tyha tre, *towards Home.*

Tyle, *Mud*; *Slime.*

T Y

Tyller, *a Place*; Pl. tellyryou.

Tyllian, *an Owl.* Hal.

Tymarrhar, *a Wooer*; *a Suiter.*

Tymarrhurian, *Sweethearts.*

Tymheſtlog, *tempeſtuous*; *boiſtrous.*

Tyn, *a Paſſage over a River*, or *Arm of the Sea*; *alſo a Hill.*

Tyner, *tender.*

Tyſtio, *to bear Witneſs.*

Tythar, *a Place*; py tythar bynnag, *what Place ſoever.* See Tyller.

Tythy, *from thence.*

Tyuldar, *Darkneſs.*

V.

N. B. No Corniſh Word begins primarily with a V, but either with B, F, P, or M, all which in Compoſition will change into a V; as, Bara, *Bread*; Maur, *great*; in Compoſition, ſay, Vara, Vaur, &c.

VEEN, *vain.* Ar.
Vab. See Mab.

Vabm, *the Milt*; *the Spleen.* Lh.

Vac, *impeached.* Ar.

Vadna, *will.* See Vedna.

Val, *a Peſt*, or *Plague.*

Vam. See Mam.

Vanaff, *I will*; ny vanaff, *I will not.*

Vanah, *a Fellow*; *a Paramour*; qua. for Manah.

Uar (for uarth), *in*, or *upon*; as, uar an diuadh, *in the End.*

Uarler, *after* (uarlyrch, id.), ſometimes divided by a Pronoun, as, uar-i-ler, *after him*; uardhalyrk, *after.*

Uarnach (uarno, id.), *on you*; uarnaz, id.

Uarnan, *upon us.*

Uarnodho, *of or concerning him*; anodho, id.

Uarnydzhanz, *over or upon them*; uarnedhe, id.

Uarrah, *higheſt*; *ſummus.* L.

Varth, *Wonder.* See Marth, id.

Varuo. See Maruo.

Uaruolez, *below.*

Uary, *Licenſe*; *Liberty*; *Play.*

Vas, *good*; *enough.* See Mat, or Maz.

Vaſe, *ſee*; fas, id.

Vaulz, *a Reaping Hook*; *Falx.* L.

Uauſſow, *Cliffs*; qua. Pl. ab aules (vel owel, vel owels), *a Cliff*; where the U ſeems to be prefixed as it were for Sound-ſake.

Vâw, *a Boy.* See Maw.

Vay, *a Kiſs.* See Baye.

U C

Uchel, *high.* See Ughel.

U D

Udzhe, or udzha, Lh. *afterwards*; udzhe henna, or udzhe hedda, id. *after this*, or *that*,

Udzheon, *a Bullock*; udgian, & odion, id.

U E

Ve, *I*; *me.*

Veam, *ſhould I.* V.

Vean (for bêan, or bychan), *little.*

Uedhu, *a Widow.*

Vedn, *will*; V. na vedn ſinzhy, *will not hold*; me vedn kерz, *I had rather.*

Vehegar, *a Bondman.*

Vel, *like*; *as it were*; *than*; *far.*

Velen, *vilely*; mar velen, *ſo vilely.*

Velha, *longer*; *farther off than.*

Velhuez. See Melhuez; cu idydh (f. eu idyn), id.

Ueli, *ſee*; ti a ueli, *thou wilt ſee.* Vid. Guelaz.

Uellyn, *yellow.* See Mellyn.

Ven, *that were*; it. *ready.*

Vendzha, *will*; *would*; *did*; *could*; me vendzha a henz, *I had rather.*

Venedh, *a Mountain.*

Veneffre, *never.*

Vennyn, *would*; *could.*

Venons, *ſpilt*; *came*; *come.* V.

Venſy, *to chaſtiſe*; *deſtroy*; *vindicate.*

Venyn, *Women*; Pl. à Benen.

Veôr, *great*; as, Treveor, *the great Town*; qua. pro Vaûr.

Veras, *looked*; *admired*; viraz for miraz, id.

Vernans. See Mernans.

Verth, *Strength*; nerth, id.

Verwy, *to die*; Merwye, id.

Vês, *out*; vês guris, *put out*; mes, id. aves, it. *out of Doors.*

Veſtl, *Gall.* Ar.

Vêſtry, *Maſtery*; *Strength*; *Victory*; à meſter.

Vet, *ſtay*; me avet, *I will ſtay.* it. *from*; as, golou vet an tuyldar, *Light from the Darkneſs.*

Veth, *ſhall be*; as, vethaff, *I ſhall be*; it. *Sorrow*; it. *a Time*, or *Turn*; as, dyweth, *twice*; biſguetn, *never*; it. pro bedh, *a Houſe*, or *Grave*; it. *any.*

Vethough, *take ye Care.*

Vetye, *to meet*; qua. à metye.

Veughe, *Lives*; V. à beu.

Vewns, *a Dream.*

Veyll, *extremely.*

Veyn,

V E

Veyn, *a Stone; Stones;* for meyn.
Vez, *loft; wafted; outward;* as, gweal an vez, *the outward Field.*

U F

Ufern, *the Ancle-bone.* Ar.

U G

Uge (auch, T. T.), *over, from above.*
Ughel, *high; loud* (ughan, & aughan, f. Ir. id.) *fupream.*
Ughelder, *Height.*
Ughelles, *extolled; praifed; hallowed.*

U H

Uhal, *hard; difficult;* hual, id. it. pro ughel.

V I

Ui, *an Egg;* oi, id. Ar.
Vî, *I; of me; to me.*
Via, *had;* na via, *had it not been.*
Uibren, *a Cloud,* or *Mift,* Lh.
Vichan, *little;* as, vean, bechan, &c.
Vidn, *Sorrow.*
Vihith, *Care; Heed;* dho kymeras vihith, *to take Heed.* Lh.
Vilekur, *a Parafite.*
Vindrau (*Torpor; Digitus,* L.), *a Numbnefs; Stupidity; Infenfibility.*
Vinny, *thou wilt.*
Vîr, *Truth;* en uir, *verily.*
Viraz, *to behold;* for miraz, id.
Vifkuethek, *everlafting.* See Bifgueth.
Vifnans, *Lances; small long Fifhes taken out of the Sands.*
Vith, *any;* vyth, *none.*
Viz, *a Month;* miz, id.

U L

Ula, *an Owl;* Ind. f. tre-ula; hule, id.
Ulair, *a Mantle; a Veil.*
Ulamy, *to accufe;* à blamye.
Ulano, difklien, Cott. *a Quaternion.*
Ulaz, *a Country;* ulaz ma, *this Country;* wlas, id. wlad, W. id.
Ullia, *to howl; to make a Noife.*
Ulos, *Sight,* welas, id.

U M

Umdowla, *Wrestling;* ymdoula, id.

U N

Un, *a;* as, un pols, *a while.*
Uncorn, *an Unicorn.*
Undamfi, *a Client; Clientulus.* L. dencofcor, id. Cott.
Ungarme, *a Lamentation.*
Ungle, *a Colewort;* ind. f. treungle.
Unfa, *to have;* unfa moy joy, *to have more Joy.*
Unfcogyon, *unwife;* mifcogyon, id.
Untye, *to anoint; Ointment; anointed.*
Unver, *a Bargain.*

V O

Voel, *a bleak Hill; a Cliff;* Pl. uaffow. See Moel, & Owel, id.
Vold, *courageous; bold.*
Volder, *Leave; Pardon;* dry volder, *by Leave.*
Uole, *to weep;* krio, id. Lh.
Voleythy, *to curfe.*
Uolhya, *to wafh;* for golhya.
Uolou (for golou), *Lights.*
Vols, *a Vault;* voffa, *to vault,* or *bow.*
Vôn, *furthermoft; hindmoft;* as, y vôn ynys, *the furthermoft Ifland;* vôn lâz, *the Land's-end.*
Vones, *Money;* vone, id.
Vons, *they be;* vonas, *he fhould be.*
Uor, ur, uyr, Pa. of the irregular Verb, guodhaz, or kodhav, *to know;* as, evaur (or uyr), *he knoweth.*
Vor, *a Way;* as, vorlas, *the green Way.*
Voreth, *Sorrow.*
Vork, *a Fork.*
Vork, trivork, *a Trident.*
Vorn, *an Oven.* See Forn.
Uorh, *from; by; in; to; unto.*
Uorto, *to,* or *unto him.*
Vôs (for fôs), *a Ditch, Wall,* or *Fence;* as, penvôs, *Head of the Trench;* marhas an vôs, *the Market on the Fofs;* Pl. vofou, as, Caervofou.
Vos, *to be;* vo, *it was; was;* vofe, *to be.*
Vofogyon, *the Poor;* bofogyon, id.
Voth, *the Will.*
Uouiz, *a Hook;* voulz, id.
Vounder, *a Lane;* vounder vôr, *the Lane-way.*
Uour, *a Hufband* (f. pro gur), dha uour, *thy Hufband.*
Voufy, *were; they were.*
Vownas, *was.*
Voxcufy, *buffeted.*
Uoze, *after.*

U P

Uppa, *here;* for omma.

U R

Ur, *a Man;* Ar. Ir. fear, id. L. Vir.
Ur, *an Hour.*
Vrac, *Malt.*
Vrafter, *Pride.*
Ureha, *to fow,* or *plant.* Lh.
Urellon, *we fhall do.*
Vrês, *Judgement; Sentence.* brês, id.
Ureth, *ftay.*
Vrinkak, *French Tongue;* W. Frennig, id.
Urma, *now; at this Hour;* yn urma, id. pel dhan urma, *long fince;* Lh. bet an urma, *thus far; to this Time or Place.* Lh.
Urna, *that Time; that Hour;* yn urna, id. Ar. urou, *sometimes.*
Urria, *to honour; worfhip.*
Vry, *Account; Price; Efteem.*
Uryffo, *I fhall do.*
Urylli, *thou fhalt do;* uryffys, id.
Urylliff (urello, id.), *he fhall do.*
Urellon, *we fhall do.*
Urz, *Borders.* Ar.

U S

Ufair, *a Veil.* Cott.
Ufion, *Chaff; Straw.*
Ufye, *ufed.*

U T

Uter, *dreadful.*
Utetha, *to fow;* fero. L.
Uther, *a Club.*
Uun, *a Downs;* as, chiuun, *a Houfe on a Downs;* for guun.

U Y

Vy, *I; me; us.*
Uy, or guy, *a Termination of Names, ufually fignifying Water;* as, dourduy, W.—and C. id. as, Treth-uy, and Trevarguy (al. Trewergy), i. e. *the Town above,* or *upon the Water,* or *River.*
Vya, *it were;* vye, *fhould be.*
Vygyans, *Suftenance.*
Vyin, *Stone* (meyn, id.), fôs a vyen, *a Stone Wall.*
Vyl, *fee;* tî a vyl, *thou wilt fee.*
Vylen, *villainoufly.*
Vyllyk (yvyllyk, id.), *they fhall lament.*
Vynaff, *I will.*
Vynna, *would;* vynnas, *will;* ti a vin, *thou wilt.*
Vynfe, *would;* vyfe, id.

U Y

Uynyn, *one* ; kynifer uynyn, *every one*.

Vyo, *might be*.

Vyru, *dead* (ef a ven vyru, *he will die*) ; verou, id.—for merow.

Vyſk, *a Flail*.

Vyth, *none* ; byth, id.

Vyttyn, *Morning* (metin, id.), kyns vyttyn, *before Day*.

Vyvyan, *Little Water*.—Name of a Family.

U Z

Uz, *Age* ; *a Time* ; huys, id. Lh.

Uzell, *Soot*, Ar. uzill, id.

W.

For the Letter W, Lhuyd uſes generally U, with a Pick under it, and the Cott. MS. the Saxon W. See Gu, U, F, Hu, and Ou.

W, was not introduced into the Britiſh Alphabet till A. D. 1200.

Wan, *weak* ; mar wan, *ſo weak*.

Wane, *to pierce* ; y wane the gollon, *to pierce him to the Heart*.

War, *upon*.

Warbarth, *altogether* ; *on every Side*.

Warſe, *did* ; *put* ; dell warſe, *they ſo put*.

Warlyrgh, *after that* ; warler, id.

Warol, *Merchandize*. Cott.

Warnough, *on ye*.

War-rag, *forward*.

Wartha, *upon high* ; yn nef wartha, *in Heaven above*.

Warthellurgh, *backwards*.

Warwoles, *below*.

Wary, *Liberty* ; *Play* ; the-wary, *out*.

Warybyn, *againſt* ; *near* ; *over-againſt him* ; warben, id.

Wathyll, *to make* ; wuthell, id.

Waz, *a Fellow* ; waz teble, *a wicked Fellow*. See Guaz.

W E

Weath, *below* ; *behind* ; awheath, id.

Wecor, *Courage* ; wecor gwan, *weak Courage* ; *faint Heart*.

Weffra, *for ever*.

Weilgi, *the Sea* ; Gw. See Lh.

Welen, *a Rod*. See Guelen.

Weles, *Seats*, or *Dwellings*. R.

Well, *have* ; a well had ; wull, id.

Wellas. See Guelas.

W E

Welth, *a Work* ; whêl, id.

Wen, or gwen, *white* ; *beautiful*.

Wens, or Wenze. See Guenz, *Wind* ; as, boſwens, chy an guenz.

Weres, *Help* ; rag ym weres, *for his Help*.

Werthys, *ſold* ; guerthy, id.

Weth, *is* ; *alſo a Time* ; *a Turn* ; often annexed to Nouns of Number, as, deweth, *twice* ; milweth, *a thouſand Times*.

Wethan. See Guethan.

Wethough, *ye felt*.

Wethyl, *to do*.

Wetras, *ſtooped*.

W H

Whad, *ſix*.

Whans, *Deſire* ; *Luſt* ; *Coveting*.

Whare, *anon* ; *but* ; yn whare, *in Account*.

Whath, *yet*.

Whefes, *the ſixth* ; whefes dydth, *the ſixth Day*.

Whegoll, *dear* ; vam whegoll, *dear Mother*.

Wheh, *ſix*.

Whek, *ſweet* ; *dear*.

Whekter, *Sweetneſs*.

Whelough, *ſeek ye*.

Wherthen, *to laugh*.

Wheſe, *Sweat* ; whes, id.

Whethe, *to blow* ; whethe the gorn, *to blow the Horn*.

Whiggian, *Pillis* ; *a Seed*.

Whole, *wept*.

Whurts, *Hurtleberries*.

Why, *you* ; *ye*.

Whyrvyth, *they ſhall ſee* ; à merow, or miraz.

Whyth, *to breath* ; *blow* ; whethe, id.

W I

Wibanor, *a Slipper*. Cott.

Widnak, *whitiſh*.

Wigan, *the ſoft Part of a Loaf of Bread* ; *the Crumb*.

Willen, *Fringe* ; f. pillen.

Win, *Wine* ; guin, id. Cott.

Winaz, *Nails of the Fingers*.

Wingarly, Qu. f. *faint*, *ſick*.

Wiſkis, *cloathed*. See Guiſkis.

Withell, *a Lion* ; withellonack, id.

Wlano-diſclien, *Quaternio*. L. Cott.

W O

Woky, *churliſh*. See Goky.

Wolas, *could*.

Wole, *to weep*.

Wolhas, *waſhed* ; walthas. id.

W O

Wollos, *below* ; wolaz, id.

Wolſowas, *to hear* ; golſowans, *let him hear*.

Won, *were ye* ; ny won, *they were not* ; it. *to know*.

Wonys, *to faſhion* ; it. *to till*, or *ſow*.

Woolac, *Reſpect* ; woolac da, *good Reſpect*. See Guelas.

Wor, *to* ; wos, id.

Woras, *put* ; gora, id.

Wornyas, *gave Notice* ; *warned*.

Woromynys, *ſent*. Pa.

Worrians, *I can*.

Worthenys, *Miſeries*.

Worte, *them*.

Worthe, *of* ; *from* ; *over* ; *while* ; dywort, *from*.

Worthebys, *anſwered*.

Worthoſow, *Thighs* ; *Legs*.

Worthe, *to worſhip*.

Worthyans, *Glory*.

Wortos, *to ſtop* ; *to ſtay*.

Worty, *your Huſband* ; gwyrti, id.

Wos, *Cold* ; it. *ſince* ; *ſeeing that*.

Wos, *to be* ; *a wos*, *that he be*.

Woteveth, *at laſt*.

Wothaff, *I knew*.

Wothe, *could*.

Wottenſe, *them* ; a wottenſe, *to them*.

Wovente, *concerning*.

Wour (worc, id.) *know* (f. won), *can* ; dell wour, *as I can*.

Wovynnys, *aſked*.

Wow, *grumbling* ; heb wow, *without grumbling* ; qua. a *now*.

W R

Wre, wra, *did* ; *cauſed* ; wraſys, *didſt come*.

Wrath, *a Giant* ; ind. Wrath's *Hole in St. Agnes*.

Wreſſens, *they made* ; wryſſens, id.

Wrenſe, *was*.

Wrowethe, *to lie along*.

Wryk, *did* (for rig, as), me re wryk ſkrife, *I did write*.

W U

Wuthell, *to do* ; *make* ; *frame*.

W Y

Wyber, *a Serpent*. R.

Wyn, *bleſſed* ; *white* ; wyan, id. gwydyn, pro gwyn. id.

Wynnough, *will ye* ; *ye will*.

Wyr, *true*. See Gwyr.

Wys, *becomes* ; awys thy, *it becomes thee*.

Wys, for Guyz, *a Sow*. See Guyz.

Wyſkens

W Y

Wyſkens, *ſtruck*; gwyſkys, id.

Wyth, *a large Field.*

W Z

Wz. See Uz.

Y.

Y, *He; his; him; that; ſhe; a; the;* as, y mawna, *that Boy,*

Y, *to;* as, y ſedha, *to ſit.*

Yau, *a Yoke;* yeu, id. Ar.

Yakh, *healthy; well;* yechet, *Health,* Ar. id.

Yâr, *a Hen;* Pl. yêr.

Yaz, *Health.*

Y B

Ybba, *here;* ubba, obba, hubba, id.

Y D

Yd, *Corn;* iz, id.

Ydd, *a Plural Termination of Britiſh Words,* as nentydd, *Fountains;* coedydd, *Woods.*

Ydnek, *eleven.*

Ydnhakvas, *the eleventh.*

Ydhyn, *a Bird.*

Ydhoz, *thou art.*

Ydnungk, *a young Bird;* ebol, id.

Ydn, *one;* ydnger, *one Word.*

Ydzhi, *he is.*

Ydzhiz, *I am.*

Y E

Yea, *ſo; yes;* L ita; imo; îa, huâth, id. Lh.

Yeghys, *called.*

Yeigen, *a Ferret;* yeugen, id.

Yein, *cold; Ice;* yên, Ar. id.

Yeinder, *Stiffneſs; Rigor;* L. *Cold; Roughneſs;* Lh.

Yenter tor, *the Back;* Cott. halen, id.

Yermis-priv, *a Rat.* ib.

Yerres, *a Boar; Pig; Verres.* L.

Yerues, *a Ram.*

Yet, *a Gate.*

Yeveren, *public Matters.*

Y F

Yffran, *Hell;* yfarn, id.

Y G

Yg, *a Hook.*

Y K

Yk, *alſo.*

Y L

Ylaſt, *ſcalding;* wylaſt, id.

Yll (yl, id.), *may,* or *can;* yll gwelas, *may ſee.*

Ylla, *he could.*

Ylly, *might.*

Ylly, *Ointment;* len a ylly, *full of Ointment.*

Ylwis, *cried.*

Yma, *there is.*

Ymbithionen, *Paper;* L. *Scheda.*

Ymdoula, *to wreſtle;* qua. ab emdal, *to ſtrive.*

Ymdoulur, *a Wreſtler; a Champion.*

Ymdwyn, *to behave well,* or *ill.*

Ymeirio, *to brawl,* or *chide.*

Ymgachu, *to defile;* concaco. L.

Ymlàdd, W. *a Battle,* or *Combat.*

Ymma (omma, id.), *here;* ſuffixed, as, chymma, for chy omma, *this Houſe here.*

Ymonz, *they are.*

Ymyl, *a Border.*

Y N

Yn, *in; to; then;* yn meath, *then ſaid;* it is alſo a Sign of an Adverb, as, yntebel, *wickedly.*

Ynbarth, *within; inſide.*

Yndan, *under.*

Ynikorn, *that hath but one Horn.*

Ynion, *Right.* Lh.

Ynir, *honorius;* L. enir, or henir, id.

Ynmes, *out; in the Middle.*

Ynn, *a Spear;* Celtic; onn, id.

Ynne, *in; within;* en, id.

Ynno, *him;* ynna, *he.*

Ynnon, *in us.*

Ynnos, *in thee.*

Ynnyas, *inſiſted; cried out.*

Ynolwedi, *behind.*

Ynta, *well;* ynta a wothe, *well knew.*

Yntebel, *wickedly.*

Ynten, *together; upright.*

Yntre, *among;* yntrethow, *among you.*

Yntyen, *entirely.*

Ynven, *earneſtly.*

Ynweth, *alſo.*

Ynyough, *charge ye; cry out to.*

Ynz, *they are;* monz, id.

Y O

Yoch, *a Pig.* Cott.

Youll, *Deſire; Wiſh.*

Yonk, *young.*

Yontye, *to anoint.*

Y O

Yorkh, *a Roe;* Cott. *Caprea.* L.

Y R

Yr, *are; her;* as, yr goar, *her Huſband.*

Yrat, *Ointment.*

Yrchys, *commanded;* as, del yrchys ev, *as he commanded;* yrges, id.

Yredy, *already; readily; indeed.*

Yrhian, *the Brim of any Thing; the Borders or Frontiers.*

Yrvyz, *armed;* Pa. ab arv.

Y S

Ys, *them; to them; than;* as, ys kyns, *than before.*

Yſbrychu, *to beſmear.*

Yſcaun, Lh. *an Elder Tree.*

Yſcod, *a Shade.* Cott.

Yſcren, *Bones.*

Yſcubell, *a Beſom.*

Yſely, *his Arms.*

Yſgal, *a Baſon.*

Yſgobeth, *a Bench,* or *Chair.* Lh.

Yſgol, W. *a Ladder; a Stile;* A. deredh, id.

Yſgubo, *to bruſh.*

Yſguydh, *a Shield.*

Yſgwydarf, *to brandiſh.*

Yſigo, *to bruiſe.*

Yſkrybl, *a labouring Breaſt;* yſgrybl, W. id.

Yſkynne, *to aſcend;* yſkunncs, *Let him mount.*

Yſkys, *ſoon.*

Yffilli, *Limbs; Members.*

Yffu, *to burn.* R.

Yſtafel gwelu, *a Bride-chamber.*

Yſtig, *ſtudious; careful.* Lh.

Yſtlym, *a Bat,* or *Dormouſe.*

Yſtuucc, *a Bucket;* kibal, id.

Yſtyn, *to reach;* yſtyn thym, *reach to me.*

Yſwil, *baſhful;* mûl, id.

Yſwilio, *to bluſh.*

Yſy, *he is.*

Y T

Ytterevis, *ſtirred up.*

Yth, *in thy;* yth ſervis, *in thy Servic.*

Y U

Yvabm, *the Spleen.*

Yves, *ſo; as.* Ar.

Yuggye, *to judge.* Lh.

Yuh, *above;* yuh an môr, *above the Sea.*

Yuhal, *high; tall.*

Yurl, *a Count; Earl,* or *Conſul.*

Yvuru, *To-morrow;* W. y vory, A. archoadh, id. Lh.

Yuzia, *to be accuſtomed;* ſoleo. L.

Yw,

Y W

Yw, *am ; is ; are.*
Yweges, *a Steer ; an Ox.*

Y Z

Yz, *Corn.*
Yzouch, *ye are.*

Z.

ZABAN, *a Pine*; avelzaban, *a Pine-apple*; plankys za-ban, *Fir-timber.* Lh.
Zadarn, *Saturn*; ind. Treza-darn, *Town of Saturn.*
Zâh, *a Sack ; dry*; zahaz, *Thirst.* Lh.
Zal, *Salt*; peſk zal, *Salt-fiſh.* Lh.
Zalla, *to ſalt.*
Zans, *a Saint.*
Zanz, *a Bay*; ind. f. Penzanz, alias Penſans, *Holy Head*, or *Promontory*; it. *a Saint.*
Zar, *a Turky.*
Zart, *an Urchin*, or *Hedge-hog.*
Zawn, *a Creek.*

Z A

Zaznak, *Engliſh*; Zouznak, id.
Zhaff, *a Cable Rope.*

Z E

Zeage, *Grains*; lacka vel zeage, *worſe than Grains.*
Zeah, *dry*; it. *an Arrow*; parc zeah, *a dry Field*; zeh, id. zeth, *Drowth.*
Zeath. See Zeth.
Zehar, *Drought*; zeha, id.
Zehez, *Thanks.*
Zheibio, *to bewitch*, or *inchant.*
Zeithan, *a Week*; ſeithan, id.
Zen, *for ; to ; ours*; as, zen enevou, *to our Souls.*
Zeth, *an Arrow ; a Pot*; ſeth, id. zethan, id. Lh. *an Archer.*
Zethar, *a Sea Mew*, or *Gull.*
Zeval, *to ſtand*; ſeval, id.

Z I

Zîan, *the Sea-ſide ; Shore*; Lh. inde f. Marhazian, *the Market by the Sea Side.*

Z I

Zighyr, *ſlow*; zighirna kuſga, *this lazy Fellow ſleeps*; zigur, *idle.*
Zillan, *Scilly Iſlands.*
Zilli, *an Eel.*
Zingy, *to hold, draw*; ſynſy, id.
Zîu, *a large Kind of Breme-fiſh*; Pl. zivion ; ziew, id.

Z O

Zoha, *a Plow-ſhare*; zôh, id. Lh.
Zhoi, *to beſtow.*
Zona, *to charm.*
Zoul, *Stubble*; W. ſovol, id. *Straw for Thatch.* Lh.
Zoulz, *a Shilling.*
Zouz, *an Engliſh Man.*
Zouzn, *Saxons.*
Zouznak, *Engliſh.*

Z Y

Zylgueth, *a Sunday.*

DEO GLORIA.